Modern Embedded Computing
Designing Connected, Pervasive, Media-Rich Systems

Modern Embedded Computing
Designing Connected, Pervasive, Media-Rich Systems

Peter Barry

Patrick Crowley

AMSTERDAM • BOSTON • HEIDELBERG • LONDON
NEW YORK • OXFORD • PARIS • SAN DIEGO
SAN FRANCISCO • SINGAPORE • SYDNEY • TOKYO

Morgan Kaufmann Publishers is an Imprint of Elsevier

Acquiring Editor: Todd Green
Development Editor: Robyn Day
Project Manager: Andre Cuello
Designer: Joanne Blank

Morgan Kaufmann is an imprint of Elsevier
225 Wyman Street, Waltham, MA 02451, USA

Notices

Knowledge and best practice in this field are constantly changing. As new research and experience broaden our understanding, changes in research methods or professional practices, may become necessary. Practitioners and researchers must always rely on their own experience and knowledge in evaluating and using any information or methods described herein. In using such information or methods they should be mindful of their own safety and the safety of others, including parties for whom they have a professional responsibility.

To the fullest extent of the law, neither the Publisher nor the authors, contributors, or editors, assume any liability for any injury and/or damage to persons or property as a matter of products liability, negligence or otherwise, or from any use or operation of any methods, products, instructions, or ideas contained in the material herein.

Library of Congress Cataloging-in-Publication Data
Application submitted

British Library Cataloguing-in-Publication Data
A catalogue record for this book is available from the British Library.

ISBN: 978-0-12-391490-3

For information on all MK publications visit our website at www.mkp.com

To Viviane, Brianna, and Jason
—Peter

To Laura, Sophia, and Alice
—Patrick

Contents

PART 2 EMBEDDED SYSTEMS ARCHITECTURE AND OPERATION

Preface

We began writing this textbook with two high-level goals in mind:

1. to introduce students to what we consider to be modern embedded systems, and
2. to show how to understand and program such systems using a concrete platform built around a modern embedded processor like the Intel Atom.

Embedded computing has changed dramatically in recent years, and we have found that academic text books do not reflect this fact. Mindful of the growing importance of embedded systems overall, we saw a need to address the discrepancy between the state of embedded computing and the state of academic textbooks in the area. Hence, this textbook.

Key Insight

How have embedded systems changed dramatically in recent years? Traditionally, embedded systems courses and textbooks take as their foundation microcontroller-based systems used primarily in industrial control applications.

However, many classes of embedded systems today—such as consumer electronics, handsets, and mobile media devices—exhibit the following characteristics.

1. Network connectivity. Nearly all embedded systems include IP networking stacks and enable network connectivity via a combination of wired and wireless network interfaces.
2. Media-rich user interfaces. Many embedded systems include graphical user interfaces built with high-resolution 2D and 3D graphics, as well as displays, inputs, and outputs supporting standard and high-definition video and audio.
3. Aggressive platform integration. For reasons of power efficiency, performance, and size, chips and chipsets for embedded systems are highly integrated, with on-die implementations of memory and I/O controllers, accelerators for computationally intensive tasks such as encryption and compression, and multiple programmable processor cores.

Modern embedded systems are connected, media-rich, and highly integrated. This core insight inspired the development of the book, and distinguishes it from existing texts.

Target Audience

This textbook is designed to form the basis of a semester-long laboratory-based undergraduate embedded design engineering course. The text is also suitable for similar courses offered in the context of continuing education. The primary audience is undergraduate engineering students in computer engineering, electrical engineering, computer science, and embedded system design.

From a technical perspective, embedded systems programmers are the primary audience of the book. Secondary audiences include embedded platform designers and SoC/CPU architects. The chapter outline of the book, and the core content of each chapter, is primarily designed to meet the needs of embedded systems programmers, and therefore emphasize how to develop systems and application software for embedded computing systems.

Our Approach

This undergraduate textbook delves into all aspects of modern embedded systems. It is designed to educate undergraduate engineering students in the principles of embedded system architecture and design. Most principles are further illustrated in a concrete way with examples using the Intel Atom processor.

The book is organized into three parts. The chapters in Part 1 introduce the principles of modern embedded systems. Part 2, which comprises the majority of the text, explores in detail the architecture and operation of embedded systems. The chapters in Part 3 explore detailed, real-world aspects of developing embedded systems, including sample platform descriptions, debugging, and performance tuning.

The text describes example embedded platforms, interfaces, peripherals, processors and operating systems associated with embedded systems, a comprehensive view of the software framework being developed around embedded SOCs, including open source firmware, power management, networking, multimedia and middleware. The text is replete with examples, which are provided to facilitate a comprehensive understanding of the overall platform architecture of modern embedded computing systems.

Beginning with a discussion of embedded platform architecture and Intel Atom-specific architecture, modular chapters cover system boot-up, operating systems, power optimization, graphics and multi-media, connectivity, and platform tuning. A companion reference design platform and an embedded design example case study will enable a laboratory component complimenting the chapters

Online Resources

The book's companion web site provides instructor-controlled access to chapter-specific homework problems and laboratory exercises. These, in combination with the use of the reference hardware platform, enable hands-on embedded design experiences.

Visit booksite.mkp.com/9780123914903 to access ancillaries, and textbooks.elsevier.com/9780123914903 for instructor's materials.

Foreword

While I am not sure where I first heard it, I have increasingly grown fond of this quote: "Architecture is art in structure." It inspires an arc one can follow that is characterized by a fascinating combination of creativity (art) and engineering discipline (structure). The latter creates bounds, the former looks for ways to fly away from it. One focuses on the function, the other is interested in creating a differentiating form. Just when one wonders if the focus on usability or function may enforce a break-no-rule regime, desire to achieve a distinguishing form opens the door for the innovation to step right in! Achieving the right balance between the seemingly contradictory tendencies of form and function requires the imagination and courage to break the mold while understanding and appreciating the rationale behind it.

The term "architecture" entered the computer vernacular in the early 1960s as the developers of mainframe computers at IBM attempted to describe data formats, instruction types, and other hardware parameters and enhancements. However, I would argue that it was probably not until the early 1980s—after the arrival of Intel's 8086 microprocessor and the IBM PC built around it—that the interesting interplay of form and function (art and structure) mentioned above began in earnest in the world of computing. The personal computer (PC) brought the power of computing to the masses, ushering in a new era of innovation and productivity improvements unimaginable in the past. Developers around the world started developing hardware platforms and software applications on top of the foundation the PC laid. As businesses around the world recognized the value of the PC toward improving productivity and eventually their bottom line, there was an obvious desire to do more with the PC. There was just one problem. The PC was not designed with such widespread applicability and usage in mind! Thus, while people explored how to extend its value, some of the fundamental tenets of the platform were already in place. Changing this foundation to allow for a more purposeful build-out would have not just risked slowing down the pace of innovation, but could possibly have undermined the value that was already realized.

In my view, this is where Moore's Law and Intel's relentless pursuit of it came to the rescue. As a lifelong Intel technologist, my view on the value of Moore's Law may appear tainted, but this is not a new claim I am putting forth. How the computer industry has ridden Moore's Law to its phenomenal expansion since the late 1980s has been well documented in trade journals, books, and academic papers. I want to connect it to the interplay of art and structure I alluded to earlier. With the key tenets of the PC architecture in place—the instruction set architecture (ISA) of the IA-32 CPU, key system-level attributes of how CPU, memory, and I/O subsystems interacted, and several platform details in terms of devices, memory map, etc.—the challenge was how to enhance the platform value without undermining these foundational pillars. In Moore's Law, what the developers found was an obliging benefactor that doubled the resources (transistors) at their disposal roughly every two years without incurring a substantial financial downside. So, the stage was set for the creativity to flourish within the guardrails established by the PC platform architecture.

The Intel386™ processor marked the first major breakthrough in this quest to innovate within the confines of the established architecture. With its 32-bit architecture, memory protection schemes, and paging architecture for virtual memory, it paved the way for supporting more sophisticated operating systems. And this was done while retaining backward compatibility with the 8086 architecture. The Intel386 processor established the playbook on how to bring new innovations to the CPU and platform architecture while protecting the investments developers had made in the prior generation platforms.

Through the various generations of Intel's IA-32 processors (later renamed to Intel® Architecture, or IA), more and more sophisticated architectural constructs—various hierarchies of caches, superscalar pipelines, out of order execution with increasingly more efficient branch prediction, hyper-threading and on-chip multicore, virtualization, power saving states, etc.—have been added. Not only that, IA product roadmap evolved to include not just CPUs optimized for the desktop and notebook computers, but also high-end servers (Intel Xeon® processors) as well as lower-power, battery-operated hand-held devices (Intel Atom™ processor). Similarly, there were several enhancements to the platform architecture as well; Advanced Peripheral Interrupt Controllers (APIC) and higher-precision event timers, Peripheral Component Interface (PCI) and subsequent PCI express, Universal Serial Bus (USB) interface, various memory interfaces to support higher bandwidths, and platform-level power management, to just name a few. Over the years, the term Intel Architecture has somewhat become synonymous with a certain platform architecture that ensures the backward compatibility mentioned above. It provided the foundation on top of which a plethora of operating systems, middleware, tool chains, and of course, applications were successfully developed and deployed with relative ease. The history of the evolution of IA is a testament to the creativity of several generations of innovators across the industry that blossomed to embrace and enable unimaginable usage scenarios, the constraints of its foundation notwithstanding!

Not surprisingly, the Intel Architecture, with all the attractive CPU and platform architecture features, found its way into embedded systems over the last three decades. Whether it was a point of sale terminal in a retail segment, an industrial PC in an industrial control segment, a firewall or security appliance in an enterprise segment, or a gaming kiosk, IA provided a ready-to-deploy platform with the most varied software ecosystem to suit different needs of developers in these segments, not to mention the guarantee of the Moore's Law cadence that would sustain predictable and straightforward performance upgrade cycles. Over the last decade the expansion of the IA product portfolio has helped extend its reach within the embedded space. For example, the advent of multi-core Intel Xeon processors has strengthened the IA position in the ever-performance-hungry communications infrastructure sector. On the other hand, the introduction of the Intel Atom processor, with its lower power and lower cost envelopes, has generated tremendous interest in IA in embedded segments—like print imaging, industrial PLC controllers, and in-vehicle infotainment—that were previously out of reach for IA.

It is against this rich and immensely productive backdrop of IA history in embedded systems that I watch with fascination the emerging phenomenon of Internet of Things (IOT)—a world of intelligent systems, including remote wireless sensor nodes, multi-protocol gateways, and smaller ("edge") clouds at the periphery, working seamlessly and in real time with the cloud infrastructure to collect, organize, and analyze massive data and derive knowledge, which then leads to a wise action. While embedded devices connecting to the Internet undoubtedly opens up exciting and enticing new opportunities to fundamentally change the way we live, work, and interact with our surroundings and each other, it also poses a slew of challenges in terms of how to secure and protect these devices as well as how to manage them through their life cycle. If one were to believe the enormous numbers projected for the "connected devices" (a majority of which will be embedded), one could easily surmise that, given the scale, deployment and management of these devices need to become much more simplified than what historically has been the case with PCs and cellular phones. This is where I believe the maturity of IA platforms with respect to the connected paradigm (IA-based clients and servers not only have been at the heart of the Internet build out, but also serve as the development platforms for practically all other platforms) and the richness of its software ecosystem, coupled with lower power and lower cost envelopes of Intel Atom architecture, can facilitate a easier and technically sound migration to the vision of the IOT.

This book is aimed at providing foundational instruction in the key technology building blocks one needs to master in order to contribute to this new world of embedded systems. I am delighted that the authors of this book not only bring many years of experience in embedded systems, networking, Intel Architecture, and systems engineering, but also represent the visionary technical leadership we will require if we were to successfully take on the challenges of the changing landscape in embedded systems. I know in my heart that this book will greatly serve the young and curious minds who we collectively will count on to change the face of embedded computing in profound ways, ultimately resulting in a better and more meaningful human experience!

—Pranav Mehta
Sr. Principal Engineer & CTO
Embedded & Communications Group
Intel

Acknowledgments

We owe a debt of gratitude to a large number of people for their help and encouragement while writing this book. We would like to thank Pranav Mehta for conceiving the original concept of the book and supporting our work.

We would like to thank the following people for their significant contribution to specific chapters: Max Domeika and Lori Matassa—Embedded Processor Architecture supplement. Pete Dice, Jenny Pelner, and James Pelner—Embedded Platform Boot Sequence. Vasco Santos, David Martinez-Nieto, Julien Carreno, and Ken Reynolds—Digital Signal Processing. Ee Khoon Yap Ee—Graphics and Multimedia. Kevin Bross—Platform Examples. Ger Hartnett—Platform Tuning.

We'd like to thank all of the people who reviewed this book and provided us with much valuable feedback: Sunil Agrawal, Steve Doyle, Ramesh Abel Edgar, Linda Fellingham, Susan Foster, Celeste Fralick, Kevin Gambill, Mylinh Gillen, William Handley, Nee Shen Ho, Muthurajan Jayakumar, Erin Jones, Asad Khan, Tomasz Kilarski, Ray Kinsella, Scott Krig, Micheal Langman, Todd Langley, Matthew Lee, Suresh Marisetty, Krishna Murthy, Bryan O'Donoghue, TJ O'Dwyer, Subhankar Panda, Marc Pepin, Richard Purdie, Mo Rooholamini, Joy Shetler, Benjamin Silva, Jay Simonetta, Brian Skerry, David Stewart, Tat Kin Tan, Tian Tian, Stephanie Wang, Brian Will, and Chris Wojslaw.

We would also like to thank Shrikant Shah, Edward Pullin, and David Clark for their significant attention to detail and whose reviews and edits greatly improved the accuracy and readability of the book.

Principles of Modern Embedded Systems

Embedded Systems Landscape

We are in the midst of an extraordinary technology transformation. Most classes of electronic devices will soon be Internet-accessible with software-defined feature sets—not just computers and mobile phones, but nearly all forms of electronics. In other words, most classes of electronics are becoming embedded computer systems, and the consequences of this transition will be substantial.

This trend can be seen plainly in current commercial offerings, across a wide range of product types, where most new product lines are built around processor-based integrated circuits that enable Internet connectivity. Consider the following examples.

- *Consumer electronics.* The most competitive and innovative categories of consumer electronics—examples include high-definition television sets, digital cameras, video game consoles, and media players—are all designed around processor-based systems-on-a-chip and rely on Internet connectivity.
- *Telephony.* From mobile handsets designed primarily to connect to cellular access networks, to VoIP phones that enable not only voice calls, but also instant messaging, video chat, and integration with social network contacts, most modern telephony platforms are designed to be extensible through software feature sets. Moreover, they are increasingly designed to connect opportunistically to a user's network of choice.
- *In-vehicle information systems.* Today's onboard automotive information systems provide compelling applications such as GPS navigation, rear/obstructed view cameras, voice communications, and audio/video playback in an integrated fashion.

For the embedded systems programmer, the consequences of this trend are considerable. Foremost, there will be a great many more embedded computer systems in the future than there have been in the past, so skilled designers and programmers have a future of stable employment ahead of them. From a technical perspective, the nature of embedded systems design is changing to reflect the large numbers of systems that are connected and have rich media interfaces. The vast majority of embedded developers have been trained with 8-bit microcontrollers in mind, and the world has clearly moved on.

In this book, you will explore the design of modern embedded computer systems and learn many of the principles and skills needed to develop and program them effectively.

Our goal in this chapter is to establish the appropriate context. The world of embedded systems is vast and changing rapidly, so we will begin by sharing our view on what modern embedded systems are all about, and why their importance and popularity have been increasing so dramatically.

WHAT IS AN EMBEDDED COMPUTER SYSTEM?

Embedded systems are computers with constraints. While the design of all engineered devices involves trade-offs to some degree, general-purpose computers have historically been designed with comparatively few constraints. Since general-purpose computers are the most widely understood class of computing systems, it is instructive to compare and contrast their constraints with those of embedded systems. Indeed, embedded computer systems are different, both from one another and from general-purpose systems, by virtue of the design trade-offs and constraints they embody.

In particular, embedded computer systems have distinctive constraints with respect to intended applications and form factors, power, system resources and features, and assumptions about user behavior.

Applications and Form Factors

Unlike general-purpose machines, embedded systems are typically designed for one target application, or class of target applications. The intended use of an embedded computer system drives many of its design constraints and tradeoffs.

The size and physical form factor are often a natural consequence of a system's intended use. For example, continuously tethered medical devices, worn by patients, have shape and weight constraints that follow from the human body and its movements. Mobile handsets, by convention, are sized to fit in a (sometimes large) pocket. And embedded networking devices, such as wireless access points, are typically larger than human-centric devices, but have size and shape constraints of their own.

A system's intended use defines its physical packaging constraints, and many other design constraints follow from these. Notably, embedded computer systems have required a higher degree of system-level integration—that is, the integration of system-wide functionality onto one or a small number of semiconductor devices—in order to meet tight size, cost, and power constraints.

Power

In embedded and general-purpose systems alike, power has become the predominant design constraint. In general-purpose systems, such as laptops and servers, power dissipation limits, expressed in terms of thermal design power (TDP), have ranged from tens to hundreds of watts, respectively. Relative to embedded systems, general-purpose platforms support a comparatively small number of ranges of TDP, which have evolved over time subject to the operational context of each particular platform. Laptop TDPs are largely a consequence of an expected battery life of between 4 and 8 hours; modern server TDPs are a consequence of the power density per unit volume that machine rooms and data centers are provisioned to dissipate (which were, in turn, based on the TDP of the previous generations of server equipment).

For the most part, embedded systems have considerably lower-power design points, ranging from a few watts to microwatts. While some high-performance contexts, such as network routers and telecommunications equipment, have power profiles more or less the same as servers, most embedded computer systems are designed to operate in smaller spaces, often on battery power, and without the benefit of mechanical heat dissipation mechanisms such as fans or other forms of active cooling.

As a result, embedded computer systems have historically been designed with comparatively aggressive dynamic power management mechanisms. In recent years, however, dynamic power management in general-purpose CPUs has become sophisticated, with the goal of switching between high-performance, high-power modes and low-performance, low-power modes without disturbing either user-perceived latency or system performance on marketing-oriented industry benchmarks.

Relative to the general-purpose scenarios, embedded computer systems exhibit a much more heterogeneous array of power design perspectives. As will be discussed in greater detail later, embedded computer systems span a wide range of use cases, from high-performance systems to battery-operated systems designed to operate in wireless sensor applications for years with a single battery.

As such, embedded computer systems rely on power management schemes and features that vary with the target application.

System Resources and Features

General-purpose and embedded computer systems differ most in the variability of system resources and features rather than in their quantity. Embedded computer systems are typically designed and deployed with a relatively static and predetermined set of system resources and features.

This fact simplifies systems software and certain system processes, such as booting the system or diagnosing problems. For example, the boot process for an IA-32-based general-purpose computer, and the design of the software that implements that process, must be organized to contend with an unpredictable set of memory and I/O resources when the system starts. This resource uncertainty is not present in most embedded computer systems; hence, embedded system boot processes are shorter and simpler.

User Assumptions

General-purpose computers enjoy generous assumptions about the behavior of users. In fact, few classes of electronics have a user profile more convenient than that of the computer user. Outside of microwave ovens and A/V remote controls, few electronics products place such a substantial burden on the user to work around system problems and inefficiencies. While the user experience has improved dramatically in recent years, the typical computer user is prepared to experience routine system failures, frequently reinstall or update software packages, experience compatibility problems following installations and updates, wait patiently for inexplicable hourglasses to disappear, and, generally speaking, learn a great deal about how to use the system and cope with its deficiencies.

On the other hand, most embedded systems have a much narrower range of assumptions about user behavior. Most embedded systems are parts of devices or infrastructure and are expected to function reliably and deterministically. Users expect devices such as media players and telephones to respond without any latency. Infrastructure and industrial equipment are often designed to reliably honor service-level agreements. These tighter usage requirements impact systems software and overall system feature selection, as we will discuss in detail in later chapters.

WHY IS THIS TRANSITION INEVITABLE?

Of course, in this day and age, it is easy for many to accept without argument that all electronics will be connected and software based. But why is this so? Does my light switch need an IP address? Isn't it hard to write bug-free software? So why pollute the everyday reliability of traditional electronics with unpredictable software bugs?

Perhaps the most persuasive explanation comes not from a technical perspective but from considering some of the business dynamics that influence electronic product development. Technological progress in the presence of genuine commercial competition demands that, over time, new products increase in value while maintaining, or reducing, the price for those products. In the computer business, for example, it is easy to see that average sales price points have been declining over time as performance has increased. New products must, quite literally, do more for less. (Why? Because if you do not offer new features at better prices, then your competitors will put you out of business.)

How is this economically sustainable? This trend—doing more for less—is only economically sustainable if new features can be developed and deployed profitably, that is, if new features can be developed and added at an aggregate cost that is less than the increase in revenue that results from the new features. In business terms, profitability is a synonym for economic sustainability.

How can new features be developed profitably in a context of declining prices? In a word: reuse! Reuse the results of prior development to lower or eliminate the cost of future development. And no technology enables reuse quite like software.

If past development investments can be amortized into the future, across future product generations, then marginal investments can fund feature development. This is precisely what software enables under ideal circumstances. A software-based, extensible product core enables past development effort to be amortized across future offerings, while enabling the cost-effective development of new features and services. Software-defined feature sets enable electronics of all kinds to exhibit qualitatively superior cost savings relative to hardware-based feature sets.

And what about deploying new features? This is an important aspect of Internet connectivity. As an example, consider that recent generations of set-top boxes and game consoles have demonstrated the dramatic effectiveness of being able to enable new features in deployed systems.

As of January 2010, all three of the major current-generation video game consoles provide access to the Netflix[†] video streaming service via the Internet. However, none of these platforms initially shipped with this capability, nor, apparently, had any business arrangements between Netflix and the console vendors been made or discussed during the console design phases. With Internet connectivity and a software-based feature set, there is no need to work out all such arrangements in advance of the deployment of the hardware; such agreements can be made and enacted according to the flow of business, provided that the platform has a software-defined feature set with Internet connectivity.

Of course, Internet connectivity enables not just feature deployment, but all other communications-oriented activities. Cameras can upload data directly to online storage accounts. Video games can be structured to provide online play features, such as access to new content or multiplayer modes. Medical devices, industrial equipment, and building automation systems can receive control commands and report back periodically with data and diagnostics information.

More broadly, Internet connectivity enables the command and control of deployed electronics. In many cases, this enables a qualitatively better mechanism for resource control. Take as an example building automation, in which systems such as lighting, climate, and security can be monitored and managed remotely. Lights can be turned off and temperatures can be adjusted in rooms and buildings that are known to be empty, without requiring a physical presence in the room.

When applied broadly across many types of electronics, the remote monitoring and control of resources can have a wide impact on resource management.

WHAT RANGE OF EMBEDDED SYSTEMS EXISTS?

In this book, we take what we consider to be a modern definition of embedded computer systems, one that is somewhat wider in scope than those found previous books.

In particular, our definition of embedded computer systems as computers with constraints admits considerably more high-performance systems than most embedded systems textbooks would include in the scope of their discussion. Most embedded textbooks have their roots in small-scale, micro-controller-style systems. Our perspective is oriented toward larger-scale systems with feature sets and ambitions more aligned with general-purpose computers than with microcontrollers.

For the purpose of illustration, Table 1.1 includes some examples of embedded systems and their corresponding descriptions.

Table 1.1 Samples of Embedded Applications

Embedded Application	Sample Description
Digital signage	Public video displays, primarily for advertising or entertainment
Digital storage	Network-attached, power- and area-efficient storage for enterprises, small business, and homes
Factory automation	Management and control of manufacturing facility assets
Gaming	Video game and other leisure gaming platforms
Building automation	User-facing controls for residential and commercial building systems such as climate, lighting, air quality, and security
In-vehicle infotainment	Converged platform for GPS navigation, A/V entertainment, climate control, and external communications
IP camera	Feature-enhanced video security system
IP media phone	Telephony device with converged messaging, contacts, audio and video communications, and web/media display
Medical	Platforms for medical imaging and managing patient records
Military/Aerospace	Ruggedized, standardized computer, communications and storage elements amenable to interoperability and large-scale systems integration
Point of sale	Connected cash registers, ATMs, and transaction terminals
Printers	Support connected operation and converged fax, scan, and conversion features
Robotics	Control and operation of industrial and retail robots
Network infrastructure	Routers, firewalls, intrusion detection and prevention systems
Sensors	Environmental and industrial process quality control sensors
Transportation	In trains, for example, control of power train along with in-cabin climate control, data communications, and media display
Wireless infrastructure	Modular compute, communications, and storage elements for extensible wireless infrastructure

WHAT TO EXPECT FROM THE REST OF THIS BOOK

The stage is set. Modern embedded systems are computers with unique constraints. The continuing industrial trend toward designing electronic devices around embedded computer systems will result in a sustained and dramatic increase in the number of Internet-connected devices with software-defined feature sets.

Developers and programmers of these systems face a new set of opportunities and challenges. The remainder of this book explores both the principles that form the foundation of modern embedded systems design and the detailed skills and knowledge required to design and program these systems effectively.

Wherever possible, we will keep the discussion concrete. To do so, we illustrate concepts and provide software that targets the Intel® Atom™ embedded processor. The Intel Atom is a relatively recent entrant in the world of embedded systems, but it, in our opinion, best illustrates the challenges and opportunities that follow from our view of modern embedded computer systems.

This book contains a considerable amount of source code that may prove useful in your projects. In order to make it easy to follow along, we have also made available a reference hardware platform; it is the system we have used to develop the software, so it is the platform we recommend using as you work your way through the text.

Attributes of Embedded Systems

With such a wide range of computer platforms with vastly varying performance and I/O capabilities, in this chapter we will define some key attributes of *embedded systems*. A key characteristic of all embedded systems is that they are designed to perform a specific task or function. The software developed for the platform is specific to the function of the overall device. In many cases the compute capability of the device is invisible to the end user; the function provided by the device is all that matters. In contrast to the rapidly growing application-centric ecosystem developing in the smartphone ecosystem, End users of embedded systems do not generally install application software on such devices (although they may have limited ability to upgrade the software).

Embedded systems cover the entire landscape of devices and products. As shown in Figure 2.1, many consumer devices are embedded compute platforms. Internet-enabled TV, Blu-ray[†] players, video game consoles, streaming Internet TV devices, and printers are just a few consumer devices that are characterized by a fairly high level of performance.

On the communications side, embedded devices are deployed throughout the infrastructure at every level. Consider the varied devices that work in unison to enable your Internet experience. For example, when visiting a web page, TCP/IP packets are generated on your device and sent out on the wireless interface (e.g., Wi-Fi). The packets are picked up by the wireless router that is connected to your broadband access device (such as an ADSL or cable modem). Once the packets leave the modem, they travel along the Internet infrastructure. On the infrastructure side, your packets will be routed through a digital subscriber line access multiplexer (DSLAM), then on to Internet network IP routers. The packets are then routed to the web server hosting environment, where the packets pass through firewalls and web load balancers and finally to the web server. Figure 2.1 shows the overall flow.

Another pervasive application of embedded control systems is in the automated manufacturing of goods. These industrial applications require a wide range of control elements with compute capabilities including motor controllers, actuators, sensors, advanced programmable logic controllers (PLCs), robotics, and control panels with user interfaces (HMIs).

In the automotive domain, the capabilities being offered are increasing at an aggressive pace. What has traditionally been a media playback system (radio, CD, DVD, MP3) and simple navigation capability has been rapidly evolving into a highly graphics intensive platform, providing realistic 3D cityscape navigation while connected to the Internet, offering streaming media capability, location-based services, live map updates, and remote car diagnostics. In addition, the domain of driver assistance is becoming increasingly important, with systems such as collision avoidance (braking assist), lane departure warnings, driver alertness indications, night vision, object identification, and trajectory warnings (such as pedestrians). There are also a number of government-sponsored efforts to create intelligent transport systems (see http://www.its.dot.gov/).

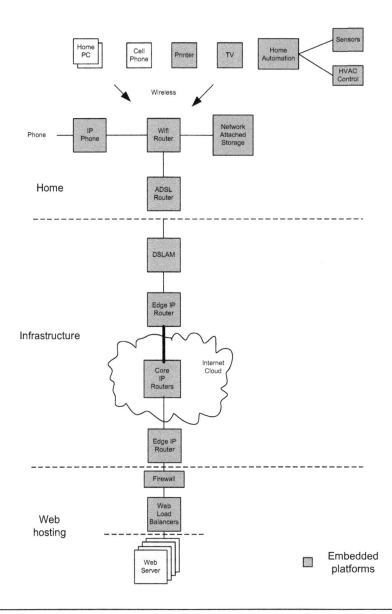

FIGURE 2.1

Internet-Embedded Devices.

Embedded systems can range from a simple stand-alone device to a chassis of networked cards to a system composed of many separate networked embedded elements. They all work collaboratively to achieve the objectives of the overall system. Such systems operate largely autonomously once set up. A chassis-based system is a common configuration for telecommunications and data communications equipment. In some cases the chassis form factor is defined by a standard such as the Advanced Telecommunications Computing Architecture (ATCA), an example of which is shown in Figure 2.2.

In some cases, embedded systems are referred to as cyber-physical systems, where the system exercises significant physical interactions in the real world. Much of the critical infrastructure in our society is controlled by embedded systems, termed supervisory control and data acquisition (SCADA) systems. Given our increasing dependence on connectivity and increased security threats to such systems, the security features of embedded devices are also becoming a critical attribute to comprehend.

Embedded systems often have specific real-time constraints that must be adhered to. In many cases, when an embedded system interfaces with the real world (physically), there are tight real-time responses demanded. These domains can place design constraints on all aspects of the system design, from the peripheral interfaces and quality of service in the system on chip to the operating system selection and the application design.

FIGURE 2.2

Chassis-Based Router.

We have just touched on a tiny fraction of the many varied roles for embedded computing; the overall spectrum covers an enormous dynamic range in terms of performance, power, connectivity, and usage models. However, the trend is toward higher compute and connectivity demands for many embedded systems.

This chapter illustrates the high-level concepts with discussion of a particular device/platform. When introducing each component/subsystem/capability, we will explicitly reference the chapter that describes it in detail. The system description shall serve as a reference to the remainder of the book.

EMBEDDED PLATFORM CHARACTERISTICS

This section describes some critical attributes of embedded systems and identifies some of the dynamic range for the capabilities identified.

Central Processing Unit (CPU)

As the examples of embedded systems in Figure 2.1 show, it is clear that there is an enormous range of compute capabilities in embedded systems.

The number of bits assigned to registers within the integer pipeline 8, 16, 32, or 64 is the first CPU characteristic to focus on. Although mainstream PC CPUs have been running 32-bit for many years, and more recently 64-bit is the standard desktop platform, and there remains a very large number of 8-bit and 16-bit CPUs in many simple control applications. For example, Atmel makes a product line of 8-bit controllers known as Atmel AVR Microcontrollers. These parts run up to the 20–30 MHz range and include integrated flash, RAM, and peripherals. In the 16-bit space, PIC microcontrollers are widely used (predominantly) from MicroChip. These platforms are very low power and can often be run from an AA battery for extended periods. In the case of 8-bit controllers, connectivity options such as IP over Ethernet require additional devices to handle the communications stack, while on 16-bit controllers limited low-speed connectivity is offered (for example, a 10-Mb Ethernet connectivity). In many cases these devices do not run any operating system, although a simple real-time operating system (RTOS) such as FreeRTOS is available.

While 8-bit and 16-bit devices will remain in use for quite some time, it's clear that there is also a large need for 32-bit devices in the embedded space. In many cases the vendors offering 8-/16-bit controllers have also introduced 32-bit variants of their product line. There are also ARM licensees introducing ARM M3–based microcontroller devices.

The devices mentioned above are generally classified as microcontrollers. Although they occupy a large portion of the embedded space, we will not focus on this class of device in this book. Instead, we are going to focus on a generally higher performance class of device, with sophisticated connectivity and graphics that, generally speaking, relies on a RTOS or a full-featured operating system such as an embedded Linux distribution. As the expectations placed on embedded systems grow exponentially, the ability to ensure that the software scales with these expectations is critical. In such cases full-featured operating systems such as Linux offer compelling capabilities.

These higher-performance devices are generally known as embedded microprocessors, as distinct from microcontrollers, and are dominated by 32-bit CPU architectures at this time. This class of processors is used in all of the embedded examples shown in Figure 2.1. In some cases, the processor provides a supervisory control function for the system; in other cases, it performs the entire application and data path workload.

Given the wide range of applications, the clock speed of the processor is an important consideration; the range of an embedded microprocessor system is from the low hundreds of megahertz (200 MHz) to over 1GHz. Clock speed is an important attribute because it is the first order indicator of performance; however, the overall architecture of the processor and the inclusion of caches (and their size) are critical aspects that contribute to overall system performance. In fact, the faster the processor speed, the more important it is to have some form of fast memory close to the processor (with cache being the easiest to take advantage of).

Another important characteristic is the level of parallelism offered by the processor. Instruction-level parallelism, where the CPU performs a number of operations simultaneously, is quite common. A wide range of processor microarchitecture techniques can improve instruction-level parallelism, such as instruction pipelining, superscalar execution, and out-of-order execution. Processors also offer instructions that are single instructions, multiple data (SIMD) to optimize the execution of algorisms that exhibit data-level parallelism. Some processors also allow for thread-level parallelism, known as symmetric multithreading, where with the addition of a relatively small amount of logic, the processor presents two separate logical cores (to the operating system). While one logical core is blocked, perhaps waiting for a memory fetch, the other logical core makes use of the arithmetic logic units.

Many embedded applications require the use of floating-point arithmetic. If floating-point operations are not an insignificant portion of the application workload, the process should include a hardware-based floating-point unit. If the floating-point unit is provided as a hardware function, it is ideal if it conforms to the IEEE Standard for Floating-Point Arithmetic (IEEE 754); otherwise, you have to become very familiar with the deviations from such a standard.

As a reference data point in terms of capabilities, the current Intel® Atom™ core in the E6XX services processor is dual superscalar, with in-order execution and data-level parallelism supported by Intel Supplemental Streaming SIMD Extensions 3 (Intel SSSE3. IEEE 754 compliant hardware), has a hardware floating-point unit, and supports two hardware threads per core. It is offered with speeds from 600 MHz to 1.6 GHz. It provides 32-kB four-way level 1 instruction cache, 32-kB six-way level 1 data cache, and a 512-kB level 2 (unified) cache.

Integration Level

The increasing demand for lower-cost, higher-density platforms and smaller form factors has driven the need to increase the level of integration for each of the devices that makes up the embedded platform. Initially, embedded platforms were composed of separate discrete components. The processor was a separate component with just a memory bus interface, and all peripherals were attached to this bus.

As integration levels increase, more and more logic is added to the processor die, creating families of application-specific service processors. The term system on chip (SOC) is often used to describe these highly integrated processors. These SOCs include much of the logic and interfaces that are required for a range of specific target applications. The silicon vendors that develop these SOC devices often create families of SOCs all using the same processor core, but with a wide range of integrated capabilities.

SOCs integrate capabilities to connect the SOC to external memory devices and nonvolatile storage devices using glue-less interfaces. Glue-less is a term used to indicate that there is no additional logic needed to connect the two devices, for example, connect the SOC to DDR DRAM.

In addition to attaching to memory devices, an SOC provides segment- or application-specific interfaces. Examples of integrated devices are general purpose input/output pins, interfaces such as Ethernet, USB, PCIe, serial ports, I2C, expansion parallel buses, and integrated display controllers. Many of these devices interface to nonvolatile storage such as NOR Flash via Serial Peripheral Interconnect (SPI), and native bus interface types are described in Chapter 4.

As a general rule, these integrated items are predominantly digital logic elements. Because we need to add analog capabilities, features such as flash memory and digital/analog converters are common, but these capabilities require special features of the silicon manufacturing process. As you review the capabilities of embedded microprocessors you may notice that, as the performance range of the processor increases, there is less likelihood that the device will include such analog capabilities. This is due to the tension in creating a silicon process that is optimized for both high-speed digital logic designs and the mixed signal analog domain. This boundary is always changing but is an important dynamic in what capabilities are viable for integration into any SOC device.

Power Consumption

The power consumed by the devices is measured in many different ways. The traditional power quoted for embedded devices provides the typical power consumption of the device. This is measured by running an application on the processor that exercises a representative portion of the I/O capabilities. The current into the device is measured using the current and supply voltage. The power can be calculated using Power = Current (I) × voltage (V). In many cases there are actually several different voltage rails in use, so this must be summed across all power supplies.

Many silicon vendors also provide the total device power figure (TDP). TDP is the maximum amount of power the cooling system is required to dissipate. This does not mean that the system needs active power cooling, such as a fan. In many embedded cases a heat sink is all that is required. The TDP is used as part of an overall thermal design that must ensure that the CPU/SOC does not overheat. There can be a considerable delta between the average power dissipation of a system and the figures quoted for TDP. TDP is and must be an extremely conservative figure. When choosing a system where power is an important attribute, make sure the datasheet comparisons are comparing the same type of figure.

Power figures are often highly dependent on the activity level of the system. Many processors systems have very low power idle states. In order to develop efficient power aware systems, it is often beneficial for an embedded application to group work into bursts of activity with the processor running at full clock rate followed by periods of processor idle states. For example, duty cycles of much less than 10% (full activity 10%, sleep/idle for 90% of the time) are not uncommon in some sensor type applications.

The power of the system must also include loss in conversion of power from the primary single supply into the power rails needed by all components in the system; an efficient conversion of 60–80% would be normal.

A platform power measurement is not just the power of the processor/SOC; other aspects of the system can contribute significantly to the power. Rich, colorful displays, for example, are often one of

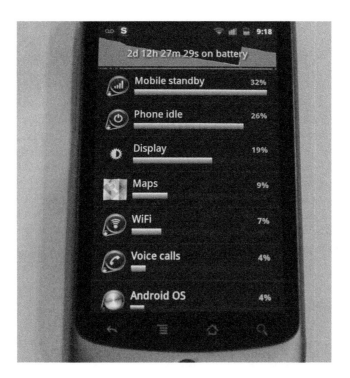

FIGURE 2.3

Android[†] Battery Information.

highest power-consuming devices. Although we are not focused on mobile cell phone embedded systems in this book, Figure 2.3 is a snapshot from an Android phone (battery information).

Overall, platform power comparisons are nuanced, and an awareness of the overall application and how it behaves over time as well as the activity level of other devices on the platform is critical in assessing the overall actual power of the system. We discuss power analysis and optimization in Chapter 9, "Power Optimization."

Form Factor

The form factors for embedded systems are as diverse as the embedded use cases themselves. A large number of embedded systems are composed of a single PCB and are often called single-board computers (SBCs). The platform provides a power connect for a single input voltage (for example, 12V) and provides connectors for devices such as mass storage SATA/SDIO, USB, and displays. These connectors are not necessarily those found in standards-based platforms such as the PC (this is especially the case for the display). Single-board platforms are the most cost-effective way to produce an embedded platform design for a specific target use case, but the platform is not readily upgradeable over time.

In many cases, considerable effort is expended in designing a core compute module that can be employed in a number of different product lines with varying I/O or interface capabilities. In such cases it is often more cost-effective to develop a single daughterboard that provides the key compute capability; this board can be mounted on a motherboard where the application-specific embedded capabilities (and I/O) are instantiated.

Given that many people and companies have a need for a generic compute module, there are a number of standard form factors and connector formats for such modules. Also given that the connector and form factor is standardized, there is a rich ecosystem that develops such boards for reuse by other companies. In this case, you just have to create the daughterboard required for your target embedded application, or often you can use a generic carrier motherboard provided by the same vendors.

The PC/104 Consortium (http://www.pc104.org) has developed a number of standards. The first PC/104 is a stacked format where the compute module can be stacked on top of a number of different I/O carrier boards. The latest standard specification included PCIe between boards. The specification can be found at http://www.pc104.org/pci104_Express_specs.php.

- Compact, 3.6 × 3.8 inch (90 × 96 mm) module size
- Self-stacking: expands without backplanes or card cages
- Rugged, reliable connectors: reliable in harsh environments
- Four-corner mounting holes: resistance to shock and vibration
- Fully PC-compatible: reduced development costs and time to market

The PC/104 organization also standardized the ECPI and EBC form factors, widely used by many vendors (not IA-32 CPUs, despite the PC moniker). COM Express is a computer-on-module (COM) form factor

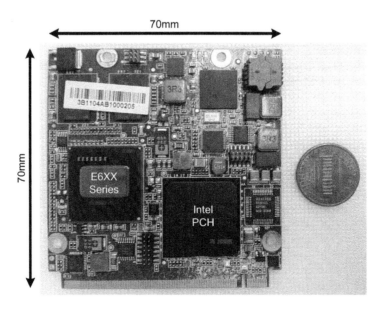

FIGURE 2.4

Intel E600 Series Q7 Module (by InForce Computing).

(http://www.picmg.org). Another standard is the Qseven standard (http://www.qseven-standard .org/). An Intel Atom E600 Q7 module is shown in Figure 2.4. The module contains all the required logic for a complete IA-32 Intel architecture system.

Many of these standards are supported by module and SBC manufacturers such as Kontron (http://us .kontron.com/products/computeronmodules/) and Congatec AG. Many vendors provide multiple versions of each module with different compute processors used from Intel, ARM-based SOCs, and others.

Expansion

An attribute often sacrificed in designing embedded systems is the ability to expand hardware capabilities over time. Given that the platform has a specific purpose, the designer has the ability to dimension the platform for the specific usage. The DRAM and nonvolatile memory are usually soldered down on the platform. There are generally no expansion slots to add additional hardware.

Software capabilities are, however, often added over time. Perhaps all the software features were not ready at the time of product launch, or the marketing team came up with a killer new feature—either way you now have to ensure that you can add these capabilities to a system that cannot be expanded. If you are fortunate, the platform designers shipped the system with a margin of DRAM and flash. As a general guideline, use no more than 70% of the installed DRAM/flash at the time the product is released if you plan on adding software features over time. Leaving a margin for additional features is a difficult embedded systems trade-off. There is a cost associated with providing additional resources that may or may not actually be used. In many cases, it is best to provide the margin in the first release of the product and subsequently create versions with a reduced margin over time. These are known as cost reduction cycles and are quite common. Naturally, CPU headroom is another key consideration in ensuring that sufficient headroom is left to add software features over time.

Application-Specific Hardware

Given the tremendous range of embedded applications, there is a likelihood that there aren't any system-on-chip devices that perfectly suit your needs. In some cases it is simply not economically viable for a silicon provider to add such a capability due to a limited market size; in other cases, the intellectual property is not available, and in fact the capability that has been added is a part of your company's "secret sauce."

To meet this need, you can add capabilities by adding a field-programmable gate array (FPGA) or by developing an application-specific integrated circuit (ASIC). The trade-offs between these two options usually have to do with cost and level of risk. The development cost of an ASIC will be higher, but the cost to manufacture will be lower (this is volume-dependent), and vice versa for FPGAs, depending on the volume of the production.

PCI Express (PCIe) is the interface of choice used to connect between the SOC and an FPGA/ASIC. FPGA vendors such as Altera (http://www.altera.com) and Xilinx (http://www.xilinx.com) provide PCIe capabilities for the FPGAs. This PCIe is usually a "hard" capability and does not use up any of the programmable resources you would need for your application.

Figure 2.5 shows multiple IP blocks behind the PCIe endpoint. It is important (for software) that separate capabilities be exposed as separate PCIe functions. Hardware aspects of PCIe are discussed in Chapter 4 and software aspects in Chapter 8.

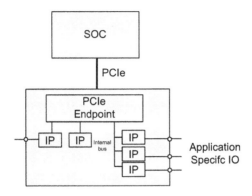

FIGURE 2.5

FPGA Expansion.

Naturally, you could extend the platform through other interfaces such as USB, SDIO, I2C, or a general expansion bus, but PCIe provides excellent general purpose interconnect capabilities, and most operating systems have a very well-defined device driver model for PCIe devices.

Certification

An important aspect of many embedded systems is that they form part of a system that itself must be certified. The certification requirements are usually industry specific, but a range of cross-industry certifications may apply to the system. For example, if your device uses wireless connectivity that uses licensed radio spectrum it must be certified by the Federal Communications Commission for sale in the United States. Your company may not have RF expertise; in this case we recommend using pre-certified wireless modules since your system must still be certified but it takes less time. It is important to be aware of such certification considerations early in the design of your embedded system, and you should plan for the certification timeline in your product release schedule.

There are many safety and security standards that may be applicable to the industry you work in, such as multilevel secure (MLS), Safety Integrity Level (SIL), and Federal Information Processing Standards Publications (FIPs). Many of these standards influence every detail of the embedded system you are developing and the processes you use to develop it. A brief mention of such considerations is provided here, but these topics are outside the scope of this book.

Reliability/Availability

Many embedded systems must remain running for significant amounts of time without any intervention (often years). In such cases small bugs that may not be apparent in desktop type applications can become debilitating over time. A simple small memory leak (failure to free previously allocated memory once it is no longer needed) may not affect the operation of a program that is executed once a day, but could consume all available heap memory over time in an embedded system. It is important to validate and test your system by running your system for several days and reviewing such resources. It's not a good idea to assume your system will be restarted regularly.

In many cases you must provide a handler to catch fatal errors (such as no more memory) and trigger a system restart; this is a failsafe option but does result in a loss of system availability during restart.

Additionally, it's good to partition the system so that subsystems can be restarted without having to restart the entire system. For example, if a Linux system is providing packet routing in the kernel but an application has become unresponsive, a better strategy is to restart the application and not the entire system. Features such as control groups (cgroups) in Linux provide an excellent mechanism to improve the robustness of systems that must have high availability (not just embedded systems).

There are also features such as error-correcting-code (ECC) memory, which automatically corrects single bit errors and detects multiple bit errors in memory.

User Interfaces

There is tremendous variability in the user interface requirements of embedded systems. There are two general classes of embedded devices, *headed* (those providing a display) and *headless* (those without a display).

For headless devices, the system must still be managed or controlled by a user, and the device usually provides a command console or simple web interface to the device, as shown in Figure 2.6.

However, many devices are now headed devices with display capabilities. There are many display types, from a simple two-line monochrome LCD screen to an HD 1920 × 1080 pixel widescreen

FIGURE 2.6

Web Interface for DD WRT Router Firmware (http://www.dd-wrt.com).

FIGURE 2.7

Meego IVI Example Home Screen User Interface.

Source: https://meego.com/devices/in-vehicle/ivi-screenshots

display. When users directly interact with the display-based embedded device there are increasingly higher expectations placed on the user experience, in term of ease of use, high quality graphics, and touch screen controls.

Chapter 10 provides detail on embedded graphics and multimedia acceleration. Figure 2.7 shows a rich user interface for an embedded automotive head unit based on Meego.

Connectivity

A dramatic increase in the level of connectivity for all embedded devices is expected. There are many industry reports that claim that there will be about 15 billion Internet-attached devices by 2015 (http://www.bbc.co.uk/news/technology-13613536). Many of these will be embedded devices. The embedded platforms must support the latest IP stacks in particular. Finally, a transition to IPv6 is likely.

From a physical connectivity view, many wired and wireless interfaces are used. Ethernet is the ubiquitous wired interface available on many platforms. For wireless interfaces, 802.11 and Wi-Fi[†] are the most prevalent. Other wireless technologies such as Bluetooth[†] and those based on IEEE 802.15.4 such as Zigbee[†] are provided, depending on the application.

Wide area wireless technologies such as those based on 3G/4G cellular technologies are also an important growing area of connectivity for remote managing of devices for which mobility is important, such as vehicle fleet management, but not exclusively for such cases—they are also employed, for example, in vending machines or ATMs.

Security

The security of embedded systems is becoming an increasingly critical aspect. Security covers a very broad range of topics. In many embedded cases today, there is no attention paid to security aspects, which leaves systems vulnerable to compromise and attack. The security of embedded systems used in key infrastructure elements within countries is becoming a particular focus of governments (http:// www.truststc.org/scada/).

You many think this does nót apply to your system, but there are many examples of compromised embedded systems. In one such case the DNS settings on wireless routers were updated (by a Windows-based worm) (http://voices.washingtonpost.com/securityfix/2008/06/malware_silently_ alters_wirele_1.html). There is also a much more sophisticated and widely published case known as Stuxnet, which is perhaps the first known malware that was designed to propagate and then target a specific Supervisory Control and Data Acquisition system (SCADA). The malware propagated through systems and only activated itself when it identified a particular SCADA configuration. The malware then altered the control functions in the programmable logic controller (PLC) to physically destroy the equipment. This is the earliest (at this time) known case of a malware causing a cyber-physical attack.

No matter how secure you believe your platform is, you should assume that you have released a platform with vulnerabilities. Embedded systems are often deployed and never updated, even if vulnerabilities are later detected. It is critical that embedded devices have an active life cycle, where security-related updates are pushed to the devices just as they are in the desktop environment. Even if you believe your software to be without vulnerabilities, it is rare that you have written all the code. For example, you can track Linux security vulnerabilities at http://cve.mitre.org. The http://www .linuxsecurty.com web site also has many tips on avoiding common bugs that can lead to serious vulnerabilities.

There is also considerable industry effort in developing white list–based systems to lock down the activity of the embedded system. This will reduce the likelihood of malware being able to attach to the device, but can put a validation burden on the development of system.

In addition to the security of the platform and designing software to reduce the number of vulnerabilities, there is also a class of content security known as Digital Rights Management (DRM), which is required on devices that present media that has specific licensing constraints (such as Blu-ray movies) or streaming media content such as that provided by Netflix. In Chapter 15 we provide some insights into this topic.

SUMMARY

This chapter has provided insight into the overall landscape and characteristics of embedded systems. The remainder of the book will delve into detail on many different aspects of such embedded devices. We believe that, overall, embedded devices are becoming more sophisticated, and connectivity (local and Internet) is an increasingly important attribute of the system. Where specific examples are needed we will use the Intel Atom platform to illustrate our point. However, in most cases the points being made are applicable to a more general embedded context.

The Future of Embedded Systems

3

The preceding chapters have rightly focused on embedded systems as they exist today. However, as with all areas of science and technology, engineers must be looking to the future in order to increase the odds that their products and technologies will be designed and implemented with durable value. We now look forward, to explore the trends and expectations that are likely to shape embedded systems in the near future.

To do so, we will consider the following three topics:

- *Technology trends.* What resources will be available?
- *Issues, applications, and initiatives.* What issues and societal transformations are likely to receive sustained attention and investment?
- *Challenges and uncertainties.* What nontechnical issues are likely to have a substantial impact on the future of embedded systems?

Our ambition here is not to predict the future. Rather, our aim is to articulate and understand the issues that we expect will influence the design and deployment of future embedded systems.

Since it is impossible to predict the future in any reliable way, the best we can do is prepare ourselves for the full range of situations that we can foresee. We may not be able to precisely describe what the future will bring, but we can make plans that will increase our odds of success based on our best understanding of what future scenarios are likely.

TECHNOLOGY TRENDS

At any point in time—today, for instance—the capabilities of embedded systems are determined by the available technology. By looking backward from a given point and considering how technology has evolved to lead to it, we can establish trends. Such trends can be the basis for forecasts of what the future might bring.

Of course, technology forecasting is a difficult business. Many have earned regrettable reputations as a result of popularized forecasts that end up being dramatically wrong. Easily the most famous such forecast is attributed to Thomas J. Watson, the iconoclastic president of IBM, who in 1943 was quoted as saying, "I think there is a world market for maybe five computers."

This sounds ridiculous to us today, when each of us brings on the order of five computers with us when we travel, but it would not have been out of place in the 1940s. Interestingly, despite the popularity of this quote, it seems that Watson never said it. Evidently, technology-related trends can be difficult, even when you do not make them! Doubly surprising, as noted by Gordon Bell in his 1997

23

keynote address at the annual Association for Computing Machinery. conference, is that even if Watson had said this, he would have been right for the next 10 years!

We recommend basing predictions on measureable trends. Doing so at least provides a rationale for predictions, and one that can be revisited through time. We will now consider a few technical directions and their evident trends.

Computation

We begin with the most critical component of technology, computation. The foundation of the digital revolution is due to the remarkably reliable progress made by the semiconductor manufacturing industry, which has in turn enabled the development of all of the digital chips, including CPUs, memory, and systems-on-a-chip that form the core of electronics.

In 1965, Gordon Moore wrote an article predicting that the natural economics of integrated circuit manufacture would lead to an annual doubling of transistor densities. The paper is notable for both its charmingly unassuming title—"Cramming more components onto integrated circuits"—and its readability. It is under four pages in length and easy to read. The following quote from the article is the genesis of what is known today as Moore's Law.

> *The complexity for minimum component costs has increased at a rate of roughly a factor of two per year. Certainly over the short term this rate can be expected to continue, if not to increase. Over the longer term, the rate of increase is a bit more uncertain, although there is no reason to believe it will not remain nearly constant for at least 10 years. That means by 1975, the number of components per integrated circuit for minimum cost will be 65,000.*

> *I believe that such a large circuit can be built on a single wafer.*

In this article, Moore anticipated an annual doubling of transistor density in integrated circuits. Ten years later, Moore revisited this topic publicly and offered a revised prediction of a doubling every two years from 1975 on.

So how accurate has Moore's Law been? Figure 3.1 plots one perspective, by showing transistor counts for chips in their year of release.

The results are impressive. The solid line tracks a doubling of transistor density every two years, and, as can be seen, the individually plotted chips support the availability of transistor densities as predicted by Moore's Law.

Moore's Law has been reliable for two reasons. First, Moore was right! But secondly, and much more importantly, it has been a sort of self-fulfilling prophecy. Moore's prediction was taken up by the semiconductor manufacturing industry as a goal to be achieved. The industry set it as a benchmark of achievement, and it has driven capital investments and design specifications. At the 2007 Intel Developer's Forum, Moore was quoted as confirming the reliability of Moore's Law for a further 10 to 15 years. Beyond that, either CMOS chips will get bigger or alternatives to CMOS semiconductors will become mainstream.

For embedded systems, the health of Moore's Law implies that at a fixed cost (that is, a fixed chip size), the logic and memory resources available for general purpose computing, hardware-specialized processing, and on-chip memory will continue to double every two years. And viewed from another perspective, the cost of a fixed design (that is, a fixed chip design) will halve every two years.

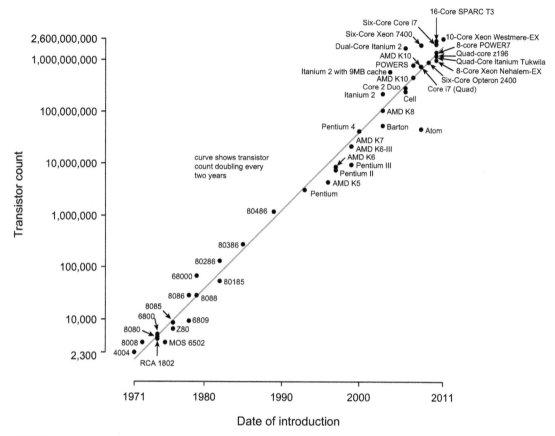

FIGURE 3.1

Trend for Moore's Law.

Connectivity

As we have discussed, connectivity has become a defining requirement of modern embedded systems, and digital systems more broadly. As such, we have every expectation that digital connectivity will continue to grow.

Unlike the case of computation and the reliable progress of Moore's Law, we have no industry-wide trend to guide or predict technical progress. However, we can explore an annual report published by Cisco systems, called the Visual Network Index, or VNI, which aggregates a staggering amount of global market research describing the adoption of various forms of digital communication into a single report and searchable database. Each year, a new report and configurable database can be found at the URL http://www.ciscovni.com.

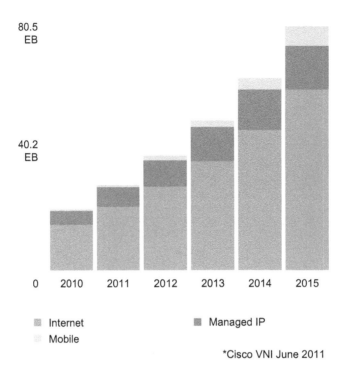

FIGURE 3.2

Current and Projected Global Data Bandwidth.

Figure 3.2 illustrates the projection for global data bandwidth growth from 2010 through 2015. As can be seen, Cisco projects that bandwidth will grow by a factor of 4 by 2015, relative to the 2010 figure. And while mobile data bandwidth is the smallest category, it is predicted to experience the greatest percentage growth, from under 250 petabytes (PB) in 2010 to more than 6200 PB in 2015.

While it should be noted that Cisco has a vested interest in the growth of network bandwidth (since it sells networking gear), it is unreasonable to think that the VNI has any market-moving ability. Thus, in our view, it is reasonable to consider Cisco's VNI to be a reasonable forecast.

To get a sense of how the VNI can be used for more focused investigations, consider Figure 3.3, which illustrates the projected growth in wireless bandwidth according to application.

This figure reveals the core of the VNI prediction: an annual doubling in the video traffic carried across wireless networks. As it happens, this assumption of rising video traffic is the basis for most predictions of traffic growth, regardless of network type. In years past, file sharing has been the dominant application in Internet traffic, but the gap narrowed to a rounding error in 2010 as video caught up. The VNI predicts that video will have easily eclipsed file sharing beginning in 2011.

Of course, bandwidth is just one measure of the growth of connectivity. Another is the number of connected devices. Once again, Cisco has a prediction to offer. At the 2010 Cellular Telecommunications Industry Association (CTIA) meeting, Cisco CTO Padmasree Warrior said:

... By 2013, the number of devices connected to the Internet will reach 1 trillion—up from 500 million in 2007. We're heading into the Internet of Things.

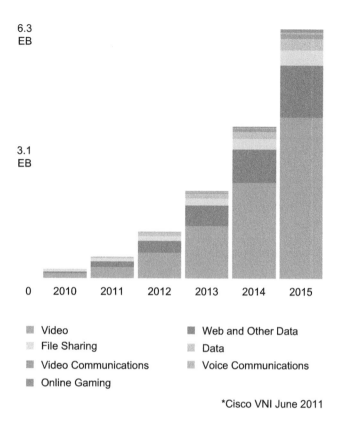

6.3
EB

3.1
EB

| 0 | 2010 | 2011 | 2012 | 2013 | 2014 | 2015 |

- Video
- File Sharing
- Video Communications
- Online Gaming
- Web and Other Data
- Data
- Voice Communications

*Cisco VNI June 2011

FIGURE 3.3

Current and Projected Global Wireless Data Bandwidth, by Application.

It is reasonable to ask how such numbers are generated. While each prediction has its own unique basis (which, like Warrior's, are not always explained), you can only realistically get to a number as big as a trillion by adding up nearly all categories of consumer electronics, industrial systems, and computer systems.

Cost trends for connectivity are even more difficult to discern in an unambiguous way. Annually, the Organization for Economic Cooperation and Development (OECD) Directorate for Science, Technology and Industry releases a global survey of broadband penetration and price. By considering one slice of the survey data from 2010, we can get a glimpse of global broadband costs and the variation between nations.

As Figure 3.4 shows, most nations have average monthly broadband subscription costs in the range of 20 to 50 U.S. dollars (USD). The true costs at any point in time are heavily influenced by currency fluctuations and government subsidy, both of which can vary dramatically from country to country and over both short and long timescales.

To the extent that anecdotal experience in North America can be considered a reliable guide, these Internet access prices are about right, and have been fairly stable over the years as the access bandwidth provided at that rate has increased. Nevertheless, compared to technology trends, no one should expect that price/performance of Internet connectivity will change as dramatically.

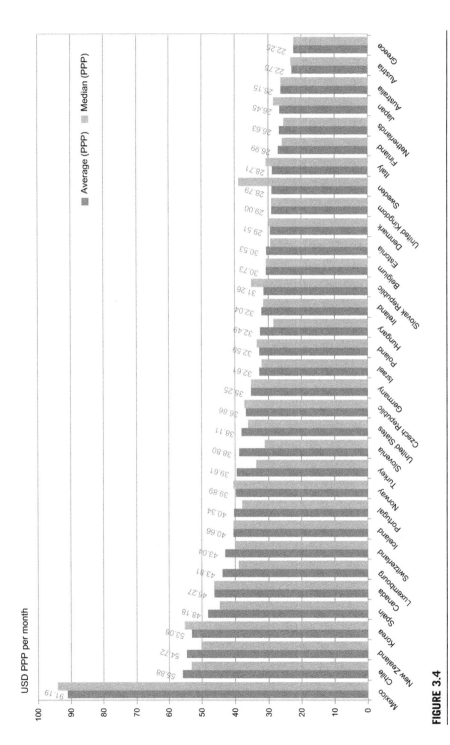

FIGURE 3.4

Average Monthly Subscription Prices for Connections between 2.5 and 15 Mbps, from September 2010.

Source: http://www.oecd.org/dataoecd/22/46/3957020.xls.

Storage

For individual consumers of computer technology, no price/capacity trend is more obvious and apparent than the cost of hard disk drives. As of early 2011, 1-TB hard disk drives were commonly available for under USD 100.

Magnetic hard disk drives have always been the dominant form of nonvolatile memory for personal computers. Their cost per unit of storage has approximately halved every 15 months since the 1980s. This dramatic and sustained improvement of price/capacity has greatly abetted the digitization of modern life.

Despite this impressive trend, the development of alternative forms of nonvolatile memory technologies is ongoing. The reason for this is their mechanical nature. Hard disk drives have motors and physical parts that move, so these aspects of their construction operate in timescales orders of magnitude slower than their electronic counterparts.

In recent years, nonvolatile memories based on flash memory, which are based on CMOS technology and hence have no moving parts, have emerged as the dominant form of storage for consumer electronics such as cameras, mobile phones, and tablets. With capacities of up to tens of gigabytes, these devices are a competitive solution. As indicated in Figure 3.5, however, their price per gigabyte is still one or two orders of magnitude greater than magnetic disk drives.

This suggests that while flash-based solid state disk drives may find niche uses, they are unlikely to displace magnetic disk drives as the standard nonvolatile storage for computer systems. However, for embedded computer systems whose physical form factors are smaller or more rugged than a standard laptop computer and are therefore less suitable for magnetic disks, one can expect that flash-based devices will continue to provide sufficient capacity.

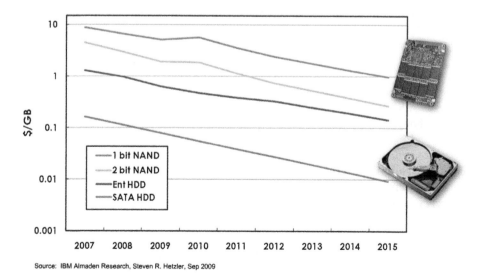

Source: IBM Almaden Research, Steven R. Hetzler, Sep 2009

FIGURE 3.5

Price Trends for Nonvolatile Storage Technologies.

Sensing

Over the past decade, mobile phones have evolved substantially and are viewed by many to be general purpose computers of limited capacity that fit in a pocket. From most perspectives, the mobile phone is a restricted incarnation of a computer: smaller screen, less capable processor, less storage, and so on. In one aspect, however, mobile phones are dramatically superior: The mobile phone platform has emerged as the most capable sensing device ever to ship in substantial volumes. Smart phones today ship with several types of sensors.

*   *Digital cameras.* One or more digital cameras for still and video photography are standard issue. Increasingly, recent model phones are capable of recording HD video.
*   *Microphones.* Handsets include both handset microphones and ambient microphones for hands-free operation and environmental recording.
*   *Accelerometers.* To detect orientation and to enable another input modality, handsets and many other forms of handheld electronics, such as game systems and controllers, include one or more accelerometers.

It is widely expected that future handsets may include additional environmental sensors, such as those that enable temperature, humidity, and air quality monitoring. Additionally, GPS radios, while not exactly sensors, provide a location sensing service, which in combination with environmental sensing has the potential to enable unique and widespread opt-in monitoring of environmental conditions.

ISSUES, APPLICATIONS, AND INITIATIVES

It is clear that the march of Moore's Law will continue to enable the development of new systems and technologies with improved capability and efficiency. Computational resources, connectivity, storage, and sensing capabilities will continue to advance and experience improved price/performance.

Indeed, even today, technological resources seem plentiful. In retrospect, it is easy to see that exponential growth in the computational resources available at a fixed price can easily outpace demand for those resources.

Given that technological resources will continue to be plentiful, how might societal trends and grand challenges evolve to put them to use? By taking a step back and considering this perspective, we can explore just how important future embedded systems will be if the world is to meet its important challenges.

What are those challenges? While a comprehensive list of societal challenges would perhaps be entertaining to read and discuss, we instead focus on the ones for which there is a broad consensus of importance and a seemingly inevitable need for substantial innovation and change. We will consider just three: energy, security, and health.

Energy

There are many interesting aspects to the world's energy challenge, but the most significant is due to supply and demand. There is a growing global demand for energy resources, and if the world per capita average of energy consumption rises to anywhere near the levels in the United States, it is not clear whether an effective supply is available.

Table 3.1 Global Energy Consumption in Regions of the World, 2008		
Region	**kWh/capita**	**Population (M)**
USA	87,216	305
Europe	40,821	499
Middle East	34,774	199
China	18,608	1,333
Latin America	14,421	462
Africa	7,792	984
India	6,280	1,140
Average	21,283	6,688

To see why this is the case, we can consider statistics gathered by the International Energy Agency. First, consider the per-capita energy consumption in the regions of the world from 2008, which is the latest year's data published in IEA's 2010 report, shown in Table 3.1.

Per-capita energy consumption in the United States is just over four times the world average. Since the U.S. population is around 4.5% of global population, if the world average per-capita energy consumption were to rise to roughly that of Europe, which is about half that of the United States, then global energy generation would need to increase by 114 terawatt hours (TWh). In 2008, global energy production was estimated to total 144 TWh. In other words, global energy output would need to nearly double.

Is that in any way feasible? To consider the question, we can examine energy sources. Perhaps a resolute focus on renewable energy sources will fit the bill.

Alas, as of 2008, over 80% of global energy production was due to nonrenewable fossil fuels, as can be seen in Table 3.2. Hydroelectric and other environmentally sustainable renewable sources, such as geothermal, solar, and wind, accounted for just 3% of global energy supply in 2008. Given the current and projected rates of energy production, we cannot expect to see anything like a doubling of supply in the foreseeable future.

Table 3.2 Global Energy by Power Source, 2008		
Source	**TWh**	**%**
Oil	47,704	33.2
Coal	38,872	27.0
Gas	30,384	21.1
Nuclear	8,283	5.8
Hydro	3,208	2.2
Combustible renewables	14,409	10.0
Others	991	0.7
Total	143,851	100.0

If the available supply of energy is in question, the only substantive recourse is to lower demand. And, since demand has historically tracked economic development, efficiency must be the goal. (One way to dramatically reduce energy consumption would be to dramatically cripple civilization.) The largest and fastest growing economies must accelerate the efficiency of their energy consumption; they must do more with less.

In this direction, embedded systems will surely play a substantive role. From smart grid technologies that improve the efficiency of energy distribution to smart appliances and building climate control systems that adapt operations to both user-driven need and the cost of energy to the interactive interfaces that close the energy consumption loop for users to help guide informed consumption, the rise of embedded systems will be a primary enabler of future energy efficiency initiatives.

Security

The rise of Internet-connected embedded systems, and Internet communications in general, comes with a substantial irony. While these technology developments have transformed much of modern life in industrialized countries, they have also introduced substantial new risks.

These Internet-related security risks derive from two important characteristics of information. First, it can be quite valuable. Second, it is inexpensive to duplicate, store, and transfer.

One consequence of the Information Age is that many of the world's most valuable assets are pure information. In bygone days, nearly all valuable assets had physical manifestations. Today, for example, your bank account and the financial assets of your employer exist merely as bits of information, susceptible to digital manipulation. In modern manufacturing, the design of products is typically of greater value than the physical materials used in construction; this can be seen in the decoupling of manufacturing resources from the companies that design and sell products. The latter is a much more lucrative undertaking and the former has become commoditized. Hollywood films require massive development and marketing investments, but once they are created and digitized, they are simply information.

And since these valuable assets are just information, they can be manipulated digitally. With the advent of the Internet, access to remote data and machines has very little cost, and the incentives for criminal activity can be very high. Whether they be criminals or nation-states, those who desire unauthorized access to digital assets often have a much easier time than those who seek physical assets. Consider that real-world criminals must physically visit 100 homes to attempt 100 home burglaries; on the Internet, however, cybercriminals can attempt to burgle hundreds of remote networks without leaving the comfort of their own couch.

So, while the Internet and its constituent embedded systems have brought great transformations to modern life, they have also brought new risks. These risks increasingly drive the design requirements of new products and systems, and, in fact, whole categories of security-focused embedded systems have arisen as a result.

While it may appear circular, and it may indeed be circular, one of the greatest challenges confronting our digital infrastructure is the risk that the infrastructure poses to itself via misuse. Ensuring the security and reliability of information infrastructure is a major societal challenge, and one that will substantially influence the design and application of future embedded systems.

Health

In a rational world, all forms of technological development would have as their ultimate purpose to improve quality of life. While we cannot say one way or another whether we live in a rational world, we can say with great confidence that health and wellness are supremely important contributors to quality of life.

Embedded systems today find application in many areas of health and wellness, and more are surely on the way. One of the more interesting and high-impact examples of embedded technologies improving health and quality of life can be seen in therapeutic technologies, such as those used in treating type 1 diabetes.

Type 1 diabetes, also known as juvenile diabetes, is an autoimmune disease that destroys the body's ability to produce insulin. (Type 2 diabetes, which is caused by lifestyle conditions rather than autoimmune deficiency, is a superficially related condition in which poor diet blunts the effectiveness of insulin.) Insulin is the hormone that regulates the metabolism of blood sugar; insulin enables carbohydrates and fats to be transferred into muscle and liver tissue for use and is also central to vascular health and cognition. In a healthy child, the body automatically produces the right amount of insulin needed to support the amount of food eaten or the amount of physical activity at any point in time. In a diabetic person, insulin must be delivered externally, via a subcutaneous injection, in an amount judged to be proportional to food intake, physical activity, and current blood sugar densities. In practical terms, diabetics must measure their blood sugar density, count carbohydrates, and administer insulin every time they eat.

Type 1 diabetes is a comparatively common disease, inflicting about 1 in 400 children and adolescents. Since there is no cure, those diagnosed undergo a lifelong course of therapy consisting of measuring blood sugars, typically via "finger poke," and delivering via syringe injection appropriate amounts of insulin.

Embedded systems have already had a major impact on easing the burdens of type 1 diabetes therapies. As one example, consider the OmniPod from Insulet Corporation, shown in Figure 3.6. The OmniPod completely replaces the use of syringes for insulin delivery.

The OmniPod consists of two devices. The Personal Diabetes Manager, or PDM, is a PDA-like device that is used to control both the automatic and manual delivery of insulin. The PDM also has an integrated blood glucose monitor. The second device is an insulin pump that is worn on the body. The pump is worn for up to three days at a time, after which it is replaced with a new one, and consists of a spring-loaded cannula that is inserted subcutaneously when attached to the body, an insulin reservoir, a motor and pump for pushing insulin doses from the reservoir through the cannula into the skin, and an onboard controller and radio.

The PDM and pump communicate wirelessly. The PDM is typically programmed to provide a background dose of insulin and is used manually to administer insulin doses whenever food is eaten.

Particularly for children, the transition away from four or more syringe injections daily to the wearing of the digital OmniPod is an exciting and time-saving one. In addition to reducing the complexity and burden of insulin therapy, some evidence suggests that children using pumps like this have a higher-quality diabetes management result overall.

Juvenile diabetes is but one example of a medical condition that is ameliorated by emerging embedded systems. Other examples include hearing aids, cochlear implants, pacemakers, and digital

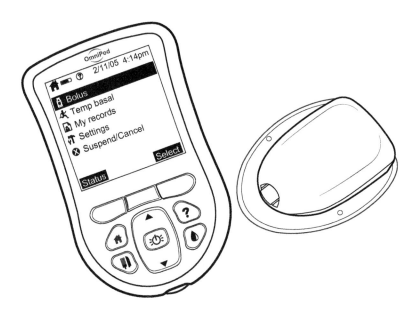

FIGURE 3.6

Insulet Corporation's OmniPod Diabetes Therapy System.

prosthetic limbs. You can be sure that the future will bring a dramatic increase in the number of medical devices and therapies built with embedded systems.

CHALLENGES AND UNCERTAINTIES

With respect to technology and societal trends, the overall outlook for embedded systems is very bright. However, there are substantial challenges and uncertainties that may play equally significant roles in shaping the future of embedded systems. We consider a few of these below.

Open Systems, Internet Access, and Neutrality

The personal computer and Internet revolutions share an important bond of openness. The advent of the personal computer was a startling example of what happens when large numbers of people are given access to a technology and are then encouraged to tinker and enhance it. There was a time not that long ago when nearly all computer users were computer programmers. This created a sense that computer users were invited, if not required, to develop new software for their machines.

Quite naturally, over time, as PC adoption grew, nonprogrammer users came to dwarf the numbers of programmers, even as the absolute number of programmers worldwide increased.

Today, some fear that the rise of Internet devices, such as phones, tablets, and video game systems, is having the unintended consequence of narrowing the pipeline of the future of computer programmers and innovators. The reasoning goes something like this. Twenty years ago, most children and new users of computers got their start by using general purpose personal computers on which it was comparatively easy to learn a little something about programming. These days, video game systems and mobile phones have all the new user appeal, but have no ability to introduce new users to programming. Hence, we can expect fewer numbers of programmers in the future.

There does not appear to be any evidence to support this line of reasoning, but it is a credible concern. Moreover, many new classes of computer systems, including most embedded systems, offer no opportunities at all for user-driven programming. In many ways, this development is positive because, for example, such systems are often simpler and more intuitive for end users.

On the other hand, if the future of software innovation does rely on large numbers of tinkering programmers, then growth among the young in device usage at the expense of growth in computer usage may be a warning sign.

In a related way, the dramatic growth of the Internet and the innovation ecosystem it supports is due in large part to its openness and the ease with which large numbers of people can create new things.

Inherent to the Internet is the ability of any machine with an IP address to communicate to any other machine with an IP address. This fact makes it possible for services and sites that did not exist yesterday to become popular today, because no permission is needed, just popularity.

As the commercial success of the Internet and its services has grown, so too has the range of opinions on what openness really means. In recent years, much has been said about the so-called net neutrality issue. The simplest statement of net neutrality is that all packets are created equal and should be treated as such. In particular, net neutrality advocates do not want Internet service providers to have the right to unilaterally apply classes of service to subscriber traffic. For example, an ISP may wish to prioritize latency-sensitive traffic such as your interactive voice-over-IP traffic over latency-insensitive traffic such as file downloads on your network link. Doing so would violate net neutrality according to most advocates.

Why is this an issue? While this example may sound harmless to most, many net neutrality advocates see such traffic manipulation as a means by which ISPs can charge remote service providers, such as streaming video providers, for use of ISP resources. Right now your ISP charges you for service, and many net neutrality supporters think that your ISP would like to charge certain types of bandwidth-intensive service providers for the right to reach you.

There are many perspectives, and each has at least some merit. While it is beyond our scope to settle the debate once and for all here, we can see that the issue has the potential to disrupt the tradition of innovation that the Internet has enjoyed to date.

Privacy

In the near future, when most forms of consumer electronics are Internet-connected and we are surrounded by an environment filled with visible and invisible devices with cameras and microphones, what will happen to individual privacy?

Already, much of what we consider to be the sum of human knowledge is available at our fingertips via our Internet-connected devices. How many more iterations of Moore's Law are required before the same thing is true of our dynamic personal information, our location, appearance, and activities?

It is a cultural issue, to be sure, and one that is to be decided by people in the context of their societies. However, there is every possibility that both within societies (and across generation gaps, young versus old, for instance) and between societies, privacy norms will begin to differ, which may in turn lead to legal and regulatory restrictions on technology to either encourage or discourage aspects of personal privacy.

For instance, imagine the effect on the development of embedded systems if some form of prohibition were enacted governing digital cameras or social networking services.

It is impossible to say how likely such developments are, but we can see that the potential exists for legal interventions to alter the capabilities and features of future systems.

Successful Commercialization

All technological progress hinges on successful commercial activity. At the macro scale, new technologies are ultimately funded via the displacement of the existing technologies that they render obsolete.

For example, one reason the world could begin to afford automobiles was that it stopped spending so much money on horses and carriages. Likewise, the demise of minicomputers and workstations funded the rapid growth of personal computers and their technology components. In the Internet, Google and other advertising-based services have been funded by siphoning off money that would otherwise have been spent on traditional forms of advertising.

While this fact seems fundamental to economic and technological development, there is a wrinkle that we feel is worth considering. The desirable economics of digital systems is based on the advance of Moore's Law, which is in turn based on growing volumes of ever larger semiconductor devices. With each new semiconductor generation, new fabrication facilities, or *fabs,* must be created, and these fabs have staggering investment requirements that easily reach into the billions of U.S. dollars today. There is a sort of virtuous pipeline that is formed in that the previous generation's cutting-edge fabrication facilities can be repurposed and used to manufacture the second most important class of products. For example, last year's leading server CPU fab can be next year's embedded processor fab. In this way, the original fab investment can be amortized over several years and classes of technology. However, enormous investments in new fabs can only be justified based on growing volumes.

And what would happen if something happened to volumes? What if, one day, the world needed fewer square feet of next-generation silicon than it needed in the preceding year? We can't say what might trigger such a development, but if anything were to threaten the front end of the technology pipeline, then big changes would emerge throughout.

In fact, this is what happens when high-growth industries become stable. Automobile engines, for example, are rarely designed to include more than 8 or 12 cylinders. Engine advancements come from efficiency gains rather than capability gains. Should the computer industry ever make such a transition, the likely effects on the broader ecosystem would be profound.

SUMMARY

In this chapter, we have taken a step back and considered some factors that are likely to influence the future of embedded systems. By discussing technology trends, societal challenges, and threats and uncertainties, we have sought not to make specific forecasts, but to consider trends and issues that are likely to remain important and influential over many years.

And while many of the specific facts and figures reported here have a limited shelf life, their sources are typically refreshed annually. So even if you are reading this chapter several years after its original publication, odds are you can revisit the sources identified here and compare the 2010/2011 forecasts with the present ones.

Embedded Systems Architecture and Operation

Embedded Platform Architecture

What makes an embedded platform? In this chapter we describe the constituent components that make up an embedded platform, providing details of each component and its role in the provision of an overall target solution. From the point of view of the system programmer, the focus is on the system details that are important to the embedded programmer specifically, so that the programmer can subsequently be in a position to work with a system designer in making trade-offs.

As a software developer working on embedded systems, it is very likely that you have at least a high level of familiarity with the platform, and often a very high level of detail down to the schematic level, particularly if you are developing the driver software for the target device.

Once you understand how blocks within the embedded platform are physically connected, you need to understand the view of those same components from the software/processor viewpoint. The key to understanding how the software interacts with the underlying platform devices is the system memory map and the associated register maps of the devices. Some devices are directly visible to software and mapped to physical addresses in the processor's address space, and other devices are attached over a bus, which introduces a level of indirection when we wish to access the device registers.

In this chapter we describe the building blocks of an embedded system.

PLATFORM OVERVIEW

Embedded platforms cover an enormous range of devices, from the residential broadband wireless router in your home to the sophisticated navigation and multimedia system in your car and the industrial control system controlling the robot that built the car. The capabilities have a broad range of interfaces and performance requirements. In the development of an embedded system you will most likely be selecting between system-on-chip devices that incorporate as many of the key peripherals your application needs. In this section we focus on the key devices required to support the operating system.

Figure 4.1 gives an overview of some of the platforms discussed in the chapter.

Processor

Embedded systems have at least one processor. The processor is the primary execution environment for the application. The processor usually runs an operating system, and the operating system hosts the applications required to run on the platform.

In modern systems, an embedded SOC sometimes contains additional processing elements that are designed for a more specific function in support of the application. Consider a modern smartphone; the

41

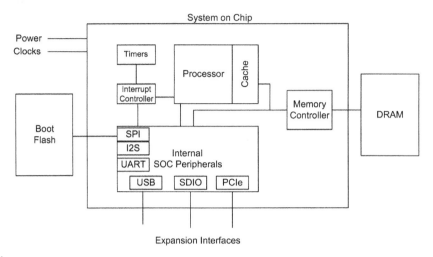

FIGURE 4.1

SOC System Overview.

application processor is the processor that runs the software visible to the user, the user interface, or one of the many thousandths of applications such as web browser, or angry birds, mapping applications and the like. There is often another processor running the wireless stack; this is sometimes known as the *baseband processor*. On other platforms specific processors may process audio and camera images. The software running on these adjunct processors is often called firmware. The software execution environment for this firmware is usually specific to the target function; often they do not run an operating system. As the application power/performance efficiency and the ability to partition the application processor to run multiple execution environments (with robust quality of service) continues to improve, the trend will be to consolidate these workloads on the central processing unit.

The processor is clearly at the center of the platform. The processor in modern systems is typically 32 bit, which means that all the registers within the processor are a maximum of 32 bits wide. That includes data and address registers. Low performance embedded systems often use 16-bit micro-controllers, but the increased workload and connectivity required by such systems are driving a migration to 32-bit processors. Similarly, when high performance or large amounts of memory are required, 64-bit systems are gaining in the market.

The instruction set of the processor may be classified as either Complex Instructing Set Computing (CISC) or Reduced Instruction Set Computing (RISC). The Intel® architecture processors are all CISC-based Instruction Set Architecture (ISA), where the ARM, MIPS, and PowerPC are all considered to be RISC architecture. A CISC instruction set usually contains variable length instruc-tions that allow for more compact encoding of the instruction. RISC, on the other hand, usually has fixed size instructions (for example, all instructions are 4 bytes long on PowerPC architecture). Some architecture, such as ARM, has introduced processors that support a subset of the original instruction set, which is recoded to improve the code density. At this point in time, from the programmer's perspective, the distinction is less meaningful. A primary consideration is the performance achieved by the implementation.

Another aspect of the processor is whether it is scalar or superscalar. These are attributes of the microarchitecture of the processor. A superscalar-based processor supports the parallel execution of instructions by having multiple copies of key functional units within the CPU. For example, the Intel Atom™ microarchitecture contains two arithmetic logic units. The replication of key features allows the processor to sustain execution of more than one instruction per clock cycle depending on the applications and cache hit rate. The trend in embedded processors has been toward superscalar implementations, where historically many implementations were scalar.

The processor itself needs support hardware for it to perform any useful work. The key capabilities required to support the execution of a multitasking operating system on the processor are as follows:

- A memory subsystem for initial instruction storage and random access memory.
- An interrupt controller to gather, prioritize, and control generation of interrupts to the processor.
- A timer; multitasking operating systems (noncooperative) typically rely on at least one timer interrupt to trigger the operating system scheduler.
- Access to I/O devices, such as graphics controllers, network interfaces, and mouse/keypads.

The processor sits at the center of the platform and interacts with all the other devices on the platform. The locations of the devices are presented through the memory map.

System Memory Map

A key to understanding any embedded system starts with a thorough understanding of the memory map. The memory map is a list of physical addresses of all the resources on the platform, such as the DRAM memory, the interrupt controllers, and I/O devices. The system memory map is generated from the point of view of the processor. It's important to note that there can be different points of view from different agents in the system; in particular, on some embedded devices the memory map is different when viewed from I/O devices or from devices that are attached on an I/O bus, although this is not the case on Intel platforms.

IA-32-based platforms have two distinct address spaces, memory space and input/output space. The memory space is actually the primary address space and it covers the DRAM and most I/O devices. It occupies the entire physical address space of the processor. For example, on a 32-bit system the memory space ranges from 0 to 4 GB, although not all addresses in this range map to a device or memory. Access to memory space is achieved by memory read/write instructions such as MOV. The I/O space is far smaller (only 64 kB) and can only be accessed via IN/OUT instructions. Since accesses to I/O devices through I/O space are relatively time consuming, most cases avoid use of the I/O space except for supporting legacy features (Intel platform architecture features that have been retained through the many generations of processors to ensure software compatibility). Many other embedded processor architectures such as ARM or PowerPC have only a memory address space.

When the processor generates a read or write, the address is decoded by the system memory address decoders and is eventually routed to the appropriate physical device to complete the transaction. This decision logic might match the address to that of the system DRAM controller, which then generates a transaction to the memory devices; the transaction could be routed to a hardware register in an Ethernet network controller on a PCI bus to indicate that a packet is ready for transmission.

The address map within the memory address space on Intel systems (and in fact in most systems) is split into two separate sub ranges. The first is the address range that when decoded accesses the

DRAM, and the second is a range of addresses that are decoded to select I/O devices. The two address ranges are known as the Main Memory Address Range and the Memory Mapped I/O (MMIO) Range. A register in the SOC called TOLM indicates the top of local memory—you can assume that the DRAM is mapped from 1 MB to TOLM. The IA-32 memory map from zero to 1 MB is built from a mix of system memory and MMIO. This portion of the memory map was defined when 1 MB of memory was considered very large and has been retained for platform compatibility. The Memory Mapped I/O Range in which I/O devices can reside is further divided into subregions:

- *Fixed Address Memory Mapped Address.* There are a number of hard coded address ranges. The map is fixed and does not change. The address in this range decodes to the flash device (where BIOS/firmware is stored), timers, interrupt controllers, and some other incidental control functions. This portion of the memory map has evolved very slowly; from Intel platform to Intel platform there is a large amount of consistency.
- *PCIe BUS.* We provide more detail on this later, but there is a range of Memory Mapped I/O Address that will all be directed to the PCI/PCIe bus on the system. The devices that appear on the PCIe bus have configurable address decoders known as Base Address Registers (BARs). The BARs and hence the addresses occupied by the devices on the PCIe bus are provisioned as part of a bus enumeration sequence. On Intel platforms a PCIe bus logical abstraction is also used for internal devices. That means that devices within the SOC are also presented and discovered to the system software in the exact same way an external PCIe device is discovered/decoded, even though the internal devices are not connected to the processor using a real PCIe bus. For example, the graphics controller in the Intel E6xx Series SOCs appears as a PCIe device in the MMIO address space of the processor. The process of discovering and setting up the address decoders on this address range is the same for internal or external devices. There is another range of MMIO addresses, called PCI Express extended configuration register space, that can be used to generate special configuration transactions on the PCI bus so that the devices can be discovered and the BARs provisioned.

Figure 4.2 shows an overview of the system memory map for an Intel architecture platform.

The PCIe bus portion of the memory map above is not fixed. The system software (BIOS/Firmware and/or the operating system) writes to the base address register within the device at system initialization time. By contrast, in many embedded systems, the address map (within the SOC) is static. All devices are assigned an address at the time of SOC design. This does simplify the hardware design, but the system software must now be aware of the static addresses used to access each device. That usually entails building a specific target image for the target SOC. In this model it can be a little more difficult to build a single software image that supports a number of different SOC devices. Having said that, in many cases the embedded systems software is targeted and tuned to a specific device.

Interrupt Controller

The processor requires the ability to interact with its environment through a range of input and output devices. The devices usually require a prompt response from the processor in order to service a real world event. The devices need a mechanism to indicate their need for attention to the processor. Interrupts provide this mechanism and avoid the need for the processor to constantly poll the devices to see if they need attention. Given that we often have multiple sources of interrupt on any given platform,

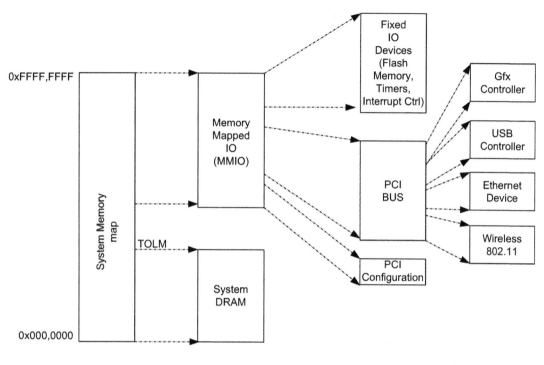

TOLM: Top Of Low Memory

FIGURE 4.2

Memory Map Representation for an Intel Platform.

an interrupt controller is needed. The interrupt controller is a component that gathers all the hardware interrupt events from the SOC and platform and then presents the events to the processor. At its fundamental level, the interrupt controller routes events to the processor core for action. The interrupt controller facilitates the identification of the event that caused the interrupt so that the exception processing mechanism of the processor can transfer control to the appropriate handling function. Figure 4.3 shows the simplest possible form of interrupt controller. It consists of three registers that can be read from or written to from the processor. The registers are composed of bit fields with a single bit allocated for each interrupt source within each register. The first is an interrupt status register. This reflects the current pin status for the incoming interrupt line. It will be set when the interrupt request is active and clear (0) when there is no pending interrupt from the device. The second register is an interrupt mask register. Pending interrupts from the device can be prevented from getting to the processor core through the use of the interrupt mask. If the interrupt bit is set in the interrupt mask register, no interrupts from the source will reach the processor interrupt line. The interrupt status register shows the unmasked state of the interrupt line. Any of the active unmasked interrupts are capable of generating an interrupt to the processor (all signals are logically ORed together).

In this simplistic case, we have a single interrupt line to the processor. When the interrupt line becomes active, the processor saves a portion of the processor's state and transfers control to the vector

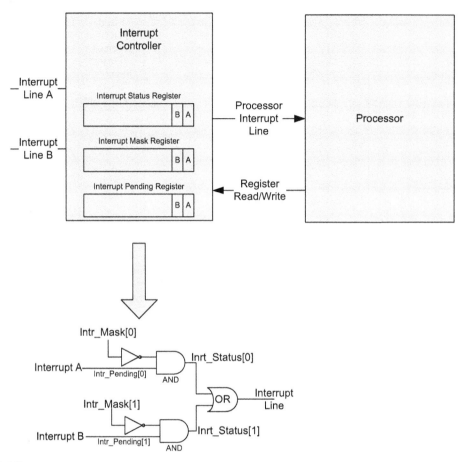

FIGURE 4.3

Basic Interrupt Controller Functions.

for external processor interrupts. This example is quite common in ARM architecture devices. The interrupt handler reads the interrupt status register and reads the active status bits in a defined priority order. A common implementation is to inspect the interrupt status bits from least significant bit to most significant bit, implying that the interrupts routed to the least significant bits are of higher priority in servicing than the other bits. The priority algorithm is under software control in this instance, and you may restructure the order in which interrupt status bits are checked.

The interrupt pending registers often take the form of a latched register. When an unmasked interrupt becomes active, the bit associated with the interrupt in the interrupt pending register becomes set (one). Then even if the interrupt signal is removed, the interrupt pending bit continues to be set. When the interrupt handler comes to service the interrupt, the handler must write a logic one to the bit it wishes to acknowledge (that is, indicate that the interrupt has been serviced). Bits with this behavior within a device register are known as Write One to Clear.

The processing of searching for the highest priority in the system by scanning bits adds to the time required to identify that highest priority interrupt to service. In embedded systems we are typically trying to reduce the overhead in identifying which interrupt we should service. To that end, a hardware block is introduced that takes the unmasked active interrupt sources and generates a number derived from a hardware-based priority scheme. The number reflects the highest-priority interrupt pending. The objective is to use this hardware generated number to quickly execute the appropriate interrupt handler for the interrupting device(s). This interrupt number can be obtained by one of two mechanisms. In the first mechanism, the interrupt software handler reads the register, the register value is used as an index into a software-based vector table containing function pointers, and the interrupt handler looks up the table and calls the function for the incoming vector. This scheme is frequently used in ARM devices where the architecture defines a single interrupt request line into the processor. The second mechanism used is one in which the CPU hardware itself generates an interrupt acknowledge cycle that automatically retrieves the interrupt number when the interrupt has been raised to the processor. This interrupt number is then translated to the interrupt vector that the processor will transfer control to. The interrupt handler is called in both cases; there is a level of software interaction in the first case that is avoided in the second implementation. The process of reading the interrupt vector number from the interrupt controller whether it was done by software or hardware may form part of an implicit interrupt acknowledgment sequence to the interrupt controller. This implicit acknowledgment indicates to the controller that the processor has consumed that particular interrupt; the interrupt controller then re-evaluates the highest priority interrupt and updates the register. In other controller implementations the device source of the interrupt must be first cleared and the highest priority interrupt will automatically update. Figure 4.4 shows the two schemes discussed.

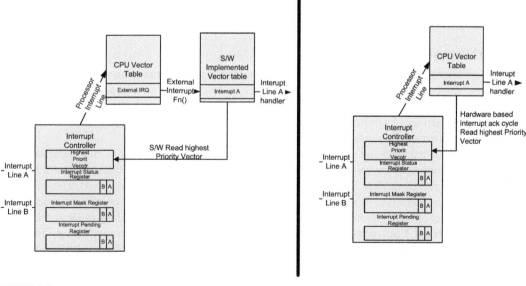

FIGURE 4.4

Interrupt Acknowledgment and Priority Schemes.

The interrupt signal designated in Interrupt A and B in Figure 4.4 may be an interrupt generated by an internal peripheral or an external general-purpose input/output (GPIO) that has interrupt generation capability. The interrupt lines typically may operate in one of the following modes:

- *Level-triggered,* either active high or active low. This refers to the how the logic level of the signal is interpreted. A signal that is high and is configured as active high indicates that the interrupt request is active; conversely, a low signal indicates that there is no interrupt request. The opposite is the case for an active low level triggered interrupt. Level triggered interrupts are often used when multiple devices share the interrupt line. The interrupt outputs from a number of devices can be electrically connected together and any device on the line can assert the interrupt line.
- *Edge-triggered,* rising edge, falling edge, or both. In this case, the transition of the interrupt line indicates that an interrupt request is signaled. When an interrupt line transitions from a logic low to a logic high and is configured as a rising edge, the transition indicates that the device has generated an interrupt. In the falling edge configurations, the opposite transition indicates an interrupt.

As you may imagine, the system (and device drivers) must handle each interrupt type differently. A level-triggered interrupt remains active and pending to the processor until the actual signal level is changed to the inactive state. The device driver handling the level-triggered interrupt may have to perform specific operations to ensure the input signal is brought to the inactive state. Otherwise, the device would constantly generate interrupts to the processor. Edge-triggered interrupts, on the other hand, effectively self-clear the indication to the interrupt controller. In many cases devices have a number of internal events that cause the device to generate an interrupt. For edge-triggered interrupts, the interrupt handler must ensure it processes all interrupt causes from the device associated with the interrupt. Level-based interrupts, on the other hand, automatically re-interrupt the processor if the driver does not clear all of the internal device interrupt sources. Level-triggered interrupts can also be shared using wired-or configuration where any device attached to the line can bring the line interrupt request line active.

Intel Architecture Specifics

The Intel architecture platform has evolved over many years and has maintained backward compatibility for a number of platform features, not just the instruction set architecture. As a result, two different interrupt controllers are available on Intel platforms. The first mechanism is the 8259 Programmable Interrupt Controller, and the second, more modern controller is known as the Advanced Programmable Interrupt Controller (APIC).

The APIC accepts interrupt messages from I/O devices (within the SOC and external PCIe devices). These messages are known as message signal interrupts (MSIs). Message signal interrupts are used by modern PCI devices (both logically on the platform and external devices). The APIC has replaced the use of 8259 PIC in most use cases, but the 8259 PIC still exists on all platforms and is often used by older operating systems. The use of the 8259 PICs is known as legacy mode at this point.

Legacy Interrupt Controller. The 8259 PIC consist of eight interrupt request lines. This was soon found to be insufficient, so the traditional configuration is to have two PIC devices, arranged in a cascaded fashion. This results in support for a total of 15 interrupt request lines. The arrangement is known as master and slave. The master PIC is wired to the processor, and the slave interrupt out signal is wired as an input to one of the master IRQ lines (IRQ2). Figure 4.5 shows cascading 8259 PICs.

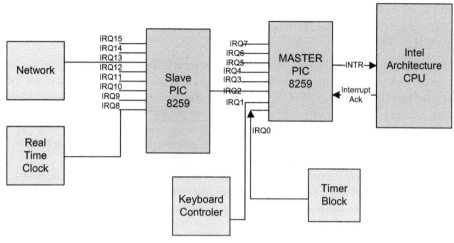

FIGURE 4.5

Cascaded 8259 Interrupt Controllers.

When an interrupt arrives at the PIC (let's use the master for the example), the PIC updates an internal interrupt vector register and raises the interrupt to the processor. The vector register contains the value of the base vector plus the IRQ number. The base vector is a value the software has previously written as part of the interrupt controller initialization. The base line value is usually set to 0x20 to avoid the lower processor interrupts.

When the master PIC raises the interrupt request line to the processor, the processor automatically responds with a query to identify the vector through the use of an interrupt acknowledgment cycle. This is a hardware-generated sequence that prompts the interrupt controller to provide the interrupt vector to the processor. The processor then transfers control to (take) that interrupt vector, saving any required processor state as needed.

The interrupt must also be acknowledged by the software. This is carried out by writing to EOI register in both the master and slave PICs. Each interrupt controller uses two addresses in the I/O space. The I/O addresses to access the PIC(s) are

- Master PIC Command address – 0x0020
- Master PIC Interrupt Mask – 0x0021
- Slave PIC Command address – 0x00A0
- Slave PIC Interrupt Mask 0x00A1

A number of registers are associated with the interrupt processing; they are an example of a specific implementation that is similar to the examples described above in general form.

- *Interrupt Request Register (IRR).* The IRR is used to store all the interrupt levels that are requesting service.
- *Interrupt In-Service (ISR).* The ISR is used to store all the interrupt levels that are being serviced.

- *Interrupt Mask Register (IMR).* The IMR stores the bits that mask the interrupt lines to be masked. The IMR operates on the IRR. Masking of a higher priority input does not affect the interrupt request lines of lower priority.

There is a block that prioritizes the presentation of the interrupts. It determines the priorities of the bits set in the IRR. The highest priority is selected and strobed into the corresponding bit of the ISR during the interrupt acknowledgment cycle (INTA). The vector corresponding to this highest priority interrupt is presented to the processor. The priority encoded has a simple priority (lower number, higher priority) and a rotating priority scheme that can be configured.

The PICs can be disabled by writing 0xFF for the PIC data output address for both PIC devices. The PIC must be disabled in order to use the APIC interrupt model.

The 8259 PIC model has a number of limitations in the number of interrupts it supports and poor support for interrupt control and steering for multicore platforms. The latency of delivery of interrupt is relatively higher than other methods since it takes a number of steps before an interrupt is finally delivered to CPU.

Advanced Programmable Interrupt Controller. The Advanced Programmable Interrupt Controller or APIC was first introduced in the Intel Pentium® processor. The APIC consists of two separate key components. The first is one or more local APICs, and the second is one or more I/O APICs. The local APIC is an integral part of the each processor (for hyper-threaded processors each hardware thread has a local APIC). The local APIC performs two primary functions for the processor:

- It receives interrupts from the processor's interrupt pins, from internal sources, and from an I/O APIC (or other external interrupt controller). It sends these to the processor core for handling.
- In multiple processor (MP) systems, it sends and receives interprocessor interrupt (IPI) messages to and from one or more logical processors on the internal or bus. IPI messages can be used to distribute interrupts among the processors in the system or to execute system-wide functions (such as booting up processors or distributing work among a group of processors).

The I/O APIC is integrated into Intel Atom–based SOC devices such as the Intel Atom Processor E6xx Series. Its primary function is to receive external interrupt events from the system and its associated I/O devices and relay them to the local APIC as interrupt messages. In MP systems, the I/O APIC also provides a mechanism for distributing external interrupts to the local APICs of selected processors or groups of processors on the system bus. The ability to steer interrupts to a target processor is often a key in embedded systems, where you are trying to carefully balance loads on the system. Figure 4.6 shows the configuration of the local and I/O APICs (although most SOC implementations do not expose the LINT0/1 pins).

Each local APIC consists of a set of APIC registers (see Table 4.1) and associated hardware that control the delivery of interrupts to the processor core and the generation of IPI messages. The APIC registers are memory mapped and can be read and written to using the MOV instruction.

Local APICs can receive interrupts from the following sources:

- *Locally connected I/O devices.* These interrupts originate as an edge or level asserted by an I/O device that is connected directly to the processor's local interrupt pins (LINT0 and LINT1) on the local APIC. These I/O devices may also be connected to an 8259-type interrupt controller that is in turn connected to the processor through one of the local interrupt pins.

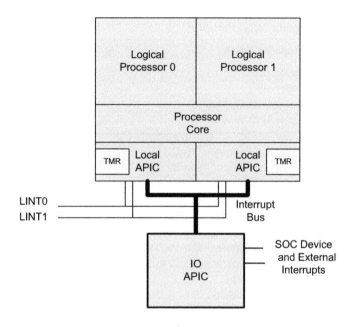

FIGURE 4.6

Local and I/O APIC Layout.

- *Externally connected I/O devices.* These interrupts originate as an edge or level asserted by an I/O device that is connected to the interrupt input pins of an I/O APIC. Interrupts are sent as I/O interrupt messages from the I/O APIC to one or more of the processors in the system.
- *Interprocessor interrupts (IPIs).* An IA-32 processor can use the IPI mechanism to interrupt another processor or group of processors on the system bus. IPIs are used for software self-interrupts, interrupt forwarding, or preemptive scheduling.
- *APIC timer–generated interrupts.* The local APIC timer can be programmed to send a local interrupt to its associated processor when a programmed count is reached.
- *Thermal sensor interrupts.* Pentium 4 and Intel Xeon™ processors provide the ability to send an interrupt to the processor when the devices thermal conditions become critical.
- *APIC internal error interrupts.* When an error condition is recognized within the local APIC (such as an attempt to access an unimplemented register), the APIC can be programmed to send an interrupt to its associated processor.

Of these interrupt sources, the processor's LINT0 and LINT1 pins, the APIC timer, and some of the other events above are referred to as *local interrupt sources*. Upon receiving a signal from a local interrupt source, the local APIC delivers the interrupt to the processor core using an interrupt delivery protocol that has been set up through a group of APIC registers called the *local vector table* or *LVT*. A separate entry is provided in the local vector table for each local interrupt source, which allows a specific interrupt delivery protocol to be set up for each source. For example, if the LINT1 pin is going to be used as an NMI pin, the LINT1 entry in the local vector table can be set up to deliver an interrupt with vector number 2 (NMI interrupt) to the processor core. The local APIC handles

Table 4.1 Local APIC Register Map (Portion)

Address	Register Name	Software Read/Write
FFE0 0000h	Reserved	
FFF0 0010h	Reserved	
FFF0 0020h	Local APID ID Register	Read/Write
FFF0 0030h	Local APIC Version	Read only
...	Other registers such as task priority, EOI	
FFF0 0100h	In Service Register – Bits 0:31	Read only
FFF0 0110h	In Service Register – Bits 32:63	Read only
FFF0 0120h	In Service Register – Bits 64:95	Read only
FFF0 0130h	In Service Register – Bits 96:127	Read only
FFF0 0140h	In Service Register – Bits 128:159	Read only
FFF0 0150h	In Service Register – Bits 160:191	Read only
FFF0 0160h	In Service Register – Bits 192:223	Read only
FFF0 0170h	In Service Register – Bits 224:255	Read only
...	Other registers	
FFF0 0320h	LVT Timer Register	Read/Write
FFF0 0330h	LVT Thermal Sensor Register	Read/Write
FFF0 0340h	LVT Performance Register	Read/Write
FFF0 0350h	LVT Local Interrupt 0 – LINT0	Read/Write
FFF0 0360h	LVT Local Interrupt 1 – LINT1	Read/Write

interrupts from the other two interrupt sources (I/O devices and IPIs) through its IPI message handling facilities.

The following sections describe the architecture of the local APIC and how to detect it, identify it, and determine its status. Figure 4.7 gives a functional block diagram for the local APIC. Software interacts with the local APIC by reading and writing its registers. APIC registers are memory-mapped to a 4-kB region of the processor's physical address space with an initial starting address of FEE00000H. For correct APIC operation, this address space must be mapped to an area of memory that has been designated as strong uncacheable (UC).

The 8259 interrupt controller must be disabled to use the local APIC features; when the local APIC is disabled, the processor LINT[0:1] pins change function to become the legacy INT and NMI pins.

In multiprocessor or hyper-threaded system configurations, the APIC registers are initially mapped to the same 4-kB region of the physical address space; that is, each process can only see its own local APIC registers. Software has the option of changing initial mapping to a different 4-kB region for all the local APICs or of mapping the APIC registers for each local APIC to its own 4-kB region.

As you may have noticed, there is similarity between the 8259 and Advanced Programmable Interrupt Controllers, namely, the In-Service Interrupt Request registers. The registers, however, are much wider on the LAPIC than on the legacy interrupt controller, supporting the full range of vectors from 0 to 255. The registers are directly memory mapped (each register has a unique address in the

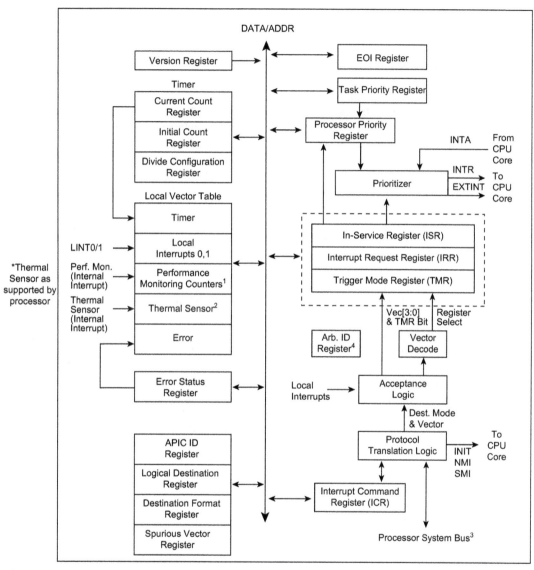

FIGURE 4.7

Local APIC Details.

processor memory map) and not indirectly, as is the case for the 8259-based interrupt controller. To illustrate the point, a portion of the memory map is shown in Table 4.1.

A number of interrupts are mapped directly to the local APIC; these must be assigned vectors for each source. The local APIC contains a local vector table (LVT) that associates an interrupt source with a vector number, which is provided to the processor during the interrupt acknowledge sequence.

Register names that begin with LVT in Table 4.1 are used to configure the vector and mode of operation for the local interrupts, which are directly wired to the APIC.

By way of example, Figure 4.8 shows the bits definition of the LVT local interrupt 0/1 registers.

As an example, setting the LVT LINT0 register value to 0x000,0020 will cause a processor interrupt with vector 32 to be generated when the processor's local interrupt pin 0 transitions from a low to high value (active high, edge triggered).

The local APIC also accepts interrupts routed to it from PCIe devices. The PCIe devices can generate messages known as Message Signaled Interrupts. The interrupts generated by PCIe devices contain the interrupt vector to be signaled to the processor. It's important to note that many of the internal devices on Intel systems present themselves as integrated PCIe devices. The devices themselves do not sit on a real PCIe bus, but the discovery logic and interrupt allocation mechanism do not distinguish external or internal "PCI" devices. There is more on PCIe devices later in the chapter.

Up to this point we have concentrated on the local interrupt scalability of the local APIC, but the local APIC provides a critical mechanism for other interrupt controllers in the system: a way to send interrupt requests to the processor. The I/O APIC is one such interrupt controller that is integrated into the SOC. The I/O APIC interrupt controller on Intel SOCs collects interrupt signals from with the SOC and routes the interrupt to the local APIC.

A key portion of the local APIC accepts interrupt messages from the I/O APIC. The I/O APIC on the SOC provides 24 individual interrupt sources. The I/O APIC interrupt sources are actually used within the SOC; none of the sources are brought out on pins for use as an external interrupt source. For example, the 8254 timer is connected to the I/O APIC IRQ2 pin internally. Most other pins are routed to serial interrupt request lines. The serial interrupt line is a single pin with a specific data encoding that simple devices can use to raise an interrupt. A number of devices can be daisy-chained on to the serial interrupt line and used for low pin count, low frequency interrupts. The translation between the I/O APIC interrupt source and the vector generated is contained in the I/O APIC interrupt redirection table. The table entries are similar to the LVT interrupt entry in the local APIC, but obviously reside in the I/O APIC (see Figure 4.9). There is one critical additional entry in the I/O APIC redirection table: the specification of a targeted local APIC. This allows a particular interrupt vector to be routed to

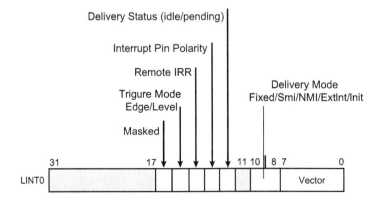

FIGURE 4.8

LVT Local Interrupt Register Definition.

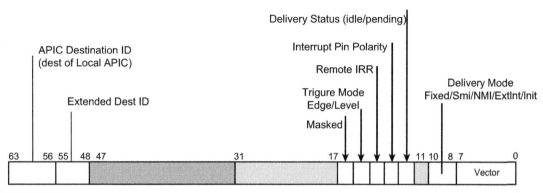

FIGURE 4.9

I/O APIC Redirection Table Entry.

a specific core or hyper-thread. The vector range for the I/O APIC is between 10h and FEh. In multiprocessor systems, the interrupts can be sent to "any" local APIC, where either core can respond to the interrupt.

The I/O APIC provides just three registers that are memory-mapped to the core. Two of the three registers provide an indirect mechanism to access the registers inside the APIC. The first register is an Index register at address 0xFEC00000. This 8-bit register selects which indirect register appears in the window register to be manipulated by software. Software will program this register to select the desired APIC internal register. The second indirect register is the Window register located at address 0xFEC00010. This 32-bit register specifies the data to be read or written to the register pointed to by the Index register. This mechanism of using a few memory-mapped registers to access a larger bank of internal device registers is a common design pattern used in IA-32 systems. The third register is the EOI register. When a write is issued to this register, the IOxAPIC will check the lower 8 bits written to this register and compare it with the vector field for each entry in the I/O Redirection Table. When a match is found, the Remote Interrupt Request Register (RIRR) for that entry will be cleared. If multiple entries have the same vector, each of those entries will have RIRR cleared. Once the RIRR entry is cleared, I/OAPIC can resume accepting the same interrupt.

Figure 4.10 shows the interrupt hardware hierarchy for a uniprocessor system. The interrupts come from many different sources, and all converge at the processor with an interrupt vector number.

The software must acknowledge level-triggered interrupts by generating an EOI by writing memory-mapped EOI register in the LAPIC. The LAPIC subsequently broadcasts EOI message to all IOxAPICs in the system. The local APIC LVT registers are directly mapped, whereas the I/O APIC registers are indirectly mapped As a result, the act of writing to the local APCI LVT registers is more efficient in software.

Timers

Hardware-based timers are critical to all computer systems. A hardware-based timer generally consists of a hardware counter that counts down from a provisioned value and triggers an event such as an interrupt to the CPU when the counter reaches zero. The timer usually automatically restarts counting

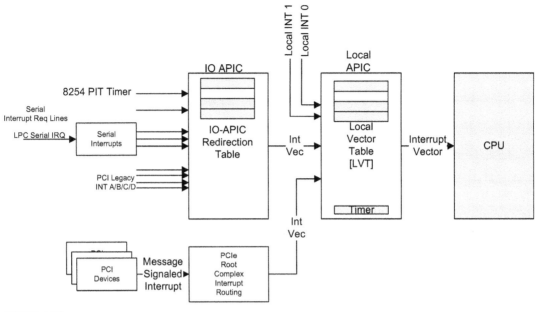

FIGURE 4.10

Interrupt Controller Hierarchy.

from the provisioned value (free-run). At least one timer is required for the operating system, particularly if it is a preemptive operating system (which most are). The operating system timer is often called the OS tick. The interrupt handler for the OS tick triggers the operating system scheduler to evaluate whether the current process should be suspended in favor of executing another ready task.

You should be aware of a number of attributes of a timer when programming it:

- *Clock source*. The clock source dictates the countdown interval of the timer. The clock source to a timer is usually derived by dividing one of the system clocks by a hardware divider, which can be programmed.
- *Timer accuracy*. The timer accuracy is largely dictated by the accuracy of the underlying clock or oscillator used to feed the timer. The accuracy of the original source is defined in parts per million (PPM). Platforms with oscillators are generally much more accurate than those that use crystals to generate the clock source. In embedded systems, the operating system tick may be used to keep track of the time of day; in this case the accuracy of the oscillator or crystal is very important. For example, a crystal source with 100 PPM will have an accuracy of $100/10^{\wedge}6$, which is 0.01%. Given that there are 86,400 seconds in a day, a ±100 PPM crystal could be out by ±8.64 seconds per day. A good rule of thumb is that 12 PPM corresponds to approximately 1 second per day. You should note that the accuracy can vary with temperature (but within the PPM bounds specified by the manufacturer). In Intel systems, a separate real-time clock (RTC) is available. A key attribute of the RTC is that time can be maintained when power is removed from the system through the use of a battery backup. However, in deeply embedded systems

a battery backup is often not used, as it would need to be replaced at some point. If the PPM of the crystal/oscillator is too high and the accuracy not acceptable, embedded platforms often rely on some external agent to provide a more accurate time of day. The Network Time Protocol is a protocol often used to acquire and maintain an accurate time of day on an embedded system. Global positioning systems also provide an accurate time stamp capability, which can be used to maintain a highly accurate time of day on the platform.

- *Free run/one shot.* This attribute defines the behavior of the timer itself. A free-running timer will start from a reference value and count down to zero; once the counter reaches zero the counter is reloaded with the reference value automatically and continues to count down from the reference value. The timer can be programmed to trigger an event such as an interrupt when the counter reaches zero. A one-shot timer, on the other hand, stops counting once it reaches zero. The timer must be explicitly restarted by software. Free-run mode is also referred to as periodic mode, and one shot is referred to as non-periodic mode.
- *Count direction.* Timers can count either down or up. The event generation value is zero for countdown timers and the reference value for count up timers.
- *Counters.* In this context a counter counts the clock input to the counter. The counters run freely and don't restart automatically. The counter will start at zero and simply roll over when the counter value saturates at "all ones" in the register; that is, a 32-bit counter will roll over from 0xFFFF,FFFF to zero. Some counter registers are wider (in terms of bits) than software can read in one single read operation. For example, a 64-bit counter is often read as two individual 32-bit reads. In this case, you have to be cautious that the counter has not rolled over during the two reads. In some timer implementations a command can be issued to latch the current timer into a latch register(s). This prevents the contents from changing as the value is being read.
- *Watchdog timers.* These are a special class of timer. A watchdog timer (WDT) is a timer like the others, but it can usually generate an event such as a non-maskable interrupt (NMI) or reset to the hardware if the timer expires. The WDT is used to ensure that the system is restarted if the software is deemed to be nonfunctional for some reason. The software must service the WDT at adequate intervals to prevent the WDT from expiring. Embedded software uses many different strategies to make sure the overall system is operating appropriately. The simplest is to have a dedicated process that sleeps for a period, wakes up, and services the WDT. Setting the priority of this task is always tricky; under heavy loads the system may be behaving perfectly normally but does not have time to schedule the watchdog process/task. More sophisticated strategies use operating system task context switch information and software-based notifications from applications tasks to assess whether the system is behaving well. WDTs are usually set to expire in 1–2 seconds. In order to prevent the accidental servicing (such as errant software writing to a single restart register) of a watchdog timer, the timer usually requires several different register writes in a specific order to service the timer and prevent its expiration.

Figure 4.11 shows the logical configuration for a generic timer block.

Hardware timers are often read in a tight busy loop by software delay routines. Especially if the delay is short, for longer delays it is best to call the appropriate operating system service to allow the operating system schedule some useful work while the thread is delayed.

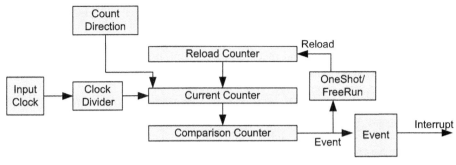

FIGURE 4.11

Logical Timer Configuration.

Intel Timers/Counters

The timer infrastructure, like most parts of the IA-32 platform, has been built up as the platform has evolved. All modern Intel architecture platforms provide the following timer capabilities:

- *253/4 Legacy PIT timer block.* This timer capability has been on IA-32 platforms almost since the beginning; it has been preserved on IA-32 platforms largely for legacy compatibility but is still extensively used.
- *High Precision Event Timers (HPET).* This is a block of timers that are wider in resolution (32/64 bit) and directly memory-mapped to the processors address space.
- *Local APIC interrupt timer* that is part of the logical core.
- *Watchdog timer.*

The original timer component on IA-32 systems was known as the 8253/4. It was an external IC device on the motherboard. This external component has long since been integrated into the chipset, and in Embedded Atom SOCs it has been provided on the SOC as part of a legacy support block. It is known as the Programmable Interrupt Timer (PIT) and is often still used to provide the OS tick timer interrupt, although we recommend migration to the high precision event timers at this point. The PIT timer is sourced by a 14.31818 MHz clock. The timer provides three separate counters:

- *Counter 0.* System timer.
- *Counter 1.* Refresh request signal; this was at one point in time used to trigger the refresh cycles for DRAM memory. It is no longer used.
- *Counter 2.* Simple PC speaker tone.

As we mentioned, counter 0 is the key timer used for the OS tick. The control registers listed in Table 4.2 are provided in the 8253/4.

This counter 0 functions as the system timer by controlling the state of IRQ0. There are many modes of operation for the counters, but the primary mode used for operating system ticks is known as mode 3: square wave. The counter produces a square wave with a period equal to the product of the counter period (838 nanoseconds) and the initial count value. The counter loads the initial count value one counter period after software writes the count value to the counter I/O address. The counter initially asserts IRQ0 and decrements the count value by two each counter period. The counter negates

Table 4.2 PIT Timer Registers—In/Out Space

Port	Register Name	Software Read/Write
40h	Counter 0 Interval Time Status Byte Format Counter 0 Counter Access Port Register	Read/Write
43h	Timer Control Word Register Commands: Timer Control command Word Register read back command Counter Latch command	Read/Write

IRQ0 when the count value reaches zero. It then reloads the initial count value and again decrements the initial count value by two each counter period. The counter then asserts IRQ0 when the count value reaches zero, reloads the initial count value, and repeats the cycle, alternately asserting and negating IRQ0. The interrupt is only actually caused by the transition of the IRQ0 line from low to high (rising edge).

The counter/timers are programmed in the following sequence:

1. Write a control word to select a counter; the control word also selects the order in which you must write the counter values to the counter.
2. Write an initial count for that counter by loading the least and/or most significant bytes (as required by control word bits 5, 4) of the 16-bit counter.

Only two conventions need to be observed when programming the counters. First, for each counter, the control word must be written before the initial count is written. Second, the initial count must follow the count format specified in the control word (least significant byte only, most significant byte only, or least significant byte and then most significant byte).

Writing to the timer control register with a latch command latches (takes a snapshot copy of) the counter value so it can be read consistently, while providing a consistent copy for software to read.

The high precision event timers (HPET) are a more modern platform timer capability. They are simpler to use and are of higher precision—usually 64-bit counters. The Embedded Atom SOC platform provides one counter and three timers. The HPET are memory-mapped to a 1-kB block of memory starting at the physical address of FED00000h. Table 4.3 lists the key HPET registers.

The HPET counter typically runs freely and always increments; the value rolls over to zero after the 64-bit value reaches all ones. If a timer is set up for periodic mode (free run), when the main counter value matches the value in T0CV, an interrupt is generated (if enabled). Hardware then increases T0CV by the last value written to T0CV. During runtime, T0CV can be read to find out when the next periodic interrupt will be generated. A timer may also be configured as a one-shot timer; this mode can be thought of as creating a single shot. When a timer is set up for nonperiodic mode, it generates an interrupt when the value in the main counter matches the value in the timer's comparator register. On Intel Atom E600 Series timers 1 and 2 are only 32 bit, and the timer will generate another interrupt when the main counter wraps.

The next category of timer is that provided in the local APIC. The local APIC timer can be programmed to send a local interrupt to its associated processor when a programmed count is reached.

Table 4.3 HPET Registers (Subset)

Offset Address	Register Name	Description
0000h	General capabilities and identification	The 64-bit value provides the period of the clock as input to the counter, the number of timers, and the precision of the counter.
0010h	General configuration	Controls the routing of some default interrupts for the timers and a general timer enable bit.
0020h	General interrupt status	In level-triggered mode, this bit is set when an interrupt is active for a particular timer.
00F0h	Main counter value	Counter value: reads return the current value of the counter. Writes load the new value to the counter.
0100h	Timer 0 config and capabilities	The register provides an indication of the capabilities for each timer. Not all timers have the same features. The register provides control for the one-shot/free-run mode and interrupt generation capability. Some of the timers are 64 bit, while others are 32 bit.
0108h	Timer 0 Comparator Value (T0CV)	When set up for periodic mode, when the main counter value matches the value in T0CV, an interrupt is generated (if enabled). Hardware then increases T0CV by the last value written to T0CV. During runtime, T0CV can be read to find out when the next periodic interrupt will be generated.

The local APIC unit contains a 32-bit programmable timer that is available to software to time events or operations. This timer is set up by programming four registers: the divide configuration, the initial-count register, the current-count register, and the Local Vector Table (LVT) timer register. The time base for the timer is derived from the processor's bus clock, divided by the value specified in the divide configuration register. The timer can be configured through the timer LVT entry for one-shot or periodic operation. In one-shot mode, the timer is started by programming its initial-count register. The initial-count value is then copied into the current-count register and countdown begins. After the timer reaches zero, an timer interrupt is generated and the timer remains at its 0 value until reprogrammed.

In periodic mode, the current-count register is automatically reloaded from the initial-count register when the count reaches zero and a timer interrupt is generated, and the countdown is repeated. If during the countdown process the initial-count register is set, counting will restart, using the new initial-count value. The initial-count register is a read-write register; the current-count register is read-only.

The LVT timer register determines the vector number that is delivered to the processor with the timer interrupt that is generated when the timer count reaches zero. The mask flag in the LVT timer register can be used to mask the timer interrupt. The clock source to the local APIC timer may not be constant. The CPUID feature can be used to identify whether the clock is constant or may be gated while the processor is in one of the many sleep states. If CPUID Function 6:ARAT[bit 2] = 1, the processor's APIC timer runs at a constant rate regardless of P-state transitions, and it continues to run at the same rate in deep C-states. If CPUID Function 6:ARAT[bit 2] = 0 or if CPUID function 6 is not supported, the APIC timer may temporarily stop while the processor is in deep sleep states. You need to know the behavior if you are using times to benchmark/time events in the system. The Atom processor timers continue to run even in the deep power-saving sleep states.

The IA watchdog timer provides a resolution that ranges from 1 µs to 10 minutes. The watchdog timer on the Embedded Atom SOC platform uses a 35-bit down-counter. The counter is loaded with the value from the 1st Preload register. The timer is then enabled and it starts counting down. The time at which the watchdog timer first starts counting down is called the first stage. If the host fails to reload the watchdog timer before the 35-bit down-counter reaches zero, the watchdog timer generates an internal interrupt. After the interrupt is generated, the watchdog timer loads the value from the second Preload register into the watchdog timer's 35-bit down-counter and starts counting down. The watchdog timer is now in the second stage. If the processor still fails to reload the watchdog timer before the second timeout, the watchdog triggers one of the following events:

- *Assert a General-Purpose Input/Output Pin* (GPIO4 on Intel Atom E600 Series). The GPIO pin is held high until the system is reset by a circuit external to the SOC.
- *Warm Reset.* This triggers the CPU to restart from the startup vector.
- *Cold Reset.* This is a reset of the SOC device and the CPU restarts from the startup vector.

The process of reloading the WDT involves the following sequence of writes, as we mentioned to reduce the likelihood of an accidently servicing the timer.

1. Write "80" to Watchdog Reload Register zero.
2. Write "86" to Watchdog Reload Register zero.
3. Write "1" to the Reload Register.

When a watchdog restart event occurs, it is very useful for the software to understand if the watchdog timer triggered the restart. To that end, the watchdog controller has a bit that indicates if the last restart was caused by a system reset. The bit itself is not cleared as part of the system reset.

Timer Summary

The hardware timers all provide a similar set of capabilities; the mechanism of setup and control all vary depending on the platform, but at heart they are all the same. The operating system will take ownership of at least one timer in the system for its uses. The application software then most often uses operating system timer services that are derived from this single source. In some cases you will write your own software for a particular timer; then you have to develop the setup code as well as, critically, the software to handle the interrupt generated by the timer expiration. In many cases you may just want to read the counter value to implement a simple delay function that does not depend on the frequency of the processor or speed of executing a particular code sequence.

VOLATILE MEMORY TECHNOLOGIES

A complete embedded system is composed of many different memory technologies.

Intel platforms have two distinct address types. The first is for I/O devices; this is read using either IN/OUT assembly instructions or, more likely, using normal MOV instructions to a dedicated part of the address map known as memory-mapped I/O space (MMIO). When a program reads to an MMIO space it is routed to a device. The other key address space is memory. The memory space is mapped to memory devices on the platform such as the DRAM on the platform, a flash ROM device, or, in some SOCs, local on-die SRAM memory. The hardware block that converts internal memory transactions to access the memory device is known as a memory controller. We discuss some key attributes of the DRAM memory controller in this section.

DRAM Controllers

Dynamic random access memory is a form of volatile storage. The bit value at a memory location is stored in a very small capacitor on the device. A capacitor is much smaller than a logic gate, and therefore the densities are greater than memory technologies using logic such as caches for the processor or SRAM block on an SOC. The ratio is significant. For example, a level two cache of 1 MB is reasonably large for a cache on an embedded device, whereas a device such as the Intel Atom Processor E6xx Series supports up to 2 GB of DRAM.

Although the densities are considerably higher, the price per bit is lower. However, there is a system trade-off that takes place. The DRAM read time is usually far slower than memory that is made from logic gates, such as the CPU cache or SRAM devices (both internal or external).

The read latency is a key performance attribute of memory. Although many strategies are used in processor and cache design to reduce the effect of read latency to memory, in many cases it will directly impact the performance of the system. After all, eventually the processor will have to wait for the result of the read from memory before it can continue to make progress. In order to read a DRAM bit, a logic device must check the value stored on the capacitor for the bit. This is done using a sense amplifier. The sense amplifier takes a little time to figure out whether the bit has a charge or not.

Another key performance attribute is the overall bandwidth or throughput supported by the DRAM devices. Whereas the read latencies of DRAM technology have not been reduced at nearly the same pace as the increase in density or overall throughput performance, the throughput performance has increased dramatically over time. The key improvements in throughput performance of DRAM are accomplished by pipelining as many read and write requests to the memory devices as possible. The DRAM device duplicates many of the logic resources in the device to have many concurrent lookups (sensing) occurring. Figure 4.12 shows the increased performance through multiple parallel requests to the DRAM. DDR memories have separate requests and response lines; this allows the requester interface to enqueue multiple requests while waiting for the response to review requests.

It is important that memory interfaces are standardized to allow many different manufacturers to develop compatible devices for the industry. At the time of writing, DDR2 SDRAM is the predominant DRAM type used in embedded platforms. DDR3 is becoming the DRAM technology used on mainstream compute platforms. The adoption of memory technologies in embedded platforms usually lags behind the adoption of the technology in mainstream platforms. This is often due to a price premium for the memory when it is first introduced into the market.

The DRAM interface as well as many physical attributes are standardized by JEDEC. This organization is the custodian of the DDR1, 2, and 3 SDRAM standards. These devices are known as synchronous DRAMs because the data are available synchronously with a clock line. DDR stands for double data rate and indicates that data are provided/consumed on both the rising and falling edge of the clock. As we mentioned above, the throughput of the memory technology can be increased by increasing the number of parallel requests to the memory controller. Both the depth of pipelining and the clock speed have increased from DDR1 to DDR2, and DDR3 has resulted in a significant increase in throughput throughout the generations of DRAM (see Table 4.4).

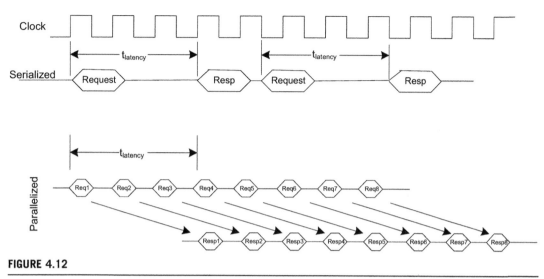

FIGURE 4.12

Increased Performance through Pipelining.

The memory controller on the Intel Atom Processor E6xx Series supports DDR2-667 and DDR2-800 megatransfers per second (MT/s).

Unlike mainstream computers, embedded platforms usually solder the memory directly down on the printed circuit board (PCB). This is often due to the additional cost associated with a module and connector, or mechanical/physical concerns with respect to having the memory not soldered to the platform. Clearly, if the memory is directly soldered to the platform, there is limited scope for upgrading the memory after the product has been shipped. The ability to expand the memory in an embedded system post-shipment is not usually required. When the memory is directly soldered down, the boot loader or BIOS software is typically preconfigured to initialize the exact DRAM that has been placed on the board. However, when modules are used such as the dual in-line modules (DIMM) prevalent on mainstream computers, the BIOS or boot loader has to establish the attributes of the DIMM plugged in. This is achieved by a Serial Presence Detect (SPD) present on the DIMM modules. The SPD is an EPROM that is accessed via a serial interface SPI explained later. The EPROM contains information about the DIMM size and memory timing required. The BIOS takes this information and configures the memory controller appropriately.

The memory cells within the DRAM device are organized in the device in a matrix of rows by columns, shown in Figure 4.13. A memory transaction is split into to two phases; the first is called the

Table 4.4 DRAM Performance		
DRAM Tech	**Memory Clock Speeds**	**Data Rates**
DDR2	100–266 MHz	400s–1066 MT/s
DDR3	100–266 MHz	800–2133 MT/s

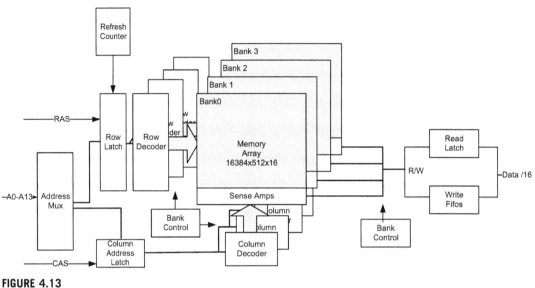

FIGURE 4.13

DDR Overview.

Row Address Strobe (RAS). In this phase an entire row of address bits is selected from the matrix; all the bits in the row are sent to the bit sense amplifiers and then into a row buffer (also called a Page). The process of reading a row of data from the capacitors is actually destructive, and the row needs to be written back to the capacitors at some point. Before entering the second phase for the transaction, the memory controller must wait for the RAS to CAS Latency, called RAS CAS Delay (tRCD). The second phase of the transaction is called the Column Address Strobe (CAS). In this phase the word being read is selected from the previous row selected. The CAS Latency (tCL) is often a figure quoted; it is the time from the presentation of the column address strobe to getting the data back to the memory controller. It is measured in memory clocks, not nanoseconds. Once the memory transaction has been completed, a command called Precharge needs to be issued unless the next request falls in the same row. Precharge closes the memory row that was being used. RAS Precharge Time (tRP) is the time taken between the Precharge command and the next active command that can be issued. That is, the next memory transaction generally won't start until the time has been completed (more on that later). As you can see, the overall latency performance of the memory device consists of three separate latencies. If we can continue to make use of the row that has been loaded into the sense amplifier logic, then we can get subsequent data with much lower latency. To this end the memory devices and controller support a burst memory command. This is where the subsequent data are provided with much lower latency. The typical burst size supported is 4. Given that modern processors have a cache subsystem, the burst memory command is a very useful transaction to exchange data between the cache and memory.

The normal burst mode support expects the initial address to be aligned to the size of the burst; for example, if the DRAM were a 32-bit device with a burst size of 4, the initial address for a burst would have to be 0xXXXX,XX00. The initial data returned would be for the first double word, then 0xXXXX,XX04, 0xXXXX,XX08, and lastly 0xXXXX,XX0C. If, however, the processor were waiting for the last double word in the burst (0xXXXX,XX0C), then using a burst command would decrease the performance of the processor waiting for the read result. To mitigate this, many memory controllers support a feature called Critical Word First. This CRW feature provides the data that the processor are actually waiting for first and then returns the other data elements of the burst. In the example above, the device would return the data for 0xXXXX,XX0C, 0xXXXX,XX00, 0xXXXX,XX04, and finally 0xXXXX,XX08. This would reduce the overall latency experienced by the processor but would still make use of data locality to load the cache line while the DRAM row was still active.

Another optimization to the DRAM subsystem is to have a policy on how long to keep the row buffer (page) active. As we mentioned, subsequent access to an active or open page takes less time than that required to load a new row. Given that programs often have high degrees of spatial and temporal locality, it is often best for the controller to keep a page open until a new row is accessed. This does, however, delay the time to open the new row when a new row is needed. Keeping a row active until a request is made outside that row is known as a page open policy. If the controller proactively closes the page once the transaction is complete, it is known as having a page close policy. The page sizes are relatively large; on Embedded Atom SOCs the memory controller supports devices with 1-kB, 2-kB, and 4-kB pages. Since there can be a considerable advantage to reading from an open page, the DRAM devices are partitioned into independent banks, each with its own page (row buffer) support. The SOC supports 4- and 8-bank DRAM devices. With 4–8 banks, memory controllers can thus keep multiple pages open, improving chances of burst transfers from different address streams.

In an embedded system you often have more flexibility and control over how memory is allocated and portioned in the system. A reasonable performance advantage can be seen by allocating different usage patterns to different banks. For example, a gain of approximately 5% can in some cases be achieved in a simple network router where the memory allocated to the network packets, operating system code space, and applications were all allocated from a separate banks.

The memory devices come in varying bit densities and data bus widths (x4, x8, x16, x32). The total memory required can be built up using any number of options. For example, one could use a 256-Mb device that has a 32-bit interface or two 128-Mb devices each with a 16-bit interface connected to the memory bus. The DRAM controller needs to be set up with the appropriate configuration to operate correctly. The rationale for determining the appropriate configuration usually comes down to the size of the devices on the platform and the amount of space available, as fewer higher density devices are required. The decision also has an economic dimension; higher-density memories are usually more expensive than lower-density ones.

No discussion of DRAM is complete without mentioning the refresh cycle. The DRAM cells are made up of tiny capacitors, and because a capacitor's charge can leak away over time, this could ultimately result in in a 1 bit turning into a 0 bit. Clearly, this is not acceptable. Each row in each device must go through a refresh cycle with sufficient frequency to guarantee that the cell does not discharge. Generally, each DRAM device must be entirely refreshed within 64 ms. If a device has 8192 ROWs, then the refresh cycle must occur every 7.8 µs. The refresh cycle consists of a CAS before RAS cycle where the ROW address to memory array determines the row to be refreshed. Some DDR devices have their own refresh counter, which updates ROW address during refresh cycle; the DRAM controller just triggers the refresh cycle and does not have to keep track of refresh ROW addresses. Some platforms support a DDRx's self-refresh capability; in this case the DRAM device performs the refresh cycle while the device is in low power mode with most of its signals tristated. This is usually used to allow the memory controller to be powered down when the system is in a sleep state, thus reducing the power required by the system in this state. The ability of a capacitor to retain charge is temperature dependent; if you develop a platform that supports an extended temperature range, the refresh rate may need to be increased to ensure data retention in memory cells. It is important to refresh with the required interval. Most of your testing will probably be done at normal room temperature, where the chance of a bit fading is relatively low. However, when your platform is deployed and experiences real-world temperatures, you really don't want to be trying to debug the random system crashes you might experience. I've been there, and it's no fun at all.

Even if the DRAM is being refreshed with the required interval, there is a small probability that a capacitor may spontaneously change its value, or an error in the reading of a bit may occur. These errors are known as *soft errors* and are thought to be the result of cosmic radiation, where a neutron strikes a portion of the logic or memory cell. To mitigate the effects, designers add a number of extra redundant bits to the devices. These extra bits record the parity of the other bits, or an error correcting code covering the data bits. Parity protection requires just a single bit (for 8 bits of data) and allows the controller to detect a single bit error in the memory. It cannot correct the bit error, as there is insufficient information. When a parity error is detected, the memory controller will typically generate an exception to the processor, as the value read from memory is known to be bad. Using additional protection bits, single bit errors in the data can be corrected, while double bit errors can be detected. The most popular protection used today is known as Error Correcting Code (ECC). The scheme uses 2 bits per 8 bits covered. When the memory controller detects a single bit error, it has enough redundant information to correct the error; it corrects the value on the fly and sends the corrected value to the processor. The error may still exist in the memory, so the controller may automatically write back the correct value into the memory location, or in some systems an interrupt is raised and the software is responsible for reading the address and writing back the same value (while interrupts are disabled). A double bit error cannot be corrected and will raise an exception to the processor. When any new data are written to memory, the controller calculates the new ECC value and writes it along with the data. During the platform startup, there is no guarantee that the error bits in the device are consistent with the data in the device. The boot code or in some cases the memory controller hardware has to write all memory locations once to bring corresponding ECC bits to the correct state before any DDR location is read. Since ECC has the ability to correct a single bit error, it is prudent to have a background activity that reads all memory locations over a period of time and self-correct memory location if a single bit soft error is encountered. Such a process is known as scrubbing. Since fixing single bit errors obviously prevents a double bit error from occurring, scrubbing drastically reduces memory data loss due to soft errors.

SRAM Controllers

Static random access memory is a volatile storage technology. The technology used in the creation of an SRAM cell is the same as that required for regular SOC logic; as a result, blocks of SRAM memory can be added to SOCs (as opposed to DRAM, which uses a completely different technology and is not found directly on the SOC die). The speed of SRAM is usually much faster than DRAM technologies, and SRAM often responds to a request within a couple of CPU clock cycles. When the SRAM block is placed on die, it is located at a particular position in the address map. The system software and device drivers can allocate portions of the SRAM for their use. Note that it is unusual for the operating system to manage the dynamic allocation/de-allocation from such memory; it is usually left up to the board support package to provide such features. SRAM memory is commonly allocated for a special data structure that is very frequently accessed by the processor, or perhaps a temporal streaming data element from an I/O device. In general, these SRAM blocks are not cache-coherent with the main memory system; care must be taken using these areas and they should be mapped to a noncached address space. On some platforms, portions of the cache infrastructure can be repurposed as an SRAM, the cache allocation/lookup is disabled, and the SRAM cells in the cache block are presented as a memory region. This is known as *cache as RAM*; some also refer to this very close low-latency RAM (with respect to the core) as *tightly coupled memory*.

The cells in a CPU cache are often made from high-speed SRAM cells. There is naturally a trade-off; the density of SRAM is far lower than DRAM, so on-die memories are at most in the megabyte range, whereas DRAMs is often in gigabytes.

Given that the read/write access time of SRAM memory is far faster than DRAM, we don't have to employ sophisticated techniques to pipeline requests through the controller. SRAM controllers typically either handle one transaction at time, or perhaps pipeline just a small number of outstanding transactions with a simple split transaction bus. There is no performance advantage from accessing addressing in a line as is the case for DRAM.

You should understand the memory sub-word write behavior of the system can be lower than you might expect. As the density of the memory cells reduces, they can fall victim to errors (as in the case of DRAM), so in many cases the SRAM cells have additional redundancy to provide ECC error bits. When the software performs a sub-word write (such as a single byte), the SRAM controller must first perform a word read, merge in the new byte, and then write back the update word into the SRAM with the correct ECC bits covering the entire word. In earlier SRAM designs without ECC, the SRAM often provided a byte write capability with no additional performance cost.

NONVOLATILE STORAGE

All embedded systems require some form of nonvolatile storage. Nonvolatile storage retains data even when the power is removed from the device. There are a range of technologies with varying storage capacities, densities, performance reliability, and size. There are two primary nonvolatile storage technologies in use today: the first and most prevalent for embedded systems is solid state memory, and the second is magnetic storage media in the form of hard drives.

Modern solid state memory is usually called flash memory. It can be erased and reprogrammed by a software driver. Flash memory read speed is relatively fast (slower than DRAM, but faster than hard drives). Write times are typically much slower than the read time. There are two distinct flash memory device types: NOR flash and NAND flash. They are named after the characteristic logic gate used in the construction of the memory cells. These two device types differ in many respects, but one key difference is that NAND flash is much higher density than NOR devices. Typically, NOR flash devices provide several megabytes of storage (at the time of writing, Spansion offered 1-MB to 64-MB devices), whereas NAND devices provide up to gigabytes of storage (devices in the 512-MB range are typical). Most commercial external solid state storage devices such as USB pen drives and SD cards use NAND devices with a controller to provide access to the device. In embedded use cases, it is usual to directly attach the flash devices to the SOC through the appropriate interface and solder the devices directly to the board.

NOR Flash

NOR flash memory devices are organized as a number of banks. Each bank contains a number of sectors. These sectors can be individually erased. You can typically continue to read from one bank while programming or erasing another. When a device powers on, it comes up in read mode. In fact, when the device is in read mode, the device can be accessed in a random access fashion: you can read any part of the device by simply performing a read cycle. In order to perform operations on the device, the software must write specific commands to specific addresses and data patterns into command registers on the device. Before you can program data into a flash part, you must first erase it. You can perform either a sector erase or full chip erase. In most use cases you will perform sector erases. When you erase a sector, it sets all bits in the sector to one. Programming of the flash can be performed on a byte/word basis.

An example code sequence to erase a flash sector and program a word is shown below. This is the most basic operation, and there are many optimizations in devices to improve write performance. This code is written for a WORD device (16-bit data bus).

```
//Sector Erase
// ww(address,value) : Write a Word
// See discussion on volatile in GPIO section below
unsigned short sector_address
ww(sector_address + 0x555), 0x00AA); // write unlock cycle 1
ww(sector_address + 0x2AA), 0x0055); // write unlock cycle 2
ww(sector_address + 0x555), 0x0080); // write setup command
ww(sector_address + 0x555), 0x00AA); // write additional unlock cycle 1

ww(sector_address + 0x2AA), 0x0055); // write additional unlock cycle 2
ww(sector_address) ,0x0030); // write sector erase command */
.. you should now poll to ensure the command completed succesfully.

// Word Program into flash device at program_address
ww(sector_address+ 0x555), 0x00AA); // write unlock cycle 1
ww(sector_address+ 0x2AA), 0x0055); // write unlock cycle 2
ww(sector_address+ 0x555), 0x00A0); // write program setup command
ww(program_address), data); // write data to be programmed
// Poll for program completion
```

When programming a byte/word in a block, you can program the bytes in the block in any order. If you need to program only one byte in the block, that's all you have to write to.

A parallel NOR interface typically consists of the following signals:

- Chip Enable: a signal to select a device, set up by an address decoder.
- Output Enable: used to signal that the device place the output on the data bus.
- Address bus: A0.A20 required number of address bits to address each byte/word in the device (directly).
- Data bus: D0–D7, (and D8–D15 for word devices). The data for a read/write are provided on the data bus.

- Write Enable: signaled when a write to the device is occurring.
- Write Protect: if active it prevents erase or writes to the flash device. As a precaution, this is hardwired on the board (perhaps with a jumper switch) or connected to a general-purpose output pin under software control.

The cycles used to access the device are consistent with many devices using a simplified address and data bus.

In order to discover the configuration of a flash device such as size, type, and performance, many devices support a Common Flash Interface. A flash memory industry standard specification [JEDEC 137-A and JESD68.01] is designed to allow a system to interrogate the flash.

Many flash devices designate a boot sector for the device. This is typically write-protected in a more robust manner than the rest of the device. Usually it requires a separate pin on the flash device to be set to a particular level to allow programming the device. The boot sectors usually contain code that is required to boot the platform (the first code fetched by the processor). The boot sector usually contains enough code to continue the boot sequence and find the location of the remaining code to boot from, and importantly it usually contains recovery code to allow you to reprogram the flash remainder of the flash device.

The initial program of flash devices that are soldered on to a platform is usually carried out through the JTAG chain. This is presented through a connector that can be attached to a JTAG programmer or ICE (see Chapter 17, "Platform Debug"). The device has access to the flash device directly and can program it by emulating the behavior of a host processor in read/writing the device.

On Intel platforms, the initial instructions fetched (BIOS or boot loader) are usually stored on a NOR flash device. The flash devices can provide either a serial or parallel interface. In most cases, a serial interface is used on Intel platforms, although many others use a parallel interface.

There are some reliability differences between NOR and NAND flash devices. NOR devices are more reliable and less susceptible to bit loss. As a result, NOR flash devices are often considered the safest memory type for storing the initial program sequence for the processor (although NAND devices do have techniques to mitigate this by duplicating copies of the boot block and adding additional ECC bits to the sectors).

With random access read/write capabilities, the NOR flash more naturally supports a mode of operation called eXecute in Place (XIP). This is where a program can run directly from the flash (without first copying the data from flash to DDR memory).

Flash devices are characterized by the number of erase cycles a device supports before it starts to fail. Current devices support up to 100,000 erase cycles per sector. If flash memory is being used for a file system or to store logs of frequently changed data, then the sectors are frequently erased and reprogrammed. Software drivers must ensure that all the activity is not focused on a small number of sectors. This strategy is known as wear leveling, and all flash file systems support the principle.

The Linux kernel uses the Memory Technology Device (MTD) interface. MTD provides a generic interface for flash devices. This layer manages the individual devices at the lowest level. There are a number of flash file systems that are also provided (with differing characteristics) built up on top of the MTD layer. The most commonly used at present is the Journaling Flash File System 2 (JFFS2).

We mentioned that erasing a block sets all bits to 1. Through programming you can convert any bit with a value of 1 to zero. You can even do this without erasing. You can never convert a 0 bit to a 1 without an erase cycle. Many flash file systems make use of this attribute to help to maintaining metadata associated with a file system.

In addition to programmable storage, many devices (NOR and NAND) offer One Time Protect/ Programmable (OTP) storage. This is used to store permanent information such as a serial number IMEI/ESN information, secure boot code, or SIM-Lock. The OTP bits are programmed at the time of manufacturing and cannot be updated.

NAND Flash

In contrast to the NOR flash, NAND flash does not provide a direct random access address interface. The devices work in a page/block mode. To read the device the driver must first request a page before the data from the page can be accessed. This is not unlike other secondary storage mechanisms such as disk drives, and as such it is relatively straightforward to build a file system on top of NAND devices. Erasing and programming occur in block modes. Unlike the NOR device, the programming of a block must occur in serial fashion (incremental address programmed in order). Each block has a number of pages. The page size is typically 2 kB. The time taken to load the page into the page register is relatively slow in comparison to the subsequent reads from the page register. To improve performance, many divides contain a number of page registers.

NAND (and to a lesser extent NOR) devices may contain bad pages. These bad pages must be managed by the controller (hardware or software) that provides the interface to the device. To improve the yield of NAND devices, the devices may be released with marked bad blocks. NAND devices may start life with bad blocks and further degrade over the lifetime of the device. The bad blocks found during manufacture are typically marked in spare bits within each block. You must not erase or program pages that are marked as being bad. Also, the increased density of the NAND devices brings with it some compromises, such as a possibility of a spontaneous bit change. To ensure correct overall operation, a number of additional bits are set aside for error correct control (ECC).

A native NAND physical interface typically consists of the following signals:

- Chip Enable: a signal to select a device, set up by an address decoder.
- Write and Read: to indicate direction of access.
- Command Latch Enable: latch a command on the I/O pins.
- Address Latch Enable: latch the address.
- I/O 0–7 (0–15 for 16-bit devices): this is a multiplexed command, address, and data protocol.
- Write Protect: if active it prevents erase or writes to the flash device.
- Busy indication: used to indicate if the device can accept a command.

A NAND read operation consists of loading a page from the flash array and then reading the data from the page register. Figure 4.14 shows the representation of the page register and blocks.

The following steps are required to read from the device:

1. Issue a Read Command by placing 0x00h on I/O[0:7]. Bring command latch signal and write enable active.
2. Issue the address to read by placing each byte of the address on the I/O[0:7] bus, activating the address latch and write enable for each byte of address.
3. Issue the second cycle of the read command by placing 0x30h on the I/O[0:7] while activating the command latch and write enable signals.

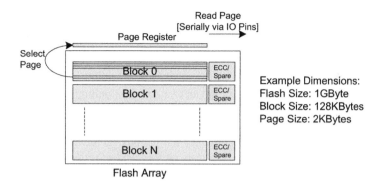

FIGURE 4.14

NAND Device Representation.

4. The busy line should now go active while the flash array is being read and places the contents in the page register.

5. Data can now be clocked out of the page register; by issuing subsequent Read Enable signals, the device places data on the I/O pins.

There are device optimizations to improve the performance, but this is the general process of accessing the device. As you can see, it really is block oriented.

In order to reduce the need for both NAND and NOR devices in a system, some NAND devices provide a special boot block. The boot block is designed to be as reliable as a traditional NOR device (using additional ECC or reduced density or an actual NOR partition). This boot page is automatically placed in the read page buffer, so that a processor can start random accesses to this page when the system first boots.

NAND Interfaces

When NAND devices were first introduced into the market, no standard interface was defined. The Open NAND Flash Interface (OnFi) industry workgroup was formed in 2006 to drive the standardization for raw flash devices. The OnFi workgroup has developed a number of specifications since 2006 (http://www.onfi.org):

- *ONFi 1.0* defines a standard electrical and protocol interface, including the base command set.
- *Block Abstracted NAND 1.0* defines a managed NAND solution that utilizes the raw NAND interface.
- *ONFi 2.0* defines a high-speed double data rate interface (synchronous) of up to 133 megatransfers/ second.
- *NAND connector 1.0* defines a physical connector that supports a DIMM type form factor. This allows for upgrade of density/devices, and so on.
- *ONFI 2.1* increased bus speed to 200 megatransfers/second.
- *ONFI 2.2* includes interruptible read/erase to allow support for high-priority reads.

Some SOCs provided a "native NAND" interface. In many cases the SOC incorporates an NAND controller, and the NAND devices are connected to the SOC via an ONFi standard interface. In other cases the interface (especially the asynchronous model) uses low level software to manage the flash transactions at a low level. In the simplest form (and probably the lowest performance) the interface can be driven by GPIO pins, as you can review in a Linux kernel driver (linux/drivers/mtd/nand/gpio.c).

NAND Controllers

As you can see, the interface to the NAND devices is complex enough that a NAND controller is required, especially if high performance is needed. The NAND controllers are usually within the SOC. A controller generally supports a DMA engine that takes a block read request and a pointer to the buffer. Then the controller issues the commands to the NAND device using the ONFi-defined mechanism, performs the NAND register read, places the results in the target memory buffer, and raises an interrupt to indicate the page has been read. An example of such a driver can be found in linux/drivers/mtd/nand/denali.c.

In many cases, the SOC does not include a NAND controller or direct support for ONFi standard NAND devices. In this case the SOC usually provides an alternative interface known as Multi-MediaCard (MMC). MMC memory usually takes the form of MMC cards. The definition is now standardized under the stewardship of the JEDEC organization (http://www.jedec.org/). The definition includes a flash memory controller and the flash memory devices. Of particular interest to embedded applications is the Embedded MMC (eMMC) specification (http://www.jedec.org/standards-documents/docs/jesd84-a441). In some cases eMMC devices can be soldered down onto the motherboard. The eMMC devices consist of a controller and memory. The controller offers a higher level application interface to the SOC. The driver for MMC devices can be found in Linux/drivers/mmc. The code is split into a card-specific folder, general host files, and files specific to the MMC controller. Secure Digital (SD) memory interface is the new flash interface standard based on MMC. The standard MMC/SD host controller interface is defined by the SD Association. Most controller covers operation with SD and MMC/eMMC devices/cards. The Linux kernel supports a device driver for the SDHC host controller in linux/drivers/mmc/host/sdhc.c. The driver provides access routines to file systems such as FAT32 on the device. The I/O hub device in the Intel Atom E600 Series design provides a standard-compliant SDHC controller.

Hard Disk Drives and Solid State Drives

Hard disks have been a traditional low-cost form of mass storage in platforms for many years. The hard disk drive is a device where data are stored on circular magnetically coated platters. This form of storage has the least cost per bit of all storage types considered. There are mechanical and environmental considerations that you must consider for these forms of mass storage device, and the environmental conditions associated with embedded devices often precludes their use. Because the media is revolving on a spindle, they are sometimes known as spindle-based drives. As the cost of NAND devices has come down, a new type of storage known as the solid state drive (SSD) has become cost-effective in many embedded cases. The SSD is a drive that is made up of NAND devices and a sophisticated NAND controller. The NAND controller presents a traditional hard disk drive interface to the host. The controller takes care of all the low-level flash management including wear leveling.

The latest drive interface is Serial Advanced Technology Attachment (SATA). It is defined by the Serial ATA International Organization (www.serialata.org). It is an interface used to connect host controller adaptors to mass storage devices. It is the natural evolution of the previous Parallel ATA

Table 4.5 Summary of NAND and NOR Flash and SSD

NAND Flash	NOR Flash	SSD
Lowest cost per bit	Higher cost per bit	Cost per bit similar to NAND
Slow random access	Random access	Faster than magnetic drives
Fast writes	Slower writes	Drive performance is based on NAND devices and controller algorithms
Fast erases	Slower erases	Drive performance is based on NAND devices and controller algorithms
Page writes only	Byte writes	Block-based device
Sustained sequential read performance similar to NOR	Sustained sequential or random read performance is similar	Drive performance is based on NAND devices and controller algorithms
Aligns with file system block semantics	Supports execute in place, similar to ROM	Supports standard file systems through traditional mass storage interfaces
Controller must perform some sanity checks before it can be used	Available instantly after power on	The controller must perform some NAND integrity checks before it is used

standard. In most platforms the host controller follows a standard register level interface known as AHCI. The AHCI standard is defined by Intel (http://www.intel.com/technology/serialata/ahci.htm).

Most controllers can be configured in legacy Parallel ATA mode or the more advanced native interface. The native high-performance mode should be used for SATA drives. This native interface is a hardware mechanism that allows software to communicate with Serial ATA devices. AHCI is a PCI class device that acts as a data movement engine between system memory and SATA devices. The host bus adaptor (controller) supports programmed I/O mode, DMA modes (which are akin to the original legacy modes on PATA devices), and a mode known as native command queuing for SATA devices. The vast majority of operating systems provide some level of support for SATA drives, especially since the controller supports the most basic of operating modes (PIO). The source for the SATA drivers can be found in Linux/drivers/ata/*ahci*.c.

Table 4.5 summarizes some of the relative attributes for each mass storage device.

DEVICE INTERFACE—HIGH PERFORMANCE

In many cases an SOC needs additional capabilities such as an external application-specific I/O device. The device interface consists of a device interface controller and a defined external interconnect to attach to an external device.

A peripheral bus interface requires a number of capabilities:

- Transaction mapping from the processor to the device address space—The device controller captures transactions directed to the memory address of the external bus and associated device, and translates the transaction (read or write) into the appropriate transaction on the expansion bus. The translation may involve adaption due to bus width changes (such as 32-bit to 16-bit), or byte order (such as endian conversions).

- Inbound transactions—For high-performances interfaces, it is important that the expansion interface allow the external devices to read and write resources in the SOC. This is often called *bus mastering*. This is primarily used to access memory so the device can read and write data. Without the ability to read or write system memory, the processor or a DMA controller on the device would need to move data to and from the device. When transactions are generated by the device the transaction contains an address, the address space may be different from that used by the processor; you should be aware of the system address map as viewed by the device. The address on the device interconnect is usually known as the bus address. Your software must translate the host system address to bus address if you want the DMA engine on the device to read the system address. The device interface block in the SOC will translate the inbound bus address to the system address.
- Interrupts—Interactions with a high-performance device require the ability to route interrupts from the device to the processor. This can be used to simply indicate events on the I/O device, but most frequently it is used to send service events from the DMA engine on the device. The interface ideally includes assignment and routing of interrupts as an integral part of the capability. In simple bus interfaces the interrupts are usually routed as signals on the side, in this case general-purpose I/O signals that are configured to generate interrupts.
- Physical standard—Some interface definitions also include a physical connector standard, such as card size. A physical standard allows the system to be expanded with many different capabilities. The Peripheral Component Interconnect (PCI) is an excellent example of this. There are other expansion connector standards that cover much more than a device interconnect such a ComExpress (http://www.picmg.org) (although this standard includes a PCI bus among others as part of the interconnect). In some cases, the interface supports removable/reinsertion of devices while the system is active. This is usually known as *hot plug* and can be key to maintaining high availability on platforms.

There are many different bus definitions, from well-standardized Peripheral Component Interconnect (PCI) to de facto standard parallel address and data bus interfaces.

Peripheral Component Interconnect (PCI)

The predominant high-performance external interface standard is PCI. PCI has been on Intel platforms for many years and has evolved from a 32-bit parallel bus to a high-speed lower-pin-count serial bus (with many lanes to scale performance). Although the PCI standard has significantly increased I/O performance with every PCI generation, the logical view of the PCI system has been kept very consistent throughout the evolution of the standard. The approach to discover and access the device has remained the same, allowing full software compatibility over PCI generations.

PCI Express (PCIe) is the third generation of the PCI standard. It is a higher-performance I/O bus used to connect peripheral devices to compute systems. PCIe is the primary peripherals interconnect used on Intel architecture systems, but it has become popular on many platforms. The PCIe standard is developed by the PCI-SIG (http://www.pcisig.com).

The PCIe standard provides the capability to identify devices attached to a PCIe bus at runtime. Once these devices are discovered, the system software can allocate resources to these devices dynamically. This process is called *bus enumeration.* The enumeration process allocates a range of addresses in the system address map to access the device, as well as one or more interrupt vectors. To facilitate the enumeration process, there is a special PCIe bus space known as configuration space. The PCIe configuration space size is a total of 256 MB. The bus supports device discovery and initial configuration by responding to special configuration space transactions on the bus. The configuration space is partitioned into PCIe busses (up to 256), devices per bus (up to 32), and functions within a device (up to 8 per device). This three tuple address is known as the Bus Device Function (BDF) address. The BDF address for a device depends on where it is connected to on the PCIe fabric. The function is dedicated by the design of the device. For example, if a Ethernet card has two separate Ethernet interfaces, it will mostly likely present two separate functions. The process of enumeration is a runtime search through the PCI configuration space looking for devices. Figure 4.15 shows the physical topology of a PCIe system.

The head of the PCIe hierarchy is known as the root complex. The root complex takes processor read/write transactions and routes them to the appropriate transaction type in the PCIe fabric. The root fabric takes upstream transactions from PCIe devices and routes them to the host memory. It also routes interrupts from the devices to the appropriate processor. Devices can also be integrated into the root complex; in this case the devices are presented in exactly the same way as devices that are attached via external physical PCIe links. This provides a consistent approach to discovering internal and external devices.

Each device has a configuration space header. Each device configuration space can be up to 256 bytes. A device can optionally have an extended capabilities register at offsets in range 256 to 4095. A total of 65,536 devices are theoretically supported on PCI. Processors cannot natively generate a PCI configuration cycle; the PCI configuration space transactions can be generated by either of the following mechanisms (on Intel architecture systems):

- *Indirect mode:* Use a sequence of I/O transaction to write to address port at I/O address 0xCF8 followed by read/write to Data Port register at I/O address 0xCFC. The address register is written with the PCI configuration address to read, and then content is read/written to by accessing the data port register. This mechanism allows accessing of first 256 configuration registers; extended capability registers in range [256–4095] can be assessed only through the MMIO mechanism described next.
- *MMIO:* Up to 256-MB (max 4K per device * 65,536 devices) configuration space is mapped into the processor's memory-mapped address space. Reads or writes to this address space generate the configuration transactions on the PCI bus.

The enhanced MMIO mode of configuration can directly access all registers of any device on the PCI bus. The MMIO address bits are built up from the following bit fields:

- A[32:28] = MMIO configuration space: base of which is set by the MMBAR register
- A[27:20] = PCI bus number
- A[19:15] = Device number on bus
- A[14:12] = Device function number (up to 8)
- A[11:8] = Extended register
- A[7:2] = Register number
- A[1:0] = Byte select for a register

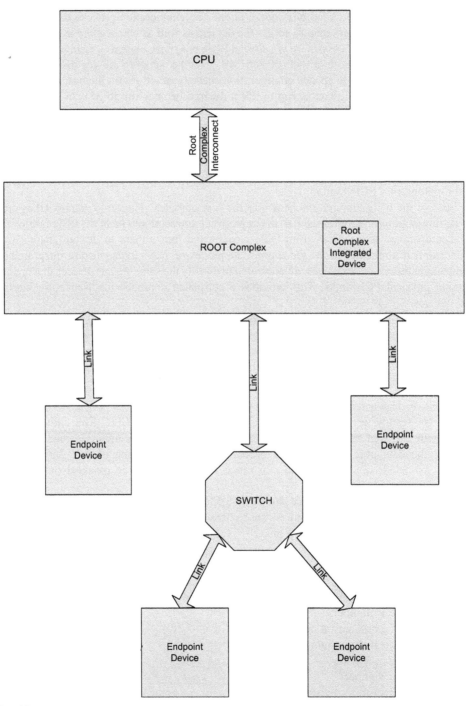

FIGURE 4.15

PCIe Physical Hierarchy.

Each device must have a base configuration header. Figure 4.16 shows a base configuration header. It allows the system software to identify the device type and to assign memory and interrupts to the device.

The vendor ID identifies the manufacturer of the function. The IDs are assigned by the PCI-SIG. The vendor ID assigned to Intel devices is, somewhat humorously, 8086h. The device ID is assigned by the manufacturer and is used to indicate the device type. This device ID is usually used by operating systems to find the appropriate device driver to load and associate with the device. The device revision can be used to adapt the driver for specific versions of the device. The Class code can for some generic devices be used to provide a generic device driver support for a device. In this case the device ID is ignored and the operating system assigns the device driver based on class code. An example where a class code for a generic device is used is a simple VGA adaptor.

PCI devices are composed of two different register spaces, the configuration space and device registers. The configuration space is primarily used as part of the enumeration and allocating the driver to the device. The configuration space contains a number of base address registers. These base address registers are programmable decoders that are used to decode access to the actual device registers.

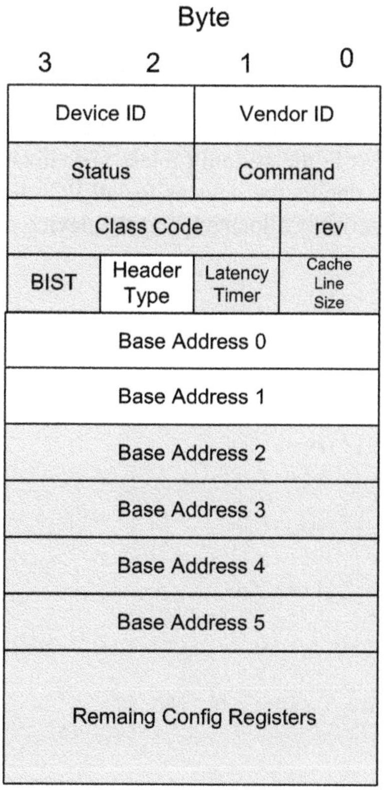

FIGURE 4.16

PCI Configuration Header.

There are six 32-bit or three 64-bit base address registers. The base address register contains some read-only low-order bits set to zero. When you write all ones to the base address register and read back the value, the enumeration software establishes the size of memory the enumeration software must allocate. For example, if the software writes 0xFFFFFFFF to a base address register but reads back 0xFFFF000, then the device is requesting a space of 4 kB. The enumeration software allocates all the memory for the devices "requested" by the enumeration process and writes to all the device base address registers. The lower byte of the base address register has some special meaning; it indicates whether the base address is to allocate memory or I/O space, although the vast majority of devices now limit the registers to memory-mapped only. It also includes an prefetchability attribute—it indicates if the memory space for the device is prefetchable. This is an important classification for I/O devices. Registers on a device must not be prefetchable of a speculative read by the processor; this has a side effect on the hardware. Consider a processor speculative read of a hardware FIFO. In this case the value is read, but it may not be used by the software: the data are lost. This bit has no special significance for Intel hardware since the Intel CPU does not do speculative prefetch to MMIO space, which is normally mapped into the uncacheable region.

When the base address register is written, all memory transactions generated to that bus address range are claimed by the device. The addresses are assigned to be in noncacheable memory-mapped I/O space by the bus enumeration software at startup. The registers allocated via the bar address registers are specific to the device and not standardized in any way by the PCI-SIG.

The addresses used on the bus are known as bus addresses. On Intel platforms there is a one-to-one correspondence between the host physical address and the address used on the bus. There is no translation of the outbound address in the system (unless virtualization is being used in the system).

In Linux the lspci command details the devices for all PCI devices in the system. It shows the device types, the memory and interrupts allocated, and the device driver attached to the device.

```
>lspci -v (sample of results)
00:03.0 Multimedia video controller:
 Intel Corporation Device 8182 (rev 01)
 Subsystem: Intel Corporation Device 8186
 Flags:bus master, fast devsel, latency 0, IRQ 11
Memory at d0300000
   (32-bit, non-prefetchable) [size=512K]
   I/O ports at f000 [size=8]
Memory at b0000000
   (32-bit, non-prefetchable) [size=256M]
Memory at d0380000
   (32-bit, non-prefetchable) [size=256K]
02:0a.2 Serial controller:
 Intel Corporation Device 8812
 (prog-if 02 [16550])
 Flags:bus master, fast devsel, latency 0, IRQ 19
 I/O ports at e040 [size=8]
Memory at d0149000
   (32-bit, non-prefetchable) [size=16]
Kernel driver in use: serial
02:00.1 Ethernet controller:
```

```
Intel Corporation Device 8802
Flags:bus master, fast devsel, latency 0, IRQ 25
Memory at d0158000
(32-bit, non-prefetchable) [size=512]
Kernel driver in use: ioh_gbe
```

The interrupts vectors are also assigned during the enumeration process. Each PCIe device provides configuration registers to support a feature known as MSI/MSI-X. There are two key register types: the first is an address register and the second is a data register. The address is a special address in the system, and it is the targeted interrupt controller for which the interrupt is being sent to. Each processor hardware thread has an individual target address, so MSI/MSI-X interrupts can be steered to a specific hardware processor thread (mechanism for any processor to handle the thread are also defined). The data register is the vector for the interrupt that is assigned to the device. The device can request multiple interrupt vectors, and the enumeration process attempts to satisfy all device requests with individual interrupt vectors. In cases where there is oversubscription of interrupt vectors versus device requirements, (i.e. the system cannot allocate all the vectors requested by the device), some vectors must be shared among different functions within a device. Having many separate vectors for a device can improve the performance of an interrupt handling routing, as it does not have to read device status registers to find out the cause of the interrupt.

Not all operating systems support MSI-X; fallback legacy interrupt support mechanisms provide emulated wired interrupts.

Bus Mastering

The ability for a PCI device to read and write payloads (descriptions of work, data to be transmitted, and so on) is very important, especially for high-performance interfaces or devices. The ability for a device to read or write host memory is known as *bus mastering*. A device can generate read and write transactions on the PCIe bus. These transactions are routed to the root complex and then to the system memory controller. The bus address used in an Intel system corresponds to host physical addresses in the system (unless virtualization is being used). The device has access to the entire physical memory space of the host. It may directly access memory with high performance. A common PCI communication pattern is to provide circular buffers of work to send to a device in host memory. The device contains head and tail pointers for the host memory resident circular buffer, and these pointers are mapped via the base address registers. The circular buffer contains the description of the work requested of the device (for example, "transmit the packet pointed to by the descriptor"). Let's discuss the case of a network interface card. The software first sets up the descriptor with a pointer to the packet to be transmitted. Then the tail pointer is updated in the device. This indicates to the device that there is something to do. The device reads the descriptor and finds a pointer to a packet to be transmitted. The device then directly accesses the packet from host memory to internal FIFOs for transmission on the line. A similar process occurs in reverse for reception of packets. The device driver can also update the circular buffer multiple times before writing the tail pointer to send a batch of work to the device. The pointers written to the device (such as the pointer to packet) must all be specified as PCIe bus addresses. In the case of Intel architecture systems this is the same as physical addresses, but not all systems are like that so you should use bus to physical address conversion routines provided by your operating system. If you are using virtual memory, you must convert from virtual to bus address when populating any address in a device that it will subsequently access directly.

Transaction Ordering

When a device has the capability of directly accessing host memory, it becomes very important to understand the memory transaction ordering rules for these host memory accesses. Consider a device that has received a packet from the network. The device issues a number of memory writes to update the packet in memory and raises an interrupt to the processor. Depending on the bus and SOC topology, the interrupts may follow a different path than the memory writes. On PCI there are very well-defined rules for transaction ordering. The interrupt indication (when MSI and MSI-X is used) follows the same logical ordered path as the memory writes, and the interrupt cannot pass the memory writes until they are globally visible to the processor. That means than when the driver eventually receives the interrupt you can be sure that the memory has been updated with the correct values from the device (or if not actually in memory, the right data values are returned if the processor performs a read of the address). On many SOC devices this is not as rigorously defined, and ordering of transactions and interrupts is loosely defined. In such cases, the software may operate on inconsistent memory contents partially updated by the device; in many cases, reading the device ensures that the memory is fully up to date.

UNIVERSAL SERIAL BUS

The Universal Serial Bus (USB) is a low-voltage differential pair serial bus that was designed to connect computer peripherals to PC platforms. The USB is standardized by the USB Implementers Forum, Inc. (www.usb.org). It has been designed to support real-time data transfer of video, audio, and data. The USB is composed of a tiered star physical topology. At the top of the hierarchy is the host root hub. There is a single USB host in the USB hierarchy; the USB host contains the USB host controller. In some cases, the host controller has an integrated hub to expand the number of connectors on the host controller. There are two types of USB device, hubs and functions. Hubs provide additional fan-out for the bus, and functions provide a capability such as a mass storage or mouse.

Each physical link consists of four wires. A pair of differential signal wires, D+ and D-, are used to carry the data to and from the device. The wires are effectively half duplex. In addition to the data wires, there is a 5 V power supply and a ground pin. The data is carried using an NRZI line encoding, and a special sync sequence is sent at the start of all the packets to allow the receiver to recover a clock. This scheme removes the need for a separate clock wire.

As the USB standard has grown in its use, the trend has been to miniaturize the USB connector standard, from the traditional PC/laptop USB connector to the micro USB connector found on many cell phones.

The USB bus is hot-pluggable, which means that the device can be added or removed from the system without any electrical considerations. When a device is inserted into the platform, a change in the electrical characteristics is detected by the host. This triggers the discovery process.

As we mentioned, the USB provides a 5 V power supply. It is provided for use by the peripherals being attached to the platform. The current supply is relatively low, from 100 mA to 500 mA. This is adequate for peripherals such as mice, touch screens, and pen drives, but not for a peripheral such as a printer.

Different speeds have been standardized; these allow for quite significant data transfer capabilities over the bus:

- Low speed: 1.5 Mbps. This is standardized under the USB 1.0/1.1 specification, and included in the USB 2.0.
- Full speed: 12.0 Mbps. USB 1.0/1.1 and 2.0.
- High speed: 480 Mbps. This data rate is only available under the USB 2.0 standard.

The speed of the bus should not be confused with sustainable throughput of the bus after all the bus and protocol overheads have been taken into account. For example, on a bulk endpoint there is a maximum payload size of 512 bytes. A reasonable sustained user payload throughput of about 400 Mb/s or 50 MB/s is available for a high-speed device when overheads are included. Actual devices may be lower due to its own hardware limitations.

Compatibility is a key feature of the USB standard; a USB device compliant with an older version of the standard can be inserted into a platform supporting a newer standard and operate at its originally supported speed. The bus limits the transactions seen by a device to ensure this compatibility: high-speed transactions are only distributed to high-speed devices, full-speed transactions are distributed to full-speed devices and low-speed transactions are distributed to full- and low-speed devices.

There are two sides to a USB link; one is known as the host side and the other as the device side. The host port is the primary driver of the USB bus. There can only be one host port in a USB hierarchy, as shown in Figure 4.17. There can be up to 127 devices on a Universal Serial Bus. This fan-out is supported by a hierarchy of simple hub devices.

There are many cases where an embedded system may want to behave as a USB device in one use case and as a USB host in another use case. For example, when a mobile phone is connected to a PC to

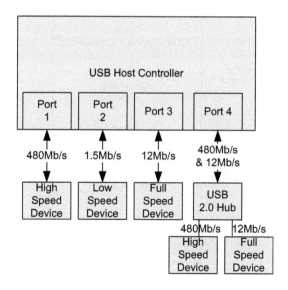

FIGURE 4.17

USB Hierarchy Examples.

change and synchronize the contacts, the PC acts as the USB host and the mobile phone acts as a USB device. However, when the phone is connected to a peripheral such as a printer or audio speakers via USB, the mobile phone now acts as a USB host and the peripheral attached acts as a USB device. A good example of this can be found in the current Android-based handsets that support the Android@ Home APIs. In order to support this, a mode known as USB On-The-Go (USB OTG) has been developed. It is a supplement to the USB 2.0 specification. A USB controller that supports USB OTG can act as a device or host. This also allows you to connect two devices of the same type, where one becomes the host and the other becomes the device; the roles are defined by the cable.

Any time a device is inserted into the bus it is detected in real time, or the host is powered on and a bus enumeration occurs. This allows the host software to assign each device in the USB hierarchy a device address. The bus protocol itself is robust with a built-in error handling/fault recovery mechanism.

The USB specification outlines the data flow between host and devices, as well as scheduling of traffic to and from the devices, as illustrated in Figure 4.18. The protocol supports isochronous and bulk data transfers across the bus.

The USB is a polled bus; the host controller initiates all data transfers between the host and devices.

Most bus transactions consist of three separate packets transmitted on the bus. The host controller starts by generating a token packet; this packet indicates the type and direction of the transaction. It also contains a device and endpoint address. The endpoint is a logical channel identifier at the device. There can be up to 15 endpoints within a device. After the token has been received by the device, the data transaction is generated either by the host or by the device depending on the direction specified. Once the data transaction is complete, the handshake packet is generated. The ACK packet is

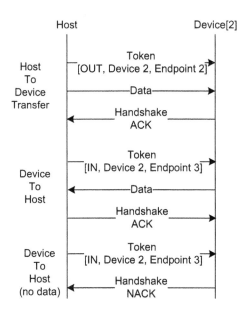

FIGURE 4.18

Transaction Phases for USB Transfer to and from a Device.

generated by the device of the data flow from the host to device (OUT transfer) or by the host to indicate that the host has received an error-free data packet from the device. IN and OUT are defined from the host controller view; an OUT token indicates that data will be sent from the host to the device, and an IN token solicits data from the device to the host.

The USB supports data and control exchange among the USB host and devices across a set of logical pipes. A pipe is a logical association between a logical endpoint and the host device. These pipes can be unidirectional or bidirectional. Pipes are used to present a logical connection between a software element running on the host and an endpoint in a device. From the software view this is a direct connection and hides the details of the bus hierarchy.

In order to support many different device types and use cases on the USB, four fundamental types of data transfer have been defined:

- *Control Transfers.* These are used to configure the device when it is initially discovered in on the bus. Control transfers are usually used to set up the other endpoints (e.g., a bulk endpoint) on the device.
- *Bulk Data Transfers.* These are used for large-scale transfer of data to and from the device. They are used when no special latency constraints exist in the transfers to or from the device. The data exchange is reliable. The bandwidth occupied by bulk transfers can vary depending on the other bus activities; these transfers are the lowest priority.
- *Interrupt Data Transfers.* These are used for timely delivery of data to and from the device. These can be used for events such as mouse movements, or they can be used from a device that wishes to indicate that data are available for a bulk transfer (avoiding constant polling of the a bulk endpoint).
- *Isochronous Data Transfers.* These transfers are allocated a guaranteed bandwidth and delivery latency constraint. They are continuous and occur in real-time. Dedicated bandwidth is set aside on the bus for isochronous data. They are usually used for real-time transfers of audio and video.

Transfer types cannot be mixed on the same pipe. The bandwidth is allocated among pipes. Depending on the configuration of the pipe, bulk data transfers can occupy any remaining unassigned bandwidth.

Devices are assigned an address during a bus enumeration process. This process occurs when the host controller is first initialized or when devices are inserted (hot-plugged). All devices support at least one endpoint: endpoint zero. Endpoint zero contains a control pipe. The control pipe on endpoint zero provides a standardized mechanism to interact with the device. The control endpoint must support standard requests: set_address, set_configuration, get_descriptor for device and configuration descriptors. The standard information that can be obtained for all USB devices is

- Vendor identification
- Device class
- Power management capabilities
- Endpoint description with configuration information

In addition to this standard information, further information that is specific to the class can be provided. After that, vendors can provide additional information, but there is no standardization of this information.

The information provided by the control endpoint is provided as a series of descriptors. The command below shows a subset of the data provided by the Linux `lsusb` command. It shows the device, configuration, interface, and endpoint descriptors for a USB pen drive.

```
>lsusb -v
Bus 001 Device 002: ID0781:5406 SanDisk Corp. Cruzer Micro U3
Device Descriptor:
   bcdUSB          2.00
   bDeviceClass       0 (Defined at Interface level)
   bDeviceSubClass  0
   bDeviceProtocol  0
   bMaxPacketSize0  64
   idVendor        0x0781 SanDisk Corp.
  idProduct       0x5406 Cruzer Micro U3
Configuration Descriptor:
   bmAttributes       0x80    (Bus Powered)
  MaxPower        200mA
Interface Descriptor:
   NumEndpoints       2
   InterfaceClass     8 Mass Storage
   InterfaceSubClass  6 SCSI
   InterfaceProtocol  80 Bulk (Zip)
Endpoint Descriptor:
   EndpointAddress    0x81 EP 1 IN
      Transfer Type   Bulk
      Synch Type      None
      Usage Type      Data
      MaxPacketSize   0x0200 1x 512 bytes
Endpoint Descriptor:
   EndpointAddress    0x01 EP 1 OUT
      Transfer Type   Bulk
      Synch Type      None
      Usage Type      Data
      MaxPacketSize   0x0200 1x 512 bytes
```

The pen drive is one of the simplest USB devices; it only used two bulk endpoints. A similar command issued for an Apple iPhone™ 4 shows far more extensive use of the USB capabilities. Table 4.6

Table 4.6 Apple iPhone 4 Configuration and Endpoints

Configuration	Endpoints/Type	Usage
PTP	2 bulk endpoints (IN /OUT) 1 interrupt endpoint	Still image capture using Picture Transfer Protocol
iPod USB Interface	1 isochronous (IN) 1 interrupt	Audio control - Streaming audio - HID
PTP + Apple Mobile Device	2 bulk + interrupt 2 bulk (IN/OUT)	PTP Vendor-specified protocol
PTP + Apple Mobile Device + Apple USB Ethernet	2 bulk + interrupt 2 bulk (IN/OUT) 2 bulk (IN/OUT)	PTP Vendor-specified protocol Vendor-specified protocol

is a summary of the endpoints on such a device as listed by `lsusb`. There are four different configurations supported with the device we queried. Only one of these configurations is active at a time.

For a particular configuration, a device's descriptors contain a list of interface classes (and subclasses). The interface classes are mapped to endpoints with the required capabilities. The interface classes have been standardized for a number of common use cases. If an interface conforms to the standard, then the device does not require a special device driver to operate with the host—it can in most cases rely on the OS class driver for the capability. If the device does not support the standard class, the platform will require a special driver to interact with the device. The following is a list of classes that are supported:

- Bluetooth
- Chip/smart card interface
- Hub
- Human interface device
- Mass storage
- Printing
- Scanning/imaging (PTP)
- Media transfer (MTP)
- USB audio
- Modem
- Video

The USB organization standardizes the class specifications. The standard covers items such as the required descriptors and endpoints, and, most importantly, it specifies the format for the payloads that go across the endpoints.

Many concurrent users of the bus are carried over the various pipes between each of the devices and the host controller. Each of the pipes has specific bandwidth requirements and latency bounds. The host controller controls the allocation of bandwidth across the bus. It manages when the host and each individual pipe are allowed to transmit data. The maximum size of a packet that a device can transmit or receive is provided in the endpoint descriptor. The USB bandwidth is allocated on the bases of 1-ms frames, with microframes of 125 µs. Each microframe can contain multiple USB transactions. The USB host controller software schedules transactions to be performed during each frame by building up a list of transfer descriptors. Linked lists of transfer descriptors called a frame list are fetched by the host controller for each USB frame. The host controller makes sure that that the microframes are packed with transactions, but no transaction can cross the microframe boundary.

Programming Interface

The programming interface for USB host controllers has been standardized. These standards define the register maps for the controller and the descriptor formats for the data when they are transmitted and received on the bus. Three standards are in existence:

- UHCI – Universal Host Controller Interface standardized by Intel and used for USB 1.x controllers.
- OHCI – Open Host Controller Interface for USB 1.x. This standard was developed by Compaq, Microsoft, and National Semiconductor (ftp://ftp.compaq.com/pub/supportinformation/papers/hcir1_0a.pdf). The OHCI specification expects more capabilities in the hardware over that expected by a UHCI controller.

- EHCI – Extended Host Controller Interface. This is used for USB 2.0 device controllers on Intel platforms (http://www.intel.com/technology/usb/ehcispec.htm).
- USB OTG – As we mentioned, there is no standard host controller interface standard for the device model.

Most devices support both 1.1 and 2.0 devices by instantiating both a UHCI and EHCI controller. This is often done for expedience; the two controllers can coexist and a multiplexing function can be placed between the devices and each controller.

Depending on the source of the IP in the embedded SOC device, the register map and descriptor format may not follow these standards.

Figure 4.19 shows the components of a software stack on top of the EHCI controller.

The EHCI host controller manages the transmission and reception of frames on the bus. The Enhanced USB host controller contains two sets of software accessible hardware registers, memory-mapped registers, and optional PCI configuration registers. The PCI configuration registers are required if the host controller is implemented as a PCI device. The PCI registers contain the PCI header and some additional configuration registers required to allocate the appropriate system resources during enumeration. The PCI registers are not used by the USB driver after enumeration.

The memory-mapped registers are divided into two sections:

- *Capability registers* are a set of read-only capability registers. The capability registers specify the limits, restrictions, and capabilities of a host controller implementation. These values are used as parameters to the host controller driver.

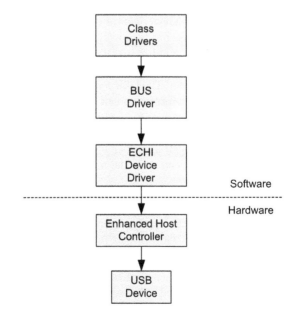

FIGURE 4.19

Software Stack on ECHI Controller.

- *Operational registers* (which are read/write). The operational registers are used by system software to interact with the operational state of the host controller. The operation registers contain pointers to lists in host memory that are used to define the traffic to be transmitted and received.

Figure 4.20 shows the register structure for a PCI ECHI controller.

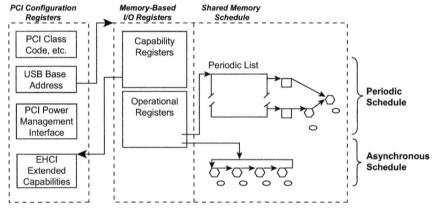

FIGURE 4.20

EHCI Register Classification.

Source: http://www.intel.com/technology/usb/download/ehci-r10.pdf

The EHCI provides support for two categories of transfer types: asynchronous and periodic. Periodic transfer types include both isochronous and interrupt. Asynchronous transfer types include control and bulk. Figure 4.20 illustrates that the EHCI schedule interface provides separate schedules for each category of transfer type. The periodic schedule is based on a time-oriented frame list that represents a sliding window of time of host controller work items. All isochronous and interrupt transfers are serviced via the periodic schedule. The asynchronous schedule is a simple circular list of schedule work items that provides a round-robin service opportunity for all asynchronous transfers.

> **Note**
> Wake on USB: The ECHI specification often describes the physical location of the registers within the device. Different parts of the ECHI controller are powered by different supply voltages within the SOC. As a result, some sets of registers retain their values during different CPU power states. These features are provided to support wakeup events from a USB device. Consider the case where your laptop is in a sleep state (suspended); moving the mouse can trigger a wakeup event to the platform, but in order to do so the ECHI controller must remain powered.

The ECHI controller generates interrupts to the processor based on a number of events. One such interrupt is generated at a point in the processing of the asynchronous lists. This is configured when the list is generated by the driver to provide enough advanced notice for the driver to add more work to the list. Another interrupt is generated when the period frame list rolls over; this again is to ensure that the driver supplies data for subsequent frames.

As we mentioned, there are two key lists managed by the driver and consumed by the host controller: the periodic frame list (for isochronous and interrupt traffic) and the asynchronous list (control and bulk transfers). We'll discuss the asynchronous list first. The list is only processed when the host controller reaches the end of the periodic list, the periodic list is disabled, or the periodic list is empty. That is, it has the lowest priority of all traffic and will only be sent on the bus when there is no other work to do. The asynchronous list is pointed to by a control register: AsyncListAddress. The list is a circular list of queue heads. The controller cycles through each element in the list (in a round-robin fashion), processing each queue head as it goes. One queue head is used to manage the data stream for one endpoint. The queue head consists of a queue element transfer descriptor. The queue head structure contains static endpoint characteristics and capabilities. It also contains a working area from where individual bus transactions for an endpoint are executed. Each queue element transfer descriptor represents one or more bus transactions, which is defined in the context of this specification as a transfer. A descriptor has an array of buffer pointers, which is used to reference the data buffer for a transfer. Figure 4.21 shows how the elements described above are linked together.

The USB UHCI device driver provides services to the individual class drivers, which make use of the bus drive to transmit and receive data.

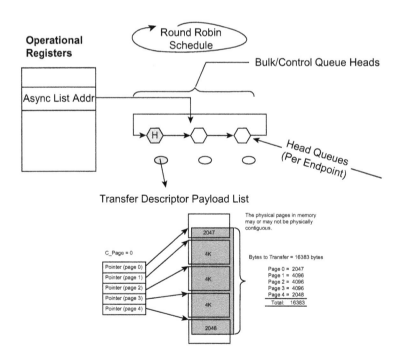

FIGURE 4.21

Async List Address, Head Queues, and Payload Description.

Source: EHCI Intel Spec.

Linux Driver

- The Linux USB driver is split into a core and set of class drivers. The core driver provides capabilities to read and write to an endpoint (among other things). The core driver provides a very simple mechanism to access the bus. The steps are as follows (http://lxr.linux.no/linux+v2.6.35.7/drivers/usb/usb-skeleton.c):
- Allocate a USB Request Block (URB) using `usb_alloc_urb()`.
- Allocate a DMA buffer data.
- Copy data into the allocated DMA buffer.
- Initialize the URB with device, endpoint, and data buffer pointers, and a function pointer to a callback routine using the call `usb_fill_bulk_urb()`.
- Submit the URB using `usb_submit_urb()`. The interface to the USB host controller is asynchronous, which means that the call `usb_submit_urb()` returns straightaway and does not block to caller.
- The USB driver will call the callback function associated with the URB once the transmission of the data associated with the URB is complete.

That describes the basic mechanism of sending data on the bus, but it is agnostic as to the payload being sent or received. The USB class driver for the device actually formats the payload that sent on the endpoint. For example, a USB pen drive uses the USB mass storage class device driver. Reference source code for the USB mass storage driver can be found at Linux/drivers/usb/storage/.

DEVICE INTERCONNECT—LOW PERFORMANCE

There is a wide range of low-speed, low-pin-count, low-performance interface types. These are used to control sensors, flash devices, simple LCD displays, and the like. In this section we discuss the following interface types:

- Inter-Integrated Circuit (I^2C) bus
- System Management Bus (SMB)
- Serial Peripheral Interface (SPI) bus
- Inter IC Sound (I^2S)
- Universal Asynchronous Receiver/Transmitter (UART)
- High-Speed Serial

Inter-Integrated Circuit Bus

One of the most prevalent of these buses is known as the Inter-Integrated Circuit bus, or I^2C bus. It was invented by Philips (now NXP) in the 1980s. The specification can be found at http://www.nxp.com/documents/user_manual/UM10204.pdf.

The bus standard allows for multiple masters on the bus (however, in many use cases it runs as a single master with multiple slaves attached). It is a simple two-wire bus consisting of a serial clock line (SCL) and a serial data line (SDA). Figure 4.22 shows the interconnection between devices on an I^2C bus.

Each wire (SDA and SCL) is bidirectional. They are driven by open collector gates on each of the devices. Open collector gates allow any device to bring a pin to zero. You may have noticed the pull-up

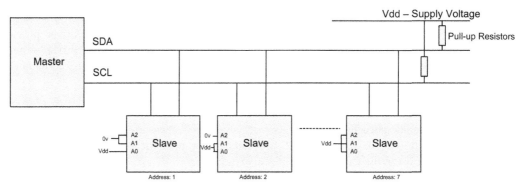

FIGURE 4.22

Single Master I²C Bus.

resistors in the diagram; these are typical when open collector outputs are used, and they bring the default bus value to Vdd—a logic one. The protocol is quite simple and is often driven by software directly controlling two general-purpose I/O pins. Each device has a 7-bit address so that transactions can be directed to a particular slave device from the master. The addresses are hard-coded by pull-up/pull-down pins on the device such as A[0-2] in Figure 4.22. Although the bus supports up to 112 devices, most devices export a low number of address bits such as 3 bits. The 3 bits that are selected with the board straps form the lower-order address bits of the device. The higher-order address bits (for example, the remaining 4) are assigned to the device type and built in to the device. The result is that you can have up to eight devices of the same type on a bus, as other devices will contain different high-order address bits.

The bus is controlled by the master device. The master device generates the serial clock, controls bus access, and controls the stop and start conditions. The clock speeds are relatively low, from 10 kHz to 100 kHz and 400 kHz to 2 MHz. The bus follows the following state transitions:

- Bus Not Busy – When both SDA and SCL are high (logic one).
- Start Bus Transfer – A high to low transition of SDA while SCL is high. All commands must start with a start transfer signal.
- Data Transfer – The data line must be set to the required value when the SCL line is low; when the SDL line is high, the data line value is considered to be valid.
- The first byte of data transfer after the start bus transfer consists of 7 bits of slave address and 1 read/write bit to indicate the type of transfer.
- An acknowledge bit/cycle is required after every byte; generally, the slave addressed will generate an acknowledge cycle. This allows the slave to indicate it has accepted the byte. The master releases the SDA line during the acknowledge clock pulse so the slave can pull the SDA line low; it must remain low during the high period of this clock pulse (still generated by the master). If the SDA line remains high during this clock phase, it is treated as a not acknowledge (NACK).
- Stop Bus Transfer – A low to high transition of SDA while SDL is high indicates that the bus transfer has completed, and the bus returns to Not busy.

The format of the data after the address transfer (first byte after a start bus transfer) is dictated by the actual device you connect, for example, a serial EEPROM (http://ww1.microchip.com/downloads/en/devicedoc/21189f.pdf). To perform a byte write to the device, the two bytes following in the device address specify an address to write within the device, and the following byte is the byte we wish to write to the address within the device. Read in the device can take two forms; the first is a current address read capability. The device has an address counter that starts at zero. Each read of the device provides a byte back to the master and the counter is incremented. This is the easiest way to read out the EEPROM contents. There is also an address specific read, but this is accessed by setting the counter using a device write sequence, then reading back the current address value. This is just an example; the actual interactions with the device are defined by the vendor.

System Management Bus (SMBus)

The System Management Bus is a two-wire bus used for host-to-device and device-to-device communications (http://smbus.org/specs/). It was originally invented by Intel, but its principles are similar to that defined by the I^2C bus. It is ubiquitous on modern PC motherboards and is used to control the power supply on/off, temperature sensors, fan control, read the configuration from the memory DIMMs, and the like. Intel devices such as the Intel Atom Processor E6xx Series integrate the SMBus host controller, which acts as a master and communicates to slave devices on the motherboard. SMBus specification 2.0 permits a bus speed for an SMBus of between 10 Khz and 100 KHz. The SMBus specification defines a number of commands for use with devices:

- *Quick Command* – This is the simplest message that can be sent to a device; the only data communicated is the address byte (see I^2C) where the read/write bit is only data indication. It can be used to simply turn the device on or off.
- *Send Byte* – A simple device will recognize its slave address and process the subsequent data byte as a command.
- *Receive Byte* – Similar to send byte, but gets a data byte from the device. When the device is read it provides a single byte. This could be a temperature reading from a device.
- *Write Byte/Word* – The first byte of a Write Byte/Word sequence is the command code. The next one or two bytes are the data to be written to the device.
- *Read Byte/Word* – To read a byte from the device, the host must first write a command to the slave device. Then the host must follow that with repeated START commands to denote a read from the slave; the slave returns one or two bytes of data.
- *Process Call* – This sends data to the slave device and waits for a response byte based on the data sent to the device.
- *Block Read/Write* – This is an extension of the read/write byte where a number of bytes to be sent or received is added is indicated after the command byte.
- *Block Write-Block Read Process Call* – This is an combination of block write and process call: it allows for the transmission of multiple bytes as the "argument" to the process call. The response can also be a variable number of bytes.

The commands described above are all quite similar to the semantics used in an I^2C bus, but SMBus has also defined a mechanism for a slave to send a notification to the host (not unlike an

I²C slave device becoming the master for a particular transaction). The SMB notification is often used by devices to alert the host processor of a particular condition. For example, an SMBus motherboard temperature sensor could be programmed to generate an alert if the temperature were to go above a critical threshold. In this case, the system software would program the device to send the alert. The system software would not be required to poll the device to check the temperature. However, if the temperature crossed the threshold, the system would be notified. Many devices have a separate alert pin that is asserted to raise a non-maskable or system management interrupt. The system software can generate a broadcast call to read all slave devices that have current alerts active (the address used is the "alert response address"). There are many manufacturers of SMBus devices, such as the Nation Semiconductor LM75. The Linux lm-sensors project provides software that can be used to manage the hardware sensors on an Intel-based motherboard. A comparison between SMBus and I²C can be found in Application note 476, www.maxim-ic.com (direct link does not work).

Serial Peripheral Interface (SPI)

Serial Peripheral Interface (SPI) is a four-wire bus. It consists of a serial clock, master output/slave input, master input/slave output, and a device select pin. The speed of the bus range is much higher than that found in I²C or SMBus; speeds up to 80 MHz are not uncommon. There are variants that provide multiple bits for the transfer (up to 4). These additional data bits dramatically increase the performance. There is no standard specification defined for SPI—it is a de facto standard. The SPI bus is used to connect to serial flash parts that provide the initial boot code for Intel platforms, as shown in Figure 4.23.

The effective throughput of a 80-MHz 4-pin serial peripheral interface to a NOR flash device is approximately 40 megabytes per second. This is faster than many parallel interfaces to older NOR flash devices. Intel SOC and chipset integrate SPI host controller, which offloads the processor from driving the SPI protocol on SPI bus.

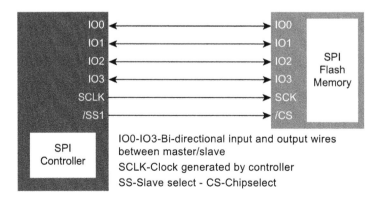

FIGURE 4.23

SPI Interface to Flash Parts.

Audio Buses

Audio buses differ from the low-pin-count buses we have described so far. They typically run continuously, providing audio samples between devices. The most common use case is to connect a codec (analog device with d/a and a/d converters) to a digital SOC where the samples are processed or generated. The Intel-based SOC devices typically use a High Def Audio bus (http://www.intel.com/design/chipsets/hdaudio.htm).

A typical configuration can carry 16 channels per stream, 32-bit audio samples at a sample rate of 192 kHz. The HD audio controller provides DMA engines that manage the transmission and reception of audio samples across the bus with low processor overhead.

Inter IC Sound (I²S)

The I^2S bus is another bus defined by Philips (http://www.nxp.com/acrobat_download2/various/I2SBUS.pdf). The bus was designed to transfer audio samples between integrated circuits. The bus is a three-wire bus: a continuously running clock, a data line, and a word select line to allow for the selection of two channels (left/right for stereo), which are time-multiplexed on the data pins.

Universal Asynchronous Receiver/Transmitter

A universal asynchronous receiver/transmitter (UART) is a device that transmits and receives data between a peer UART across a serial line. There are a number of EIA standards, RS-232, RS-422, and RS-485, that define the data format, signals, and electrical voltages on the wires and connector format. The COM port (if it still has one) on PC computer platforms is an RS-232 port. The simplest form of serial communication requires just three wires: a transmit wire, a receive wire, and an electrical ground wire (by which the signals are referenced). To connect two systems together via the serial port, you need to cross over the Tx and Rx wires so the Tx of one port is connected to the Rx of the other port and vice versa. This is known as a null modem cable. There are other wires that can be defined on the serial port connector. There are hardware flow control signals and indications associated with analog modems that are no longer that prevalent. The most standard form is the simple three-wire Tx/Rx and Ground.

A serial port is one of the most basic items you can find on an embedded system. It is quite simple to program and can provide a simple command console and boot indication on when to bring up the system. If the device SOC has a UART, you should definitely make it accessible on your system. In many cases the UART signals are not electrically compatible with the RS-232 standard, and you must use a level shifter to be compatible with an actual RS-232 standard. A Maxim MAX232 is a common level shifter part used to convert the logic levels coming from the UART port to the RS-232 levels.

The asynchronous nature means that there is no separate clock signal to indicate the bit transitions on the Tx and Rx wires. The line encoding used is sufficient for the bits being transmitted to be detected. The transmission consists of a start bit, 5 to 8 data bits, an optional parity bit, and then 1, 1.5, or 2 stop bits. The most ubiquitously used format is No-Parity, 8 data bits, and 1 stop bit. This is usually written as N81.

There are many different speeds supported on UARTS: 300, 600, 1200, 1800, 2400, 4800, 7200, 9600, 14,400, 19,200, 38,400, 57,600, and 115,200 baud. The most common speed used by default on systems is 9600. If the UART is used for heavy data transfer such as downloading images to a platform, a faster baud rate such as 115,200 or higher is used.

When transferring data across the serial port, some form of flow control is often needed. Flow control allows the receiver of the data to indicate to the transmitter than it cannot process additional data sent to it. There are two forms of flow control: hardware and software. The hardware flow control uses additional signal wires (Request to Send and Clear to Send for five-wire RS-232) between the transmitter and receiver to delay the transmission of data to the receiver. More frequently used is software flow control, where the receiver sends a special data value to the transmitter to request that the transmitter pause transmission, and another code to resume the transmission. The characters used are XON/XOFF; XOFF corresponds to the Ctrl-S character and XON corresponds to the Ctrl-Q character. These key sequences can still be used on Linux terminals to pause and resume the terminal.

In some cases, the serial port is used to transfer binary data. In these cases the binary data must be altered and sent in a special format, as it cannot be transmitted directly (imagine XON/XOFF was one of the binary values to be transmitted). A common binary to serial (escaping) format is that provided by a protocol known as kermit (http://www.columbia.edu/Kermit/). Kermit is a terminal emulation program that provides a binary file transfer mechanism. However, the protocol is used more widely than the program itself, especially in embedded systems.

The UART device is a relatively simple device. It provides control registers to set for format (such as N81), clock dividers to set the baud rate, simple transmit and receive FIFOs, and interrupt triggers based on the levels of occupancy within these FIFOs. The model used (register set, behavior, and so on) by the vast majority of UART devices in systems was based on a device known as the 16550A UART, which was originally made by National Semiconductor. There are some limited variations used; one common variation is the size/depth of the FIFO. When the part was originally developed, baud rates supported were relatively low and the size of the corresponding FIFO was quite small; in later revisions or instantiations the FIFO grew to a nominal size of 16 bytes.

The Linux serial driver can be used to start a login shell on a serial port. The serial driver is located in kernel/drivers/serial/8250.c. It supports the 8250 (the 16550A predecessor) and 16550A UART devices. The driver does its best to probe the hardware to identify which variant of UART is there. The serial devices are presented to the system via the /dev/ttyS handle, for example, /dev/ttyS0 for serial port 0 (usually COM port 0 on PCs), /dev/ttyS1 for serial port one, and so on. The Linux boot arguments can specify that a login console be brought up on a specific serial port as follows.

```
Kernel /vmlinux-2.6.34 ro root=LABEL=/ console=ttyS0,38400
```

The kernel arguments are specified by the bootloader configuration files. Bootloaders such as Grub, readboot, and uboot all support passing arguments to the kernel.

As the baud rates have increased, there can be some limited performance concerns due to the interaction model with the de facto standard 16550A UART model. In this model the FIFOs must be read by and written to by software byte by byte. In order to reduce the software overheads in handling UARTS, some UART controllers provide a DMA mechanism to transfer the serial characters received from the FIFO to contiguous memory buffers provided by the device driver (similar structure for Transmit). In these cases the interrupt indication is usually based on filling the supplied buffer or a timeout after the last character has been received. This significantly reduces the software overheads associated with transferring data over the serial port. It should be noted that the speeds are still very low in comparison to the relative performance of the processor, and large FIFOs are more common than DMA capable UARTS.

Bluetooth Usage Model

In the previous section we focused on using the UART to interact with a user for debug or a device console provisioning, and so forth. In many platforms the UART is used as a data channel to other devices on the platform. For example, many Bluetooth devices provided a UART interface for connection to the device. For example, the Infineon Bluetooth module (PMB 8763) provides a UART interface Host Controller Interface (HCI) and a Pulse Code Modulation (PCM) interface for audio connections/routing. The HCI transport layer is defined by the Bluetooth organization (www .bluetooth.com). The specification provides for the transmission of commands, events, and data packets between the Host and the Host Controller (Bluetooth device). The specification defines a number of physical interconnects, namely, UART, USB, Secure Digital, and three-wire, that can be used. In many embedded use cases the UART physical interconnect is used, whereas for aftermarket PC designers the USB interface is used. The Bluetooth stack is configured to run over a particular physical interface. There are a number of Linux commands, such as `hciattach`, `hcitool` scan, and `hcidump`, that can be used to discover, attach to, and control Bluetooth devices. The tools are user space tools that communicate with the Bluetooth stack, known as BlueZ (on Linux distributions). You should note that although the UART is a very simple physical interface, a sophisticated multiuse protocol stack can be built on top providing transfer of audio, packet data, contact information, and so on, as shown in Figure 4.24.

The Bluetooth air interface can run to several megabits per second (consider a tethered use case where Bluetooth is used to connect to the cell phone, which in turn provides data connectivity at 3G or 4G speeds). As the air interface capabilities have improved, so too must the speed of the UART to

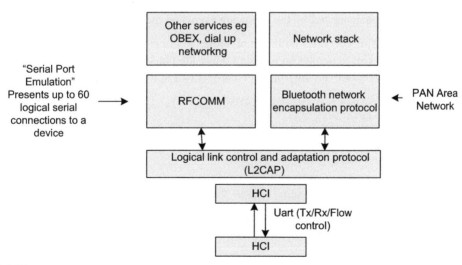

FIGURE 4.24

Bluetooth Protocol Stack.

connect to Bluetooth radio. As we mentioned above, as the speed increases you may need to make use of DMA features (if they exist) on the UART to reduce the overheads in communicating with the radio.

GENERAL-PURPOSE INPUT/OUTPUT

General-purpose input/output (GPIO) pins are external pins on an SOC device that are under direct control of software. The pins can be typically configured as an input pin or an output pin, or tri-stated.

The value (one or zero) of an output pin is controlled by the value of a specific bit in a control register. In some cases there is also control of the current that the pin can source (called *drive strength*). The output pin can be connected to any logic device on the platform. A very common use is to tie it to an LED to provide some form of user indication.

There is also a configuration known as *open collector*. An open collector output can be connected to other open collector outputs from other devices. In this configuration the line is typically pulled up to high with a resistor connected to the supply voltage. In this case any device can drive the line low. This is also known as wired AND for positive TRUE logic.

When the GPIO pin is configured as an input, the logic value on the external pin is reflected in a bit within a register. As the external value changes, it is updated automatically in the register.

In some configurations the input pin logic can be attached to the pin after the output driver so the software can read the actual pin value even though the pin may also be driven by the software. This can be useful for reading the logic state value of an open collector bus, ensuring that the value on the pin reflects the output value, or referencing the value written to output previously. Such feedback logic can also help detect a short on pin or some output contention, where multiple devices are driving different logic values onto the wire (this should not occur but it happens).

It is common to provide some interrupt processing logic that can be assigned to the input pins. An interrupt can typically be generated by the following events on the GPIO pin:

- *Active Low Level* – This generates an interrupt while the pin signal is low.
- *Active High Level* – This generates an interrupt while the pin signal is high.
- *Rising Edge* – This generates an interrupt when the GPIO pin transitions from a low to high signal value.

```
struct gpio_ctrl {
  unsigned long gpio_input_reg;
    . . .
}
unsigned read_gpio_pin_a(void)
{
unsigned bit;
struct gpio_ctrl *addr = GPIO_REG_ADDRESS;

  bit = ((read_word(addr->gpio_input_reg) & GPIO_BIT_A) >>
         GPIO_BIT_A;
  return bit;
}
```

FIGURE 4.25

GPIO Read Pin Example.

- *Falling Edge* – This generates an interrupt when the GPIO pin transitions from a high to low signal value.
- *Any Edge* – This generates an interrupt when the GPIO pin toggle its states, that is, transitions from a low to high or a high to low signal value.

When controlling the GPIO pins through software, the software will have a number of registers that are memory mapped. Given that the register value may change as a result of change in GPIO pin status, you must ensure that the actual hardware is read. It used to be common to use the C keyword *volatile* when using pointers to access hardware registers; it is recommended that you use functions supplied by the operating system to read/write to the hardware. These functions ensure that the compiler does not optimize away the access. Figure 4.25 shows a simple example to read a bit value.

A discussion kernel position on *volatile* can be found in the kernel tree Kernel/Documentation/volatile-considered-harmful.txt.

The I^2C bus we described earlier can be implemented using two GPIO pins and a software driver that drives the clock pins and configures the data pin as an output, toggles it in line with the clock output toggles, and then changes the direction of the data pin to an input to receive the data from the bus while continue toggling the clock pin, all through software control.

POWER DELIVERY

The details of the power deliver mechanism are not critical to understand as a software developer, but one topic may be relevant, and that is the management of power failure events. In many cases systems provide an indication that the power is about to fail. In this scenario, the platform has a very limited amount of time to perform critical save operations. The interrupt should be handled with the upmost priority; usually, the software flushes cached elements from RAM to nonvolatile storage (such as flash).

A subset of power fail scenarios is known as brown-outs. These are cases where the power supply drops below its normal operating level but not completely off. Think of an engine cranking in your car; this is such a heavy electrical load that the power to some of the electronics can drop momentarily. Managing these scenarios is beyond the scope of this book, but rest assured there can be significant effort expended in testing these scenario; in particular, the integrity of the nonvolatile storage file systems needs particular attention. The technique often requires fail-safe file system updates that can easily be rolled back in the event of corruption due to brown-outs. It is important to have robust brown-out detection circuitry on such platforms. Bear in mind that nothing can be trusted in this grey zone of operation.

SUMMARY

As you can see, an embedded platform consists of a wide range of peripheral types with many different characteristics. Many of the peripherals we mentioned are now integrated as part of modern SOC devices, while others remain as part of the platform board. We have shown how many of the interfaces are used to expand the capabilities of the SOC device.

Embedded Processor Architecture

How do we go about classifying an embedded processor? The traditional embedded CPU market is generally divided into microprocessors, microcontrollers, and digital signal processors. Microcontrollers are typically 8-/16-bit processors with a number of input/output (I/O) peripherals, and they are usually self-sufficient in terms of ROM and RAM. Microprocessors, on the other hand, traditionally comprise a 32-bit processor with a number of onboard peripherals. As the transistor continues its reduction in size every year, it has become more and more cost-effective to develop large-scale System-On-Chip (SOC) devices. The majority of SOCs today contain a 32-bit microprocessor integrated with a broad range of additional capabilities alongside the processor. The ability to expand the capabilities of an SOC by integrating industry standard interfaces is an important attribute of developing embedded systems.

The embedded industry currently uses 8-, 16-, and 32-bit processors, continually evolving the performance and applications supported. As applications have steadily evolved well beyond simple control functions, there is a significant migration to 32-bit microprocessor SOCs, as a result we will focus its attention on 32-bit microprocessor based systems. The capabilities of the processors used in the embedded market have typically lagged behind those found in the mainstream processors' environments. As embedded applications have become more and more complex, requiring higher performance and using larger data sets, this lag is quickly diminishing.

A number of embedded applications incorporate digital signal processing (DSP) algorithms. Consequently, a number of embedded microprocessors incorporate capabilities that are optimized for DSP algorithms. In this book, we discuss processor extensions that are designed to support DSP operations (Chapter 11), but coverage of discrete digital signal processor devices is beyond the scope of this work.

This chapter covers a range of concepts associated with the processor within the SOC, with a focus on topics that are of particular interest when developing embedded systems. Where examples are required we make reference to the Intel® Atom™ processor, and where appropriate make comparisons to other embedded processor architectures.

BASIC EXECUTION ENVIRONMENT

All processors provide a register set for use by the programmer. We consider a subset of the registers in a processor to be architecturally defined. Architecturally defined registers are persistent across many specific implementations and generations of the architecture.

All processors provide a general-purpose register file—these registers hold the data to be operated on by the processor. Processors provide a rich set of instructors to operate on these registers; the most basic functions that can be performed are loading to and from memory and logical and arithmetic operations.

99

The register file on some processors such as ARM™ and PowerPC™ is completely generalized, and most registers can be used as source or destination operators in any of the instructions, whereas other processors impose limitations on the registers that can be used in a subset of the instructions.

The Intel processors provide eight general-purpose registers and six segment registers. The general-purpose registers are known as EAX, EBX, ECX, EDX, ESI, EDI, EBP, and ESP. Although all registers are considered general purpose, some instructions are limited to act on a subset of the registers.

The general-purpose registers are either 32 bits or 64 bits wide, 32 bits when the CPU is configured in IA32 mode and 64 bits in EM64T mode. We will concentrate on 32-bit operation in this chapter, as at the time of writing it is the most widely deployed configuration for Atom-based processors. On Intel processors, naming conventions are used to access the registers in 16- and 8-bit modes. The naming conventions used by mnemonics to access portions of the 32-bit register are shown in Figure 5.1.

Each processor architecture and programming language has conventions that assign specific uses for particular registers. The general-purpose registers can attain a specific meaning for many reasons, perhaps because the operation is particularly fast with the designated register or more commonly through conventions established by high-level languages. Conventions established by high-level languages are known as application binary interfaces (ABIs). The ABI is a specification (sometimes de facto) that describes which registers are used to pass function variables, manage the software stack, and return values. The ABIs are always architecture specific and often also operating system dependent. As an embedded systems programmer, it's quite beneficial to know these conventions for your target architecture/operating system/language combination. We describe ABIs in more detail in the section "Application Binary Interface" later in this chapter.

The segment registers on Intel architecture processors are worth a brief discussion. Both the Intel architecture and the operating systems that run on it have evolved over many years. This evolution has allowed the Intel architecture to keep pace with advances in software architectures and best in class operating system design, moving from 16-bit single-thread real-memory models under MS-DOS to multi-threaded protected mode 32- and 64-bit applications under a variety of modern operating system kernels, such as Linux. Features such as segmented memory solved the need of 16-bit applications to access more memory than a single 16-bit register could address. Segment registers

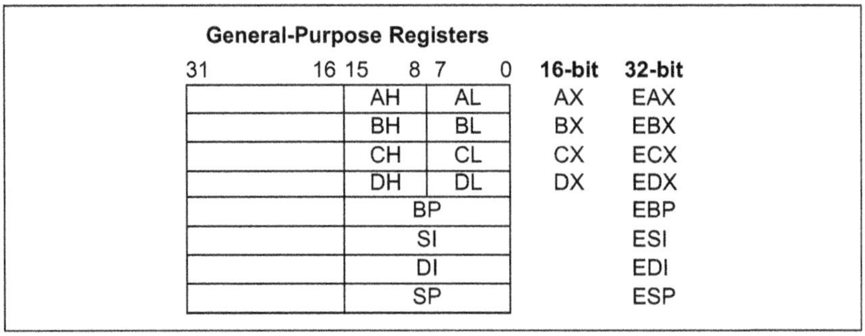

General-Purpose Registers

31	16	15	8	7	0	**16-bit**	**32-bit**
		AH		AL		AX	EAX
		BH		BL		BX	EBX
		CH		CL		CX	ECX
		DH		DL		DX	EDX
		BP					EBP
		SI					ESI
		DI					EDI
		SP					ESP

FIGURE 5.1

Intel Architecture Register Naming in 32-Bit Mode.

were first introduced to allow the generation of a linear address greater than 16 bits. The segment register was shifted and added to a 16-bit register to generate a logical address greater than 16 bits. Intel processors provide three primary modes of operation, namely, Flat, Segmented, and Real 8086 modes. However, today the predominant configuration mode of the processor is the Flat Memory mode. In this mode a selection of bits within the segment registers provide indexes into a table, which selects a segment descriptor. The segment descriptor then provides a base address for the segment. The base address is added to the contents of the register to create the linear address for the memory reference. The segment base addresses are configured by the operating system; they are set to zero for Linux User Space, Linux™ kernel space, and VxWorks™. Some operating systems (such as Linux) use the FS and GS segment registers to access application thread-specific data or OS-specific data in the kernel. The GCC compiler may use GS to implement a runtime stack protector or as a base pointer for Thread Local Storage (TLS).

The key point is that for most Intel environments today you don't have to worry about the segmentation model to any great extent, as most environments have migrated to a linear 32-bit flat memory model.

In addition to the general-purpose register file, the processor maintains an instruction pointer, flags, stack, and frame pointers:

- *Instruction pointer.* All processors provide a register that contains the current instruction pointer. The instruction counter is mostly maintained by the processor and updated automatically as the processor executes instructions. The program flow may be altered from its normally increasing (words) sequence through call, branch, conditional instructions, exceptions, or interrupts. On some architecture such as ARM, instructions are provided to directly alter the instruction pointer itself.
- The instruction pointer on Intel architecture is called the Extended Instruction Pointer (EIP). The EIP is a 32-bit register unless the processor is in one of its extended 64-bit modes. There are no instructions that can be used to directly read or write to the EIP. The EIP can only be modified using instructions such as JMP (jump to an address), JMPcc (conditionally jump to an address), CALL (call a procedure), RET (return from a procedure), and IRET (return from an interrupt or exception).
- *Flags.* All processors provide a register that contain a set of flags. The bits within a flag register on a processor can usually be broken down into two groups. The first are status flags. Status flags are updated as a result of an instruction that operates on one of the general-purpose registers. Examples of instructions that update the status flags are ADD, SUB, and MUL. Status flags can be used by subsequent instructions to change the flow of the program, for example, to branch to a new program address if the zero flag bit is set. Most processors offer a similar set of status flags, sometimes known as condition codes. Intel processors provide the following status flags: Carry, Parity, BCD Carry/Borrow, Zero, Sign, and Overflow.
- Along with the status flags, processors usually have a number of additional bits providing information to the programmer and operating system; these bits are usually specific to the processor architecture. They typically provide information on the privilege level of the processor, a global mask for interrupts, and other bits used to control the behavior of the processor for debugging, legacy support, and so on. The full list of flags in the EFLAGS register is shown in Figure 5.2.

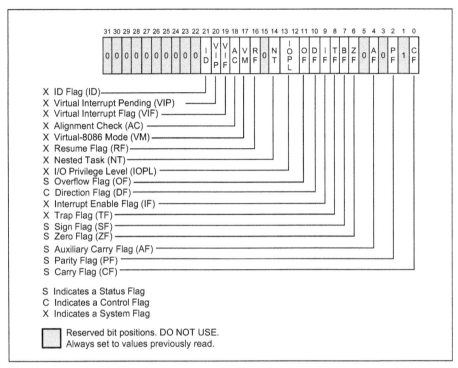

FIGURE 5.2

Intel Architecture EFLAGS Register.

- *Stack pointer.* In higher-level languages such as C, The program stacks are created in system memory. The stack can used to store local variables, allocate storage, and pass function arguments. It is typical for processors to provide dedicated registers to hold the stack pointer and specific instructions to manipulate the stack. The Intel processor provides PUSH and POP instructions, which operate on the ESP register. Depending on the processor architecture, stacks grow up or grow down as entries are added; which way they grow is a largely arbitrary and up to the architecture creators. In Intel processors, the stack frame grows down.
- *Base pointer.* In conjunction with the stack pointer, higher-level languages create what's often known as a stack frame. The base pointer allows the program to manage the function calling hierarchy on the stack. Using a memory dump of the program stack, the base pointer, and stack pointer, you can identify the calling sequence of function calls that occurred before the current function. Some processors provide a dedicated base register, and others just define a specific register by ABI convention. The Intel processor ABIs designate the EBP register as the base pointer. The base pointer is also referred to as a frame pointer in other architectures.

Figure 5.3 brings together the basic view described above and adds some conventions for registers use cases.

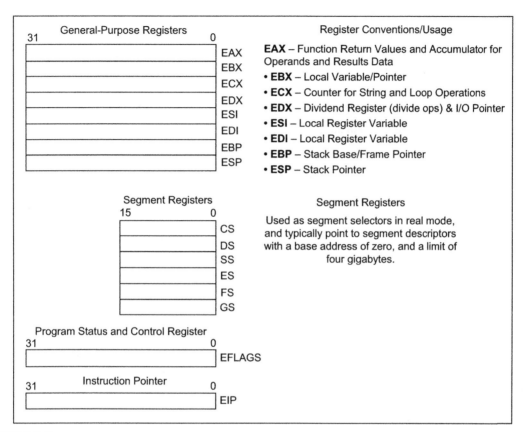

FIGURE 5.3

Basic 32-Bit Execution Environment.

Privilege Levels

All modern embedded processors provide a mechanism to allow portions of the software to operate with differing levels of privilege. The current privilege level is used by the system to control access to resources and execution of certain instructions. The number and specific use of privilege levels are architecture specific, but most architectures support a minimum of two privilege levels. The highest privilege level is usually reserved for the operating system. User programs and applications typically run with a lower privilege level. The use of privilege levels increases the robustness of the system by reducing the ability of an application to interfere with system-wide resources. For example, the ability to disable interrupts is a privileged instruction and ideally not accessible directly by an application.

Intel processors provide four privilege levels, although in practice level zero and level three are predominantly used. The current privilege level (CPL) of the processor is stored in the lowest 2 bits of the code segment selector (CS). The highest privilege level is number zero. This level is commonly known as Kernel Mode for Linux and Ring 0 for Windows-based operating systems. A CPL of three is used for user space programs in both Linux and Windows.

Many processors simply grant privileges to execute system level instructions or access system level resources by being at a privileged supervisor level. However, on Intel architecture processors some further details are required to understand how an Intel processor decides whether an operation is allowed. Whether an instruction has sufficient privilege to perform a specific operation is established by comparing the CPL to the active I/O Privilege Level (IOPL) The IOPL is stored in bits 12 and 13 of the FLAGS register and its value is controlled by the operating system. If the CPL is less than the current IOPL, then the privileged operation is allowed; if greater than or equal to IOPL, then a privileged operation will fail. On an Intel processor the CPL value is stored in the low 2 bits of the Code Segment register. Most operating systems set the IOPL value to three, thus having a CPL value of three corresponds to the lowest privilege level allowed in the system, and a CPL value of zero is the highest privilege level. As an embedded systems programmer, you might often require direct access to a hardware resource from your application. Most operating systems provide a mechanism to alter the privilege level, and a root privileged application, for example, can call the IOPL() function on Linux to altar the IOPL flags. To increase the security of your application you should minimize the time where the code executes with higher privilege level, and you should not run the entire application with increased privileges.

Floating-Point Units

Floating-point mathematical operations are required in a wide range of embedded applications, such as control systems and digital signal analysis. Where an application does require floating point, the performance targets often dictate the need for a hardware-based floating-point unit. Most embedded processor SOCs offer a version that provides hardware-based floating point. A key attribute of a floating point acceleration function associated with the processor is whether the floating-point unit is compliant with the IEEE Standard 754 for Binary Floating-Point Arithmetic. The precision of the floating-point unit (single/double) is also an important attribute in developing the floating-point algorithms.

Intel processors have two floating-point units. The first and probably best known is the x87 Floating-Point Unit (FPU). The x87 FPU instructions operate on floating-point, integer, and binary-coded decimal (BCD) operands. It supports 80-bit precision, double extended floating-point. The FPU operates as a coprocessor to the instruction unit. The FPU instructions are submitted to the FPU and the scalar (main processor) pipeline continues to run in parallel. To maximize overall application performance it is important to ensure that the processor's main execution flow can perform useful work while the FPU performs the floating-point operations. To that end it is usually best to use a compiler to generate the target code to ensure efficient instruction scheduling.

Not all floating-point operations can be completed; for example, dividing a number by zero results in a floating-point fault. The following floating-point operations result in faults: all invalid operations, for example, square root of a negative number, overflow, underflow, and inexact result. The operating system provides an exception handler to handle the floating-point fault exceptions. In the case of Linux, the kernel catches the fault and sends a user space signal (SIGFPE, signal floating-point exception). The application will be terminated unless the application has chosen to handle the exceptions. The C language specification as defined by the ISO C99 (ISO/IEC 9899:1999) standardizes a number of functions to control the behavior of floating-point rounding and exception handling. One such function is fegetexceptflag().

Intel processors also have a Single Instruction Multiple Data (SIMD) execution engine. The Intel Atom processor supports the Supplemental Streaming SIMD Extensions 3 (SSSE3) version of the SIMD instructions, which support integer, single, and double precession floating-point units.

The Intel Atom processor has a rich set of floating-point coprocessor capabilities. As a result, a particular algorithm could be implemented in a number of ways. The trade-offs for the use of each floating-point unit for a particular operation are described in Chapter 11, "Digital Signal Processing."

The floating-point units are resources that contain a number of registers and some current state information. When different software threads wish to use the resources, the kernel software may have to save and restore the registers and all state information during operating system context switches. The Intel processor provides FXSAVE and FXRSTOR to save and restore the required state and register information of FP and SSE units. These operations can be costly if performed on every task transition, so Intel processors provide a mechanism to help the kernel identify whether an FPU was actually used by a particular process. The TS flag in the control register zero (CS0.TS) provides an indication that the floating point unit has been used. The kernel can clear the value when it performs a context switch, and check if the bit has been set during the execution of the process (indicating the process used the FP unit). The operating system can be configured to save the registers and state on transition from a thread that used the resource or alternatively raise an exception when a new thread attempts to use the resource after a previous thread has used it. If the real-time behavior of your FP/SSE code is important, you should look into the detailed operating system behavior. You may have to take special steps if you want to use floating-point or SSE units from within the kernel. For example, in Linux you have to call `kernel_fpu_begin()` and `kernel_fpu_end()` around the code that uses the FP/SSE units. This will save and restore the required state.

Processor Specifics

Practically all embedded processors have been in existence for a number of generations, though none of the existing embedded processors quite match the longevity of the Intel architecture. As each product generation evolves, new capabilities are introduced, and as an embedded systems developer you will need to establish exactly which features are supported on the particular version you are working with. Having mechanisms to identity product capabilities at runtime facilitates the development of code that will run on a number of different generations of the part without modification. The information is typically provided by special registers that are accessed via dedicated instructions. For example, on ARM platforms, there are a number of co-processor registers one of which is the System Control co-Processor. The system control coprocessor is known as CP15 and provides information and controls the processor behavior. On Intel platforms, a number of control/information registers, CR0, CR1, CR2, CR3, and CR4, and a special instruction (CPUID) are available. The CPUID instruction and registers describe capabilities of the processor and also provide some current processor state information. The CPUID instruction provides detailed information on the executing processor. The output from the CPUID instruction is dependent upon the contents of the EAX register; by placing different values in the EAX register and then executing the CPUID instruction, the CPUID instruction performs the function defined by the EAX value. The CPUID instruction returns the requested values in the EAX/EBX/EDX and ECX registers. The code segment below uses GCC compiler inline assembly code to dump all the CPUID values available on an Intel Atom platform.

```
long maxCpuId=0 , long cpuid;
long eax = 0, ebx = 0, ecx=0, edx=0;
eax = 0;  /* Get the maximum CPUID range */
/*
 * Input:Loads eax input register with eax variable value
 * Call CPUID instrucion
 * Output:Ensure EAX/EBX/EXC and EDX registers are mapped
 * the variables with the corresponding name.
 */
__asm__ __volatile__
("CPUID"
 :"=a"(eax), "=b"(ebx), "=c"(ecx), "=d"(edx)
 :"a"(eax)
);
maxCpuId=eax; /* Get the maximum value for EAX*/
for ( cpuid=0; cpuid <= maxCpuId ; ++cpuid)
{
  eax = cpuid;
  __asm__ __volatile__("CPUID"
           :"=a"(eax), "=b"(ebx), "=c"(ecx), "=d"(edx)
           :"a"(eax)
    );
  printf("CPUID [%2X] = %08X, %08X, %08X, %08X \n",cpuid, eax,ebx,ecx,edx);
}
```

The code above displays the various CPUID values, which can be decoded to provide detailed information about the processor. A good example of the type of information provided is the processor feature list. This is provided by calling CPUID with an EAX value of 01h. The processor features capabilities listed on an Atom processor returned the following values: EDX[31:0] = 0xBFE9FBFF and ECX[31:0] = 0x0040C3BD. Decoding the bits set in EDX/ECX indicates the following feature set on the Intel Atom processor: Floating-Point Unit, Time Stamp Counter, Physical Address Extension, Local Interrupt Controller (APIC), Cache Line Flush, Model Specific Registers, FXSAVE/FXSTOR, MMX, SSE, SSE2, SSE3, SSSE3, Thermal Management, Multi-Threading – (Hyper thread). The support for 64-bit operation (EM64T) is also indicated through the CPUID feature.

It is often useful to have an awareness of the cache structures on your platform, especially when it comes to performance tuning or at least understanding the behavior of your application and the correlation between application data set size and overall cache sizes. Chapter 18, "Platform Tuning," provides more specific details on tuning your system. The CPUID provides cache structure details of the processor. The decoded values returned from the current Intel Atom processor are as follows:

- L1 data cache: 24 kB, six-way set associative.
- L1 instruction cache: 32 kB, eight-way set associative.
- L2 cache: 512 kB, eight-way set associative.

The Linux command `cat/proc/cpuinfo` provides similar details relating to the CPU. A portion of the details presented is obtained by issuing using the CPUID instruction.

The provision of free running counters and hardware timers is required by most operating systems to provide the operating system "Tick," timed delay loops, code performance measurements, and the like. Intel Atom platforms provide a wealth of timers and counters on the platform. A very useful free running time stamp counter is provided on Intel platforms. It is simply accessed by using the RDTSC instruction. The instruction returns the number of ticks at maximum processor frequency (resolved at boot up) since reset. The tick represents the length of time for one duty cycle of the CPU clock, so for a processor running at 1.6 GHz, a tick would represent 0.625 ns. The value is very reliable, but you should be aware that in some system interactions may skew some measurements, such as when the processor's actual speed is slowed due to power-managed controls, although this is not the case for Atom processors. The code segment below shows how the time stamp counter can be read from a C program. The embedded assembly is written to be compiled by the GCC compiler.

```
long long timeStamp;

__asm__ __volatile__
 ("RDTSC"            ; Mnemonic to read counter
  :"=A"(timeStamp)  ; Map 64bit timeStamp to EDX/EAX
  :
 );
```

In addition to the free running counter, embedded platforms will make use of hardware-based timers. The timers on the Intel Atom platform are described in Chapter 4, "Embedded Platform Architecture."

APPLICATION BINARY INTERFACE

As an embedded software developer, you will develop most of your software in higher-level languages. It is less likely that you have to develop large portions of your code in assembly language. However, it is very important that you are conversant with assembly language and how assembly and high-level languages interact, particularly when it comes to debugging the platform. For embedded systems it is not unusual to have to "root cause" a system crash with information saved at the time of the system crash. A common example of this is debugging Linux Kernel Oops (http://www.kerneloops.org). The crash logs provide register values, stack frames, and software versions at the time of the crash. Understanding the register usages and calling convention of the high-level language is critical to debugging such logs. There is little formal standardization of the calling conventions but in general two de facto standard conventions predominate. The open source Gnu Compiler (GCC) conventions are used on Unix-like operating systems and most real-time operating systems, whereas the Microsoft Compiler calling conventions are used by compilers and tool chains on Windows-based operating systems. The best source of information on Linux/Unix type ABIs is located at http://refspecsfreestandards.org; consult http://msdn.microsoft.com for Windows-based platforms. As an indication of the fragmentation that arises, the Intel C++ Compiler provides an -fabi-version option, which allows you to select between *most recent ABI*, *g++ 3.2 and 3.3 compatible*, or *compatible with gcc 3.4 and higher*.

The calling conventions define the following aspects of the code generated by compilation:

- Data representation
- Data alignment and packing
- Stack alignment

- Register usage
- Function calling conventions
- Relocation/relative addressing
- Name mangling

The width (number of bits to represent) of data types is largely standard across all compilers and in general is intuitive. The alignment and packing behavior, on the other hand, can vary significantly and cause difficulty when debugging the stack trace associated with a crash. In general, data types are aligned to the width of the data type. A 4-byte integer is aligned to a 32-bit address; this is also known as double word aligned. The number of bits in a word, double word, and quad word is itself a convention specific to the processor architecture. On IA-32 processors, a 16-bit value is a word, a 32-bit value is a double word, and a 64-bit value is a quad-word. ARM and PowerPC architectures were defined later and word size changed to 32 bits, therefore making 16-bit values half words and 64-bit values double words.

The compilers also provide compiler options and pragmas that can be used to change the alignment of basic types and structure members. The most common option to change the way elements in a structure are aligned is the __PACKED__ pragma or equivalent command line compiler option. In this case all members of a structure are packed together, leaving no unused memory space. The alignment of members may not be on their natural boundary. This mechanism is often used in embedded systems where we want to share information between different systems or overlay a structure over the register map of a device. When sharing information across processors within a system or between systems, this approach may suffice, but it is not very rigorous. When sharing data across embedded systems, it is important to format the data in a formally agreed-upon standard for transmission; this removes all packing and endian issues that may arise. Common packing standards are eXternal Data Representation (XDR) and, more recently, XML.

The stack alignment is typically double word (4-byte) aligned for 32-bit operating systems and 16-byte aligned for 64-bit operating systems. The compiler will often have an option to set the alignment. An example of such an option is `-mpreferred-stack-boundary=value`, which is available when using a GCC compiler. The alignment of the stack is useful to know when debugging stack traces.

The processor's register usage by high-level languages can be divided into a number of categories:

- *Caller saved registers.* A number of registers may be altered (such as scratch registers) when a function is called; if the caller needs to retain this value, the caller must save the contents of these registers on the stack to facilitate restoration after the function returns.
- *Callee saved registers.* This is the list of registers the called function must restore to their previous value when the function returns.
- *Function argument passing registers.* Arguments are passed to a function either in registers or on the stack, depending on the number and type of arguments. For 32-bit IA-32 ABIs, all function parameters are passed on the stack; for 64-bit ABIs, a combination of registers and stack is used.
- *Function return value registers.* Function that returns a value does so in a register.

The IA-32 registers for the GNU compiler Linux 32-bit ABI are shown in Table 5.1. At the time of writing, a new draft ABI for use on Intel EM64T-capable processors is known as X32-ABI (https://sites.google.com/site/x32abi/). It maximizes the use of the registers available while enabled in

Table 5.1 ABI Register Calling Conventions—32-Bit Linux/Windows

IA-32 Register	32-Bit Linux GNU/Windows
EAX	Scratch and return value
EBX	Callee save
ECX	Scratch
EDX	Scratch and return value
ST0-ST7	Scratch/ST0 return float
ESI	Callee save
EDI	Callee save
EBP	Callee save
XMM0-XMM7	Scratch registers
YMM0-YMM7	Scratch registers—256 bit on AVX-capable processors only

EM64T mode, yet retains pointer, long, and integer sizes as if it were a 32-bit machine. This is a best-case hybrid for 32-bit applications.

A key aspect of the calling conventions is the creation of a stack. The stack is built up from a number of stack frames. Each stack frame consists of memory that is allocated from the program stack. The stack frame consists of parameters to the function being called, automatic stack variables, saved scratch registers, and callee and caller saved register values. A number of conventions specify where the stack cleanup operations must take place. These are known as cdecl, stdcall, and fastcall. The cdecl is the default calling convention and requires the calling function to perform the stack cleanup. The cdecl calling convention supports functions with a variable number of arguments such as printf. The stdcall calling convention supports a fixed number of arguments for a function and the stack cleanup is performed by the called function. The majority of embedded systems use the C default cdecl convention. Windows libraries primarily use the stdcall convention. The fastcall convention is an additional convention supported by Linux and Windows to increase the performance of the function call. It is critical that the caller and callee use the same convention—if not, the stack program will undoubtedly crash.

The following sequence of actions is performed as part of a function call:

- Save scratch registers in the caller.
- Push the function arguments onto the stack from right to left.
- Call the function, and the call instruction pushes the Instruction Pointer (EIP) onto the stack and transfers control to the function. The EIP value contains the address of the next instruction, and therefore the stack will contain the address of the instruction after the call.
- Save the base pointer (pushed onto the stack) and update the base pointer with the current stack pointer. The base pointer can now be used to reference the calling arguments. The first argument of the function is referred to by 8(%EBP); the second argument is accessed by 12(%EBP).
- Save scratch registers (caller save) used by this function.
- Grow the stack for local variables, simply by decrementing the ESP by the amount of space needed. Local variables are typically accessed by relative reference from the EBP.
- Do some useful work.

- Free the local stack storage, by adding the appropriate value to the ESP.
- Restore the scratch registers.
- Restore the base pointer, using POP.
- Return from the function, using RET. This moves the previously pushed address off the stack and transfers control to the instruction after the call.
- As this is the cdecl convention, the caller now frees the stack of the calling arguments, typically discarded by adding the required value to the ESP, or if the variables are reused, the values are moved into registers with POP for reuse.

The following section shows a simple C function call and the corresponding assembly.

```
main()
{
 int a = 1; x = 100; y = 150;
 int z;
  z = fool(a,x,y);
  printf("Z fool:%d\n", z);
}
int fool(int a, int x, int y)
{
 int z;
  z = a + x + y;
  return(z);
}
```

This produces the following assembly code using GNU disassembly format. The code is produced by calling gcc with the -S option. The GNU tools command objdump (called with argument -s) is very useful command in studying study the assembly code of an object or executable.

```
1  main:pushl  %ebp           ; Save the base pointer
2  movl        %esp, %ebp     ; Set the stack = base
3  andl        $-16, %esp     ; Allocate stack -16
4  subl        $32, %esp      ; Allocate stack -32
5  movl        $1, 16(%esp)   ; Put 01h into variable a
6  movl        $100, 20(%esp) ; Put 100h into variable x
7  movl        $150, 24(%esp) ; Put 100h into variable y
8  movl        24(%esp), %eax ; Get y into eax
9  movl        %eax, 8(%esp)  ; Put y onto stack
10 movl        20(%esp), %eax ; Put x into eax
11 movl        %eax, 4(%esp)  ; Put x onto stack
12 movl        16(%esp), %eax ; Put a into eax
13 movl        %eax, (%esp)   ; Push a onto stack
14 call        fool           ; Call the function
15 movl        %eax, 28(%esp) ; Put return z onto local stack
16 movl        28(%esp), %eax ; Move local variable into eax
17 movl        %eax, 4(%esp)  ; move return z into call stack
18 movl        $.LC0, (%esp)  ; move pointer to printf str
19 call    printf             ; call printf
```

```
20 leave                            ; Set ESP to EBP, POP EBP
21 ret                             ; return from function.
22 ...
23 foo1:
24 pushl    %ebp                    ; Save the base pointer
25 movl     %esp, %ebp              ; Set the stack = base
26 subl     $16, %esp               ; Grow stack by 16 bytes
27 movl     12(%ebp), %eax          ; Get x from stack into eax
28 movl     8(%ebp), %edx           ; Get a from stack into edx
29 leal     (%edx,%eax), %eax       ; Add edx+eax into eax
30 addl     16(%ebp), %eax          ; add y to eax
31 movl     %eax, -4(%ebp)          ; put Z local regstack
32 movl     -4(%ebp), %eax          ; put local Z into return reg
33 leave                            ; Sets ESP to EBP and POPs EBP
34 ret                             ; Return from function
35
36 .section    .rodata
37 .LC0:
38 .string "Z foo1:%d\n"           ; String for printf
```

The stack dump below in Table 5.2 is a snapshot of the stack when the processor is executing from line 32 above. The table shows the different stack values, parameters, local variables, and return addresses.

The code generated for this simple function is far from optimized, and was generated with the default compiler options. The instruction count for the function foo() above is 11 instructions, with the average optimization (GCC option −O2), the code generated is reduced to 7 instructions. The optimized code will make more efficient usage of the stack as well.

Table 5.2 Detailed Example Stack Snapshot

	Stack Address	Stack Contents	Comment
	0xbffff1d8:	0x00000096	Local y
		0x00000064	Local x
		0x00000001	Local a
		0x002ebff4	Padding/align
	0xbffff1c8:	0x00000096	[EBP + 16] = Arg2 = y
		0x00000064	[EBP + 12] = Arg1 = x
		0x00000001	[EBP + 8] = Arg0 = a
		0x0804841b	Return address from foo in function main()
EBP->	0xbffff1b8:	0xbffff1e8	Contents previous EBP
		0x000000fb	Local Z
		0xbffff1f8	Alignment
		0x080482c0	Alignment
ESP->	0xbffff1a8:	0xbffff1b8	Previous EBP

PROCESSOR INSTRUCTION CLASSES

In this section, we outline the general classes of instructions available in most processors. This is by no means a complete list of instructions; the goal is to provide a flavor of the instruction classes available. As an embedded programmer, this is often the level of detail you will require; you should be familiar enough to read assembly code, but not necessarily proficient at writing highly optimized large scale assembly.

First, a brief segway to discuss the symbolic representation of instructions. The actual representation is defined by the assembler used, but not all assemblers use the same presentation for instructions. In the context of this book, the following representation is used:

`label: mnemonic argument1, argument2, argument3`

- Label is an identifier that is followed by a colon.
- A mnemonic is a reserved name for a class of instruction op-codes that have the same function.
- The operands argument1, argument2, and argument3 are optional. There may be zero to three operands, depending on the op-code. When present, they take the form of either literals or identifiers for data items. Operand identifiers either are reserved names of registers or are assumed to be assigned to data items declared in another part of the program.

When two operands are present in an arithmetic or logical instruction, the right operand is the source and the left operand is the destination (same order as the mathematical assignment operator (=)). For example:

`LOADREG: MOV EAX, SUBTOTAL`

In this example, `LOADREG` is a label, `MOV` is the mnemonic identifier of an op-code, `EAX` is the destination operand, and `SUBTOTAL` is the source operand. The direction of the assignment is just a convention set out by the assembler. We'll call the convention above the Intel convention; the opposite assignment is also used on Intel platforms and it's known as the AT&T convention. The `LOADREG` instruction would be shown as follows:

`LOADREG: MOV SUBTOTAL, EAX`

The Intel Compiler and Microsoft compilers use the Intel convention. The GNU tool chain (including debuggers) uses the AT&T convention by default. However, we use the Intel convention throughout this book, unless it's an example segment to be used by a GNU tool chain.

The types and number of operand supported by a processor instruction set are architecture specific; all architectures allow operands that represent an immediate value, a register, or memory location. Intel architecture machine instructions operate on zero or more operands. Operands are specified explicitly and others are implicit. The data for a source operand can be found in one of the following:

- The instruction itself (an immediate operand)—The number of bits available in the op-code for an immediate value depends on the processor architecture; on Intel processors an immediate value has a range of 2^{32}. RISC processors such as ARM have a fixed size op-code and as a result support immediate values with a reduced range of 2^{16}. As a result, RISC processors generally use literal pools to load 32-bit values into a register.
- Register.

- Memory location.
- An I/O port—The Intel architecture supports 64K 8-bit I/O ports that can be written to and read from using the OUT/IN instructions. These ports are now mostly used to provide simple debug output on Intel reference platforms; most will provide a two-character eight-segment LED display to show the values written to I/O PORT 80h and 84h.

When an instruction returns data to a destination operand, it can be returned to:

- A register.
- Memory location—In limited cases the Intel processor supports direct memory to memory moves, this is typically not supported on RISC processors.
- An I/O port.

The size of the instruction is worth a brief mention. Most RISC processors such as ARM and PowerPC use fixed size instructions, typically 32-bit instruction word. The Intel processors use variable sized op-codes ranging from a single byte op-code to a theoretical maximum of 17 bytes. When using a debugger to display the raw assembly of a program, the address provided to the decode command must be aligned to an instruction boundary. This can take some practice, although it is pretty obvious when you get it wrong, as the command will display quite a few invalid op-codes.

Immediate Operands

Some instructions use data encoded in the instruction itself as a source operand. The operands are called immediate operands. For example, the following instruction loads the EAX register with zero.

```
MOV EAX, 00
```

The maximum value of an immediate operand varies among instructions, but it can never be greater than 2^{32}. The maximum size of an immediate on RISC architecture is much lower; for example, on the ARM architecture the maximum size of an immediate is 12 bits as the instruction size is fixed at 32 bits. The concept of a literal pool is commonly used on RISC processors to get around this limitation. In this case the 32-bit value to be stored into a register is a data value held as part of the code section (in an area set aside for literals, often at the end of the object file). The RISC instruction loads the register with a load program counter relative operation to read the 32-bit data value into the register.

Register Operands

Source and destination operands can be any of the follow registers depending on the instruction being executed:

- 32-bit general purpose registers (EAX, EBC, ECX, EDX, ESI, EDI, ESP, or EBP)
- 16-bit general purpose registers (AX, BX, CX, DX, SI, SP, BP)
- 8-bit general-purpose registers (AH, BH, CH, DH, AL, BL, CL, DL)
- Segment registers
- EFLAGS register
- MMX
- Control (CR0 through CR4)

- System Table registers (such as the Interrupt Descriptor Table register)
- Debug registers
- Machine-specific registers

On RISC embedded processors, there are generally fewer limitations in the registers that can be used by instructions. IA-32 often reduces the registers that can be used as operands for certain instructions.

Memory Operands

Source and destination operands in memory are referenced by means of a segment selector and an offset. On embedded operating systems, the segment selector often results in a base address of zero, particularly if virtual memory is used, so the memory address specified by the operand degenerates to being the offset value. The segment selector is automatically chosen by the processor, but can be overridden if needed. The following instruction moves the value in EAX to the address pointed by EBX, assuming the data segment selector contains zero. It is the simplest memory operand form.

MOV [EBX], EAX

The memory operand can also specify offsets to the base address specified in the memory operand. The offset is added to the base address (the general-purpose register) and can be made up from one or more of the following components:

- Displacement—An 8-, 16-, or 32-bit immediate value.
- Index—A value in a general-purpose register.
- Scale factor—A value of 2, 4, or 8 that is multiplied by the index value.

So we have a memory operand that can consist of

$$\text{Memory Operand} = \text{Segment Selector} + \text{Base Register}$$
$$+ (\text{Index Reg} \times \text{Scale}) + \text{Displacement Value}$$

Since the segment selector usually returns zero, the memory operand effective address becomes the following:

$$\text{Memory Operand} = \text{Base Register}$$
$$+ (\text{Index Register} \times \text{Scale}) + \text{Displacement Value}$$

The compiler will make best use of these modes to de-reference data structures in memory or on the stack. The components of the offsets can be either positive or negative (two's complement values), providing excellent flexibility in the memory operand address generation.

Data Transfer Instructions

All processes provide instructions to move data between registers, memory, and registers, and in some architectures between memory locations. Table 5.3 shows some instruction combinations.

There is also a set of instructions that provides hints to the underlying hardware to help manage the cache more efficiently. The MOVNTI (store double word using non-temporal hint) instruction is

Table 5.3 Data Transfer Instructions

Instruction Mnemonic	Example	Description
MOV	MOV EAX,EBX	Move contents between registers. Note that register may be ALU register, segment register, or control registers such as CR0
MOV	MOVEAX,0abcd00h MOV EAX,[EBX -4]	Load a register from memory. Effect address defined by the addressing modes discussed above
MOV	MOV [EBX],EAX	Write register contents to memory
MOV	MOV EAX,12345678h	Load an immediate value into a register
MOV	MOV EAX,[4*ESI][EBX+256]	Load memory at 4*ESI + BX + 256 to register ax
MOV	MOVS EDI,ESI	String move memory to memory
PUSH	PUSH EBP	Push ECX value onto stack. Update EBP
POP	POP ECX	Pop ECX, update EBP
XCHG	XCHG EBX, ECX	Swap register values
XCHG	XCHG [EAX],EBX	Swap contents at memory location with register value in atomic fashion
CMOVcc	CMOVE EAX,[EBX]	Move if Flags show equal (ZF = 1)

designed to minimize cache pollution; by writing a double word to memory without writing to the cache hierarchy, it also prevents allocation in the cache line. There are also PREFETCH instructions that perform memory reads and bring the result data closer to the processor core. The instruction includes a temporal hint to specify how close the data should be brought to it. These instructions are used when you are aggressively tuning your software and require some skill to use effectively. More details are provided in Chapter 18, "Platform Tuning." These hints are optional; the processor may ignore them.

Arithmetic Instructions

The arithmetic instructions define the set of operations performed by the processor Arithmetic Logic Unit (ALU). The arithmetic instructions are further classified into binary, decimal, logical, shift/rotate, and bit/byte manipulation instructions.

Binary Operations

The binary arithmetic instructions perform basic binary integer computations on byte, word, and double word integers located in memory and/or the general-purpose registers, as described in Table 5.4.

Decimal Operations

The decimal arithmetic instructions perform decimal arithmetic on binary coded decimal (BCD) data, as described in Table 5.5. BCD is not used as much as it has been in the past, but it still remains relevant for some financial and industrial applications.

Table 5.4 Binary Arithmetic Operation Instructions

Instruction Mnemonic	Example	Description
ADD	ADD EAX, EAX	Add the contents of EAX to EAX
ADC	ADC EAX, EAX	Add with carry
SUB	SUB *EAX*, 0002h	Subtract the 2 from the register
SBB	SBB *EBX*, 0002h	Subtract with borrow
MUL	MUL EBX	Unsigned multiply EAX by EBX; results in EDX:EAX
DIV	DIV EBX	Unsigned divide
INC	INC [EAX]	Increment value at memory eax by one
DEC	DEC EAX	Decrement EAX by one
NEG	NEG EAX	Two's complement negation

Table 5.5 Decimal Operation Instructions (Subset)

Instruction Mnemonic	Example	Description
DAA	ADD EAX, EAX	Decimal adjust after addition
DAS	DAS	Decimal adjust AL after subtraction. Adjusts the result of the subtraction of two packed BCD values to create a packed BCD result
AAA	AAA	ASCII adjust after addition. Adjusts the sum of two unpacked BCD values to create an unpacked BCD result
AAS	AAS	ASCII adjust after subtraction. Adjusts the result of the subtraction of two unpacked BCD values to create a unpacked BCD result

Logical Operations

The logical instructions perform basic AND, OR, XOR, and NOT logical operations on byte, word, and double word values, as described in Table 5.6.

Table 5.6 Logical Operation Instructions

Instruction Mnemonic	Example	Description
AND	AND EAX, 0ffffh	Performs bitwise logical AND
OR	OR EAX, 0ffffff0h	Performs bitwise logical OR
XOR	EBX, 0ffffff0h	Performs bitwise logical XOR
NOT	NOT [EAX]	Performs bitwise logical NOT

Table 5.7 Shift and Rotate Instructions

Instruction Mnemonic	Example	Description
SAR	SAR EAX, 4h	Shifts arithmetic right
SHR	SAL EAX,1	Shifts logical right
SAL/SHL	SAL EAX,1	Shifts arithmetic left/Shifts logical left
SHRD	SHRD EAX, EBX, 4	Shifts right double
SHLD	SHRD EAX, EBX, 4	Shifts left double
ROR	ROR EAX, 4h	Rotates right
ROL	ROL EAX, 4h	Rotates left
RCR	RCR EAX, 4h	Rotates through carry right
RCL	RCL EAX, 4h	Rotates through carry left

Shift Rotate Operations

The shift and rotate instructions shift and rotate the bits in word and double word operands. Table 5.7 shows some examples.

The arithmetic shift operations are often used in power of two arithmetic operations (such a multiply by two), as the instructions are much faster than the equivalent multiply or divide operation.

Bit/Byte Operations

Bit instructions test and modify individual bits in word and double word operands, as described in Table 5.8. Byte instructions set the value of a byte operand to indicate the status of flags in the EFLAGS register.

Table 5.8 Bit/Byte Operation Instructions

Instruction Mnemonic	Example	Description
BT	BT EAX, 4h	Bit test. Stores selected bit in Carry flag
BTS	BTS EAX, 4h	Bit test and set. Stores selected bit in Carry flag and sets the bit
BTR	BTS EAX, 4h	Bit test and reset. Stores selected bit in Carry flag and clears the bit
BTC	BTS EAX, 4h	Bit test and complement. Stores selected bit in Carry flag and complements the bit
BSF	BTS EBX, [EAX]	Bit scan forward. Searches the source operand (second operand) for the least significant set bit (1 bit)
BSR	BTR EBX, [EAX]	Bit scan reference. Searches the source operand (second operand) for the most significant set bit (1 bit)
SETE/SETZ	SET EAX	Conditional Set byte if equal/Set byte if zero
TEST	TEST EAX, Offffffffh	Logical compare. Computes the bit-wise logical AND of first operand (source 1 operand) and the second operand (source 2 operand) and sets the SF, ZF, and PF status flags according to the result

Branch and Control Flow Instructions

We clearly need instructions to control the flow of a program's execution. The branch and control flow instructions fall into two primary categories. The first is unconditional changes of program flow to a new program counter address. This occurs when a jump or call instruction is encountered. The second category of branch or control flow instructions are conditional branches or conditional execution of an instruction. The conditional execution of an instruction is dictated by the contents of bits within the EFLAGS register, or for some instructions the value in the ECX register.

Jump operations transfer control to a different point in the program stream without recording any return information. The destination operand specifies the address of the instruction we wish to execute next. The operand can be an immediate value, a register, or a memory location. Intel processors have several different jump modes that have evolved over time, but a number of modes are no longer used. The *near* jump is a jump within the current code segment. As we mentioned earlier, the current code segment often spans the entire linear memory range (such as zero to 4 GB). So all jumps are effective within the current code segment. The target operand specifies either an absolute offset (that is, an offset from the base of the code segment) or a relative offset (a signed displacement relative to the current value of the instruction pointer in the EIP register). A near jump to a relative offset of 8 bits is referred to as a short jump. The CS register is not changed on near and short jumps. An absolute offset is specified indirectly in a general-purpose register or a memory location. Absolute offsets are loaded directly into the EIP register. A relative offset is generally specified as a label in assembly code, but at the machine code level it is encoded as a signed 8-, 16-, or 32-bit immediate value. This value is added to the value in the EIP register. (Here, the EIP register contains the address of the instruction following the JMP instruction). Although this looks complicated, in practice the near jump is a simple branch with flexibility in specifying the target destination address. Intel processors also includes FAR jumps, which allow the program to jump to a different code segment, jump through a call gate with privilege checks, or a task switch (task in the IA-32 processor context). Table 5.9 shows the different instructions with examples.

Call gates are sometimes used to support calls to operating system services; for instance, this is a configuration available in VxWorks for real-time tasks when calling operating system services. However, operating system calls are more usually provided via the software interrupt call.

Table 5.9 Program Flow—No Saved Return State

Instruction Mnemonic	Example	Description
Jmp	JMP target_label	Jumps unconditionally to the destination address operand
JZ	JZ target_label	Jumps conditionally to the destination operand if the EFLAG. Zero bit is set
JNZ	JZ target_label	Jumps conditionally to the destination operand if the EFLAG. Zero is not set

LOOP	MOV ECX,5
	LoopStart:
	  XXX
	  YYY
	LOOP LoopStart
		Decrements the contents of the ECX register, then tests the register for the loop-termination condition. If the count in the ECX register is non-zero, program control is transferred to the instruction address specified by the destination operand

Calling subroutines, functions, or procedures require the return address to be saved before the control is transferred to the new address; otherwise, there is no way for the processor to get back from the call. The CALL (call procedure) and RET (return from procedure) instructions allow a jump from one procedure (or subroutine) to another and a subsequent jump back (return) to the calling procedure. The CALL instruction transfers program control from the current procedure (the calling procedure) to another procedure (the called procedure). To allow a subsequent return to the calling procedure, the CALL instruction saves the current contents of the EIP register on the stack before jumping to the called procedure. The EIP register (prior to transferring program control) contains the address of the instruction following the CALL instruction. When this address is pushed on the stack, it is referred to as the return instruction pointer or return address. The address of the called procedure (the address of the first instruction in the procedure being jumped to) is specified in a CALL instruction in the same way it is in a JMP instruction (described above).

Most processors provide an instruction to allow a program to explicitly raise a specified interrupt. The INT instruction can raise any of the processor's interrupts or exceptions by encoding the vector number or the interrupt or exception in the instruction or exception, which in turn causes the handler routine for the interrupt or exception to be called. This is typically used by user space programs to call operating system services. Table 5.10 shows the instructions that affect the program flow.

On Intel platforms there is quite a lot of history associated with the INT calls. Legacy (non-EFI) BIOS supports a number of INT calls to provide support to operating systems. An example of a well-known INT call is the E820. This is an interrupt call that the operating system can use to get a report of the memory map. The data are obtained by calling INT 15h while setting the AX register to E820h. For embedded programmers, there is an ever-decreasing dependence on the INT service provided by the BIOS. The Linux kernel reports the memory map reported by the BIOS in the `dmesg` logs at startup.

The BIOS environment is transitioning from a traditional legacy BIOS, which was first developed a few decades ago, to a more modern codebase. The newer codebase is known as Unified Extensible Firmware Interface (UEFI). At the time of writing, many products are transitioning from this legacy BIOS to EFI. More information on this topic can be found in Chapter 6.

Structure/Procedure Instructions

Modern languages such as C/C++ define a frame structure on the stack to allocate local variables and define how parameters are passed on the stack. The IA-32 provides two instructions to support the creation and management of these stack frames, namely, ENTER and LEAVE. The stack frame is discussed as part of the Application Binary Interface discussed earlier in this chapter.

Table 5.10 Program Flow with Saved Return State

Instruction Mnemonic	Example	Description
CALL	CALL target_label	Saves the return address of the stack and jumps to subroutine
RET	RET	Returns to the instruction after the previous call
INT x	INT 13h	Calls software interrupt 13
IRET	IRET	Returns from the interrupt handler

SIMD Instructions

Several classes of embedded applications are a mix of traditional general-purpose (scalar) workloads with an additional moderate digital signaling workload. Most embedded processors provide extensions to their core instruction set to support these additional workloads. These instructions are known as Single Instruction Multiple Data (SIMD). On Intel platforms the extensions are known as Intel Streaming SIMD Extensions (Intel SSE). Other processors have more basic extensions to provide single multiply-and-accumulate (MAC) operations. This operation is the basic building block for a large number of simple DSP algorithms. Over time the range of SSE instructions has grown significantly, and in fact they can bring substantial performance benefits to a wide range of workloads:

- Speech compression algorithms and filters
- Speech recognition algorithms
- Video display and capture routines
- Rendering routines
- 3D graphics (geometry)
- Image and video processing algorithms
- Spatial (3D) audio
- Physical modeling (graphics, CAD)
- Workstation applications
- Encryption algorithms
- Complex arithmetic

Generally, code that contains small-sized repetitive loops that operate on sequential arrays of integers of 8, 16, or 32 bits, single-precision 32-bit floating-point data, and double-precision 64-bit floating-point data are a good candidate for tuning using SSE instructions. The repetitiveness of these loops incurs costly application processing time. However, these routines have the potential for increased performance when you convert them to use one of the SIMD technologies.

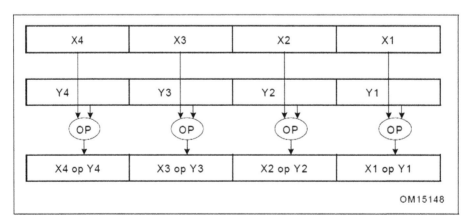

OM15148

FIGURE 5.4

Typical SIMD Operation.

On the Intel Atom processor, the SSSE3 SIMD instructions are supported and the instructions operate on packed byte, word, and double-word integers, as well as single-precision floating point. A key efficiency of the SIMD instructions is the fact that a single instruction operates on a number of data elements in parallel. If your data structures can be structured to make use of SIMD instructions, significant improvements in performance can be obtained. Figure 5.4 shows a typical SIMD operation.

The following code sequence is an example of how to get the data into the XMM registers and have the SIMD operation performed. It is written in the Intel Compiler format to incorporate assembly into C code.

```
1 void add(float *a, float *b, float *c)
2  {
3    __asm {
4      mov eax, a
5      mov edx, b
6      mov ecx, c
7      movaps xmm0, XMMWORD PTR [eax]
8      addps xmm0, XMMWORD PTR [edx]
9      movaps XMMWORD PTR [ecx], xmm0
10   }
11
```

The first three instructions get pointers for a, b, and c into EAX, EDX, and ECX registers, respectively. The MOVAPS instruction in line 7 above moves four quad-words containing four packed single-precision floating-point values from memory pointed to by EAX (128 bytes) into the XMM0 register. The ADDPS instruction performs a SIMD add of the four packed single-precision floating-point values in XMM0 with the four packed single-precision floating-point values pointed to by the EDX register. The final MOVAPS instruction saves the XMM0 (128-byte contents) to the memory pointed to by the ECX register. This is far more efficient than the traditional scalar equivalent.

EXCEPTIONS/INTERRUPTS MODEL

Integral to all processors is the ability for the processor to handle events that are orthogonal to the execution flow of the program. All modern processors have a well-defined model to signal and prioritize these events. The processor can then change the flow of the executing instructions sequence to handle these events in a deterministic manner. The event is typically handled by transferring execution from the current running task to a special software routine. The software routines are called interrupt or exception handlers. The processor will save sufficient processor state information to allow the processor to return to the currently executing task when the interrupt or exception was raised. The resumption of the interrupts task happens with no loss in program continuity unless the exception is not recoverable or causes the running program to be terminated. To aid in handling exceptions and interrupts, each architecturally defined exception and each interrupt condition requiring special handling by the processor is assigned a unique identification number, called a vector.

Interrupts are divided into two types—hardware and software. Hardware interrupts are typically generated as a result of a peripheral (external to the processor core) that needs attention. Peripherals both within the SOC device and on the platform can raise an interrupt to the processor. The processor then transfers control to the appropriate interrupt handled for the specific device interrupt. The allocation and sharing of interrupt vectors is performed by the operating system. A simple example of a peripheral is a timer block, used to "kick" the operating system timer.

Software interrupts are typically triggered via a dedicated instruction such as INT #vector on Intel processors and SWI on ARM architectures. The execution of a software interrupt instruction causes a context switch to an interrupt handler in a fashion similar to an external hardware interrupt. Software interrupts are most often used as part of a system call. A system call is a call to an operating system kernel in order to execute a specific function that controls a device or executes a privileged instruction. The Linux operating system uses INT 0x80 for service calls.

Interrupts can be classed as maskable or non-maskable, though not all processors make provision for non-maskable interrupts. Non-maskable interrupts, as the name suggests, are interrupts that are always serviced. There is no ability to prevent or delay the recognition of a non-maskable interrupt. Non-maskable interrupts are themselves uninterruptible, with at most one non-maskable interrupt active at any time.

Exceptions are events detected by the processor. They are usually associated with the currently executing instruction. A common exception supported by all processors is "Divide by Zero," which is generated as a result of a DIV instruction with a denominator of zero. Processors detect a variety of conditions including protection violations, page faults, and invalid instructions. The processor also monitors other processor conditions that may not be strictly correlated to the current instruction being executed. On the Intel platform these are known as *machine check* exceptions. Machine check exceptions include system bus errors, ECC errors, parity errors, cache errors, and translation lookaside buffer (TLB) errors. The machine check details are recorded in machine-specific registers.

Precise and Imprecise Exceptions

Exceptions can be categorized as precise or imprecise. Precise exceptions are those that indicate precisely the address of the instruction that caused the exception. Again, the divide-by-zero exception is an excellent example of a precise exception because the faulting instruction can be identified. Imprecise exceptions, on the other hand, cannot directly be associated with an instruction. The processor has continued execution of an indeterminate number of instructions between the time the exception was triggered and when the processor processed it; alternatively, the exception was generated by an event that was not due to an instruction execution. An example of an imprecise exception is the detection of an uncorrectable ECC error discovered in a cache. Imprecise exceptions are not generally recoverable; although the Linux machine check handler does all it can to avoid a kernel panic and the resulting reboot, imprecise exceptions are referred to as *aborts* on Intel architectures. Precise exceptions fall into two categories on Intel architectures, *faults* and *traps*:

Faults. A fault is an exception that can generally be corrected and that, once corrected, allows the program to be restarted with no loss of continuity. When a fault is reported, the processor restores the machine state to the state prior to the beginning of execution of the faulting instruction. The return address (saved contents of the CS and EIP registers) for the fault handler points to the faulting instruction, rather than to the instruction following the faulting instruction.

Traps. A trap is an exception that is reported immediately following the execution of the trapping instruction. Traps allow execution of a program or task to be continued without loss of program continuity. The return address for the trap handler points to the instruction to be executed after the trapping instruction. Traps are generated by INT 3 and INTO (overflow) instructions.

You may have noticed that the fault handler points to the faulting instruction for faults; this is because the handler is likely to rerun the faulting instruction once the underlying reason for the fault is resolved. For example, if a page fault is generated, the operating system will load the page from disk, set up the page table to map the page, and then rerun the instruction. Instructions that generate a trap, on the other hand, are not rerun. On other embedded platforms such as ARM, the fault address recorded on the exception is always that of the next instruction to run. However, when all instructions are the same size (32-bits) it's a trivial matter to establish the faulting instruction; it's not quite as straightforward with a variable size instruction set. The list of exceptions and interrupts that a processor supports is part of a processor's architecture definition. All exceptions and interrupts are assigned a vector number. The processor uses the vector assigned to the exception or interrupt as an index into a vector table. On Intel architectures this vector table is called the Interrupt Descriptor Table (IDT). The table provides the entry point to the exception or interrupt handler. IA-32 defines an allowable vector range of 0 to 255. Vectors from 0 to 31 are reserved for architecture-defined exceptions and interrupts. Vectors 32 to 255 are designed as user-defined interrupts. The user-defined vectors are typically allocated to external (to the processor) hardware generated interrupts and software interrupts. Table 5.11 is a partial list of the IA-32 Protected mode exceptions and interrupts. See Chapter 5 of *IA-32 Intel Architecture Systems Programming Guide.*

In summary, exceptions and interrupts can come from a wide range of sources from the processor core, caches, floating-point units, bus interfaces, and external peripherals. Figure 5.5 shows the wide range of sources.

Table 5.11 Abbreviated IA-32 Exceptions and Interrupts

Vector Number	Description	Type	Source
0	Divide error	Fault	DIV and IDIV instructions
2	NMI	Interrupt	Non-maskable external interrupt
3	Breakpoint	Trap	INT 3 instruction
4	Overflow	Trap	INTO (overflow) instruction
6	Invalid op-code	Fault	Reserved op-codes
13	General protection	Fault	Any memory reference or other protection checks
14	Page fault	Fault	Any memory reference
16	X87 FPU floating-point	Fault	Exception from the FP unit
17	Alignment check	Fault	Misaligned data references in memory
18	Machine check	Abort	Model specific faults
32–255	User-defined Interrupts	Interrupt	External interrupt or INT n instruction

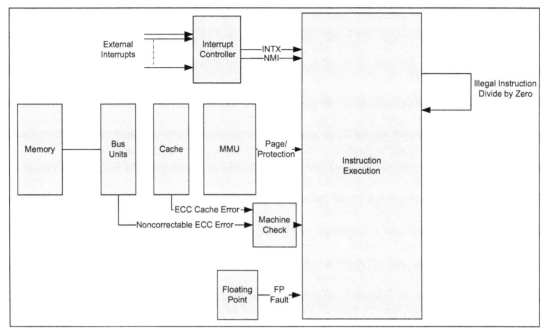

FIGURE 5.5

Exception and Interrupt Sources.

VECTOR TABLE STRUCTURE

All processors provide mechanisms to translate an interrupt or exception into a handler for the interruption. Different processor architectures provide differing levels of hardware support in identification of the underlying hardware exception. As we mentioned above, external hardware interrupts are assigned a vector. PowerPC and some ARM architectures have a single IRQ line to the processor. The exception handler must then resolve the underlying cause of the interrupt, look up a software-based vector table, and transfer control to the interrupt handler. On Intel processors, the processor hardware itself identifies the underlying cause of the interrupt and transfers control to the exception handler without software intervention. An Intel processor takes a number of steps in the transition to the interrupt handler. Figure 5.6 shows the structures and registers that are used in the process.

The IA-32 processor automatically takes several steps in transfer of control to the exception function handler. The hardware interrupt controller sends an interrupt N message to the CPU. The interrupt controller is called the Local Advanced Peripheral Interrupt Controller (Local APIC) on Intel processors. The CPU reads the interrupt descriptor from the interrupt descriptor table (IDT). The interrupt descriptor table is located in system memory. The IDT stores a collection of gate descriptors that provide access to interrupt and exception handlers. The linear address for the base of the IDT is contained in the interrupt descriptor table register (IDTR). The IDT descriptor can contain one of three types of descriptor: task gate, interrupt gate, and trap gate. The IDT contains either an

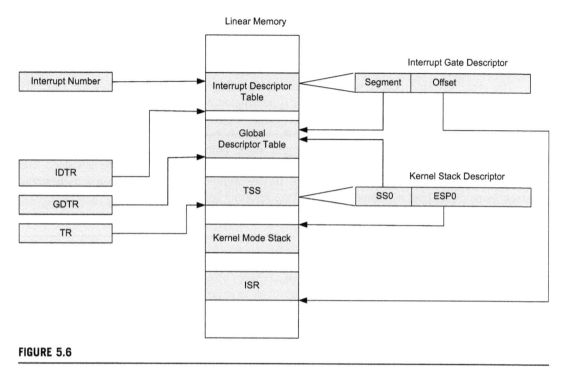

FIGURE 5.6

Interrupt Descriptor Dereferencing.

interrupt gate or trap gate descriptor for external interrupts. The difference between an interrupt gate and a trap gate is its effect on the IF flag: using an interrupt gate clears the IF flag, which prevents other interrupts from interfering with the current interrupt handler. The interrupt gate contains the following information:

- *Segment selector.* The segment selector selects a segment in the global or local descriptor table; this provides a base address for the IRQ handler table.
- *Segment offset.* This offset is added to the base address found in the referencing of the segment selector to produce the linear address of the ISR handler.
- *Privilege level.* This is usually set to zero (same privilege level as kernel mode code).

The address of the actual interrupt service routine is

```
ISR Linear Address =
 GDT[(IDTR[Vector Number ].SegmentSelector)].BaseAddress +
IDTR[Vector Number].SegmentOffset
```

For Linux the values populated in the tables degenerate to the following (the processor still performs the lookups but the value returned is zero):

```
ISR Linear Address =
    IDTR[Vector Number].SegmentOffset
```

Before the processor transfers control to the ISR, it must identify the appropriate stack to use to save registers. Two situations can occur. The first is when the interrupt privilege is the same level as the currently executing code. This occurs when an interrupt occurs while the processor is running kernel mode software. In this scenario the processor saves the EFLAGS, CS, and EIP registers on the current stack. The other situation occurs when the interrupt privilege level is lower than the currently executing code, for example, when the processor is interrupted while running user mode application code. In this case the segment selector and stack pointer for the stack to be used by the handler are obtained from the Task State Segment (TSS) for the currently executing task. On this new stack, the processor pushes the stack segment selector and stack pointer of the interrupted procedure. The processor then saves the current state of the EFLAGS, CS, and EIP registers on the new stack. The processor then transfers control to the interrupt service routine. The following sections describe the stack frame established by the processor and the resulting software handlers.

EXCEPTION FRAME

A considerable amount of data must be saved when an exception or interrupt occurs. The state is saved on a stack, and the format of the saved data is known as an *exception frame,* as shown in Figure 5.7. The exception frame can be split into two distinct portions: the first is the portion saved automatically by the processor, and the second is the set of additional registers that are saved by operating system interrupt service routine before it loads the software handler that deals with the actual device interrupt.

Some processor-generated exception frames include an error number on the stack. For example, a page fault will provide an error code on the stack frame. These error codes provide additional information such as whether the fault was due to a page not being present or a page-level protection violation.

The actual IRQ function call is usually written in assembly language. The function is then responsible for saving the registers that may be destroyed in the handling of the interrupt. For example, the MACRO SAVE_ALL defined in the Linux kernel file `entry_32.s` saves all the required registers as part of interrupt handler call. Once the interrupt has been processed, the system must return to normal execution. The IRET instruction will restore the processor to the same state prior to the interrupt (once the software saved state is also unrolled). In a simple embedded system this is the normal mechanism used to return to the pre-interrupt operation; however, in a multitasking operating system environment, the operating system may not necessarily return directly to the task that was interrupted. For example, if the operating system timer IRQ *fires* while a user process is running, the operating system will save the user space process registers into a process-specific storage area, execute the interrupt handler, and then identify what code should run next. It most likely will execute the kernel scheduler function. The kernel scheduler identifies the process to continue with, and transfers control to that process.

MASKING INTERRUPTS

As we discussed, interrupts fall into two classes, maskable and non-maskable interrupts. Processors provide a control mechanism to disable the servicing of interrupts received by the processor core. For Intel CPUs the Interrupt Enable (IF) flag in the EFLAGs register provides the control. If the flag is set,

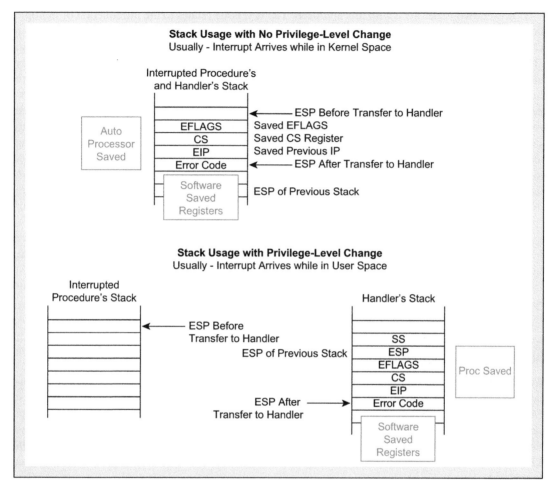

FIGURE 5.7

Stack Frames.

then the processor will service interrupts. If the flag is cleared, the processor will not service maskable interrupts. A number of mechanisms can be used to control the state of the IF flag. First, there is an instruction specifically assigned to allow you to set and clear the flag directly. The STI (set interrupt enable flag) instruction sets the flag, and the CLI (clear interrupt enable flag) clears the flag.

The use of STI/CLI (or its equivalent on other processors) has been quite prevalent in embedded systems to provide a low-cost method of mutual exclusion. For instance, if two threads were working with a linked list, it was quite common to disable interrupts while the pointer updates associated with link element insertion took place. Then the interrupts were re-enabled. This allowed the multiple pointer updates associated with a linked list insertion to be atomic. The mechanism has also been used between interrupt handlers and threads used for deferred processing.

However, two issues arise with this approach. The first issue relates to the introduction of multiple hardware threads in processors (multiple processor cores, or hardware threading on a single core). The STI/CLI instructions mask interrupts on the hardware thread that issued the instruction (the local CPU). Interrupts can be processed by other hardware threads. As a result, the guarantee of atomicity has been lost. In this case other synchronization mechanisms such as locks may be needed to ensure that there are no race conditions. The second issue arises because masking of interrupts can affect the real-time behavior of the platform. Masking interrupt introduces non-determinism associated with the overall interrupt latency performance. In embedded systems, having a deterministic latency time to service specific interrupts can be very important. For both these reasons and others, directly enabling and disabling of interrupts to provide mutual exclusion should be avoided. A case in point: the Linux kernel 2.4 had a significant number of sti/cli calls in the device drivers. The introduction of version 2.6 kernels was aligned with multi-core processors being much more prevalent, and correspondingly there are almost no driver calls left in the drivers for the 2.6.* Linux kernel. In fact, function wrappers for sti()/cli() have been removed from the kernel.

The interrupt flags can also be affected by the following operations: the PUSHF instruction saves the flags register onto the stack where it can be examined, and the POPF and IRET instructions load the flags register from the stack, and as a result can be used to modify the interrupt enable flag.

The interrupts are automatically masked when you enter an interrupt handler, and the driver or operating system will re-enable interrupts.

ACKNOWLEDGING INTERRUPTS

When a device indicates an interrupt request to the interrupt controller, the interrupt controller typically latches the request in an interrupt status pending register. The interrupt handling software must eventually clear the interrupt in the device and also indicate to the interrupt controller that the interrupt has been serviced. The device driver is typically responsible to consume all events that are associated with the interrupt and explicitly clear the source on the device. The interrupt controller (such as 8259/IOAPIC) must also be notified that an interrupt has been processed so the interrupt controller state can be updated.

The device interrupts on Intel systems may be presented to the interrupt controller as either edge- or level-triggered interrupts. For level-based interrupts, the device will de-assert the interrupt line once the underlying device event has been acknowledged. Level-triggered interrupts consist of a message sent to the interrupt controller that an interrupt has been raised. The actual interrupt line is now represented by a message being routed on a bus. There is no message signal to indicate that the interrupt has been cleared. The legacy (8259) interrupt controller has a register known as the End of Interrupt (EOI) register. The system interrupt handler may have to write to this register depending on the configuration.

INTERRUPT LATENCY

It is important to understand both the latency and the jitter associated with interrupt latency on embedded systems, as shown in Figure 5.8. The interrupt latency is defined as the time from when the

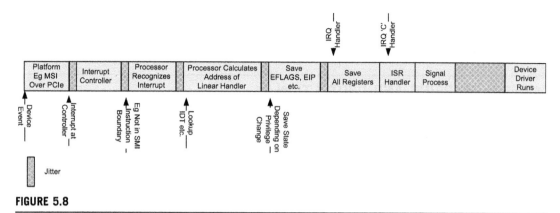

FIGURE 5.8

Components of Interrupt Latency.

hardware event occurred to the time when the software handler starts to execute. The contributions to the overall latency (and its variability) are:

- Hardware detection of the interrupt and its propagation to the processor core.
- Waiting for the interrupt to be at the appropriate level, for example, waiting for a current interrupt handler to complete.
- Recognition by the processor either by waiting for the current instruction to complete or by interrupting the current instruction at the next available cycle.
- The processor must identify the linear address of the interrupt handler. On Intel processors this requires reading the GDT and IDT tables, which could result in cache and translation look-aside buffer misses.
- The processor saves critical registers and transfers control to the interrupt handler.
- The interrupt handler then saves the remaining registers before the tradition C interrupt handler is called.

As you can see, quite a few steps are involved between the interrupt event and the actual transfer of control to the handler. In most operating systems the first handler must do very little work directly. Typically, the interrupt is just acknowledged and a signal to another thread or context is generated. The rest of the interrupt processing then takes place in the signaled task. This latency before this next task executes is generally larger than the original latency between events and interrupt handler. At a platform level, additional latencies such as system management interrupts, power-saving sleep states, and CPU frequency throttling can all affect the jitter of the interrupt response.

As soon as you start to discuss interrupt latencies in a system, the question of real-time behavior arises. Is your system hard real time or soft real time, for instance? It depends on your target application and the expected deadlines imposed by the application and how it interacts with the interrupt events. For real-time platforms, the actual delay between interrupt and service routine, consistency of time delay, and a maximum upper bound are all important criteria. As you can see in Figure 5.8, there can be a number of delays before the interrupt is called. The nominal interrupt latency delay for between the raising of an interrupt to the execution of the handler is on the order of microseconds.

MEMORY MAPPING AND PROTECTION

For the most trivial of embedded processors, the address space that the processor runs in is the same as the physical addresses used in the system. That is, the pointers used by your program are used directly to decode the physical memory, peripherals, and external devices. These systems are known as Memory Management Unit (MMU)-less processors, to which category the ARM M3 and older ARM7 TDMI belong. All programs and processes live in the same overall address space. The executable running on such a device is typically a monolithic image (all linked together). Most of the system runs either a single program or an RTOS. It is unusual to run a general-purpose operating system such as Linux, although a limited version of Linux is available for such devices, known as uCLinux.

In MMU-less devices, there is often the need to provide some form of protection between different aspects of the system. This level of protection is provided by the provisions of a memory protection unit (MPU). The MPU defines the portions of the system memory map that are valid and provides different access control for system and user processes. On some SOC devices the MPU also controls whether a memory region is cacheable. The MPU typically supports a limited number of defined regions.

Given the increasing complexity of the software running on embedded systems, it is increasingly likely that the SOC has a significantly more capable protection mechanism known as a memory management unit (MMU). The MMU provides protection and a fine-grained address translation capability between the processor's address space and the physical addresses used throughout the system. The processor address space is known as the linear address space on Intel processors and is often referred to as virtual address space by other architectures. The MMU has support for different translations based on the currently active process. This allows each process to live in the same linear address space, but actually be resident in different physical address spaces. The MMU is also a fundamental building block that allows a processor to support a virtual memory system. A virtual memory system allows the operating system to overcommit the amount of memory provided to applications by having a mechanism to move data in and out from a backing store typically on a disk. This mechanism is known as paging.

Embedded systems do not typically employ the use of virtual memory paging. For a number of reasons, embedded systems shy away from the use of virtual memory paging: paging can introduce significant non-determinism to the behavior of the system, and page faults can take a significant number of processor cycles to handle. A page fault requires copying the processes' virtual memory page from a disk to an allocated physical memory page, an operation that is tens of thousands of times slower than accessing memory. If a process triggers a page fault, it is suspended until the page fault handler completes the data move. While embedded systems do require nonvolatile storage, it is unlikely that a traditional spinning hard disk medium is used due to environments, cost, serviceability, and power considerations. Flash memory is the predominant nonvolatile storage mechanism used in embedded systems, and a paged virtual memory system would generate a significant number of transactions to the flash-based file system. Given that flash-based nonvolatile storage lifetime is measured in terms of erase cycles, paging could adversely affect the product's longevity. Most real-time operating systems do not actually support paging for the reasons mentioned above. The Linux operating system does support paging (also known as swapping) by default. It can be disabled at kernel build time by setting the CONFIG_SWAP=N. Swapping can also be disabled at runtime using the root command `swapoff -a`, but the swap partition or file will remain and consume storage resources.

PROTECTION ON INTEL ARCHITECTURE

The IA-32 architecture has been one of the most consistent and pervasive architectures to date. The earliest products in the architecture (8086 and 80286) provided memory protection by way of segmentation. Given that Intel architecture has always been backward compatible, the segmentation features remain. However, most operating systems use the MMU capabilities for protection (as well as address translation).

MEMORY MANAGEMENT UNIT

The memory management unit logically sits between the processor internal bus and the memory hierarchy—the first level of the hierarchy is most likely the processor's first level cache on modern embedded processors. The MMU provides the following key features:

- *Address translation.* The MMU provides per process address translation of linear (virtual) address to physical addresses.
- *Protection.* The MMU entries provide privilege checking and read/write protection of memory. Privilege checking ensures that the processor has the correct privilege level to access a particular memory region.
- *Cache control.* Different memory regions requires different cacheability attributes.

When using the MMU, the memory map is divided into pages (typically 4 kB each). The operating system maintains a page directory and a set of page tables to keep track of the pages. When a program (or task) attempts to access an address location in the linear address space, the processor uses the page directory and page tables to translate the linear address into a physical address and then performs the requested operation (read or write) to the memory location, as illustrated in Figure 5.9.

The design of the MMU translation structure must optimize for lookup efficiency and overall table size. To meet these goals, both table-based lookups and hashed data structures are used in processors today. On IA-32 architectures the MMU use a page table structure to look up a page descriptor associated with a virtual address. In a 32-bit system, with a page covering 4 kB of physical memory, the MMU table would require 1,048,576 contiguous entries to cover entire 4 GB addressing if the table were constructed as a simple lookup table using high-order address bits of the linear address. Processes generally only use a small fraction of the available 4 GB virtual address space. In addition, the page table structures are replicated once for the kernel and for each process in the system. So using a simple lookup table for paging would be very costly in memory usage. IA implements the paging tables as a sparse data structure with a page table hierarchy consisting of two levels of indirection.

The base physical address of the page directory value is specified in the control register CR3 [31:12]. The lower 12 bits of the address are zero, which means the page directory must be aligned on a 4-kB boundary. The CR3 register also contains some cacheability information for the directory itself.

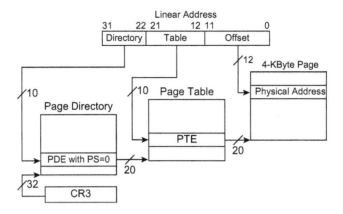

FIGURE 5.9

Liner Address Translation.

A page directory comprises 1024 32-bit entries. The Page Directory Entry (PDE) is selected using the high-order address bits (31-22) from the linear address along with a base address provided by CR3. The page directory entry contains the two following fields—a page present indicator and the base address of a page table that is the next level of the sparse table hierarchy (if the PDE contains an entry for 4-kB pages).

When the page present bit is set, it indicates that the base address is valid. The page directory entries are created and managed by the operating system. Table 5.12 shows the bit definitions for the directory descriptor entry.

If a memory access is generated to a memory region without a valid page descriptor (including "non-present"), the MMU generates a page fault exception. The page fault is a precise exception and

Table 5.12 Directory Descriptor Entry

Descriptor Bit	Bit Name	Description
bit 0	Present	1 if the page descriptor is present and valid
bit 2	R/W	Read/write; if 0, writes may not be allowed to the 4-MB region controlled by this entry
bit 2	U/S	User/supervisor; if 0, accesses with CPL $= 3$ are not allowed to the 4-MB region controlled by this entry
bit 3	PWT	Page-level write-through; indirectly determines the memory type used to access the page table referenced by this entry
bit 4	PCD	Page-level cache disable; indirectly determines the memory type used to access the page table referenced by this entry
bit 5	A	Accessed; indicates whether this entry has been used for linear-address translation
bit 6	D	Ignored
bit 7	PS	If CR4.PSE $= 1$, must be 0
bits 8–11	Ignored	Should be zero
bits 12–31	Addr	Physical address of 4-kB aligned page table referenced by this entry

Table 5.13 Page Table Entry (That Maps a 4-kB Range)

Page Descriptor Bit	Bit Name	Description
bit 0	Present	1 if the page descriptor is present and valid
bit 2	R/W	Read/write; if 0, writes may not be allowed to the 4-kB region controlled by this entry
bit 2	U/S	User/supervisor; if 0, accesses with CPL = 3 are not allowed to the 4-kB region controlled by this entry
bit 3	PWT	Page-level write-through; indirectly determines the memory type used to access the 4-kB page referenced by this entry
bit 4	PCD	Page-level cache disable; indirectly determines the memory type used to access the 4-kB page referenced by this entry
bit 5	A	Accessed; indicates whether software has accessed the 4-kB page referenced by this entry
bit 6	D	Dirty; indicates whether software has written to the 4-kB page referenced by this entry
bit 7	PAT	If the PAT is supported, indirectly determines the memory type used to access the 4-kB page referenced by this entry
bit 8	Global	Global; if CR4.PGE = 1, determines whether the translation is global
bit 9-11	Ignored	Should be zero
bit 12-31	Address	Physical address of 4-kB aligned page referenced by this entry

the instruction pointer of the memory access can be identified in the exception handler. When using an RTOS, this is often a result of not defining the memory map correctly or general program errors.

The next level in the hierarchy are the page tables. If the page directory entry contained a valid page table entry, then the MMU looks up the page table entry by means of a page table lookup using bits 12 to 21 from the linear address. Table 5.13 shows a page table entry for a 32-bit system.

The key field in the page table entry is the physical address of the 4-kB page being looked up; this address provide bits 31:12 of the actual physical address, while the remaining bits 11:0 are provided by bits 11:0 from the virtual address, which are used as an offset into the 4-kB physically addressed page.

This is a summary of the address translation for valid entries using 4-kB pages.

```
Directory Base Physical Address = (CR3 & ~0xFFF)
Page Table Base = Directory Base Physical Address[Linear Address[31:22]].Addr
4KPageBase = Page Table Base[Linear Address[21:12]].Addr
Physical Address = 4KPageBase + Linear Address[11:0]
```

The section above concentrated on the translation function provided by the MMU, but the descriptor and page table entries provides a number of other data elements that warrant further discussion:

- *Write protection.* The MMU will generate a general-protection fault if an attempt is made to a write to a protected page. The operating system would normally treat this as a program fault. Write-protected pages are also used to implement "copy on write" strategies in an operating system. For example, when a process forks in Linux, the forked process is logically a full copy of the forking process along with all its associated data. At the start of the forked process all of the data are identical to the process that carried out a fork, so instead of a new physical pages for the forked process, each physical page in the process is marked as write protect and mapped to each copy of the forked processes. When any of the processes actually updates a page, the write protection fault triggers the operating system to actually make a copy of the page for the process that triggered the fault. This effectively maximizes the number of identical shared virtual pages mapping to the same physical page and only allocates memory for pages that are different between the forked processes. This technique is known as "copy on write" (COW).

- *Privilege.* The MMU can allow the kernel process to have full visibility of and access to the user space pages, while preventing user space programs from accessing kernel structure (unless mapped to the user space program). Specifically, if the U/S (User/Supervisor) bit in the page table is zero, then user space (CPL = 3) processes cannot access the memory covered by this page.
- *Accessed.* The MMU updates the accessed bits within the page descriptor if the processor has accessed a memory location in the page. The accessed bit in the page descriptor can be used to identify the "age" of a page table entry. The operating system swap process periodically resets the accessed bits in the page tables. Then when a process accesses a page, the processor can identify which pages have been used since the values were last reset. On Linux this forms the basis of a least recently used (LRU) algorithm that selects the candidate pages that may be swapped to mass storage.
- *Dirty.* The MMU updates the dirty bit of a page if it has been written to any address in this page since the bit was last cleared. This is used with the operating system's paging/swapping algorithm. When a page is first swapped in from disk to memory, the dirty bit is cleared by the operating system. If a process writes to this page subsequently, the dirty bit is set. When the time comes to swap out the page, the dirty bit is tested. If the page is dirty, which means one or more locations in the page are updated, then the page must be written back out to disk. If, however, the dirty bit is zero, then the page does not have to be written out to the disk because the backing store is still valid.
- *Memory cache control.* On Intel architectures, the control of the caches and memory ordering is a complex area. The page tables contribute page-granular control of this cacheability and memory ordering behavior. The cacheability can also be defined by Memory Type Range Registers; when a conflict arises the most conservative configuration will be selected. For example, if the page table indicates that the area is cached but an MTRR indicates un-cached, un-cached is the safest, most conservative option. The processor caches are described later in this chapter.
- *Global pages.* These are pages that are usually active for operating system contexts (kernel and all processes). It facilitates optimization in translation cache behavior, as described in the following section.

The MMU can also prevent execution from data pages, but this feature is only available in PAE or 64-bit mode.

The Intel architecture supports three different modes for the MMU paging, namely, 32-bit, Physical Address Extension (allows a 32-bit CPU to access more than 4 GB of memory), and 64-bit modes. In the context of embedded platforms we will focus on the 32-bit configuration. The nominal page size is 4 kB; 2-MB and 4-MB (often called large page) pages are supported depending on the mode.

Translation Caching

As you may predict, the translation from a virtual address to a physical address would be a very costly event if it were required for every single memory transaction. For the Intel architecture each translation could result in two dependent reads. To reduce the impact of translation, processors generally employ techniques to cache the translation and additional details it provides in a translation cache. This is usually very effective given that page table access exhibits excellent temporal locality. These are generally known as translation look-aside buffers (TLBs). The TLB is typically constructed as a fully or highly associative cache, where the virtual address is compared against all cache entries. If the TLB hits, the contents of the TLB are used for the translation, access permissions, and so on. The management of the TLB is shared between the operating system and hardware. The TLB will allocate space automatically for new entries, typically by employing a (Least Recently Used) LRU policy for replacement. There is no hardware coherency enforcement between the TLBs and the page tables in memory. If software modifies a page or table entry (e.g., for resetting Accessed bit or changing the mapping) directly, then the TLBs must be invalidated. Otherwise, there is a risk that an out-of-date translation is used. The INVLPG instruction invalidates a single TLB entry; software writes to the CR3 register can be used to invalidate the entire TLB. On some processors, the TLB is managed in software with hardware-assist functions to perform the page walks.

An optimization can improve the effectiveness of the TLB during process context switches (kernel/user and user/user). The page tables provide a Global bit in the page entries. If this is set, then the page table entry is not flushed on a global TLB flush event.

The current Intel Atom processor has a number of separate TLB structures:

- Instruction for 4-kB page: 32 entries, fully associative.
- Instruction for large pages: 8 entries, four-way set associative.
- Data 4-kB pages: 16-entry-per-thread micro-TLB, fully associative; 64-entry DTLB, four-way set associative; 16-entry page directory entry cache, fully associative.

As an embedded software developer, you may find yourself tuning the overall platform execution. High TLB miss rates can contribute to poor overall system performance. It is prudent to review performance counters in the platform and focus on the overall TLB miss rate. There are a few strategies to reduce the overall system TLB miss rate. The first is to consolidate program and data hot spots into a minimum memory footprint, which reduces the number of pages and subsequently TLB entries needed during the hot spot execution of the platform software. This can be achieved by linking the hot spot objects close together. An additional technique to consider is using large pages to cover hot spot areas. The ability to use pages other than the standard 4 kB is dependent on the operating system providing such control. A Linux kernel feature known as *HughTLB* provides a memory allocation mechanism that allocates a contiguous piece of physical memory that is covered by a single large TLB entry. If you have an application that jumps around (a nontechnical term for *exhibits poor locality*) a large data structure, using a large page entry could significantly reduce the TLB misses.

MMU AND PROCESSES

Thus far, all the discussion on the memory management unit has been relatively static and to a single set of translation tables. Each time the operating system makes a transition between processes (between user and kernel, or between user and user space process) the active page tables must be changed. The transition between processes is known as a context switch. For example, each user space program "lives" in the same virtual address space, which maps to the process-specific physical RAM pages; therefore, we need to apply a different translation from virtual to physical pages when the new process executes.

A processor can use a number of mechanisms to incorporate the processes' specific information in the address translation. On some architecture, the translation tables contain process identification information within the table; on Intel architectures the MMU uses the contents of CR3 as the base pointer to the active page table. The operating system updates the CR3 register each time the operating system changes process space. When the CR3 register is written to, any cached translations in the TLB are for the most case invalid, the act of writing to the CR3 register invalidates ... all but nonglobal TLB entries. The global entries are entries that are guaranteed to be consistent for all processes (by operating system convention).

Although it is becoming less common due to robustness and security concerns, embedded systems often set up very simple memory maps where processes live in the same linear address space. In this case the vast majority of TLBs may be made global to reduce the cost of flushing the TLBs; however, processes can subsequently see other processes' memory.

On ARMv4™ and ARMv5™ (such as Intel XScale) processors, the cache is virtually indexed and virtually tagged. The index and tag fields are both derived from the virtual address. This means that the cache can be looked up without looking up the TLB. The TLB translation search can happen in parallel to the cache lookup. The downside of this approach is that the cache is generally invalidated on a context switch. On ARMv6™ and ARMv7™ processors caches may be virtually indexed and physically tagged. This reduces the number of cached invalidates, but the cached lookup mostly occurs after the virtual to physical address translation occurs. To support multi-processor or hardware coherency, the caches are physically indexed and tagged (as is the case for Intel architecture).

MEMORY HIERARCHY

Providing a higher-performance memory subsystem is critical in maximizing the performance of the CPU. If the memory subsystem does not complete transactions quickly enough, the processor eventually stalls. There are many microarchitecture techniques that strive to keep the processor doing useful work while memory transactions are in flight, but it is impossible to always keep the processor busy at all times. When the processor is waiting for the memory subsystem, the processor stalls and is no longer doing useful work. These stalled cycles have a direct impact on the effective clocks per instruction (often called CPI) taken by your application; that is, stalls directly impact the performance of the system.

The processor may stall on both read and write operations. Stalling on reads is relatively intuitive; the program cannot make forward progress until the memory read provides the required value in the register in order for the program to progress. Stalls caused by memory writes are less likely but can still occur. The processor may stall on writes when the processor generates memory write transactions at a rate that is higher than the ability of the memory subsystem to consume the memory writes. The microarchitecture of the processor will typically have several stages of write buffering to ensure that the processor does not stall. This write buffering also serves to allow the memory subsystem to prioritize memory reads over writes. In general, the memory subsystem always prioritizes reads over writes until write transactions build up to such an extent that the processor stalls on writes. You may have noted that the prioritization of reads over writes in the memory subsystem causes reordering of the memory transactions. Naturally, reordering transactions without any regard to the program order of the memory transactions would have a catastrophic effect on program execution. To resolve this, key program order guarantees are maintained. For example, if a read follows a write to a memory address and the write command is still in a write buffer, the write buffer must be snooped and provide the value for the read. We discuss ordering of transactions and how they interact with the I/O subsystem later in the chapter.

We have briefly touched on the effects of not matching the memory system performance to that of the CPU. The strategies for maximizing the performance of the memory subsystem come from the optimization of subsystem design and economics. The ideal device would provide large amounts of the extremely fast memory technology tightly coupled to the processor core. Unfortunately, the highest density and fastest memory technology typically has the highest cost associated with it. The following are different types of memory, as illustrated in Figure 5.10:

- *Logic gate memory.* This is typically used for intermediate buffering, such as write buffers.
- *Static RAM (SRAM).* SRAM cells are used on devices for caches and small amounts of RAM that is close to the processor. Access time for SRAM/caches would be in the order of 1–2 CPU core clocks.

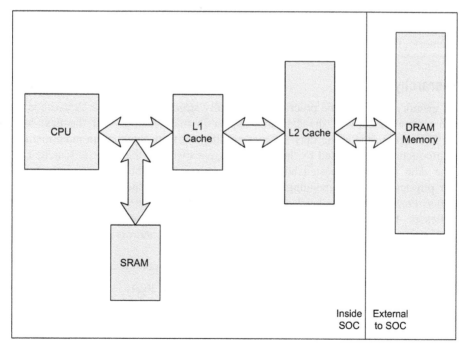

FIGURE 5.10

Memory Hierarchy.

The caches are also broken down into separate levels (such as Level 1 and Level 2) with increases in access latency and increasing density as the levels increase.

- *Dynamic RAM (DRAM).* DRAM technology provides the bulk of the memory requirements for embedded systems. Typically access cycles are 100ns. The technology required to create high-density DRAM devices is not the same as the silicon process technology required for high-speed logic or SRAMs. As a result, DRAM memory is usually external to the SOC. In some limited cases, the DRAM is placed in the same package as the processor/SOC, but at the time of writing it is a costly operation and not common.
- *Mass storage.* When mass storage is used as part of the paging virtual memory system. Access to mass storage even for SSD-based media requires thousands of CPU cycles.

Local Memory

On some embedded SOC devices dedicated SRAM is provided on die. The SRAM device is mapped to a unique address in the memory map and must be explicitly managed by the application or operating system. This is usually achieved by using a specific tool chain linker section and mapping specific data structures with your application to this tool chain linker section. The access times are usually similar to that of an L1 cache (perhaps a little faster because there are no tag lookups required). The contents that you place in these RAM devices are really a function of the application; they are often used to increase the determinism of interrupt handing software because access to the memory cannot miss, as is the case for caches. These embedded SOC SRAMs are not usually coherent with the remainder of the I/O system. This local memory is sometimes called tightly coupled memory (TCM).

Cache Hierarchy

The fastest memory closest to the processor is typically structured as caches. A cache is a memory structure that stores a copy of the data that appear in main memory (or the next level in the hierarchy). The copy in the cache may at times be different from the copy in main memory. When a memory transaction is generated by the processor (reads/writes), the cache is searched to see if it contains the data for the requested address. The address used in the cache structure may be a virtual or physical address depending on whether the cache is situated before the MMU translation or after. For example, the level one cache of the Intel XScale processor is addressed using virtual addresses. Caches in the Intel Architecture processors are all addressed with physical addresses. The term *tag* is used to refer to the fields within the address that are used to search the cache for a match.

Caches are structures that take advantage of a program's temporal and spatial locality:

- *Temporal locality.* If a memory location was accessed then it is likely to be accessed again soon (in time).
- *Spatial locality.* A program is likely to access a memory address close by shortly after the current access.

The caches themselves are often organized in a hierarchy, again with increasing access times and increased size. Even though the technology of the SRAMs is usually similar for L1 and L2 caches, the

L2 cache takes longer to return the contents of a hit as it is farther from the core, and it takes longer to search a larger cache. The L1 cache is usually close to the same frequency as the core, whereas the L2 is often clocked at a slower speed.

Theoretically, cache structures can be organized in many different forms. Two extreme implementations are the following:

- *Direct mapped.* The tag is used to perform a direct lookup in the cache structure. The contents of the cache for the virtual address can reside in exactly one location within the cache.
- *Fully associative.* The tag is used to search the cache for a match; however, any cache location may contain the entry. Unlike the direct mapped implementation where no comparisons must be made, every entry in the fully associative cache must be compared with the tag. Comparing the tag with all entries requires complex combinational logic whose complexity grows the larger the cache size. This is sometimes known as content addressable memory.

In reality, neither approach is feasible; the cache structures are a hybrid of both the direct mapped and fully associative. The structures created on Intel processors are N-way set associative, where N is a different number based on the product and level of the cache. The (physical) address used to look up a set associative cache is divided into three separate fields:

- *Tag.* The tag field within the address is used to look up a fully associative set. The set consists of N ways, which all must be matched against the tag. The tag field is usually composed of the upper address bits within the physical address.
- *Set index.* The cache is split into M sets, and this index is used to directly select the set, which is then searched with the tag.
- *Offset/displacement.* Each cache entry is called a line. The offset selects the actual word within the cache line to return.

Figure 5.11 shows the logical structure of a 24-K Intel Atom instruction cache.

As a software designer, the cache structure can be largely transparent; however, an awareness of the structure can help greatly when you start to optimize the code for performance. At a minimum, be aware of the cache line size and structure your data such that commonly used elements fall within the same cache line. The Intel Atom platform has the following caches, all with a cache line size of 64 bytes:

- 32-K eight-way set associative L1 instruction cache.
- 24-K six-way set associative L1 data cache.
- 512-K eight-way set associative unified instruction and data L2 cache.

Allocation Policy

The cache allocation policy dictates whether the cache should allocate space based on the transaction type from the processor. Two primary modes of operations are supported by embedded processors. The first is read-only allocate; this occurs when the processor performs a memory read that misses the cache. The cache will identify which line to evict from the cache, usually based on a least recently used (LRU) algorithm. This process identifies which *way* to evict from the set. The data will be fetched from the next level memory hierarchy and both placed in the cache and returned to the processor. In addition to allocation on read, some embedded processors also support allocation on a write transaction. In this case a similar set of events occurs; a line must be evicted, the contents of the associated cache line are

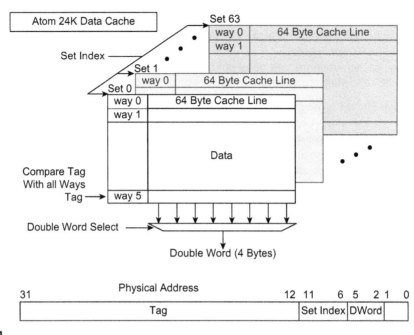

FIGURE 5.11

Six-Way Set Associative 24-K Data Cache.

populated from the next level of the memory hierarchy, and then the processor write data are merged into the cache line in the cache. There is an additional policy that dictates whether the data will also be written to memory (as well as the cache) immediately; this is known as write-through. The normal cache mode for the Intel Atom processor is write allocate.

When a cache miss occurs, the full cache line must be brought into the cache. This requires a cached line memory read to occur. This transaction generally appears as a burst read to the memory. The normal operation is for the memory controller to return the words in ascending memory order starting at the start of the cache line. Some platforms support a feature known as Critical Word First (CWF). In this mode, the memory controller first returns the actual requested contents of the memory location that missed the cache (the word), followed by the remainder of the cache line. The CWF feature reduces the latency to the processor for the missed transaction.

The Intel platforms generally have larger cache structures than competing products in the same segment. Larger caches have a lower miss rate, and as result the SOCs based on the Intel Atom do not provide this feature.

Exclusivity

If there are multiple levels of cache in a system, the question arises, can any entry reside in a number of levels of the cache at the same time? Inclusive cache hierarchies ensure that data that is in a level one cache will have a copy in the level two cache, whereas non-inclusive caches will guarantee that data will be resident in only one level at any time. SOCs based on the Intel Atom make no such guarantees and are neither exclusive nor inclusive, although the likelihood is that data in the level one cache would usually also reside in the level two cache.

Whether the caches L1, L2 (and Last Level Cache) are mutually exclusive, mutually inclusive, or a mixture of both depends on the micro architecture of the processor and is not usually architecturally defined. In any respect, the hardware will ensure cache consistency and the correct program behavior.

Memory Types

Different regions of system memory on a platform require different attributes when the memory system interacts with them. For example, portions of the memory map that contain peripheral devices (within or outside the SOC) must not be marked as a cache region. Similarly, general-purpose memory for the operating system, applications, and such is mapped as cacheable. Most systems often provide a register-based mechanism to provide course grained memory attributes. The register typically consists of a base address, range of the register, and the attributes to set for access to memory covered by the register. In the Intel processors, the Memory Type Range Registers (MTRRs), which are machine specific, are provided. In more advanced cases the memory management page tables, as described in the previous section, are used in addition to the MTRRs to provide per page attributes of a particular memory region. Processors such as the Intel XScale enable application memory type classification using the MMU page tables.

On Intel architectures, there are five types of classification that can be assigned to a particular memory region:

- *Strong Un-cacheable (UC).* System memory locations are not cached. All reads and writes appear on the system bus and are executed in program order without reordering. No speculative memory accesses, page-table walks, or prefetches of speculated branch targets are made. This type of cache control is useful for memory-mapped I/O devices. When used with normal RAM, it greatly reduces processor performance.
- *Un-cacheable (UC-).* Has the same characteristics as the strong un-cacheable (UC) memory type, except that this memory type can be overridden by programming the MTRRs for the write combining memory type.
- *Write Combining (WC).* System memory locations are not cached (as with un-cacheable memory) and coherency is not enforced by the processor's bus coherency protocol. Speculative reads are allowed. Writes may be delayed and combined in the write combining buffer (WC buffer) to reduce memory accesses. If the WC buffer is partially filled, the writes may be delayed until the next occurrence of a serializing event, such as a serializing instruction such as SFENCE, MFENCE, or CPUID execution, interrupts, and processor internal events.
- *Write-Through (WT).* Writes and reads to and from system memory are cached. Reads come from cache lines on cache hits; read misses cause cache fills. Speculative reads are allowed. All writes are written to a cache line (when possible) and through to system memory. When writing through to memory, invalid cache lines are never filled, and valid cache lines are either filled or invalidated. Write combining is allowed. This type of cache control is appropriate for frame buffers or when there are devices on the system bus that access system memory but do not perform snooping of memory accesses. It enforces coherency between caches in the processors and system memory.
- *Write-Back (WB).* Writes and reads to and from system memory are cached. Reads are fulfilled by cache lines on cache hits; read misses cause cache fills. Speculative reads are allowed. Write misses also cause cache line fills, and writes are performed entirely in the cache. When possible write

combining is allowed. The write-back memory type reduces bus traffic by eliminating many unnecessary writes to system memory. Writes to a cache line are not immediately forwarded to system memory; instead, they are accumulated in the cache. The modified cache lines are written to system memory later, when a write-back operation is performed. Write-back operations are triggered when cache lines need to be reallocated, such as when a new cache line must be allocated when the cache is already fully allocated (most of the time). This type of cache control provides the best performance, but it requires that all devices that access system memory on the system bus be able to snoop memory accesses to ensure system memory and cache coherency. This is the case for all systems based on Intel architecture.

- *Write Protected (WP)*. Reads come from cache lines when possible, and read misses cause cache fills. Writes are propagated to the system bus and cause corresponding cache lines on all processors on the bus to be invalidated. Speculative reads are allowed.

The majority of embedded systems provide simple cache/not-cached memory type attributes. At first look, the Intel architecture capabilities appear overly complex, but the fine-grained approach affords selection of optimal behavior for any memory region in the system with the effect of maximizing the performance.

For a 2.6.34 kernel running on an Intel Atom platform with 1 GB of memory, the following Linux command shows the MTRR settings.

```
ubuntu-atom1:/proc$ cat /proc/mtrr
reg00: base=0x00000000 ( 0MB), size=1024MB: write-back, count=1
reg01: base=0x3f700000 (1015MB), size=  1MB: uncachable, count=1
reg02: base=0x3f800000 (1016MB), size=  8MB: uncachable, count=1
```

The first region sets the DRAM as write-back cacheable, the typical setting. The Linux /var/log/Xorg.0.log file indicates that the graphics frame buffer is at 0x3f800000.

```
(EE) PSB(0): screnIndex is:0;fbPhys is:0x3f800000; fbsize is:0x007bf000
(--) PSB(0): Mapped graphics aperture at physical address 0x3f800000
```

Linux has set up the third MTRR (reg02) to provide the attributes for graphics aperture. However, the page tables have set up the region as write-combining, overriding the MTRR UC- setting.

Cache Coherency

A number of agents other than the processor access system memory. For example, a peripheral such as a network interface must read and write system memory through direct memory access to transmit and receive packets. When the processor generates a network packet to be transmitted on the network, the system must ensure that the DMA engines of the network interface get the most recent consistent data when it reads system memory for the packet. Conversely, when a processor reads data written by the network card, it should get the most recent content from the memory. The mechanism that manages the data consistency is known as cache coherency.

To ensure that the contents read by the DMA engine are correct, there are two approaches. The first is to ensure that the system memory contents reflect the latest payload before the NIC issues the DMA read. The NIC driver could use software instruction to flush all cache lines associated with packet. This is a costly operation, but not untypical on some embedded SOC platforms. The second approach calls for dedicated logic to search the cache when other agents are reading and writing to system memory.

Managing coherency using software is the responsibility of each device driver on the platform. The operating system typically provides calls that the driver must call to ensure consistency. For an example of an Ethernet device driver that manages coherence in software, you can review the Linux Coldfire fast Ethernet Driver linux-source-2.6.24/drivers/net/fec.c. The following code segment flushes the dcache lines associated with the packet to ensure memory is consistent before transmission.

```
flush_dcache_range((unsigned long)skb->data,
            (unsigned long)skb->data + skb->len);
```

On Intel platforms, the hardware maintains coherence by snooping the memory transactions to ensure consistency. The processor maintains cache consistency with the MESI (Modified, Exclusive, Shared, Invalid) protocol. Cache consistency is maintained for I/O agents and other processors (with caches). MESI is used to allow the cache to decide whether a memory entry should be updated or invalidated. Two functions are performed to allow its internal cache to stay consistent:

- *Snoop cycles.* The processor snoops during memory transactions on the system bus. That is, when another bus master performs a write, the processor snoops the address. If the cache(s) contain(s) the data, the processor will schedule a write-back. The agent performing the read will get the up-to-date values.
- *Cache flushing.* This is the mechanism by which the processor clears its cache. A cache flush may result from actions in either hardware or software. During a cache flush, the processor writes back all modified (or dirty) data. It then invalidates its cache (that is, makes all cache lines unavailable).

These mechanisms ensure that data read or written to the system memory from an IO agent are always consistent with the caches. The availably of hardware-managed coherence greatly simplifies software development of the operating system device drivers, especially when it comes to debugging—it's tricky to debug cache coherence issues. Newer ARM Cortex™ A9 processors have introduced a Snoop Control Unit for use with Multicore designs. See http://www.arm.com/products/processors/cortex-a/cortex-a9.php for more details.

You should be aware that even though the system may support cache coherence, it is not sufficient to guarantee that writes issued by the processor can be snooped by the snoop logic. The write may be in a write buffer on the way to the cache or memory subsystem. It may still be important that the driver issues a memory barrier before the hardware is notified that it can read any data. The smp_wmb() in Linux performs this function; if the barrier is not needed on a target system it will degenerate to be a null operation. In the case of PCIe™ devices, device drivers usually perform a read from the device. This is a serialization event in the processor and ensures that all memory writes are visible to any snoop logic.

The Linux kernel has a number of APIs that should be used to manage memory that is coherent with the I/O subsystem. For an example of pci_alloc_consistent() refer to Chapter 8.

MESI

Although largely transparent to the programmer, the cache coherence protocol used is worth a brief mention. In processors that support Symmetric Multi Processing (SMP), the behavior of writes in the system depend on the cache states of other caches in the system, For example, if there is a copy of a memory location in another processor's cache, then each cache entry associated with the memory location will be in a shared state. When any of the processors write to a cache line in the shared state, the write must be written through to the system bus so that other caches can invalidate their copy (it is no longer valid). The multicore processors use the MESI protocol to ensure that all the caches in the system are coherent and consistent, and ensure that no two valid cache lines can have a different copy of the same address. The MESI protocol's name comes from the states that each of the cache lines may be in at any point in time: Modified, Exclusive, Shared, and Invalid.

- Modified: The cache line is only present in the current cache and has been modified (is dirty) from the value held in memory. The data must be written back to memory at some point. If another processor attempts to read the data from memory before it has been written back, this cache must "snoop" the read and write back the data as part of a snoop response. If the data has been written back to memory, the state transitions to exclusive.
- Exclusive: The cache line is present in the current cache and is clean, has not been modified, and is the same as the copy in memory. It will be updated to shared if another processor also obtains a copy.
- Shared: Indicates that this cache and others have a copy of the cache line. The cache line is clean and all copies are identical to the copy in memory.
- Invalid: Indicates that the cache line is not valid.

Table 5.14 shows the cache line states and the associated behavior.

MESI is a very common cache coherence protocol used in multiprocessor designs, including Intel architectures, ARM11™, and ARM Cortex-A9 MPCores.

Bus Addresses

Externally attached devices are typically attached through a bus, usually PCIe or expansion bus interfaces. These external buses most often support direct memory access from the device to system memory. You should note that a device also has a system memory map relative to the bus mastering agent; that is, the memory map as viewed from a device may be different from that as viewed by the processor. When the devices generate addresses for reads or writes, they generate bus addresses, which are then converted to a physical system address at the bus interface point, such as an expansion bus controller or the PCIe root complex. Device drivers use APIs to convert virtual memory addresses to physical system addresses and then to device-relative bus addresses. These bus addresses are populated in the device DMA engines. For traditional 32-bit Intel architecture systems the PCIe bus

Table 5.14 MESI Cache Line States

Cache Line State	M (Modified)	E (Exclusive)	S (Shared)	I (Invalid)
This cache line is valid	Yes	Yes	Yes	No
The memory content for this cache line	Stale	Valid	Valid	–
Copies exist in caches of other processors	No	No	Yes	Maybe
A write to this line	Does not go to the system bus	Does not go to the system bus	Causes the processor to gain exclusive ownership of the line	Causes RFO transaction to memory (WB memory type)

address maps 1:1 with the physical address used. On most SOCs, however, either there are changes in the size of the address space or translation between bus addresses and system addresses. You should be aware of such translation and abstract the translation when developing your device driver software.

System Bus Interface

In previous generations of embedded systems the processors or system bus was externally exposed on the device, and the system bus was routed throughout the printed circuit board. However, with advances in integration the system bus is now an internal (to the SOC) interconnect. The processor bus within some Intel Atom devices is a derivative of the previously exposed Front Side Bus (FSB). The FSB was the bus that connected the CPU to the Memory Controller Hub (MCH) in older generations of Intel platforms. The memory controller hub feature set is now integrated into the SOC; as a result, the memory controller interface is exposed for direct attachment to the memory devices. On the Intel Atom-based SOC, a bus similar to the FSB logically remains within the SOC.

Memory Technology

At the time of writing the memory technology attached to the processor is usually Double Data Rate Synchronous Dynamic Random Access Memory (DDR3 is common on desktop platforms, while DDR2 is still prevalent on embedded systems). The interface for DDR is defined by the JEDEC organization (reference: http://www.jedec.org). Both the density and bandwidth of the dynamic memory technology have increased considerably over time; however, the latencies associated with memory access have not declined at nearly the same rate. The memory controller and memory devices are highly pipelined. Attributes of the memory hierarchy described above are all structured to try to ensure that the application does not directly experience the latency of a DRAM transaction. To that end, in addition to the cache structure, some platforms have pre-fetchers. A pre-fetcher is a piece of logic that attempts to predict future memory access that will be made based on the history of the application. It then issues a speculative read transaction to the memory controller to bring a likely entry closer to the processor before it is actually needed.

The memory controller can operate in burst and single-transaction mode. Burst mode transactions are significantly more efficient than the single transaction. This burst mode transaction matches well to the cache line fill/write-back behavior of the caches.

More details on the memory interfaces are provided in Chapter 2.

INTEL ATOM MICROARCHITECTURE (SUPPLEMENTAL MATERIAL)

The primary view by which a software designer understands a processor-based system is through its architecture definition. From a software viewpoint, the architecture definition is a contract between the platform and the software. The platform behaves in a guaranteed manner in compliance with the architecture definition. The architecture of the CPU in particular changes infrequently over time, and there are relatively few of them in existence. For example, in the embedded processor space the primary architectures are IA-32, ARM, MIPS™, and PowerPC. The architecture itself can evolve by adding capabilities; each architecture has differing approaches to the growth and management of the architecture over time. The IA-32 architecture takes one of the most rigorous approaches to ensure that software written for any previous microarchitecture continues to run on the latest microarchitecture. Other architectures such as ARM have chosen to allow for forward compatibility only. For example, the ARM Cortex M3 runs a subset of the ARM ISA known as Thumb2, so code compiled for an ARM Cortex M3 will run on an ARM Cortex A9 but not vice versa. Each approach brings about its own trade-offs in silicon complexity and reuse of software.

The microarchitecture of a product is not part of the architectural contract with the software. It is a specific implementation that complies with the architecture. The microarchitecture of a product changes more frequently than the architecture and represents a specific implementation that is tuned to fulfill specific optimizations such as core speed, power, or both. The IA-32 architecture includes Intel486®, Pentium® processors, Intel Core, Core 2, and Intel Atom microarchitecture. The microarchitecture defines attributes of the implementation such as in-order/out-of-order instruction processing, the depth of the instruction pipeline, and branch prediction. In particular, the software designer should be aware of the microarchitecture of the CPU when tuning the system to maximize its performance or power for the target architecture. The architecture definition will guarantee that your software will always execute. Awareness of the microarchitecture (especially in the compiler) will help ensure that the code runs optimally. To ensure optimal execution on all platforms, the Intel Performance Primitive have a code path for all supported microarchitectures, each specially tuned. A CPU dispatch block establishes the best code path to execute depending on the CPU identifier.

Microarchitecture

The Intel Atom processor microarchitecture consists of the set of components on the processor that enables it to implement and provide support for the IA-32 and Intel 64 ISA. Embedded software developers need a basic understanding of the microarchitecture if they are engaged in low-level assembly language programming, such as developers working on device drivers or performance-critical portions of an application. Embedded software developers focused on utmost performance must also understand the microarchitecture and its implications for high-performing assembly or machine language. The ability to inspect assembly language code or a disassembly of an application and to understand the difference between high-performing and low-performing code sequences when executing on the Intel Atom processor is critical for product success. This section provides the basic understanding of the microarchitecture required to do so.

Figure 5.12 is a high-level depiction of the Intel Atom processor microarchitecture. At a first level, the microarchitecture of the initial Intel Atom processor is classified as an in-order, superscalar pipeline. The term *in-order* means that the machine instructions execute in the same order that they appear in the application. The term *superscalar* means that more than one instruction can execute at the same time. The Intel Atom processor is classified as *two-wide superscalar* since it has the ability to execute and retire two instructions in the same clock cycle. Modern processors are pipelined, which allows multiple instructions to be in different stages of processing at the same time.

The integer pipeline for the Intel Atom processor is detailed in Figure 5.13. The pipeline is divided into six phases of instruction processing:

• Instruction Fetch
• Instruction Decode
• Instruction Issue

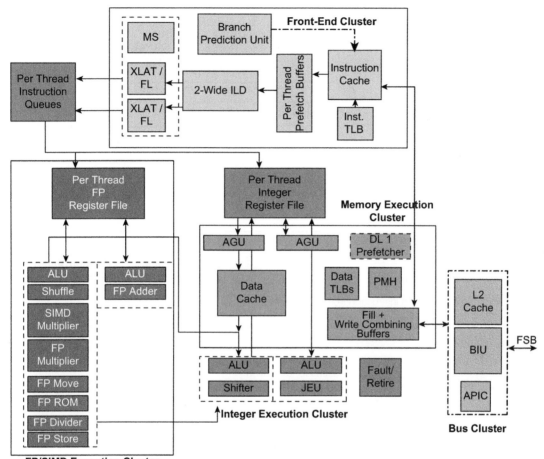

FIGURE 5.12

Intel Atom Processor Microarchitecture.

- Data Access
- Execute
- Write Back

The integer pipeline consists of 16 stages and the floating-point pipeline consists of 19 stages. In normal pipeline operation each stage takes one cycle to execute. The number of stages for each phase is detailed in Table 5.15. Note that each phase is pipelined; for example, it is possible for three instructions to be in the different stages of the instruction fetch phase (IF1, IF2, and IF3) at the same time.

For the integer pipeline, the instruction fetch phase is three stages and the instruction decode is three stages. Instruction issue consists of three stages and data access consists of three stages. Instruction execution consists of one stage and write back consists of three stages. For floating-point instructions, the instruction fetch consists of three stages and instruction decode consists of three

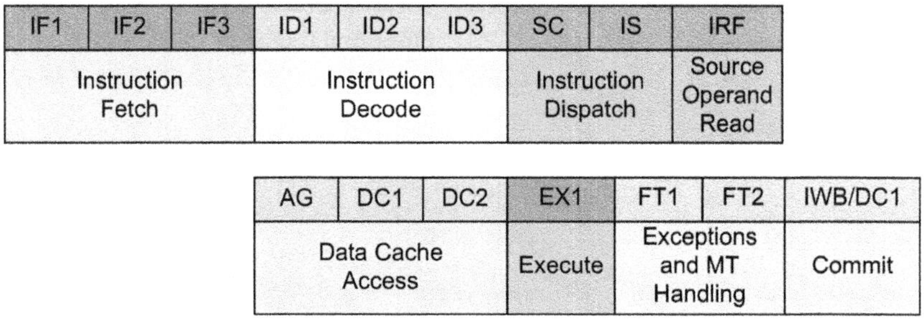

IF1	IF2	IF3	ID1	ID2	ID3	SC	IS	IRF
Instruction Fetch			Instruction Decode			Instruction Dispatch		Source Operand Read

AG	DC1	DC2	EX1	FT1	FT2	IWB/DC1
Data Cache Access			Execute	Exceptions and MT Handling		Commit

FIGURE 5.13

Integer Pipeline.

Table 5.15 Intel Atom Processor Pipeline

Pipeline Phase	Description	Integer: Number of Stages	Floating-Point: Number of Stages
Instruction Fetch	Obtains instruction from instruction cache	3	3
Instruction Decode	Understands instruction	3	3
Instruction Issue	Checks and satisfies dependencies, reads registers, and issues for execution	3	3
Data Access	Generates address if needed and accesses data cache	3	3
Execute	Execution of the operation	1	7
Write Back	Checks for exceptions and commits results	3	1

stages. Instruction issue consists of three stages and data access consists of three stages. Instruction execution consists of seven stages and write back consists of one stage. There are many exceptions when an instruction can take longer to execute than 16 or 19 cycles; examples include division operations and instructions that decode in the microcode sequencer.

As mentioned previously, the Intel Atom processor microarchitecture is in-order. You can understand what in-order means by comparing it to an out-of-order microarchitecture such as the Intel Core i7 processor. Consider the sequence of instructions listed in Figure 5.14, which has the following program-specified dependencies:

- Instruction 2 is dependent on the result of instruction 1.
- Instruction 3 is dependent on the result of instructions 2 and 1.
- Instruction 5 is dependent on the result of instruction 4.
- Instruction 6 is dependent on the result of instructions 5 and 4.

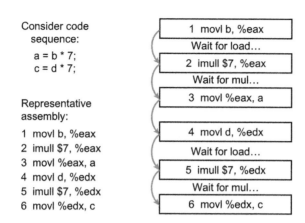

Consider code sequence:

a = b * 7;
c = d * 7;

Representative assembly:

1 movl b, %eax
2 imull $7, %eax
3 movl %eax, a
4 movl d, %edx
5 imull $7, %edx
6 movl %edx, c

FIGURE 5.14

In-Order Execution.

An in-order processor would execute the instructions in the order the instructions are listed. In an in-order superscalar processor such as the Intel Atom processor with two execution pipelines, instruction 2 would attempt to execute at the same time as instruction 1, but due to the dependency, the pipeline would stall until the result of instruction 1 were ready. Instruction 3 would not start executing until instruction 2 had the result from instruction 1. Instruction 4 could start execution as soon as instruction 2 finished; however, instruction 5 would be stalled until instruction 4 had a result ready.

An out-of-order processor allows independent instructions to execute out of order as long as the instruction's dependencies have been fulfilled. On an out-of-order processor with sufficient execution resources the instruction schedule is more efficient. Instruction 4 can execute at the same time as instruction 1. Instruction 5 can execute at the same time as instruction 2. Instruction 6 can execute at the same time as instruction 3. The results are still written in program order; however, superscalar execution enables more efficient usage of process resources.

This is a fundamental difference between the Intel Atom processor and other modern out-of-order processors. One method of addressing this disadvantage is to use a compiler that schedules for the Intel Atom processor. If the compiler laid out the instructions in the order specified in Figure 5.15, many of the same benefits of out-of-order execution would result when executing on the Intel Atom processor.

Front End

The components that comprise what is termed the front end of the processor are charged with finding and placing the instructions into the execution units. The components that comprise the front end of the processor and their functionality are the following:

- *Branch Prediction Unit.* Predicts the target address for branches.
- *Instruction TLB.* Translates virtual to physical addresses.
- *Instruction Cache.* Fast access to recently executed instructions.
- *Prefetch Buffer.* Holds instruction bytes ready for decoding.

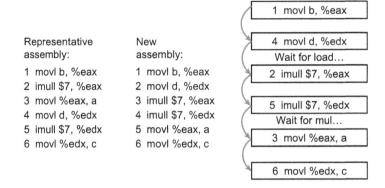

Representative
assembly:
1 movl b, %eax
2 imull $7, %eax
3 movl %eax, a
4 movl d, %edx
5 imull $7, %edx
6 movl %edx, c

New
assembly:
1 movl b, %eax
2 movl d, %edx
3 imull $7, %eax
4 imull $7, %edx
5 movl %eax, a
6 movl %edx, c

FIGURE 5.15

Instruction Schedule for In-Order Execution.

- *Decode.* Performs the decode.
- *Microcode Sequencer.* Complex instruction decode.

The front end of the microarchitecture performs the instruction fetch and instruction issue phases of the pipeline. The first action in placing an instruction into the pipeline is to obtain the address of the instruction. This address comes from one of two places. If the current instruction that is just entering the pipeline is not a branch instruction, the next instruction is equal to the address of the current instruction plus the size of the current instruction. If the current instruction is a branch, the next instruction is determined by the branch prediction unit that caches previously seen branches and provides a prediction as to the direction and target of the branch. The instruction TLB translates the virtual address used by the program into the physical address where the instruction is actually stored. The instruction cache is used to keep recently executed instructions closer to the processor if those particular instructions are executed again. The instruction cache is 24 kB.

Predecode Bits

The instruction cache contains predecode bits to demarcate individual instructions to improve decode speed. One of the challenges with the IA-32 and Intel 64 ISA is that instructions are variable in length. In other words, the size of the instruction is not known until the instruction has been partially decoded. The front end contains two instruction decoders that enable up to two instructions to be decoded per cycle, and this is consistent with the Intel Atom processor's dual instruction execution architecture. These decoders assume the boundary of an instruction is known, which is a change from previous decoders used in Intel architecture processors. Previous processors buffered bytes into a window that was rotated from instruction to instruction. The front end also contains two queues to temporarily hold decoded instructions until they are ready to execute. Two queues service the two threads of execution available due to support for Intel Hyper-Threading Technology.

Instruction Decode

During instruction decode, the IA-32 and Intel 64 instructions are decoded into another instruction that drives the microarchitecture. In previous IA-32 and Intel 64 architecture processors, the decode phase broke instructions into micro-operations characterized as very simple. For example, an addition operation that referenced and wrote to memory would be broken down into four micro-operations for execution by the microarchitecture. In the Intel Atom processor, the two decoders are capable of decoding most instructions in the Intel 64 and IA-32 architecture. The microarchitecture does make a distinction between instructions that are too complicated to execute in the pipeline and simpler instructions, and has a fallback mechanism, a microcode sequencer. The microcode sequencer is used to decode the more complex instructions into a number of smaller operations for execution in the pipeline. The drawback to the microcode store is that these instructions decode slower and break down into more than one operation in the pipeline.

Decode Stage to Issue Stage

The decode stages can decode up to two instructions to keep the two-issue pipeline filled; however, in some cases the decoder is limited in only being able to decode one instruction per cycle. Cases where the decoder is limited to one instruction per cycle include x87 floating-point instructions and branch instructions. The Intel Atom processor is dual-issue superscalar, but it is not perfectly symmetrical. Not every possible pairing of operations can execute in the pipeline at the same time. The instruction queue holds instructions until they are ready to execute in the memory execution cluster, the integer execution cluster, or the FP/SIMD execution cluster.

Memory Execution Cluster

The memory execution cluster provides the functionality for generating addresses and accessing data. Components of the memory execution cluster and their functionality include the following:

- *Address Generation Unit.* Generates data address composing base address, scale, and offset.
- *Data TLB.* Translates virtual address to physical address.
- *Data Cache.* Holds recently accessed data.
- *Prefetcher.* Predicts future access and fetches by analyzing previous accesses.
- *Write-Combining Buffers.* Allows grouping of individual write operations before being sent on to the cache; enables more efficient memory bandwidth utilization.

In the optimum case for a data access, the data are resident in the L1 cache; however, if the data are not resident there, an L2 cache request is made. One architectural optimization is the inclusion of a data prefetcher that analyzes historical access patterns and attempts to fetch future data in advance of reference.

Common to many architectures, the memory subsystem supports store forwarding, which takes a result of a previous store and forwards the value internally for use in a proceeding load operation. This forwarding eliminates potential pipeline stalls because the load instruction does not need to wait until the stored value is committed to the cache. A special case of forwarding results from operations that affect the flags and instructions dependent upon them. Branch operations have an implicit one-cycle penalty. All other instructions have a two-cycle bubble.

One common occurrence in instruction sequences is the computation of an address for use in subsequent instructions. For example, Figure 5.16 shows an instruction sequence where the second instruction depends on an address calculation from the previous instruction. This dependency would cause a three-cycle stall because the second instruction cannot execute until the result of the first

Instruction							
subl $4, %esp	IRF	AG	DC1	DC2	EX1	FT1	
movl %ebx, (%esp)		IRF	stall	stall	stall	AG	DC1

FIGURE 5.16

Address Generation Stall.

instruction is known. Figure 5.16 shows the impact on the pipeline as there is a bubble between the AG and EX pipeline stages.

Integer Execution Cluster

The integer execution cluster features two arithmetic/logic units (ALU) enabling joint execution of many instructions. Dual execution in the execution cluster has some limitations.

FP/SIMD Execution Cluster

The floating-point execution cluster executes x87, SIMD, and integer multiply instructions. The cluster contains two ALUs and supports limited combinations of dual execution. The second execution unit is limited to floating-point additions. Integer multiplies take more than one cycle in the execute stage and effectively stall subsequent instructions until after the multiply is finished with the execute stage. The only exceptions to this are for subsequent integer multiplies, which can be effectively pipelined in this stage.

Safe Instruction Recognition

One microarchitectural issue specific to the Intel Atom processor is that the integer pipeline is shorter than the floating-point pipeline. Floating-point exceptions can occur in an instruction that is programmatically before an integer instruction, but takes longer to retire. A straightforward solution would be to delay retirement of integer instructions until preceding floating-point instructions in the pipeline retire. This solution would effectively add a multicycle delay to integer instruction retirement. Instead, a safe instruction recognition algorithm is employed that detects whether it is possible for a floating-point instruction to fault. In only those cases, a restart of preceding integer instructions from the scheduler would be issued.

Bus Cluster

The bus cluster is the connection from the processor to the memory subsystem and contains a 512-kB, eight-way L2 cache. The bus cluster also contains the Bus Interface Unit (BIU) and Advanced Programmable Interrupt Controller (APIC).

Embedded Platform Boot Sequence

The boot sequence of embedded processors varies very little regardless of the class of device and the storage media available. This chapter outlines the sequence required to execute user code in a platform, with particular reference to Intel® architecture platforms.

Before we look at various steps and stages of the boot flow, let's talk about the two most important technologies on the system for consideration: the processor and the storage devices. The processor, which could be composed of multiple logical and physical cores, provides the execution engine. The storage devices, ranging from small NOR flashes to multi-terabyte hard disk drives, provide the code to be executed.

MULTI-CORE AND MULTI-PROCESSOR BOOT

Multi-core and multi-processor systems are becoming more and more pervasive in embedded systems. A variety of multi-processor configurations exist, such as multiple logical cores in a CPU, multiple cores in the same package, and multiple processors in separate packages on the platform. In this section we discuss the boot sequences for Intel Architecture–based systems. For Intel architecture–based systems, all configurations are logically identical and the discussion applies to any of the multi-core configurations. Given the range of different configurations, here are some definitions.

- *Thread*—A thread is a logical processor that shares resources with another logical core in the package. Typically, there may be two threads per core of the Intel Atom™ cores. This could also be called a hardware thread. For Intel Architecture processors this is referred to Symmetrical Multi-Threading (formerly Hyper Threading).
- *Core*—A processor core can coexist with other cores in the same package. There is no sharing of the core resources between cores, but they may share higher levels of cache (such as L2 cache).
- *Package*—A package is a chip that contains one or more cores; each core may provide one or more thread.
- *System on Chip*—A package that contains one or more CPUs/cores, along with memory controllers, interfaces, and peripherals all integrated on the same device.

When the reset signal is released to the processors, a hardware arbitration process starts off. This hardware arbitration process picks one of the processors as being the bootstrap processor (BSP). All other processors are known as application processors (APs). There is no physical difference between the processors; the assignment of one of the processors as the bootstrap processor is a process developed to facilitate the boot sequence of a multicore system. For processors with multiple hardware

153

threads, the multi-processor initialization protocol treats each of the logical processors as a separate processor. During boot-up, one of the logical processors is selected as the BSP and the rest of the logical processors are designated as APs. The nominated BSP is Intel architecture generation and platform dependent. Each processor has a local interrupt controller (LAPIC). The BSP bit is set in the LAPIC for the BSP and cleared for all other processors.

The BSP is the first processor to start executing code, which it fetches from the reset vector. The BSP BIOS/UEFI startup code initializes the APIC and sets up all system-wide BIOS/UEFI data structures. The application processor, on the other hand, performs processor self-tests and then waits for a signal for what to do next from the BSP. This is the Wait for Startup Inter Processor Interrupt, referred to as the WAIT-for-SIPI state. The BSP sends a Startup Inter Processor Interrupt (SIPI) message to all the APs indicating that the targeted processor should start execution from a physical address provided in the SIPI message. The address must be within the first megabyte of the address space and must be aligned on a 4-kB boundary.

The SIPI message is broadcast to all APs in the system. The SIPI message contains a vector to the BIOS/UEFI AP initialization code. The vector is defined as 0x000VV000, where VV is the vector contained in SIPI message. The first action of the AP initialization code is to set up a race (among the APs) to a BIOS/UEFI initialization semaphore. The first AP to the semaphore begins executing the initialization code. As part of the AP initialization procedure, the AP adds its APIC ID number to the ACPI and MP tables as appropriate and increments the processor counter by 1. At the completion of the initialization procedure, the AP clears interrupts and halts itself. When each of the APs has gained access to the semaphore and executed the AP initialization code, the BSP establishes a count for the number of processors connected to the system bus, completes executing the BIOS bootstrap code, and then begins executing operating system bootstrap and startup code. While the BSP is executing operating system bootstrap and startup code, the APs remain in the halted state. The BSP has access to complete PCI configuration space of the platform, that is, it can initialize all SOC resources as needed. The APs are now waiting for an INIT message. Most BIOS/firmware continues to run only on the BSP; that is, it is single hardware threaded. Once the firmware is ready to attempt to boot an OS, all AP processors must be placed back in their power-on state ("Wait-for-SIPI"), which can be accomplished by the BSP sending an INIT ASSERT IPI followed by an INIT DEASSERT IPI to all APs in the system (all except self).

This multiprocessor boot sequence allows a single standardized multiprocessor capable boot image to discover and initialize all the processors on the system, without knowing in advance the exact configuration of the system. While multi-processor boot may add more time to the overall boot process, the OS is able to take full advantage of the additional processing power, without requiring it to be re-written for all the different possible architectures.

BOOT TECHNOLOGY CONSIDERATIONS

The selection of boot technologies for an embedded system must take into account a number of factors for the boot device. The key factors are the following:

- *Time to availability*—Indicates how much time elapses after power-on or restart before the technology can be safely read from. Depending on which part of the boot code is stored on the media, it may have an impact on how fast the system boots. The availability may be dictated by mechanical aspects such as a disk drive spindle spin-up that can take a number of seconds or error integrity checks for consistency on NAND-based memory devices.

- *Performance*—Clearly, read performance of the initial boot media will have an impact on boot performance. The read performance of the device will be a combination of the underlying technology and how it is attached to the SOC; for example, a native SOC interface such as SATA will have far higher performance than a low-pin-count interface such as Serial Peripheral Interconnect (SPI), such as may be the case when the OS is stored in the flash device with the firmware.
- *Robustness*—Each technology has a mean time between failure defined. For solid state media such as those based on NAND or NOR Flash memory, the reliability is dictated by the number of times the sectors on the device are erased. On the other hand storage devices based on magnetic media such as traditional hard disks are sensitive to environmental conditions such as vibration and temperature.
- *Price/density*—Generally, the higher the density of the media, the lower the price per megabyte. Magnetic-based media has the lowest cost per megabyte, followed by SSD, NAND flash, and then NOR flash devices.

The storage technologies prevalent at the time of writing are:

- *NOR flash memory devices*—Nonvolatile storage devices made up of floating gate transistors. The flash memory of the memory cells acts like a logical NOR gate. NOR memory has the highest reliability of all memory types and is the most prevalent for storing the initial boot code, that is, the storage for the instructions that are fetched when the processor comes out of reset. Executing the code directly from the flash device is known as eXecute in Place (XIP). The flash devices usually provide specific boot sectors that can be locked to prevent loss. NOR flash devices are normally attached via an SPI interface on Intel Architecture platforms; in other SOC devices a parallel interface of either 8 bits or 16 bits is more commonplace.
- *NAND flash memory devices*—Nonvolatile devices that are made of floating gate transistors. Each memory cell behaves like a logical NAND gate. The layout of the devices generally allow for much higher density devices than NOR devices. The devices are also more prone to bit errors caused by writes, retention due to loss of charge, and read-disturb errors. The bits are typically protected by ECC. The ECC bits added cover a block of the device, for instance, a 512-byte block. At startup, the controller will often validate the integrity of all blocks. This validation step delays the availability of the device. NAND flash devices come in a range of form factors and interface types:
  - Natively attached to the SOC using Open NAND Flash Interface (ONFI). This requires a NAND controller integrated into the SOC or attached to the SOC.
  - Secure Digital I/O (SDIO) is an interface typically used for consumer devices, such as memory cards for cameras, phones, and so on. Many embedded SOC devices have a native SDIO interface that allows the platform to use SDIO devices for storage.
  - Multi Media Card (MMC), as in the case of SDIO; a controller interface is often integrated.
  - USB interface to NAND, normally found in a USB key storage device.
- *Solid state drives*—Storage devices that are developed using NAND flash memories with a standard hard drive controller interface presented to the platform. This is typically a SATA interface. The controller must perform low-level NAND integrity tests when the platform boots.

Table 6.1 Image Storage Boot Considerations

Storage Type Heading	Availability	Read Performance
NOR 8-bit Interface	0 s	12.5 MB/s (80 ns read)
1xSPI NOR Flash[1]	0 s	2.5 MB/s (~6 MB/s at 50 MHz)
LPC NOR Flash[2]	0 s	1.7 MB/s (16 MBs)
SDIO NAND Flash[3]	~1 s	3/12/50 MB/s (x1, x4, x8 data bus)
Raw NAND[4] – ONFI	100 µs	16/32 MB/s (8x, 16x data)
SATA SSD[5]	~1 s	100 MB/s[6]
SATA HD[5]	2-4 s	60 MB/s[6]

[1]64-byte block, single-channel, 20 MHz clock (50–70 MHz recommended): ~2 MB/s.
[2]LPC running at 33 MHz, non-DMA mode, 8-bit cycles are supported on Poulsbo (128-byte burst reads not supported).
[3]Four-bit SDIO mode throughput 100 Mb/s (416 Mb/s for 8-bit mode); RV: 8-bit; TC-STM:4-bit SDIO.
[4]Sixteen-bit interface, 30-ns clock, 2-kB page, sequential read mode.
[5]2.5-inch disk from Fujitstu.
[6]Actual read performance is dictated by the SATA interface version and the sequential/random access pattern.
Source: http://spansion.com/Products/Documents/Spansion_MirrorBit_SPI_MIO_backgrounder.pdf.

- *Magnetic media hard drives*—These devices need no introduction; they are a commonplace form of mass storage. There is a delay in the availability of the media; at a minimum the hard drive spindle must spin up to the required speed. This can take a second or two.

Table 6.1 summarizes the performance and availability of each of the technologies.

As you can see, the performance of the device comes down to not only the underlying read performance of the technology but also the interconnect used between the technology and the processor/SOC. Intel architecture–based systems tend to use a low-pin-count interface such as SPI to connect to the initial NOR-based flash device and boot the OS from a mass storage device such as an SSD. However, for embedded platforms such as that supported by the Intel Atom Processor E6xx Series, booting from interfaces such as SDIO and MMC is also accommodated. Other embedded SOC platforms with a smaller overall footprint often just support a NOR flash interface via an expansion bus (such as an 8-bit or 16-bit parallel) interface.

NOR flash devices are still predominantly used for the initial boot-up code in embedded systems where failure to boot due to the loss of the initial boot-up code is not at all acceptable. Even if follow-on memory technologies used for the remainder of the boot sequence lose the image contents, the NOR-based image is provisioned to support re-flashing or recovery of the other images in the system.

HARDWARE POWER SEQUENCES (THE PRE-PRE-BOOT)

When external power is first applied to a platform, the hardware platform must carry out a number of tasks before the processor can be brought out of reset. The first task is for the power supply to be allowed to settle down to its nominal state; once the primary power supply settles, there are usually a number of derived voltage levels needed on the platform. For example, on the Intel architecture reference platform the input supply consists of a 12-volt source, but the platform and processor require

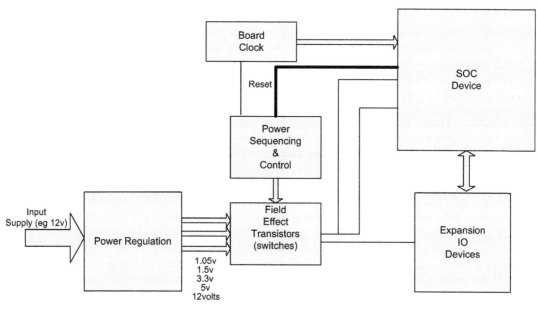

FIGURE 6.1

Power Sequencing Overview.

a number of different voltage rails such as 1.3v, 5v and 12 volts. The platform and processor also require that the voltages are provided in a particular sequence. This process is known as power sequencing. The power is sequenced by controlling analog switches (typically field effect transistors). The sequence is often driven by a complex programmable logic device (CPLD). The platform clocks are also derived from a small number of input clock and oscillator sources. The devices use phase locked loop circuitry to generate the derived clocks used for the platform. These clocks also take time to converge and become stable. When all these steps have occurred, the power sequencing CPLD de-asserts the reset line to the processor. Figure 6.1 shows an overview of the platform blocks described.

RESET: THE FIRST FEW STEPS AND A JUMP

Once the processor reset line has been de-asserted, the processor will begin fetching instructions. The location of these initial processor instructions is known as the reset vector. The reset vector may contain instructions or a pointer to the actual staring instruction sequence. The location of the vector is architecture specific and usually in a fixed location depending on the processor. The initial address must be a physical address, as the MMU (if it exists) has not yet been enabled. The following lists some specific examples:

- Intel Architecture—Starts fetching instructions from 0xFFF,FFF0. Only 16 bytes are left to the top of memory, so these 16 bytes must contain a far jump to the remainder of the initialization code.

- ARM Architecture—Starts fetching instructions from 0x000,0000 or 0xFFFF,0000 depending on the SOC and configuration. The reset vector is directly followed by other interrupt vectors, so the instruction found at the reset vector must be a jump instruction.
- PPC Architecture—Starts to fetch instructions from 0x0000,0100 or 0xFFF0,0100 on most implementations. The selection of a low or high vector is dictated by an IP status bit in the processors Machine State Register (MSR).

On embedded systems we often have to distinguish between hard and soft resets. Hard resets are resets due to a power-on event, whereas soft resets are as a result of the reset line being asserted but no loss of power has occurred. The soft reset may be generated under software control or due to the expiration of the watchdog timer. The hard reset is a relatively clean start to the system, but a soft reset may have been asserted for many reasons. Normally, a reset is triggered by an explicit restart event driven by the software, firmware, or BIOS, for example, reset, S3/S4 restart. On the other hand, the event may have been triggered by an abnormal event such as a watchdog timeout. A watchdog is usually a hardware device on the SOC or platform that must be written to frequently to show the software is operating within some normal limits. When a watchdog timer expires, the device generates a reset event. When the system software is booting, it should check the reason behind the reset. If the reset was due to a watchdog timer, the system software should record the event as abnormal in the system logs. In an effort to help debug such errors, embedded software often keep logs as the platform is running, for example, the process/task identifier of the currently running process. If a watchdog timer expires, the system software can include this information in the logs when the system is coming back up. Logs with such details are invaluable in identifying the errant software. On Intel E600 Series platforms the watchdog timer provides a WDT_TIMEOUT bit to indicate if a watchdog timeout triggered the reset.

When the processor starts executing instructions from after a reset, the processor is placed in a well-defined architectural state. All processor resources are reset. The MMU and caches are disabled, and all register contents are undefined. The processor often has many different operating modes. The platform usually starts off with a high privilege level (for example, supervisor mode). On Intel architectures there are three primary modes that a processor can operate in:

- Real mode
- Flat protected mode
- Segmented protected mode

The processor starts executing the initial instructions in real mode with paging disabled. Real mode runs 16-bit code with 16-bit registers. The physical address is calculated by (Stack Segment << 4) + Instruction Pointer. Real mode only allows access to the lowest 1 MB of memory. The processor boots continues to boot in real mode today; this ensures that the platform can boot legacy code written many years ago. The first power-on mode is a special subset of the real mode. The top 12 address lines are held high, thus allowing aliasing, where the processor can execute code from the nonvolatile storage (such as flash) located within lowest 1 MB as if from the top of memory. Normal operation of the firmware (such as BIOS) is to switch modes to flat protected mode as early in the boot sequence as possible. Once the processor is running in protected mode, it is usually not necessary to switch back to real mode unless executing a legacy option ROM, which makes certain legacy SW interrupt calls. The flat mode runs 32-bit code and the physical addresses are mapped one to one with the logical addresses (paging off). The interrupt descriptor table is used for interrupt handling. This is the recommended mode for all BIOS/boot loaders to operate in. The segmented protected mode is not used for the initialization code as part of the BIOS sequence.

The steps above are somewhat specific in Intel processors, but the key point is that all processors will start to boot in an architectural defined state, and the only valid memory space at startup is usually the nonvolatile storage from which the first instruction sequence is actually hosted.

There are a number of phases associated with a generalized boot sequence for embedded processors:

- *Early Initialization.* CPU and memory controller initialization.
- *Advanced Init.* Platform related initialization, peripheral-specific.
- *Handoff.* Identifying the image for the next phase and transferring control to the image.

Figure 6.2 shows the overall boot flow described in much more detail.

EARLY INITIALIZATION

The early initialization phase readies the bootstrap processor (BSP) and I/O peripherals' base addresses needed to configure the memory controller.

In an UEFI-based system BIOS, the Security (SEC) and the pre-EFI initialization (PEI) phases are normally synonymous with "early initialization." It doesn't matter if legacy or UEFI BIOS is used; the early init sequence is the same for a given system. The detailed initialization steps are particular to the SOC architectures; the Intel architecture system consists of the steps outlined in the following sections.

CPU Initialization

This consists of simple configuration of processor and machine registers. There is no DRAM available, so the code may have to operate in a stackless environment. On most modern processors there is an internal cache that can be configured as RAM (cache as RAM or CAR) to provide a software stack. Developers must write extremely tight code when using CAR, as an eviction would be paradoxical to the system at this point in the boot sequence; there is no memory to maintain coherency with at this time. There is a special mode for processors operate in cache as RAM called "no evict mode" (NEM), where a cache line miss in the processor will not cause an eviction. The motivation for having a stack frame is to be able to run C code, hence all the code that runs without stack would use register-based calling conventions. Developing code with an available software stack is much easier, and initialization code often performs the minimal setup to use a stack even prior to DRAM initialization.

IA Microcode Update

The processor may need a microcode update. Microcode is a hardware layer of instructions involved in the implementation of the machine-defined architecture. It is most prevalent in CISC-based processors. Microcode is developed by the CPU vendor and incorporated into an internal CPU ROM during manufacture. Most processors allow that microcode to be updated in the field either through a firmware

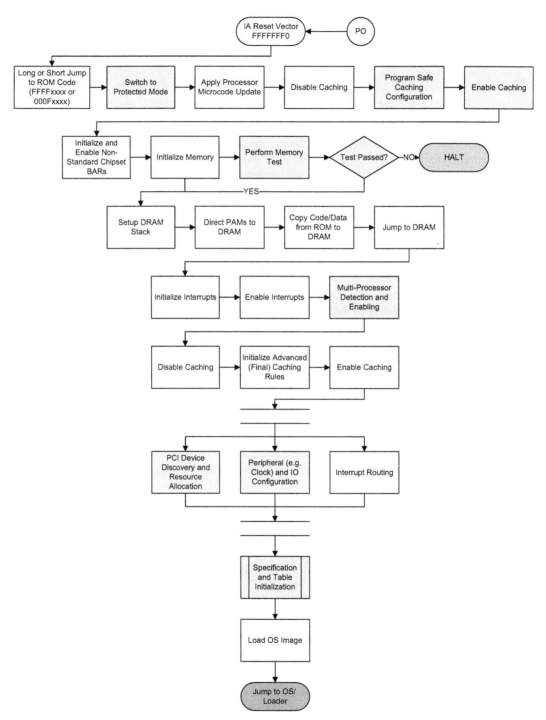

FIGURE 6.2

Detailed Boot Sequence Flow.

update or via an OS update of "configuration data." Intel can provide microcode updates that must be written to the writable microcode store. The updates are encrypted and signed by Intel such that only the processor that the microcode update was designed for can authenticate and load that update. On socketed systems, the BIOS may have to carry many flavors of microcode update depending on the number of processor steppings supported. It is important to load the microcode updates early in the boot sequence to limit the exposure of the system to any known bugs in the silicon.

Device Initialization

The device-specific portion of an Intel architecture memory map is highly configurable. Most devices are seen and accessed via a logical PCI bus hierarchy, although a small number may be memory-mapped devices that have part-specific access mechanisms. Device control registers are mapped to a predefined I/O or MMIO space and can be set up before the memory map is configured. This allows the early initial firmware to configure the memory map of the device needed to set up DRAM. Before DRAM can be configured, the firmware must establish the exact configuration of DRAM that is on the board. In most embedded cases the memory is soldered down on the board and the firmware is configured with the appropriate memory configuration with an initialized data structure. The Intel architecture reference platform memory map is described in more detail in Figure 6.3. SOC devices based on other processor architectures typically provide a static address map for all internal peripherals, with external devices connected via a bus interface. The bus-based devices are mapped to a memory range within in the SOC address space. These SOC devices usually provide a configurable chip select register set specifying the base address and size of the memory range enabled by the chip select. SOCs based on Intel architecture primarily use the logical PCI infrastructure for internal and external devices. The location of the device in the host memory address space is defined by the PCI base address register (BAR) for each of the devices. The device initialization typically enables all the BAR registers for the devices required as part of the system boot path. BIOS will typically assign all devices in the system a PCI base address by writing the appropriate BAR registers.

Memory Configuration

The initialization of the memory controller varies considerably depending on the DRAM technology and the capabilities of the memory controller itself. The information on the DRAM controller is often proprietary for SOC devices, and in such cases the initialization reference code is typically supplied by the SOC vendor. This is the case for Intel platforms, and you will have to contact Intel to request access to the low-level information required. There is a very wide range of DRAM configuration parameters, such as number of ranks, 8-bit or 16-bit addresses, overall memory size, constellation, soldered down or add-in module (DIMM) configurations, page closing policy, and power management. Given that most embedded systems populate soldered down DRAM on the board, the firmware may not need to discover the configuration at boot time. These configurations are known as memory-down. The firmware is specifically built for the target configuration. At current DRAM speeds, the wires between the memory controllers behave like transmission lines; the SOC may provide automatic calibration and runtime control of resistive compensation (RCOMP) and delay locked look (DLL) capabilities. These capabilities allow the memory controller to change elements such as the drive strength to ensure error-free operation over time and temperature variations.

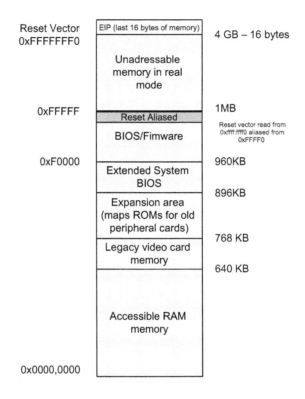

FIGURE 6.3

Intel Architecture Memory Map at Power-On.

If the platform supports add-in modules for memory, there are a number of standardized form factors for such memory. The small outline dual in-line memory module (SODIMM) is one such form factor often found in embedded systems. The DIMMs provide a serial PROM. The serial PROM devices contain the DRAM configuration data. The data are known as serial presence detect data (SPD data). The firmware reads the SPD data to identify the device configuration and subsequently configures the device. The serial PROM is connected via I2C/SMBUS; thus the I2C device must be available in this early initialization phase, so the software can establish the memory devices on board. In most cases where the memory is soldered down, the BIOS is configured with the memory configuration; however, it is also possible for memory-down motherboards to incorporate serial SPD PROM to allow for multiple and updatable memory configurations to be handled efficiently by a single BIOS algorithm.

Post-Memory Setup

Once the memory controller has been initialized, a number of subsequent events take place. The first (optional) item is to run a memory test. The memory test is best performed at system startup and in particular on cold start of the platform. Unfortunately, memory tests can take quite a long time, and the more thorough the testing, the longer the test takes. The embedded designer must make the trade-off between the robustness of the memory test and the delay in boot time it introduces. Some embedded devices use error correction codes (ECC) memory, which may need extra initialization. After power up, the state of the error correction codes may not reflect the contents of the other memory bytes and all memory must be written to; writing to memory ensures that the ECC bits are valid and sets the ECC bits to the appropriate contents. For security purposes, the memory may need to be zeroed out manually by the BIOS, or in some cases a memory controller may incorporate the feature into hardware to save time.

Shadowing

From the reset vector, execution starts off executing directly from the nonvolatile flash storage (NVRAM). This operating mode is known as execute in place (XIP). The read performance of nonvolatile storage is much slower than the read performance of DRAM. So most early firmware will copy code from the slower nonvolatile storage into RAM. The firmware starts to run the RAM copy of the firmware. This process is sometimes known as *shadowing*. Shadowing involves having the same contents in RAM and flash; with a change in the address decoders the RAM copy is logically in front of the flash copy and the program starts to execute from RAM. On other embedded systems, the chip selects ranges that are managed to allow the change from flash to RAM execution. Most computing systems run as little as possible directly from flash. However, some constrained (in terms of RAM) embedded platforms execute all the application in place (directly from Flash memory). This is generally an option on very small embedded devices. The Intel architecture platforms generally do not execute in place for anything but the very initial boot steps before memory have been configured. The firmware is often compressed. This allows reduction of the NVRAM requirements for the firmware. Clearly, the processor cannot execute a compressed image in place.

There is a trade-off between the storage requirements of a uncompressed firmware image and the time it takes to decompress the image. The decompression algorithm may take much longer to load and execute than it would for the image to remain uncompressed. Prefetchers in the processor, if enabled, may also speed up execution in place, and some SOCs have internal NVRAM cache buffers to assist in pipelining the data from the flash to the processor.

Figure 6.3 shows the memory map at initialization in real mode, which can only access 1 MB of memory.

AP PROCESSOR INITIALIZATION

Even in SOCs, there is the likelihood of having multiple CPU cores. While the BSP starts and initializes the system, the application processors (APs) must also be initialized with identical features enabled to the BSP. Prior to memory, the APs are left uninitialized. After memory is started, the remaining processors are initialized and left in a "Wait for SIPI" state. For more information, see the IA32 Software Development Manual, Volume 3.

ADVANCED INITIALIZATION

The advanced device initialization follows the early initialization and basically ensures that the DRAM is initialized. This second stage is focused on device-specific initialization. In a UEFI-based BIOS solution, advanced initialization tasks are also known as Dynamic Execute Environment (DXE) and Boot Device Selection (BDS) phases. The following devices must be initialized in order to enable an embedded system. Not all are applicable to all embedded systems, but the list is prescriptive for most and is particular to an Intel architecture–based SOC.

- GPIO—General-purpose I/O
- Interrupt controller
- Timers
- Cache initialization (could/should be done during early initialization)
- Serial ports
- PCI bus initialization
- USB
- SATA storage
- Network controller

General-Purpose Input/Output

System-on-chip devices are designed to be used in a large number of configurations, with the devices often having more capabilities than the device is capable of exposing on the I/O pins concurrently. That is because several functions are multiplexed to a particular I/O pin. The configuration of the pins must be set before use. The pins are configured to either provide a specific function or to serve as a general-purpose I/O pin. I/O pins on the device are used to control logic or behavior on the device. General-purpose I/O pins can be configured as input or output pins. The status and control are provided by GPIO control registers.

Interrupt Controller

An interrupt controller multiplexes a number of possible interrupt sources on the platform for presentation to the processor. The interrupt controller in embedded systems must be configured to prioritize and route interrupts from devices within the SOC and externally attached devices. The Intel architecture–based SOC uses the traditional Intel architecture interrupt processing capabilities. This section outlines some of the low-level configuration items associated with the Intel architecture interrupt controllers; however, details of the interrupt controller are specified in Chapter 4.

The requirement to ensure backward-compatible software on Intel architecture platforms extends far beyond the instruction set architecture; Intel has gone to extreme lengths to ensure that legacy software can continue to run on new generations of processors. To this end, a number of interrupt controllers are instantiated on Intel architecture platforms. The most basic is known as the 8259. The 8259 Peripheral Interrupt Controller (PIC) was first developed for the 8086 16-bit processor. The controller is very simple to set up and control, but at this point new software should not and in general does not set up the platform to use it. The modern interrupt controller on the Intel architecture platform is known as the local Advanced Peripheral Interrupt Controller (APIC) and I/O APIC. The local APIC is contained within the processor and controls the delivery to the processor. The local APIC is memory mapped to a physical address of 0xFEE00000. In a system with multiple logical processors, there is one local APIC per logical processor. A single processor with symmetric multithreading (SMT) consists of two hardware threads within one core. The local APIC will always appear in the same location for each processor, but each processor accesses its own local APIC. Each local APIC provides a local vector table (LVT). The LVT specifies the manner in which the interrupts are delivered to the core. The IOxAPIC is outside the CPU and integrated into the SOC or chipset; it expands the number of interrupt lines to 24. Each interrupt controller line has a redirection table. The interrupt descriptor tables provide a vector number for the associated interrupt request line. The combination of the local APIC and IOxAPIC on the platform allows interrupts from the devices to be assigned to a specific interrupt vector and targeted CPU core. A vector-based interrupt controller improves the efficiency of interrupt processing, as the CPU core can quickly start execution of the appropriate interrupt processing routine. Non-vector-based interrupt controllers usually require the CPU to query the interrupt controller to establish which interrupt to process. The latest ARM processor cores (M3) have introduced a vectored interrupt controller to reduce the overheads traditionally associated with interrupt processing.

When the Intel architecture processor is running in protected mode, the CPU uses the interrupt descriptor table (IDT). The IDT is a table of 256 vectors for exceptions and interrupts.

Timers

As is the case for the interrupt controller, the Intel architecture platforms provide a Programmable Interrupt Timer (PIT) and a High-Precision Event Timer (HPET). The PIT timer is known as the 8254 and was introduced quite some time ago. The PIT timer can be used by firmware to provide simple timer features; a common timer function for low-level software is to provide timeouts. The HPET is generally not used by firmware and is left for use by the operating system.

Embedded platforms often require the ability to keep track of the system time and data. A real-time clock (RTC) provides the system time in seconds, minutes, and hours. If the RTC is incorporated in the SOC, the RTC must remain powered even if the main SOC has been powered off. As an example, the RTC clock can be used by the firmware to record boot times.

Cache Control

The default setup of caching behavior for different memory regions is platform specific. It's best if you start off with a very conservative configuration during early software development, and then optimize the setup once your firmware/software is stable. There's nothing worse than chasing cache-related software bugs while also debugging new software. The most conservative setting for an Intel architecture–based system during firmware development is shown in Table 6.2.

It is particularly important to set up the cache coherence as conservatively as possible on platforms that do not provide hardware cache coherence for device driver DMA accesses.

The sooner cache is turned on after shadowing, the better. It is possible that the legacy option ROM space may not be needed if using an UEFI-only BIOS solution. In such cases, the BIOS may relocate option ROMs to other areas of memory to make caching easier.

Table 6.2 Conservative Cache Control for Memory Regions

Address Space	Cache Setup	Comment
Default	Un-cached	Any memory address not specified below is not cached.
0x00000000-0x0009FFFF	Write back	
0x000A00000-0x000BFFFF	Write combined/Un-cached	
0x000C0000-0x00FFFFFF	Write back or write protected	
0x00100000-Top of memory	Write back	
TSEG	Un-cached	This is a memory region above 1 MB. It is known as SMRAM and is used by the system management mode.
Graphics stolen memory	Write combined or un-cached	
Hardware memory-mapped I/O	Un-cached	

UART Serial Ports

A universal asynchronous receiver/transmitter is a simple device that enables character reception and transmission over a three wire (Transmit, Receive, and Ground). It is simple and perhaps the first employed communication port to get debug output from an embedded device. The UART device is usually configured and used in a polled mode (that is, no interrupts) during the early boot-up phases. The use of UARTs for debug and simple console access is particularly important for headless systems (without displays). The UART output levels are typically low-voltage outputs and need to be level-shifted to provide an EIA RS-232 standard interface.

The traditional legacy PC–based platform provides a UART via a Super I/O device attached over the low pin count (LPC) interface. If the UART is only required during debug, it's not unusual to have the UART pins and a power supply pin be put on the board. A small breakout board can then be used to convert to the appropriate RS-232 levels. For the Intel Atom Processor E6xx Series–based reference platform the UART is part of the IOH device. The de facto standard complies with the register definition of the 8250 or Motorola 16550A. The Linux kernel continues to support the serial driver and the driver can be found in the Linux driver file linux/drivers/serial/8250.c. The kernel also supports complete headless boot and login consoles (tty) over serial ports.

Debug Output

Although we discussed early debug in the context of UART serial ports, platforms (particular debug platforms) may provide a LED/LCD display that is used to capture output from the Intel architecture OUT port 80h and 84h. Port 84h was claimed by another company for proprietary usage, so most people refer to the post codes as coming from "port 80h." It is also useful for debugging prior to the enablement of the UART. The majority of BIOS platforms output code though these legacy IO ports to indicate progress or errors in the boot sequence. An example of a LCD debug display is shown in Figure 6.4.

FIGURE 6.4

Example I/O Port 80h/84h Debug Display.

Configuration Storage

The BIOS is never completely hard coded for a particular board. A small amount of storage is embedded in the system for some basic configuration variables that can be set dynamically through setup menus or altered by various diagnostic or OS level drivers. The CMOS configuration system must be available very early in the boot sequence. The configuration must be stored in nonvolatile storage. The primary nonvolatile storage is provided by flash. The firmware must provide routes to read and write the firmware flash sector dedicated to the low-level configuration items. Intel platforms also provide a CMOS/RTC device; the nonvolatile storage in the CMOS/RTC device is usually maintained by battery backed up configuration and may not be used in embedded systems. Flash-based storage is by far the most common approach. A small portion of the flash is dedicated to the management of this configuration data. For robustness, two copies can be maintained, validated by a checksum/CRC. The firmware validates the "latest" copy and at all times has a backup copy in case power is lost during updates. All BIOS solutions require some form of non-volatile storage to save configuration items and the like. Historically the CMOS battery-backed RAM was used to store basic configuration items, but with such limited space, most BIOS now uses the flash device to store configuration items.

PCIe Bus Initialization

The firmware and BIOS must perform PCIe device discovery. The device discovery identifies integrated devices within the SOC and outside the SOC that are attached via PCIe. Once the devices are discovered the firmware must assign resources to the devices. This process is known as PCIe enumeration.

The resources that must be allocated are memory-mapped I/O space (MMIO), I/O space, and interrupt request lines. Most modern devices only require MMIO space and interrupt allocation. When the device is allocated MMIO space, it places the registers in the memory map of the processor. The device registers are then simply read from and written to by reading and writing to the memory allocated to it.

The enumeration process is described in more detail in Chapter 4. It has been designed to accommodate the plug and play installation of PCIe and PCIe cards into a platform such as a PC. However, for some embedded platforms the firmware is only really required to allocate resources to devices that are required during the boot path. The devices are usually reallocated when the operating system boots up. The enumeration process is designed to scan the bus and identify the populated devices; this can take some time and is not necessary if the firmware is prebuilt with the configuration information for a closed box design. In this case, the scan time can be eliminated and the devices are allocated fixed (hard coded) resources. If any expansion slots are available in the design, even a single PCIe x1 slot, then a partial bus scan may be mandatory.

Image Storage

Once the early firmware/BIOS completes enough of the previous steps, the next task is to identify the OS image location. The next stage may be a OS boot loader, or in some cases direct launch of the RTOS or OS kernel image.

Potential locations of the next stage boot loader, operating system, or application image are described in the following sections. As I/O devices are always expanding, there will likely be other boot device targets.

USB

Depending on the capabilities of the platform and dependencies on USB peripherals, the early initialization software may not do any USB initialization beyond PCI enumeration of the integrated USB controller. If required, Intel architecture BIOS/firmware may provide software drivers to support USB keyboard and mouse operation in this early boot phase. USB may be used as a debug port as well.

Another use case of the USB interface that is more likely in an embedded system is to allow the user to attach a USB mass storage device, for example, a USB pen drive. This is highly advantageous in the early development of software for an embedded platform. The USB device can be formatted to provide simple data storage options, or perhaps the required OS boot loader and operating system.

This may be the most cost-effective option for production, and may be either internal or through an exposed port.

SATA

For larger amounts of mass storage, SATA is the primary interface type for both spindle based and solid state drives. The firmware can initialize the SATA controller without advanced features to simplify implementation. The firmware reads the boot loader (next stage) from a well-defined location on the mass storage device and executes the commands.

SDIO

SDIO is not a typical boot target, but it is possible to have an SDIO card used as a formatted boot device. The performance of the interface and devices is lower than what can be achieved by a SATA interface device.

The BIOS can have a combination of the above support built in and can dynamically scan all available ports for boot partitions, which has advantages for developers, but can take a very long time for production. A hard coded boot path to a known location (perhaps with a single backup for recovery purposes) is the fastest solution for highly embedded systems.

LEGACY BIOS AND UEFI FRAMEWORK SOFTWARE

The early initialization code has evolved very significantly on Intel architecture platforms. For many years, legacy-based system BIOS has been the standard firmware running on every Intel architecture platform developed from the inception of the very first 8086-based systems. It has served the platforms well, but the time came to move beyond the legacy BIOS and introduce a framework much more scalable for today's platform technologies. BIOS's replacement is known as Unified Extensible Firmware Interface (UEFI) and the UEFI framework. It is absolutely impossible to do this domain any real justice in a subsection of our book; it is more fully covered in several books, including *Beyond BIOS*. We try to provide a brief overview of some of the current landscape. The transition from legacy BIOS to UEFI has taken some time and at the time of writing is still in progress. The difficulty not only arises due to the challenges in introducing a fairly complex new software code base and the required drivers for all the new platforms and devices, but a significant interdependency exists among the firmware, boot loader, and operating systems. To help decouple some of the dependencies between the BIOS, expansion ROMs, OS loaders, and operating systems, most UEFI-based platforms currently provide a Compatibility Support Module (CSM). The CSM provides some of the legacy software interrupt and system BIOS features in the context of an UEFI-based platform; at some point all dependencies will have migrated away from the legacy services modeled.

In the BIOS industry, there is a classification for various advancements of BIOS/OS interface and support.

Class 1: Legacy OS interface only (SW interrupts Int 10h, Int 13h, etc).

Class 2: Hybrid systems that have a CSM and a UEFI interface. Most IA systems in the mainstream today support both because developers may not know what the end user will choose to install or run on these open box systems. This class also provides the most flexibility for hardware choices depending on the expansion ROM support for either legacy interface or UEFI.

Class 3: Today, it is possible to have a completely legacy-free pre-boot space, especially in a closed box. UEFI-only "class 3" systems are intended to boot only UEFI-supported BIOS, expansion ROMs (UEFI drivers), UEFI boot loaders, and UEFI operating systems.

At the highest level, both legacy BIOS and UEFI-based BIOS initialize the platform and put it in a known state. They identify the boot device and transfer control to the next agent in the boot process: either an OS boot loader or the operating system directly. In addition to the transfer of control, the firmware can provide services that the OS boot loader or operating system can use. A significant amount of platform information is also provided to the operating system so it does not have to scan/establish the details.

Legacy Operating System Boot

A legacy operating system as defined in the context of firmware is an operating system that is non-UEFI compliant. The implementing of the firmware can be either legacy BIOS or UEFI with a CSM (class 2 system). The BIOS boot specification specifies the handoff behavior for legacy BIOS in detail, but be warned that it is not 100% and people can always deviate from the standards as needed on embedded products. The following section is a very brief overview of the process.

The BIOS carries out some or all the initialization steps mentioned above, and at the end of this sequence the boot device is identified, or it may be hard coded. BIOS loads and executes the boot sector, which in turn has responsibility of starting the OS or a more sophisticated boot loader. Legacy BIOS supports loading from mass storage devices, from the NVRAM storage where the BIOS is held, and/or via code in option ROMs. For example, downloading an operating system via an Ethernet port is normally supported via a PXE (preboot execution environment) option ROM. The option ROM provides the code that the BIOS calls to get the operating system downloaded to memory. PXE may be stored in an actual ROM device on an add-in card, or if the motherboard has an Ethernet controller built on board, the option ROM code is built into the BIOS flash image.

The most typical location for the operating system is on some form of mass storage device (USB, SATA, SDIO, etc.). If the drive is formatted and configured to be booted from, then the sector 0 of the drive will contain the Master Boot Record (MBR). The MBR is a 512-byte boot sector and the first sector of a partitioned mass storage device such as a hard disk drive (HDD). Solid state drives (SSDs) can be formatted to mimic a spindle drive. If the drive isn't configured for booting, no such record will exist and the BIOS will proceed to the next boot target on its priority list, or simply not boot. The first 446 bytes are the primary boot loader, which contains both executable code and error message text. The next 64 bytes are the partition table, which contains a record for each of four partitions (16 bytes each). The MBR ends with 2 bytes that are defined as the magic number (0xAA55). The magic number serves as a validation check of the MBR. The BIOS code copies 446 bytes of data from the MBR to the memory location 0x0007C00, and the BIOS jumps to that address while in real mode. We mentioned briefly that the processor boots in real mode, but that the BIOS will operate in protected mode as much as possible. If required, the BIOS must revert back to real mode for this transition; again, this is primarily to support backward compatibility. Legacy BIOS may be called upon to boot older OS loaders or operating systems. When control is transferred to the memory copy of the initial loader, additional information is also passed:

- Registers ES:DI—Pointer to PnP installation check structure.
- Register DL—Drive number to select to OS boot from.

There is a natural size limit to the MBR of 2.2 terabytes in a partition. While this was unheard of when DOS was the mainstream OS back in the age of dinosaurs, today such large drives can be purchased regularly. UEFI-based BIOS and OSs offer another table called a global partition table (or GPT) that supplies a much larger boot capacity.

Once the BIOS transfers control to the OS loader, the BIOS continues to provide legacy services to the loader. The services are provided by making software interrupt (INT) calls to access the services. Some of the common services defined are

- INT 10h—Video support.
- INT 13h—This provides a disk I/O service; the OS loader uses this service to load the remainder of the boot-loader/operating system into memory.
- INT 14h—Serial port transmit and receive, ideal for headless devices.
- INT 18h—This is the recover service; if the OS fails to boot, the boot loader calls this service. The behavior is BIOS dependent; it may try to boot from the next device and eventually restart.
- INT 19h—Service to start the loading of the operating system.

At the time of writing, The GR and Unified Bootloader (GRUB 2) supported booting from a legacy BIOS and has introduced booting from UEFI firmware. For legacy boot mode the code that resides in the MBR can be found in the grub-1.98/boot/i386/pc/boot.S.

It should be noted that most Windows operating systems up to Windows* XP–based machines also boot via the legacy OS interface. While the Microsoft OS after that (Windows Vista SP1 through Windows 7) have supported a UEFI OS boot interface, it has not been completely legacy free. Int 10h support is still required through Windows* 7.

Most of the Linux boot loaders do not support UEFI. This will likely change over time as other OSs gradually convert.

The overall system requirements and developer capabilities will dictate what choice of BIOS and OS is optimal.

OS Boot Loader to OS Handoff

In an effort to abstract platform knowledge to the lowest level of the boot hierarchy, the operating system may have dependences on a number of table structures depending on the target operating system. The following are some tables that the OS may depend on:

- Memory Map—The legacy BIOS exports a memory map via the legacy INT 15h function E820h service.
- Programmable Interrupt Routing—The $PIR table and interrupt-based memory map used by some older OSs.
- Multi-Processor Specification—The multiprocessor tables needed for multiprocessor or SMT/hyper-threaded systems. The existence of a standard interface between the hardware and the OS makes it easy for the software and operating systems to be developed for platforms. For Intel platforms the tables are defined by the Multiprocessor Speciation (MP Spec). This mechanism is no longer in active development.
- Simple Firmware Interface—SFI tables are provided information such as GPIO configuration and UART devices, and in general the information provided augments the system knowledge that can be acquired via PCI enumeration.
- Advanced Configuration and Power Interface (ACPI)—A specification that defines platform-independent interfaces for hardware discovery, configuration, power management, and monitoring.
- UEFI tables do exist that replace the legacy-based tables and add to the ACPI tables.

In reality, only a small proportion of embedded Intel architecture developers will ever have to work on the BIOS or UEFI firmware. The summary above gives a general sense of the normal Intel architecture landscape; optimization for embedded specific boot is described below.

OS Boot Loaders

In the context of a legacy Intel architecture boot-up from a mass storage device, the MBR contains the initial code sequence to the next boot stage. The boot loader is primarily responsible for getting the operating system from wherever it is stored and copying it to memory to launch. The OS boot loader must be aware of the local file system if the operating system is stored on a mass storage device. For example, a common file system format is FAT32; if you wish to use a USB key to load/store the OS, then the boot loader must have support for the target file system. There are a number of Intel architecture boot loaders:

- GRUB2—A GNU unified boot loader, build time support for legacy and OS. It supports the selection of which of the installed operating systems to boot (multiboot). The boot loader supports a wide range of file systems and boots a number of operating systems.

- VxWorks™—This is a widely used real-time operations system; we will cover the boot sequence in more detail below.
- Syslinux—A boot loader for the Linux operating system that operates off an MS-DOS/Windows FAT file system.
- Eboot—The Microsoft WinCE boot loader.

To give an idea of what issues are involved in implementation, we will describe the VxWorks boot loader further. The VxWorks RTOS supports a wide range of embedded architectures such as ARM, Intel architecture, MIPS, and PowerPC. The general debug deployment model is to use a bootROM image, which then downloads the kernel image; the bootROM image can load the kernel image from a number of locations either on a local file system or frequently over the network for debug environments.

VxWorks provides a bootsect.bin binary file. The file must be copied to the MBR of the boot mass storage device. The MKBT program (which works on Windows) can be used to copy the bootsec.bin file. You could use the Linux dd command for the same action. The bootsect.bin initial bootstrap loads the bootrom.sys file. The bootROM sysfile is the VXWorks boot loader, which can then load the OS. The VxWorks boot loader can support either legacy or UEFI by replacing a single INT 13h command with the equivalent UEFI command. The same steps are applicable for all environments; on Intel architecture the steps are partitioned into one additional step (Kernel Copy) since the actual boot loader(s) in the sequence may not all fit on the SPI flash image. Figure 6.5 shows examples of the different stages and location of images.

Although the BIOS has a provision for transferring memory map and other platform details to the boot loader and on the target operating system, real-time operating systems such as VxWorks provide the flexibility to reuse the settings established during the BIOS phase or to have a pre-defined memory map and re-probe the platform capabilities. The RTOS may be configured to re-enumerate the entire PCI bus as part of the driver initialization sequence. For example, the Intel Atom Processor E6xx Series reference platform VxWorks BSP has a defined INCLUDE_MTRR_GET to true. This has the behavior of loading a copy of the MTRR registers set by the

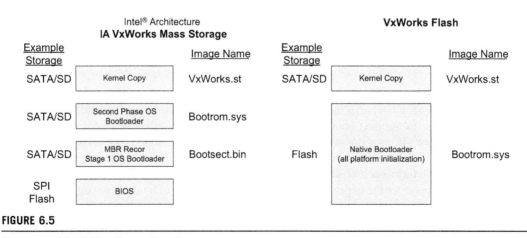

FIGURE 6.5

Examples of Boot Stage Image Locations.

BIOS. Alternately, the BSP can statically allocate a table to set up the cache control in the MTRR tables. The normal/safest option is usually to rely on the BIOS set values, but you may want to have more control in an embedded OS.

ARM-based platforms also typically use a boot loader to initialize the platform directly from the reset vector and launch the OS. There are many loaders for embedded systems, of which Redboot and DAS U-Boot loaders are quite commonly used. They perform basically the same behavior as we described above except when it comes to the information exchange and services offered to the booting operations system. In general, an embedded boot loader will set up the hardware, initialize data tables to provide information exchange, and then transfer control. Once control is transferred, no further use of the boot loader is made. The transfer of information is far simpler than those that have evolved in the Intel architecture environment. The Intel architecture platform has evolved to have platform-specific firmware, table-driven boot loaders, and operating system initialization. This allows the industry to keep a very significant proportion of the platform changes as data table updates in firmware, and makes it less likely to have to make code-specific updates in the boot loaders or operating systems.

As a general rule, on other embedded platforms you must make modifications to the boot loader for each SOC or platform. The communication of information between the boot loader and the operating system is limited. For example, Redboot provides a memory map, and some other platform-specific knowledge is provided using ATAG_*** parameters. You may also need to make kernel platform modifications; for example, Linux requires many runtime changes for `machine_type()` calls for specific platforms. This can be problematic for maintenance and the development of board support packages (BSPs). To get an indication of the differing approaches and the resultant changes that can be seen in the Linux kernel tree, the linux/arch/arm contains no less than 59 machine directories and 12 platform sub-trees. Naturally, not all variations are due to the boot model, but the partitioning of initialization between boot loaders and kernel is an aspect.

Extensible Firmware Interface

The Unified Extensible Firmware Interface (UEFI) specification defines a model for the interface between operating systems and platform firmware operating system boot. The interface consists of data tables that contain platform-related information, boot service calls, and runtime service calls that are available to the operating system and its loader. These provide a standard environment for booting an operating system and running pre-boot applications.

A number of implementations of the specification exist, and reference implementations are available. At the time of writing, the EFI Development Kit (EDK I) hosted at SourceForge is classified as an official level project. EDK II was released in 2010 under the package known as UEFI Development Kit (UDK2010). The EDK II project provides build tools to allow you to build your own UEFI applications. The UEFI project is architecture-agnostic, and there are ports for Intel architecture as well as ARM platforms. The Extensible Firmware Interface describes a programmatic interface to the platform; the platform includes the CPU and all devices, within the SOC and on the platform. UEFI makes provision for the execution of pre-operating system agents. A pre-operating system agent might be an OS loader, a diagnostics application, or a native application written to use UEFI runtime services to get access to console/network interfaces or hardware.

The UEFI platform supports launching UEFI OS images, formatted in the PE/COFF executable format as defined by the Microsoft PE and COFF Specification. This specification describes the structure of executable (image) files and object files under the Windows family of operating systems. These files are referred to as Portable Executable (PE) and Common Object File Format (COFF) files (http://msdn.microsoft.com/en-us/windows/hardware/gg463119).

The UEFI images can be one of three types, UEFI applications, UEFI boot service drivers, and UEFI runtime drivers. The UEFI applications are only run in the context of the framework and destroyed once control is transferred to the operating system. The UEFI boot service driver images run in the pre-OS environment and continue to offer services in the OS loader. The OS loader makes a call to the UEFI function `ExitBootServices()` to allow the UEFI framework to release resources allocated (such as memory) to the boot service driver. Finally, the UEFI runtime drivers provide UEFI services to the UEFI-aware operating system. The introduction of UEFI in embedded systems has lagged behind the mainstream computer industry. In the case of Intel architecture, the config-uration is entered by pressing a key during boot (such as F1). The menus presented by either legacy or UEFI-based BIOS take the same familiar form, but the UEFI-based BIOS may offer a "Boot to UEFI Shell" command prompt. This provides access to the UEFI shell, where you can execute UEFI applications you have developed. The tools required to develop UEFI applications can be found at the UEFI web site.

While UEFI is relatively new in comparison to the legacy BIOS it replaces, most BIOS provided on Intel's embedded platforms have transitioned to using UEFI, although they all still ship with the compatibility support module to ensure backward compatibility and the ability to boot any existing OS/RTOS. A number of UEFI-based boot loaders have already been deployed at the time of writing, namely:

- GRUB2—A GNU unified boot loader thatsupports both legacy and UEFI boot, although you have to configure it at build time for one or the other.
- VxWorks—Provides both a legacy and an UEFI boot loader.
- eLilo—The UEFI version of the LILO boot loader.

GRUB2 UEFI Boot

When the multiboot GRUB2 boot loader is configured in UEFI mode, the boot loader makes extensive use of the UEFI boot service calls. The grub file located at grub-1.98/kern/efi/efi.c is an excellent place to review the service called and how to actually call the services. The runtime services are provided at a set of function pointers from a base efi_system table. Examples of services used are:

- Page Allocation Service—Allocates memory into which an image can be loaded
- Disk Input/Output
- Console Input/Output
- Image Load—Loads an UEFI image into the allocated memory
- Start Image—Transfers control to an image
- Reset System, Cold/Shutdown
- Set Virtual Address Map
- Get Time
- Stall (sleep for a period of time)

One OS of note that has been UEFI compliant for quite some time, although not considered an embedded OS per se, is Apple Mac OS X™.

VxWorks UEFI

At the time of writing, a number of Intel architecture VxWorks BSPs are being developed to use UEFI services. The boot process has been adapted to use the UEFI boot process. In the context of the RTOS deployment, the UEFI firmware provides boot services and runtime services. The boot services are not available once the VxWorks kernel is launched. When the platform boots, the firmware will search for an OS loader application; the OS loader will then identity the location of the operating system, load it, and call `ExitBootServices`. For VxWorks, the UEFI loader application is called vxWorks _osloader. efi. You can call the loader application from the UEFI shell:

```
Shell>vxworks_osloader.efi
```

The UEFI services are used to obtain the memory map and the contents of the EFI system tables (such as ACPI). The VxWorks OS image uses the runtime services to obtain these details during the boot sequence. The VxWorks BSP function `uefiPhysMemTop()` calls a UEFI service to obtain the memory map and does not actually return the top of physical memory. It automatically reserves a small portion of memory for the UEFI firmware and data. Table 6.3 shows a sample UEFI VxWorks memory map.

The UEFI services also provide APIs to reset the platform. The VxWorks RTOS configured to use UEFI runtime services provides a `uefiSysReset` service, which is bound to the OS reboot APIs.

eLILO

eLILO is the UEFI version of the LILO boot loader. It is generally used to boot Linux operating systems.

Native Boot Environments

At this point, you have been given a glimpse of the features offered by the UEFI loaders. They are quite sophisticated and can form the basis of an application environment for the end user. The book *Harnessing the UEFI Shell* is recommended reading if you plan on developing applications for execution within the UEFI shell.

Table 6.3 Sample VxWorks Image with UEFI Support

Start Address	Size	Use
0x0	0x3FFF	Unusable by VxWorks
0x4000	0x9C000	UEFI runtime code, data, and VxWorks DMA buffers
0xA0000	0x60000	Video RAM and so on
0x100000	0x100000	Boot ROM for UEFI
0x20000	sysPhysMemTop – 0x200000	Upper memory for VxWorks, UEFI runtime code, data

Embedded Considerations

As an embedded programmer, the platforms you deploy on vary greatly. An embedded system may be a small single-board computer with only one storage medium or a large system composed of many cards in a chassis, with functions dedicated to specific cards. For data communicators and telecommunications applications, the shelf or rack typically has a redundancy controller and a large number of "line" cards that perform specific functions such as packet routing. The application images (including operating system) on these cards must be managed. Images are often stored on the controller cards and downloaded to the line cards on power-on or restart. These kinds of deployments may require you to manage the boot sequence quite differently from the simple single-board computer. It may be critical to ensure fail-safe upgrades of images, again requiring design of the overall platform level boot sequences. In these contexts, using a UEFI-based system offers a great deal of flexibility in how applications are deployed on to your platform at runtime. Figure 6.6 shows a possible incarnation of a multi-card deployment. A multi-card deployment scenario may consist of a chassis/shelf that contains a number of cards: one may be the master controller for the shelf, and the other could be data cards. Such a configuration is very common in telecommunications equipment.

To support network download, all required services such as a TCP/IP stack and packet transmission and reception on the local network interface are normally provided by the UEFI framework, including IPv4 and IPv6 in EDK II solutions. In such embedded systems, you may have a proprietary interface used on the backplane between the cards. You would have to develop the appropriate PXE backplane or network driver to support image download over this proprietary bus in such cases.

COLD AND WARM BOOT

Typically, when referring to cold boot we refer to the sequence of taking the system from the S5 sleep state in ACPI (or soft-off), where power has been supplied into S0 or the fully awake/active state where the system is available to the application.

While a "cold boot and constant run" mode does apply to most embedded applications, it is not an option for Intel platforms. There are two ACPI-defined sleep states, namely, S3 sleep (suspend to RAM) and S4 hibernate (suspend to disk), where the boot times and boot sequences can be dramatically reduced.

In the S3 state, the system is consuming refresh power in the DIMMs and enough power to react to a wake event in the I/O hardware. The boot sequence for Intel platforms from S3 is the basic initialization outlined above and a short boot script to restore the register contents in the I/O that may have been lost. The advanced initialization and device selection process is skipped. The OS drivers need to be restarted (not loaded and started). This results in a several orders of magnitude speedup when compare to a cold start. The applications do not need to be restarted, but are all active within a few hundred milliseconds of the wake event. As always, the system requirements will dictate how power and response time can be optimized.

In S4, the system is consuming near zero power if the wake events are limited to something akin to the S5 boot. The kernel does not have to be fully loaded. The OS drivers do not have to be loaded/

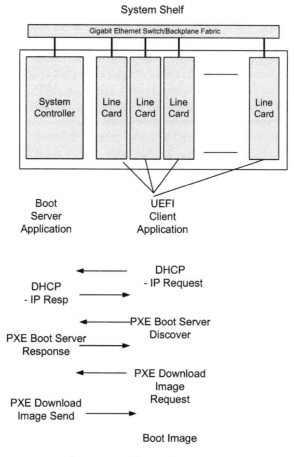

FIGURE 6.6

Multi-Card PXE Download Scenario.

started, as is required in the cold boot case. The applications are already running when in the state prior to hibernate. From a boot perspective, it is normally thought that that S4 boot path is equal to the S5 boot path, but in reality most of the advanced initialization steps can be skipped completely.

SUMMARY

The standard IA boot sequence of embedded processors has been partitioned into three distinct phases. The first is the initial code that starts to execute from the processor's reset vector. This code must initialize the processor and a subset of the platform required to load the second stage. On Intel architecture platforms, this is known as BIOS or firmware. The firmware supports loading the OS boot loader from a storage device. The OS boot loader is responsible for loading the operating system in memory and transferring control to the OS. In some embedded systems, the firmware and OS boot loader are merged into a single image known simply as the boot loader.

The Intel architecture–based firmware has been developed to pass a significant amount of platform-specific information to the booting operating system (such as ACPI tables and multi-processor configuration). The provision of this data to the OS simplifies the OS boot-up and significantly reduces the amount of conditional architecture-specific code in the OS.

The selection of boot device is determined by many criteria: the time the device is available and its read performance, robustness, and price/density. All these aspects must be evaluated in selecting the appropriate boot media.

Operating Systems Overview

An operating system provides multiplexed access to shared resources that include peripherals, CPU, and memory. Multitasking creates the illusion that many concurrent threads of execution are running on the processor when in reality the operating system kernel interleaves their execution on the basis of a scheduling policy. This is effectively time division multiplexing of the CPU. The operating system provides mechanisms to interact with services through an application interface. It provides process management (creation, deletion, and so on) and schedules the execution of the processes. It provides memory management, thread synchronization primitives, and time of day services.

As an embedded systems designer you will also have to be aware of the device driver model supported by the operating system. Each operating system has its own pattern to implement a device driver, but they have many traits in common. This chapter describes each of these topics in detail, and where appropriate we will use examples from VxWorks and Linux to illustrate our points.

APPLICATION INTERFACE

The operating system provides a series of service calls that allow applications to interact with the kernel. In many cases application writers do not make direct system calls, but instead rely on a set of libraries that provide a broad range of services to applications. Some of these libraries depend on making kernel services calls, while others do not require any interaction with the kernel.

The C library is a good example. The C libraries are defined by the C Library Standard under ISO/IEC 9899:1999 (commonly referred to as C99). The library provides functions such as string manipulation and parsing, memory copy, memory allocation, print formatting, and file I/O. Functions such as string and memory copy do not require any operating services; however, `malloc()` and file I/O such as `printf()` do require the use of OS services. A C language application can perform many functions without resorting to using any OS service calls directly. The most common implementation of the C library on Linux systems is the GNU C Library (GLIBC). In addition to complying with C99, the library provides services compatible with POSIX.1c, POSIX.1j, POSIX.1d, and Unix98, Single Unix Specification.

OS Application Interface

Let's look at an example of implementation of `malloc()` found in GLIBC (http://www.gnu.org, glibc/malloc/malloc.c). The `malloc()` function maintains a number of buffers in fast bins. These are a small number of fixed buffer pools from which memory can be allocated when an application requires memory without having to make a system call. If the bins are empty or an allocation size request is larger than that supported by the bins, the `malloc()` function must make a request to the operating system to extend the process data segment. This is carried out by calling the `sbrk()` function, which is a wrapper to the system call `brk()`. The `brk()` call changes the location of the program break, which is defined as the end of the process data segment. This effectively allocates memory to the process. In some cases, the `brk()` call fails and the `mmap()` service call is used to request a number of pages allocated by the kernel and mapped to the process space. The `malloc()` call then allocates memory from this mapped pool for requests. Figure 7.1 shows the interaction between the application, library, and service calls.

The mechanism shown in Figure 7.1 is one of the most advanced scenarios; in embedded systems running an RTOS the implementation is simpler. For example, in VxWorks™ at the time of system initialization the malloc() library creates a number of fixed-size buffers pools. The malloc() call attempts to allocate from one of these buffer pools, and if this fails it will attempt to allocate from the system pool.

OS Service Calls

The operating system services are exposed through function wrappers provided as part of the POSIX/C Libraries. The general design pattern used for service calls is as follows (using Linux as an example).

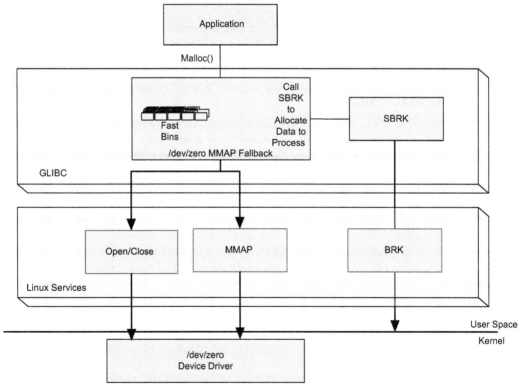

FIGURE 7.1

GLIBC and Service Calls.

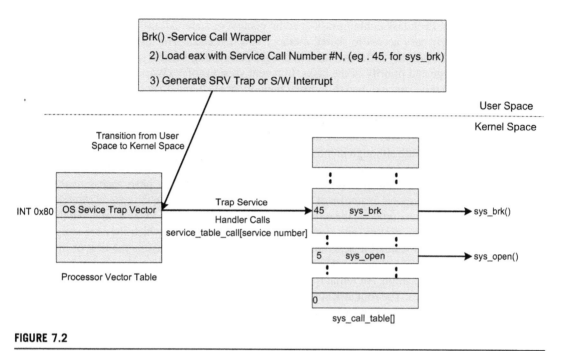

FIGURE 7.2

Service Call Design Pattern.

1. Each service call has a user space library wrapper providing a function for each call.
2. Each service call is assigned an operating system service identifier in the form of an integer. The assignment of numbers for each service call is done by the maintainer of the operating systems. The previously allocated numbers do not change or get reassigned because doing so could break existing applications or libraries, that is, it would break backward compatibility
3. The service wrapper call pushes the calling arguments on to the stack, loads a register (eax for IA-32 platforms) with the service number for the call, and issues a service trap (or software interrupt depending on the target processor architecture).
4. The trap is an instruction that causes transition from the current user space execution to the function in the exception vector table, with the associated increase in privileges.
5. The system services trap handler dereferences a system call table using the service call number and transfers control to the function bound to the table.
6. At this point, the processor is executing the kernel system call function with kernel privileges.

Figure 7.2 shows the design pattern used by most operating systems when providing service calls.

PROCESSES, TASKS, AND THREADS

An operating system defines a minimal execution context that can be scheduled. Depending on the operating system, they are called tasks or threads. In an RTOS, the system is normally composed exclusively of tasks. Each task contains task-specific context or state. All tasks are generally globally visible with relatively easy access to shared memory between tasks. The task view is flat across the operating system; the primary difference between tasks performing kernel type work and application work are the privilege and priority of the tasks. In recent versions of VxWorks a process concept was introduced in which tasks are assigned to a virtual memory context and do not have global visibility of memory. In the case of more general-purpose operating systems one or more threads are incorporated to execute under a user space process. Threads within a process share the same memory space, descriptors for access to system resources, and the like. In Linux, threads are created within a process through the fork system call, although in most cases programmers use the `pthread` library to create and manage threads. The kernel threads are not unlike the task equivalent in the VxWorks RTOS case; there is no protection mechanism between the kernel threads and they have access to the kernel memory map. Figure 7.3 shows examples of the differing configurations. In the case of threads created as part of a user space Linux process, the threads are similar to those found in the kernel, but they share the memory space, file descriptors, and signal handles of the process to which they are assigned.

In both VxWorks and Linux the scheduling unit in the operating system is the task or thread.

In the case of VxWorks and many other real-time operating systems the task creation is explicitly under control of the application. An initial root task is created by the kernel. The kernel root task starts with the highest privileges. The root task subsequently creates a number of other task and then deletes itself (frees all resources associated with it). Each of the threads can create new threads using the `taskOpen()` function call. The `taskOpen()` function call takes the following arguments:

- Name—A character string that can be displayed by debug functions or used to obtain a handle for a task. There are public and private task name spaces.
- Priority—A value ranging from 0 to 255, with 0 being the highest priority.
- Task options—Indicate whether the task uses floating point, private or public task, some stack fill and protection options, and a flag to indicate whether the thread should start on creation or be created in a suspended state to be started explicitly later.
- Mode—Indicates whether a new task is to be created or just a search for an existing task.
- Stack base—Allows the stack to be placed at a particular address; if NULL is specified, the kernel will allocate stack space. In embedded systems, this is often useful as you may place the stack for a real-time process in a dedicated on-die SRAM. This improves determinism and is often important for interrupt tasks.
- Stack size—This is the size of the stack to be used for the task; if stack base is NULL, this will be allocated. As resources can be quite limited in embedded systems, the maximum size of the task must be specified at the time the task is created and it is allocated at that time.
- Context—This is a pointer to an object that is stored by the kernel for this task. VxWorks does not use it directly. You should consider this to be a cookie; it can be used to store application-specific data for this task. This design pattern is often used in embedded systems.
- Function pointer—Starting function address for the task. When the task first starts to execute it will start to execute at this address.
- Arguments to task—The call supports providing up to 10 integer arguments to the task. The arguments are available to the function once the function is started. This allows you to create a number of different threads using the same function but have them behave differently depending on the arguments supplied.

VxWorks Global Memory Context

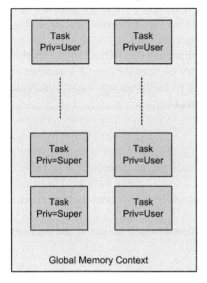

VxWorks Process Memory Context

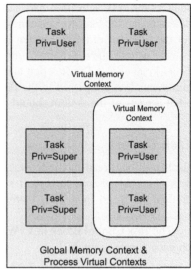

Linux Process and Thread Context

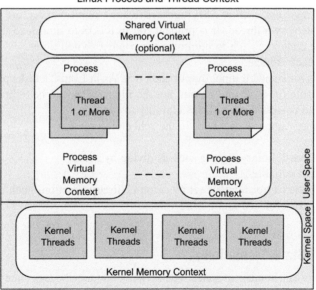

FIGURE 7.3

Tasks, Threads, and Processes.

The function returns a `TaskID` number. This task ID can be used for many low-level control functions such as the task activation call `taskActivate()` or other control functions to change priority, task deletion, and the like. As you can see, the creation of a task in an RTOS offers considerable flexibility for the behavior of the task when it is created and subsequently once it exists.

The pattern above is quite common for operating systems; the equivalent call in the Linux kernel is `kernel_thread()`. The function takes a function pointer for the entry point to the thread, a number of arguments that are passed to the threads entry point, and a number of configuration flags to indicate what aspects of the system should be shared (such as memory space).

Task Context

Each task or thread has a context store; the context store keeps all the task-specific data for the task. The kernel scheduler will save and restore the task state on a context switch. The task's context is stored in a Task Control Block in VxWorks; the equivalent in Linux is the `struct task_struct`.

The Task Control Block in VxWorks contains the following elements, which are saved and restored on each context switch:

- The task program/instruction counter.
- Virtual memory context for tasks within a process if enabled.
- CPU registers for the task.
- Non-core CPU registers, such as SSE registers/floating-point register, are saved/restored based on use of the registers by a thread. It is prudent for an RTOS to minimize the data it must save and restore for each context switch to minimize the context switch times.
- Task program stack storage.
- I/O assignments for standard input/output and error. As in Linux, a tasks/process output is directed to standard console for input and output, but the file handles can be redirected to a file.
- A delay timer, to postpone the tasks availability to run.
- A time slice timer (more on that later in the scheduling section).
- Kernel structures.
- Signal handles (for C library signals such as divide by zero).
- Task environment variables.
- `Errno`—the C library error number set by some C library functions such as `strtod()`.
- Debugging and performance monitoring values.

Task State and State Transitions

A task can be in one of a number of states. The kernel maintains the task state and transitions from one state to another. In the case of VxWorks, a task initially starts in the *suspended* state. When the task is activated it transitions to the *ready* state. The ready state does not mean the task is actually running; it is available to be run by the scheduler. Table 7.1 shows the task states that are supported by the VxWorks kernel but are representative of other operating systems.

The state transitions are managed by the kernel. Figure 7.4 shows the state transitions and a selection of events that trigger the state transitions in normal operating (non-debug) scenarios.

Table 7.1 RTOS States

State	State Description
Ready	The task is not waiting for any resource other than the CPU.
Pending	The task is blocked due to the unavailability of some resource. For example, the task could be blocked waiting for the release of a semaphore from another task, or waiting for input.
Delayed	The task is waiting on a timeout and is sleeping.
Suspended	The task is unavailable for execution (but not pending or delayed). This state is used primarily for debugging. Suspension does not inhibit state transition, only execution. Thus, pending-suspended tasks can still unblock and delayed-suspended tasks can still awaken.
Stop	The task is stopped by the debugger.
Pending + T	The task is pending with a timeout value.
Other state combinations with Suspend and Stop	The kernel maintains a number of combination states that are combined with Stop and Suspend states, for example, Stop + Pending + Stopped, indicating the task is pending, suspended, and stopped by the debugger.
State + Inherited Priority	All states can be augmented with an inherited priority. The kernel supports a mechanism to increase of priority to prevent a condition known as priority inversion, described later in the scheduling section.

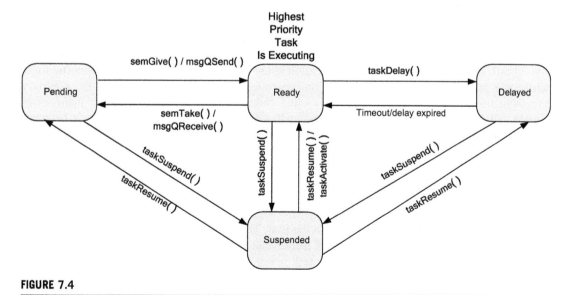

FIGURE 7.4

RTOS State Transitions.

The transition between ready and pending is the most common transition for a task in an embedded application. Examples are given in the diagram of the use of semaphore and message queues. The `semTake` call attempts to get a semaphore. If the semaphore can be acquired (no other task has acquired it), then the task continues without blocking. If, however, another task has ownership of the semaphore, the task will block and be placed into the pending state. When the owner of the semaphore releases it, it allows the requesting task to transition to the ready state. At some point the kernel will schedule that ready task for execution. The message send and receive has a similar state transition sequence. A receiving task will typically make a blocking call to a message queue receive function. The task will block (be placed into the pending state) if there are no messages in the queue. When another task places a message in the queue, the message receive task will transition from pending to ready. Each state is typically maintained as a queue data structure, where tasks/threads in each state are in the appropriate queue; for example, the Ready Queue contains all tasks/threads that are in the read state.

SCHEDULING

The scheduler in the operating system selects a task/thread from the available list of ready tasks and starts the execution of the task. A number of different scheduler types are used in operating systems with varying characteristics. We will discuss the simple scheduler, round-robin scheduler, preemptive priority scheduler, and completely fair scheduler.

Simple FIFO Scheduler

The most basic scheduler selects a task from the top of a ready queue and transfers control to the task. No scheduling decision is made until the running task relinquishes control by generating an event that causes the task to block (no longer ready) or the task explicitly yields the CPU using a yield call. A yield call is an explicit notification to the scheduler that it can take an opportunity to reschedule another task if one is ready. The operating system does not preempt the currently executing task; this scheduling schemes is often called cooperative scheduling. In many cases a yield call is implemented as a system delay call with a timeout of zero. When a task becomes ready it is simply added to the end of the ready queue. The scheduler picks the task from the top of the queue to run. Simply put, the first task to enter the ready queue is the first to be scheduled (first in, first out, or FIFO). The coding of such tasks requires detailed knowledge of all other tasks in the system if appropriate system behavior is to be achieved. This scheme works on only the simplest of systems. Figure 7.5 shows the wide range of times that are allocated to each task due to the sequence blocking and yield calls.

This form of scheduling was prevalent in the past. The code was often developed by the system developer and no use of an RTOS/OS was made. The execution time of a task in this model is completely dependent on the time when the task is run to the time it blocks or yields. Tuning such a system to ensure the appropriate system behavior can be very challenging; the introduction of a new task can perturb the other tasks' behavior to an extent that the system no longer functions as required.

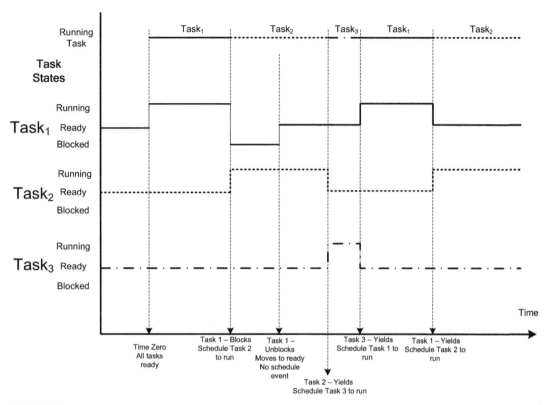

FIGURE 7.5

Nonpreemptive FIFO Task Scheduling.

Round-Robin Scheduler with Priority and Preemption

A priority-based preemptive scheduler preempts the currently executing task when a task of higher priority than the current task running transitions to the ready state. Thus, the kernel ensures that the CPU is always allocated to the highest-priority task that is ready to run. When a higher-priority task (than the current running task) changes state from blocked to ready, it will start executing. The transition from blocked to ready may be due to reception of a message in the queue, acquiring a semaphore, a timeout event, or reception of some data from an I/O device. In all such operating system events the scheduler evaluates the task states and priorities. The disadvantage of this scheduling policy is that when multiple tasks of equal priority must share the processor, if a single task is never blocked it can usurp the processor. Thus, other equal-priority tasks are never given a chance to run.

In order to ensure that equal-priority tasks are guaranteed to share the processor, an extension of the priority scheduler is introduced, namely, round robin. The round-robin scheduler shares the processor using a time-slicing algorithm between the equal priority tasks. When the OS timer expires, the scheduler is executed. The scheduler switches between equal priority tasks (unless a higher-priority task becomes ready) on each OS time slice. The time slice corresponds to one or more OS timer periods and is configured as part of the RTOS. Note that the OS timer also causes an evaluation of the operating system timers, and an expired timer could result in a task moving from blocked (pending timeout) to ready, and if this is the highest-priority task, it will run. No task gets a second slice of time before all other tasks in the priority group have been allowed to run.

The selection of the OS timer period is a critical aspect in an embedded operating system. The typical timer period in an RTOS is 1 ms; that is, the timer frequency is 1000 Hz. The equivalent timer period on a general purpose OS is usually less. The Linux kernel as of 2.6.36 provided configuration options for 100 Hz, 250 Hz, 300 Hz, and 1000 Hz, with the default option set to 250 Hz.

The combination of both preemption and round-robin scheduling provides very effective control of the behavior of a real-time system; however, the selection of priorities for the tasks is a skilled exercise

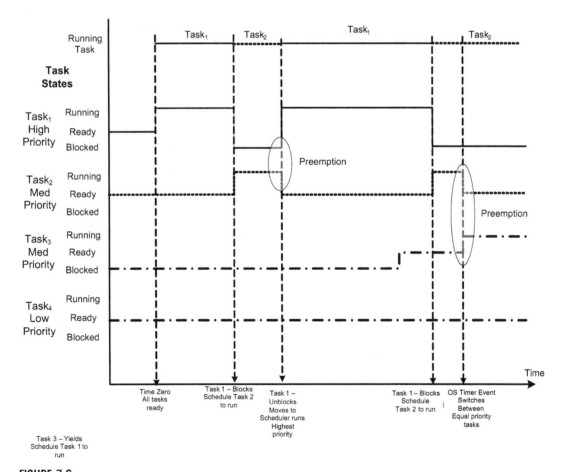

FIGURE 7.6

Round-Robin Scheduler with Preemption and Priority.

to ensure the appropriate behavior of the system. Figure 7.6 shows an example of the task states and run order.

The round-robin scheduler with preemption and priority is the traditional schedule enabled in VxWorks by default.

> **Note**
>
> Protection of data structures: if two tasks have access to a shared data structure (such as a linked list), it is important to always protect access to the structure by using synchronization primitives to ensure atomic updates. Operating system preemption could cause a context switch at any point in the data structure update, which could result in an incorrect update.

Linux Kernel's Scheduler

The Linux scheduler has to support a very wide range of scenarios, from single-processor to multi-processor systems, from workstation high-compute workloads to the low-latency interactivity requirements for user interfaces and a wide range of processor performance ranges. The scheduler has continued to evolve to meet this broad range of requirements. The original Linux 2.4 scheduler was nonpreemptible and only supported real-time scheduling with a separate patch. As the kernel transitioned to 2.6, the scheduler was enhanced to support preemption and real-time tasks; the latest change has been the introduction of the completely fair scheduler (CFS) in version 2.6.23 of the kernel. The completely fair scheduler is primarily a "desktop" scheduler, although it has many mechanisms to control its behavior (http://lxr.linux.no/linux+v2.6.37/Documentation/scheduler/sched-design-CFS.txt#L214).

The following function controls the behavior of processes scheduling discipline:

```
int sched_setscheduler(pid_t pid, int policy,
                       const struct sched_param
                       *param);
```

There are real-time and non-real-time disciplines. For the non-real-time processes, you can select one of the disciplines that are scheduled by the CFS:

- SCHED_NORMAL—The standard round-robin time-sharing policy, used for regular tasks.
- SCHED_BATCH—For batch-style execution of processes. It is does not preempt as often as a NORMAL task, allowing them to run longer; this has an impact on the overall interactivity of the system.
- SCHED_IDLE—For running very low priority background jobs.

The vast majority of threads in a system are scheduled under one of the disciplines defined by the completely fair scheduler. Threads can also be scheduled under one of the real-time disciplines. All ready real-time threads are scheduled to execute before NORMAL/BATCH and IDLE threads. There are two real-time disciplines that can be selected:

- SCHED_FIFO—A first in, first out policy
- SCHED_RR—Round-robin policy

The priority of a process scheduled with SCHED_FIFO and SCHED_RR dictates when a thread will be scheduled, with priorities ranging from 1 (low) to 99 (high) priority. The priority of these real-time processes is always higher than the NORMAL/BATCH and IDLE scheduled processes. For embedded applications it is important to use the appropriate scheduling discipline and thread priorities.

Real-time processes are always scheduled to run over any "normal" process, simply because the priority is not zero. As soon as any real-time process becomes ready it will preempt the normal process (SCHED_OTHER). The SCHED_FIFO discipline is a very simple scheduling algorithm. It does not time slice between processes at the same priority. When a SCHED_FIFO process first becomes ready, it is placed at the end of the run queue for that particular priority. Processes of higher priority preempt lower-priority process. A preempted process will still be at the head of the ready queue when the higher-priority process blocks. A yield call will place the currently executing process at the end of the run list for its priority level. The process remains available to run unless it blocks. The SCHED_FIFO_RR is similar to the SCHED_FIFO; however, execution of a SCHED_FIFO_RR process is allocated a time quantum. When the quantum expires, the scheduler de-schedules the process and puts it at the end of the run list for that priority level. The process remains ready to run. If a SCHED_FIFO_RR process is pre-empted by a higher-priority process, its quantum counter is suspended, and it will be allowed to execute the remainder of its quantum when the higher-priority process blocks. See the Linux main page for `sched_setscheduler` for more details.

Although the Linux kernel (as of 2.6) is often stated to be preemptible, the behavior of the scheduler is in actuality configurable. The kernel has three options to control preemption.

- CONFIG_PREEMPT_NONE—This sets the scheduler as nonpreemptible and is often set for servers where we want to maximize the overall work done by the CPU by reducing context switches. In this case kernel processes are not subject to preemption.
- CONFIG_PREEMPT_VOLUNTARY—This allows kernel threads to voluntarily be preempted. This controls the behavior of the `might_preempt()` call.
- CONFIG_PREEMPT—This makes kernel threads fully preemptible, unless a thread is holding a kernel lock.

POSIX-Compliant Scheduler

POSIX standardized a wide range of service APIs, and APIs are defined to create POSIX threads; the standard defines how the threads should be scheduled. The POSIX:2008 standard the Open Group Base Specifications Issue 7IEEE Std 1003.1™-2008 can be found here: http://pubs.opengroup.org/onlinepubs/9699919799/.

As in Linux, the scheduling disciplines are SCHED_FIFO, SCHED_RR, and SCHED_OTHER. In the SCHED_FIFO the thread waiting the longest is processed first; for the SCHED_RR thread, the behavior is the same as that defined by the Linux kernel. VxWorks also offers a POSIX-compliant scheduler (although it is not the default configuration).

Scheduler Complexity

The time taken to select the next task/thread to run with respect to the number of tasks in the system is an important characteristic of a scheduler. As with many algorithms, big O notation is used to describe this aspect of a scheduler.

- O(1) scheduler—This scheduler takes a constant amount of time to select a task to run regardless of the number of tasks/threads to select. The scheduler used in Linux versions prior to 2.6.23 used a O(1) order scheduler.
- O(log N) scheduler—The scheduler evaluation time increases with the log of the number of tasks. The Linux scheduler post 2.6.23 is known as the completely fair scheduler. The selection of the run tasks occurs in O(1); however, the tasks are placed into a red-black self-balancing binary tree that takes O(log N) time, so the algorithm is considered to be of O(log N) complexity.

Note that no specific performance attributes are associated with the classification; it merely represents the relative performance of the scheduler as the number of tasks increases.

MEMORY ALLOCATION

All systems provide a mechanism to allocate memory to an application. Functions are provided to allocate and free memory from the system heap. In the case of the C language, the C language library provides the functions to manage the memory allocation. In this case the calls are `malloc()` and `free()`.

An embedded system may support individual heaps per process, with separate maximum heap sizes assigned to each process. Other configurations have a single heap in the system, where all tasks may allocate from and free to. In the case of the process view, the memory allocation functions return a virtual address that is only valid for the process making the call. In a flat model, the memory allocated is globally visible. It is not uncommon for embedded applications to pass messages between tasks that contain pointers to memory that is allocated using `malloc()` calls. To access memory allocated by another task, the system must use a flat memory model or use special shared memory APIs to facilitate the sharing of allocated memory across tasks.

The memory allocation system has no prior knowledge of the sequence of memory allocations and frees that might be requested by applications. The allocator algorithms attempt to maximize the size of contiguous blocks within the heap over time to ensure that the heap does not get fragmented. A fragmented heap is one in which a significant amount of memory is free but the size of any contiguous section is small. In this case an application request to allocate memory can fail. Allocator algorithms can help significantly to reduce fragmentation. Figure 7.7 shows an example of how a heap may be fragmented through a series of allocation and free calls.

To help achieve this many memory allocations, schemes partition the heap into a number of fixed-size pools and a single large variable-size pool as shown in Figure 7.8. The pools are often referred to as power of two pools, as the entry sizes increase with power of two (for example, 32, 64, 128 bytes).

When an application makes a request for a number of bytes, for example, 64 bytes, the allocator first attempts to allocate from the 64-byte pool. If that fails, it tries the next size pool, and so on. If allocation fails for all the fixed-size pools, then the allocator allocates from the variable-size heap. The number of fixed-size pools, the size of the entries in a pool, and the number of entries in each pool are configurable and should be tuned for your embedded application. In embedded applications it is very important to manage possible heap fragmentation. Embedded systems can remain running without restarting for very long periods of time (up to years). The `mallopt()` call in the C library can be used to tune the behavior of `malloc/free`.

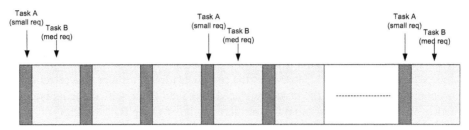

Heap State: Series of small requests from Task A and medium requets from Task B (no frees)

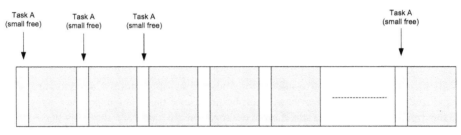

Heap State: Task A frees all previously allocated memory

Maximum contiguous size available for allocation

FIGURE 7.7

Fragmented Heap (Zebra Pattern).

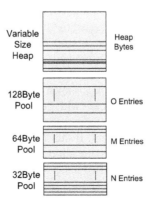

FIGURE 7.8

Power of Two Heap.

Despite the techniques described here, over time the pattern of allocation and free may result in fragmentation of the variable-size heap. For embedded systems, it is best practice to pre-allocate all memory requirements for applications at the time of startup and subsequently manage the allocated memory in the form of memory pools. Many real-time operating systems provide APIs to create and manage such pools; it is strongly advised to use such techniques in embedded systems. The Linux kernel uses such techniques in the `slab` memory allocator.

Virtual Memory and Protection

When process level memory protection is employed, the memory addresses allocated to the process are virtual addresses in the process space. The memory management unit (MMU) and associated page tables manage the translation between code, data, and heap process memory to the underlying physical memory. Each process appears to live in the same virtual address space, but actually resides in different physical areas of memory. Figure 7.9 shows how memory regions in a process are mapped to physical memory.

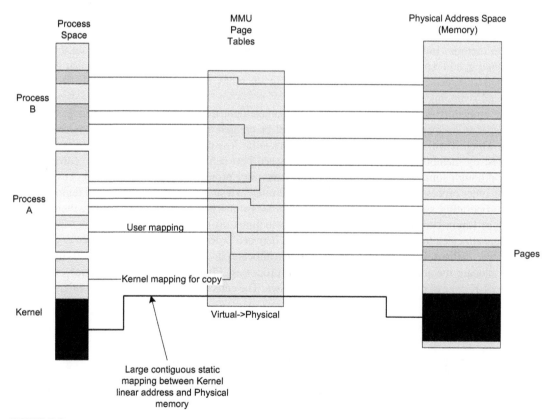

FIGURE 7.9

Address Space Mapping to Physical Memory.

The operating system manages the page tables based on process creation and underlying kernel services calls. Each process has an active page table in context when the process is executing. The CPU contains a process ID register (CR3 on Intel architecture) that is used to select the appropriate tree within the page table hierarchy. One of the tasks the operating system performs is to update the CR3 value in the CPU during context switches. The mapping between process address space and physical pages is often highly fragmented; there is no mathematical correlation between the virtual and physical address (it must be identified via page table lookup). On the other hand, in many systems, the page tables configured to map kernel space usually map a large, virtually contiguous area within the kernel to a large, physically contiguous area in physical memory. This simplifies the calculation/translation between kernel virtual and physical address for the kernel mappings. The addition/subtraction of an address offset can be used to convert between kernel virtual and physical addresses. However, this should not be relied upon. You must always use OS-provided functions to translate addresses. This attribute is a system optimization to make the translation as efficient as possible.

In full-featured operating systems, the physical memory pages may be copied to a storage device. This process is known as *swapping*. The virtual to physical mapping for the process physical page will be removed. When an application attempts to access the virtual address that previously had a physical page mapped, the MMU will generate a page fault. The page fault handler copies the page from the drive into memory (not likely to be the same physical memory used previously), sets up the correct page mapping, and returns from the page fault exception, at which point the instruction that generated the fault is re-executed, this time without faulting. In many embedded systems, there is no swap storage and swapping is disabled.

Some embedded systems have no memory management unit. In this case the virtual and linear address spaces are mapped 1:1. Each process must be created and linked to a target physical address range in which it will reside during runtime. There is far less protection (code from one process can access/destroy memory belonging to another process) between processes if there is no MMU in the system, although some systems do implement a memory protection unit to prevent processes from accessing other processes' memory, but these are limited to a small number of protection regions. Most real-time operating systems support embedded processors with or without an MMU; there is also a variant of Linux known as uCLinux (http://www.uclinux.org) that does not require an MMU.

Buffers allocated to a process cannot be shared between processes, as the physical memory backing the `malloc()` call is only allocated to the process that allocates it. There is also a series of calls that can be used to allocate memory that is shared between processes. Figure 7.10 shows the series of calls to allocate a 4-K page of memory between two processes. The calls must be coordinated by both processes.

```
int memDesc;
void *virt_addr;

/* Open Shared memory descriptor for "shared_memory" */
memDesc = shm_open ("shared_memory", O_CREAT|O_RDWR, 0);
/* Map one page */
ftruncate(memDesc, 4096);
virt_addr = mmap(0, 4096, PROT_WRITE, MAP_SHARED, memDesc, 0);
```

FIGURE 7.10

Shared Memory Allocation.

The shared memory is set up by creating two different contiguous virtual memory mappings for one set of physical memory pages.

Freeing Memory

In embedded systems the memory allocated by a task may not be automatically freed based on the deletion of that task; this is in contrast to a process model in an operating system such as Linux where all memory associated with a process is automatically returned to the kernel when a process is terminated. For embedded tasks, it is important to keep track of all the memory allocated by the task if you expect to be able to destroy and restart it. In many cases, a memory allocation wrapper is used. The wrapper places the pointer allocated to the task in a linked list that can be used to ensure that all resources are freed when the task is destroyed.

Swapping Memory

On most desktop systems, the memory associated with a process may be swapped out to mass storage when the process is not active. It allows the system to allocate more virtual memory to applications than the total amount of physical memory. In fact, the space allocated for swapping memory pages from an application is usually set to twice the amount of physical memory. The swapping process only applies to user-level applications. Kernel memory is never swapped.

Memory swapping is rarely used in embedded systems, because it introduces additional wear on the file system (often based on flash solid-state devices) and also introduces a level of non-determinism to applications. Few real-time operating systems actually support swapping, and swapping can be disabled in Linux by not setting the Linux kernel build option CONFIG_SWAP. The function `mlockall()` can also be used to lock all pages mapped into the address space of the calling process.

CLOCKS AND TIMERS

Timer and clock services are capabilities offered by an operating system. In embedded applications a task may need to issue a delay/sleep for a period of time or manage the generation of events at a particular rate. To facilitate such cases, the platform provides counters and timers. A timer is typically a hardware resource that generates an interrupt to the processor at a periodic rate. Counters are hardware resources that are clocked at a particular rate and can be read by the software to establish the amount of time that has passed.

All operating systems make use of at least one timer called the system tick. This timer is used to trigger timer callback functions and provide the time base to support time slicing of tasks by the OS scheduler.

Synchronous Execution

Many OS service calls provide an argument to specify a timeout. The execution context is delayed or suspended for a period of time. For example, OS calls used to wait for events such as a message on a queue or a socket select call provide an argument to timeout and return without having received any data. The VxWorks call to wait for a message on a queue is as follows.

```
int msgQReceive(
    MSG_Q_ID msgQId,/* message queue from         */
    char * buffer,  /* buffer to receive message */
    UINT maxNBytes, /* length of buffer          */
    int timeout )   /* ticks to wait             */
```

The operating system also provides calls such as sleep(), nanosleep(), uDelay(), and mDelay() that delay the calling task by a specified amount of time. If the time is long enough the call may actually de-schedule the task, and the operating system will place it on the ready queue after the specified delay. In simple executives, a sleep(0) call is the same as a yield() call explicitly requesting that the OS scheduler review the list of ready tasks and reschedule if appropriate.

Asynchronous Execution

Operating systems also provide services to cause the execution of a function asynchronously to the main tasks after a defined delay. For example, user space applications in Linux/VxWorks can request that a SIGNAL be sent to an application (task) after a specified period of time using the alarm() call. The application must register a callback function for the SIGALARM signal. The operating system generates a SIGALARM to the application after the specified number of seconds expires. This mechanism only offers granularity of one second and is not very useful for embedded application use.

In the case of the Linux kernel and many real-time operating systems, a generic service is provided to schedule a callback function after a specified delay or periodically. The operating system maintains a list of callback functions and an associated timeout time in the future. Each time the OS tick timer expires, the timer list is reviewed and any callbacks that have an expiry time that is less than or equal to the current time count are called. The callback functions are often called in the context of the timer interrupt or timer thread. It is good practice to limit the amount of time spent in these callback functions, as lengthy callbacks affect the execution of the other callbacks. In most cases the callback is used to indicate to another thread that the timeout has occurred. For example, the callback function could send an event to another task or release a semaphore held by another task.

The Linux kernel offers timer services using the init_timer(), add_timer(), and del_timer() calls. The init_timer call is provided with a function pointer, a delta expiry time in jiffies, and data to pass to the callback function when the timer expires. In Linux a jiffy is the unit of time the scheduler operates on, by default 4 ms when the system is configured to schedule at 250 Hz. The add_timer() call schedules the timer to expire in the future at delta expire jiffies from when the add_timer() call occurs. The timer callback function is called in a separate context to the add_timer() call. These calls can be used by device drivers to perform simple polling behavior of a device, such as to check the link state of an Ethernet cable.

Depending on how the timer callback service is implemented, the calling context for the callbacks may have restrictions on what behavior is allowed within the function. In the case of Linux, in_interrupt() and in_atomic() are two calls you can use to establish whether you can make certain OS calls in the callback. In many embedded cases, you will know the context at design time and ensure the callback does not call any inappropriate calls. Although it is a good idea to use calls such as `in_interrupt()` for debug images, the system may evolve over time. If the underlying OS assumptions change, it is very difficult to debug cases where the callbacks make calls that are not allowed in the calling context.

Time of Day

Most operating systems provide time of day services. This is the real-world date and time of the platform. The operating system can maintain this in one of two ways. The first is to read a Real-Time Clock (RTC). A RTC is a hardware timer that is typically backed up by a battery and is maintained even when the platform power is removed. The RTC provides date, time, and alarm services. The second option is where the time is maintained by the CPU while the CPU is running. In this case the operating system uses a timer interrupt (perhaps the operating system tick timer) to count interrupts and increment the time. The time and date value must be seeded when the platform first starts-ups as it is not retained when no power is applied. In embedded systems, the initial time may be seeded using the RTC mentioned above or it may be acquired from an external source. A platform can acquire time from many external sources; the most frequent method is to obtain the time from a network source using Network Time Protocol (NTP). This protocol allows a network time server to provide time updates to clients with very high precision. The NTP is used not only to seed the initial time on a platform but also to ensure that an accurate time is mainlined over time (bearing in mind that the local oscillators on an embedded platform may not be very accurate.). In mobile systems, a very accurate time may be obtained from the cellular radio network.

The concept of time on Unix/Linux systems is represented by a counter that counts seconds since the epoch. The epoch is defined (by POSIX 2008 standard) as midnight Coordinated Universal Time (UTC) of January 1, 1970. The POSIX function `time_t time(time_t *tloc)` returns a type `time_t`, which represents the number of seconds since the epoch. Most operating systems provide functions to convert this value into other forms, such as the function `asctime()`, which converts the time in seconds to a string.

The granularity of time offered by the `time()` API is seconds. In many cases you will require a more precise copy of time, such as microseconds. The POSIX standard defines the following APIs to address this requirement:

- `clock_getres()` returns the resolution for a particular timer source, for example, the `CLOCK_REALTIME` (system time).
- `clock_gettime()`/`clock_setime()` get and set the time source specified in the API (for example, the real-time clock).

These calls both indicate the resolution and return the time to the appropriate resolution. At the time of writing, Linux 3.x reported a resolution of 1 ns, as shown by the code in Figure 7.11.

MUTUAL EXCLUSION/SYNCHRONIZATION

In many cases it is critical to ensure serialized atomic access to resources such as data structures and/or physical device resources. There are many mechanisms to ensure mutually exclusive access to

```
#include <stdio.h>
#include <stdint.h>
#include <time.h>
struct timespec res;
    clock_getres(CLOCK_REALTIME, &res);
    printf("Real Time Clock Resolution: %ju Sec:%ld
            nanoseconds\n",(uintmax_t)res.tv_sec,
            res.tv_nsec);
    clock_gettime(CLOCK_REALTIME, &res);
    printf("%ju Sec %ld nanoseconds since Epoch\n",
            (uintmax_t)res.tv_sec,
            res.tv_nsec);

Output:
Real Time Clock Resolution: 0 Sec:1 nanoseconds
1295499450 Sec 472094648 nanoseconds since Epoch
```

FIGURE 7.11

Get Resolution of Time on Platform.

a resource. The first is to serialize access to the area where atomic updates must occur. An example of a critical section is when the execution context updates a counter in memory or performs pointer updates associated with insertion/removal of a node in a linked list.

When an execution context is performing the atomic update to a resource, it must prevent execution of any other context that might update the resource.

The simplest mechanism is to prevent the scheduling of any other execution context while the update is occurring. In many simple embedded systems, this was often carried out by disabling interrupts. This is not recommended, as it perturbs real-time behavior, interacts with device drivers, and may not work with multi-core systems. Disabling interrupts effectively prevents an operating system–triggered rescheduling of the task running in the critical section. The task must also avoid any system calls that would trigger execution of the OS scheduler. There may also be an operating system call to suspend scheduling of other tasks. Such mechanisms are blunt instruments to ensure mutual exclusion, as they may have a broad system wide impact. These techniques also do not work when being used by user- or de-privileged contexts such as a POSIX thread.

In many systems a hardware mechanism is provided to perform an atomic update in system memory. Processor architectures provide instructions to build mutual exclusion primitives such as Compare and Swap (CAS) and Compare and Exchange (CMPXCHG) in Intel Architecture and load-link/store-conditional instructions on PowerPC, ARM and MOPS architectures. These are sometimes referred to as atomic test and set operations. As an example, we describe how the CAS instruction can be used to perform an atomic update from two execution contexts. The CAS instruction compares the memory location with a given value. If the value at the memory location is the same as the given value, then the memory is updated with a new value given. Consider two execution contexts (A and B) attempting to update a counter: context A reads the current value, increments the current value by one to create the new value, then issues a CAS with the current and new values. If context B has not intervened, the update to the new value will occur, as the current value in memory is the same as the current value issued in the CAS. If, however, context B reads the same current value as context A and issues the CAS instruction before context A, then the update by context A would fail, as the value in memory is no longer the same as the current value issued in the CAS by context A. This collision can be detected because the CAS instruction returns the value of the memory; if the update fails then context A must try the loop again and will mostly likely succeed the second time. In the case described above, context A may be interrupted by an interrupt and context B may be run in the interrupt handler or from a different context scheduled by the operating system. Alternatively, the system has multiple CPUs where the other CPU is performing an update at exactly the same time.

Using a technique similar to the one described above, we can implement a construct known as a spin lock. A spin lock is where a thread waits to get a lock by repeatedly trying to get the lock. The calling context busy-waits until it acquires the lock. This mechanism works well when the time for which a context owns a lock is very small. However, care must be taken to avoid deadlock. For example, if a kernel task has acquired the spin lock but an interrupt handler wishes to acquire the lock, you could have a scenario where the interrupt hander spins forever waiting for the lock. Spinlocks in embedded systems can create delays due to priority inversion and it would be good to use mutexes where possible.

In reality, building robust multi-CPU mutual exclusion primitives is quite involved. Many papers have been written on efficient use of such resources to update data structures such as binary counters, counters, and linked lists. Techniques can be varied depending on the balance of consumer versus producer contexts (number of readers and writers).

The mechanism described above does not interact with the operating system scheduling behavior and the mechanism is not appropriate if the work to be performed in the critical section is long or if operating system calls are required. Operating systems provide specific calls to facilitate mutual exclusion between threads/tasks. Common capabilities provided include semaphores (invented by Edsger W. Dijkstra), mutexes, and message queues.

These functions often rely on underlying hardware capabilities as described above and interact with the operating system scheduler to manage the state transitions of the calling tasks.

Let's describe a time sequence of two contexts acquiring a semaphore. Assuming context A has acquired a semaphore and context B makes a call to acquire the same semaphore, the operating system will place task B into a blocked state. Task B will transition to a ready state when task A releases the semaphore. In this case the system has provided the capabilities for the developer to provide mutual exclusion between task A and task B. Figure 7.12 shows the timeline associated with semaphore ownership.

As you can see, the operating system scheduler ensures that only one task is executing in the critical section at any time. Although we show task A continuing to run after the semaphore is released until it is preempted, in many operating systems the call to release the semaphore also performs a scheduling evaluation and the transition to task B (or other task) could occur at that point.

Note

Priority inversion is a situation that can occur when a low-priority task is holding a resource such as a semaphore for which a higher-priority task is waiting. The high-priority task has effectively acquired the priority of the low-priority thread (thus the name priority inversion). Some operating systems automatically increase the priority of the lower-priority thread to that of the highest-priority waiting thread until the resource is no longer owned by the low-priority thread.

In the case of VxWorks, the mutual-exclusion semaphore has the option SEM_INVERSION_SAFE. This option enables a priority inheritance feature. The priority inheritance feature ensures that a task that holds a resource executes at the priority of the highest-priority task blocked on that resource.

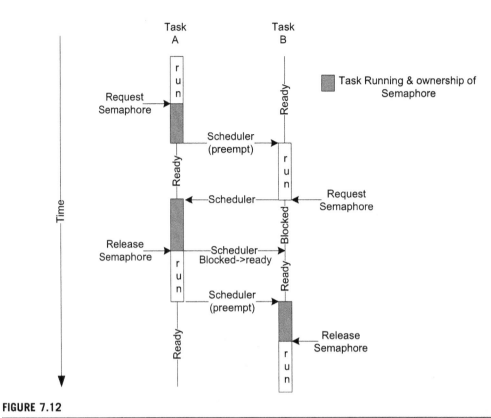

FIGURE 7.12

Semaphore Timeline.

There are two different types of semaphore, namely, binary and counting. Binary semaphores are restricted to two values (one or zero) acquired/available. Counting semaphores increment in value each time the semaphore is acquired. Typically the count is incremented each time the semaphore is acquired or reacquired. Depending on the operating system the semaphore can only be incremented by the task/thread that acquired it in the first place. Generally speaking, a mutex is the same as a binary semaphore. Although we have discussed semaphores in the context of providing mutual exclusion between two threads, in many real-time operating systems a semaphore can also be used to synchronize a task or thread, and in essence indicates an event. Figure 7.13 shows a simple case where a task is notified of an event by an interrupt handler (using VxWorks calls).

As an embedded programmer, you have to be very aware of the services you can use in an interrupt handler. The documentation associated with your RTOS/OS should be referenced; making an OS call in an interrupt handler that is illegal can result in very strange behavior at runtime.

A common alternative to using mutual exclusion primitives to serialize access to data structure is to nominate a single entity in the system with responsibility to perform the updates. For example, a database structure can be abstracted by a messaging interface to send updates and make inquiries. Since only one thread is operating on the data at any time, there is no need for synchronization to be

```
// Task A Context
// create a binary semaphore
sema = semBCreate (SEM_Q_FIFO, SEM_EMPTY);
while ( TRUE ) {
  semTake (sema, WAIT_FOREVER); //wait for event to occur
  // Do Work based on event.
}
// Interrupt Context
...
semGive (sema); /* Send task A "event" */
```

FIGURE 7.13

Task Synchronization.

used within this thread. This can be a beneficial approach especially if the software was not originally designed to be multi-thread safe, but it comes at the higher cost of messaging to and from the owning thread. This technique can also be used to create a data structure that is optimized for a single writer and multiple readers. All writes to the data structures are carried out by a single thread that receives messages to perform the updates. Any thread reading the data structure uses API calls to directly read the data structures. This single write/multi-reader pattern allows for high-performance locking approaches, and it is a common design pattern. Figure 7.14 shows a simple message queue–based interaction between two tasks.

Figure 7.14 uses VxWorks API's calls to demonstrate the example. Two noteworthy arguments are in the calls (in addition to the message-related calls). The first is the blocking behavior: the example in Figure 7.14 blocks the calling thread forever when the task is waiting for a message; that is, the task is placed in the blocked state when no are messages in the queue and transited to ready when messages are in the queue. Similarly, on the msgQSend() call, the sending task may block if the queue is full, and

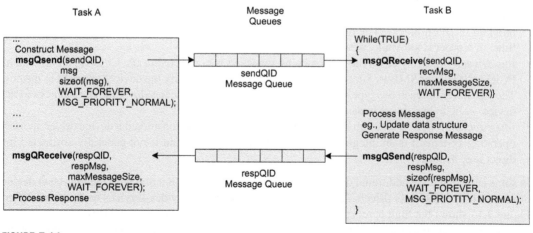

FIGURE 7.14

Message Queues.

the receive task does not draw down the messages. Balancing task priorities and message queue sizes to ensure that the system does not block or give unusual behavior is a task you will have to perform as an embedded software designer using an RTOS.

DEVICE DRIVER MODELS

A function of the operating system is to provide arbitrated shared access to I/O devices in the system. Applications do not directly interact with the I/O devices but instead make use of operating system services to access them.

A number of different device driver models may apply to differing device classes. Some device drivers provide services to other elements with the operating system, while other device drivers provide access to user space applications and the devices are managed directly by the application. A general classification of drivers is as follows:

- *Serial port drivers*—Many embedded systems provide a UART interface that is connected to a host or debug system through a RS232 serial cable. The UART device driver allows for character reception and transmission of octets to the serial port. The driver supports configuration of the port parameters such as baud rate and flow control. The driver usually presents a /dev/ttyN node, which can be opened using the POSIX open() call. Once the file descriptor is obtained from the open call, calls to read()/write() data from/to the serial port.
- *Network device drivers*—The device driver interacts with the network interface, such as an Ethernet or Wi-Fi™ interface. The network device driver connects to the TCP/IP stack within the operating system and offers user level services through the BSD sockets API.
- *Serial ATA*—Most disk drives (both solid state and magnetic hard disk) are attached via serial ATA. The SATA interface defines an advanced host controller interface (AHCI). The driver provides block services to a file system driver. The file system driver provides the file system capability to the operating system.
- *Flash*—Flash storage is a special class of block driver. The flash driver must manage, erase, and program the flash blocks. The driver must ensure that all blocks of the flash device are used over time, in a process known as wear leveling.
- *Bus drivers*—In many cases the device being managed is connected to the CPU via a bus such as PCIe™, USB™, or SMBus. Such buses have mechanisms to identify the devices attached to the bus. The bus driver for each bus type scans the bus for devices and allocates the required resources to the device. A PCIe bus driver is described below.
- *Interrupt controller*—Although the interrupt controller could be considered a device driver, in most operating systems it is an integral part of the operating system and is not generally abstracted for direct user access.

In some cases there are additional device drivers that operate in conjunction with the low-level device driver, such as USB class drivers. The low-level device driver provides services to the class driver. Figure 7.15 shows the high-level relationship between devices, drivers, and services.

As you can see, the hierarchy in Figure 7.15 demonstrates a significant amount of abstraction of the device and allows for the provision of many services across many physical interfaces. Let us consider storage as an example. An application uses traditional C library/POSIX calls to open, close, read, write

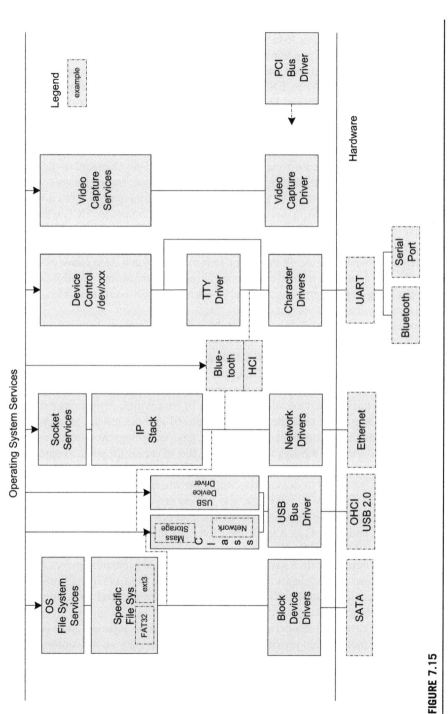

FIGURE 7.15

Device Driver Relationships.

calls to the selected file descriptor which subsequently operates on a file on the file system. The operating system provides generic service calls to facilitate these C library/POSIX calls. These calls are the contract between the operating system and applications. The file system receives generic service calls, then calls file system–specific calls to read and write files. There are many different file system types, such as File Allocation Table 32 (FAT32), EXT2/3, and Journaling Flash File System 2 (JFFS2). The file system–specific handlers then call a block level device driver interface. The block device driver manages the block device, which could be a SATA drive connected over a SATA interconnect, or the file system could be connected to a USB mass storage class driver managing an external USB drive. In all cases, there is tremendous freedom to evolve each individual capability without changing the application interface. For example, there has been a great deal of innovation and development in the Linux file systems since its inception, each with increasing robustness, performance, and resilience.

In Figure 7.15, we also show a sample flow for a Bluetooth™ device. Bluetooth devices are often connected via a high-speed UART. The UART provides a host controller interface (HCI) where the serial stream is formatted in accordance with the Bluetooth standard HCI definition. The HCI driver connects to the UART driver connected to the device. The Bluetooth stack provides a number of Bluetooth control services and connects to the TCP/IP stack to provide Personal Area Network (PAN) IP services between devices. Again, this example serves to show the tremendous capabilities and innovation that result from achieving the appropriate level of abstraction between subsystems in the operating systems.

As you have seen, there are a number of different device driver models in place. In many cases the driver provides services to other modules within the operating system. Also, the entry to the device driver often provides a reentrant API; this means that the API can be called from multiple contexts and it is the driver's responsibility to ensure that data structures are protected from concurrent access. The driver typically relies on synchronization principles (such as mutexes) to ensure safe concurrent access to the actual device or data structures associated with the device. To ensure high-performance drivers, it is important to minimize the amount of time the driver is serialized in these critical sections.

A device driver must manage the memory associated with the payload being sent or received from the device. The device driver or the device through DMA must be able to access the payload data being sent or a receive buffer for data being received. There are a number of scenarios that relate to the accessibility of this memory by the driver or device, depending on where the buffer is residing.

In a flat memory system with no process separation, the buffers are always resident in memory. This is the simplest case to handle for the device driver writer. The driver is executing in the same memory context as applications and drivers; as a result the driver can directly read from/write to the buffer. The buffer is resident in DRAM and the device may also use direct memory access (DMA) to and from the buffer. The biggest concern with a flat memory system with no separation is security and robustness of the system. Because any application can read/write data from other applications or device drivers, the application could obtain information or accidently destroy data structures if the application had defects (and of course, all software has some defects).

In operating systems including real-time operating systems that provide separate address space between user process and the kernel, buffers provided to the device driver may be resident in kernel memory. The driver is running in the same process space (kernel) and has direct access to the buffer. The kernel buffer is not subject to paging and will always be accessible until the driver frees the buffer or returns the buffer to an upper layer. You may have considered that if there are defects in the driver and it runs in the context of the kernel, then defects in the kernel can have a significant impact on the robustness and security of the system. This is true—a buggy device driver will likely crash the entire system, and, to make matters worse, such crashes are difficult to debug if the driver has corrupted a kernel data structure. In some operating systems, there is a trend to move device drivers (or portions thereof) to user space to increase the robustness of the system.

In the case of operating systems that support process separation, the device driver may be providing a direct interface to user space applications (such as `/dev/tty` in Linux). In this case the top layer of the driver is called with a memory descriptor with references to the user space buffer in the call. The driver must perform buffer copies between user mapped buffer and an allocated kernel buffer. The remainder of the driver then operates on the kernel buffer. There are also techniques for mapping the user space buffer to kernel space; more details can be found in the NMAP section in Chapter 10, "Embedded Graphics and Multimedia Acceleration."

The case where memory buffers are originating from a user space application is an important one, and we will provide more details. A buffer that has been allocated to a user space process is a virtually contiguous buffer. The buffer has a base address and a length, and the length can be very large (as large as the system can allocate to a process depending on system resources). The memory management system (using the MMU) maps the large virtually contiguous buffer to a number of physical pages in memory. The buffer may or may not be physically contiguous. The user space buffer is represented as a list of physical pages. The device driver uses a system call to copy data from the user-mapped virtually contiguous buffer into kernel buffers. The kernel buffers themselves have a maximum contiguous size, although it is best to assume that the maximum contiguous kernel memory you can allocate is one page. In order for the copy to take place, the kernel must provide a kernel virtual mapping to allow the CPU to read the data and allocate a kernel buffer. Given that, the virtually contiguous user space data is copied into a number of kernel buffers. Linux kernel provides functions such as `copy_from_user(to_kernel_pointer, from_user_address, size)`. The function copies size bytes from the user address to the kernel address pointer. The function actually executes in the context of the user space process, in that the page table mappings for the user space pointer are valid.

Some operating systems (BSD and VxWorks) have optimized the exchange of network buffers through the provision of zero-copy memory buffers. In this case the application writes directly into the network buffer structure and can submit the packet to the stack without a copy operation.

Given that data elements within the kernel are composed of a list of physical pages, the operating systems often defines a construct for a *scatter gather list*. A scatter gather list is a mechanism defined and supported by an operating system to represent a list of data that is not physically contiguous. The scatter gather list is operating system–specific, and when available it should be used to pass data elements that are larger than the contiguous elements in the system (usually a page). The Linux kernel makes extensive use of scatter gather lists and defines structures and management functions in `/linux/include/scatterlist.h`. The TCP/IP stack incorporates a scatter gather list representation into the stack buffer known as an `SKBUFF`. The device driver must iterate through the scatter gather list and write to the devices' data registers or create device descriptors that point to the scatter gather list as it is submitted to the hardware. The scatter gather list is usually represented as an array of pointers to data elements, or alternately the scatter list can be represented as a linked list structure. The best structure depends on the access pattern of the driver/stack. The array-based approach is best if the CPU needs access to an element down the list (for example, the third buffer is the start of the IP packet in a packet list). However, since the maximum array size is often fixed, the linked list approach can support a very long list of buffers, but the list traversal can take some time. Figure 7.16 shows examples of both

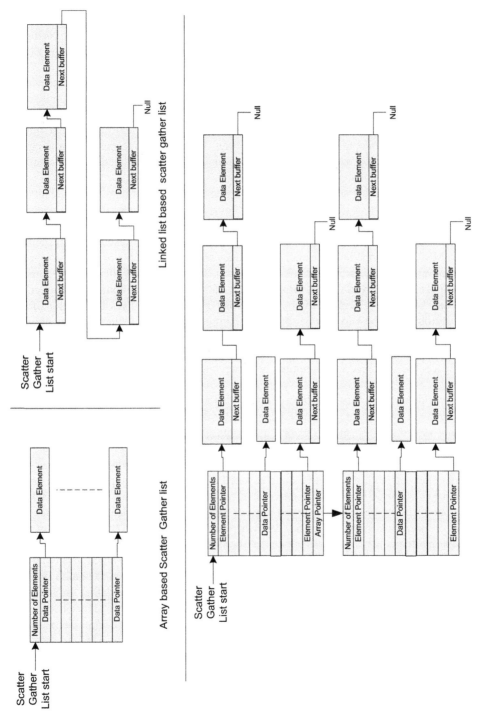

FIGURE 7.16

Scatter Gather Structures.

array-based and linked-list–based scatter gather lists and a combination structure used in Linux. The data payload pointed to by the data pointer should be viewed as logically contiguous data but is likely to be physically discontiguous.

The Linux scatter gather list is a combination of both an array and linked list. The determination of which format will actually be used is made at runtime by the design of the software using the scatter gather list.

Low-Level Data Path

There are two distinct aspects of the data path for most device drivers. At the lowest level, the device driver directly interacts with the registers and descriptors associated with the device. At the higher level, the device driver presents an interface to the operating system or to the applications.

The device driver is called with data to submit to the device; this is often called the transmit or device send call. The transmit function contains a pointer to the data to be transmitted. The data structure containing the data is directly accessible by the driver code; that is, the driver can access the data in the transmit call. The interaction model is dictated by the presence or absence of DMA capability in the device. For the simplest case, the device contains a memory-mapped first in, first out (FIFO) register. Data written to the register will be transmitted on the device interface. The device provides indications when the FIFO is full. When the FIFO is full, the device driver must not write to the FIFO and wait for the device to drain the FIFO. In the context of the transmit function, if data remain to be transmitted, the device driver may poll the device status register until the FIFO has room, at which point the driver writes data to the FIFO. If the driver send function does not return until all the data have been written to the FIFO, it is considered to be a blocking call. Return from the driver indicates all data have been sent to the FIFO. In some cases, the driver may also wish to ensure that the data have actually been drained from the FIFO and transmitted (for example, a flush). In this case the driver call blocks until the FIFO indicates that it is empty. Blocking calls such as the one described are often used during the early part of a boot phase; polling the device is not a recommended design when the operating system is up and running with interrupt support. Most devices can be configured to generate interrupts when different state changes occur in the FIFO. The common interrupt triggers would be transitions to Full, Empty, Nearly Full, and Nearly Empty, to avoid polling and support a nonblocking interaction with the device. Consider a call where we are asked to transmit 1 kb of data, with a FIFO depth of 32 bytes. The device driver first fills the FIFO until the FIFO is full (as indicated by the FIFO status). The transmit function then places the transmit data buffer into a deferral queue, with an indication of how much data remain to be transmitted. The device is configured to generate interrupts when the FIFO transitions to nearly empty (for example, the FIFO contains 8 bytes to be transmitted). The device interrupt handler inspects the interrupt status register and identifies that the device's Nearly Empty FIFO interrupt event is active. The interrupt handler consumes the buffer from the deferred transmit queue and writes data to the FIFO until it is full again. The buffer is then returned to the deferred transmit queue. These steps continues until all the data has been consumed from the buffer. At this point the buffer must be returned to the pool from which it was allocated, typically by calling a transmit complete callback with the buffer. As the transit call is now asynchronous, there may be additional transmit calls while the driver is still processing previous submissions. In this case, all the data requests are added to the tail of the deferred transmit queue. Using a Nearly Empty FIFO interrupt instead of a FIFO Empty interrupt improves the likelihood that the device will transmit data continuously, if the nearly empty threshold is configured to allow sufficient time for the CPU to be interrupted and to refill the FIFO before the FIFO goes empty. This can often be a critical factor depending on the device usage model. Figure 7.17 shows the interactions between the different elements described above.

In the case of the receive path, two patterns are frequently used; the first is driver polling and the second is to use interrupts to indicate when data is received (in some cases a hybrid of the two is used—see NAPI below).

In a device poll receive call, a receive function is called with a pointer to a buffer where the receive data is to be placed. The device status register is read to assess if there is any receive data available in the receive FIFO. If the status register indicates that the FIFO is not empty, then the device driver can read data from the receive FIFO and place it in the receive buffer. The receive function continues in a loop until the receive buffer is full or no more data are in the FIFO, at which point the polled receive function returns with an indication of how much data has been placed in the receive buffer. More likely, a device driver will be interrupt driven. In this case, a receive buffer must be provided to the low-level driver prior to the reception of data. When

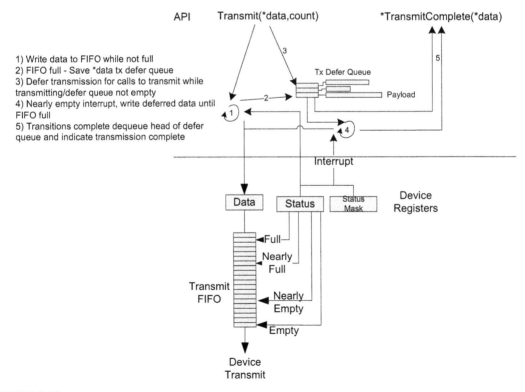

FIGURE 7.17

Low-Level Transmit Driver Path.

a buffer is provided, the device receive interrupts are enabled. For example, the device could be configured to generate an interrupt when the FIFO status transitions from Empty to Not Empty. The interrupt hander reads the receive FIFO until the FIFO is empty or the buffer provided is full. Once this occurs, the interrupt handler calls a receive callback function (previously registered function pointer) with a pointer to the buffer just populated with receive data. Figure 7.18 shows the sequence just described.

Direct Memory Access

The low-level data path described above assumed that the CPU wrote to and read from the data registers on the device. This is generally a poor use of the CPU, and the CPU utilization associated with device input/output increases substantially as the device interface speed increases. A device driver design that is reasonable to handle a low-speed UART (for example, 38,400 baud) is no longer viable at higher speeds (such as 4MBits). A more efficient design is to allow the device to read and write buffers directly in system memory. A device with the capability to directly read and write system memory is

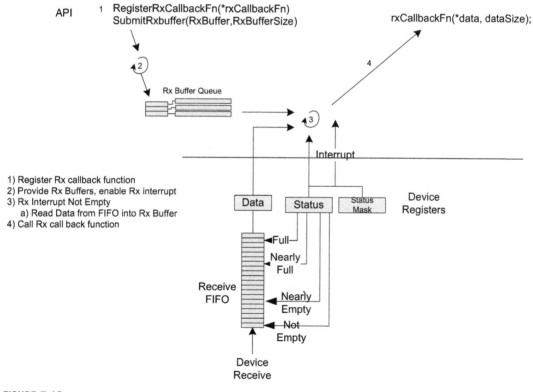

FIGURE 7.18

Low-Level Receive Data Path.

said to be Direct Memory Accessible (DMA) capable. Practically all modern I/O devices make use of DMA to read and write system memory. In this case the CPU writes the system physical address of the data to be transmitted or the physical address of a receive buffer into registers within the device. Instead of the CPU moving the data to and from the FIFO to memory, the device automatically moves the data and then provides an indication that the data transfer is complete—primarily through the generation of a transmit complete interrupt or a receive data interrupt.

The use of DMA for data payload is far more efficient than using the CPU to move data, but the CPU still interacts with the device writing buffers to the hardware transmit FIFO and writing receive buffer pointers to the receive FIFO hardware. Interacting directly with hardware device registers is typically a slower operation than reading or writing to system memory, so an extension of the technique above is to create transmit descriptor rings and receive descriptor rings in system memory and only read or write head/tail pointers when necessary. In most cases this reduces the level of direct CPU-to-device interaction, and system memory is used as an intermediary. The descriptors can be extended to provide commands to the transmit function or provide status information for data received. Figure 7.19 shows the memory structure and example contents for a transmit descriptor ring. Logically, the CPU is a producer of transmit data on the ring, and the device is a consumer of data from the descriptor ring. The device maintains the head pointer to indicate the current transmit buffer, and the CPU must write to the tail pointer when the CPU has updated the transmit descriptors in memory. The CPU may update multiple descriptors for each tail pointer update, and this greatly improves the efficiently of the device driver.

The following is a sample sequence of events to transmit data using a transmit descriptor ring.

1. The first step is to initialize the hardware registers with the base address in system memory of the descriptor ring, along with the number of descriptors. The device uses the number of descriptors to allow the hardware to automatically wrap around the head pointer.
2. For each payload to be transmitted, the driver must write to the transmit descriptor. The driver updates the payload data pointer, data length, and sets the data valid bit.
3. After one or more descriptors have been updated, the tail pointer must be updated in the device. This is carried out by writing the device tail pointer register. This write event triggers the hardware device to read (via DMA to system memory) the descriptors between the head of the ring and newly updated tail of the ring. For each valid descriptor (with buffer status = 1) the device will read the data pointed to by the transmit descriptor and transmit the specified (len) number of bytes on the interface.
4. For each descriptor consumed, the device updates the descriptor in system memory to indicate that the device has consumed the data and transmitted it on the interface. The internal device head pointer also moves to the next descriptor to be consumed.

Figure 7.19 shows a snapshot in time for the head, tail pointers, and descriptor status.

Memory Addresses

When a device supports DMA, the address in the descriptors and registers must be populated with an address from the perspective of the device. There are three separate address types in an embedded system that supports DMA.

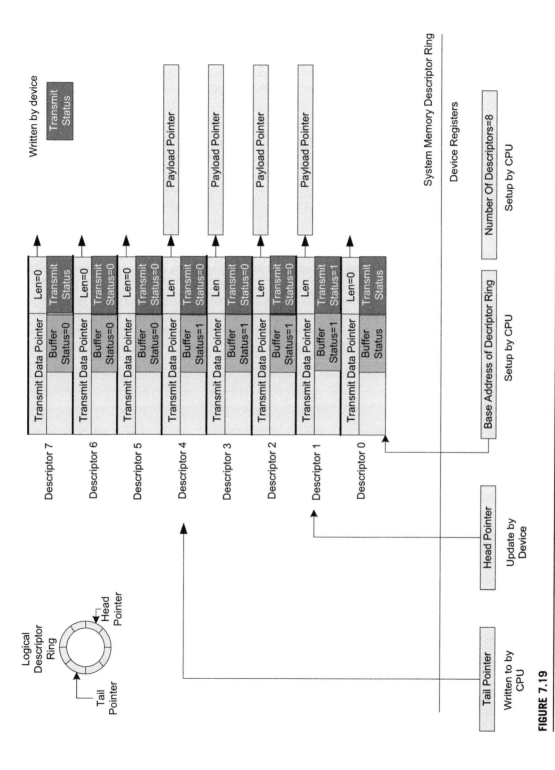

FIGURE 7.19

Example of a Transmit Descriptor Ring.

- *CPU virtual address*—This is the address of the buffer mapped to the current process space, usually that of the kernel. The device driver can read or write to these addresses.
- *Physical address*—This is the physical address in memory that corresponds to the virtual address. The MMU translates the CPU virtual address to the physical memory address when the CPU preforms a read or write.
- *Bus address*—This is the address generated by a device as DMA agent targeted at system memory.

The MMU translates between virtual and physical address (for CPU originated transactions) and the bus may convert between bus address and physical addresses (for device originated addresses). The device driver must convert any address that it writes to the device into a bus address. For example, consider the address of the base of the descriptor to be `virt_base_addr`, then the driver must use system functions to convert to an appropriate address, for example:

```
bus_addrs = phy_to_bus(cpu_virt_to_phy(virt_base_addr))
```

In many cases the physical addresses are mapped 1:1 to bus addresses, as is the case for PCIe buses on Intel platforms, but it is never a good idea to assume this. OS-provided conversion functions should always be used.

Given the frequency that device drivers may perform a virtual-to-physical-address translation for data payload, the system is often configured to have a simple mapping between the virtual and physical address for kernel space. This could be either a 1:1 mapping or, as in the case of Linux, a fixed offset between the two. Having a simple translation between the virtual address space and physical address space for the kernel makes conversion very efficient.

BUS DRIVERS

As you have seen in Chapter 4, there are a number of bus standards such as PCIe, USB, SMBus, and I2C. PCIe, USB, and SMBus all provide a mechanism to scan the bus at runtime and identify what devices are attached to the bus. This process is known as *enumeration*. The bus driver handles the enumeration of the bus and provides services to each of the devices that are attached to the bus. Each bus driver has its own pattern for supporting the attached devices. For example, a PCI bus driver performs the following steps:

- Scans the PCI configuration space for devices.
- Saves the device ID—a uniquely assigned number of the device manufacturer and specific device.
- Identifies the memory size requested by each of the base address registers (configurable chip selects) and allocates the memory space for the device.
- Assigns an interrupt(s) to the device.

Once the scan is complete, the drive initializes a device driver registered for the specific device ID. In the case of Linux the devices are probed and the `pci_dev` structure is provided, such as in the example below:

```
static int __devinit device_probe(struct pci_dev *pdev,
            const struct pci_device_id *ent);
```

The `pci_dev` structure provides many elements, but in the context of this discussion, the `resources` and `irq` entries are pertinent. The `resources` elements is a list of memory address assigned to the device. The `irq` is the interrupt vector assigned to the device (this may be shared/unique).

The bus driver provides an abstraction that allows the device to be written generically regardless of the resources allocated to the device. It allows the driver to be unaltered for devices that are actually incorporated into an SOC or on an external PCI bus.

NETWORKING

Most operating systems provide a networking stack of some kind. The most prevalent networking stack deployed is an Internet Protocol (IP) stack. The IP stack provides an application library to open/close connections to remote devices and send and receive data between the remote device. The application API is provided by a sockets library (usually BSD sockets). The APIs are consistent across nearly all platforms that provide an IP stack. Chapter 12, "Network Connectivity," provides more detail on networking.

The TCP/IP stack takes socket send and receive requests from the applications. The application may select either Transmission Control Protocol (TCP) or User Datagram Protocol (UDP). The protocol definitions are defined and maintained, along with many other networking protocol standards, by the Internet Engineering Task Force (IEFT). The protocols are identified by the RFC number. The original UDP RFC is RFC768, published in 1980.

TCP is a reliable streaming protocol with retransmission of data if it is lost across the network. UDP is an unreliable datagram protocol. The TCP/IP stack performs the required protocol level processing for the protocol type.

Aside

In embedded systems the UDP protocol is often used within systems to send messages between cards (within a single chassis). The application messages directly are mapped 1:1 to the datagram being transmitted. However, in many cases we would like to use a reliable datagram service; the Stream Control Transmission Protocol (IEFT RCF 3286) provides reliable ordered delivery of datagrams.

For outgoing packets the IP layer adds the IP header to the PDU and selects the appropriate network interface to submit the packet to. The outgoing network interface is identified by looking up the routing tables and the destination IP address for the packet. In some cases the PDU is also fragmented to PDUs that are no bigger than the Path Maximum Transmission Unit (PMTU). The PMTU is the minimum MTU of any link between the source and destination. The MTU is the maximum size in octets/bytes that a layer can forward. For example, the MTU on an Ethernet (802.3) interface is 1492 bytes (RFC 1191). Fragmentation is an expensive operation (particularly for the receive-side processing), and it is best to ensure that upper layers do not generate PDUs that require IP fragmentation.

For packets received from the network interface, the IP layer validates the header, identifies the appropriate protocol handler, and forwards the packet to the appropriate protocol hander (TCP/UPD/ICMP/other). The IP layer must reassemble any fragmented packets that arrive.

At the bottom of the stack are the network device drivers. The driver model used for networking interfaces is usually different from the generic OPEN/CLOSE/IOCTL driver model described above.

The network driver interacts with the protocol stack directly and does not generally provide any direct device interface. A network device driver is specific to the type of network interface (such as Ethernet or 802.11), the driver mode of the OS, and the network stack (such as IP). Figure 7.20 shows an overview of the stack and network interface drivers.

The following APIs are generally provided by a network driver:

- *Load/Unload*—These are services to load a dynamic driver. In many cases device driver loading is deferred until the hardware presence is established by a discovery process such as PCIe enumeration. In many cases, the network interfaces (LAN/wireless LAN) are separate devices connected to the SOC (via PCIe or USB) which makes dynamic loading useful.
- *Send/Packet Transmit*—This is a function that takes a buffer in the network stack format to be transmitted to on the network interface. The function typically populates a transmit descriptor in the network interface with a pointer to the buffer provided in the packet transmit call. The network interface sends the packet via DMA from the buffer at some point later. The transmit call does not wait for the packet to be transmitted and returns immediately.

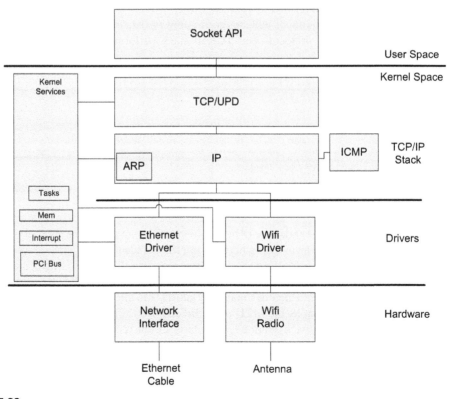

FIGURE 7.20

Network Stack and Device Drivers.

- *IOCTL*—I/O control interface is a generic control API for the driver. The IOCTL functions control behavior of the MAC such as setting the MAC address of the interface and getting device statistics such as packets transmitted/received.
- *Device Stop/Start*—These functions are used to enable or disable the device. When a device is stopped, no packets are transmitted or received. This capability is usually controlled by user space programs to bring the interface up or down.

On arrival of a packet on the network interface, the network device sends the packet via DMA into a receive buffer and interrupts the processor to indicate that a packet has arrived. The network driver then sends an event or notification to a deferred work task. When the deferred task wakes up to process the packet arrival event, it makes a call to submit the packet to the IP stack. The Linux kernel calls

```
netif_rx(struct sk_buff *skb)
netif_receive_skb (struct sk_buff *skb)
```

are used to send a packet from the driver up into the TCP/IP network stack. The function takes a pointer to an sk_buff buffer. An sk_buff buffer is a special buffer format used to carry packet data up and down the TCP/IP stack.

Buffer Management

Once the network interface has completed transmission of a packet, the network device generates an interrupt to indicate that the packet has been transmitted. The network device driver reads the transmit complete descriptor where a pointer to the buffer that was transmitted can be obtained. The driver usually frees the buffer back into a buffer pool. Similarly, in order to ensure that a buffer is available for receive packets, the device driver must populate the network interface receive buffer descriptors with buffers allocated from a buffer pool.

Some embedded systems have extensions to the socket APIs. For example, the socket library provided by FreeBSD and VxWorks provides an option to send and receive data from a user buffer without having to copy it into a kernel network buffer. This is known as a zero copy socket option, and it can improve performance for some embedded networking applications.

Polling Interface

In many cases, the network interface driver provides a mechanism to poll the network interface for received packets. The network stack may be set up to poll for network packets for two reasons. The first is to improve the overall performance of the device driver under varying packet arrival rates. When a low rate of packets arrives at the network interface, it is best for the network device driver to interrupt the processor when each packet arrives; in this case there is little delay in processing the packet that has arrived. If the network load is high and a burst of packets arrives with the minimum interpacket arrival time, it is often better to be interrupted on the arrival of the first packet and then to poll the interface a number of times before the packet related interrupts are re-enabled from the device. This has the effect of reducing the total number of interrupts processed for the bursty traffic. In some cases where the network traffic is at a sustained high rate, a scenario known as *live lock* can occur. Live lock in this case is when the CPU is spending all of the time servicing network receive interrupts but never has an opportunity to process the packets. The Linux stack implements a concept known as New API (NAPI) (http://www.linuxfoundation.org/collaborate/workgroups/networking/napi) to switch between inter-rupt driven operation and polled operation based on the network load. There are also interrupt moderation schemes developed for some network interfaces to help moderate the interrupt rate using inter packet timers and network traffic load.

The other reason to provide a network polling API implementation is to allow the network interface to be used as a debug interface when debugging the operating system. For example, you can connect to the Linux target system and use the GDB debugger to debug the kernel from a host machine across an Ethernet interface that supports the polling. Network interfaces that only operate with interrupts cannot be used for this purpose, as interrupts processing is prevented when a breakpoint is hit in the kernel.

Acceleration

In many modern network interfaces, the networking device can offload some of the work normally carried out by the IP stack. The simplest is TCP receive checksum offload. In this case the checksum for TCP/UDP checksum is validated by the network interface card. The network device descriptor indicates if the checksum is okay, in which case the driver indicates that the checksum need not be checked by setting a flag in the network packet buffer. With Linux the Sk_buff- >ip_summed flag is set to CHECKSUM_UNNCESSARY. Setting flags in Sk_buff is a common design pattern used in the network drivers to either defer work to the NIC for packets to be transmitted, or to indicate preprocessing/checking carried out on received packets.

STORAGE FILE SYSTEMS

File systems are predominantly used to provide an abstract mechanism to open and close or read and write to a storage device. The storage device may or may not be persistent. Many different file systems are implemented in modern operating systems, with a subset available for real-time operating systems. In a traditional desktop system such as Linux or Microsoft Windows, the operating system provides a mass storage file system that is applicable to a large mass storage device such as a magnetic hard disk or solid state drives. Windows provides the New Technology File System (NTFS) and FAT file system. Linux desktop distributions predominantly use EXT3/4 file systems at the time of writing. In embedded systems, there are many more, such as JFFS2, TFAT, CRAMFS, RAMFS, and INITFS (all of which we will describe later).

> Note
> The file system abstraction is also used to provide a logical namespace used to access device resources in kernel. Consider the Linux /dev/, /proc, and /sys pseudo file systems, which are mechanisms used to provide input/output and obtain information from the kernel and control functions within the kernel.

When an application performs a write to the file system, the file system must allocate blocks on the storage device and write the required contents into the blocks allocated on the storage device. This operation is typically an asynchronous operation from the perspective of the applications. The write call returns immediately (does not block the application) even though the data may not have been written to the device. The file system drivers will at some point reflect the write in the file system. There are many reasons to defer the actual writing, the primary one being performance. A sophisticated file system will consolidate file system requests from a number of applications concurrently, and it schedules (order) the requests with the purpose of maximizing the file system throughput. At the time of writing, there are four I/O scheduler options available (in Linux):

- No-op scheduler
- Anticipatory I/O scheduler (AS)
- Deadline scheduler
- Complete fair queuing (CFQ) scheduler

Given that updates to the file system occur asynchronously to the application, there are cases where the contents on the mass storage do not reflect the current logical state of the file system. At any point in time portions of the data being written to mass storage may still reside in CPU memory buffers or even in buffers within the storage device (in the drive itself). In cases where the storage media is going to be removed or the system is about to be restarted, it is critical to issue a synchronization request to the file system prior to such an event. The synchronization request flushes the data all the way out to the storage media, and the media is guaranteed to be consistent when the media is reinserted or the system restarts. I'm sure you have used the Windows option to "stop a USB device" prior to removal; this effectively ensures that any data contents still on memory are written out to the pen drive. I'm equally sure that you have at times simply removed the drive without taking the time to issue the request—and it has probably always worked, but there is a chance that the data are corrupted or, worse, the file system management structures are not consistent. In embedded systems, this could prevent a system from booting properly or an application getting incorrect data and failing to operate correctly, so it is particularly important to synchronize the file systems before shutdown, restarting, or media removal.

Two distinct file system types are in use today, journaling and non-journaling. A journaling file system maintains a record of updates or deltas to the existing state of the mass storage device. The updates, primarily to metadata, are carried out as transactions. Each transaction is an atomic operation to the file system, thus at any point the file system can be recovered to a consistent state. The journal updates are held on the storage device. When the file system is mounted the journal entries are applied to the file system baseline. This also occurs periodically during the operation of the file system. File systems with journaling capability such as EXT3 rely on a Journaling Block Device driver to provide transaction-based journaling capabilities to the underlying block devices.

A non-journaling file system such as the File Allocation Table 32 (FAT32), often used on USB pen drives, performs all updates directly to the file system management structures (such as file allocation tables). A journaling file system is more resilient to un-notified removal of device or power. The underlying structures are always consistent, and the worst case is loss of some transactions.

We should distinguish between file system consistency and ensuring that the contents of a file reflect all up-to-date application transactions. The journaling file system is very resilient and ensures consistency. However, it may lose the latest transactions depending on the scenario. In this case the application data may not have actually been made persistent on the device. There are transaction-based file systems in which the application writes a transaction that will be written as an atomic operation to the file system. The transaction will either complete in its entirety or none of the transaction will complete (if an error occurred). It allows the application to ensure data consistency by making sure the transactions are written atomically. The application can also ensure that the transaction has made its way to the mass storage device. Transaction file systems are EXT3, JFFS2, and YAFFS2.

In many embedded systems, flash-based file systems are required as the mass storage devices use flash memory. We mentioned in Chapter 4 two primary types of flash, NAND and NOR. There is still a preponderance of NOR-based flash where storage requirements are modest and reliability is paramount (many microcontrollers actually include on-die flash, and in such cases, it is generally NOR). There are two classes of file systems commonly used. The first is read-only compressed file systems, such as CRAMFS. CRAMFS is a simple file system that uses zlib compression routines to compress each file page by page. The file system can be accessed using normal file access routines, and random access is supported. A CRAMFS file system could be used to hold the root file system of an embedded system.

An alternative approach to providing the initial file system for a Linux kernel boot is to use INITRAMFS. This file system consists of an archive that is stored on the flash devices. The archive contains a gzipped cpio format image. This initial image is decompressed at startup to create a root file system (ROOTFS). The root file system is read-only, as any updates will not be written to the compressed archive. This root file system is ramfs. A ramfs file system is a RAM-resident file system with no backing store. It actually reuses much of the kernel's disk caching mechanisms.

Another file system to consider is a journaling flash file system such as Journaling Flash File System (JFFS2) or Yet Another Flash File System (YAFFS2). JFFS2 file systems operate by continuously writing to the "end" of the file system for wear-leveling purposes and as such is, strictly speaking, a log-structured file system. As the name of the first of these file systems suggests, these are file systems that support flash devices and use journaling. These flash file systems support both NAND and NOR devices. YAFFS2 provides the following features (http://www.yaffs.net/):

- NOR and NAND device support (although it appears to have been primarily designed for NAND devices)
- Wear leveling
- Fast booting from media
- Error correction for robust handling under power failure
- Small RAM footprint

To support flash file systems, a flash block driver is provided; this is a low-level interface that manages the blocks on the device. On a Linux system these are provided by MTD drivers.

Device Wear and Tear

In many embedded cases, the device will be operational for many, many years, having a life expectancy of perhaps greater than 10 years, depending on the application. In such cases, you should be cognizant of the file system activity and the resultant use of either magnetic-based media or flash devices. Where possible, the system should avoid frequent access to the mass storage device and alternatively either rely on RAM-based file systems or ensure that the applications only write to the storage devices periodically. Even with techniques such as wear leveling for solid state devices, they still have a finite number of cycles supported. If you have a device that supports 100 million cycles but performs a write every second, the device may fail in a little over three years.

Power Interactions

In embedded systems, many systems have a number of different voltages required for the platform. There are two scenarios that are important to comprehend in the design of the embedded system, both of which can have consequences to the robustness of the file system. The first is un-notified power removal. As we mentioned above, the file system or application data may not be consistent when the system restarts depending on the file system selected and what operations were being performed on that file system. In cases where resilience is absolutely required, the best approach is to avoid situations in which power can be removed from the CPU and storage device without notification. This is often accomplished by having a large capacitor and a circuit to sense the removal of the main voltage. The removal of the main supply triggers an interrupt (highest priority) to the processor. The CPU can then take the necessary operations to flush the file system data. The time available for such operations is typically very brief, as a capacitor, however large, would provide only a tiny time margin to sync the file system. In many cases, only critical file systems for platform boot are safeguarded using this mechanism. The other challenge in embedded systems is a topic known as brownout. Brownout occurs when the voltage level drops but is not completely removed. Since many systems require a number of different voltages in the system, the reduction in input voltages may cause each of the derived voltages to go out of specifications (although not all voltages go out of specification). This can cause file system consistency issues, if, for example, the flash voltage drops out but the CPU does not, or vice versa.

Figure 7.21 shows a brownout voltage diagram. It is important to validate and test your embedded system with both removal of power and brownouts while performing a significant number of file system transactions.

POWER MANAGEMENT

An ever-increasing responsibility of the operating system is to effectively manage power on the platform. Chapter 9, "Power Optimization," describes some of the overall principles in managing power. Although a number of techniques apply to changing the dynamic power of the system through changing the frequency and core voltage of the CPU, in many embedded cases, the designer is likely not willing to design a sufficient margin for the variable performance when the system is active. It is more likely that the system is designed to perform at a fixed high-performance point and to aggressively bring the system to a sleep state when there is no work to be done. In the case of the operating systems, this is usually determined by the behavior of the "idle" function. This is a function that is scheduled when there is no other high-priority work to be done. The thread may simply halt the CPU. A halt instruction typically puts the processor in a lower power state while waiting for the CPU to receive an interrupt and continue execution. In modern Intel architecture systems, the idle function uses the MWAIT instruction. The MWAIT instruction takes a CPU/platform-specific hint to the targeted sleep state of the CPU. An embedded system designer should be aware of exit latencies associated with CPU sleep states; in general, the deeper the sleep state, the longer the latency to wake up. The operating system may provide configuration of these capabilities. An example of dynamically controlling the suggested sleep state of the CPU can be found in the Linux IA-32 idle driver.

Many desktop-based operating systems support a formal transition to a suspended state, where all state information is saved into DRAM (self-refreshed) and all other aspects of the system are powered

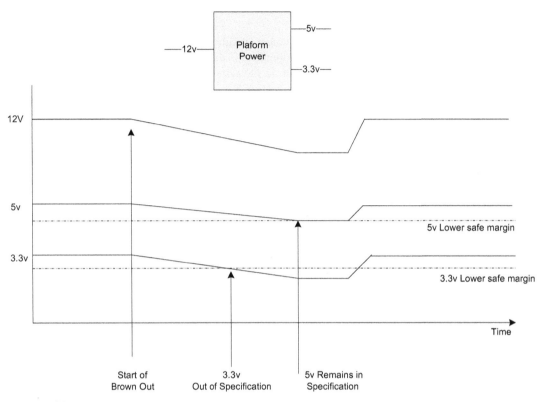

FIGURE 7.21

Brownout Events.

down: CPU, caches, and all devices not requiring monitoring for a wakeup event. This state is known as S3 on Intel platforms. When the wakeup event occurs, the operating system resumes execution and sends a notification event to each driver to reprogram the devices. Such a capability is rarely used in embedded systems where they are expected to perform the application function at all times. A further extension of the suspend to RAM (S3) operating system state is hibernation. Hibernation is similar in principal to S3 except that the contents of DRAM are saved into a hibernation file on a mass storage device. Once this is complete, power can be totally removed from the system (except for any wakeup devices, such as support for wake-on-LAN from the NIC card).

Device drivers also play a part in the power management of the system. Each device driver may be asked to place a device in a particular power state; the driver must perform the action and respond to the kernel when the task is complete.

In addition to the basic technique of controlling the idle function of the file operating system, some platforms actively manage the device's state (power and clock) depending on the current usage of the device. This is an active topic in embedded and especially mobile systems. However, few standardized approaches allow the operating system to automatically manage the overall system at this level of detail (at the time of writing).

REAL TIME

The real-time behavior of an operating system is critical in many embedded platforms. The real-time behavior is usually defined by having a deterministic bounded time from an external event such as an interrupting device to the execution of the real-time handler (task or thread) and the action resulting from the original event. This may be an output or simply data analysis of the incoming data. Figure 7.22 shows the flow from hardware event to task.

Many system aspects contribute to the latency from interrupt event to the execution of the thread to handle the interrupt.

Device Interrupt Delivery

In modern embedded systems the delivery of interrupts to the CPU is not likely to simply consist of wires with the SOC or platform. The interrupts are likely to follow an internal path and coexist with other memory-targeted traffic from the device generating the interrupt. This is particularly the case when devices are presented as logical PCI devices within the SOC. Given that the interrupt traffic is mixed with traffic from other devices, there may be congestion in the path. This can lead to increased jitter and non-determinism in the interrupt delivery. This can be alleviated by ensuring that traffic from devices that a require real-time response is allocated a prioritized channel through the fabric. This is usually controlled by registers assigned to the device.

In some designs, the interrupts are wired directly from the device to the interrupt controller. In this case there is no opportunity for delays in the I/O fabric. In many cases a device that has generated an interrupt has also generated memory write transactions (for example, DMA of data from the device

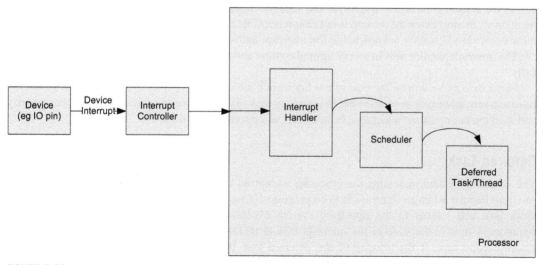

FIGURE 7.22

Interrupt Delivery to Thread Flow.

into memory). If the SOC device hardwires the interrupts, the processor may start to handle the interrupt before the memory has actually been updated (for example, when the memory write transaction has been delayed in the fabric). In this case, you should perform a device read; the data returned from the read will stall the processor until the previous data writes from the device have been pushed through the I/O fabric. The net result is that both wired or message-based interrupts have similar behavior if the interrupt handler needs to wait for system memory to be updated.

An additional consideration for an SOC design is the requirement to support multiple processors. In this case interrupt message-based interrupts are easily extended to steer interrupts to a specific core.

Processor Interrupt Handler

The processor only starts to process an interrupt on an instruction boundary; on most platforms instructions have variable execution delays and can add to the jitter associated with the transition to the first instruction of the interrupt handler. Once the interrupt has been delivered to the processor, the processor has to be in a state where the interrupt can be processed. The processor may have the interrupts disabled or processing an interrupt. If the interrupts are disabled, then all interrupts are blocked until the processor re-enables interrupts.

When the processor is processing the interrupt, the processor is generally not re-interruptible. The interrupts can be re-enabled to allow higher-priority interrupts to interrupt the processor.

Once the processor has accepted the interrupt, the processor transfers control to the vector associated with the interrupt. This is known as the interrupt handler. The interrupt handler may require the memory management unit to fetch translations via page walking, which can add to the delay/jitter in executing the interrupt handler.

The interrupt handler should perform the minimal processing possible and defer as much of the device processing to some form of deferred task. There are many reasons for this, the first is that it allows the system to re-enable interrupts and accept a higher priority interrupt if one is pending; as we mentioned, in most cases the system is not re-interruptible while in an interrupt handler. The handler in most cases should simply acknowledge the interrupt and send an event to trigger the differed task.

The interrupt handler runs in a very limited context and can access only a small subset of the kernel calls.

In the case of VxWorks, the equivalent interrupt handler might post an event to a message queue, release a semaphore, or send an event to a waiting task. The task would typically be a higher priority and start executing as soon as the scheduler has an opportunity to do so.

Deferred Task

The operating system maintains the processor exception table and calls the registered device driver interrupt handler when an interrupt is to be processed. Once the interrupt handler signals to a deferred work task and returns to the operating system exception handler, the operating system has an opportunity to save the state of the interrupt task to its task control block and schedule the highest-priority ready task. If the priority of the deferred task is high enough, then the operating system scheduler will schedule the execution of the deferred interrupt task immediately.

Figure 7.23 shows the simplest Linux interrupt handler, which simply triggers the execution of a deferred function to perform the subsequent processing for the device.

```
interrupt_handler(int irq,void *dev_id, struct pt_regs
*regs)
{
  tasklet_schedule(&int_tasklet);
  int_count++; /* count interrupts */
  return IRQ_HANDLED;
}
```

FIGURE 7.23

Interrupt Handler.

In an RTOS such as VxWorks, the deferred task can be any system task. The task is responsible for servicing the device. Linux has a number of specific capabilities that are introduced to provide a deferred interrupt processing interrupt context. This is known as a *tasklet*. The tasklet is a software interrupt context and it is scheduled by the operating system (once requested by the interrupt handler). Each specific tasklet is guaranteed not to run in parallel even on an SMP system. The system can continue process interrupts while executing a tasklet.

RTOS Characteristics

A real-time operating system or a general-purpose operating system with real-time extensions has design attributes to improve the determinism for each of the phases above. The key aspects that make an RTOS real-time are twofold; the first is to ensure that the processor can accept an interrupt for the vast majority of time, that is, there is almost no time where the operating system cannot accept an interrupt. The second is to ensure very low cycle time for the scheduler to schedule any deferred workload. This requires that the scheduler be very efficient. A dedicated RTOS such as VxWorks or Nucleus is designed from the ground up to ensure such behavior.

In many cases designers wish to make use of a general-purpose Linux and extend it to provide real-time behavior. The behavior extends the scheduler to allow the creation and scheduling of real-time user space threads. The capabilities allow for millisecond scheduling of real-time threads, which is acceptable for many applications.

In many embedded systems an executive is run underneath the full-featured operating system. Xenomai (http://www.xenoami.org) is such an implementation and is described below.

Real-Time Adjuncts

Xenoamai is a real-time framework for Linux. It is based on an abstract real-time operating system core. The core provides a basic set of generic interfaces. This core RTOS is skinned with an API personality that matches many preexisting commonly used interface such as POSIX. Applications written using the traditional POSIX calls under user space Linux can be migrated to the POSIX APIs provided by a POSIX skinned Xenoamai and run as a special higher-priority thread in the context of Xenoamai.

A Xenoamai-based system runs two kernels on the system. The Xenoamai real-time kernel schedules its real-time threads using the Xenoamai scheduler. When no real-time threads are ready to run in the Xenoamai kernel, then the traditional Linux kernel run.

In order for the Xenoamai kernel to ensure deterministic real-time response to interrupts, Xenoamai requires special support by the kernel. The kernel does not support this option by default and must be patched. The patch is known as the Interrupt pipe (I-pipe) patch.

A number of products also provide real-time behavior to Microsoft Windows. These products generally take ownership of the interrupts in the system and provide an environment where application code can execute directly as a consequence of the interrupt trigger.

LICENSING

It might seem strange to include a section on licensing in an operating system chapter, but we think a brief discussion is warranted, especially in the context of embedded systems.

In many systems, you may elect to purchase software to be included in your product. This could range from the operating system itself to special-purpose libraries or applications themselves. Such software is delivered under a license. The license dictates how the software may be used and or redistributed. Let's discuss proprietary and open source licenses.

If you purchase software for inclusion in your product, it may be provided in either binary or source form. Regardless of the form in which you received the software, it will have an accompanying license that specifies what you can do with it. The most common is that you can include it in your product but you cannot redistribute the source code. Depending on how you purchased the software, you may have made a single buyout payment where you do not have to pay for each individual instance you ship as part of your product, or you may have to make a royalty payment for each copy shipped as part of your product. It will be important for you to have processes in your software development to ensure you track the use of such software. These licenses are known as proprietary licenses and each one is different.

Another class of libraries is known as open source licenses. Many such licenses exist but the most prevalent are BSD License, Apache License, and Gnu Public Licenses (GPLv2, LGPLv2, and GPLv3). The BSD and Apache License generally allow you to reuse the code in your own system and do not make any redistribution demands on you, the user of the code. You may be required to mention the fact that you have included the software in your product. If you make changes or updates to such software you are not required to share these changes with an external party.

Gnu Public License 2 (GPL2) is a license that you can include in your product but with the requirement that you mention that you have incorporated the code in your product, and should you make any change to the source, you are also required to provide that source code to anybody who requests it. This requirement is triggered when you deliver the software or product including the code to a third party. Depending on how you link any GPL software into your product, you may also be required to redistribute the source code of your own software. In general, if you are linking to any GPL software you should pay particular attention. There is also a license known as LGPL, which is the same as GPL in the requirement to redistribute any changes you make to the GPL code in source form, but you are not required to redistribute your software if you simply link to the LGPL code. The attribute where linking GPL code to other code triggers the requirement to also release the source code of your code is known as viral license. You should also consider the implications to the entire system. Perhaps you have purchased a software library under a proprietary license. You then download a piece of open source code released under GPL license. If you link the entire software together into a monolithic application (which would not be unusual in embedded systems), then you may have triggered the requirement to publish the source code of the proprietary software—clearly, you probably don't have such rights.

This is an important area. You don't want to find that you have an issue blocking the shipment of your product just when you want to release it.

This is just an overview—don't consider it to be legal advice on this topic. You should make sure you comprehend your company's interpretation of each software license that applies to your software and external software you plan on incorporating into the system.

Embedded Linux

This chapter provides an overview of the Linux capabilities you should be familiar with in order to develop embedded Linux systems. It covers aspects such as cross-development tool chains, configuring and building the Linux kernel, development of a simple character device driver and provides an overview of some key kernel services that can be used within your device drivers.

TOOL CHAIN

In order to build the operating system and applications, you need a tool chain. The tool chain provides the assembler, compiler, and linker, along with a number of other utilities needed to develop a Linux-based system.

The most common tool chain used in Linux systems are the GNU tools. The compiler is provided by GNU Compiler Collection (GCC) (http://gcc.gnu.org/), and the assembler, linker, library, and object manipulation tools are provided by the GNU `binutils` project (http://www.gnu.org/software/binutils/). These tool chains are available in source form but in many cases are also available in binary form. It is simple to install GNU toolchains on a Linux desktop distribution. Desktop distributions include a software package manager such as `apt` for debian-based hosts or yum for rpm type distributions. The command `sudo apt-get install gcc` will install the IA-32 GCC binary tool chain for a debian/Ubuntu-based system.

When you install a tool chain as shown above, you are downloading a binary version of the tool chain from a repository. The binaries were configured and built from a source for the target system you are downloading to. This build process and hosting is carried out by the repository maintainer. Normally, the tool chain being installed has been configured to compile and build applications with the same environment (processor type, 32-/64-bit, and so on) as the host downloading the tool chain.

Let's take a moment to define host and target. The *host* machine is the machine you develop your applications on. In most cases today that will be an IA-32-based machine running a desktop distribution of Linux such as Fedora/Centos, Ubuntu, or SUSE/OpenSuse. In most examples used in the text, we have used an Ubuntu desktop distribution (with no real rationale or preference). The *target* device is the actual embedded device that you are developing the software for. The device could be based on IA-32, ARM™, MIPS™, PowerPC™, or any of the other CPU architecture supported by Linux. When the host and target architecture are the same, you are said to be doing *native development*; however, the target platform architecture does not have to be the same as the host platform architecture (for example, CPU IA-32). When the host and target platforms differ, you are said to be doing *cross-development*. In this case the tool chain that you download and run on your host must be a specialized version capable of executing on the host CPU architecture but building for the target CPU architecture. All of the GNU tools support both native host development and cross-development configurations. If your target embedded device is IA-32 and your host is IA-32, it is still advisable to create a tool chain dedicated to your target and not to rely on your host tools chains. It is convenient for early development, but can cause issues later in the development cycle.

Note

When you develop and release an embedded system, you would normally be very diligent about using a source code control system. At the point of release, you should tag the source code with a particular version. You will also be expected to rebuild the target image at a later point (to fix bugs and such). To recreate the target image, you will need to recover every aspect that went into creating the target image; that includes sources, binary libraries, and even the tool chain that you used to create the image. To facilitate that, you should also always archive the tool chain used at the time of release. If you rely on the host-based tool chains, you may have upgraded to a new version of Linux and a corresponding new tool chain. Should this occur, you will not be able to recreate the exact image you previously shipped; in some cases it may not even compile again. A number of open-source source code control systems are available, such as GIT, Subversion, Mercurial, and CVS.

Getting the Tools

You can download the source code for `binutils` and `gcc` and build the tool chain yourself. This can often be very tricky and takes many separate stages (consider the problem of creating a compiler without first having a compiler). There are a number of scripts that greatly simplify the generation of the tool chain. At the time of writing, the `crosstool-NG` is a good option if you just require a tool chain. It cross-builds the tool chain for all architectures supported by GCC. The `ct-ng menuconfig` line is where you select the target CPU architecture. Below is a Mercurial source code control command to get the source from the source repository system.

```
>hg clone http://crosstool-ng.org/hg/crosstool-ng
>./configure --prefix=/some/place>make
>make install
>export PATH="${PATH}:/some/place/bin"
>cd /your/development/directory
>ct-ng help
>ct-ng menuconfig
>ct-ng build
```

There are four key attributes of the target tool chain that must be selected:

- The target CPU architectures (for example, IA-32, ARM)
- The application binary interface (ABI)/calling conventions (for example, fastcall, X.32, System V AMD64 ABI convention, and EABI)
- Object format (for example, ELF)
- Target operating system (for example, bare metal/Linux). This is important for calling conventions used to interact with the system.

The output of the build process is placed in your home directory in an x-tools folder. Each tool chain that you select is placed in a configuration specific folder. For example, a generic IA-32 tool chain is placed in the ~/x-tool/i386-unknown-elf/ folder, and a generic ARM tool chain is placed in ~/x-tools/arm-unknown-eabi folder. In addition to the target architectures, the target application binary interface must also be selected for the tool chain to use. The ABI defines all semantics associated with the construction of binary objects, libraries, interfunction calling mechanisms, calls to operating system services, register usage, and the like.

There are two versions of ABIs in use on IA-32 systems, a 32-bit and a 64-bit version. The 32-bit version of standard can be found at http://www.sco.com/developers/devspecs/abi386-4.pdf and the 64-bit version http://www.x86-64.org/documentation/abi.pdf.

> **Note**
>
> For many years, IA-32-based processors have supported two ABIs, the 32-bit and 64-bit ABI. Work is under way to develop a hybrid of the two ABIs (called X32) to maximize the use of registers in a 64-bit CPU but avoid much of the porting difficulties when porting applications from 32-bit to 64-bit environments. When using the X32 ABI, all ints, longs, and pointers are restricted to 32 bits, even though the code will execute on a 64-bit machine. Many of the porting difficulties between 32-bit and 64-bit are as a result of the type size change. There can be a reluctance to migrate to 64-bit, particularly since the traditional advantages of moving to 64-bit do not apply to many embedded systems. In the case of IA-32, however, there are far more registers available in 64-bit mode. The X32 ABI maximizes the use of all processors' registers in the 64-bit-enabled CPU. The OS itself must be run in 64-bit mode to take advantage of this ABI. Kernel updates and so on can be found at https://sites.google.com/site/x32abi/documents. Intel® Atom™ processors support both 32-bit and 64-bit modes.

The default ARM tool chain application binary interface is the Embedded Application Binary Interface (EABI). It defines the conventions for files, data types, register mapping, stack frame and parameter passing rules. The EABI is commonly used on ARM and PowerPC CPUs. The ARM EABI specification can be found at http://www.arm.com.

The primary object format is defined by the Tool Interface Standard – Executable and Linking Format (ELF) (http://refspecs.freestandards.org/elf/elf.pdf.) The standard is composed of books that define the generic ELF format, along with extensions of processor architectures and target operating systems.

In some cases, there is no target operating system specified or used; this is in effect a generic target. Most tool chains support a non-OS-specific processor-specific target option. This is sometimes known as *bare metal*.

Tools Overview

The tools used/required in embedded systems go beyond the traditional compiler and linker. There are a number of cross-development tools generated that are part of the GCC family, as shown in Table 8.1. A review follows of the capabilities of each tool and what each is used for.

The most commonly used programs for an embedded developer are set in boldface in the table, namely, ar, as, gcc, ld, and objdump.

Once you have acquired the appropriate tools, make sure you set the path to them and archive a copy when you release your software.

Table 8.1 Cross-Tool Chain Programs.

Executable	Description
addr2line	Converts an address into a file name and file line number. It uses debug information to figure out the file name/line number from the executable. This is very useful for debugging crashes, as it can be used to narrow down and find the cause.
ar	Creates, modifies, and extracts from archives. An archive is a collection of objects or libraries. It provides a simple way to distribute a large number of objects/libraries in a single file.
as	The GNU assembler. The assembler can be used natively and is used to assembly the output of the GCC compiler.
C++filt	Demangles C++ and Java symbols. C++ and Java languages provide function overloading. This demangles the auto-generated (managed) names produced by the compiler into a human-readable form.
cpp	The C preprocessor, the MACRO preprocessor used by the C compiler prior to compilation. It expands macros, definitions, and so on in the code. The C preprocessor can also be used as a standalone tool.
gcc	The GNU C and C++ compiler. The default invocation of cc performs preprocessing, compilation assembly, and linking to generate an executable image.
gcov	Coverage testing tool. Use this tool to analyze your programs, create more efficient code, and discover untested portions of code (from http://gcc.gnu.org/onlinedocs/gcc/Gcov-Intro.html#Gcov-Intro).
gdb	The GNU debugger. It can be used for application/user space and kernel space debugging; it can also be used to communicate with target debug hardware such as JTAG ICEs. IDE wrappers such as DDD also exist to improve usability,
gprof	Display call graph profile data. Profiling allows you to examine the amount of time spent in certain functions and frequency of function calls being made.
ld	The GNU linker. The linker combines objects and archives, relocates their data, and resolves symbol references. A map file of the resulting output can be generated and is very useful in understanding the layout of the application.
nm	Lists all the symbols from objects.
objdump	Displays information from object files: `objdump -S <file>` dumps the entire object and displays the disassembly object and where possible interleaves this with the source code; `objdump -s vmlinux` generates a useful file for debugging kernel oops (at least for the statically linked kernel elements).
ranlib	Generates an index to the contents of an archive and stores it in the archive.
readelf	Displays information about ELF files, similar to objdump but displays additional information.
size	Lists the size of sections and to the total size of an object/executable. The sections are text, data, and bss. The text section is where the code resides, data is where global and static variables that are program initialized such as `char str[] = "hello world"` are stored, and bss are uninitialized variables, such as a global or statics that are not initialized or initialized to zero. The startup code for an application clears the bss section.
strings	Displays any human-readable strings from a file. For an executable or object, it displays strings in the code and any symbol strings in the object.
strip	Removes symbol information from object files.

ANATOMY OF AN EMBEDDED LINUX

There are a number of components within an embedded Linux system. The focus of this discussion will be on the aspects that an embedded developer is most likely to interact with.

The first key component is the Linux kernel itself. The source code for the Linux kernel is always available from http://www.kernel.org. The site contains both mature and bleeding edge versions of the kernel. In most cases you should pick the latest mature kernel to start your work. The kernel source tree includes all the code for the kernel itself along with device drivers and platform support code. Prior to selecting the kernel version to use you should review the major kernel features (by reading the kernel mailing lists and so on) to ensure that the major kernel features you wish to use are in the current version. Generally speaking, embedded systems are not developed using all the latest and greatest kernel features, but there could be a specific item you wish to ensure is available.

If your platform is very new, the drivers for your platform may not actually be in the mature branches of the source tree, and you may have to choose a kernel version that is a little less mature. In general, device drivers are developed and submitted for inclusion in the kernel source tree using the latest kernel version. If you choose to develop your platform on an older kernel version, you may have to "backport" the driver from the staging or later kernel versions to the one you choose. In most cases, your software development is likely to remain on the same kernel version for quite some time. In some cases there are bugs in the kernel that are discovered and fixed in later kernel versions. You should track the major bug lists/reports for the kernel to ensure that your system does not ship with a known serious bug or security issue. You should make the same changes (backport) to your kernel version (if it is possible) or upgrade. Clearly, the closer you are to shipping your embedded system, the less churn you can introduce into your system, so selective backporting is best as you approach product release.

Although the entire codebase (source code) is free to download and use, in the context of product delivery and maintenance, an embedded project team should dedicate resources to the selection and constant tracking of the kernel. Building your own kernel and maintaining it internally for your product use is known as "role your own". In some projects, you may choose to go with an operating system provider such as MontaVista, TimeSys, or Wind River. There are many aspects to the decision of whether to "roll your own" (RYO) or select a commercial offering. A lot will depend on where you and your team need to focus your resources. You should be aware that the traditional desktop distributions such as Ubuntu, Fedora, and SUSE are generally not well suited to an embedded system.

We touched on device drivers and platform support above. If you are using a device (such as a wireless chipset or SOC) that has been in the market for some time, the driver is most likely obtained directly from the kernel source tree. In some cases, you may have to obtain the driver from a silicon device manufacturer. This would be from the vendor's site or other hosting locations such as SourceForge. Failing that, or if you are developing your own hardware, you will have to develop the device drivers yourself. Once you have developed a driver for a target hardware device, you may elect to *upstream* the driver. This is a process where you submit the driver to the appropriate kernel mailing list to be vetted and approved by the subsection maintainer for inclusion. It is strongly advisable to start this process well in advance of designing your driver. There are many criteria that the upstream maintainer may apply to code that they accept; it's not advisable to go off and create a sophisticated device driver in a silo and then attempt to throw it upstream. Do your homework, read the mailing lists, look for design patterns in previously submitted/accepted drivers, and engage with the subsystem maintainers. There are a lot of long-term advantages if you upstream the driver: the code is automatically distributed with the kernel, and you may get help maintaining the driver when the kernel is updated to a subsequent revision.

Once you have the kernel and appropriate device drivers for your platform, you will need to decide on a root file system. The root file system contains the user space applications and libraries, services daemons, and initialization scripts/programs that your embedded Linux system will need. The basis format of a root file system is described below.

Much of the user space applications and libraries are packaged up using a package manager. There are two main types of package formats/tools at this time: Debian (DPKG) and Redhat (RPM). Each format allows you to combine a number of target files together and distribute them as a single entity. The package format includes details such as version, contents, and critically dependences on other packages. You can get a sense of the number of pages in the desktop build by entering >dpkg --get-selections in an Ubuntu system. At the time of writing, this command listed 1477 packages installed in an Ubuntu 11.04 release. Each of the packages describes the files associated with the package. Installing the package will install all of the files in the package in the corrected locations as specified by the package. In addition, the package manager ensures that critical dependencies are also installed if possible. For example, the bash shell output is shown below.

```
>dpkg --listfiles bash (simplified output)
/bin/bash
/etc/skel
/etc/skel/.bashrc
/etc/skel/.profile
/etc/skel/.bash_logout
/etc/bash.bashrc
/usr/share/man/man7
/usr/share/man/man7/bash-builtins.7.gz
/usr/bin/bashbug
/usr/bin/clear_console
/bin/rbash
/bin/sh
/usr/share
/usr/share/doc
/usr/share/doc/bash
/usr/share/doc/bash/CHANGES.gz
```

Even the simplest package such as bash includes many files that you would not need in an embedded system. Embedded systems should only include the capabilities needed for the function of the embedded system (and some occasional debug/diagnostics capabilities).

Each package itself may have a dependency on other packages. An easy way to visualize these dependences on Ubuntu is using a combination of debtree and dot. The following command generates a png file (shown in Figure 8.1) for the component bash: (You should try the command on more complex packages such as bluez).

```
debtree bash | dot -Tpng -Obash.png
```

Building a file system with the required packages and all of the associated dependences requires a deep knowledge of the system; it can be challenging to ensure that the entire system created is consistent. For embedded systems it is often a requirement to be able to reproduce all binaries in the system that ships in the system. This involves using the source code version of a package and generating

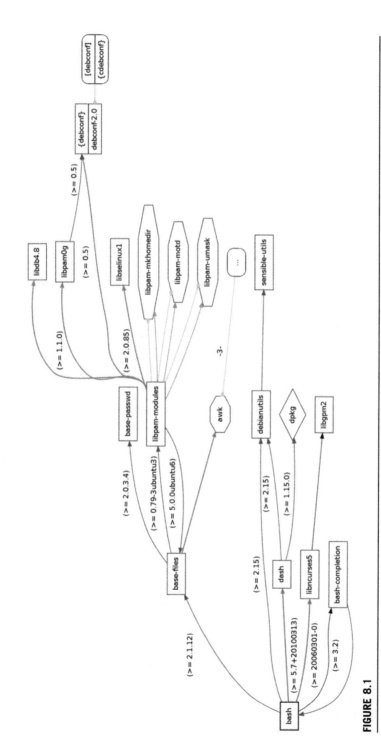

FIGURE 8.1

Package Dependencies for the Bash shell – Bash Package.

the binary package. You may already be familiar with installing binary packages on Linux systems. However, in this case a third party has taken care of building the binary packages from the source. It's a more difficult challenge to have to configure and rebuild every binary/object used in the system.

As you can see, the selection and development of an embedded system from scratch is a very challenging task. Luckily, a number of projects have been created to simplify the development and use of Linux in embedded platforms. These are not actual Linux distributions, but they allow you to tailor and define the contents of your embedded system with very fine granularity. The following are some key open source projects in use:

- Buildroot (http://buildroot.uclibc.org/) is a set of makefiles and patches that makes it easy to generate a complete embedded Linux system.
- The Yocto Project™ (http://www.yoctoproject.org) is an open source project that helps you create a custom Linux-based system. The Yocto Project is a workgroup under the Linux foundation (http://www.linuxfoundation.org/collaborate/workgroups/yocto).
- OpenEmbedded (http://www.openembedded.net) is a build framework for embedded Linux. It also allows developers to create a complete Linux distribution for embedded systems. At the time of writing, the Yocto Project and OpenEmbedded projects have converged on common build tools and core package metadata, and have some shared governance.

There also more formally supported/funded projects such as the Linaro project (http://www.linaro.org).

These projects allow you build embedded systems. In all cases they provide a wide range of board support packages that include all the required drivers for a number of existing embedded platforms. The tools also help in the creation of the root file system needed to run a Linux system.

After having acquired some insight into developing an embedded system using Linux, you should consider the most expedient path to creating your baseline system. You should also consider commercial offerings of embedded Linux distributions, where there are defined support options.

BUILDING A KERNEL

Although you may use some tools such as the Yocto Project to build your target platform images, it is a good idea to understand the underlying steps involved in configuring and building the actual kernel.

Kernel Build

Building the Linux kernel from source is a relatively straightforward process. You must first download the entire source tree for the Linux kernel. The kernel source tree consists of all the source code for the kernel and device drivers for all supported processor architectures. The original kernel was developed to support 32-bit IA-32-based systems (starting with the 80386). At this point it supports all Intel architectures from the 80486, Intel Atom, Intel Core™ family, and Intel Xeon™—in both 32-bit and 64-bit modes. The kernel itself is remarkably portable, and at the time of writing the kernel source tree supports the following systems in additional to the IA-32-based platforms: Alpha™, AXP™, Sun Spark™, Motorola 68000™, PowerPC, ARM, Hitachi SuperH™, IBM S/390/ MIPS, HP PA-RISC™, AMD IA-32-64™, ASOC CRIS™, Renesas M32R™, Atmel AVR32™, Renesas H8/300™, NEC V850™, Tensilca Xtensa™, and Analog Device Blackfin™ architectures.

Kernel Steps
1. Download the kernel source directly from kernel.org. You should pick the latest stable, then un-compress and use tar to extract the kernel.
```
> bunzip2 linux-2.6.38.4.tar.bz2
> tar -xvf linux-2.6.38.4.tar
> cd linux-2.6.38.4
> ls
 arch Documentation init lib README   sound block drivers ipc MAINTAINERS REPORTING-
BUGS tools COPYING firmware Kbuild Makefile samples usr CREDITS fs Kconfig mm scripts
virt Crypto include kernel net security
```

In addition to specifying the processor architecture that the kernel supports, specific platforms or boards are also supported in the source tree. In general, the vast majority of IA-32-based platforms are supported by default (primarily due to the platform level consistency of all IA-32 platforms). The IA-32 processor-specific source is primarily found in `linux-2.6.38.4/arch/IA-32`. For non-IA-32 architecture, the source tree usually contains a directory entry for the SOC along with board-specific variants. For example, the XScale IPX400 BSP code is primarily located in the `linux-2.6.38.4/arch/arm/mach-ixp4xx/`.

Another key directory in the kernel tree is the `linux-2.6.38.4/drivers` tree. This portion of the source tree provides device drivers. Depending the architecture, the drivers required to support an SOC device may be in the driver tree area or within the platform directories. Figure 8.2 shows a selection of the kernel source tree most likely to be updated for platform or processor changes.

Note
There are a number of very useful Linux code cross-reference web sites such as http://lxr.linux.no/linux/ and http://lxr.free-electrons.com/source/. Such sites can be used to help navigate the kernel source tree.

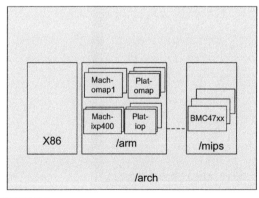 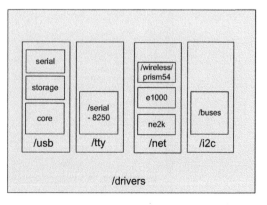

FIGURE 8.2

Sample Directories in the Kernel Tree.

Kernel Options

There is a wide range of kernel configuration items that can be selected prior to the build phase. The build system is controlled by the contents of a `.config` file in the root directory of the kernel tree. The configuration file itself can be generated by issuing the `make menuconfig` command. The configuration items can be selected using the menus presented.

Kernel Steps
2. Run the tool to create the kernel .config:
```
make menuconfig
ls .config
.config
```

Figure 8.3 shows the initial screen for the `make menuconfig`. If you simply select exit, the command will generate the default kernel configuration. There are other graphics variants that you can use to configure the kernel `make xconfig` and `make gconfig`, which just use different graphics tools kits for the menu structure.

The default .config file can also be created by issuing the `make defconfig` command.

There is truly a very large number of configuration items; the default .config currently has over 5000 entries. You should not directly edit the .config file; you should use the configuration tools to make such modifications, because the configuration tool ensures that any dependent configuration items are also configured appropriately. Making direct modifications to the .config file may result in a configuration that fails to build or even crashes at runtime.

There are three types of options generated in the configuration (`.config`) file.

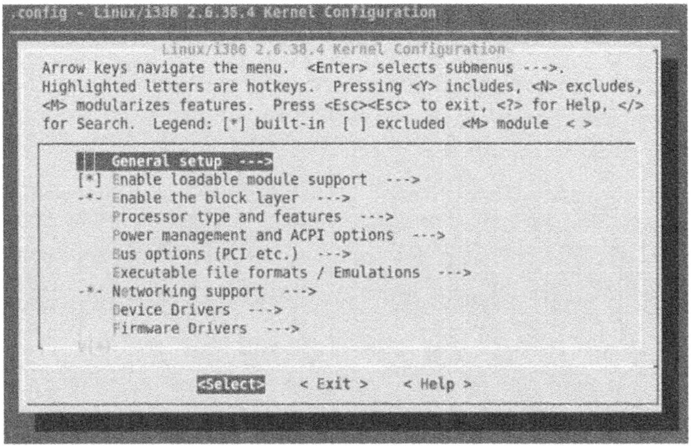

FIGURE 8.3

Screenshot of `make menuconfig` Command.

- CONFIG_FEATURE_XX=y. This means that the feature is built into the kernel at build time. The feature cannot be updated without updating the kernel itself.
- #CONFIG_FEATURE_XX is not set. The # symbol is indicates the remainder of the line is a comment; as a result the CONFIG item is not included.
- CONFIG_FEATURE_XX=m. This item includes a feature as a dynamically loaded module. The feature is not statically compiled into the kernel. The modules are stored on the root file system and loaded automatically as required during the boot sequence. They can be updated without rebuilding the kernel. Not all features can be built as a module instead of being statically linked. There can be a number of static dependences in the build that prevent you from turning a capability from a statically linked item into a dynamically loaded one. In general, the dynamically loaded modules are used for device drivers. This allows a standard kernel with dynamic support for a huge number of devices to be developed. The kernel size remains small, and the required device driver modules are simply stored on the root file system; on embedded systems you can prune the modules to just the devices that must be supported on the platform.

Note

The Linux kernel provides a dynamic loader. A *dynamic loader* is a program that takes a module and updates all the external symbol dependences to that of the currently running kernel. The module can then be used in the kernel. The kernel maintains a list of symbols and the address of each symbol to achieve this. You can display the kernel symbols using:

```
> more /proc/kallsyms
  c0100000 T startup_32
  c0100000 T _text
  c0100079 t bad_subarch
  c0100079 W lguest_entry
```

Changing a configuration option is as simple as selecting the required option in the configuration tool prior to building the kernel.

The design pattern for configuring the behavior of the system in a static manner by setting compile time variables in a configuration file is a common one. Kernel or driver code must use the resultant #defines to alter the behavior of the kernel at compile time. There are also runtime controls that may change the behavior of the system. In the case of ARM BSPs, for each ARM platform there are platform-specific definitions that are generated from definitions in the file linux/arch/arm/tools/mach-type. For example, on an XScale Intel IXP435 BSP the following run/configuration values are created:

- machine_is_ixp425() – A runtime function that is defined and will return true if the function executes on the target platform.
- CONFIG_MACH_IXP425 – A #define configuration that can be used for code that is specific to the standard IXP425 reference board.
- MACH_TYPE_IXP425 – A #define configuration that can be used at compile time to select code to run for this machine type (IXP425 reference board).

Kernel Build Steps (assuming tool chain has been installed)
3. To build the kernel (using four processes):
   ```
   Make -j 4
   ```
   This will generate a linux/arch/IA-32/boot/bzImage and a system map file in the linux direcory.
   ```
   file bzImage
   ```
   ```
   bzImage: Linux kernel IA-32 boot executable bzImage, version 2.6.38.4 (user@ubuntu)
   #3 SMP M, RO-rootFS, root_dev 0x801, swap_dev 0x3, Normal VGA
   ```

The bzimage file consists of a compressed kernel and startup code that is used to decompress the kernel image. The map file is created for the compressed kernel image when it is decompressed into memory (shown in Figure 8.4). A map file is a list of addresses and an associated program symbols. The Linux kernel map file is system.map.

If you have ever booted a Linux kernel, especially on an embedded system, you may have seen a series of dots on the screen ("...."). This is the decompression phase of the boot sequence.

There are two reasons to compress the kernel image (and initial RAM file system). The first reason is to save on the storage requirements for the kernel. In embedded systems the kernel is usually stored on a flash device (although general mass storage is also an option). The second reason to use compression is boot speed; a compressed kernel requires less I/O to get it off the storage device into memory, and the decompression carried out by the CPU runs quickly. The time taken to read and decompress a compressed image is less than the time to read a larger uncompressed image.

There are also options in many embedded systems to keep the image uncompressed and run the kernel from flash without first copying to memory. This is known as execute in place (XIP). XIP saves

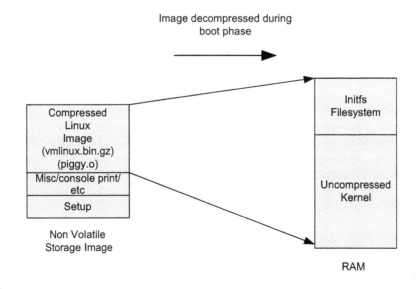

FIGURE 8.4

Linux Compressed Images.

overall RAM as the kernel remains on flash; however, since the flash image is not compressed, it requires additional flash space. The performance of such systems is often lower than non XIP based systems as read access times to flash memory are typically slower than those of DRAM.

Root File System Build

The root file system is the file system you will see if you launch a shell or login to a Linux-based system (host or target) and then change directory to the root via the command

```
cd /
```

The file system layout in most cases will follow the layout defined by the Filesystem Hierarchy Standard (FHS). The FHS is standardized as part of the Linux Standard Base (LSB) (http:// refspecs.linuxfoundation.org/fhs.shtm). If a distribution indicates that it is compliant with an LSB version, then the file system layout will also follow the specified FHS. In many embedded systems, the FHS is not followed exactly, as the root file system is trimmed significantly.

Creating a root file system for a full distribution is a very challenging task. The distribution could contain thousands of packages, all of which must be selected to ensure that all of the dependences and versions are correctly aligned. If your embedded system requires a significant number of packages and capabilities such as a window manager, graphics frameworks, and so on, you should start from an existing distribution. Meego, Yocto Linux, or Open Embedded would be good starting points for a sophisticated multimedia embedded platform. There are, of course, a number of commercially supported embedded distributions that are available, such as MontaVista Linux and Wind River Linux, all such distributions provide tools to build the root file system and manage the contents of the root file system (with an aim to tune the contents of the file system).

The FHS based file system follows the directory layout below:

- /bin – The programs that are normally accessible by all users are stored here. For example, shell-sh or busybox.
- /dev – This contains special block/character device and named pipe files. For example, the file /dev/ tty0 is a special file to access the serial port on tty0. The mknod command can be used to create these special files. When you create such a file, you must provide a device major and minor number. This can be used by the kernel, which associates a specific device driver to the special file. (More on the assignment of these numbers follows later in the chapter.) There are even special files that can be used to access the entire physical memory from user space (/dev/mem).
- /etc - This is the general configuration storage directory, such as the password file and dhcp/ network configuration information. Scripts to boot up the system are often executed by the init program (see below).
- /lib - The shared libraries for other programs are stored here. Using shared libraries significantly reduces the storage requirements on the system. If all shared library content were linked directly to each and every application (that requires a library), the file system would be significantly bloated.
- /lib/modules - This holds the loadable device drivers in the form of kernel modules.
- /proc - This is a virtual file system used to provide information about the system. For each file there is a corresponding set of functions that are called in the kernel. A device driver can install a handler for a particular file name in the /proc folder. There is a lot of interesting data that you can obtain from the /proc file system; for example, the CPU information can be obtained by issuing the cat

/proc/cpuinfo command at the console. The /proc file system can also be used to configure aspects of the kernels behavior; for example, you can enable TCP/IP forwarding between network ports by issuing the echo 1 > /proc/sys/net/ipv4/ip_forward command. The proc file system provides very accessible mechanism to control aspects of your driver at runtime as well as display information from the system in a simple way.

- /root – This is the home directory for the root user.
- /sbin – Programs that are normally run by the system, or as root, are stored here. The init program is stored here; this is the first process to be executed at startup.
- /sys – This is a virtual file system (sysfs). It provides user space access to details about devices and drivers. It was introduced in 2.6 versions of the kernel, partially because the procfs was getting too cluttered. For the devices that appear on a bus hierarchy, the directory structure will replicate that structure of the bus; for example, information about the PCI device at bus:device:function zero is located at /sys/bus/pci/devices/0000:00:00.0/.
- /tmp – Temporary files are created and stored here; they are not guaranteed to survive a system restart.
- /usr – This is where a lot of miscellaneous packages and configuration items are stored. They are general packages that are incremental to the base system.
- /var – This is for variable files; it stores files that change constantly during the operation of the system. Items such as logs are stored here. In an embedded system, you may opt to store these in a dedicated partition where you can manage how often the underlying storage device is written to (to help maintain the life of the storage device).

In embedded systems it is best to combine the root file system directly with the kernel image. This allows the system to boot quickly, and given that it is linked with the kernel, it can provide capabilities such as loadable kernel modules before a traditional file system is available. In many embedded cases, this is the only file system that is required and no further file system need be mounted.

In this configuration selected below the initial root file system is compressed and integrated into the kernel. The file system is decompressed and mounted as a RAM disk during kernel initialization. Having the kernel and file system in one image has advantages in managing/deploying the images for the embedded system. However, if the file system must be updated, the kernel must also be rebuilt and upgraded.

The Linux kernel has a built-in option to build a file system for inclusion into the kernel. The option is known as "Initial RAM File system and RAM disk." The option takes a configuration file that describes the file system as shown in Figure 8.5.

The initial RAM disk is available very early on in the boot sequence and is described in kernel/documentation/early-userspace/README. The kernel build takes an argument to a configuration file. The configuration file is a list of entries that create the underlying file system. The following is a list of commands that are used to define the layout of the initial ram disk.

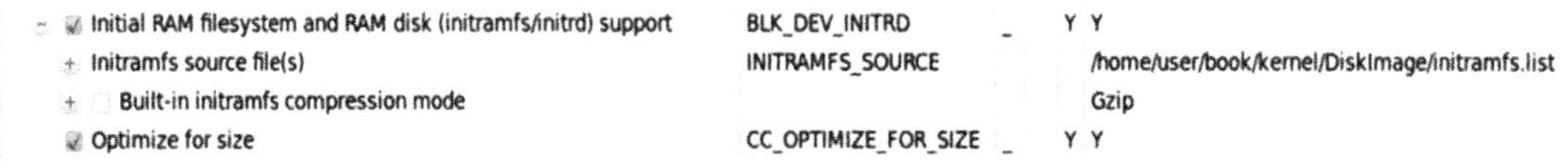

☑ Initial RAM filesystem and RAM disk (initramfs/initrd) support	BLK_DEV_INITRD	–	Y Y
+ Initramfs source file(s)	INITRAMFS_SOURCE		/home/user/book/kernel/DiskImage/initramfs.list
+ Built-in initramfs compression mode			Gzip
☑ Optimize for size	CC_OPTIMIZE_FOR_SIZE	–	Y Y

FIGURE 8.5

Kernel Configuration for an Initial RAM File System.

- `dir`, **example:**
  - `dir /bin 0755 0 0`
  - Creates a /bin directory in the root file system.
- `file`, example:
  - `file /bin/busybox /home/busybox-1.18.4/bin/busybox 0755 0 0`
  - Copies the file `busybox` into `/bin/busybox` on the `initramfs` with permission 755, root ownership, and group root.
- `slink`, **example:**
  - `slink /bin/sh busybox 777 0 0`
  - Creates a file called `/bin/sh` that is linked to `busybox`. The file permissions are 777 and owned by root, group root. A link creates the specified directory entry mapped to an underlying preexisting object (which already has a directory entry). That is, an underling object or file can have multiple directory entries by which it can be accessed.
- `nod`, **example:**
  - `nod /dev/console 644 0 0 c 5 1`
  - Creates a character device console in the `/dev` subdirectory. The file has permission 644, root ownership, root group; c indicates a character special file type (man mknod); 5 is the major device number and 1 is the minor device number.

While building the initial root file system into the kernel image has advantages, in many cases the system must mount a larger file system from a mass storage device. The kernel must include the file system driver applicable to the file system format used on the mass storage device. In order to switch the root file system from the RAM disk mounted during boot to the other mass storage based root file system we must perform a pivot root. This mounts a new root file system.

```
int
pivot_root(const char *new_root, const char *put_old);
```

Once the initial RAM disk root file system is up, the kernel executes `/init` as its first process. The `init` execute may be a binary or script. If the `busybox init` is used, it will search for scripts at defined locations and execute them. If required, this script should perform the root pivot.

Note

There are different variants of Linux man pages. The man pages used for the C library functions are usually accessed using man 2; for example, issuing `man 2 pivot_root` will provide the man page for the system call `pivot_root()`, whereas man 8 `pivot_root` provides details on the same call but it is a shell command. The man command displays the different selection options:

1. Executable programs or shell commands
2. System calls (functions provided by the kernel)
3. Library calls (functions within program libraries)
4. Special files (usually found in /dev)
5. File formats and conventions, e.g., /etc/passwd
6. Games
7. Miscellaneous (including macro packages and conventions), e.g., man(7), groff(7)
8. System administration commands (usually only for root)
9. Kernel routines [nonstandard]

The standard desktop system (for example, Ubuntu) also uses an initial RAM file system. The boot loader in the system (such as `grub2`) takes augments to the kernel and initial RAM file system to load. If you look in the root directory you will find a `vmlinux` and `initd.img` file (these are actually links to the files in /boot directory or partition.). When the `vmlinumx` and `initd` images are loaded by the boot loader, the boot loader must support the file system, on which these files are stored. This can often be problematic in some embedded systems, as the boot loader (for example, Das UBOOT) needs to support the file system used; this entails duplicate development of file system support in the boot loader and the kernel. As mentioned above, it is beneficial to link the kernel and initial root file system into a single image; this image can be stored in a simple file system, which is easily supported by the boot loader. The more sophisticated file systems such as EXT3 are supported by the kernel, this alleviates the need to develop separate code to support file system for the boot loader and kernel. It can also be difficult to reuse kernel code in a boot loader, they are often released under different licence models which precludes the reuse of kernel code in the boot loader.

You can use a platform emulator (on your host machine) such as `QEMU` to load the kernel and initial RAM disk. For example, take a copy of the kernel and `initrd` file into a local directory, then issue the command

```
>qemu -kenrel vmlinux -initrd initrd.img
```

The kernel will boot up and load the file system. It will then probably fail because there is no root file system/hard drive assigned to the qemu.

Busybox

No discussion of embedded Linux can take place without also mentioning Busybox. The most widely used shell commands in an embedded system are provided by Busybox (http://www.busybox.net/):

> Busybox combines tiny versions of many common UNIX utilities into a single small executable. It provides replacements for most of the utilities you usually find in GNU fileutils, shellutils, etc. The utilities in Busybox generally have fewer options than their full-featured GNU cousins; however, the options that are included provide the expected functionality and behave very much like their GNU counterparts. Busybox provides a fairly complete environment for any small or embedded system.

The Busybox is a single statically linked executable. Each Busybox command is created by creating a link to the Busybox executable. When the command executes, the first argument passed to program is the name of the executable. When busy box executes, the name of the executable is passed as the first argument to the executable, and as a result the Busybox image can select the appropriate behavior to provide.

Note

Compiling:
```
#include <stdlib.h>
#include <stdio.h>
int main(int argc, char *argv[])
```

```
{
  printf("Program name is :%10s\n",
  (char *)argv[0]);
  exit(1);
}
  Shell commands to run:
>gcc -o test test.c
>ln -s test test_command1
>ln -s test test_command2
>test
Program name is :test
>test_command1
Program name is :test_command1
>test_command2
Program name is :test_command2
```

There is significant space saving by using one executable to provide multiple shell commands. Each executable has a fixed overhead that would be replicated to every command. In this case, it is over 600KBytes per executable if statically linked, and 7KBytes per command if the executable were dynamically linked. A static linked file means that all of the required code is placed into the binary—that's all the startup code and library functions used—whereas a dynamically linked executable only has the application code (with some minimal startup code). The library code is loaded on demand as needed from shared libraries.

```
Note
Compiling this simplest possible executable:
 #include <stdlib.h>
 int main()
 {
    exit(1);
 }
>gcc -o test_dynamic test1.c
>gcc -static -o test_static test1.c
 >ls -l test*
 -rwxr-xr-x 1 user user   7123 test_dynamic
 -rwxr-xr-x 1 user user 615976 test_static
```

C Library

One of the key libraries in any system is the standard C library, often known simply as libc. The standard C library provides functions that are available to all C programs (and some other language bindings use the library). The library provides implementations of functions such as input/output (printf, open) and string handling functions (strlen). The international C Standard (C99) is maintained by the ISO under the ISO/IEC 9899:1999 standard.

There are many implementations of the standard C library to choose from, especially for embedded systems. The most commonly used implementation is that provided by the GNU C Library. This is a comprehensive implementation that provides all the functions defined in the standard. In fact, it complies with ISO C99, POSIX.1c, POSIX.1j, POSIX.1d, Unix98, and Single Unix Specification standards.

Given that GLIBC is so comprehensive, it can be considered too large for use in an embedded system. As a result, there are a number of lighter variants available. These variants usually remove some features not generally required by most applications. In some cases applications will need to be modified to use these embedded variants of the C library due to missing capabilities, but every effort is made to reduce the impact of such changes.

The Embedded GLIBC is a variant of the GLIBC. It is defined for use on embedded systems. It has a reduced footprint (to that of GLIBC) and provides the capability to configure individual components within the library. This is a good choice for larger embedded systems where most C library functions are required. EGLIBC strives to be both source and binary compatible with GLIBC.

Another popular C library is uClibc (μClibc). It is much smaller than the GLIBC and most functions are supported. In many cases just recompilation is required, so it is source code compatible but not necessarily binary compatible.

The core operating system within Android™ is a Linux variant. Google choose to use the Bionic C library. The library is a derivative of the original BSD standard C library. The library is not as fully featured as GLIBC. The objective in using Bionic was stated as

License: Google stated they wish to keep GPL licensed code out of the user space; Bionic uses BSD license. Size: The goal was to create a much library smaller than GLIBC, approx. ½ size of GLIBC; and speed: Allowing speed optimizations, e.g., a fast threading API (from http://www.youtube.com (17:50), Google I/O 2008 – Anatomy and Physiology of an Android).

The Bionic library is not compatible with GLIBC. All Android native code must be recompiled against Bionic. Native code will need to be updated if porting from a traditional Linux system where it uses GLIBC features which are not available in Bionic.

Boot Sequence

The Linux boot sequence is substantially more involved than that of a simple RTOS boot sequence. In the case of an RTOS it is not unusual to link the application and the kernel and even boot loader into a single monolithic image. The linking process binds both (or all three) components together. In fact, this configuration is a common one used in the deployments of the VxWorks operating system; the image contains the code required to boot up, decompress the kernel, and call an application entry point, which then starts all of the threads that are required for the application.

In the case of Linux, the system consists of four distinct capabilities that are sometimes merged, but not usually for IA-32 systems:

- *BIOS or early firmware.* Particularly on IA-32-based systems, a BIOS or early firmware first executes when the CPU comes out of reset. This firmware initializes memory and any devices that are required to find the next stage boot loader. The firmware identifies the next stage loader and transfers control to it (copies a portion of the boot loader into memory and starts execution of that image). As a general rule, the firmware could get the next stage image from the same flash part as the firmware, a mass storage device, or a network resource. The firmware is not aware of the details of the file system (such as EXT3) where the kernel and application image is stored. The firmware generates ACPI and EFI tables that can be used by the operating system to comprehend the details of the platform.

- *The boot loader (in the context of IA-32 systems).* The boot loader (often called second stage loader) on IA-32 systems is responsible for finding the kernel, copying it into memory, and transferring control to it. If the kernel image is stored on a device with a file system such as an SSD drive, then the boot loader must have a file system driver for the target file system in order to read the kernel from the storage device into memory. In other embedded systems, or where the boot time is key, the boot loader and firmware can be merged into a single image. However, maintaining a separate firmware and boot loader strategy has provided a good deal of abstraction allowing a single boot loaded (e.g. Grub2) to operate on all IA-32 platforms. The firmware takes care of platform specifics in a uniform and consistent way. Combining the firmware and boot loader can also have licensing considerations; the second stage boot loader must be file system aware and may well contain GPL code. If you link this GPL code with your boot loader/firmware, then this must also be released in source form under the GPL license.
- *Kernel image.* The kernel image may be on a mass storage device as is the case on traditional desktop Linux deployments. In this case the kernel is stored on the root file system along with the other applications and user space environment. The kernel and `initrd` images can be found in the `/boot` folder for most distributions. As mentioned, in an embedded Linux deployment, you are more likely to put the kernel in a flash area dedicated to the kernel.
- *Root file system.* This is where the applications, libraries, scripts, and initial `init` task are stored. This can be a RAM disk image linked with the kernel or a separate file system on a mass storage device.

The following is the sequence of events on an IA-32 embedded boot flow.

1. The processor comes out of reset, and the reset code within the firmware executes. This firmware initializes the memory and boot devices. The boot device loads the starting code for the second stage boot loader (for example, `elilo/grub2`), copies it into memory, and jumps to it.
2. The second stage boot loader finds the compressed kernel image file (`bzImage`) from mass storage, copies that into memory, and jumps to it.
3. The start of the kernel image contains uncompressed code. This code decompresses the compressed kernel image within the `bzImage` file into the system RAM. It then transfers control to the uncompressed kernel in memory. The kernel's main starting point is `start_kernel()` in `kernel/init/main.c`.
4. The kernel then performs all internal initialization, along with device initialization for drivers that are integrated into the kernel. The kernel then schedules the `kernel_init()` as the first thread (PID 0).
5. The `kernel_init()` function starts the user space application `init` found on the root file system (that could be the RAM disk or mass storage device depending on how the system is configured).

The `init` program or script is the first user space program that will be executed. The process id given to this process is 1, as can be seen by the following command:

```
$ ps -ef
UID  PID PPID C STIME TTY TIME   CMD
root 1   0    0 May14 ?  00:00:01 /sbin/init
```

The `init` could execute traditional bring-up scripts (as you may be familiar with in a desktop distribution, such as /etc/init.d files), or it could be an application binary that you create to run just one special dedicated application—the choice is yours as an embedded developer. Having said that, it is really convenient for debug and development if you can start a login console (using the normal `init` scripts).

While developing a system it can be very convenient to mount a network file system during boot. In this case the RAM disk would mount an NFS remote partition and then perform the root pivot. The hosting system simply exports a directory on the host, which becomes the root file system on the target. This allows you to build and update applications on the target root file system very easily. You don't have to perform any special download to the target; updates to the NFS mounted directory on the host are immediately available on the target device.

DEBUGGING

There are two distinct debug actives that you may undertake, debugging applications and debugging kernel code and device drivers.

Debugging Applications

Debugging applications is relatively straightforward. There are a number of user space debuggers available. The GNU debugger, GDB (http://www.gnu.org/software/gdb/), is still ubiquitous. GDB provides native and cross-platform debug capabilities (between host and target). GDB can be a little tricky to get used to at first, but there are many GUI wrappers to improve its usability. There are some very powerful features in GDB such as reverse debugging—this is where you can run your program backwards to help find a bug—and it is also effective for debugging multithread applications. Examples of such GUI wrappers are DDD and the KDE GDB – `kdbg`. There are also full-fledged IDEs such as KDevelop and Eclipse-based development environments that you can use. The Eclipse platform is very extensible and supports development in source languages (C, C++, Java etc.) languages. The C/C++ development environment is known as the Eclipse C/C++ Development tool. Figure 8.6 shows a snapshot of the eclipse C/C++ debugger. The example shows multiple threads within the application, disassembly of the code, the source code, and an console output.

One advantage of using Linux on your embedded target platform is that you can start to develop and debug your application on a host-based Linux system such as on a Linux desktop. In this case, you can use any of the native development and debug tools mentioned above. Once you have completed debugging on the host, you can then migrate your application to the target. If the embedded target system is high performance and provides a display, then you can continue to use a host debugger on the target, but in many cases this is not available. So you must debug the target from the host platform - this is known as cross-debugging. The debugger runs on the host system and communicates with the target either via a direct connection to the processor via JTAG/BDM (background debug mode, or over a communications port such as Ethernet or a serial port (see Figure 8.7).

The target must provide a target debugger agent. In the case of hardware-based JTAG debuggers (see Chapter 17), this agent is provided by the hardware debugger. In software-only-based target debug scenarios, the target debug agent runs on the target CPU.

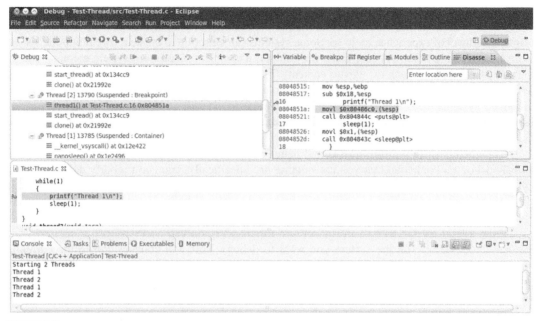

FIGURE 8.6

Eclipse Debugger.

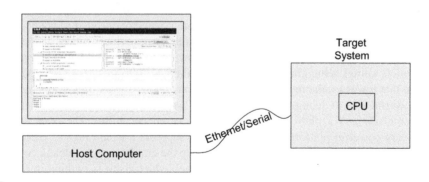

FIGURE 8.7

Cross-Target Debugging.

Kernel Debugging

The most common way of debugging a kernel is to insert strategically placed printk() messages in the kernel and device driver modules. The printk function is an implementation of printf that can be used in the kernel. printk messages are directed to the kernel debug buffer (circular) and the messages are also displayed on the console port. The Linux command dmesg can be used to dump the contents of the kernel debug buffer.

If the kernel crashes, you will be presented with a kernel oops. This is a detailed traceback of the kernel stack; it often provides sufficient information to identify why the kernel crashed, but it can take a significant level of experience to do so. Some systems can be set up to create a core dump file for the entire system (using Kdump). A core dump file contains a complete snapshot of system memory, and all relevant processor state such as register contents. The core dump file can be loaded into gdb and the system memory can be examined in detail. This can make it easier to debug a system crash, but in many embedded systems there is not sufficient local storage to save the core dump file, and relying on a mechanism (eg network stack) to send a core dump file to another system during a crash can be challenging.

Using a debugger to perform host kernel debugging brings about its own challenges. You cannot actively debug on the kernel that you are running on. Specifically, you can't modify data structures, call functions in the kernel, or use breakpoints. You can inspect the system at great length, and that can often be enough to find the issue. In order to debug any kernel you must edit the kernel configuration to compile the kernel with debugging information (turn on CONFIG_DEBUG_INFO). If you want to inspect the kernel for the host platform you are running on you can issue the gdb command >gdb vmlinux /proc/kcore (on the system you want to debug). This will connect gdb to the currently executing system. The symbols for the kernel are loaded from the vmlinux file (stored in the /boot folder). The /proc/kcore is a special driver used to communicate with the kernel debug agent from the user space gdb application.

Cross-target kernel debugging is likely to be one of the most advanced embedded debugging techniques you will have to master. The core debugger runs on your host development system. The target will require a debug agent to communicate with the debugger on the host system. In many embedded systems you will use some form of hardware probe (via JTAG or BDM). This works well at the start of a system development but is often not practical when you are getting close to releasing the system (production hardware often removes the hardware connectors needed to connect to the hardware probe to save costs). Once the system is stable enough to provide a robust data connection via Ethernet, serial ports, or even USB, a good option is to switch to a software-based target debug agent. Support for remote kernel debugging was introduced (merged) into the 2.6.35 version of the Linux kernel (prior to that it was available as a patch to the kernel). This allows for kernel target debugging.

Another powerful way to debug the kernel is to use a software emulator. An emulator consists of both a CPU emulator and a platform/board level emulation capability. The open source QEMU emulator is a very powerful platform-level emulator. It supports a wide range of CPU architectures along with a number of emulated boards. You can start up the emulator with a debug connection from GBD to a target kernel debug agent running in the kernel, which itself is running in QEMU. In this configuration you can perform kernel level debug of the kernel executing within the QEMU emulator. The only downside is that you are not able to easily debug your target hardware drivers. Having said that, if the hardware being developed is new also, it can be very useful to develop a model of the new hardware in a software environment. You could do this by looking at how devices are emulated in QEMU and create your own device model. Special modeling languages exist such as System-C, these languages can be used to develop functional simulation models. These models can be developed in advance of the actual hardware development, and can be used to develop software while the silicon/hardware is still under development. This can often accelerate the time to market by allowing you to have the software ready when the hardware/SOC is ready. Full platform-level modeling/emulation environments are also commercially available, such as Wind River Simics and Synopsis Innovator.

QEMU Kernel Debugging

QEMU supports a mechanism to connect GDB directly to the simulator. You must first start QEMU in a suspended state, with a GDB server started listening for communications from the debugger. This is a very similar process to debugging any target, except the target is an emulated instance on your host machine. As part of the Linux build, you should have a `vmlinux` file in the root directory, as we mentioned—you need to build the kernel with debugging options turned on, and this includes all the debug information in the image to allow source-level debug. When the debugger first connects to QEMU, the processor has not even started to execute its BIOS code; the debugger only has symbol information for the Linux kernel.

Build Kernel
Build the kernel as described above, including an `initramfs`.

Start QEMU
```
qemu --gdb tcp::1234 -S -kernel arch/IA-32/boot/bzImage
```
  This starts QEMU in a suspended mode, with a GDB server waiting on TCP port 1234. Add an option to add a file system device/image to QEMU if needed.

Start Debugger
```
ddd ./vmlinux
```
  Load symbol information from `vmlinux`.
  In `ddd` command window:
```
target remote localhost:1234
b kernel_start
cont
```

The commands above connect to the debug server in QEMU, set a break point at the function `kernel_start`, and runs to that point. Another interesting break point is `kernel_init`.

You can set breakpoints in the kernel and step through the boot sequence. You can test any code you have placed into a kernel using this simple technique. This mechanism works well when all of the code you wish to test has been linked into the kernel, it is a little more challenging to debug dynamically loaded modules, as modules are dynamically linked to the kernel the debugger does not have an accurate symbol table for the loaded modules.

DRIVER DEVELOPMENT

Device drivers are software components within the kernel that directly interact with a hardware device. They provide a software interface to allow other software components in the system to interact with the device. A device driver performs the following functions:

- *Abstracts the hardware.* A device driver should abstract the underlying implementations of the hardware. For example, a UART device driver should provide a consistent software interface regardless of the actual physical device specifications.
- *Manages privilege.* A driver allows an unprivileged application to interface with a device. Traditionally, the code required to manage the driver runs with kernel privileges. However, the application does not need to operate in kernel mode to make use of a device.

- *Enables multiplexed access.* In many cases a number of applications may require concurrent access to a particular device. The device driver provides mechanisms for multiple applications to use a device concurrently. This may be achieved by serializing access to the device or by merging requests from multiple driver instances to the hardware.
- *Martials data to and from an application's process space to kernel space.* A device driver will usually copy data to and from the applications process space into kernel space; kernel memory space is then accessible by the device via DMA.
- *Provides security.* A device driver may provide security features to prevent an unauthorized process from accessing a device. This capability is usually supported by the operating system.

For Linux, the vast majority of device drivers run in the context of the kernel. As described in Chapter 7, many device drivers provide services to other components in the operating system such as the TCP/IP stack or the file system drivers. In this chapter we describe a driver that provides services directly to user space applications. The device driver provides methods that can be accessed through the /dev pseudo file system and controlled using standard system calls such as OPEN/CLOSE/READ/WRITE and IOCTL. These types of drivers are called character drivers in Linux. This driver type can be used to control simple hardware and demonstrate many of the principles used on more advanced device drivers.

The vast majority of device drivers are written to execute in the kernel and are either statically linked or dynamically linked into the kernel (inserted as modules). In some cases, however, user space drivers are developed. User space drivers still rely on a helper kernel driver, but the majority of the logic is run in user space. Running more code in user space has the advantage of being more robust— an error in a user space driver is not likely to crash the system. However, errors in kernel drivers will almost undoubtedly cause a kernel oops. There are a number of disadvantages, too. The application often requires privileges, as it must map the device memory into user space. Performance is often lower due to process switches needed to access the device. At the time of writing, the XServer is still used extensively. The XServer is one of the most well-known user space drivers, and its successor, Wayland, also relies on applications using user space drivers to render content managed by Wayland.

Character Driver Model

This section provides an overview of the different aspects of a character-based device driver, discusses the user space interface provided by the driver, and the data path from submission of data by the user space application down to an underlying device.

Character Driver—User Space

In order to interact with the device from a user space application, a mechanism is needed to identify the device and subsequently interact with the device. Character device drivers are referenced through special files in the file system. The files are typically in the /dev folder. You can see the files by executing ls -l.

```
root@ubuntu:/dev# ls -l
total 0
..
crw-------  1 root root 5,  1 2011-05-14 20:31 console
crw-rw-rw-  1 root tty 5,   0 2011-06-02 07:13 tty
crw--w----  1 root root 4,  0 2011-05-14 20:31 tty0
crw-------  1 root root 4,  1 2011-05-14 20:31 tty1
```

The c in the ls listing above indicates that the file is a char device. The listing shows two numbers associated with each character file (5,1; 5,0; 4,0; 4,1). These are known as the device *major* and *minor numbers,* respectively. The major number typically indicates a device driver type, and the minor number can be used to indicate an instance of the driver. For example, above you can see two tty (terminal teletype) instances.

The major and minor device numbers can be allocated statically or dynamically. The kernel supports a mechanism to allocate such numbers on demand when the driver is initialized. However, the pseudo-character driver in the file system must correlate with these dynamically allocated entries, so you must create the special file after the driver has been initialized. For embedded systems, it is more common to use statically assigned numbers because they are incorporated into the initial RAM file system. The official registry of allocate device numbers can be found in http://www.lanana.org. You should request an allocation if you plan on up streaming your device driver. Major device number 42 is left for demos/prototyping.

The user space application can perform the traditional open/close/read/write and ioctl calls to interact with the device. For example, to open the device, use the following code sequence.

```
int fd;
fd = open("/dev/tty", O_RDWR | O_SYNC );
if ( fd <= 0 ) {
    perror("Error failed open");
}
```

The function returns a file descriptor (fd), which is then used as an argument for the other functions. The O_SYNC argument is an important option to consider when operating with devices. It indicates that the user space application will block until the data written to the device have been actually written to the hardware.

> **Note**
> Deciding between a synchronous and an asynchronous device driver is an important choice to make. A synchronous driver may block the calling application or thread until the data have been written to the device. A nonblocking or asynchronous driver will quickly copy the data from the calling application and let the calling application continue. The driver will write the data to the underlying hardware device asynchronously to the caller. If the data cannot be transmitted for some reason later the caller will not be notified.

Once you have opened the device, you can use the other calls to interact with the device. The following are the most common functions to use.

- read()—This function can be used to read data from the device.
- write()—Conversely, this function is used to write data to the device.
- ioctl()—This is a generic control function that can be used to pass setup information and configuration information to a device.

When the user space library functions are called, the kernel infrastructure directly triggers a call to the associated driver functions.

Character Driver—Kernel Module

This section shows how to create a simple character-based loadable device driver. Writing a sophisticated device driver is beyond the scope of this book; the book *Linux Device Drivers* is recommended when you are developing a more sophisticated driver (http://lwn.net/Kernel/LDD3/).

The first element is to create a simple make file. There is a standardized make file pattern that can be used to allow you to build a kernel module. You need to download kernel source code in order to build a kernel module; this is to allow you to reuse the kernel make file structure and use the appropriate header files. This kernel must also be compiled, so follow the kernel build steps mentioned above. A module must be compiled against the correct kernel version; that is, the versions must match. If you plan on testing a module on your desktop system, then you must ensure that you download the code for the kernel running on your system. You can find the version by running uname -a. Alternately, use a package manager such as Synaptic Package Manager to download the kernel source for your running system. Aligning the version of the running kernel and the source code used to build a kernel module is critically important; failing to get it right will lead to a frustrating error, "Invalid module format," when you try to install the module.

In the directory where you are creating the test module, create a make file with the following entry, assuming our module c file will be called ex_kernel_drv.c:

```
#
# Makefile for simple driver.
#
obj-m += ex_kernel_drv.o
```

Now create the actual kernel module source, shown in the following. It is a basic character device driver. The driver allows a user space program to write a string to a kernel static buffer and read back from later.

```
1 #include <linux/module.h>
2 #include <linux/moduleparam.h>
3 #include <linux/init.h>
4 #include <linux/kernel.h>
5 #include <linux/fs.h>
6 #include <linux/errno.h>
7 #include <asm/uaccess.h>
```

Lines 1–7: The header file required for a simple character device loadable kernel module.

```
8 MODULE_LICENSE("Dual BSD/GPL");
```

Line 8: A number of MODULE_* definitions are useful in declaring attributes associated with the module. This declares the license under which the module is being released.

```
9
10
11 #define MAJOR_DEVICE_NUMBER 42
12 char *kernel_data;
13 int ret_count;
```

Lines 11–13: Define the major device number for the driver and allocate a global pointer for the kernel data string that will be updated from user space.

```
14
15 int drv_open(struct inode *inode,struct file *filep)
16 {
17   printk("Example driver open\n");
18   ret_count = 0;
19   return 0;
20 }
21 int drv_close(struct inode *inode,struct file *filep)
22 {
23   printk("Example driver close\n");
24   return 0;
25 }
```

Lines 14–25: No specific data are kept when the device is open or closed. No file pointer data are kept (to simplify the example).

```
26 ssize_t drv_read(struct file *filep,char *user_buf,
27          size_t count,loff_t *offp )
28 {
29   printk("Example driver read: size:%d\n",count);
30   if ( ret_count >= strlen(kernel_data))
31   {
32    printk("Example driver read: ret_count = %d",
33        ret_count);
34    return 0;
35   }
36   if (
37   copy_to_user(user_buf,kernel_data,strlen(kernel_data))
38   != 0 )
39    printk("Kernel to user copy failed\n");
40   ret_count += strlen(kernel_data);
41   return (strlen(kernel_data));
42 }
```

Lines 26–42: This is the device function called when the device is read. The key item is the copy_to_user() call. This will copy the data from the kernel data buffer into the buffer provided by the user space read() call. The code managing ret_count ensures that the read call is terminated. The user space application will continue to read from the device until zero characters are returned.

```
43 ssize_t drv_write(struct file *filep,
44                   const char *user_buf,
45                   size_t count,loff_t *offp )
46 {
47   printk("Example driver write:Count:%d\n",count);
48   if ( copy_from_user(kernel_data,user_buf,count) != 0 )
49    printk("User to kernel copy failed\n");
50   *(kernel_data+count)=NULL;
51   return count;
52 }
```

Lines 43–52: This is the device function called when the device is written to. The `copy_from_user()` call copies data from the user space buffer into the kernel buffer.

```
53
54 /*
55  * The device operations structure.
56  */
57 static struct file_operations drv_ops = {
58    .owner    = THIS_MODULE,
59    .open     = drv_open,
60    .read     = drv_read,
61    .write    = drv_write,
62    .release  = drv_close,
63    /* .ioctl  = drv_ioctl */
64 };
65
66
67 static int __init example_drv_init(void)
68 {
69    printk("Example driver init\n");
70    kernel_data = kmalloc(132,GFP_KERNEL);
71    strcpy(kernel_data,
72      "Kernel data string not yet written to\n");
73    if ( register_chrdev(
74        MAJOR_DEVICE_NUMBER,
75        "example_dev",
76        &drv_ops))
77      printk("Device registration failed");
78    printk("Example driver init complete\n");
79    return 0;
80 }
```

Lines 53–80: The `struct file_operations` drv_ops data structure is populated with the function pointers for each operation supported by the driver. The structure contains quite a few more members, but only the members supported by the driver are set up. The format used is an extension to GCC that allows you to initialize a member by name; you do not have to be aware of the member order in the structure. The structure is defined in <linux/fs.h>. Once the structure has been initialized, it must be registered by calling `register_chrdev()`. The function takes the major device number and the file operations structure.

There is an IOCTL handler (commented on above); an implementation is not shown in this code snippet, but it is very useful to send control information.

```
81
82 static void __exit example_drv_exit(void)
83 {
84    printk("Example driver exit\n");
85    unregister_chrdev(MAJOR_DEVICE_NUMBER,
86             "example_device");
87    kfree(kernel_data);
88 }
```

Lines 81–88: Disconnect this driver from the major number. Free kernel memory allocated in init. This is called when the module is removed via the command rmmod.

```
89
90 module_init(example_drv_init);
91 module_exit(example_drv_exit);
92
93
```

Lines 89–93: These functions register the entry and exit points of the module. The function registered via module_init() is called when a module is installed, for example, via the insmod command. Similarly, the function registered via module_exit is the function called when the module is removed via the rmmod command. When we build and run we get the following input and output.

Shell Commands to Demonstrate Driver
First, we compile the kernel module.

- `make -C /usr/src/linux-source-2.6.38/ M=$PWD modules`

Next, create the device node in the /dev file system.

- `mknod /dev/new_device c 42 0`

Now, we load the kernel module (you can verify it was loaded by issuing the lsmod command).

- `insmod ex_kernel_drv.ko`

Perform a number of reads and writes to the device.

- `cat /dev/example_device`

Kernel data string not yet written to.

- `echo "Hello world driver" > /dev/example_device`
- `cat /dev/example_device`

Hello world driver.

- `echo "New string" > /dev/example_device`
- `cat /dev/example_device`

New string.
Debug messages from the module can be displayed using:

- `dmesg`

```
[46306.157051] Example driver init complete
[46309.165205] Example driver open
[46309.165317] Example driver read: size:32768
[46309.165465] Example driver read: size:32768
[46309.165482] Example driver read: ret_count = 38
[46309.165510] Example driver close
```

The character driver above demonstrates the simplest interaction model; it does not deal with any real hardware. It primarily shows an example of user space interactions with a driver module.

PCI Device Drivers

The current IA-32-based drivers present the vast majority of hardware as PCI devices. The device may be internal in an SOC or on a board via physical PCIe links, but in all cases they are presented via the logical PCIe discovery model. The kernel identifies all hardware on the system and associates it automatically with the appropriate driver. The kernel uses a combination of PCI Vendor Code and Device ID or Class ID to associate the correct driver with an associated device automatically.

Each kernel module supporting a PCIe device indicates which devices are supported by the device driver. It does so by initializing a `pci_device_id` table and declaring the structure to the kernel loader using the `MODULE_DEVICE_TABLE()` macro. A sample from an Intel Gigabit Ethernet driver – e1000_main.c is shown below.

```
static DEFINE_PCI_DEVICE_TABLE(e1000_pci_tbl)
  = {
    PCI_DEVICE(0x8086, 0x1000),
    PCI_DEVICE(0x8086, 0x1000),
   {0,}
  };
MODULE_DEVICE_TABLE(pci, e1000_pci_tbl);
```

In the initiation function you must register the drive handling functions. This is similar to the procedure shown for the simple character device.

```
static struct pci_driver e1000_driver = {
 .name    = e1000_driver_name,
 .id_table = e1000_pci_tbl,
 .probe   = e1000_probe,
 .remove  = __devexit_p(e1000_remove),
#ifdef CONFIG_PM
 /* Power Managment Hooks */
 .suspend  = e1000_suspend,
 .resume   = e1000_resume,
#endif
 .shutdown  = e1000_shutdown,
 .err_handler = &e1000_err_handler
};

pci_register_driver(&e1000_driver);
```

The probe function is particular to the PCI discovery process. The driver probe function is called with a pointer to the PCI device structure. This provides all the required information for the driver to identify the individual instance of a PCI device being initialized (for instance, there could be many NIC interfaces in the system):

```
static int __devinit
  e1000_probe(struct pci_dev *pdev,
      const struct pci_device_id *ent)
```

The probe, shutdown, and power manage handlers do not expose any specific capability of the PCI device. It could be a video capture card or a network interface, and these functions would be very similar in behavior. The following are the general steps required during this phase:

1. Enable the device. This can be done by writing to register in the configuration space. The function `pci_enable_device()` should be called. This ensures that the device is active, allocates memory, and assigns an interrupt if the BIOS/firmware has not done so yet.
2. Request memory-mapped I/O regions for use by the device. This is done using `pci_request_regions(pdev, DRV_NAME);`.
3. Set the DMA mask size (for both coherent and streaming DMA). This is accomplished using `pci_dma_set_mask()` and `pci_set_consistent_dma_mask()`. These calls inform the system about the bus mastering capabilities of the device.
4. Allocate and initialize shared control data. This is shared physical memory that can be accessed by the kernel driver and the device itself. This is usually used for driver control structures such as DMA descriptor. More detail can be found in the kernel/docs/DMA-API.txt. The function `-pci_allocate_coherent()` is primarily used.
5. Access device configuration space (if needed).
6. Manage the allocation of MSI/MSIx interrupt vectors for the device.
7. Initialize the non-PCI capabilities of the device. These are specific to the device, for example, an NIC or video capture device.
8. Register with other kernel sub systems like the TCP/IP stack and the file system.
9. Enable the device for processing. This usually involves clearing pending interrupts, populating the device descriptors with buffers, and enabling the device and associated interrupts.

These steps ensure that resources are allocated and the device is set up ready to be used.

Network Driver Specifics

In addition to the generic PCI handling and registration mentioned above, each device driver must register its services with the appropriate higher level service in the kernel. In the case of networking drivers, the driver must register functions to allow the TCP/IP networking stack to interact with the adaptor to transmit and receive packets. Again, a standard kernel design pattern is in use here, the pattern is to initialize a structure populated with pointers to functions and then register the structure with the appropriate service. In the case of an Ethernet driver (e1000) the following code snippet shows the registration of the functions to be used by the network stack.

```
static const struct net_device_ops e1000_netdev_ops = {
  .ndo_open            = e1000_open,
  .ndo_stop            = e1000_close,
  .ndo_start_xmit      = e1000_xmit_frame,
  .ndo_get_stats       = e1000_get_stats,
  .ndo_set_rx_mode     = e1000_set_rx_mode,
  .ndo_set_mac_address = e1000_set_mac,
  .ndo_tx_timeout      = e1000_tx_timeout,
  .ndo_change_mtu      = e1000_change_mtu,
  .ndo_do_ioctl        = e1000_ioctl,
  .ndo_validate_addr   = eth_validate_addr,
```

```
#ifdef CONFIG_NET_POLL_CONTROLLER
        .ndo_poll_controller  = e1000_netpoll,
#endif
};

struct net_device *netdev;
SET_NETDEV_DEV(netdev, &pdev->dev);
        pci_set_drvdata(pdev, netdev);
netdev->netdev_ops = &e1000_netdev_ops;
register_netdev(netdev);
```

Once the device has been registered via `register_netdev()`, the networking stack makes calls to the appropriate functions.

Interrupt Handling

Almost all device interactions require that the device driver operate with device interrupts. Interrupts are used to indicate that a change has occurred in the device. The driver is expected to service the hardware interrupt in a timely fashion.

The operating system provides a specific mechanism to allocate and assign a callback function to device interrupts. In IA-32-based systems, many hardware devices are presented as PCIe devices (both on the SOC and external). For such devices, three different types of interrupts support mechanisms in the hardware and are supported by the kernel. They are:

- *Legacy Interrupts, often called INTA/INTB/INTC/INTD.* These are wire-based interrupts. Each wire is usually shared between multiple devices, and each device can only generate a single interrupt type—sub-interrupts within the devices must be identified by reading an interrupt reason register in the device. This interrupt mechanism should be avoided if possible, primarily due to time spent establishing the true cause of the interrupt. In fact, a device driver using legacy interrupts and supports DMA must perform a read to the device to ensure that all data from the device have been updated in memory before the driver uses the DMA data. This interrupt is also considered to be level sensitive, so you must generally clear the interrupt source in the device at the start of your interrupt handler.
- *Message Signal Interrupts (MSI).* These allow the system to allocate a number of interrupt vectors to the device. The vectors must be contiguous. When a device generates interrupts, it can generate a specific vector to indicate a specific event in the device. For example, a specific interrupt vector can be triggered to indicate that the device has received a packet, and a separate vector to indicate less critical maintenance events such as an Ethernet link going down. This allows the driver to efficiently handle the underlying event. The MSI message is a special system message that is directed to the CPU's local Advanced Peripheral Interrupt Controller (APIC). In a multicore system, this can be directed to a specific core. All device MSI vectors must be targeted at the same core.
- *Message Signal Interrupts eXtension (MSIx).* This is an extension of MSI in that the vectors assigned to a device do not need be contiguous. Additionally, each vector allocated can be directed to a targeted core. With multi core systems, this capability allows you to affinitize interrupts for different devices (or functions within a device) to individual cores, this can greatly improve performance across the system.

The driver should enable MSI/MSIx for a device by calling `pci_enable_msi()` or `pci_enable_msix()`. This allocates CPU interrupt vectors and writes the vector data into a PCI device. The interrupt vectors allocated to the device are returned by the call. If the call fails, then the driver should revert to a legacy interrupt support and bind a single interrupt callback function to the legacy interrupt vector. For MSI/MSIx vectors, you should not assume that you obtained all the vectors that the device is capable of generating; the operating system may allocate fewer vectors (perhaps only 1) to a device if vectors are scarce (255 vectors in all). This is not very likely in an embedded system, but you must ensure that your driver handles such cases gracefully.

MSI/MSIx-based systems also follow different ordering semantics for transactions from the device (to devices which use legacy wired interrupts). When a device which uses MSI/MSIx interrupts writes to system memory and then generates an interrupt, the system memory is guaranteed to be up to date when the processor reads the data based on the arrival of the interrupt. The driver is not *required* to perform a device read to ensure memory consistency.

Once the system allocates the vectors, the driver can assign the vectors to callback routines.

```
request_irq(IRQ Number,
            callback function handler,
            irq_flags,
            name, /* show in statistics */
            data);
```

When an interrupt fires on the device, the callback function handler is called with an interrupt vector and a `void* data` pointer. The data pointer is usually set to a device driver stricture that contains all the required device instance/specific information (including a pointer to the PCI device structure for the device.). The interrupts statistics can be seen in the `/proc/interrupts` pseudo file system.

The handler runs in interrupt context. In most systems, there are significant limitations to the operating system functions that can be called from interrupt context. The `in_interrupt()` call returns true if the calling function is in the interrupt context, this call can be used to check the calling context and ensure the function does not call inappropriate services given the calling context.

The amount of work performed in the interrupt handler should be kept to a minimum; specifically, only perform the time-critical aspect of servicing the device. At a minimum, the interrupt handler runs with the current interrupt level disabled, so running too much code may affect the performance of other critical interrupt handling, specifically it can add to the jitter associated with processing other key interrupts.

All other work related to the device should be deferred in an alternative non-interrupt context. Operating systems provide a specific mechanism to defer work to a kernel task context to perform the remainder of the work. In Linux these are kernel bottom halves/tasklets, while on VxWorks you can transfer work to any system task.

Deferred Work

Three key capabilities in the kernel can be used to defer work from the interrupt handler, namely, softIRQs, tasklets, and work queues. Deferred work occurs with interrupts re-enabled and are scheduled by the operating system at a convenient time. They are often run directly after the return from the interrupt handler—the key difference being that interrupts have been re-enabled. The term *bottom-half handling* is often used to refer to this deferred work.

softIRQs. There are 32 softIRQs defined in the system. They can run concurrently in the system (in a multiprocessor system) and are statically configured at compile time in the `kernel/include/linux/interrupt.h/` file. They cannot be created dynamically. In fact, you have to modify the kernel to add to the list, so it is not really feasible for you to add them unless you are working with upstream kernel maintainers. The softIRQs form the base for other deferred work mechanisms such as tasklets. Because of the static nature of softIRQs they are not generally directly used by device drivers. There are 10 of the 32 softIRQs that are used at the time of writing. Two of the softIRQs are dedicated to the execution of tasklets (one high-priority list and one low-priority task list).

Tasklets. Tasklets are functions that are run from the context of the softIRQ. A tasklet is a function that is added to a linked list and then called when the softIRQ executes. Only one instance of a given tasklet is guaranteed to execute at any one time. Even on multicore systems, the tasklets will be serialized to ensure that they do not run concurrently. This has the advantage that you do not have to worry about locking data structures used within a tasklet on a multicore system. Tasklets are the best way to defer work from the interrupt handler (with the exception of network device drivers). Tasklets must run to completion and should not block. If the tasklet blocked, it would prevent/delay the execution of other tasklets.

Using Tasklets

```
#include<interrupt.h>
DECLARE_TASKLET(name, function, data)
```

The tasklet prototype:

```
void tasklet_handler(unsigned long data)
```

Scheduling the tasklet:

```
tasklet_schedule(&tasklet_handle);
```

Work Queues. Work queues are the final mechanism we can use to defer work. Work queue items are executed in the context of a kernel thread. The kernel thread associated with the work queue runs as a process that is scheduled. As it runs in the context of a kernel thread, it can make use of all standard kernel services, block on semaphores, allocate memory (which may not be immediately available), and sleep to poll hardware. Generally speaking, a work queue should be used if such services are required.

Note

Network device drivers defer work using the `napi_schedule()`. The `napi_schedule()` function is implemented in `linux/net/core/dev.c`. The call uses the NET_RX_SOFTIRQ softIRQ to defer network device driver–related work.

Interrupt Flow Summary

The pattern of handling interrupts in Linux is a general design pattern for handling interrupts in many embedded systems. The objective is to balance the needs of low latency interrupt service requirements of the hardware while ensuring that the overall operation of threads/tasks in the system is also accommodated. It should be noted, however, that in some special embedded cases, all of the required interrupt handling is performed in interrupt context; this is where there are very tight temporal bounds to service the hardware. However, such handlers can have adverse effects on the rest of the system unless they are well understood. Figure 8.8 shows an example of flow from hardware interrupt to user space task execution.

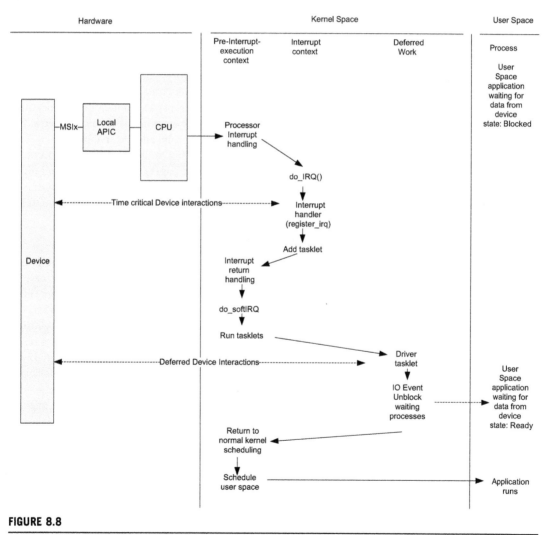

FIGURE 8.8

Interrupt Flow through Linux.

Careful attention must be paid to interrupt processing in embedded systems. You have to consider what other interrupts in the system may delay the execution of critical interrupts associated with any real-time behavior.

MEMORY MANAGEMENT

There are two distinct memory allocation domains within Linux. This section touches upon the allocation of memory for user space application, kernel space allocations, and mechanisms to share memory between user and kernel space.

User Space

The most well-known mechanism for requesting memory from user space is to call `malloc()`. This is a C library function that returns a user space pointer to the allocated memory. The pointer contains a virtual address, and the MMU system within the CPU translates access to this virtual address to an underlying physical memory location(s). The memory is contiguous as far as the user space application is concerned, however the allocation may have come from multiple physically discontinuous memory pages. The MMU tables are appropriately configured to ensure the contiguous virtual address mappings.

An important attribute to this memory is that it is subject to paging to disk if the system becomes oversubscribed (in terms of memory requests). You should note that paging is generally turned off in embedded systems due to file system wear (particularly for flash devices) and nondeterministic performance. The user space memory library often makes requests to the underlying kernel for memory.

Access to User Space memory from the Kernel

When a user space application makes a system call such as `write()` to a device, a transition from user space to kernel space occurs. The appropriate device driver write function is called (as in the case of our character driver above). The `write` function will be working on behalf of the calling user space process and as a result is said to be running in its process context. While in process context, the memory of the calling process and kernel mappings are accessible (provided no paging has occurred). In this context both the user space process and kernel virtual address ranges are available, as a result the virtual address assigned to the kernel and those assigned to processes must be unique. In a 32-bit Linux system, processes are assigned virtual addresses that range from zero to 3 GBytes, and the kernel uses virtual addresses that ranges from 3 GB through 4 GB. The Linux system calls `copy_from_user()` and `copy_to_user()` are provided to copy data between the user space pages and the kernel pages.

Function

`copy_from_user()`– Copy a block of data from user space.

Synopsis

```
unsigned long
copy_from_user (void * to,
const void __user * from,
unsigned long n);
```

Arguments

to – Destination address, in kernel space.
from – Source address, in user space.
n – Number of bytes to copy.

Context

User context only. This function may sleep.

Description

Copy data from user space to kernel space.

Figure 8.9 shows the mapping and copy. If the user space memory has been paged out, the process context is blocked until the page has been brought back into physical memory.

Kernel Allocation

The kernel manages all memory in physical page units. Each processor has a defined page size (4 K on IA-32). The kernel tracks every page in the system with page structure defined in linux/include/linux/mm_types.h.

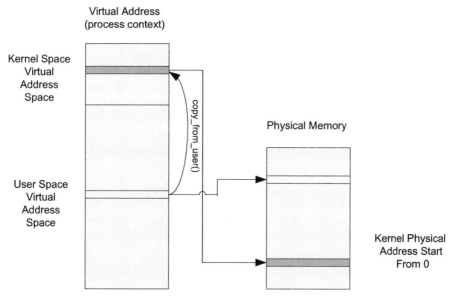

FIGURE 8.9

The copy_from_user() Function.

The following key attributes are maintained for each physical page in the system:

- *Page flags.* If the page is dirty, referenced, locked, backed by a swap copy, least recently used data. The flags are found in `linux/include/linux/page-flags.h`.
- *Virtual address.* Usually the virtual address of the page. This is valid for most of the memory in the system. However, there are cases where a physical memory location is not always mapped to the kernel, as in the case of what is known as HIGHMEM. HIGHMEM memory has a null address in the page mapping.
- *Owner.* The kernel must track available pages, particularly if they are to support allocation of such pages.

Information on the current page statistics can be found using the command `>cat /proc/meminfo`.

The kernel supports a number of different logical zones for memory allocation. The zones address ranges are processor architecture specific. The first is ZONE_DMA; when an allocation request ZONE_DMA is requested it provides pages that are guaranteed to be accessible by any DMA agent in the system. In some cases devices with DMA capability are not all capable of accessing all addresses in the system. This is set to <16 MB in IA-32 systems to cover old ISA bus devices and is rarely used at this point. ZONE_DMA2 is a zone that is supported on IA-32 systems. It is used for devices that can only access 32-bit address space but with more than 4 GB of memory populated (x64).

ZONE_NORMAL is the normal memory zone used. If used with a device, the device must be able to access all system memory (for a 32-bit device system, all 4 GB must be accessible from the device). Memory obtained from this zone has a valid virtual address that can be used to dereference the physical memory at any time. Most allocations use this zone. It's important to note that there is a fixed offset between the virtual address and physical address allocated from the normal zone. This is very important; in many cases device drivers convert from virtual addresses to physical (and then bus address) addresses when interacting with a device. It is important for the cost of such translations to be low, and having a fixed arithmetic offset between the two addresses achieves a very efficient translation at runtime. The function `virt_to_phy()` performs such a translation.

ZONE_HIGH_MEM is assigned to pages that are high in physical memory (above 900 MB). As mentioned earlier, the kernel occupies virtual address ranges from 3 GB through 4 GB. That is, it is allocated 1 GB of virtual address. Therefore, it cannot have all physical addresses mapped. In this case you can still allocate the pages, but there is no permanent virtual mapping to the physical page. These pages must be mapped if you need to read/write the memory from the kernel at run time. However these memory regions are accessible from devices via DMA without creating a kernel virtual address mapping.

Page Allocation

A number of low-level functions can be used to request memory from a particular zone. The allocations return memory that is both page-aligned and with page granularity. The lowest level page allocation function is

```
struct page *alloc_pages(unsigned int gfp_mask,
                         unsigned int order)
```

This function allocates 2 << order contiguous pages from the kernel. The function returns a page structure. The flags include the ZONE and other elements described later. The virtual address mapped to the page (for DMA_ZONE and DMA_NORMAL) can be obtained from the returned page structure by calling `page_address()`. As the physical pages must be contiguous (not the case for user space malloced memory). It is often difficult to obtain large contiguous memory regions from the kernel, especially the longer the system is up and running. In most cases you should request your large contiguous memory requests during startup to improve the likelihood of success, however in general it is better to assume you cannot guarantee large physically contiguous memory allocations. As a general rule of thumb, a 64-kB block is considered a large contiguous section to request. When large contiguous memory regions are needed, you can make a call to `alloc_bootmem()` during system startup. This has a much higher probability of succeeding, and it is used when very large buffers are needed (several megabytes).

In many cases, device drivers make use of linked lists of pages to describe incoming and outgoing data. These are arranged as linked lists of pages; each page is contiguous but the list does not need to be made up from contiguous pages. These lists are referred to as *scatter gather lists*. Corresponding to the DMA engines, a device should support a descriptor mechanism whereby a logical contiguous data block can be characterized by a list of physical pointers.

The `kmalloc()` Function

The kernel provides a function very similar to the user space counterpart `malloc()`. The page allocation routines above may be very inefficient if small allocations (below one page) are required. The kernel maintains a SLAB of buffers and can efficiently provide subpage or page size allocation.

```
Void *ptr;
ptr = kmalloc(1024,GFP_KERNEL);
..
kfree(ptr);
```

The `kmalloc` function returns at least the number of bytes requested, but they are not necessarily page aligned (often important for devices). The second argument is the `gfp_mask` flag. The flags are defined in `linux/include/linux/gfp.h and slab.h`. The mask can be broken down into two separate modifiers.

- *Zone modifiers.* These are __GFP_DMA, __GFP_NORMAL, and __GFP_HIGHMEM. You cannot use the HIGHMEM zone with calls that return a mapped virtually address such as `kmalloc`. In practically all cases the NORMAL zone is used.
- *Action modifiers.* These control the behavior of an allocation, such as whether the request can sleep waiting for memory to be available, or if the allocator can return with a failed request.

Luckily, the kernel provides a number of predefined definitions that you can use without the need to understand the lower-level details, as shown in Table 8.2.

The majority of uses of `kmalloc` simply use the GFP_KERNEL flag.

PCI Memory Allocation and Mapping

The PCI subsystem provides a number of memory allocation routines that should be used when allocating memory, which is shared between the processor and a device. There are a wide range of system combinations supported by Linux, 32-bit/64-bit CPU, 32-bit/64-bit PCI, different processor endianness, PCI bus address translation in controllers, memory coherence (between CPU and devices)—all of which lead to challenges in creating platform device drivers for PCI devices that may

Table 8.2 Flag Types (Subset).

Flag	Description
GFP_USER	Allocates memory on behalf of a user process (current process context). May sleep.
GFP_KERNEL	Allocates normal kernel memory. May sleep.
GFP_ATOMIC	Allocation will not sleep, uses emergency pools, and can be called from interrupt handlers.
GFP_HIGHUSER	Requests high memory; cannot be used with kmalloc.
GFP_NOIO	Does not perform any I/O while trying to get memory.
GFP_NOFS	Does not perform file system I/O while trying to get memory.
GFP_NOWAIT	The allocation request cannot sleep, but may fail.
GFP_THISNODE	In some SMP NUMA vases you may want to allocate memory closest to a particular processor. This makes such a request.

be used in any system. The expectation of a device driver that has been upstreamed and hosted at kernel.org is that it will operate on any supported architecture if a PCI bus is supported.

A device driver may allocate memory for use as a shared communication area between the processor and device. The device driver must have a virtual address mapping for this memory in order to write to the memory. The device must also be informed of the address in a configuration register. The address written to in the device must be the address the device puts in the PCI transactions and is called the bus address. The driver must have the physical and bus address that corresponds to the virtual address used by the driver. On older kernels this translation was achieved by calling virt_to_bus() and bus_to_virt(). However, these have been superseded by the PCI DMA interface and should not be used.

The DMA API provides allocation for two different use cases, known as *consistent* and *streaming*. Consistent mapping should be used for memory that must be guaranteed to be accessible from the device at all times. It is typically allocated and mapped during initialization. The device and CPU can access the memory concurrently. The software is not expected to perform any cache flush (for non-cache coherent architectures) for this memory space. When the CPU writes to this space, it is immediately visible to the device. There are some processor architectures where you need place a write barrier in the instruction pipeline to ensure such consistency. This can be achieved by using the write memory barrier call wmb(). The IA-32 processors are strongly ordered and do not require the wmb(). Processors such as Itanium® are weakly ordered and do require such barriers.

The call to allocate a consistent area of memory uses the following function:

```
dma_addr_t dma_handle;
cpu_addr =
dma_alloc_coherent(dev, size, &dma_handle, gfp);
```

The function returns a CPU virtual address that can be directly used by the driver to read from and write to the memory. It also returns a dma_handle. The DMA address is the appropriate bus address that can be written to the device.

The DMA Streaming API provides a mechanism to obtain bus addresses for data. The data could be allocated from the NORMAL or HIGHMEM zones. The functions used are called dma_map_single(), dma_map_page(), and dma_map_sg().

```
dma_addr_t dma_handle;
dma_handle = dma_map_single(dev, addr, size, direction);
```

The function returns the bus address for the virtual address provided. The function also performs any architecture-required cache coherence updates. You should consider the data to be "owned" by the device after a map call is made. The reciprocal `dma_unmap_single()`, `dma_unmap_page`, `dma_unmap_sg()` functions should be called once the driver is aware that the device no longer needs access to the mapped page. For example, it may be known that the device interrupts the process to indicate that the packet has been transmitted. The calls take a direction parameter to indicate whether the buffer is going to be written to or read from the device, or both.

SYNCHRONIZATION/LOCKING

All operating systems provide primitives for synchronization and locking mechanisms to develop race-free code. In this section we cover atomic updates to variables, spinlocks, and semaphores.

Atomic Operations

An *atomic operation* is an operation that runs without being interrupted. Operations on atomic integers are easy to use.

```
atomic_t atomic_var;
atomic_set(&atomic_var, 10); / set to 10
atomic_add(5,&atomic_var); // add 5 to the variable
atomic_inc(&atomic_var); // increment by 1.
```

Atomic intrinsics usually use processor atomic instructions, such as the IA-32 instruction `TSL` (test set and lock) or Locked `CMPXCHG` (locked compare and exchange), which are used to build up these underling atomic operations. These instructions can be costly and often serialize the processor's pipeline.

Atomic operations are often used to update counters, although the use of atomics for simple counters should be avoided where possible (create per CPU/context counter values).

Spinlock

In many cases, a sequence of code needs to run that must be executed in one execution context at any given time. No other context can enter the synchronized area of code until the previous context leaves the synchronized area. A simple example of such a case is to update a linked list where head/tail pointer updates must be carried out atomically.

To facilitate such serialization, the Linux kernel provides spinlocks. A spinlock can only be held/owned by one execution context (thread). If the lock has not yet been acquired, then the first thread to request it obtains the lock (with little overhead). If an execution context attempts to acquire the lock but it has already been acquired, then the calling context will simply spin in a loop until the other context releases the lock. Spinlocks are very fast and efficient in terms of acquisition cost, but the CPU running the busy loop is wasting CPU time until the contended execution context is de-scheduled (in a single-processor system).

```
spinlock_t link_lock = SPIN_LOCK_UNLOCKED;
spin_lock(&link_lock);
...
spin_unlock(&link_lock)
```

Obviously, you have to be careful to ensure that you do not create a deadlock scenario, for example, by using spinlocks between an interrupt and kernel thread. To facilitate the use of spinlocks between interrupt and kernel execution context you can use `spin_lock_irqsave()` and `spin_unlock_irqrestore()`.

Depending on the use case, the use of a generic spinlock may block threads that in reality do not need to be. The most common use case is the single writer, multiple reader design pattern. In this case the kernel provides a lock that does not block multiple readers until a thread wishes to perform an update/write. The `read_lock()` and `write_lock()` functions provide such capabilities.

Semaphore

A semaphore is a lock, but it may sleep the context that attempts to obtain a contented lock. Instead of running a busy loop waiting for the lock, the thread is placed in a not-ready state and de-scheduled. Semaphores should only be used where the expected wait time is long; spinlocks should be used in short wait use cases.

The semaphores implemented in the Linux kernel are known as counting semaphores, and the count can be specified. In many cases the count is specified as one, which makes the semaphore a binary semaphore or mutex. There is an API added for mutexes given that they are so common.

```
static DECLARE_MUTEX(link_mutex);
// attempt to get the semaphore
if ( down_ interruptible(&link_mutex))
{
  /* only case were we don't get the mutex is due to
    reception of a signal.*/
...handle signal ..
}
/* Critical section */
...
/* release the mutex */
up(&link_mutex);
```

Given that semaphores and mutexes may cause the calling context to switch, they thus cannot be used from an interrupt context.

SUMMARY

The Linux system is truly amazing. It supports a tremendous number of processor architectures and devices. The subsystems provide an excellent range of capabilities, such as networking and sophisticated file systems. There is a rich set of user space packages providing sophisticated capabilities such as immersive user interfaces and database functions. The capabilities available match well to almost any embedded class of device. The challenge is specifying and scaling the system to the appropriate footprint required by many resource-constrained embedded platforms.

Power Optimization

When embedded systems are either battery operated or deployed in large quantities, power usage is a primary concern in the design. Cost, performance, power, and size are the design considerations that must always be balanced in the design of a computer system.

In this chapter, we consider the power management features that are common to modern embedded computer system components, from CPU-specific features to platform-level industry standards for system management. Moreover, we illustrate a power optimization process that software engineers can use to manage the power efficiency of applications and systems software. While much of power management is handled in platform components, software design choices can have a considerable impact on overall power efficiency.

We begin the discussion with an overview of power consumption in electronics. We focus in particular on the principles that drive power efficiency.

POWER BASICS

Modern integrated circuits are manufactured with a complementary metal oxide semiconductor (CMOS) fabrication process. In a CMOS process, circuits are built with interconnected metal oxide semiconductor field effect transistors (MOSFETs). The power characteristics of these transistors dominate the power characteristics of modern digital electronics, including embedded systems.

Circuits of MOSFETs dissipate power actively by charging capacitors in the circuit network, and this charging happens every time the circuit switches. Active power can be modeled as $P = CV^2f$, where C is the capacitive load, V is the voltage difference across the device, and f is the switching frequency.

Circuit designers have direct control over all three contributing factors, but the capacitive load is a consequence of the physical layout of the circuit and so cannot be managed or varied dynamically. Voltage and frequency, however, can both be changed throughout the operation of the circuit, although doing so requires a substantial circuit design effort.

It is possible to design circuits, and indeed entire logic devices such as CPUs, in order to vary operating voltage and frequency in response to system policy. For example, since voltage and frequency are both first-order determinants of performance, during idle times both can be reduced. When lower performance can be tolerated, opportunities arise to reduce power consumption.

Dynamic power is not the only form of power dissipation. Static power is also consumed in between transistor switching cycles. Historically, this *leakage power* has been negligible, but two trends have pushed it to the forefront. First, in order to accommodate high frequencies, designers typically utilize transistors that operate at voltages very near the switching threshold. This enables fast operation, but increases the fraction of time during which charge can leak across the device (that is, the so-called subthreshold leakage current). Second, modern submicron CMOS processes use very thin gate insulators that make it possible for current to tunnel through the insulator. In fact, the design of highly resistant gate materials is one of the most critical advances required to keep Moore's Law on track, and recent processes have transitioned away from the use of the traditional gate dielectric, silicon dioxide, in favor of highly resistant dielectrics such as those based on hafnium. An operational system can manage leakage power by completely powering down circuits and by increasing threshold voltage (and this latter is at odds with reducing dynamic power).

Circuit designers and semiconductor process engineers have many years of innovation ahead in which they will further improve the power efficiency of integrated circuits. However, at any given time, system designers and programmers must understand the means at their disposal to influence and minimize power consumption. To do so, we now discuss the overall power context for an embedded system.

THE POWER PROFILE OF AN EMBEDDED COMPUTING SYSTEM

Embedded systems are varied, and so are their power profiles. Some embedded systems are always powered on and provide continuous operation. Many types of displays, controllers, and networking devices have usage models that demand that they provide near-peak performance, nearly all of the time.

Other types of embedded computer systems have more variable workloads. Mobile handsets and mobile computers, for example, often have very bursty workloads that vary according to user behavior. With a varying workload comes an opportunity to vary the operational characteristics of the system. In user-facing mobile systems, for example, it is often possible for system components to "sleep" at sub-millisecond frequency in order to reduce overall power consumption without impacting the user experience. Given that humans cannot perceive visual change at frequencies above 60 Hz, opportunities exist to reduce or shut down the operation of system components at frequencies beyond human perception.

It is not surprising, then, that the bulk of advanced power management techniques and features has emerged first in mobile platforms. For example, Intel SpeedStep® technology was introduced in Pentium® M processors in order to support both policy and usage-based frequency and voltage control. The Windows™ operating system has supported Intel SpeedStep technology since its inception. The operating system and CPU work together effectively in a mobile context, such as a laptop. When operating from battery power, Intel SpeedStep technology is enabled and can be configured via operating system preferences to emphasize either performance or battery life ("Max Battery"). When Intel SpeedStep technology is enabled, both clock frequency and voltage are scaled down to reduce dynamic power consumption. Using the default settings, a user benefits from the presence of Intel SpeedStep technology as a natural consequence of plugging in or unplugging the laptop.

Of course, CPUs are not the only components found in a system. Historically, CPUs have been the most intensive consumers of power, but in recent years the growing importance of mobile computing has prompted increases in power efficiency and power management in mobile CPU products. For reasons unrelated to mobile computing and more related to cost-effective power dissipation and reducing the energy contribution to total cost of system ownership, server and desktop chips have experienced similar degrees of improvement in power efficiency. Non-mobile chipsets have certainly benefitted from many of the power efficiency and power management techniques developed for mobile systems.

While CPUs have improved considerably, other system components have been slower to increase power efficiency. With CPUs now consuming a smaller portion of the overall system power budget, manufacturers of other components, such as memory, displays, and I/O devices, have found an unmistakable reason to begin improving power efficiency in earnest.

The first challenge for any system component is to maximize the range of power consumption between low-power states and high-power ones. To see why, consider that it is only beneficial to manage power actively if substantial power savings are to be had, and that the only way for a system or component to achieve substantial power savings is for it to exhibit significantly lower power consumption when idle or under low utilization as compared to the power consumed under load. In other words, if the difference between minimum power and maximum power is negligible, then power management will have a negligible impact.

To clarify this idea, we now discuss the difference between constant and dynamic power in the context of an example system.

CONSTANT VERSUS DYNAMIC POWER

When the hardware system components can operate in a range of power and performance states, from low-power and low-performance to high-performance and peak power, then the resulting power efficiency of an operational system becomes a consequence of the actions and activity of the operating system and application software. Software engineers would hope that idle software would lead to lower power consumption.

However, all systems have some degree of power consumption that is independent of system use. This constant power is drawn regardless of load.

Constant Power

An embedded computer consumes a constant, minimum amount of power when powered on, regardless of the level of system activity. Unfortunately, it is often the case that this constant power dominates the overall power budget of a system. Other than by powering a system down completely or transitioning to a sleep state, software cannot influence a system's constant power.

Dynamic Power

If most of the components in an embedded system support low-power modes, then dynamic power consumption can be significantly controlled through the careful use of resources. An operating system may either observe load or receive explicit signals from applications in order to decide to transition the machine to a lower-power, and consequently lower-performance, state. However, any benefits associated with doing so must be measured against the background constant power that is always being drawn.

To make the discussion concrete, we begin with a discussion of a platform based on the Intel® Atom processor from CompuLab, the fit-PC2. The fit-PC2 is a small-form factor computer built around the 1.6-GHz Intel Atom Z530 CPU and the Intel US15W chipset. With 1 GB DRAM, a 160-GB hard drive, and a full array of I/O channels, including six USB ports, Gigabit Ethernet, and Wi-Fi™, the fit-PC2 offers a typical low-end computing platform in a very small form factor (4.5 x 3.9 x 1.1 inches, or 115 x 101 x 27 millimeters).

Figure 9.1 reports power data for the fit-PC2 in two columns. The first column indicates the power consumption of the platform as reported by the manufacturer. The column has two stacked components. The bottom component indicates the idle power consumption; that is, the power consumed when the system is not executing any user-level application or OS-based service or maintenance task. As can be seen, the reported idle power is 6 W. The top component is the corresponding value under load, reported to be 9 W.

The second column indicates the idle and loaded power consumption as measured at the outlet (that is, by measuring "wall power") on a test system running Ubuntu™ Linux. Such measurements can easily be gathered through the use of low-cost digital power meters. As the chart reports, the measured idle and loaded power consumption rates correspond to 9 W and 11 W, respectively. Given that the combined thermal design power (TDP) for the Intel Atom Z530 and its US15W chipset is 5 W, and that TDP for these chips represents fixed upper bounds on the power that will be dissipated by these two packages, we can see that a substantial fraction of power is consumed in non-CPU and non-chipset components.

The point of this exercise is not to call attention to the difference between the advertised and measured power values. Indeed, any estimates are expected to be loose because they are usually highly dependent on the type and number of I/O devices that are present in the system, such as hard disks and USB devices.

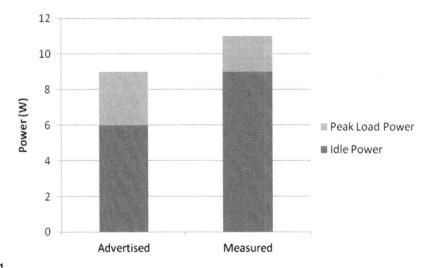

FIGURE 9.1

Advertised and Measured Dynamic Power Range for CompuLab's fit-PC2. The Advertised Power Range Covers 66% of Peak, Whereas the Measured Value, When Accounting for Active I/O Devices, Covers 81% of the Observed Peak.

The main point of this figure is to point out the difference between the constant amount of power that will be consumed by such a system regardless of the load and the peak power consumption. It is constructive to consider the ratio between the two. The estimate has a ratio of idle to peak of $6/9 = 0.66$, while the observed values correspond to a ratio of $9/11 = 0.81$.

These ratios suggest that, say, 75% of total system power consumption is completely independent of software-level activity on this platform. If the system is powered up and capable of executing software, then it will consume at least 75% of its peak power regardless of the organization and activity of the application software and of the attempts at power management made by the operating system.

In other words, when the system has 0% utilization, it will consume 75% of its peak power. Clearly, the benefits of power management are limited in this platform. Intuitively, we desire a system that consumes power in proportion to its utilization.

The obvious problem with managing power efficiency in this platform is its comparatively large constant power consumption. In order to increase the effectiveness of dynamic power management, this constant power must be reduced. Even if the peak power is unchanged, a significant lowering of the constant power will enable software engineers to better manage the power efficiency of the system.

Indeed, future computer system designs aim to improve the effectiveness of dynamic power management in this way. To explore the impact of likely advances, we can construct and explore a simple model of efficiency.

A SIMPLE MODEL OF POWER EFFICIENCY

Suppose our system is capable of linearly scaling power consumption with utilization, or load. Given a fixed constant power, which is the power consumption observed at zero load, we can define our system's *power efficiency* by taking the ratio of power usage to utilization.

Figure 9.2 illustrates an example with constant power equal to 50% of peak power. Thus, at 0% load, it consumes 50% of peak power for an efficiency of $0/50 = 0$. At 10% load, since power consumption scales linearly with load in our model, normalized power consumption is 55%, yielding an efficiency of 18%. As illustrated in the figure, the system is highly inefficient over most of its operating range and does not achieve 80% efficiency until utilization rises to 70%. Note that we do not want *efficiency* to scale with load; rather, we would like high efficiency over the entire operating range. As we will see, our simple model suggests that a dramatically lower constant power has a transformative impact on the overall power efficiency of a system. In our fit-PC2 example, we saw that constant power represented around 80% of peak power, and Figure 9.2 represents a system with a constant power that corresponds to 50% of peak power. Future systems, however, may well have substantially lower constant power profiles.

Figure 9.3 illustrates results for a system with a constant power that corresponds to 10% of peak power. As can be seen, the efficiency of the unloaded system necessarily remains 0%. However, at 10% load, the system exhibits efficiency of 52%! In fact, 80% efficiency is achieved at a load of 30%. At 50% utilization, the system is 90% efficient.

While current systems do not exhibit such low constant power, this is clearly the direction in which future system designs are heading.

It stands to reason that if an entire system is to be capable of a 10% constant power, then each major hardware component must be as well. Recall that in the fit-PC2, the Intel Atom Z530 and its US15W

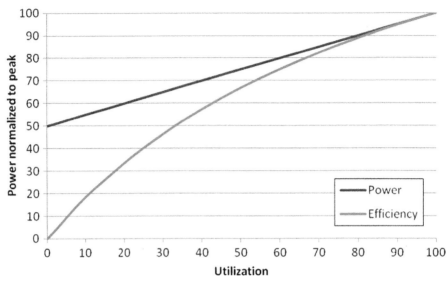

FIGURE 9.2

Power Consumption and Efficiency for a System With a Dynamic Power Range Down to 50% of Peak Performance. Power is Normalized to Peak Consumption. Efficiency is Calculated by Dividing Utilization by Normalized Power.

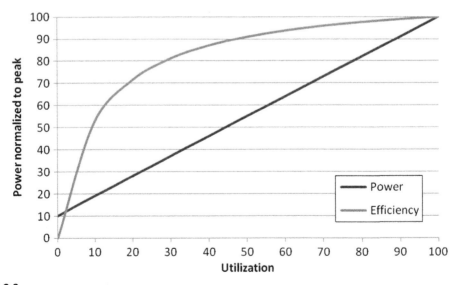

FIGURE 9.3

Power Consumption and Efficiency for a System With a Dynamic Power Range Down to 10% of Peak Performance. Power is Normalized to Peak Consumption. Efficiency is Calculated by Dividing Utilization by Normalized Power.

chipset consumed a maximum of 5 W of the peak observed 11 W of power. So more than half of peak power is contributed by non-CPU and non-chipset components.

This observation illustrates the need for comprehensive system efficiency and a power management scheme that manages power in all hardware components. However, consider the challenge involved with doing so. It is acceptable for an operating system to adapt its low-level systems software in order to accommodate the power management features of a CPU produced by companies like Intel, but only because there are so few types of CPUs that operating system vendors must be aware of! It is not so for memory and I/O device manufacturers.

So how can operating systems accommodate these non-CPU components? And, clearly, any power management scheme must be part of a strategy mediated by the operating system. For a component or device to substantially reduce its power consumption, it must be able to enter a sleep mode, and such a transition in the I/O subsystem must be apparent to the operating system for reasons of stability and performance.

To address this issue, which is in fact a reflection of the overall management requirement that must be sustained between an operating system and the system components, platform-specific industry standards have been developed that define the roles, responsibilities, and specific mechanisms provided to achieve reliable power management and system configuration.

In the next section, we introduce the current standard for managing power in computer systems, the Advanced Configuration and Power Interface (ACPI), which is used in computer systems of all scales to manage power and device configurations. ACPI represents the contemporary philosophy, and indeed the universal industrial standard among manufacturers, of how to manage power in computer systems.

ADVANCED CONFIGURATION AND POWER INTERFACE (ACPI)

ACPI is a standard that has been developed through the cooperation of a group of companies in the computer industry: Hewlett-Packard, Intel, Microsoft, Phoenix Technologies, and Toshiba. The purpose of ACPI is to provide a standard interface for computer system power and configuration management. Through ACPI, the operating system is granted exclusive control over all system-level management tasks, including the boot sequence, device configuration, power management, and external event handling (such as thermal monitoring or power button presses).

ACPI is an evolutionary development that has drawn upon a collection of earlier technologies that individually managed specific tasks. Consequently, ACPI subsumes and replaces technologies such as plug-and-play BIOS, power management BIOS routines, Advanced Power Management (APM), and multiprocessor configuration APIs.

In these previous-generation designs, spreading system configuration and power management responsibility across several different technologies within a system makes it difficult both to optimize system and power management and to develop and exploit effective new management features in system hardware components. Furthermore, since these APIs are not generally interoperable, platform- and operating system–specific development must be undertaken in order to provide support for a wide range of motherboard designs. ACPI has been designed to eliminate this fragmentation and provide robust, efficient, and extensible platform and power management.

Figure 9.4 illustrates the relationship between ACPI, its major internal components, and the rest of a computer system. Entities in red are part of ACPI proper, and while the data held within the memory

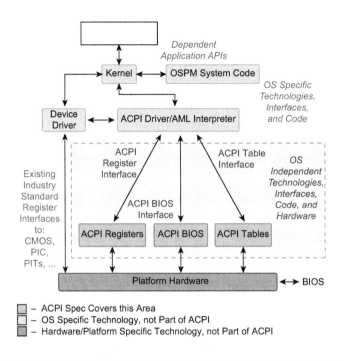

FIGURE 9.4

The Organization of ACPI in a Computer System.

From the Advanced Configuration and Power Interface Specification, Revision 4.0.

structures are specific to a platform and to a platform-instance, ACPI interfaces are used to communicate and interpret the meaning of the data.

As indicated in Figure 9.4, ACPI has three major components:

- *ACPI Registers.* These registers are well-defined locations that can be read and written to monitor and change the status of hardware resources.
- *ACPI BIOS.* This firmware manages system boot and transitions between sleep and active states. The ACPI tables are provided by the ACPI BIOS.
- *ACPI Tables.* These tables describe the interfaces to the underlying hardware and represent the system description. In order to keep hardware descriptions generic and extensible, a domain-specific language has been defined within ACPI. The language, known as the ACPI Machine Language (AML), is a compact, pseudo-code style of machine language. The operating system's ACPI driver includes an interpreter for AML. In ACPI parlance, hardware descriptions are called Definition Blocks.

ACPI is a large specification, and most of its details are beyond the scope of this book. The most important aspect for embedded systems programmers to understand is how the ACPI management strategy relates to power optimization. To gain this understanding, we must consider the state-based model that ACPI employs to relate a system's current state to the operating system and user-visible platform management goal.

Idle Versus Sleep

The two dominant forms of user-facing power management, idle and sleep, have different characteristics and motivations. Sleep states were introduced to allow laptop users to quickly power down a system and then power it up again without having to reboot the system from disk, which is a comparatively long-latency event. In sleep states, the system appears to be powered off completely, while in fact some software may periodically execute to service external events, such as network packet arrivals. Idle modes were introduced to take advantage of the variation in system utilization when the system is powered up. Transitions are made between idle modes at the granularity of seconds and less to reduce active power consumption; these transitions happen without the involvement or even awareness of the user.

ACPI develops these basic notions substantially.

ACPI System States

Figure 9.5 presents a high-level overview of how explicit states are used to implement an overall system management strategy. As can be seen, several types of related states are used to model the overall state of the system as well as the states of individual system components such as CPUs and I/O devices. The G states represent system state; within the sleep state G1, multiple levels of sleep are differentiated via S states. C states encode the state of CPUs; within state C0, P states distinguish between performance and power consumption levels. D states do the same for I/O devices. A uniform interpretation can be applied to the number scheme: the 0-level state always corresponds to a fully operational state, and the higher numbers indicate increasing deep sleep states with correspondingly lower power consumption and higher return latencies. We now briefly discuss each in turn.

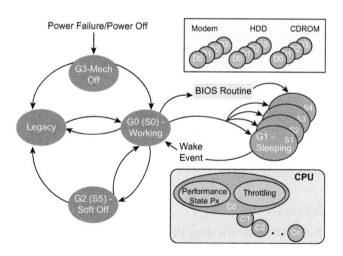

FIGURE 9.5

Relationship between Global, CPU, and Device States in ACPI.

From the Advanced Configuration and Power Interface Specification, Revision 4.0.

Global System States (G*x* States)

Global system states describe the entire system, and transitions between these states are typically obvious to the user.

G0: Working. In this state, the computer is in a normal operating mode, executing user application threads. As described next, the operating system can optionally manage the performance state of the CPUs in the system in response to system usage and policy. Similarly, the power state of peripheral devices can be managed.

G1: Sleeping. When sleeping, the system appears to be powered down. Applications do not execute, but the system may awaken on its own in response to an external event such as a timer or network packet arrival, depending on the system policy as interpreted by the operating system. It is expected that the G1 state consumes less power than G0. Several sleep states can be specified, and these are represented with the S states discussed below. Both the amount of power consumed and the time needed to awaken vary with the S state. In many sleep states, the system can be awoken without rebooting the operating system because the hardware stores system context. The G1 state is used to implement "instant on" boot behavior and often corresponds to "suspend mode" in laptops.

G2 (S5): Soft Off. While technically a sleep state, this "soft off" state is distinguished from the others and is considered a global system state. The mode consumes nearly zero power but can boot to a working state following an electrical signal. In other words, no physical action is necessary to exit the state. No system context is saved, so a complete operating system reboot is necessary.

G3: Mechanical Off. G3 is the genuine "off" state that corresponds to an electrical disconnection mediated via a mechanical action, such as the opening of a physical switch. Likewise, a mechanical action is required to exit this state. States G3 and G2 are distinguished for practical reasons, including some international legal requirements that computing equipment provide a mechanically driven shutdown mechanism. No system context is retained, so a complete operating system reboot is required upon state exit.

S4: Nonvolatile Sleep. Also a sleep state, this nonvolatile sleep mode has a name that directly suggests its purpose. When entering S4, the operating system stores all system context in an image file written to a nonvolatile storage device. Upon state exit, this system context is retrieved and resumed. Exiting S4 is considerably slower than the other states. Under some circumstances, it is possible for a booting operating system to discover the presence of a context that has been written to nonvolatile memory and use it upon entry to G0. For this to be feasible, the system configuration at boot time must be the same as it was at the time of the system image capture. Because the state S4 relies on nonvolatile storage, it is in principle possible for the system to sleep for periods of years without difficulty. S4 typically corresponds to "hibernate mode" in laptops.

Sleep States (S*x* States)

Within the global sleep state G1, several S sleep states are available. Multiple sleep states are needed in order to accommodate lulls in system activity across multiple time scales. We now briefly describe each state.

S1. Among sleep states, S1 provides the lowest waking latency. All system context is maintained by hardware upon entry to S1, including main memory, cache contents, and chipset state.

S2. Sleep state S2 is similar to S1, but differs in one significant detail: the operating system is responsible for storing and restoring CPU and cache hierarchy context. Upon entry to S2, CPU and cache state is lost.

S3. S3 powers down more internal units than S2 but has the same operating system storage requirements. The only difference visible to systems software has to do with the corresponding state levels of I/O devices. Some I/O paths are unavailable in S3, hence more I/O devices need to be in deeper sleep states in order to transition to sleep state S3. Consequently, some wake events are available in S2 but not S3. DRAM, however, is maintained in S3.

S4. As previously discussed, state S4 writes all system states, including main memory, to non-volatile storage. All devices are powered down. Power consumption is very low, but waking latency is high relative to lower sleep states.

S5. As mentioned above, the S5 sleep state does not store system context. Rather, it enables the system to be powered on electronically. State is similar to the S4 state except that the OS does not save any context. With BIOS support, it is possible to resume from S5 with a stored image provided that the system configuration does not differ from the configuration in place at the time the image was captured.

Device Power States (D*x* States)

Device power states are the most unwieldy to discuss in a generic way. For example, consider how similar the power management requirements of, displays, audio devices, and network devices are. In any case, ACPI has created a device class–specific approach to power management that at least allows devices of the same type to be treated in the same way. The device classes defined by ACPI are as follows:

- Audio Device Class
- COM Port Device Class
- Display Device Class (includes CRT monitors, LCD panels, and video controllers for those devices)
- Input Device Class (includes input devices that enable human input, such as keyboards, mice, and game controllers)
- Modem Device Class
- Network Device Class
- PC Card Controller Device Class
- Storage Device Class (includes ATA hard disks, floppy disks, and CD-ROM drives)

The device power states allow for the states to be interpreted or excluded in a class-specific way. A brief summary of the four D states follows.

D0 (Fully On). D0 corresponds to the fully powered-up, fully operational state. In this state, the device offers continuous availability and maintains its own internal context. It is expected to be the state with the highest power consumption.

D1. D1 is the initial sleep state for a device. D1 does not provide normal service, but in many cases is capable of waking itself or the entire system in response to an external event, such as the arrival of a packet on a network link.

D2. D2 is an incremental sleep state beyond D1. The specific differences vary according to the device class, but, generally speaking, the D2 state operates at a lower power, requires a greater waking latency, and is more likely to lose its device context. In the event of lost context, the CPU must either replenish it or reboot the device upon awakening. D2 is also typically capable of waking itself and the rest of the system.

D3hot. The D3hot state effectively saves a device-specific state so that it can be awakened from an otherwise fully powered down state without a complete reboot.

D3 (Off, or D3cold). D3 corresponds to a complete power down of the device. When exiting D3, no device context can be restored, and hence a complete initialization is required.

Processor Power States (C*x* States)

ACPI allows processors to sleep while in the G0 working state. The processor power states, the C states, only apply when the global state is G0. The C states are categorized as either active (C0) or sleeping (C1, C2, …). In the ACPI specification, only C0 and C1 are required; the other states are optional. In the sleeping states, no instructions are executed and the processor is expected to consume less power. Of course, the deeper the sleep state, the longer the latency required to awaken from that state.

Transitions from C0 to C1 or other C states are initiated by the operating system during idle periods. The operating system periodically checks an ACPI counter to observe what fraction of its time has recently been spent in the idle loop.

C0. In C0, the processor executes instructions and operates normally.

C1. Of the C sleep states, C1 has the lowest transition latency. In fact, it must be low enough as to be negligible and therefore not an input to the operating system's decision to transition to this state. Transition to C1 is not apparent to application software and does not otherwise alter system operation. This state is supported through a native instruction of the processor (HLT or MWAIT for IA32 processors) and assumes no hardware support is needed from the chipset.

C2. C2 is a lower-power sleep state, as compared to C1, and its worst-case transition latency can be found in the ACPI system firmware. The operating system does consider the transition latency when determining the benefits of transitioning to this state rather than another. Transition to C2 is not apparent to software and does not otherwise alter system operation.

C3. The C3 state offers great power reduction at the cost of an increased transition latency, which, like C2, is part of the explicit evaluation made by the operating system when making sleep state transition decisions. Additionally, in C3, processor caches maintain their state but do not emit cache coherence traffic; operating system software must ensure cache coherence when a processor resides in C3 by, for example, flushing and invalidating caches prior to state entry.

C4…C*n*. ACPI, Revision 2.0 introduced optional additional power states. The specific entry and exit semantics are the responsibility of the vendor, but the principles that define the relationships between the first four states—that higher state numbers imply higher transition latency and greater reductions in power consumption—apply among these states as well.

Processor Performance States (P*x* States)

Within processor power state C0, ACPI defines a range of performance states that are intended to enable a fully working system to vary its power consumption and performance by operating at different voltage and frequency levels. The operating system explicitly controls transitions between these states. If a CPU provides multiple levels of operating performance, then they can be mapped onto these P states. In multiprocessor systems, each processor must support the same number and type of processor performance state; the ACPI specification does not offer support for any degree of heterogeneity. The Px states are briefly introduced below.

P0. P0 is the maximum performance, maximum power consumption state.

P1. P1 is the next-highest-performing processor performance state and is expected to have the second-greatest power consumption.

Pn. ACPI allows for a maximum of 16 distinct performance states. The requirement is that performance and power consumption decrease monotonically with the level n. So, P0 is the highest in both performance and power consumption, and Pk, where k is the last available performance state, has the least performance and power consumption among performance states.

Enhanced Intel SpeedStep Technology

Enhanced Intel SpeedStep technology was introduced in 2003 with Pentium M architecture, and since then most of the processors support it. The technology features performance and power management through voltage and frequency control, thermal monitoring, and thermal management features.

Enhanced Intel Speedstep Technology provides a central software control mechanism through which the processor can manage different operating points.

Multiple voltage and frequency processor operating points offer various performance and power combinations.

In an FSB-based system, processors drive seven output voltage identification (VID) pins to facilitate automatic selection of processor voltages VCC from the motherboard voltage regulator. The Intel datasheet provides tables mapping VID pin values and the expected voltage values from the power circuitry.

Each core in a multi-core processor has its own MSR to control the VID value. However, each core must work at the same voltage and frequency. Processors have special logic to resolve performance requests from all cores.

OPTIMIZING SOFTWARE FOR POWER PERFORMANCE

Ultimately, embedded software engineers must influence the power efficiency of their systems through the design and implementation of their software. As described in the preceding sections, both the total amount of dynamic power efficiency and the specific mechanisms used to transition between power management states are a direct consequence of the hardware resources and the operating system power management policy. Certain coarse-grained power management preferences can be expressed to the operating system, for example, to maximize battery life or performance, but these are under the control of the user, not the application or service developer.

So how should software be constructed to maximize power performance? The overriding guiding principle is "race to sleep."

Race to Sleep

Since modern systems transition between high-performance, high-power states and low-performance, low-power ones in response to load, software should be organized to complete all available useful work in a continuous batch and then transition to an idle state and avoid unnecessary interruptions.

Of course, traditional software development tools emphasize code execution frequency and aim to point out the relative contributions to execution time that are made by program subsets. Profiling and tracing program execution can clearly indicate where time is spent within a program but do not directly indicate how often a program interferes with transitions to low-power CPU states.

The Linux PowerTOP Tool

PowerTOP was created in response to this situation. PowerTOP is an open-source power profiling tool for Linux that reports the occupation frequency of processor sleep and performance states. It also reports the overall frequency of wake-up events and keeps track of their system-wide sources. The tool can be obtained, along with installation instructions, at http://www.lesswatts.org.

Figure 9.6 presents a screen capture of the interactive PowerTOP interface, version 1.11. As can be seen, it uses a text-console interface with four distinct information regions.

The topmost region reports the system's available C and P states and their relative occupancy during the most recent observation period (the observation period can be found in the following region). In fact, using PowerTOP is among the easiest ways to discover which C and P states are supported by your CPU and operating system. Figure 9.6 reports a PowerTOP instance running on an idle fit-PC2 based on the Intel Atom Z530 CPU and Ubuntu Linux version 9.10. Because the system is idle, which means that the GUI is running but no application processes are running, the system is able to spend nearly all of its time in the C6 sleep state and the lowest-frequency 800-MHz P3 performance state.

The second region in the PowerTOP display consists of two lines. The first reports the number of wake-up events per second that have been observed during the experimental interval. Since wake-up events cause the system to transition out of lower power states, wake-up event frequency is an important contributor to overall power efficiency. The second line gives a power consumption estimate, but is typically only available on laptop systems running on battery power.

The third region of the interface lists the most frequent sources of wake-up events. As can be seen, the sources can be interrupts, operating system services, or user-level processes, and in each case the name of the source and, when available, the name of the internal function, is identified. By listing the top events and quantifying their relative frequencies, developers can direct their attention to the sources that will have the greatest impact on overall power efficiency.

The fourth and final region, at the bottom of the figure, consists of suggestions for improving power drawn from a program-resident database of known tips and tricks for improving efficiency. Based on the observed characteristics of the system, PowerTOP will display those suggestions that are most likely to lead to improvements. Most of the suggestions seem related to spurious I/O activity.

Basic PowerTOP Usage

Figure 9.6 reports data for an idle system, and while it is comforting to see that the idle system spends nearly all of its time in the lowest power states, it is more instructive and interesting to consider how to use PowerTOP to measure an active system.

File   Edit   View   Terminal   Help

```
      PowerTOP version 1.11        (C) 2007 Intel Corporation

Cn                    Avg residency        P-states (frequencies)
C0 (cpu running)         ( 2.8%)             1.60 Ghz    3.2%
polling               0.0ms ( 0.0%)          1333 Mhz    0.0%
C1 mwait              0.2ms ( 0.0%)          1067 Mhz    0.0%
C2 mwait              0.5ms ( 0.0%)           800 Mhz   96.8%
C4 mwait              0.2ms ( 0.0%)
C6 mwait              9.1ms (97.2%)
Wakeups-from-idle per second : 107.8     interval: 15.0s
no ACPI power usage estimate available

Top causes for wakeups:
  41.1% ( 62.1)          <interrupt> : eth0, psb@pci:0000:00:02.0
  21.4% ( 32.4)          <interrupt> : ehci_hcd:usb1, uhci_hcd:usb2, ra0
   8.9% ( 13.4)   USB device  2-2 : Microsoft Wireless Optical Mouse® 1.00 (Micr
   8.6% ( 12.9)        <kernel core> : hrtimer_start (tick_sched_timer)
   6.6% ( 10.0)        <kernel core> : add_timer (rtmp_timer_MlmePeriodicExec)
   5.4% (  8.1)        <kernel core> : usb_hcd_poll_rh_status (rh_timer_func)
   3.8% (  5.8)        <kernel core> : hrtimer_start_range_ns (tick_sched_timer)
   1.2% (  1.8)     gnome-terminal : hrtimer_start_range_ns (hrtimer_wakeup)
   0.6% (  0.9)               Xorg : psb_xhw_ioctl (process_timeout)
   0.4% (  0.6)               Xorg : queue_delayed_work (delayed_work_timer_fn)
   0.2% (  0.3)        <kernel core> : add_timer (rtmp_timer_AsicRxAntEvalTimeout)
   0.2% (  0.3)            nautilus : hrtimer_start_range_ns (hrtimer_wakeup)
   0.2% (  0.3)    update-notifier : hrtimer_start_range_ns (hrtimer_wakeup)
   0.2% (  0.3)     gnome-screensav : hrtimer_start_range_ns (hrtimer_wakeup)
   0.2% (  0.3)         gnome-panel : hrtimer_start_range_ns (hrtimer_wakeup)
   0.1% (  0.2)          <interrupt> : pata_sch
   0.1% (  0.2)     gnome-settings- : hrtimer_start_range_ns (hrtimer_wakeup)
   0.1% (  0.1)               Xorg : hrtimer_start (it_real_fn)
   0.1% (  0.1)          ssh-agent : hrtimer_start_range_ns (hrtimer_wakeup)
   0.1% (  0.1)     gnome-power-man : hrtimer_start_range_ns (hrtimer_wakeup)

Suggestion: increase the VM dirty writeback time from 5.00 to 15 seconds with:
  echo 1500 > /proc/sys/vm/dirty_writeback_centisecs
This wakes the disk up less frequently for background VM activity
  Q - Quit   R - Refresh   W - Increase Writeback time
```

FIGURE 9.6

Screen Capture of the PowerTOP Interactive Console Interface.

Furthermore, since our system is not a laptop, PowerTOP cannot provide us with power consumption estimates, so it is impossible to see how the power state occupancies translate to overall system power consumption. To measure system power, we can use an inexpensive power meter (typically available for around USD 20), such as the Kill-a-Watt meter from P3 International, to measure wall power. Note that the use of a wall power meter like this requires manual recording of power consumption, and, as a result, requires that measurements be taken over reasonably long time scales, ones no shorter than a few seconds.

To get a sense of how PowerTOP can be used to explore the power consumption consequences of normal use behavior, we will consider a few Web browsing scenarios. We begin with an idle system, with a Firefox™ version 3.5.4 browser window open with a single tab pane displaying a static web page. In this condition, PowerTOP reports that C6 is active 97.7% of the time, with 120.1 wake-ups per second. During this period, the wall power meter indicates that 9 W (the minimum) are drawn in steady state.

The same configuration used to stream a standard-definition video from YouTube™ reports occupancies for C0 and C6 as 82% and 13%, respectively, with the remainder balanced between C2 and C4. Around 70 wake-ups per second are observed, along with a steady state wall power of 10 W. Curiously, after the video is stopped but before the browser is closed, the system exhibits C0 and C6 occupancies of 18% and 72%; although the system is idle, and there is no visible activity on the screen, the pane displaying the web page generates enough wake-up events to keep the system from fully utilizing its low-power state.

Using PowerTOP to Evaluate Software and Systems

The previous example illustrates how a running system can be studied, but how can PowerTOP be used to measure and improve the performance of code as you write it? To illustrate one way of doing so, we have created a simple measurement harness that can be used to explore the power efficiency of pieces of code as they are being written.

The measurement harness is implemented in Python. To begin, the developer identifies the target code for measurement, which we refer to as the code-under-test (CUT). The basic operation of the harness proceeds in three phases.

Phase 1. Discover the maximum rate of execution of the CUT. In other words, how many times can the CUT be executed per second on an unloaded system? This notion is easy to understand for code that is run in an event-handling context. Not all code fits this model directly; for example, some code sequences have side effects such as file I/O that may interfere across iterations, but we find that most code can be made to fit in the harness with modest effort. The point of discovering the execution rate of the CUT is to accurately identify its maximum rate of power consumption, which corresponds to the power consumed during a substation period of its peak execution rate. The harness automatically discovers the CUT's maximum execution rate by calculating the execution time per iteration across rounds of iterations whose lengths vary by orders of magnitude. Multiple rounds are used to ensure that the observed execution rate scales linearly with the number of iterations. This ensures that startup or shutdown effects do not disturb the measurements.

Phase 2. Measure the power efficiency at the maximum execution rate. Once the CUT's maximum execution rate is found, PowerTOP is used to measure the power efficiency of the CUT during a sustained period of maximum rate execution. The resulting measurements indicated what level of power efficiency the CUT would achieve if it ran continuously.

Phase 3. Measure the power efficiency as the execution rate is scaled down from the maximum. Given the peak power consumption as a baseline, the harness varies the execution frequency of the CUT to explore the impact on power efficiency. We vary two key parameters to explore reduce execution frequency. First, we explore the total fraction of "sleep" time during the experimental observation period. Sleep time refers to time the process spends suspending, awaiting a timer interrupt to resume normal execution. At the maximum execution rate, the sleep fraction is zero. Suppose, however, that 10% of the total observation period was spent sleeping. Would this change result in a gain in power efficiency? If so, then by how much? The answer also depends on the second parameter, which is the duration of an individual sleep interval. If 10% of the total observation period is sleep time, then it is possible to achieve by using a single long sleep interval, or many shorter ones. In the measurement harness, both of these parameters are varied automatically to measure the resulting change in power efficiency.

Note that our interest is in steady-state power consumption and not in the total amount of power consumed to complete a given amount of work; if there is a fixed amount of work to do, it is probably best to complete it all in one high-performance burst if possible. Our interest is in exploring the power efficiency of code as its execution frequency changes, as this can be useful information when deciding to further optimize or set maximum execution frequency limits.

We will now consider an explicit example and explain the test harness code as we proceed. The measurement harness script begins by including libraries and defining the code-under-test.

```
1 import random, sys, time, os
2
3 random.seed()
4
5 #Define the code-under-test
6 def CUT():
7     a = random.random() * random.random()
8     b = a**2
9     c = random.random()*a + b
10
```

Let's look at what is going on in this code.

Lines 6–9: This CUT example is a simple numerical computation that makes use of several random number library function calls.

The program continues with the implementation of phase 1.

```
11 # Phase 1: Discover CUT max execution rate
12
13 # The basic strategy is to measure the time needed
14 # to execute a range of known iterations and make
15 # sure that performance scales linearly with iterations
16 # over the range.
17
18 iters = [10000, 100000, 1000000, 2000000]
19 elapsed = {}
20
21 for icount in iters:
22     #Record start counter
23     start = time.time()
24     for lcv in range(icount):
25         CUT()
26     #Record stop counter
27     stop = time.time()
28     #Record elasped time
29     elapsed[icount] = stop - start
30
31 rates = []
```

```
32 for val in elapsed.keys():
33     rate = val/elapsed[val]
34     rates.append(rate)
35
36 rates.sort()
37 print "Observed rates:", rates
```

Lines 18–37: As can be seen, the CUT's runtime is measured over several rounds of iterations, ranging from 10,000 to 2,000,000. The loop beginning on line 21 records the time before and after the iterations are completed. Given the elapsed time and the number of iterations, the average time per iteration can be calculated (in lines 31–34) and sorted (line 36). The rates are then printed to the console, where the user can inspect the values and modify the iterations if necessary (that is, if the stable average isn't found over the range). For this particular CUT, the maximum observed rate on our Intel Atom system is approximately 216,000 iterations per second.

```
38
39 #Phase 2. Measure C levels, P levels, and IPS at max rate
40
41 # Use max observed rate, but reduce it by 10% to be safe
42 maxrate = int(0.9*rates[-1])
43 print "Maximum CUT rate: ", maxrate
44 obsperiod = 10
45 sleeptime = 0
```

Lines 38–45: Next, phase 2 begins. The maximum rate is defined to be 90% of the peak average execution rate from the observed trials. Ninety percent is an arbitrary scaling factor to account for the overhead our test harness imparts. The rates list is in order from lowest to highest, and the [-1] subscript returns the last element. The observation period is set to 10 seconds, and sleeptime is set to zero since we are about to measure the power efficiency of our peak performance.

```
46
47 def run_and_measure():
48     # Now run at proper rate and measure with powertop.
49     # Use a forked process. Run the code in the child,
50     # and start a background powertop proc in the parent.
51
52     pread, pwrite = os.pipe()
53     pid = os.fork()
```

Lines 47–53: The function run_and_measure() uses two processes to simultaneously execute the CUT and measure it with PowerTOP. Line 53 spawns the additional thread, and from this point on two distinct threads of control exist. The parent process receives the process ID of the child process, whereas the child process has a zero value written into its copy of the process ID variable. Thus, the ID variable can be used to control the flow of execution in each process.

```
54     if pid > 0:
55         # This is the parent. Run powertop here.
56         os.close(pwrite)
```

```
57          if not sleeptime:
58              os.system("powertop -d --time=%i >/ powercut_max.txt" % (obsperiod/2))
59          else:
60              os.system("powertop -d --time=%i >/ powercut_%f_%f.txt" % (obsperiod/2,
61                          sleeptime,
62                          pctsleep))
63          os.waitpid(pid, 0)
```

Lines 54–63: Only the parent process has a nonzero process ID variable, and the parent process will invoke the PowerTOP tool. The `sleeptime` variable is used to control whether the maximum rate is being measured or whether some fraction of time will be spent sleeping. In the PowerTOP system calls, the `-d` parameter instructs PowerTOP to run in batch mode and simply dump its output to standard out. The `-time` parameter sets the observation period and is here set to be one-half of the overall observation period. The CUT is executed for more time to make sure that PowerTOP measures during steady-state execution and not a portion of the program exit. Each PowerTOP invocation writes its results to a file named to reflect its parameters. After the measurement harness has completed its work, these output files can be parsed with scripts (such as the one included in the directory with the source code) to gather and analyze the measurements. Once the system call has been invoked, the parent process waits for the child to complete.

```
64
65    else:
66          # This is the child process. Run code here.
67          os.close(pread)
68          if not sleeptime:
69              for i in range(maxrate * obsperiod):
70                  CUT()
71          else:
72              for j in range(sleepintervals):
73                  for i in range(iters_per_interval):
74                      CUT()
75                  time.sleep(sleeptime)
76
77          os._exit(0)
78
79 run_and_measure()
```

Lines 65–79: The CUT executes in the child process. If the `sleeptime` variable is zero, then the code is measuring the efficiency of the maximum execution rate, so the loop iterates often enough to sustain the maximum rate for the duration of the observation period. Otherwise, some number of sleep intervals will be employed, with a corresponding change in the number of execution iterations per interval. These values are calculated below. The child process exits upon complete. On line 79, the function is invoked in order to measure the efficiency of the maximum execution rate.

```
80 #Phase 3. Vary sleeptimes.
81
82 #We will evenly space our executions. How long does
```

```
83 #one iteration take?
84 itlen = 1.0/float(maxrate)
85
86 sleeptimes = [0.1, 0.01, 0.001]
87 sleeppcts = [0.2, 0.4, 0.6, 0.8, 0.9, 0.99]
```

Lines 80–87: The purpose of phase 3 is to explore a range of lower-rate execution scenarios. Two parameters determine precisely how the execution rate of the CUT is reduced, and they both involve putting the process to sleep. The sleep time is the duration in seconds of each sleep interval; three values are explored here. The sleep percentage is the overall percentage of the observation period that is spent sleeping; six values are evaluated. In these observation periods, we spread the sleep periods evenly; this is not the only possible distribution, of course. These two parameters, along with the known duration of a single iteration of the CUT, can together be used to structure the activities of an observation period. In this measurement harness, we will investigate all combinations of these two sleep parameters, meaning that we will have 18 total experiments.

```
88 for sleeptime in sleeptimes:
89     for pctsleep in sleeppcts:
90         print
91         print "Beginning sleeptime=%f and pctsleep=%f" %\ (sleeptime,
92     pctsleep)
93         print
94         maxsleeprate = 1.0/sleeptime
95         # Calculate total sleep time
96         totsleep = obsperiod*pctsleep
97         totrun = obsperiod*(1.0-pctsleep)
98         #How many sleeptime intervals?
99         sleepintervals = int(totsleep/sleeptime)
100        runinterval = totrun/sleepintervals
101        iters_per_interval = int(runinterval*maxrate)
102
103        print "Observation period:", obsperiod
104        print "Sleep percentage: ", pctsleep
105        print "Total sleep time:", totsleep
106        print "Time length of a sleep interval",/ sleeptime
107        print "Total run time:", totrun
108        print "Time length of a run interval:",/ runinterval
109        print "Iterations per interval:",/ iters_per_interval
110        print "Sleep intervals:", sleepintervals
111
112        run_and_measure()
```

Lines 88–112: The experiments are carried out within a doubly nested loop. Lines 94–101 calculate the durations and ratios that are used within the run_and_measure() function described above to execute the proper number and type of intervals.

To see how the measurement harness can be used to understand the performance of this particular CUT on our test system, consider that PowerTOP reports that C0 was occupied 100% of the time at the maximum execution rate of 217,000 iterations per second. With an overall sleep percentage of 60%, meaning that process was sleeping for 60% of the observation period, the occupancy of C0 varied moderately with the sleep interval value. In particular, C0 occupancy was 41.6%, 49.8%, and 56.7% for sleep intervals 0.1, 0.01, and 0.001, respectively. However, C6 occupancy, the deep sleep state, differed more dramatically: intervals 0.1 and 0.01 had C6 occupancies of 58.3% and 49.5%, respectively, while 0.001 had a C6 occupancy of 1.5% (it spent 41.7% of its time in C2).

This particular trend was robust across nearly all experiments. Millisecond sleep times were too brief and would not allow substantive occupancy in the C6 sleep state. Even when 80% of the observation period was spent sleeping, a sleep interval of 1 ms led to a 57.3% occupancy in C2 and 35.3% in C0.

SUMMARY

In this chapter, we have explored the basics of power dissipation in semiconductor devices, the significance of constant and dynamic power consumption in a computer system, the ACPI standard for power management, and software techniques for measuring and managing power consumption.

Through careful system configuration and disciplined use of power measurement tools such as PowerTOP, it is possible to make maximum use of the available dynamic power range in order to minimize power consumption. Unfortunately, most present-day systems offer narrow dynamic power ranges in comparison to their levels of constant power consumption. So while there are many steps that can be taken to reduce dynamic power consumption, the benefits must always be weighed against the total effect on system power consumption.

It is certain that future systems will lower their constant power consumption and widen their range of dynamic power consumption. The methods discussed in this chapter will take on even greater significance as these system characteristics improve in mainstream platforms.

Embedded Graphics and Multimedia Acceleration

10

In this chapter we will describe frame rendering and layer mixing techniques to provide a simple human–machine interface (HMI) in addition to multimedia rendering on displays. We briefly touch on graphics application programming interfaces (APIs) and their use in composing images for embedded displays.

Given that embedded applications often mix low power requirements and high-quality media, SOC devices often include dedicated hardware acceleration functions to support real-time decoding and encoding of high-definition compressed media streams such as MPEG4. In this chapter we will describe the frameworks and APIs for video capture, encoding, and decoding.

We make no attempt to cover the actual graphics APIs or detailed 2D/3D rendering techniques; the topic itself is the subject of many books. The chapter provides some insight into aspects of the graphics and media pipelines related to embedded systems.

At its most basic instantiation, the display controller of the hardware takes the frame represented in memory and outputs it to an interface connected to the display. The memory associated with the display is known as the frame buffer. In embedded systems the frame buffer is usually allocated from system memory. The display controller copies the contents from the memory every frame (for example 30 times per second) and outputs to the display across one of the many physical interface standards. Figure 10.1 shows this transformation of memory data to the display. A pixel can be represented in memory in a number of ways; the most common is Red-Green-Blue-Alpha (RGBA), where a 32-bit memory word represents the pixel. The 32-bit value is comprised of four separate 8-bit elements, red, green, and blue obviously represent the three pixel colors, and alpha signifies the amount of opacity of that pixel. The display controller reads the memory address of the frame buffer and generates the appropriate interface signals to encode the pixel color directed to the display.

The contents of the frame buffer can be generated using a number of different hardware capabilities. In some cases the software simply writes to the frame buffer directly. There are also 2D and 3D graphics acceleration functions that take a command sequence and update the frame buffer based on these high-order commands. The 2D/3D engines rely on off-screen resources (stored in memory) to construct/update the image in the frame buffer. In addition, there is a video decode engine, where the decoded video output can be directed to the display engine, frame buffer, or an off-screen memory region to be included as part of a 3D command sequence. All these capabilities are used when creating sophisticated multimedia human–machine interfaces. The display engine needs to provide indications of the frame start, so the software and hardware accelerator updates can occur to the frame buffer when the system is not accessing data via DMA from the frame buffer. If the frame buffer is updated during the DMA sequence, tearing artifacts may appear on the screen.

The remainder of this chapter provides more detail on each of the capabilities described.

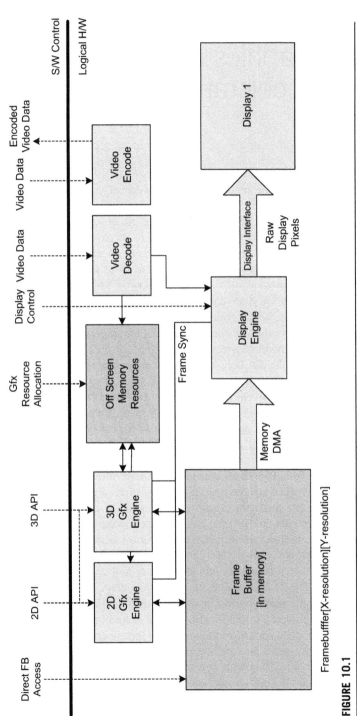

FIGURE 10.1

Graphics Overview.

SCREEN DISPLAY

There are two key techniques for rendering image and HMI data from multiple application data onto the screen. The first technique uses hardware planes to merge different image/frame sources into a single output display. Each plane consists of an individual frame buffer. The display controller blends each of the planes into a single output image. The mixing of the plane data is controlled by the display controller and the content of the per pixel alpha fields. The second technique uses software that relies on graphics processor resources to compose multiple display elements into a sophisticated screen rendering. Earlier embedded SOC devices primarily used hardware-supported layers, but now embedded low-power graphics processing units (GPUs) are being exploited to support the merging of multiple content streams to the output display.

Display Engine

The display system takes a number of input frame buffer sources and merges the frames into a single composite output frame image. The output image can then be sent to the display interfaces for transmission to the display (for example, the LCD screen). Each individual input frame source is known as a *display plane*.

There are a variety of planes (such as display, overlay, sprite, and cursor). A *plane* consists of a rectangular image that has characteristics such as source, size, position, method, and pixel format. These planes get attached to source surfaces, which are rectangular areas in memory with a similar set of characteristics. They are also associated with a particular destination pipe. A pipe consists of a blender that combines a set of planes and an independent timing generator. These timing generators provide distinct timing information for each of the display pipes. The E6xx Series SOCs have two independent display pipes that can generate two independent display streams. The individual pipes do not have to have the same timing, resolution, or refresh rate. There is also an option to clone the content between pipes so the same output goes to the two displays at the same or different resolutions. Figure 10.2 shows the relationship between the pipes and displays. When a pipe is cloned, there is a reduction in memory bandwidth (versus two non-cloned displays), and the displays may have different timing (as the pipe generates the appropriate timing for the attached display).

The use of planes and appropriate control of the blending can reduce software complexity and system bandwidth requirements to present an overall display constructed from multiple sources. Figure 10.3 shows an example of ordering of the planes for a single pipe. The display plane has the highest Z order and is normally on top. A color key can be written to any portion of the display plane; it effectively punches a hole through the display plane showing the overlay plane through the hole made in the display plane. Image rotation is often carried out by the display controller to support horizontal and vertical alignment of the screen. It is not likely that this mechanism is used in devices that change display orientation when the device itself changes orientation (such as the Apple iPhone™), as in this case the device has an elegant transition between landscape and portrait modes.

The blending functions are usually based on a principle known as alpha blending. Each pixel in the plane is represented by an alpha component or transparency value and the color component. For example, the pixels in Plane A could be presented using an encoding of RGBA: red, green, blue, and alpha, and a similar arrangement for Plane B. An alpha value of 0xFF represents a completely opaque

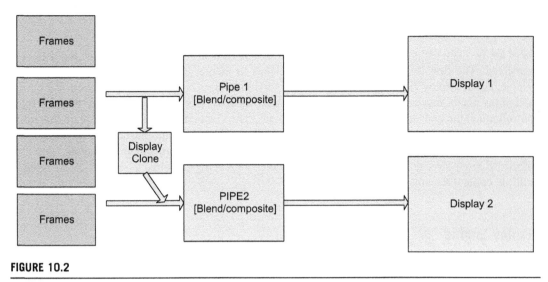

FIGURE 10.2

Display Pipes.

pixel, and a value of 0x00 represents a transparent pixel. Source Alpha (the alpha associated with the uppermost plane in Z order) is used for the alpha blending operation:

$$\text{Destination R, G, B} = (\text{Source Alpha}^*\text{Source RGB}) + ((1.0 - \text{Source Alpha})^*\text{Destination RGB})$$

There are also capabilities to crop/offset and scale an image as part of the blending function. Cropping the image is done by selecting a subset rectangle of the incoming frame rectangle. The cropped portion

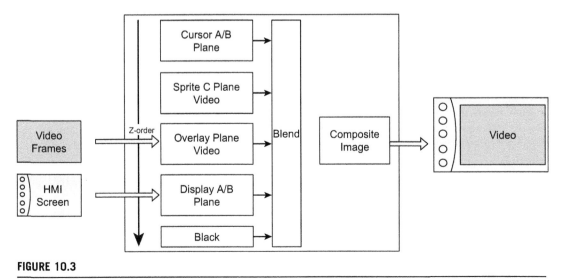

FIGURE 10.3

Plane Mapping/Blending.

of the frame can be further scaled and offsets added to relocate the image in the new frame. Figure 10.4 shows some of the options available using this very simple technique.

An example of the transform and scale example above could be used in your television satellite or cable receiver. Normally, the video stream is occupying the entire screen. When you select a program guide mode, the live video stream is put into a small window in the corner and the remainder of the display is occupied by the program guide menus and such. These techniques using a combination of cropping, offsetting, scaling, and alpha blending are employed in many devices to create relatively sophisticated user experiences.

On the Z600 Series processors, the task of the blend engine in the pipe is to combine the various planes (from different video memory surfaces) into one image to be displayed on the screen. The pipe supports a frame buffer/overlay alpha blending feature to enable the display plane to show on top of the video overlay plane. Normally, the video plane is opaque, as the frame buffer paints a color key over the overlay plane for it to show.

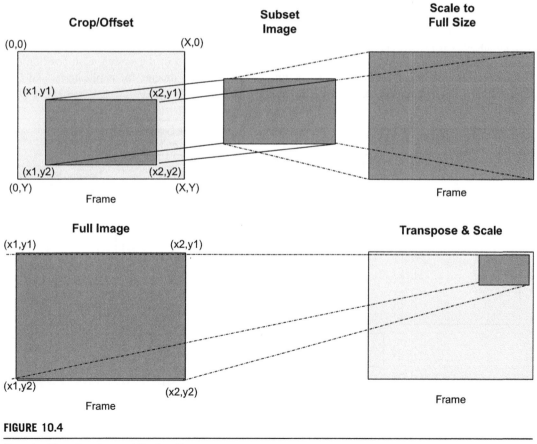

FIGURE 10.4

Cropping/Transforming and Scaling Frames.

Window Management

In order to provide multiple applications with access to the screen, most platforms provide a capability to allow applications to access the screen. In many cases each application writes to an off-screen buffer. The window manager then coordinates rendering the data to the screen. The data is often double-buffered. Double-buffering ensures that no artifacts appear on the screen due to the application updating the buffer while the display reads from the same buffer. The window manager also manages the event subsystem and sends keyboard, mouse, and touchscreen events to the application in focus. The X-Window system is predominantly used in Linux-based systems, although in some cases X-Windows is not used, and the screen is directly managed by coordinating applications or some alternate proprietary layer (logical or real) management library.

Screen Composition

The overall contents on the display are typically composed using a composition manager. A composition manager provides a buffer manager and a synchronization capability and decouples rendering from the display. Each application renders into an application-specific surface. The application can use accelerated 2D and 3D features to render into the surface. The composition manager then composes each of the application surfaces into an overall output. The composition manager itself can use 2D/3D and alpha blending GPU effects in the composition of the screen. Composition (UI composition) is the graphics process that "composes" the display images for applications and OS. Figure 10.5 shows the screen composition process.

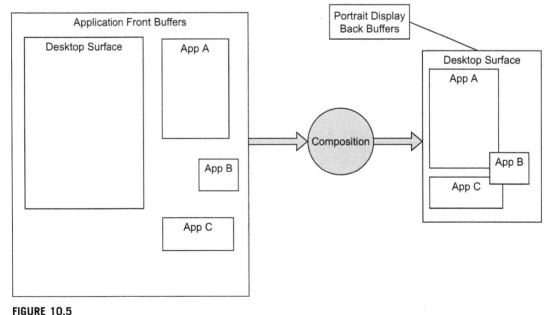

FIGURE 10.5

Screen Composition.

The composition capability is much more sophisticated than that outlined using display planes. The composition manager can add transition effects when an application surface is being presented to the user. In traditional desktop platforms the screen is managed by a window manager. There are a number of compositing window managers available for X-Window-based systems, such as Compiz Fusion™, KWin™, and Metacity™. However, in the context of embedded devices, the concept of a home screen manager is more likely. The window manager also ensures that input events are routed to the appropriate application process depending on window focus, visibility, and so on. In many embedded cases the event coordination is managed by a composition manager. For example, the Android™ operating system provides a composition manager known as Surface Flinger. It provides a system surface composer and renders the individual application frame surfaces into the frame buffer. Surface Flinger can combine 2D and 3D surfaces into a composite output. The surface manager is a native platform library. To coordinate and use the surface manager the application framework provides Window and Activity Manager APIs for use by the application.

As we mentioned above, the application renders into an application-specific buffer; in the case of direct rendering support (DRI2 Linux), the application renders into a buffer that is in video memory (as opposed to a normal host memory buffer). The application can use OpenGL calls to render into the video memory buffer. The compositor can then use the application buffer in video memory as a texture in an overall 3D rendered scene. (Note that the scene can be a flat 2D surface and still use the 3D rendering capabilities.) At the time of writing, the use of X continues to evolve and Wayland is becoming prevalent.

EMBEDDED PANELS

Although the technologies used to create standalone LCD monitors are similar to those used to create LCD panels, the mechanism to attach and LCD panels usually employs interfaces specific to embedded systems. The traditional digital connections to monitors in use today are Digital Visual Interface (DVI) and DisplayPort™, whereas Low Voltage Differential Signal (LVDS), Serial Digital Video Output (SVDO), and Embedded DisplayPort (eDP) are common in embedded systems. All formats are designed to carry digital data from the system to the display.

DVI consists of four twisted pairs of wires: red, green, blue, and clock. The color twisted pair carries a pixel bit stream with 24 bits per pixel. With a maximum clock speed, the realistic maximum supported display size is 2098 x 1311 (widescreen ratio). The DVI connector makes provision to carry an extra set of pixel twisted pairs (red, green, blue). High-Definition Multimedia Interface (HDMI) (mostly compatible with DVI) is an interface standardized to transmit both uncompressed audio and video signals. In addition to the multimedia, the link includes Consumer Electronics Control (CEC), which is a one-wire bidirectional serial bus that uses the industry-standard AV Link to control devices. The digital video format over HDMI is the same as that found in a single link DVI signal and can be converted just by using the appropriate physical adaptor.

Low Voltage Differential Signal (LVDS) is actually the electrical definition for the physical signaling on a parallel bus. Each signal wire consists of two separate wires. A small current is injected into one of the wires depending on the logical level being sent. The current flows from the transmitter to the receiver, across a sensing resistor, and back along the other (return) wire.

The receiver measures the voltage and polarity at the resistor to identify the logic level being sent. The system requires very little power to send the information and is used to connect to LCD panels in laptops, and so on. There are 18-bits-per-pixel and 24-bits-per=pixel interfaces and associated displays in common use. The pixels and control data are sent across a number of these LVDS pairs.

At the time of writing LVDS-based interconnects are starting to be superseded by Internal DisplayPort and Embedded DisplayPort under VESA. VESA is a display industry standards body (http://www.vesa.org). DisplayPort consists of one, two, or four high-speed differential pairs. The format uses a micro-packet architecture, where a packet size is limited to 64 bytes. The line encoding uses 8b:10b where the clock is embedded in the data stream. The data rate can be 1.6, 2.7, or 5.4 Gbps per lane. Auxiliary data channels are also supported to identify and manage the display and remote command capabilities. Embedded DisplayPort is based on the standard DisplayPort, with some minor changes. The number of link lanes can be reduced to match the capabilities of the actual display (for example, one lane supports 1680 x 1050 18-bit color at 60 Hz). A simple display authentication is introduced that simplifies the circuitry of the source and sink function. A fast link retraining sequence ensures fast display resume times. Embedded DisplayPort brings a significant reduction in wires from that found in LVDS-based displays (for example, from 18 down to 5 for a 1680 x 1050 panel with 18-bit color). The micro-packet architecture allows the DisplayPort cable to carry many logical channels within the cable; it can carry video, audio, and bidirectional control channels to multiple displays.

The LCD panel itself cannot be driven directly by the digital interface used to carry the pixel stream; it is attached to a timing controller (TCON). An embedded display port system is shown in Figure 10.6.

The Mobile Industry Process Interface Alliance (MIPI) has developed a number of interface specifications for displays in mobile devices. The design goal is to provide a low-power, low-cost interface to the display.

Serial Digital Video Out (SDVO) is a proprietary technology developed by Intel. SDVO is a digital display channel that serially transmits digital display data to an external SDVO receiver device. The SDVO device accepts this serialized format and then translates the data into the appropriate display output format: TMDS, LVDS, and TV-Out.

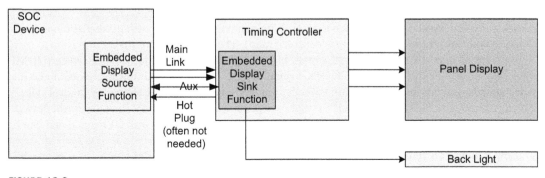

FIGURE 10.6

Embedded Display Connection to LCD Panel.

SVDO converters are available from a number of vendors, and the Intel® Atom™ Processor E6xx Series' device integrates both an LVDS display controller and an SDVO port.

Display Query and Timing

In order to operate with an embedded panel, the display timing must be established. In many non-embedded cases the display timing and other information are stored in a serial EPROM associated with the display. A number of standardized mechanisms are available to read the data. The most common is through the use of an Enhanced Display Data Channel, which provides display data defined by the Enhanced EDID (E-EDID) standard. The standard defines the format and content of the data structure when queried. The contents include display manufacturer and the detailed panel timing.

In many embedded use cases, the display is an integral part of the design, and the software may have to query the display data from using the Display Data Channel. However given that the display is not usually changed in an embedded system the graphics driver provider will provide tools to hard-code the panel information. For example, the Intel Embedded Graphics Driver (IEGD) provides such an application called the Configuration EDitor (CED) to configure the driver (http://edc.intel.com/ Software/Downloads/IEGD/#download). Pre-provisioning the panel data has the added advantage of improving the boot time of the system by eliminating the delay for the display configuration to be read.

Copy Protection

In many cases the embedded system will be rendering content that is protected under some form of digital rights management (DRM) scheme; a good example of protected content is a movie on a Blu-ray™ disk. In order to play back this content it is usually required that the link to the display be encrypted. High-bandwidth Digital Content Protection (HDCP; http://www.digital-cp.com/) is a digital copy protection protocol. HDCP can operate over DVI, HDMI, and DisplayPort. The latest specification has broadened to include encryption over any physical interface via Interface Independent Adaptation.

The HDCP protocol first requires that the display device (HDCP receiver) be authenticated to the HDCP transmitter. Each device has a set of 56-bit keys assigned by the Digital Content Protection LLC. The keys are used as part of an authentication process when they established shared symmetric keys to encrypt the pixel stream.

The deployment also allows for the revocation of device keys if they have been compromised. A HDCP transmitter will not transmit to a device with a revoked key.

GRAPHICS STACK

Computer graphics and the associated APIs is an extremely broad and in-depth topic in its own right; in this section we are going to briefly describe the capabilities and APIs to expect as part of a modern embedded SOC.

The graphics stack and associated APIs provide many levels of abstraction to allow the programmer to create sophisticated scenes on the display. The most basic capability is the ability to render a bitmap on to the screen, rendering directly into the frame buffer of the display. This is often called software bit blitting—bit block transfer. Bit blitting is the combination of bitmap images using simple logical operations to create the overall frame which is rendered.

Currently, most graphical user interfaces use 2D primitives to create the interface. The 2D primitives are accessed using a vector graphics API such as the Cairo Vector Graphics Library™ or the OpenVG™ API (http://www.khronos.org). In many embedded cases the 2D vector graphics are accelerated in hardware (GPU). In addition to the use of 2D rendering, 3D capabilities are required for high-end applications such as navigation applications, games, and sophisticated HMIs. OpenGL™ (http://www.opengl.org) is the most commonly used API, and Direct3D is the 3D API/library provided on Microsoft-based systems (although an OpenGL implementation also exists to run on Windows platforms).

The following open APIs are generally offered in embedded systems, although many embedded systems do not support the full OpenGL and the SOC vendors chose to implement a subset of OpenGL known as OpenGL ES.

- OpenGL—This is the most widely used library providing 2D and 3D APIs. The functions typically make use of hardware capabilities in the GPU. The standard also includes a shader language. The OpenGL Shading Language allows application programmers to express processing that occurs at programmable points within the OpenGL processing pipeline.
- OpenGL ES—Standard for Embedded Accelerated 3D Graphics—A royalty-free, cross-platform API for full-function 2D and 3D graphics on embedded systems. It consists of well-defined subsets of desktop OpenGL. OpenGL ES includes profiles for floating-point and fixed-point systems in the EGL™ specification. OpenGL ES 1.X is for fixed function hardware and offers acceleration, image quality, and efficient embedded performance. OpenGL ES 2.X enables full programmable 3D graphics.
- OpenVG—This is an API for hardware accelerated 2D vector and raster graphics. It provides a device-independent and vendor-neutral interface for sophisticated 2D graphical applications, while allowing device manufacturers to provide hardware acceleration on devices ranging from wrist watches to full microprocessor-based desktop and server machines.
- EGL (*Khronos* Native Platform Graphics Interface)—EGL provides mechanisms for creating rendering surfaces onto which client APIs such as OpenGL ES and OpenVG can draw, creates graphics contexts for client APIs, and synchronizes drawing by client APIs as well as native platform rendering APIs. This enables seamless rendering using both OpenGL ES and OpenVG for high-performance, accelerated, mixed-mode 2D and 3D rendering.

Figure 10.7 shows the overall interaction between the different APIs in the context of an Intel Atom™ Processor E6xx driver suite.

The graphics APIs mentioned above are prevalent in systems today; the OpenGL ES API is the most popular as it requires fewer resources (than OpenGL) in both hardware and software to implement, although Intel platforms often provide implementations that support the full OpenGL standard to allow for code portability from desktop environments for some applications. The OpenGL (ES) APIs are standard on a wide range of operating systems from Linux to QNX. OpenVG is an acceleration API used by a number of applications such as Adobe Flash™ rendering.

Microsoft products provide graphics APIs under the DirectX collection of APIs. These APIs are only available on recent Microsoft operating systems, introduced with Windows XP; however, OpenGL APIs are also available on Microsoft platforms. The choice of APIs to use for your application is most likely dictated by the target operating system and APIs supported by the platform.

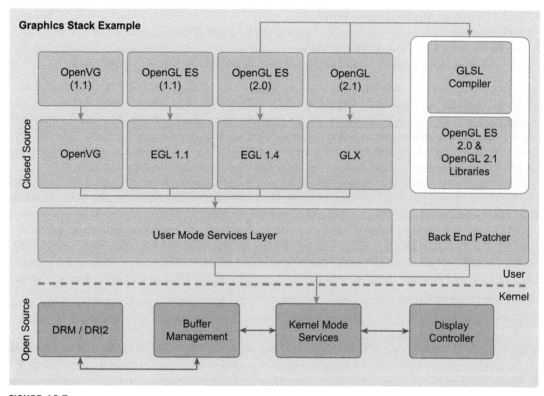

FIGURE 10.7

Graphics Stacks—Linux X.org Context.

ACCELERATED MEDIA DECODE

Raw video content is quite voluminous in terms of the data required to fully represent it, as a result in order to efficiently transport and store video content, it is generally compressed. There are two aspects to the transport/storage of video content. The first is the container format, and the second is the encoder format. A media encoder takes an uncompressed source and compressed format.

The container defines the structure of the media. The media formats typically include a number of video streams encoded with a video codec(s) and one or more synchronized audio streams encoded using audio codec(s). In some cases the container also includes synchronized subtitles or other metadata. The video and audio formats do not have to use the same formats. The following are common container formats and examples of file extensions used for files with that particular container format.

- MPEG4—.MP4
- 3GPP—.3GP

- WMV, Windows Media Video—.WMV
- MPEG Transport Streams—Streaming format used by Digital Video Broadcast (DVB standards)
- Adobe Systems Flash Video (FLV)—.F4V
- Ogg—A free, open standard container format maintained by the Xiph.Org Foundation.

The container formats are standardized by the standard owner, such as the 3GPP organization, Adobe Systems, International Standards Organization (http://www.iso.org/iso/home.htm), Microsoft, and Xiph.Org Foundation in the cases above. At the time of writing the Flash video format is commonly used; a detailed description can be found at http://download.macromedia.com/f4v/video_file_format_spec_v10_1.pdf. Although with the rapid adoption of HTML5, Video streaming and rendering using HTML5 Canvas features has promoted video to a first class capability in web protocols.

There is a wide range of constantly evolving audio and video codecs, although a few are noteworthy due to their extensive use, such as MPEG2, VC-1, H.264/AVC MPEG4, and MP3. MPEG4/H.264 are video codecs; MP3 is an audio codec. We are not going to go into the details of how a codec actually encodes the media source; rather, we will discuss how to incorporate media into embedded systems. The decode of media requires a codec decoder incorporated into the media playback pipeline. Media decoding (both video and audio) can be performed using software-based codecs or hardware-assisted codecs. There are three reasons an SOC designer might elect to include a hardware-based decoder in the design:

- Power efficiency—Using dedicated hardware to decode media is generally more efficient in terms of the power consumption than running the equivalent codec using software in the processor.
- Performance—Codecs (video in particular) are computationally expensive, so the SOC can balance the performance of the system by including a hardware video decode accelerator as part of the SOC.
- Media protection—In many cases the copyright owners and distributors of premium media content (such as movies) place special requirements for media decode. In general, the unencrypted decoded media stream must not be accessible by the host processor.

However, using a hardware-based decoder may have a drawback in terms of the ability to play new codec formats. It can be difficult to forecast which codec format will become widely deployed in the market. In this case it is can be useful to have enough compute power on the general-purpose processor to employ software-based decoding.

As an example, the Intel Atom Processor E6xx Series devices incorporate a video decode engine to hardware-accelerate the video codecs listed in Table 10.1.

Table 10.1 Hardware-Based Video Decoding Support

Codec Standard	Profile	Typical Picture and Frame Rate
H.264	Baseline/Mid/High	1080p at 30 fps, 720p at 60 fps
MPEG4	Simple/Advanced	720p at 30 fps
VC-1	Simple/Advanced	1080p at 30 fps, 720p at 60 fps
WMV9	Simple/Main	1080p at 30 fps, 720p at 60 fps
MPEG2	Simple/Main	1080p at 30 fps, 720p at 60 fps

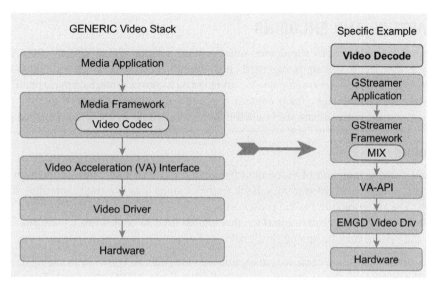

FIGURE 10.8

Media Video Decoding Stack.

In order to make use of the hardware-based decoder, a driver must be provided. In the case of the Intel Atom Processor E6xx Series, the graphics driver provides access to the hardware encoding and decoding engine. This driver then connects to a generic video acceleration API known as the Video Acceleration API (in Linux). The hardware acceleration codec then uses VA API (http://www.freedesktop.org/wiki/Software/vaapi) services to provide a codec level interface to the accelerator. The codec itself is then "plugged in" to a media framework such as GStreamer. The codec plug-in format is specific to the actual framework. The codec for the hardware accelerator and all items below are generally provided by the SOC provider. Figure 10.8 shows the overall hardware accelerated decode stack.

Lip Syncing

The close synchronization of video and audio playback is critical for the viewer. Even minor discrepancies are easily identified. This is particularly the case when watching people speak. The common term for ensuring video and audio synchronization is lip syncing. When audio and video decode functions are performed in different parts of the SOC (for example, the accelerator and processor), the media framework must pay particular attention to synchronizing the media video rendering on the display and audio playback on the device. The video decoder provides detailed timing information about the video frame decode and rendering. The media framework must then delay the audio for the appropriate time to result in synchronization. This problem can be exasperated we subsequently transmit the video and audio over network or wireless interfaces. Consider transmitting video to a display and using Bluetooth wireless headphones. In such cases the delay variation between the differing paths must be accommodated.

VIDEO CAPTURE AND ENCODING

In many embedded applications the device must acquire a video signal directly from an attached camera. Once this video stream is captured, it is usually compressed. This reduces the storage requirements and allows the video content to be streamed on a network interface more readily. A typical uncompressed video stream for 1080p content requires a data rate of several gigabits per second, whereas a compressed video stream using a MPEG4 encoder peaks at about 50 megabits per second.

Video Capture

Video capture is the acquisition of video data from a camera into a software application. The video source consists of a series of video frames. Each frame of video data is a single snapshot in time of the video stream. The video capture system presents the series of frames in data buffers to the application.

Different forms of video camera interface that can be used to connect to a platform. The camera interface to the system may be analog or digital:

- Analog cameras—These are cameras that capture the video data and provide an analog interface to the system. The format of the analog signal is typically either NTSC (National Television System Committee) or PAL (Phase Alternate Line). These formats are commonplace analog television transmissions standards although they are being phased out in many areas of the world. In order for a system to acquire video source from an analog camera, it must be converted into digital form. This is carried out by a video decoder such as the Analog Devices ADV7403. This device converts analog signal into a digital data stream using analog to digital converters and frame processing logic.
- Digital interface—The International Telecommunication Union (ITU), which is part of the United Nations, has standardized a digital video interface known as BT656 (http://www.itu.int/rec/R-REC-BT.656/en). The interface consists of a stream of active video samples (8- or 10-bit) blended with

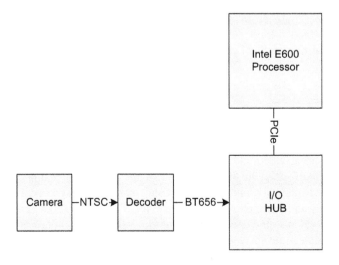

FIGURE 10.9

Video Capture Hardware Path.

Start of Active Video (SAV) and End of Active Video (EAV) codes transmitted at a rate of 27 Mb/s. The digital stream consists of horizontal scan data for the video field. NTSC and PAL sources consist of odd and even fields that combine to make a single fame of data. The individual pixel data are represented using a 4:2:2 YCrCb pixel format. See the pixel encoding discussion below for some detail. There are also low-cost CCD sensor devices that directly connect to the BT656 interface.

- USB camera devices—Many low-cost USB camera solutions can be directly connected to the platform.

Figure 10.9 shows a simple hardware connection of an analog camera device.

Color Space

Many different encodings can be used to represent pixel data. The most common in computer systems is RGB, which is red, green, blue. Each color is usually assigned an 8-bit value, which in total requires 24 bits to represent the pixel color. Given that most systems represent a word as 32 bits, many systems assign the last byte to a transparency (alpha) value for the pixel. The alpha value is used when blending overlays together and represents the transparency of the pixel. RGB is a color space.

The human eye is more sensitive to variations in brightness than to that of color; for each pixel, a differing number of bits can be assigned to represent brightness and color. A common representation of a video signal is YCrCb. The luma or brightness component is Y, and Cr and Cb are the red and blue difference chroma components. The encoding 4:2:2 YCrCb has the advantage of assigning fewer bits to the color component and requires two-thirds less bandwidth than its corresponding RGB-encoded signal. YCrCb is not a color space but a compressed representation of RGB.

Color encoding or color space is the mechanism to represent color in the system. Red/green/blue is the most common color space used in digital systems, but there are many variants. The variants usually take advantage of the human visual system to improve the pervaded quality or reduce the required bandwidth. For example, YUV 4:2:2 uses twice the number of bits to represent the luminance signal. Accurate conversion between the color schemes requires floating-point arithmetic, but in many cases simplified, less accurate integer arithmetic is used due to performance considerations.

You need to be very aware of the color encoding used at each step on your video capture or processing pipeline, as many software and hardware accelerated blocks have limitations in the types of pixel format supported. Conversion between the formats can be relatively expensive, especially in software, so ideally you will set up the whole pipeline to use the same format.

Video Capture Drivers

The Linux operating system provides a video capture subsystem known as Video for Linux 2, or V4L2. V4L2 supports capture by a wide range of capture (http://lwn.net/Articles/203924/) devices and presents the frame data to a user space application. The V4L2 components support a general video capture framework requiring device drivers to interact with the actual capture device. The drivers support the following capture mechanisms:

- USB camera interfaces
- Video capture PCI cards such as those created by Hauppauge
- Digital Video Broadcast standard devices (DVB-S, DVB-T, and so on)

Upstreamed Linux video capture drivers are normally available in the kernel source Linux/Drivers/media/video.

In many cases the video capture hardware requires some control functions. The BT656 standard is a video input stream only and does not provide any control capability for attached devices. Usually, the control of devices attached to the BT656 interfaces provides an I2C interface. The functions controlled by the overall device driver manage the capture and control aspects of the device.

The IOH video capture driver consists of three main components:

- V4L2 (Video for Linux 2)—Video driver. When installed, the /dev/videoX device node is created.
- DMA driver—A shared DMA driver is instantiated in the IOH and is used to transfer data via DMA from the IOH video capture engine.
- I2C/GPIO—A driver to control the camera sensors (e.g., Omnivision VGA sensor ov7620 and 1.3-megapixel sensor ov9653).

The V4L2 device drivers create a character device that supports `ioctl` commands to control the device. The devices typically provide two mechanisms to get frame data from the device:

- Device `read()` calls—These calls follow the traditional I/O model device driver. Frame data is copied into the user space buffer provided to the read buffer. The driver must continuously DMA from the device to a kernel buffers until it is read by the application via the `read()` call.
- Streaming mode—There are two separate modes for streaming, `V4L2_MEMORY_MMAP` and `V4L2_MEMORY_USERPTR`. In the case of the MMAP mode, the video frame buffers are allocated in kernel space. The application maps the buffers into its address space using the `mmap()` system call. In the case of the USER pointer mode, as the name suggests, the application allocates user space buffers. The capture device fills the user space buffers directly by employing DMA from the device into the buffer. This is often more complicated to support in hardware, as the applications allocate virtual memory, which can be composed of a number of physical pages. The DMA engine must DMA into multiple physical memory buffers per frame.

MMAP

MMAP is a service in Linux to provide a two separate virtual address mappings to the same physical location in memory. The memory is first allocated by the kernel; this creates the kernel virtual-to-physical address mapping. The memory is then prevented from being swapped to mass storage by a process known as *pinning*. A MMAP call is then carried out on behalf of a process. This associates a new process-specific virtual address with the same physical memory. When a device uses DMA to access the physical memory buffer, it is also directly visible to the application. This removes the normal data copy between a kernel driver and a user space application and is particularly useful for high volumes of data. In this case, however, it is difficult to share the device with more than one application. MMAP is usually used when a single application takes ownership of the device, as in the case of video capture.

In the streaming mode the buffers are supplied in advance of the video frame being received, and the V4L2 driver uses DMA from the device directly into the user space buffer. The coordination still occurs via `ioctl()` calls to the device, but the frame data (which can be quite voluminous as it is uncompressed) is transferred directly to the application buffers. The application must ensure that a continuous supply of frame buffers is provided to sustain a drop-free video capture. A selection of the capture reference example code is shown in Figure 10.10.

The `ioctl()` call to the V4L2 driver with argument `VIDIOC_REQBUFS` causes the driver to allocate the kernel memory required for the frames. The kernel memory is not visible to the user space application. The `MMAP` call returns a virtual address for this process that corresponds to a buffer allocated in the kernel. The application should request enough buffers to ensure that drop-free operation occurs while the application is processing the buffers.

The video capture processing loop would be as shown in Figure 10.11.

Once the buffers have been allocated, the user space application must queue up the drivers to accept captured data. This is carried out with an `ioctl()` call specifying VIDIOC_QBUF.

```
/*
 *   V4L2 video capture example
 */
#include <linux/videodev2.h>struct buffer {
        void *                 start;

        size_t                 length;

};
// Map a number of buffers into USER space
static void init_mmap_to_userspace(fileDesc)
{
  struct v4l2_requestbuffers buf_req;

  struct buffer *buffers  = NULL;

 ZERO (buf_req);

  buf_req.count   = 64;
  buf_req.type  = V4L2_BUF_TYPE_VIDEO_CAPTURE;
  buf_req.memory  = V4L2_MEMORY_MMAP;
  ioctl (fileDesc, VIDIOC_REQBUFS, & buf_req);

  buffers = calloc (buf_req.count, sizeof (*buffers));
  for (n = 0;n  <  buf_req.count; ++n) {
    struct v4l2_buffer buffer;
    ZERO (buffer);
    buffer.type       = V4L2_BUF_TYPE_VIDEO_CAPTURE;
    buffer.memory     = V4L2_MEMORY_MMAP;
    buffer.index      = n;
    ioctl (fd, VIDIOC_QUERYBUF, & buffer);
    buffers[n].length = buffer.length;
    buffers[n].start =
      mmap (NULL ,
          buffer.length,
          PROT_READ | PROT_WRITE
          MAP_SHARED
          fileDesc, buffer.m.offset);
  }
}
```

FIGURE 10.10

Video for Linux MMAP Buffer Mapping.

```
buf.type = V4L2_BUF_TYPE_VIDEO_CAPTURE;
buf.memory = V4L2_MEMORY_MMAP;
ioctl (fd, VIDIOC_DQBUF, &buf
process_image (buffers[buf.index].start);
ioctl (fd, VIDIOC_QBUF, &buf))
```

FIGURE 10.11

Video for Linux Capture Loop.

The `ioctl()` with VIDIOC_DQBUF de-queues a buffer from the video capture driver. The buffer itself is not copied; rather, the call returns the index of the buffer that has valid frame data and can be consumed by the application. The process image call is a generic call to the application, and finally the `ioctl()` with VIDIOC_QBUF indicates to the driver that the buffer has been processed and can be filled in with new frame data.

We will show how to use the GStreamer framework to capture and encode a video stream later in the chapter.

Video Encoding

The video stream captured by the video capture device can be quite voluminous, and it is common practice to compress this data stream. For example, a relatively low definition 640 x 480 image at 30 frames per second requires a bit rate of 9.2 Mb/s. There are a number of compression standards in use such as Moving Picture Expert Group 2 and 4—MPEG2 and MPEG4. These are known as video codecs, and there are many more. These compression standards are designed to efficiently decode the image; the corresponding encoding process is usually far more computationally expensive (than the decode). As a result, it is common to provide a hardware-based video encoder, especially in low-power embedded systems. For example, encoding a 640 x 480 video stream to MPEG4 requires approximate

Table 10.2 Hardware-Based Video Codec Support

Codec Standard	Level	Max Bit Rate	Typical Picture and Frame Rate
H.264	1b	128 kb/s	Quarter Common Intermediate Format (QCIF) at 15 fps
H.264	L1.1	192 kb/s	QCIF at 30 fps
H.264	L1.2	384 kb/s	Common Intermediate Format (CIF) at 30 fps or Quad Video Graphics Array (QVGA) at 30 fps
H.264	L2.0	2 Mb/s	CIF at 30 fps or QVGA at 30 fps
H.264	L3.0	10 Mb/s	720 x 480 at 30 fps, 720 x 576 at 25 fps, Video Graphics Array (VGA) at 30 fps
H.264	L3.1	14 Mb/s	1280 x 720 at 30 fps
MPEG4	L0/L1	64 kb/s	QCIF at 15 fps
MPEG4	L5	8 Mb/s	720 x 480 at 30 fps, 720 x 576 at 25 fps, VGA at 30 fps
MPEG	L6	16 Mb/s	1280 x 720 at 30 fps
H.263	L60	8 Mb/s	720 x 240 at 60 fps, 720 x 288 at 50 fps
H.263	L70	16 Mb/s	720 x 480 at 60 fps, 720 x 768 at 50 fps

five times fewer CPU cycles to encode using a hardware accelerator than that required by a software encoder. This ratio is even greater for higher frame resolutions. The Intel Atom Processor E6xx Series SOC provides a hardware video encoder that can encode an uncompressed video stream into the following codec standards (subset shown in Table 10.2).

The bit rate output from the codec can be either a constant or variable bit rate (CBR/VBR), or no rate control. In most cases, VBR encoding is now used, as it generally results in a more efficient bit stream for the same quality level.

The video software stack for hardware-based video acceleration requires a video acceleration driver, an abstraction interface to support video encode capabilities, a video codec, and a media framework. The organization is shown in Figure 10.12.

The media encoding stack shown is similar to the decoding stack shown in Figure 10.8. The GStreamer plug-in, however, is an encode codec.

The stack consists of the following components:

- Media application—Many applications have a need to compress a captured media stream. One example is a video security application where the camera data are stored on a local media device or streamed to a central observation center.
- Media framework—Provides an infrastructure to manage the capture, processing, and rendering of media.
- Video encode codec—A video codec plugs into a media framework and converts a stream format from an uncompressed form to a compressed format. The codec can be software only or use the hardware accelerator features of the SOC. As many of the codec standards are encumbered by patent rights, the codecs are usually supplied by a company that has the appropriate business

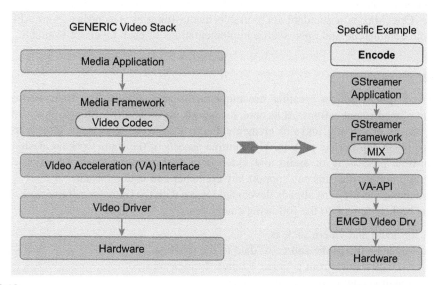

FIGURE 10.12

Media Video Encoding Stack.

agreements in place to license the codec. This is the case for hardware or software implementations. Codecs usually employ a lossy form of compression algorithm (such as H.264).

- Video acceleration interface—LIBVA library and the VAAPI provide both encode and decode acceleration capabilities (http://freedesktop.org/wiki/Software/vaapi). The VAAPI provides an abstraction for hardware-accelerated video decode/encode at various entry points (VLD, IDCT, Motion Compensation, and so on) for the prevailing coding standards today MPEG-2, MPEG-4 ASP/H.263, MPEG-4 AVC/H.264, and VC-1/VMW3.
- Video encode driver—The video encode driver could be stand-alone or integrated into the overall graphics driver depending on how the video encoder is exposed as a device by the hardware.
- Encode hardware—This is the actual hardware accelerator. The hardware is designed to encode to a number of video codec standards. The hardware is targeted to specific standards or portions of the codec function for a standard.

We discussed codec formats above. We should note that there are also container formats. A container is the definition of the transport format for the data. It contains both the audio and video streams as well as metadata such as subtitles information, or additional audio streams. The container should not be confused with the codec format. Some common container formats used at present are 3GP, AVI, FLV, and MPEG-2 transport.

MEDIA FRAMEWORKS

A number of media frameworks are in common use in embedded platforms today, namely, Gstreamer, OpenHelix and frameworks based on the OpenMax defined APIs. Gstreamer is an open source multimedia framework for constructing filter graphs and media processing components using a plug-in architecture. OpenMax is a standard for portable media libraries. OpenMax is an API definition; however, both commercial and open source implementations of each layer are available.

GStreamer

GStreamer is a framework for creating streaming media applications. The framework enables the development of media applications. At its core, it supports the creation of filter graphs. A filter graph is made from source, processing, and sink elements. Each of these elements in the filter graph is created and provided by an appropriate plug-in. The runtime aspects of the framework are designed for low-latency real-time processing of audio and video (and its associated synchronization). GStreamer through the appropriate plug-ins can support any container and codec format.

There are numerous plug-ins already developed for use with the Gstreamer framework. The plug-in types can be broken down into the following categories:

- Sources: for audio and video, such as
  - filesrc—opens a file as the source of data to the pipeline.
  - v4l2src—reads frames from a Video 4 Linux 2 video source.
  - alsasrc—audio capture from an alsa device.
- Formats: parsers, formatters, muxers, demuxers, metadata, and subtitle, such as oggdemux, used to separate audio and video streams from an incoming container. Ogg is a free, open standard

container format maintained by the Xiph.Org Foundation. The creators of the Ogg format state that it is unrestricted by software patents and is designed to provide for efficient streaming and manipulation of high-quality digital multimedia.

- Codecs: coders and decoders that compress and decompress audio/video sources using standardized lossy coders such as OGG/Vorbis and MPEG. Vorbis is an open source non-royalty–bearing audio codec. Similarly, Theora is an open source video codec. These open source royalty-free codecs are not yet widely deployed, and as such hardware acceleration for them is not yet commonplace.
- Filters: converters, mixers, effects such as the geometric transform plug-in.
- Sinks: for audio and video, similar to the source plug-ins, file and network sinks are provided. For network sink capabilities the RTP sink capability is most notable. Simple network sink functions pump the data into a TCP/IP socket.
- Protocol plug-ins: these handle low level protocols such as file I/O and http.

The overall framework is represented in Figure 10.13.

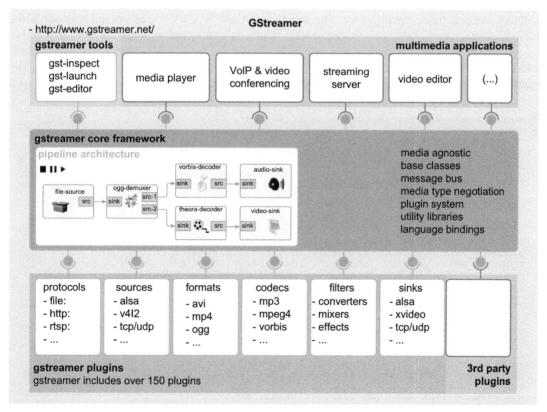

FIGURE 10.13

GStreamer Overview.

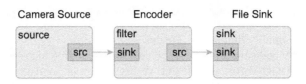

FIGURE 10.14

Simple GStreamer Graph.

A GStreamer-based application is characterized by first defining the data flow. The data flow is structured as a filter graph. A filter graph describes the source of data, processing of data, and sinking of the output data. An example of a trivial filter graph for a video capture application is shown in Figure 10.14.

The equivalent source code developed using the GStreamer framework is shown in Figure 10.15.

The processing in Figure 10.15 first involves creating the required elements of a pipeline. These elements include the video source, which is a V4L2 video source. The capture mode is set to use memory-mapped frame data transfer. The format is YUV2 or UYVY. The second element is the hardware-accelerated codec MixVideoEncoder, which is configured to generate a H.264 output format. The final element is the file data sink. The output is written to a file. Then all the elements are added to the pipeline using `gst_bin_add_many()`. The elements are then linked to form a graph. The example above does not consider possible color conversion steps that may be needed. Depending on

```
source = gst_element_factory_make ("v4l2src", "src0");
g_object_set (G_OBJECT (source), "location",
"/root/Vid_Raw/video_data.raw", NULL);
g_object_set (G_OBJECT (source), "use-mmap", TRUE, NULL);
g_object_set( G_OBJECT(v4l2src), "device", "/dev/videoX", NULL);
g_object_set (G_OBJECT (source), "blocksize", 518400, NULL);
caps = gst_caps_new_simple ("video/x-raw-yuv",
                "width", G_TYPE_INT, 720,
                "height", G_TYPE_INT, 480,
                "framerate", GST_TYPE_FRACTION, 30, 1,
                NULL);
encoder = gst_element_factory_make ("MixVideoEncoder", "mix-video-encoder");
g_object_set (G_OBJECT (encoder), "bit-rate", 1000000, NULL);
g_object_set (G_OBJECT (encoder), "h264-delimiter-type", 1, NULL);
g_object_set (G_OBJECT (encoder), "need-display", 0, NULL);
filesink = gst_element_factory_make ("filesink", "file-sink");
 g_object_set (G_OBJECT (filesink), "location", "video.h264", NULL);
/* we add all elements into the pipeline */
/* file-source | mix-video-encoder | file-sink */
gst_bin_add_many (GST_BIN (pipeline), source, encoder,
                    filesink, NULL);
/* we link the elements together */
/* file-source | ffmpegcolorspace | mix-video-encoder | mix-video-sink */
gst_element_link_filtered(source, encoder, caps);
gst_caps_unref (caps);
gst_element_link_many (encoder, filesink, NULL);
```

FIGURE 10.15

Code Flow for GStreamer Graph Setup.

the video capture device and the currently supported color formats of the encoder, you may need to call `ffmpegcolorspace()`; however, it is much better (in terms of CPU performance) to select a color space that is matched throughout the graph.

For very simple use cases the gst-launch application can be used to create a filter graph without the need to create a stand-alone application. This can be very useful in creating/testing an application before you develop the code, as with the following GStreamer launch application:

```
Linux>gst-launch-0.10 v4l2src ! video/x-raw-yuv,width=640,height=480 ! xvimagesink
```

GStreamer provides a very effective framework to build up multimedia applications. The hardware-accelerated video encoding and decoding are easily integrated into the processing pipeline.

OpenMAX™

OpenMAX is a standard from the Khronos group. It covers API standards for differing portions of a multimedia stack.

- OpenMAX AL (Application Layer)—Provides an application-level multimedia playback and recording API for embedded devices.
- OpenMAZ IL (Integration Layer)—Provides an interface for audio, video, and imaging codecs.
- OpenMAX DL—Provides a set of building block APIs that provide low-level media functions.

The following sections provide more details on each area.

OpenMAX AL

The OpenMAX Application Layer (AL) provides a set of APIs used between the application and multimedia middleware. The APIs define objects and associated control APIs for the objects. An example object might be a camera or media player object. Objects can be linked to create an overall multimedia application, or may be linked to form a media playback or record application. Figure 10.16 shows an example of how the objects may be configured together to form an audio player application.

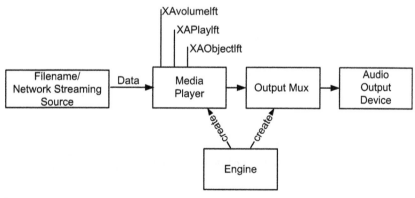

FIGURE 10.16

OpenMAX AL Audio Playback.

The broad range of objects defined in OpenMAX AL facilitates the creation of many multimedia applications such as media players and recording applications.

OpenMAX IL

The OpenMAX Integration Layer (IL) provides an interface for audio, video, and imaging codecs. It provides multimedia frameworks a consistent API to access both hardware- and software-based codecs. An open source implementation of OpenMAX IL can be found in the Bellagio open source package. A system may use the IL integration layer without using OpenMAX AL. For example, a GStreamer plug-in can be employed to use OpenMAX AL–based codecs in a GStreamer filter graph (http://www.khronos.org/files/openmax/whitepapers/OpenMAX_IL_with_GSstreamer.pdf). At the time of writing at wildly deployed multimedia framework is OpenCore which is employed in Android systems, OpenCore uses the OpenMAX IL interface for codecs.

OpenMAX DL

The OpenMAX DL provides an API standard for the creation of low-level functions that provide optimized media processing to the higher layers. The API definition includes audio signal processing such as fast Fourier transforms, filters, color space conversion, and video primitives that can be used to implement codecs. It is often very useful to tune these functions for the target CPU architecture and platform features. Although not aligned with OpenMAX DL API, the capabilities are not unlike those provided by Intel(r) Performance Primitives (described in Chapter 11). The development layer also

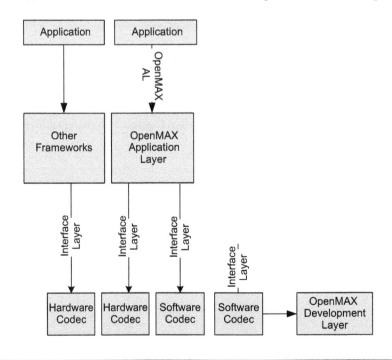

FIGURE 10.17

OpenMAX Capabilities Can Be Used at Any Layer.

provides a pattern for asynchronous APIs. Asynchronous APIs are very important when using fixed-function hardware accelerators or DSP functions to perform an operation. It allows the CPU calling the function to continue to perform useful work while the hardware codec performs its conversion in parallel.

OpenMAX Summary

Figure 10.17 illustrates the overall OpenMAX stack showing the different layers.

Each of the layers can be used by layers above it or natively, by applications or non-OpenMAX frameworks.

Framework Summary

A wide range of multimedia frameworks are available for embedded systems. The GStreamer-based framework is widely used in Linux systems but does not provide a platform-independent codec abstraction for codecs to the same extent as defined by OpenMax. Hardware-based codec support generally comes from the silicon provider, and the frameworks supported by the silicon provider often depend on the target market and the prevalent framework in use for that market.

SUMMARY

The graphics and multimedia subsystems are becoming more and more important aspects of embedded systems. The capabilities integrated are comparable to those found in recent desktop systems. At this point users have extremely high expectations in terms of the user experience interacting with embedded devices. Sophisticated and esthetically pleasing HMIs incorporating smooth 3D transitions and effects are now commonplace and must be provided with the underlying hardware capabilities to ensure that such expectations are met even on embedded devices.

Digital Signal Processing Using General-Purpose Processors

Digital signal processing is a distinct subset within the broader field of signal processing. Digital signal processing (DSP) is concerned with the digital representation of signals and the subsequent transformation of these signals with software or digital hardware implementations of signal processing algorithms. DSP techniques are applied to a wide range of applications in everyday use—audio codecs such as the ubiquitous MP3, speech codecs used in your cell phone such as the Adaptive Multi-Rate Audio Code (AMR), signal processing implementations of the physical layers of communications technologies such as WiMAX™ or 3G networks, medical ultrasound applications—the list is endless.

Digital signal processing algorithms may be run on standard general-purpose processors, specialized digital signal processors, FPGAs, and ASICs. With this broad range of applications comes a very wide range of computational demands. The increased level of specialization from general-purpose processors to ASICs typically brings with it significantly more computational power for the target application; however, this increase in performance brings with it increasing specificity at the expense of generality. This chapter primarily focuses on describing application workloads and techniques that apply to the execution of digital processing algorithms on primary general-purpose processors. Although embedded processors are general purpose, many architectures include some level of hardware support to facilitate the execution of DSP algorithms. The use of a general-purpose processor, albeit with extensions, may not be a solution suitable for all applications. This approach of developing DSP algorithms on standard embedded processors is more applicable to specific DSP workloads and performance requirements, or where the overall system architecture opens up the possibility of efficiencies by managing the mix of DSP and general-purpose processing to be carried out. This approach does not negate the need for DSPs, FPGAs, or ASICs in the overall domain of digital signal processing, but suggests the possibility of developing efficient designs that take advantage of the performance and enhanced capabilities of embedded architectures to consolidate applications where appropriate. It is not a goal of this chapter to provide a great deal of depth in the vast topic of DSP. This chapter intends to provide sufficient information to the developer so that intelligent system-level architectural options regarding embedded processor capabilities and extensions can be taken into consideration when developing signal processing applications.

This chapter considers the algorithm and application implementation options of DSP on general-purpose embedded platforms.

OVERVIEW

This section provides an overview of signal capture and definition of basic processing in the digital domain. This overview primarily examines time domain processing.

Analog signals typically vary continuously with time; however, in order to process analog signals with a CPU, we must first acquire digital samples to be processed. When samples of a continuous input signal are captured as digital data, a waveform is considered a discrete time signal. Figure 11.1 shows the sampling of a continuously varying signal.

The signal Sig(t) is sampled at regular periodic intervals, T0, T1, and so forth. The set of digital samples comprises the discrete time signal version of the original signal. The discrete signal are denoted by Sig[n], where $n = 0, 1, 2, ...7$. The sampling process is carried out by an analog-to-digital converter.

The time between the samples is known as the sampling period. The sampling period is usually constant for a particular signal being sampled. The reciprocal of the sampling period is known as the sampling frequency f_s. The sampling frequency is a very important principle in digital signal processing; the sampling frequency must be at least twice the bandwidth of the signal being processed according to the Nyquist sampling theorem. In the case of a baseband signal that starts at zero, the bandwidth is equal to the maximum frequency of the signal. Choosing a sampling frequency greater than or equal to the Nyquist rate prevents a condition known as aliasing, which would cause distortion of the original signal such that the sampled signals would not correctly represent the continuous signal. The following are some examples of maximum frequencies of common signals and their Nyquist frequencies and sampling periods:

- Traditional telephony signals: 4 KHz, $f_s = 8$ KHz, samples every 125 μs
- Wideband telephony signals: 8 KHz, $f_s = 16$ KHz, samples every 62.5 μs
- CD audio signals: 22 KHz, $f_s = 44$ KHz, samples every 27 μs

Signals

We take a moment to define some commonly used signal constructs in signal processing. These signal constructs are used to excite the DSP system and then to consider its response to the signals stimulus.

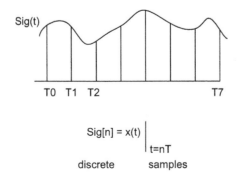

FIGURE 11.1

Discrete Time Signals.

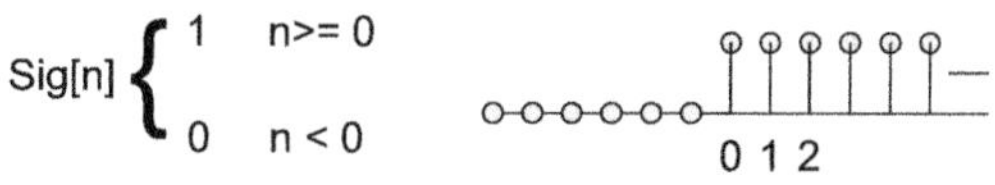

FIGURE 11.2

Step Function.

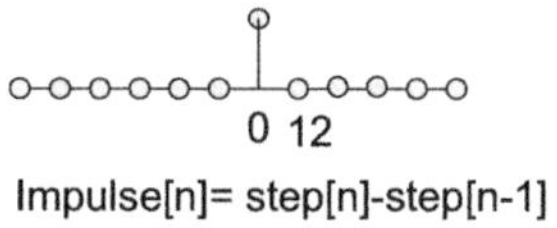

Impulse[n]= step[n]-step[n-1]

FIGURE 11.3

Impulse Function.

This provides a common representation of the behavior of the signal processing system. The first signal we cover is step discontinuity. This signal has a value of zero for samples before T0 and a unit value of 1 for all samples after time zero, as shown in Figure 11.2.

Another common signal construct is the impulse signal. It is one of the most useful signals, which can easily be derived by simply subtracting two step-discontinuity functions, one of which is delayed in time one sample unit.

Figure 11.3 shows an impulse function in the time domain. The signal is useful because it contains an infinite number of frequencies (in the frequency domain).

DSP Building Blocks

Digital signal processing algorithms are typically built up from three basic functions: Add, Multiply, and Delay. The functions are applied in combination to build up complex algorithms in discrete time systems. The Multiply and Add functions are known as operations or ops. The raw performance needs of a particular DSP algorithm are usually quoted in terms of the number of ops the algorithm requires to execute at the required sample frequency. The total number of operations is simply the ops required for a single sample multiplied by the sampling frequency f_s.

The first function is an adder; it adds samples of two or more discrete time signals. Samples are added for all values of n, as shown in Figure 11.4.

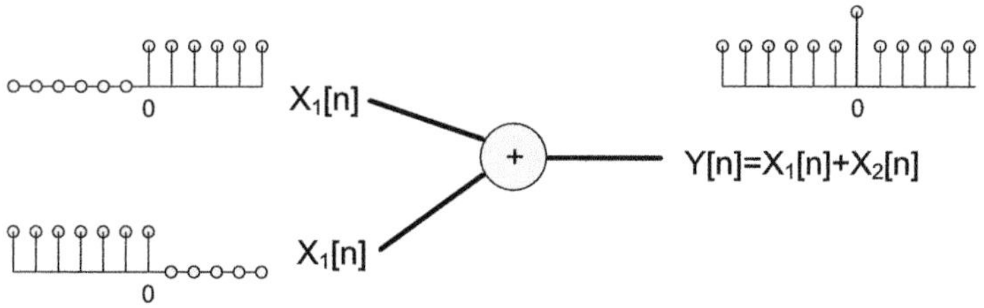

FIGURE 11.4

Add Function.

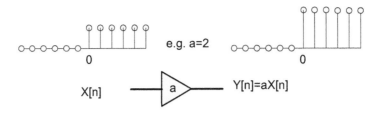

FIGURE 11.5

Multiply Function.

The second function is the multiplier; the multiply block scales all samples in the discrete time signal by the same scaling factor, as shown in Figure 11.5.

The third key building block for a DSP algorithm is a delay function. The delay function shifts the samples to the right. The delay is symbolically defined as Z^{-1} for a delay of 1, Z^{-2} for a delay of 2, and so on. Figure 11.6 shows the delay function.

A discrete time system with combinations of multiply, add, and delay can be described as a difference equation, such as:

```
y[n] = a.x[n] + b.x[n-1] + c.x[n-2]
```

This equation is symbolically represented as shown in Figure 11.7.

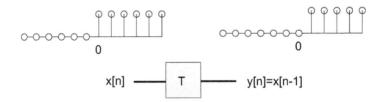

FIGURE 11.6

Delay Function.

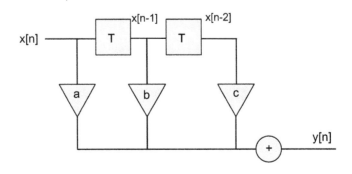

FIGURE 11.7

Feedforward System.

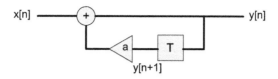

FIGURE 11.8

Feedback System.

This system shown in Figure 11.7 is feedforward. As the system only uses input samples, it is defined as a static or memory-less system. An alternative, the feedback system, is shown in Figure 11.8.

Combination of these two system constructs can be used as needed to develop any discrete difference equation.

For a discrete time system, the input signal can be represented by a series of time-shifted, weighted impulse signals. The response of a system (output) to the impulse signal gives a complete characterization of the system. The response to an arbitrary input signal x[n] is calculated as a convolution of the input signal (represented as series of scaled delayed impulse signals) and the impulse response of the system.

Data Acquisition

The DSP subsystem operates on the series of samples, which are typically captured from the analog world. The underlying data are captured using an analog to digital converter (A/D). The A/D converts the sample analog signal and provides an integer value representing the signal sampled. There are a wide range of A/D converters available with varying resolutions. The resolution is defined by the number of bits used to represent the full range of the sampled signal; common resolutions are 8, 10, 11, 12, 14, 16, and 24 bits. The samples may, for example, be acquired by a directly attached A/D converter or as samples sent in a data packet over the network. For audio sample acquisition on Intel Embedded Atom SOCs, a component known as a codec (*co*de, *dec*ode) is attached via the HD audio interface. This is a digital interface with a clock and data lines. Samples are captured and transferred to and from the codec to memory by an HD interface block within the SOC. The RealTek ALC888 Codec is such a device that can be used to convert between the analog audio domain and the digital domain of the processor. The codec itself performs a number of functions in addition to the simple capture of samples. The ALC888 provides acoustic echo cancellation (AEC), beam forming (BF), and noise suppression (NS) technology; these are DSP functions in themselves. Figure 11.9 shows the connection between the Intel® Atom™ Processor E6xx Series device and the hardware codec.

In this application the signals are encoded as 24-bit integer values. This bit range gives a theoretical dynamic range of 144 dB (using a simplified formula of 6 dB per bit), but in practical terms, the actual signal-to-noise ratio limits the performance to about 90 dB. Similar dynamic signal power ranges are specified for the A/D converter in the Realtek codec referenced above.

An important aspect of signal acquisition and the associated digital signal processing relates to the real-time behavior of the overall system. In the case where we are implementing DSP functions on

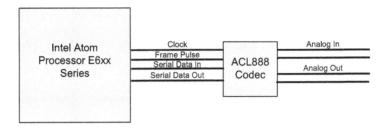

FIGURE 11.9

Codec Connection to an E6xx Series Device.

a general-purpose processor, it is likely that we are doing so because the application contains a general-purpose application in addition to the moderate DSP workload. As a result, it is quite likely that the CPU is running an operating system. The operating system may be a real-time operating system such as VxWorks™ or often it may be running a Linux distribution. Chapter 8 goes into some additional detail on using Linux in real-time scenarios.

Fixed-Point and Floating-Point Implementations

DSP algorithms may be implemented in fixed-point or floating-point arithmetic. The fixed-point implementation uses integer values for all of the mathematics processing within the DSP algorithm. Fixed-point integers can be used to represent a limited dynamic range. For example, a 16-bit integer can represent a maximum range of 65,536. Floating-point implementations, on the other hand, can represent a much larger dynamic range, as floating-point representations are designed to represent both very small and very large numbers. A number of floating-point binary representations exist, but the most common is that standardized under the IEEE 754-1985. Under this standardized definition a 32-bit floating-point (single precision) positive number has a range of 2^{-149} to 3.403×10^{38}. The range for a double-precision floating-point is even larger, at approximately -10^{-308} to $+10^{+308}$.

Analog world signals have infinite precision, and the first step in most of the cases is to build infinite precision versions of the digital signal processing algorithms. Floating-point better mimics the "infinite" range of analog signals; the floating version of the algorithm is basically the same as the original (perhaps with some scaling).

Even though the incoming samples are in the form of fixed-point integers (for data coming from the analog world), the algorithms are more naturally implemented with floating-point arithmetic. In particular, it helps avoid rounding and overflow errors, as each phase of the algorithm is executed. When developing an algorithm using fixed-point representations, the implementer must constantly be aware of the range of the intermediate values' output during the calculations. The output of a multiply and add stage might easily saturate the output and can result in erroneous behavior of the algorithm. The range of values available in floating-point representations removes this problem and as a result using floating-point greatly simplifies the software implementation.

If it's far easier to implement an algorithm using floating-point, why wouldn't a developer always use floating-point implementations? The issue often comes down to the cost, availability, price, and performance of the hardware-based floating-point implementation on the platform. Traditional DSPs produced by companies such as Texas Instruments provide DSP processors that are designed around fixed-point or floating-point implementations. The fixed-point implementations often offer parallel data paths where two 32-bit numbers can processed at the same time. The floating-point devices offer far more computational power overall than the fixed-point equivalents. In the past, there was significant difference in die size between fixed and floating-point, but the trend to include more devices with the DSP in an SOC has reduced the overall relative increase of a floating-point DSP core. At this time fixed-point DSPs have an edge in cost, but floating-point DSPs have the edge when it comes to ease of use. The application itself can also significantly influence the need for a floating-point DSP capability. High-fidelity audio applications require floating-point to ensure that intermediate products and coefficients are adequately represented. Audio applications often cascade a number of filtering operations, where errors are propagated through to the output; using floating-point generally minimizes these errors at all stages. The ear is particularly sensitive, and accuracy of the signal is important at low levels; these applications also benefit by a floating-point representations of the signal processing. Similarly, medical imaging and military applications often have very wide dynamic ranges of signals that must use floating-point implementations.

Choices between fixed and floating-point may also be affected by the precision required. Thirty-two-bit floating-point implementations provide more precision than 16-bit fixed-point; however, 32-bit fixed-point may have better precision than 32-bit floating-point. The mantissa in 32-bit floating-point has only 24 bits. Floating-point representation offers good precision for small signal values but poorer precision for larger values, using the same number of bits. Furthermore, an addition in fixed-point doesn't lose precision, but it may in a floating-point implementation. An application with very large magnitude differences (such as military radar) will probably require floating-point, because the equivalent range in fixed-point would be prohibitive.

As you can see from the building DSP blocks section above, a number of algorithms consist of the multiplication of a sample by a coefficient and then adding it to an accumulated value. This step is often referred to as a Multiply Accumulate operation (MAC). Dedicated DSPs usually offer an MAC instruction.

Embedded processors often provide a simple integer MAC function. The ARM family of devices optionally offers a MAC that provides 16 x 16 and 32 x 16 integer MAC implementations. In addition, the ability to run multiple operations at the same time is made available through a series of SIMD instructions, which is further extended with ARM's NEON technology. The ARM NEON technology supports operations on data packed data types consisting of 8-bit, 16-bit, 32-bit, 64-bit integers and single-precision floating-point.

When it comes to Intel architecture, the instruction set has been extended to offer high-performance parallel multiplication and addition of either integer or floating-point values as part of the Supplemental Streaming SIMD Extensions 3 (SSSE3) instruction set. Intel has introduced a fused multiply and add (similar in scope to a MMAC) in the follow-on to the SSSE instruction set known as AVX. The Intel SIMD instruction set continues to evolve to bring a mix of DSP capabilities to the general-purpose Intel architecture cores. On Intel architecture, SIMD floating-point code is almost on par as fixed-point (performance-wise, for the same data width), and may even be faster depending on the implementation overheads associated with the latter, so in a number of cases the trade-offs we discussed above are no longer necessary.

SINGLE INSTRUCTION MULTIPLE DATA

SIMD Microarchitecture and Instructions

Although DSP algorithms tend to be mathematically intensive, they are often fairly simple in concept. Filters and fast Fourier transforms (FFTs), for example, can be implemented using simple multiply and accumulate instructions. Modern general purpose processors use single instruction multiple data (SIMD) techniques to increase their performance on these low-level DSP functions. The principal concepts of SIMD operation are shown in Figure 11.10. Let's say four single-precision (32-bit) floating-point numbers need to be multiplied by a second value. Rather than doing four sequential multiply operations, all four numbers are loaded into a single 128-bit SIMD register. Then the multiply operation is done on all four numbers in a single processor clock cycle.

Intel SIMD instructions are known as Intel Streaming SIMD Extensions (Intel SSE). There have been six generations to Intel architecture SIMD instructions since they first released with the Intel Pentium® II Processor and Intel Pentium Processor with MMX™ technology. These new instructions have added SIMD operations for both integer and floating-point data elements. Processors based on the Intel Atom microarchitecture currently support SSSE3, whereas Intel Core™ i7 processors implement Intel SSE4.2. The code developed for earlier versions of SSE is always forward-compatible with later versions.

Operating System

Streaming SIMD instructions require OS support to save and restore the register state across OS context switches. The same provision has been required since the early inception of SIMD instructions, and we have discussed the principle in Chapter 6. In addition to the generic save/restore requirements, a number of the SSE instructions may generate numeric exceptions (SIMD floating-point). The operating system must provide IEEE-754-compliant event handlers for these post-compute exceptions. Most operating systems on Intel architecture currently support the save/restore model and require exception handlers.

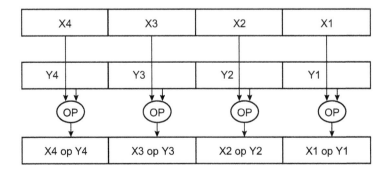

FIGURE 11.10

SIMD Instruction.

MICROARCHITECTURE CONSIDERATIONS

The overall microarchitecture of the processor can have a significant impact on the performance and ease of use for DSP applications. One large impact is the relative large cache sizes and clock speed of the processors.

Memory organization on a DSP differs from that found on Intel architecture processors. On traditional DSP architectures, the developer manually partitions the memory space in order to reduce the number of accesses to external memories. Program, data, temporary buffers, and look-up tables all need to be allocated carefully, as accessing the external memory is costly in terms of latencies introduced.

By comparison, Intel architectures are populated with large amounts of cache while DSPs traditionally include dedicated internal memory. On one hand, the large cache structures overcome the strict separation of fast/slow memory devices, enabling more "transparent" memory management strategies. On the other hand, all data, look-up tables, and programs are originally located in "far" memory. Applications may need to warm the cache with the appropriate data at start-up. To maximize platform performance, it is also important to understand the differences between local and shared caches, as well as cache coherency, especially in the context of multi-threaded applications that span multiple processor cores.

To further reduce the latency penalties due to cache misses, output data should ideally be generated sequentially, or at least in a way in which concurrent threads' output do not generate cache line invalidations; that is, threads working on the same cache line should be executed in the same core. Accessing memory in a scattered pattern across multiple pages should be avoided whenever possible.

IMPLEMENTATION OPTIONS

There are a number of ways you can go about implementing your DSP algorithms on an Intel processor.

- Intrinsic—Develop C code that calls special built-in compiler capabilities that map closely to the underlying SSE instruction set.
- Vectorization—Use the compiler to apply vectorization techniques to loops within the data processing iterations. The compiler identifies opportunities to convert loops that operate on a single set of operands within a loop to a vector-based implementation where multiple pairs of operands are operated on at once. The compiler task is quite difficult, and it is often important to guide the vectorization process through the use of compiler directives such as pragmas.
- Intel Performance Primitives—The Intel Performance Libraries provide highly optimized implementations for a number of domains, such as audio codecs, image codes, image processing, string processing, data compression, and a list of general-purpose DSP building blocks. Such libraries take full advantage of the CPU and SIMD instruction set (many are hand written for performance). Other vendors offer similar optimized libraries to take advantage of the underlying SIMD capabilities within the processor.

INTRINSICS AND DATA TYPES

The C language as defined by the C ANSI standard does not make any provision for wide data types typically used by SIMD engines. Similarly, the wide range of SIMD instructions is not easily automatically generated by the traditional language structure. To avoid having to write the native SIMD assembly code, most compilers that support Intel SIMD instructions provide a set of intrinsics to make the task of using the SIMD engine much more straightforward. Intrinsics are like function calls that perform the required behavior, but they are built into the compiler. They typically map to a single instruction, although there are some composite intrinsics. Intrinsic functions provide an intermediate abstraction level between assembly code and higher-level C code. The abstraction level at which the programmer works is low, allowing vector operations, but some details like register allocation are hidden from the developer. Also, the compiler can still perform optimizations over the code that uses intrinsics (in contrast with inline ASM).

The SIMD engine contained on Intel architectures has grown in width over the many generations of its evolution. There are eight 128-bit SSE registers (XMM0–XMM7). GCC, the Intel C Compiler (ICC), and others provide the following data types that can be used for SIMD instructions and allow the compiler to manage the allocation of the XMM registers. Because each of these registers can hold more than one data element, the processor can process more than one data element simultaneously. This processing capability is also known as single-instruction multiple data processing (SIMD). The following data types are added to compilers that support Intel architecture.

- The __m64 data type is used to represent the contents of an MMX register, which is the register that is used by the MMX technology intrinsic. The __m64 data type can hold eight 8-bit values, four 16-bit values, two 32-bit values, or one 64-bit value.
- The __m128 data type is used to represent the contents of an Intel Streaming SIMD Extension register used by the Intel Streaming SIMD Extension intrinsics. The __m128 data type can hold four 32-bit standard precision floating-point values.
- The __m128d data type can hold two 64-bit floating-point values.
- The __m128i date type can hold 16 8-bit, eight 16-bit, four 32-bit, or two 64-bit integer values.

These data types are not basic ANSI C data types. You must observe the following usage restrictions:

- Use data types only on either side of an assignment, as a return value, or as a parameter. You cannot use it with other arithmetic expressions (+, −, and so on).
- Use data types as objects in aggregates, such as unions, to access the byte elements and structures.
- Use data types only with the respective intrinsics described in this documentation.

As the data types are not true compiler native data types, you must use intrinsic commands to pack and unpack the data. For example, to pack a 128-bit SIMD register with four separate 32-bit standard precision floating-points, you can use the following code segment.

```
float a[4] = {1.0, 2.0, 3.0, 4.0};
__m128 t = _mm_load_ps(a);
```

The packed values are represented in right-to-left order, with the lowest value being used for scalar operations. The call shown above assumes that the argument (a) is aligned to a 16-byte boundary.

Significant performance gains (up to 2x) can be achieved be paying particular attention to data alignment. If the argument (a) is not known to be aligned then the `_mm_loadu_ps()` should be used.

Once you have the appropriate values loaded or packed into the SIMD register, you can use a range of different intrinsic types to operate on the data. The following list is classifying the different intrinsic operation types that are provided by the Intel Compiler.

- Arithmetic (fixed- and floating-point)
- Shift
- Logical
- Compare
- Set
- Shuffle
- Concatenation

The intrinsics can be used to operate on the SIMD register directly. For example, the following code segment adds the four FP values packed into a and b. It performs four additions in one instruction.

```
__m128 _mm_add_ps(__m128 a, __m128 b)
```

The corresponding segment for multiplication is

```
__m128 _mm_mul_ps(__m128 a, __m128 b)
```

Another key aspect of the SSE instructions is the ability to shuffle data around in the registers. This is important while processing a streaming input data sequence. For example, the following sequence shuffles bytes from a depending on the contents of the register b.

```
extern __m64 _mm_shuffle_pi8 (__m64 a, __m64 b);
```

The code segment in Listing 11.1 replicates the shuffle behavior.

```
for (i = 0; i < 8; i++) {
    if (b[i] & 0x80)
    {
    r[i] = 0;
    }
    else
    {
    r[i] = a[b[i] & 0x07];
    }
}
```

LISTING 11.1

Shuffle Behavior.

The code in Listing 11.2 presents an example of SSE intrinsic programming that calculates the complex reciprocal (conjugate of the number divided by the squared modulo) of a series of 32-bit floating-point input samples. The complex reciprocal is used for channel estimation or signal equalization. Four input samples are processed at the same time in order to take best advantage of the SIMD arithmetic units. The shuffle behavior is quite an important capability to be familiar with; moving data around is a key capability used in arranging the data for the subsequent arithmetic operations.

```
/* load data - assumes all data is 16byte aligned */
sseA[0] = _mm_load_ps(&a[i+0]);
sseA[1] = _mm_load_ps(&a[i+2]);
/* Negate Imaginary part */
sseA[0] = _mm_xor_ps(sseA[0], NegFx);
sseA[1] = _mm_xor_ps(sseA[1], NegFx);
/* multiply to calculate real and imaginary squares */
sseM[0] = _mm_mul_ps(sseA[0], sseA[0]);
sseM[1] = _mm_mul_ps(sseA[1], sseA[1]);
/* real and imaginary parts are now squared and placed
 * horizontally. Add them in that direction */
sseI = _mm_hadd_ps(sseM[0], sseM[1]);
/* calculate the four reciprocals */
sseI = _mm_rcp_ps(sseI);
/* reorder to multiply both real and imag on samples */
sseT[0] = _mm_shuffle_ps(sseI,sseI,0x50); // 01 01 00 00
sseT[1] = _mm_shuffle_ps(sseI,sseI,0xFA); // 11 11 10 10
/* multiply by conjugate */
sseY[0] = _mm_mul_ps(sseT[0],sseA[0]);
sseY[1] = _mm_mul_ps(sseT[1],sseA[1]);
/* store */
_mm_store_ps(&y[i+0], sseY[0]);
_mm_store_ps(&y[i+2], sseY[1]);
```

LISTING 11.2

Complex Reciprocal Using Intrinsics.

The complex reciprocal is often used in channel estimation or in signal equalization.

VECTORIZATION

Efficiently taking advantage of the vector processing units on modern CPUs can be accomplished by assembly-level programming. The instruction set reference and optimization manuals detail the necessary low-level functionality description and performance provided by the underlying processing units. Although low-level programming potentiates a higher performance level, effective code portability, maintainability, and development efficiency can only be attained by using higher-level languages.

Automatic vectorization is available on mainstream compilers such as GCC and ICC and consists of a series of methods that identify and implement vectorizable loops according to the version of the

SIMD instruction set specified. Although it works transparently to the programmer, increasing the percentage of code amenable to vectorization requires developers to be aware of issues related to the automatics vectorization of the code, for example, data dependence and memory alignment.

In cases where it is not possible to resolve data dependence or memory alignment, compilers may automatically add test code constructs prior to the loop. To work around data dependence, both vectorized and nonvectorized versions of the loop are implemented, and the selection of which version to run is based on the test results. To circumvent memory misalignment issues, the compiler may "peel" a number of iterations off the loop so that at least part of it runs vectorized. Besides obvious increases in program size, these overheads also affect overall loop performance. The use of special #pragma directives and other keywords can guide the compiler through its code generation process, avoiding these overheads.

The following code fragments are different versions of a simple vector multiply-accumulate function, where the use of #pragma directives gives hints to the compiler regarding vectorization.

The first code segment in Listing 11.3 is a the baseline function with no specific considerations for vectorization.

```
void vecmac( float* x, float* a, float* y, int len )
{
    /* The loop below is already vectorizable as-is. */
    int i;
    for( i = 0; i < len; i++ )
      y[i] += x[i] * a[i];
}
```

LISTING 11.3

Simple Vector Multiply Loop.

The section shown in Listing 11.4 includes a pragma to specifically avoid the vectorization of the code sequence.

```
void vecmac_nv( float* x, float* a, float* y, int len )
{
    int i;
    /* Do not vectorize loop */
    #pragma novector
    for( i = 0; i < len; i++ )
      y[i] += x[i] * a[i];
}
```

LISTING 11.4

Explicitly Don't Vectorize Loop.

The code fragment in Listing 11.5 includes a pragma to specifically request the compiler to attempt to vectorize the loop following the pragma, with the assumption that the vectors are aligned correctly.

```
void vecmac_al( float* x, float* a, float* y, int len )
{
   int i;
   /* Assume data is aligned in memory. An exception is caused if this assumption is not
      valid. */
   #pragma vector aligned
   for( i = 0; i < len; i++ )
     y[i] += x[i] * a[i];
}
```

LISTING 11.5

Aligned Vectors.

The code fragment in Listing 11.6 tells the compiler that there are no input to output data dependencies, that is, the y[] array does not overlap with x[] nor a[].

```
void vecmac_iv( float* x, float* a, float* y, int len )
{
   int i;
   /* Discard data dependence assumptions. Results may
      differ if arrays do overlap in memory. */
   #pragma ivdep
   for( i = 0; i < len; i++ )
     y[i] += x[i] * a[i];
}
```

LISTING 11.6

Vectorized Assuming No Data Dependency.

The code fragment in Listing 11.7 combines both the vectorization hint and the notification that there are no data dependences in the loop.

```
void vecmac_al_iv( float* x, float* a, float* y, int len )
{
   int i;
   #pragma vector aligned
   #pragma ivdep
   for( i = 0; i < len; i++ )
     y[i] += x[i] * a[i];
}
```

LISTING 11.7

Memory Alignment Property and Discarding Assumed Data Dependences.

Table 11.1 Code Size Generated and Performance

Code Fragment	Arrays Aligned	# Instructions	Relative Performance
vecrmac_nv	No	68	1 (reference)
Vecmac	No	118	2.31x
Vecmac_iv	No	84	2.32x
Vecmac_nv	Yes	68	1.00x
Vecmac	Yes	118	2.88x
Vecmac_iv	Yes	84	2.9x
Vecmac_al	Yes	89	3.71x
Vecmac_al_iv	Yes	47	3.75x

Comparison on both generated assembly (ASM) code size, and performance was carried out for the different versions of the vecmac function, on an Intel Core 2 Duo platform (2.533 GHz, 6 MB L2 cache) running Linux 2.6.18 and ICC 11.0. Table 11.1 summarizes the results obtained for random input vectors with *len* = 1000. The impact of memory alignment is also included in the performance numbers, which are normalized to the vecmac_nv version having nonaligned input data.

The insignificant performance impact in using the #pragma ivdep directive is due to the fact that, in this case, there is no overlap (aliasing) between the memory regions occupied by x[], a[], and y[]. A vectorized version of the loop is always run, even when this hint is not given to the compiler. The only difference is the initial overlap tests performed to these arrays, hence the differences in resulting assembly code size.

The effect of having the arrays aligned in memory is visible in the performance values for the vecmac and vecmac_iv implementations. Although the loop is still vectorized in both versions, nonaligned memory access introduces performance penalties.

Finally, it is seen that fully vectorized versions of the same loop outperform the nonvectorized code by close to four times, as initially anticipated for 32-bit floating-point processing.

PERFORMANCE PRIMITIVES

Efficiently taking advantage of the vector processing units on modern CPUs can be accomplished using pre-built high-performance libraries for use on target platforms. Most vendors will provide a library of higher-level functions optimized for specific tasks. These are tasks that are commonly used within a specific application domain and are typically tuned to take maximum advantage of the underlying hardware capabilities. The Intel Integrated Performance Primitives (Intel IPPs) are libraries optimized for performance on Intel-based products; some of the libraries are efficient implementations of DSP algorithms. The libraries are split according to specific domains. In addition to taking advantage of the SSE units available on a particular platform, the libraries are threaded and can obtain performance gains by parallelizing the algorithm and executing it on several cores at the same time, although this aspect is not applicable for all algorithms. The domains covered by the Intel IPPs are

- Signal processing
- Image and video processing
- Small matrices and realistic rendering
- Cryptography

The signal processing library provide a wide range of basic DSP functions, such as add multiple and normalize, windowing functions based on a number of algorithms such as Hamming window, and statistics functions such as mean and standard deviation. The filtering functions are of most interest given the other discussions in this chapter. The filtering functions provided are

- Convolution and correlation
- Finite impulse response (FIR) filter
- FIR coefficients generation function (to create a low pass filter)
- Infinite response filter (IIR)
- Transforms, such as Fourier, discrete cosine, and Hilbert

We show an example of using the IPPs to create a FIR filter in Listing 11.10.

The libraries can be linked to your application and you specify the precise target Intel SSE version on your platform. Often you will wish to produce a single application that can run on a number of Intel architecture platforms that span many versions of Intel SSE, for instance, SSSE3 on Intel Atom or Intel SSE 4.2 on the Intel Core family of devices. In this case, you link a "fatter" library that contains highly optimized versions for all current Intel SSE generations; the library selects at runtime the most optimized instruction path for the target version of Intel SSE. For further information and to get access to the libraries go to the Intel web site for Intel IPPs. If you are going to be developing with Intel IPPs, we recommend that you get a copy of *Optimizing Applications for Multi-Core Processors, Using the Intel IPPs* by Stewart Taylor.

FINITE IMPULSE RESPONSE FILTER

In this section, we will show the code for a simple finite impulse response filter. We will cover the simple C code example and then a highly optimized version using Intel SSE instructions. FIR filters are used in a large percentage of DSP algorithms. They can be easily vectorized since there is no dependency between the calculation of the current frame and the output of the previous frame. This makes them perform very well on SIMD processors. On the other hand, when contiguous input/output interdependence exists (as in recursive filter implementations), efficient vectorization is not always possible. In some cases, however, a careful analysis of the algorithm may still reveal opportunities for vectorized processing.

The FIR filter is an example of a feedforward discrete time system described as a difference equation, for example:

$$y[n] = a.x[n] + b.x[n-1] + c.x[n-2]$$

The number of stages in the FIR equation above is three, with tap coefficients of a, b, and c.

FIR Example: C Code

The finite response filter is one of the most basic building blocks. The code segment in Listing 11.8 shows a FIR function call. This implementation is for demonstration purposes only; it does not account for any coefficients' symmetry, which would be quite common for FIR filters. The input array (x) contains samples that are older in time as the index increases; for example, x[0] is the oldest sample, x [1] is the sample after that, x[2] is the sample afterwards is x[1], and so on up to the latest sample, which is x[len−1]. The arguments to the function are X-array if input samples, Y-array if output samples, and c-array if coefficients, with *nc* being the number of coefficients in the FIR and len the number of samples in x and y.

```
// 32-bit floating point FIR
void fir_filter_flt( float* x, float* y, float* c, int nc, int len )
{
  int k, n;
  float acc;
  for( k = 0; k < len; k++ ) {
    acc = c[0] * x[k];
    for( n = 1; n < nc && n <= k; n++ ) {
      acc += c[n] * x[k - n];
    }
    y[k] = acc;
  }
}
```

LISTING 11.8

FIR Filter C Code Example.

In the following sections we show the use of performance libraries and intrinsics to provide the same capability shown in Listing 11.8.

FIR Example: Intel Performance Primitives

The same example using performance primitives is trivial in comparison to the hand-coded intrinsic-based sequence. We have left out some of the `include` statements and memory allocation calls. It might be worth noting that the code is thread safe, as all structures are allocated outside of the IPP library.

```
Ipp32f coeffs[] = { -0.5f, 0.0f, 0.5f };
Ipp32f delay[] = { 0.0f, 0.0f, 0.0f};
IppsFIRState_32f *pFIRState;
    ippsFIRInitAlloc_32f( &pFIRState, coeffs, 3, dlyl );
    /// filter the signal by the FIR filter
    ippsFIR_32f(pSrc, pDst, len, pFIRState );
```

LISTING 11.9

FIR Using Intel Performance Primitives.

The code sequence in Listing 11.9 calls a FIR filter with three taps, and the coefficients are specified in the `coeffs` array. The initial state of the filter is set up with the delay array. The delay array holds the initial values in reverse time order.

This is just one simple example of how to use an Intel IPP call for your application. A rich set of optimized functions are available. The next section shows to code an FIR example using intrinsics.

FIR Example: Intel SSE

The C code example above does not make any use of the SSE SIMD capability. The use of SIMD takes some skill, in particular, ensuring that the required data is shuffled into the appropriate register field before the operations. The optimal performance gain is achieved when the code is operating on data chunks that fit into the width of the SSE registers, for example, processing four single-precision floating-point values in one 128-bit SSE register, or eight 16-bit integer numbers packed into one 128-bit SSE register. It is often more efficient to use regular C code for that start and end processing of a data stream until the function is processing aligned at multiples of the number of entries packed into the SSE registers. The code fragment below uses 32-bit floating-point numbers; it assumes that the input vector is x, the output vector is y, coefficients' c length is a multiple of 4, and vectors are memory-aligned to 16-byte values. The function below takes an input vector x of length len, a coefficients' vector with nc entries, and outputs an output vector of y with len entries.

```
1 fir_filter_flt( float* x, float* y, float* c, int nc, int len )
2 {
3  int k, n, j; float acc;
4  __m128 curr_x; // holds the 4 most recent values of 'x'
5  __m128 prev_x; // holds the 4 previous values of 'x'
6  __m128 eff_x; // holds the 4 effective inputs (blend of 'curr_x' and 'prev_x')
7  __m128 coefs; // holds 4 coefficient values
8  __m128 coefs_exp; // holds expanded values of coefficients read
9  __m128 acc_reg; // 4 parallel accumulators
10 // first nonvectorized 'nc' iter fill the filter delay line
11 for( k = 0; k < nc; k++ ) {
12   acc = c[0] * x[k];
13     for( n = 1; n <= k; n++ ) {
14       acc += c[n] * x[k - n];
15     }
16   y[k] = acc;
17 }
18 // subsequent iterations are fully vectorized
19 for( k = nc; k < len; k += 4 ) {
20   acc_reg = _mm_setzero_ps();
```

LISTING 11.10

FIR Using Intel Performance Primitives.

```
21    prev_x = _mm_load_ps( &x[ k - 4 ] );
22    for( n = 0; n < nc; n += 4 ) {
23    // assuming memory alignment to 16-byte boundary
24     curr_x = _mm_load_ps( &x[ k - n ] );
25     coefs = _mm_load_ps( &c[ n ] );
26     // 1st coefficient of batch of 4
27     eff_x   = curr_x; // load inputs
28     // same coefficient for all inputs
29     coefs_exp = _mm_shuffle_ps( coefs, coefs,
30          _MM_SHUFFLE( 0, 0, 0, 0 ) );
31     // Multiply
32     coefs_exp = _mm_mul_ps( coefs_exp, eff_x );
33     // Accumilate
34     acc_reg  = _mm_add_ps( acc_reg, coefs_exp );
35      // 2nd, 3rd and 4th coefficients
36      for( j = 0; j < 3; j++ ) {
37      // 'rotating' values to the left
38      eff_x = _mm_shuffle_ps( eff_x, eff_x,
39           _MM_SHUFFLE( 2, 1, 0, 3 ) );
40      // 'rotating' values to the left
41      prev_x = _mm_shuffle_ps( prev_x, prev_x,
42           _MM_SHUFFLE( 2, 1, 0, 3 ) );
43      // 'rotating' values to the right
44      coefs = _mm_shuffle_ps( coefs, coefs,
45           _MM_SHUFFLE( 0, 3, 2, 1 ) );
46      // same coefficient for all inputs
47      coefs_exp = _mm_shuffle_ps( coefs, coefs,
48           _MM_SHUFFLE( 0, 0, 0, 0 ) );
49     // replacing only the rightmost value of 'eff_x'
50      eff_x = _mm_move_ss( eff_x, prev_x );
51      // multiply packed register.
52      coefs_exp = _mm_mul_ps( coefs_exp, eff_x );
53      // accumulate
54      acc_reg = _mm_add_ps( acc_reg, coefs_exp );
55      }
56     prev_x = curr_x;
57    }
58    // store the 4 results
59    _mm_store_ps( &y[ k ], acc_reg );
60  }
61 }
```

LISTING 11.10

(continued).

The code above requires some explanation, particularly in terms of the swizzling behavior. One key aspect of the design is that is it cheaper to swizzle the contents of an SSE register than to load the data multiple times from memory.

The series of calculations required for an 8 tap FIR filter are as follows:

$$Y_0 = a.X0 + b.X - 1 + c.X - 2 + d.X - 3 + e.X - 4 + f.X - 5 + g.X - 6 + h.X - 7$$
$$Y_1 = a.X1 + b.X0 + c.X - 1 + d.X - 2 + e.X - 3 + f.X - 4 + g.X - 5 + h.X - 6$$
$$Y_2 = a.X2 + b.X1 + c.X0 + d.X - 1 + e.X - 2 + f.X - 3 + g.X - 4 + h.X - 5$$
$$Y_3 = a.X3 + b.X2 + c.X1 + d.X0 + e.X - 1 + f.X - 2 + g.X - 3 + h.X - 4$$
$$Y_4 = a.X4 + b.X3 + c.X2 + d.X1 + e.X0 + f.X - 1 + g.X - 2 + h.X - 3$$
$$Y_5 = a.X5 + b.X4 + c.X3 + d.X2 + e.X1 + f.X0 + g.X - 1 + h.X - 2$$
$$Y_6 = a.X6 + b.X5 + c.X4 + d.X3 + e.X2 + f.X1 + g.X0 + h.X - 1$$
$$Y_7 = a.X7 + b.X6 + c.X5 + d.X4 + e.X3 + f.X2 + g.X1 + h.X0$$

The calculations of Y_0 to Y_4 are part of the initial setup and not easily vectorizable and are calculated by lines 11–17 above. You may have noticed the pattern of execution in the above sequence once the iterations calculate Y_4 and subsequent output values. The code can be vectorized manually and makes efficient use of the SIMD capabilities. On first inspection, you might try to use the SSE registers and SIMD instructions to calculate a single output value of Y. For example, to calculate the first half of Y_4, first pack SSE register d, c, b, a, then $X_3 X_2 X_1 X_0$ and multiply the two registers, add the values in the output, and so on. In the code above, the algorithm is structured to generate outputs $Y_{n+3}Y_{n+2}Y_{n+1}Y_n$ at each iteration; the input coefficients and X values are packed and swizzled to reduce the memory loads. So let's look at the code in more detail. Let's assume we are on the iteration at the start of Y_4.

Line 20: Clear the accumulation register that will end up holding $Y_7 Y_6 Y_5 Y_4$.

Line 21: Load a SSE register (prev_x) with $X_3 X_2 X_1 X_0$.

Line 22: Walk through the coefficients in groups of four. For our example, the loop will execute twice, as we have eight coefficients. For the remainder of the explanation, assume this is the first instance through *n* is zero.

Line 24: Load the SSE register allocated to curr_x with $X_7 X_6 X_5 X_4$.

Line 25: Load the SSE register allocated to coefficients with dcba.

Line 27: Copy curr_x into eff_x, which is currently $X_7X_6X_5X_4$.

Line 29: Expand one of the coefficients into an SSE register allocated by coefs_exp. The first iteration will take the least significant element (rightmost) and create four copies of it into coefs_exp. Now coefs_exp will contain aaaa.

Line 32: This is the first SIMD multiply operation. The result will be $aX_7,a.X_6,a.X_5,a.X_4$.

Line 34: We now accumulate the output from the first multiply into acc_reg; acc_reg now equals $aX_7,a.X_6,a.X_5,a.X_4$.

Line 36: We will now iterate through the d,c,b coefficients in the for loop.

Line 38: In the first time coming into the loop, eff_x contained $X_7X_6X_5X_4$, The shuffle puts $X_6X_5X_4X_7$ into eff_x.

Line 41: In the first time coming into the loop, prev_x contained $X_3X_2X_1X_0$, The shuffle puts $X_2X_1X_0X_3$ into prev_x.

Line 44: In the first time coming into the loop, `coefs` contained dcba. The shuffle puts adcb into `coefs`.

Line 47: The element in the rightmost field of `coefs` is now equal to b and is replicated into `coefs_exp`, resulting in bbbb.

Line 50: The `eff_x` value is $X_6X_5X_4X_7$, but we need $X_6X_5X_4X_3$. So the rightmost element in `prev_x` is extracted, X_3, and merged into `eff_x`, resulting in $X_6X_5X_4X_3$.

Line 52: This is the next SIMD multiply operation. The result will be $b.X_6, b.X_5, b.X_4, b.X_3$.

Line 54: This is the next accumulate operation. The result will be $b.X_6, b.X_5, b.X_4, b.X_3 \_ + aX_7, a.X_6, a.X_5, a.X_4$.

Line 55: This will loop around to the coefficients c and d. The result in `acc_reg` will be $Y_7Y_6Y_5Y_4 = d.X_4, d.X_3, d.X_2, d.X_1 + cX_5, c.X_4, c.X_3, c.X_2 + b.X_6, b.X_5, b.X_4, b.X_3 \_ + aX_7, a.X_6, a.X_5, a.X_4$. However, the processing is not yet complete.

Line 56: Set `curr_x` equal to `prev_x` for the following loop iteration. This eliminates an unnecessary memory load.

Line 57: This will loop around to the next four samples and coefficients hgfe. The accumulator will contain the correct values for $Y_7Y_6Y_5Y_4$ as defined in the formula above.

Line 59: We now write out the $Y_7Y_6Y_5Y_4$ to the output array Y.

From the example in Listing 11.10, you can see the importance of understanding the algorithm and the runtime pattern of access to the data elements. The use of swizzle operations allows the implementation to significantly reduce the number of data reads that would otherwise occur. This shows that some skill is needed to develop algorithms using intrinsics.

APPLICATION EXAMPLES

In this section, we cover two different examples of applications running on Intel architecture processors using some of the techniques mentioned above. The first section covers codecs, while the second section covers the implementation of a basic ultrasound application.

Codec

The encoding and decoding of media is typically a computationally intensive task. For this reason, many embedded systems provide a hardware acceleration block to accelerate the encoding and decoding of audio and video processing. However, hardware-based accelerators cannot easily support every possible codec format (and it is often the case that hardware accelerators do not support new, up and coming codec that have become mainstream after the product was designed), so the optimization of software-based codecs can be very important, particularly in embedded devices where the overall compute resources are limited. There are also programmable hardware accelerators that run firmware to provide the codec acceleration. These capabilities are programmable but often rely on fixed function hardware, so there can still be issues when a new codec must be implemented.

To facilitate the creation of software-based codecs, Intel has created a set of Unified Media C++ Classes (UMC). This C++ framework was designed to simplify the development of advanced codecs and to implement some applications that demonstrate Intel IPP audio and video acceleration

Table 11.2 Voice CODEC Encode Benchmarks

Algorithm	MHz/Channel	VAD	kB/s	Narrow/Wideband
G.723.1	25.25	Disabled	6.3	Narrowband
G.723.1	17.05	Enabled	6.3	Narrowband
G.726	7.27	Disabled	16	Narrowband
GSM-AMR	27.61	Disabled	4.75	Narrowband
GSM-AFR	4.87	Disabled	13	Narrowband
GSM-AFR	5.62	Enabled Mode 1	13	Narrowband
GSM-AFR	5.35	Enabled Mode 2	13	Narrowband
G.729A-Integer	22.36	Disabled	8	Narrowband
G.729A-Integer	16.74	Enabled	8	Narrowband
G.729A-Floating-point	19.16	Disabled	8	Narrowband
G.729A-Floating-point	15.23	Enabled	8	Narrowband
G.729.1	52.64	Disabled	32	Wideband

features. This is one of the most prevalent use cases for SIMD accelerated implementations, and the code for MP3- and telephony/voice-based codecs that use the Intel IPPs to accelerate the execution can be found on the web site http://software.intel.com/en-us/articles/intel-integrated-performance-primitives-code-samples/. The results of a performance analysis of voice codecs running on an Intel Atom Processor E6xx Series platform are shown in Table 11.2. The figure of merit used for codec is the number of CPU cycles in megahertz required to encode or decode a reference audio sample. The overall processor utilization can be significantly reduced if voice activity detection (VAD) is enabled. Voice activity detection is a technique to detect when there is speech or voice present in the signal. The use of VAD increases the efficiency of the encoding process as normal speech conversations have a relatively low signal activity level (conversations are approximately

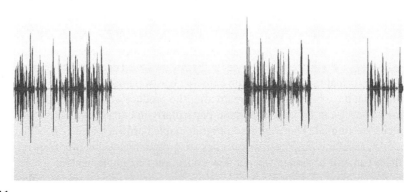

FIGURE 11.11

Input Sample Waveform for Benchmarks.

50% idle), and the use of VAD allows the codec to encode/decode silence using a much simpler algorithm than the full speech encode/decode.

Figure 11.11 shows the test waveform injected into the codec for the purpose of benchmarking. The waveform is a recording of a person talking. As you can see there is a significant percentage of silence, so the benchmarks for VAD enabled or disabled show different codec costs.

Table 11.2 provides the processor utilization in megahertz for a number of codecs performing an encode operation on 15 seconds of the input sample. The platform configuration used here to generate this analysis included an Intel Atom 1.6 GHz Core, using ICC 11.1, Intel IPP version 6.1 on a Linux kernel version of 2.6.31.

As you can see from the results given in Table 11.2, G729 is one of the most compute-intensive algorithms. Generally speaking, the more sophisticated the audio codec, the better the encoding and resultant Perceptual Evaluation of Speech Quality (PESQ) score. The PESQ score is defined by a family of standards standardized by the International Telecommunication Union under ITU-T recommendation P.862 (02/01). It describes a test methodology for the automated assessment of speech quality in a telephone system. Naturally, the improvement in resultant audio quality comes at the cost of increased compute cycles used to encode the speech.

Medical Ultrasound Imaging

Medical ultrasound imaging is a class of applications that demand a significant amount of embedded computational performance. The compute intensive requirements of these applications spans down to even the lower-end portable devices. Even though the physical configurations, parameters, and functionality may vary widely across the available device ranges, basic functions such as B-mode imaging share the same basic algorithmic pattern: beam forming, envelope extraction, and polar-to-Cartesian coordinate translation. B-mode ultrasound imaging is the traditional 2D ultrasound used in medical environments.

Figure 11.12 shows the block diagram of a typical basic ultrasound imaging implementation. The transducer array comprises a number of ultrasound emitters and receivers that connect to an analog front end (AFE) responsible for conditioning the ultrasound signals. These signals are converted to/from a digital representation by means of a series of analog to digital converters and digital to analog converters. The transmit and receive beam former algorithm calculates the components delay and weight for each of the transducer elements during transmission and reception, dynamically focusing the transducer array in a sequence of directions during each image frame, without the need for mechanical moving parts or complex analog circuitry. This does come at the cost of a significant increase in digital computational requirements. An envelope detector extracts the information carried by the ultrasound signals, which are then stored and prepared for display. Common systems also have the ability to detect and measure the velocity of blood flow, usually carried out by a Doppler processing algorithm. Image compression and storage for post-analysis is also a common feature.

The highlighted blocks in Figure 11.12 have been prototyped and measured for performance on the Intel Core 2 Duo and Intel Atom processors, looking at a B-mode imaging application. The Intel IPP libraries were used throughout this prototype. A brief discussion on the architecture, parameters, and corresponding estimated performance requirements for each of these blocks follows. Table 11.3 lists some of the overall parameter values for this prototype system; these values are common for small portable ultrasound devices.

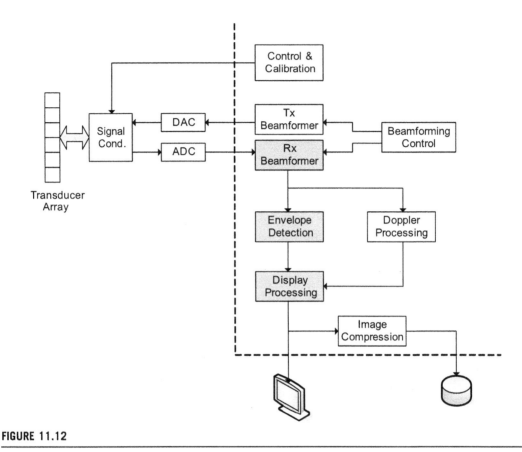

FIGURE 11.12

Block Diagram of a Typical Ultrasound Imaging Application.

All of the dimensions in Table 11.3 play a significant role in establishing the overall numeric complexity of the system. We will evaluate each step in the algorithm and identify whether its implementation in software running on the Intel architecture core is viable or whether the compute requirements are too high, in which case it is a candidate for execution in an FPGA device or external accelerator. These trade-offs are a frequent pattern of analysis when it comes to developing system architectures.

Receive Beam Former

Beam forming is a signal processing technique that uses an array of sensors. The technique relies on constructive/destructive interference to target a spatial location. It can be used with transmit and receive processing. The block described below implements delay-and-sum synthetic receive focusing with linear interpolation and dynamic apodization. Figure 11.13 shows the DSP block diagram for this module.

Table 11.3 Reference Parameters for the Ultrasound System

Reference Parameter	Value Used
Number of ultrasound transducers	128
Number of scanned lines per frame (steering directions)	128
Angle aperture	90 degrees
Number of samples acquired per transducer per line	3000
Output image dimensions	640 x 480 pixels
Target number of frames per second	30
Image resolution	8-bit grayscale
Input signal resolution	12-bit fixed-point
Output signal resolution	8-bit fixed-point
Computational precision for all stages	32-bit floating-point (single precision)

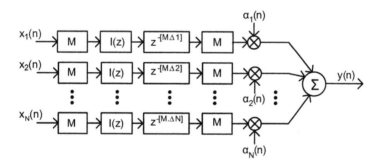

FIGURE 11.13

Block Diagram of the Receive Beam Former.

For each scan line that is acquired, each signal stream $x_k(n)$ coming from the transducer elements passes through an upsampler, an interpolation filter $I(z)$, a delay element, and a downsampler, and is multiplied by a dynamically varying apodization coefficient. The resulting signals are then accumulated and a single stream $y(n)$ is sent to the next processing stage. The delay values are pre-computed, multiplied by M, rounded to the nearest integer value (operator $[\ ]$), stored in a look-up table (LUT), and recomputed each time a new line starts to be acquired. The apodization function updates itself for each sampling period of the input streams. All its coefficients are also pre-computed and are stored in a LUT.

The interpolation filter is a first-order linear interpolating filter. If this filter is decomposed into its M polyphase components, only N/M of its taps need to be computed (N being the total number of taps). An interpolation/decimation factor of 4 was chosen for this prototype, which means that the filter has a 7-tap, linear-phase FIR configuration.

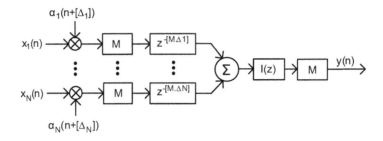

FIGURE 11.14

Simplified Block Diagram of the Receive Beam Former.

Assuming that each of the filter instances processes 2 taps per input sample, the structure of Figure 11.13 requires more than 7.3 GFLOPs (Floating-Point DSP Operations per Second) for real-time, 30 fps B-mode imaging. This performance level is difficult to achieve using typical DSP or GPP architectures. Figure 11.14 shows an alternate arrangement of the same block diagram, where the 128 parallel filters are transformed into a single filter having the same impulse response. This block diagram is roughly equivalent to the previous one. The new architecture incurs a minor loss of accuracy in the delays applied to the apodization coefficients.

Although the channel streams are accumulated at the higher sampling rate, at most the same number of additions is performed, since for each M samples of the upsampled signals, only one is not equal to zero. The interpolating filter is now a decimating filter, and an efficient polyphase implementation is also possible.

Assuming the worst-case scenario in which all delay values are the same, the number of operations for the beam forming algorithm is now 3.1 GFLOPs. Although still a high-performance target, this represents a reduction of more than 57% in computational complexity as compared to the algorithm of Figure 11.13.

Envelope Detector

The envelope detector algorithm uses a Hilbert transformer as its central building block. The incoming signals are modulated in amplitude, where the ultrasound pulses carry (modulate) the information to be displayed. Figure 11.15 shows its block diagram. The order L of the Hilbert transformer is 30.

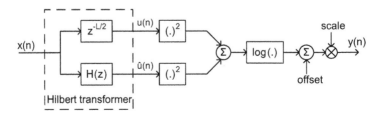

FIGURE 11.15

Block Diagram of the Envelope Detector.

The code sample for the envelope detector is shown in Listing 11.11.

```
/* Pass the signal through the Hilbert transformer and store in pOutBuf */
ippsFIRSetDlyLine_32f( envdet->pFIRState, NULL );
ippsFIR_32f( &beamf->pRxOutBuf[outIndx], envdet->pTmpBuf,
        dataset->params.numSamples + envdet->nDly,
        envdet->pFIRState );
/* Square the I and Q signals and add them */
ippsPowerSpectr_32f( &beamf->pRxOutBuf[outIndx],
            &envdet->pTmpBuf[envdet->nDly],
 &envdet->pOutBuf[outIndx], dataset->params.numSamples );
/* Avoid log of 0.0 */
ippsAddC_32f_I( 1.0e-37, &envdet->pOutBuf[outIndx],
        dataset->params.numSamples );
/* Compute the logarithm of the result */
ippsLog10_32f_A11( &envdet->pOutBuf[outIndx],
            &envdet->pOutBuf[outIndx],
            dataset->params.numSamples );
/* Offset and scale the output */
ippsAddC_32f_I( 37.0, &envdet->pOutBuf[outIndx],
        dataset->params.numSamples );
ippsMulC_32f_I( 5.0, &envdet->pOutBuf[outIndx],
        dataset->params.numSamples );
```

LISTING 11.11

Code Sample for Envelope Detector.

Assuming that the logarithm consumes 10 DSP operations per sample, the computational requirements for this block would be 437.8 MFLOPs.

Display Processing

The main function of this block is to transform the array containing all the information to be displayed from polar to Cartesian coordinates. Figure 11.16 illustrates the transformation performed in this module, in which a hypothetical scanned object (a rectangle) is "de-warped" for proper visual representation.

In Figure 11.16, θ represents the steering angle, d is the penetration depth, and x and y are the pixel coordinates in the output image.

During initialization, the application takes the physical parameters of the system and determines the active pixels in the output target frame. Using the conversion formulas in Figure 11.16, a look-up table (LUT) is built that stores all the information required for mapping between coordinate spaces. Bilinear interpolation is performed in the (d, θ) space for an increased quality of the output images.

For a 640 x 480 pixel image and for a 90 degree angle aperture, the number of active pixels is about 150,000. To obtain the output pixel amplitude values, the four nearest values are read from the

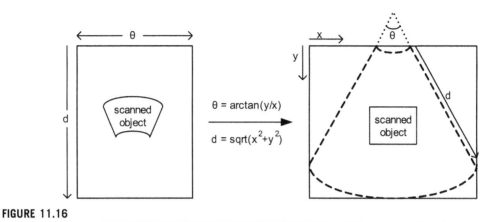

FIGURE 11.16

Polar-to-Cartesian Conversion of a Hypothetically Scanned Rectangular Object.

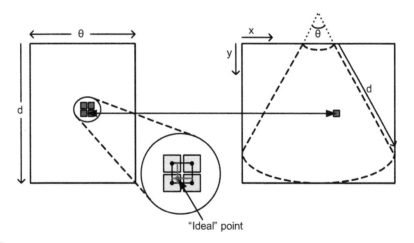

FIGURE 11.17

Illustration of the Process for Obtaining the Output Pixel Values.

polar-coordinate space, and then bilinear interpolation is performed using the mapping information computed upon initialization. Figure 11.17 illustrates this process. For each pixel, 13 DSP operations in total are performed. For a 30 fps system, 58.5 MFLOPs are required.

Performance Results

Table 11.4 and Table 11.5 show the performance results for each of the three DSP modules described above, running on Intel Core 2 Duo and Intel Atom processors. The benchmark was run on a single-thread, single-core configuration, that is, no high-grain parallelism was taken into consideration. Linux

Table 11.4 Performance: Intel Core 2 Duo (2.533 GHz, 6 MB L2 Cache)

Algorithm	Processing Requirement (MFLOPs)	Time to Process One Frame (ms)	Equivalent Processing Throughput (MFLOPs)
Rx beam forming	3098	227	453
Envelope detection	437	4.5	3207
Display processing	58	3.39	575
Total	3595	235	508

Table 11.5 Performance: Intel Atom N270 (1.6 GHz, 512 KB L2 Cache)

Algorithm	Processing Requirement (MFLOPs)	Time to Process One Frame (ms)	Equivalent Processing Throughput (MFLOPs)
Rx beam forming	3098	1177	453
Envelope detection	437	22.7	3207
Display processing	58	24.7	575
Total	3595	1224	508
Total excluding beam forming	496	47.5	348

2.6.18 was used on the Intel Core 2 Duo system (GCC 4.1.1 was used for compiling the application), and Linux 2.6.24 on the Intel Atom platform (GCC 4.2.3). Intel IPP version 6.0 was installed on both platforms.

Other than the lower clock frequency, various factors influence the lower performance values obtained with the Intel Atom processor: total available cache size and number of instructions retired per clock cycle. The Intel Atom's instruction pipeline, optimized for low-power applications, is not able to retire as many instructions per clock cycle (in average) as the Intel Core 2 Duo.

Due to its more straightforward nature of memory accessing, the envelope detector is the most efficient part of the processing chain.

The low performance values for the display processing algorithm are mostly due to the non-sequential memory access patterns. The generation of many cache line and page misses makes the algorithm unsuitable for vectorization, although it could still operate in a parallel fashion on a multi-core, multi-threaded platform.

One of the largest performance bottlenecks of the beam forming algorithm is caused by the varying delay values applied to the signals, causing many nonaligned memory access patterns. Usually due to its high performance requirements, this part of the algorithm is offloaded to external, dedicated circuitry, mostly based on FPGAs. Table 11.5 shows the benchmark results in terms of number of frames per second attainable for the platforms tested.

The Intel Atom performed reasonably, sufficient for handheld designs, but was not to be able to reach the initial 30 fps target. The Intel Core 2 Duo easily meets this target and provides enough headroom to accommodate significant other runtime control and processing tasks required of a fully functional ultrasound imaging application. It is also worth noting that opportunities for parallel processing exist in several places within the algorithm, though they were not taken into consideration throughout this study; in particular, no attempt was made to thread the applications with symmetric multi-threading enabled. Additionally, many Intel Atom–based platforms are available with multi-core Intel Atom Processors, which would make the target frame rate more than achievable. In all of the above cases reviewed, the beam former data rate and computational complexity required make it an unlikely candidate for implementation on the Intel architecture processor core.

SUMMARY

Digital signal processing is a truly expansive field, with a very wide range of precision requirements, competing complexities, architectural demands, and performance processing deadlines. The extended processing capabilities and the introduction of SIMD engines to general-purpose processors make the use of general purpose processors for many workloads that are a combination of general-purpose computing and digital signaling processing. The DSP functions within many applications can be accelerated significantly by using techniques such as vectorization, hand coding using SIMD intrinsics, or using vendor-provided signal processing libraries that maximize the use of the appropriate SIMD capabilities. These techniques may not replace the need for traditional DSPs when the compute requirements are very high, but do offer the opportunity to simplify the overall application when platforms require control, communications, and general-purpose processing combined with DSP processing. Managing a mix of these applications using common hardware and software architectures makes this a compelling avenue for system architects and developers to pursue.

Network Connectivity

Connectivity is the hallmark of contemporary digital systems. Of the many changes that have arisen in computing and embedded systems in recent decades, few can match the sweeping consequences that have resulted from the development of the Internet and from the trend toward universal, always available, connectivity for devices and, by extension, the people who rely on them.

Most of us consider the impact of the Internet from the perspective of an information consumer, and for good reason: nearly all forms of remote communications are either explicitly or implicitly Internet-based. Embedded applications and the systems that drive them have been irrevocably changed by the emergence of the Internet. Consider that entire classes of embedded communications systems—Ethernet switches, Wi-Fi™ access points, and firewall appliances, for example—are predicated on the existence of the Internet. Traditional classes of embedded systems, from printers to point-of-sale terminals, now rely on always-on network connectivity to provide their primary functions.

The impact of connectivity has, in fact, changed the nature of most embedded systems. Connected embedded systems can now report back to both owners and operators and the system manufacturers, receive updated software, have maintenance performed, and communicate explicitly; none of these were previous capabilities of traditional embedded electronics. Furthermore, feature sets no longer must be completely implemented within the embedded device itself, but can use the extension of its access to its advantage. Network connectivity, and Internet access in particular, allows some features to be implemented entirely on remote systems. The dramatic opportunities for innovation provided by network connectivity represent very strong evidence that market size and competitiveness will only expand in coming years.

Of course, network connectivity brings consequences to embedded systems beyond the technical. Communications technologies have a peculiar and relatively rare characteristic: the use of a given communications solution implies and requires a consensus among those communicating. Two parties cannot communicate with one another without using a shared protocol. This fact has created a new axis of cooperation across embedded industries and among competitors. To the extent that embedded systems developers can rally behind a networking technology, all can benefit.

This need for consensus has resulted in a large number of processes and organizations whose sole purpose is to manage and promulgate progress in networking standards. As will be seen, volunteer organizations such as the IETF and IEEE, whose membership is primarily drawn from the ranks of large equipment vendors, software vendors, and service providers, compete and cooperate to drive forward the definition of the standards that will dominate the communications in a given industry. Behind each successful networking technology is a history that explains how decisions were made and by whom; often, the specific history—the documents, e-mail exchanges, and meeting notes—are in the public domain and freely available on the Internet. Often, embedded system designers must choose from among a small set of communications and networking technologies to include in a product, with dramatic consequences in store for those who mistakenly choose a failing technology. Companies and

347

designers actively work to avoid this by sending engineers to participate in standards bodies and to pay close attention to the public record of which technologies have the greatest momentum.

In addition to considering these qualitative effects of network connectivity on embedded systems, it is possible to quantify some detailed aspects of the expanse of this connectedness. In particular, the growth in global Internet traffic is a strong indicator of how network connectivity continues to change the landscape. Each year, Cisco publishes a Virtual Networking Index (VNI), the most comprehensive and reliable estimate of both current Internet usage and future projections.

Figure 12.1 illustrates global Internet traffic by its application source from 2009 and projects its growth through 2014. First, consider the scale: in 2010, global public Internet bandwidth, excluding private IP networks and mobile networks, was approximately 16 exabytes (1 exabyte equals 1000 petabytes) and is expected to double by 2013. Second, four categories dominate the total for 2010: file sharing (5075 PB), Internet video (4725 PB), business internet, meaning traffic from business IP addresses and governments (2522 PB), and consumer web/email/data (2273 PB). It can clearly be seen that these are large numbers and they all are projected to significantly grow. Clearly, embedded systems that relate to video or networking infrastructure have a positive growth projection!

In this chapter, we will explore the key concepts and system details that developers must understand in order to integrate network connectivity into embedded systems. Because networking brings together many different concepts from distinct conceptual layers of abstraction, any overview like this

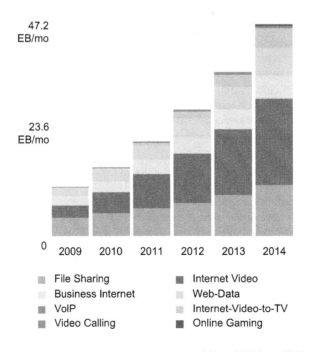

*Cisco VNI June 2010

FIGURE 12.1

Current and Projected Global Internet Bandwidth.

must choose a layered approach. In this overview, we will pursue a mostly top-down direction: we begin with a summary of the higher-level networked application structure and programmer-facing details that matter most to developers, and from there delve deeper into the details of IP networking and specific physical network technologies, in particular, Ethernet, Wi-Fi, and Bluetooth™. To see how these networking technologies are managed within the operating system, the chapter proceeds with a discussion of the systems software in using the Linux operating system that implements network connectivity.

NETWORKING BASICS

The concept of computer networking arose shortly after the advent of computers. The primary aim of computer networking as originally envisioned was to enable resource sharing and the effective use of expensive large-scale computers. Economic factors still dominate networking and computing, but nearly every aspect of computing and communications has changed since the late 1960s, when the computer networking concept emerged.

In any knowledge domain so vast and so full of detailed information, it is helpful to approach the information with a clear and structured perspective, so that the details themselves don't blur the basic concepts. At a high level, two basic concepts are important to recognize in order to establish the proper context. Modern networking technologies are based on packets and addresses. That is, devices with network addresses communicate by sending and receiving packets of data.

Modern computer networking may be approached, and indeed described, in two ways. First, *protocol layering* describes how the levels of abstraction in a computer network relate to one another. Second, *node operation* describes how network messages move through a device. These different perspectives will provide very useful in gaining a more comprehensive view of the technologies at work in a network connection.

Layering and Network Software

We will review in detail the TCP/IP protocols in further sections, but for now we note that protocols are layered and separated by well-defined interfaces. Layering helps to separate the implementation details of a given layer of abstraction from the interface, or agreement, it shares with those components it interacts with. By keeping the interface constant but allowing implementation details to change, each layer in the system can be replaced or modified without requiring coordination in layers above or below. In the absence of strict layering, changes in any level would need to be coordinated with those above and below, representing a dramatic resistance to change.

Figure 12.2 illustrates the layering present in modern networked devices. This particular representation is referred to as the Internet hourglass because it has a "thin waist," represented by the IP protocol, which is the only protocol that must be universally understood by communicating devices in an internetwork (that is, a connected group of networks that may have different link types). The IP protocol is the protocol that provides connectivity between systems featuring a variety of transport or physical layer protocols above and link types below.

The topmost layer in this figure indicates some of the user applications that communicate via the application layer as shown in the second layer. Examples of software and applications in these levels

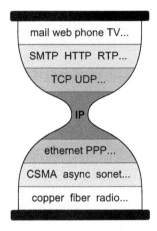

FIGURE 12.2

Protocol Layering as Embodied by the Internet Hourglass.

include web browsers and servers, instant message (IM) clients, and streaming video plug-ins. The third layer is the transport layer, where protocols are distinguished by the ordering and delivery guarantees that may or may not provide. In the middle, IP defines the packet and address structure. Beneath IP are the layers that describe the data link type and the physical medium used for communication. We will revisit layering in the context of TCP/IP in further sections.

Node Operation and Network Hardware

While helpful in illustrating the relationship between protocols, the layering model does not reveal anything about how information might flow through a computer or network device.

Organizationally, a networked device consists of a network interface, operating system, and application program. Physical I/O is provided by the network interface, such as an Ethernet adapter in a computer or an Ethernet port in a switch. In a computer, the network interface is a peripheral device, either integrated in the computer chipset or resident on an I/O bus such as PCI Express™, whose operation is determined by the device driver and its use by the host operating system. Physical buffer memories on the network interface are used to temporarily store data taken off the wire until the device driver and operating system can move the bits into a buffer in main memory. The operating system examines packets as they arrive to determine their ultimate destination. Some packets are destined for services that are part of the operating system itself, and others are destined for applications executing on the system. Application-bound packets are ultimately delivered to user-level processes through I/O libraries similar in principle, and sometimes identical, to those used to access files in a file system.

Later in the chapter, we discuss several network link types as well as the details of Linux networking. In those discussions, we will consider in greater detail the relationship between protocol definitions, device drivers, and operating system organization.

Sockets and a Simple Example

Academic networking textbooks must always strike a balance between introducing protocols in isolation and motivating protocols by demonstrating how they function in real usage contexts. Fortunately, this is not an academic networking textbook, so we can move directly to a real-world example!

While we expect that all readers have used networked applications, we do not expect that all have written networked programs of their own. We will now walk through a simple example that illustrates most of the key user-level topics that we will explore in greater detail in the remainder of the chapter.

The dominant user-level software interface used by developers is the *sockets interface.* Socket programming is synonymous with TCP/IP networking, Unix, and C programming. Sockets were first introduced in Berkeley Unix in the early 1980s, and are as a result sometimes referred to as Berkeley sockets. However, sockets libraries exist on all platforms these days.

Table 12.1 names and describes the important socket API functions. These functions provide a high-level indication of how socket programs do their work. However, to make sense of the specific parameters and associated data structures, we will first need to discuss the TCP/IP protocols.

Table 12.1 Sockets API

Socket Function	Description
`socket()`	Creates a new socket.
`bind()`	Associates a socket with an IP address and port number.
`listen()`	For connection-oriented protocols like TCP only: forces a bound socket to wait for a connection.
`connect()`	For TCP only: opens a connection to a specified IP address and port.
`accept()`	For TCP only: initializes a connection following a successful `listen()`.
`send()`, `sendto()`, `write()`, `recv()`, `recvfrom()`, `read()`	Sends and receives data, providing sockets and buffers and buffer sizes where appropriate.
`close()`	Releases the socket.
`getaddrinfo()`, `getnameinfo()`, `gethostbyaddr()`, `gethostbyname()`	Translates URLs/names to IP addresses, and vice versa. Uses `get*info()` rather than `gethostby*()` because it works for both IPv4 and IPv6; the latter is IPv4-only.
`select()`	Allows a single program to work with multiple sockets concurrently. This function takes a wait time value and three lists of sockets: a list awaiting reads, a list awaiting writes, and a list of possible exceptions. Upon return, only ready sockets remain in their respective lists.
`poll()`	A generalized version of `select()` that requires just a single list that, after return, will reflect the ready status (read, write, error) of each supplied socket.
`getsockopt()`, `setsockopt()`	Gets and sets options and information associated with a socket.

For now, however, we will proceed with a simple example of how two user-level programs can exchange information across an IP network.

Listing 12.1 shows a simple sockets program in Python that transmits a text string to port 7777 on the machine executing the program. We'll discuss host names, IP addresses, and IP ports later, so if you are unfamiliar with them, you can think of addresses and ports as pairs of numbers that we choose in advance of communicating between two machines on the Internet. Addresses identify a machine uniquely, and ports identify a process running on a machine; ports are the mechanism for multiplexing network traffic between distinct concurrent processes on a given machine.

Python provides a sockets library, and coupled with the language's concise syntax, we can quickly get an idea of how sockets programs are structured without first having to confront the many constants, data types, and structures that are present in an equivalent C program listing. We will get to those in due course, but for now our purpose is to understand how socket programs function.

In this example, the user datagram protocol (UDP) is used. UDP provides an unreliable datagram service on top of IP. This means that the message may not be successfully delivered or may be delivered more than once. The application needs to verify proper delivery. How is this useful, and why does this unreliability make sense? Well, not all applications care about ordered, reliable message delivery, and many that do have unique, application-specific requirements that the networking stack and operating system could not be expected to anticipate. The transmission control protocol (TCP) provides a generic, byte-stream delivery service (that is, your bytes will be delivered in the order you provided them, or an error will be reported), and we'll discuss it later. For now, let's look at the program in Listing 12.1.

```
1  import socket, sys
2  if len(sys.argv) > 1:
3      dst = sys.argv[1]
4  else:
5      dst = 'localhost'
6  # Create a socket
7  s = socket.socket(socket.AF_INET, socket.SOCK_DGRAM)
8  # Open a connection to the local machine at port 7777
9  s.connect((dst,7777))
10 # Send some bytes through the connection.
11 s.send("Mr. Watson--come here--I want to see you.")
12 s.close()
13 print "Message sent."
```

LISTING 12.1

Sending a UDP Packet: udp_sender.py.

In 13 lines, including comments, we have a complete sockets program. This program sends text data via UDP, and we can see precisely how by considering each section in turn.

Lines 1–5: The socket and sys libraries are imported. The program takes a single, optional command line destination argument; sys.argv is an array of strings with the program name in the first location, and each subsequent location contains the next command line parameter. If no argument is given, 'localhost' is the default.

Line 7: A new socket is created. The first parameter—`socket.AF_INET`—specifies the IPv4 protocol, and the second—`socket.SOCK_DGRAM`—indicates the UDP protocol. You can use `AF_INET6` and `SOCK_STREAM` to specify IPv6 and TCP, respectively.

Line 9: This `connect` call specifies our destination machine and port. Python makes it easy because this function call accepts either a URL (for example, `'localhost'`) or an IP address (for example, `'127.0.0.1'`); in C, `connect` only accepts an address.

Lines 10–13: The data are sent and the socket is closed. The send call used here returns an integer value corresponding to the number of bytes sent.

We now consider the corresponding receive program shown in Listing 12.2, which, as will be seen, is no more complex.

```
1  import socket
2  # Create a socket
3  s = socket.socket(socket.AF_INET, socket.SOCK_DGRAM)
4  # Bind to port 7777 on the local machine
5  s.bind(('',7777))
6  # Dump data 4KB at a time
7  while 1:
8    data, addr = s.recvfrom(4096)
9    if not data: break
10   print "From ", addr, ": ", data
11 s.close()
```

LISTING 12.2

Receiving a UDP Packet: udp_receiver.py.

Let's look at what is going on in this code. Lines 1–5: The socket is created and bound in the same manner seen in udp_sender.py. An empty bind address string implies the local host.

Lines 7–11: Within the loop, the Python `recvfrom` function returns both a string containing up to the specified number of bytes and the IP address of the sender. This infinite loop breaks (line 9) when the `recvfrom` call returns without any data; receiving an empty packet (for example, sent with `s.send("")`) would terminate the loop.

These two programs together illustrate how to send and receive basic IP traffic across the Internet in less than two dozen lines of Python source code. Of course, in demonstrating how simple sockets programs work, we have introduced and glossed over many important details. For example, nowhere in either program did we indicate whether we were going to use Ethernet, Wi-Fi, Bluetooth, or any other specific network type. Thankfully, sockets and TCP/IP make those lower-level distinctions largely irrelevant for user-level programs. To see how, we now consider TCP/IP.

TCP/IP NETWORKING

The TCP/IP protocols embody the Internet architecture, and they grew out of early ideas about packet switching and queuing at MIT and elsewhere in the early 1960s. At that time packet-switched networks did not exist, but large communication networks certainly did. The world had a very robust telephone network that operated in a circuit-based manner to provide voice telephony. To make a phone call, a circuit must be established between the handsets before any data can be sent. For voice calls, this arrangement is entirely natural for two reasons. First, there is no reason to speak before the other side picks up. Second, effectively constant bit rates are needed to sustain a conversation, so circuits along the paths between the handsets could be provisioned to provide the right amount of bandwidth for a call of acceptable quality.

Data traffic between computers, however, is not such an obvious fit for circuit-based communication. Computer data can be bursty and highly variable, and not all computer communications patterns require concurrent interaction. If data are being sent only intermittently or if only a small amount of data is being sent, then reserving an entire end-to-end circuit may be wasteful. In place of circuits, data can be fragmented into individually wrapped packets and sent across networks interconnected by switches. In such a packet-switched network, data only consume resources as they are sent, and data can be sent without first having to set up and reserve potentially long paths across a collection of networks. Early ideas in packet switching appeared improbable and ineffective from the perspective of telephony but turned out to be a perfect fit for computer communications.

Of course, a packet-switched network requires that attached hosts have addresses and that network devices know how to direct, or route, packets from source addresses to destination addresses. These two functions, addressing and routing, are the core functions of the IP protocol.

Governance, the IETF, and RFCs

Before considering the details of the protocols, it is necessary to understand how the protocols have been established and how they are specified. The Internet Society was established in the early 1990s to provide an organized corporate structure to govern the various community activities that developed in the 1980s that ultimately developed the Internet protocols. In particular, both the Internet Engineering Task Force (IETF) and the Request for Comments (RFC) process, both of which preceded the Internet Society, report to the board of the Internet Society.

The IETF consists of volunteers organized into formal working groups and informal discussion groups for the purpose of developing and promoting Internet standards. RFCs are the IETF's method of publication. Each RFC has a number and a status; most are informational and express an opinion or best practice relating to the Internet. A small number of RFCs become Internet standards, at the conclusion of the IETF-governed standardization process.

For example, RFC 1122 "Requirements for Internet Hosts—Communication Layers" and RFC 1123 "Requirements for Internet Hosts—Application and Support" were both published in 1989 and together define the standards for Internet host software. From an end-hosts role in an IP network to how correctly and incorrectly formed datagrams should be handled, RFCs 1122 and 1123 define what hosts should implement. You may wonder, since the IETF and RFCs only exist to support Internet standards, and "host software" appears to be the most important type of standard to establish, how is it possible that 1121 RFCs were created prior to these two? There are three kinds of answers. First, the Internet protocol itself was defined RFC 791, published in 1981. Second, there was much to do! In browsing the preceding RFCs, the first of which was published in 1969, you see the basic notions of common byte sizes, message definitions, and basic user-level usage models emerge. RFC 97 is "A First Cut at a Proposed Telnet Protocol" and discusses the basic ideas involved with trying to provide a remote terminal window that acts like a local one. The third answer is that many of the RFCs are nontechnical in nature: records of conversations, personal opinions, and typographical corrections to prior RFCs.

The RFCs collectively represent what is likely to be the best and most accessible (you can find them all here: http://tools.ietf.org/rfc/) engineering project record in history. It documents precisely the development activities and decisions that ultimately led to the development of the Internet. It is a tremendous asset for scholars and aspiring technologists.

Addresses, Packets, and Routes

IP addresses are numbers. In IPv4, they are 4 bytes, or octets, in length; in IPv6, they are 16 octets in length. It is common to write IPv4 addresses in dot-decimal notation, such as 128.252.73.216. Groups of addresses with a common prefix can be annotated with a trailing slash and integer, such as 128.252.0.0/16, which refers to all addresses with a prefix beginning with the 16 bits equal to 128.252.

IPv6 addresses are customarily written as eight groups of four hexadecimal digits separated by colons, such as 2002:80fc:a0ba::80fc:a0ba (one sequence of groups consisting of four 0 digits can be omitted, as in this example; leading zeros can always be omitted).

How are IP addresses obtained? Since IP addresses are globally unique machine addresses, they must be assigned to network owners by a centralized authority. The Internet Assigned Numbers Authority (IANA) manages global IP address allocation under a contract awarded by the United States Department of Commerce. IANA in turn grants IP address allotments to five regional registries:

- African Network Information Centre (AfriNIC)
- American Registry for Internet Numbers (ARIN) for the United States, Canada, and parts of the Caribbean
- Asia-Pacific Network Information Centre (APNIC)
- Latin American and Caribbean Internet Addresses Registry (LACNIC) for Latin America and parts of the Caribbean
- RIPE NCC for Europe, Central Asia, and the Middle East

An organization requests a group of IP addresses from its regional registrar. Of course, being only 32 bits in length, IPv4 addresses are running short, and this shortage was seen well in advance and represents one of the primary motivations for developing IPv6. IPv6 is well-supported in new devices and software but has not yet become a mainstream protocol. Many believe that emerging nations, such as China, and technologies, such as 4G handsets, will trigger the mainstream transition in the not-too-distant future. Network address translation (NAT) has mitigated the IPv4 address shortage problem and will be discussed later in this chapter.

Once an organization has been allocated a block of IP addresses, such as the block denoted 128.252.0.0/16, the individual addresses can be allocated to machines. This allocation can be managed *statically,* in which case a machine is, in one way or another, assigned a permanent IP address, or *dynamically,* in which case a machine uses a dynamic, broadcast-based protocol such as DHCP (discussed later) to obtain an address from a common pool.

IP packets consist of headers, which contain source and destination addresses and ports, protocols, and payloads, which contain the data being communicated.

Figure 12.3 illustrates the header format for IPv4 and IPv6 packets.

The IPv4 header fields have the following definitions. *Version* is a 4-bit field with value 4. *IHL* is the header length expressed in 32-bit words; five words is the typical length, but the presence of

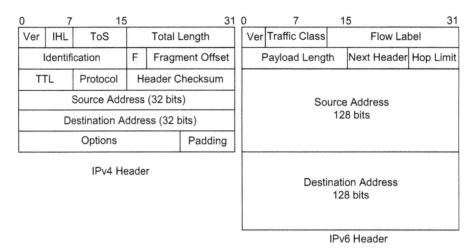

FIGURE 12.3

IPv4 and IPv6 Packet Header Formats.

options following the destination address can increase the header size to a maximum of 15 words. *ToS* stands for type of service, and has recently been replaced with the label DS, for differentiated services. The purpose of both labels is to express a relative priority or request for a typical treatment; RFC 2474 describes differentiated services and the available options. None are widely supported.

Total Length is the datagram size in bytes, header and payload included. Identification is a field containing a 16-bit value that is useful when datagrams are fragmented along a transmission path. It is possible for an IP datagram to exceed the maximum packet size of a given underlying network technology, in which case the device, be it host or switch, must fragment the datagram into multiple datagrams, each with the same identification value. Upon receipt, the identification field is used to make sure fragments from multiple original datagrams are not mistakenly reassembled.

The *F* field contains flags that can be used to disable fragmenting and to indicate whether this fragment is the final fragment in a series. The *Fragment Offset* indicates this fragment's offset within the original datagram, in units of 8-byte blocks.

The *TTL* field records the datagram's time to live. Each time the packet is forwarded through the router, the router decrements the TTL value. If a zero TTL value is reached before the packet arrives at the destination, the packet is dropped by the router. The router will usually send an ICMP (more on this protocol later) time-exceeded message when the packet is dropped. This mechanism is used to implement the traceroute tool.

The *Protocol* field indicates the protocol type of the encapsulated packet. The number 17 indicates UDP; 6 indicates TCP. RFC 790 defines the protocol numbers.

The *Header Checksum* is calculated over the IP header at each router that forwards the packet; the purpose is to verify that no errors have corrupted the header. The checksum computation is a 16-bit one's complement of the one's complement sum of all 16-bit words in the header. During the computation, the value of the checksum field is set to zero.

The *Source* and *Destination* address fields identify the IP addresses of the sender and receiver, respectively.

The *Options* field is rarely used but enables the inclusion of optional headers fields, which are typically intended to support measurement or experimental features. Options can vary in number and length, and padding must be included at the end to ensure the datagram ends on a 32-bit boundary.

The IPv6 packet format is simpler. The *Version* field holds value 6. *Traffic Class* is identical to the ToS field in IPv4. The *Flow Label* field is used to identify packets from a source that should all be treated in the same way; this was inspired by the difficulty of identifying flows in IPv4 traffic. The *Payload Length* identifies the number of bytes in the payload.

The *Next Header* field replaces protocol field from IPv4 and identifies the type of header that follows the 40-byte IPv6 header. *Hop Limit* replaces TTL from IPv4. The *Source* and *Destination* addresses identify the sender and receiver, respectively. Protocols that sit above IP, such as UDP and TCP, define headers of their own that appear at the beginning of the IP payload. Figure 12.4 illustrates the header format for each protocol.

The UDP headers are fairly simple. They include the source and destination ports, the length of the UDP datagram in bytes, and a checksum. The checksum is a bit unusual; it is calculated over a partial IP header (referred to as a *pseudo header* in RFC 768), the UDP header and the payload. The checksum calculation (which in other respects is like the one used in IP discussed previously) includes the portions of the IP header to protect against misrouted packets. In UDP, the source port and checksum fields are optional.

The TCP header and protocol are considerably more complex. Because TCP provides reliable, in-order byte-stream transport, mechanisms are needed to detect and recover from errors and losses. The

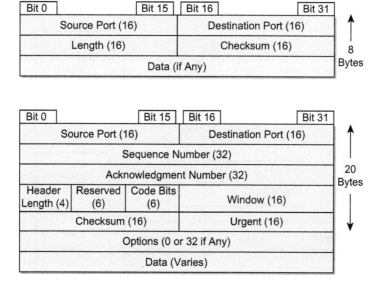

FIGURE 12.4

UDP (Top) and TCP (Bottom) Header Formats.

complete operation of TCP is outside the scope of this book; readers requiring more detail provided than the following brief overview are encouraged to consult the many online and print references available on the subject.

To ensure that both sender and receiver are prepared to communicate, TCP establishes a connection between the two hosts by way of a three-way handshake. A finite state machine is used on each side of the connection to systematically and reliably establish a connection, transfer data, and terminate a connection.

In order to make sure all bytes arrive in order, *Sequence Numbers* are used to number each byte, and the field in the TCP header is used to signal the current (that is, the sequence number for the first byte in this payload) or initial byte sequence number. The receiver advertises the sequence number it is expecting in the next packet in the *Acknowledgment Number* field; upon receipt of this acknowledgment, the sender can infer whether previous datagrams have been dropped.

Header Length encodes the TCP header length in units of 32-bit words. The Code Bits field contains eight 1-bit flags that correspond to TCP states and transitions between them.

To keep fast machines from overloading slower ones, the *Window* field reports how many bytes the host is currently willing to receive.

The *Checksum* is calculated in the same way as UDP as described above, but is not optional. Like in IP, TCP supports *optional* header fields, which are variably supported in deployed systems.

To see how these packet formats relate to application data, consider the illustration in Figure 12.5. It shows, from top to bottom, how data from an application process might first calculate and apply a UDP header, the result of which is to be contained within an IP header. Ultimately, something like an Ethernet frame is constructed and transmitted. In practical terms, this encapsulation involves prepending and appending headers and footers to data. Typically, everything beneath the application layer would be handled by the operating system and system libraries. The software that implements the operating system's networking features is called the network stack.

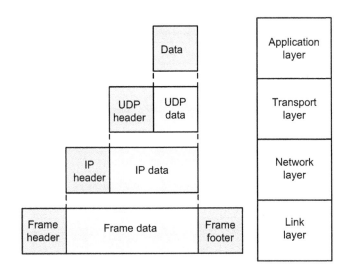

FIGURE 12.5

Encapsulation and the Four-Layer Internet Model.

We have discussed addresses and packet formats, but how does the network know where to send IP packets? Each end-host and router in an IP network has a route table containing IP prefixes indicating to which output interface a given packet should be sent. To forward a packet, the destination IP address is copied and used as a lookup key in the route table; the next-hop IP address associated with the longest matching prefix in the table is used to forward the packet. In small networks, it is possible to populate routing tables by providing entries for all hosts. In general, however, and in the Internet, a collection of higher-level, distributed routing protocols is used to calculate reasonable routes. The basic framework for these routing algorithms requires neighboring networks to publish to one another the IP address prefixes they know about, along with some measure of how efficiently they can forward to those prefixes. Most end-hosts have very small route tables with only a few default rules that forward packets to routers that server either local or remote IP addresses; routers in the core of the Internet have hundreds of thousands of entries.

Port Numbers, Byte Ordering, and OS Tools

In addition to the basic workings of the TCP/IP protocols, network system developers should be aware of the collection of enforced conventions and essential tools that exist to monitor and manage Internet devices.

Port numbers, for example, come in three varieties: well known (0–1023), registered (1024–49,151), and ephemeral (49,152–65,535). Port numbers in the first two categories are curated by IANA and officially require registration. In practice, many ports in the 1024–49,151 range have conflicting uses.

Ports identify services and application types. Port 80 is reserved for HTTP servers. Port 143 is used for IMAP email account access; port 25 is used to send email via SMTP. The full list can always be found at http://www.iana.org/assignments/port-numbers.

Another important convention concerns the order of bytes within words. Big-endian CPUs order bytes within words so that the most significant byte is stored at the lowest byte address; little-endian CPUs, including IA-32 processors, use the opposite byte placement. When communicating across a network, it is possible that two machines may use different byte orderings.

To account for this possibility, the network byte order (which happens to be big-endian) is used by convention to send network data in a manner that will be received coherently, regardless of the endianness of the sender and receiver. Sockets libraries provide helper functions to convert integers of various sizes to and from network byte order, as follows:

- `htons()`: host to network short
- `htonl()`: host to network long
- `ntohs()`: network to host short
- `ntohl()`: network to host long

All computer platforms, from embedded systems to servers, provide tools to configure and monitor the IP subsystem. To help get you started, we briefly introduce here three of the most essential.

Most embedded systems feature multiple IP network interfaces. These can be managed and queried using standard command line tools. On Microsoft Windows™–based systems the `ipconfig` utility can be used to both display and, given appropriate permissions, modify current TCP/IP configuration options for all interfaces. On Unix-like systems, the `ifconfig` utility offers the same capabilities.

It is often helpful to enumerate and examine the state of all active sockets in a system. The `netstat` program enables precisely this capability. It also can be used to gather statistics on the number of bytes and packets sent and received on individual interfaces. It can also display the content of the route table. The `netstat` utility is available on Unix-based and Windows systems alike.

Finally, packet analyzers are a class of program that allows users to capture traffic that is sent and received by the host machine. Wireshark™ is perhaps the most popular cross-platform, open source packet analyzer available today. It is a GUI-based program that very effectively identifies and parses all popular network protocols. It is commonly used to characterize network traffic, debug new network protocols, and diagnose network problems.

Supporting Protocols and Services

The Internet architecture relies on a broad array of additional protocols to function. IP, TCP, and UDP are the dominant components in data transmission, but, to be effective and productive, other protocols must help.

Translating names to addresses. The Internet was not a mainstream global technology until the World Wide Web emerged. With the web came names: domain names and URLs. The IP protocol works with IP addresses and has no means by which to express names. The domain name system (DNS) plays this role. DNS is a globally distributed, hierarchical name resolution database. Domain names are managed, like so many things, by IANA. IANA maintains and distributes the root zone database, which maps top-level domains, such as .com, .edu, and .uk, to authoritative name servers. So, a domain name such as intel.com would be resolved starting at the right most component, .com. The .com top-level domain is delegated by IANA to VeriSign, and a root zone lookup would yield the IP addresses and host names for a collection of name servers managed by VeriSign that are capable of resolving .com domains. Next, a VeriSign name server would be queried for intel.com, and the result would be a name server operated by Intel (or perhaps its ISP) that could answer specific questions about host names at intel.com.

Fortunately, very few DNS requests begin at the root zone. DNS supports query caching, so mappings for the most popular domain names are typically resident at each network's DNS server at any given time. Cache entries timeout periodically, to make sure stale name-address mappings eventually disappear. DNS is implemented atop UDP and uses port 52. Details can be found in RFC 1035.

Mapping IP addresses to link-layer addresses. As discussed previously, an IP packet is forwarded by matching a destination IP address to the longest matching prefix in the route table. The result is the IP address of the next hop along the path to the destination. How do we send to that machine? IP is layered atop a link-level protocol, but all we have is the IP address of the next hop machine. The address resolution protocol (ARP) does this job. ARP has been implemented on many types of LANs, but it is most commonly used to map IPv4 addresses to Ethernet addresses. To do this, an ARP request is broadcast on the Ethernet LAN asking, "Does anyone have an Ethernet interface associated with this IP address?" All machines on the LAN hear the broadcast, but only the machine with the interface associated with the desired IP address responds. With this response, the sender now has the correct destination MAC address and can create the Ethernet frame. To improve efficiency, ARP results are cached for future reuse.

Dynamically assigning IP addresses to hosts. Automatic assignment of addresses to hosts offers benefits of scalability, efficiency, and reliability as compared to static assignment. In IP, the dynamic host configuration protocol (DHCP) provides this service. When joining a network, the DHCP client on a host works by first broadcasting on the LAN a UDP request (with an empty source IP address) in search of a DHCP server. The DHCP responds to the source LAN address with an IP address offer (the DHCP client can also request its last known IP address; the DHCP server can also be configured to assign IP addresses based on assignments or randomly from a pool). When the host acknowledges acceptance of the offer, the address assignment is complete.

Error messages and basic connectivity. The Internet control message protocol (ICMP) is layered atop IP and provides error reporting in IP networks. Error codes are defined within the ICMP protocol to handle most forms of failures associated with the delivery of IP datagrams. ICMP is also used to implement the ping utility; ping is used in system development and network diagnosis, as well as whenever the user needs to verify that two systems are connected via IP. It is a simple but essential tool.

ETHERNET

Local area networks (LANs) emerged almost in lockstep with personal computers. Resource sharing and communications are natural tendencies, so as users began integrating PCs into daily work patterns, the benefits of connecting PCs within an organization became obvious.

Modern wired LANs are Ethernet LANs. In the past, multiple LAN technologies were commonly found interconnecting PCs in an organization, but those days are gone. If your PC has a wired network connection, it is Ethernet. Ethernet has successfully evolved and improved over the years, with periodic order-of-magnitude improvements in link bandwidth from 10 Mbps, to 100 Mbps, 1000 Mbps, 10 Gbps and beyond. Along with these improvements in performance have come substantial changes in the operation of the protocol. In fact, modern Ethernet shares a name and much of a packet format with its predecessors, but that's about all!

History

Ethernet was developed by Robert Metcalfe at Xerox PARC in the mid-1980s. The Ethernet LAN at PARC was effective, and ultimately resulted in a group of technology companies—Digital Equipment Corporation (DEC), Intel, and Xerox—developing and promoting a standard (DIX) for networking PCs. The initial data rate of each link was 10 Mbps, and, unlike today's switch-based Ethernet, each LAN was a shared medium. Metcalfe's inspiration, in fact, came from a radio-based network developed in Hawaii by Norman Abramson. The ALOHANET system was designed to provide computer connectivity to a central server from computers scattered across islands. To achieve this, each computer was equipped with a radio capable of sending on one frequency (the up link) and receiving on another (the down link). The central server received on the up link and transmitted on the down link; the opposite held for the remote computers. While the down link had only one transmitter (the central server), the up link had multiple. To cope with this, the central server would transmit an acknowledgment message each time a message was successfully received; if two or more nodes transmitted at the same time, the central server would only receive noise and would hence not acknowledge any of the transmissions. This, in turn, indicates to the senders that transmission had failed and that they would need to retry.

Metcalfe applied the same principles within the limited broadcast domain of physical Ethernet cables (that is, the radio frequencies stay within metal cables and do not propagate through free space). With a few refinements (such as listening for a clear channel before transmitting and continuing to listen during transmission), this approach is referred to as carrier sense multiple access with collision detection (CSMA/CD).

After a few years, in 1983, the DIX standard had essentially become the IEEE 802.3 standard. Ethernet quickly began to establish itself as the dominant LAN technology for PCs. Other companies backed other technologies (most notably IBM supported a token-ring LAN standardized as 802.5), but Ethernet after a relatively short time became the only LAN technology that mattered. It has continued to mature and develop and to this day completely dominates LAN installations.

Protocol Description

What follows is an overview of switched gigabit Ethernet. As illustrated in Figure 12.6, contemporary Ethernet LANs consist of hosts directly connected to switches, which are in turn connected to other switches or routers. This is the most substantial difference between modern and past incarnations of Ethernet; the network links are no longer shared in a way that allows broadcast collisions. Ethernet switches have a small amount of buffering in order to tolerate temporary congestion on a given link. For example, if two hosts on the same switch send to the same destination at the same time, one packet will be buffered temporarily in the switch while the other is transmitted. Neither end host need respond to this downstream congestion.

While nearly all LAN environments use full-duplex, point-to-point links between hosts and switches, modes for backward compatibility are typically present in Ethernet chipsets. A media access control (MAC) protocol is not needed on full-duplex, point-to-point links, but most network interfaces provide an implementation. As discussed below, Ethernet chipsets separate MAC functions from physical (PHY) device and media signaling functions; these can be separate ASICs or separate functional blocks on a single ASIC.

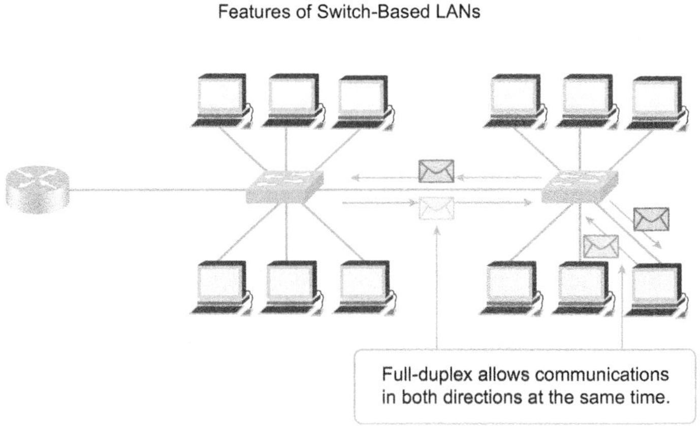

Features of Switch-Based LANs

Full-duplex allows communications in both directions at the same time.

FIGURE 12.6

Example of a Switched Ethernet LAN.

Ethernet MAC Addresses

The original Xerox Ethernet addressing scheme was adopted by IEEE in the form of IEEE 802 MAC addresses and has subsequently become the dominant address format for link-level network technologies. IEEE 802 defines addresses of two lengths, 48 and 64 bits. Ethernet uses 48-bit (6-byte) addresses.

Globally unique Ethernet addresses are typically established at the time of NIC manufacture. Each NIC has an originally assigned MAC address, the most significant 3 bytes of which uniquely identify the manufacturer, who can then make sure that the lower 3 bytes are unique for each NIC it creates. Modern NICs allow these MAC addresses to be changed by the owner, so global uniqueness is not enforceable, nor is it particularly necessary since Ethernet is a LAN technology, and the only requirement is that MAC addresses be unique within a broadcast domain.

Otherwise, MAC addresses are flat. Two bit positions have special significance. The least significant bit of the most significant byte indicates whether the address is unicast (0) or multicast (1). The second least significant bit of the most significant byte should indicate whether the MAC address is globally unique (0) or locally administered (1).

Ethernet Packet Format

The structure of an Ethernet packet is illustrated in Figure 12.7. The *Preamble* and *Start of Frame* fields are constant, well-known repeating bit patterns that enable synchronization between end points.

The *Destination* and *Source Addresses* identify the receiver and sender, respectively. The *802.1q Tag* field is optional, and is the mechanism for implementing Ethernet virtual LAN (VLAN) tagging. VLANs can be used to establish multiple, logically distinct LANs atop a shared underlying physical LAN. When an end host is part of a VLAN, the VLAN represents the extent of its broadcast domain. In this way, groups of machines and their traffic can be completely separated from one another on the same physical network. The *TPID* field contains a special pattern that signals the presence of the

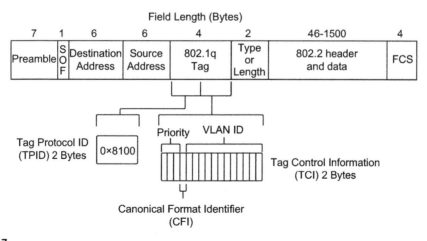

FIGURE 12.7

Ethernet 802.3 Frame Format.

optional 802.1q; the size of this field matches that of the *Type* field. The *Priority* field can be used to express which of eight levels of IEEE 802.1p priority applies. The *CFI* field indicates Ethernet (0) or Token Ring (1). The *VLAN ID* contains the 12-bit VLAN tag itself.

The *Type* field can express either the type of the encapsulated packet (such types must have values 0 x 0600 or greater) or the size of payload in bytes (assumed to be the case when the value is less than 0 x 0600).

The *802.2 header and data* field contains the payload and must be at least 46 bytes but no more than 1500.

The frame check sequence (FCS) contains a 32-bit cyclic redundancy check (CRC) value calculated over the frame. The sending NIC hardware calculates and appends the CRC, while the receiving NIC hardware verifies the value upon reception.

Other nonstandard formats exist, such as to support "jumbo" frames with payloads greater than 1500 bytes, but these are neither standardized nor widely enabled due to their violation of backward compatibility with legacy infrastructure.

A Gigabit Ethernet Controller and Its Features

The vast majority of embedded systems developers will use third-party networking silicon to support Ethernet connectivity. A gigabit Ethernet controller will implement the basic Ethernet protocol features we have described, along with a great many others.

For example, consider the Intel 82546GB dual port gigabit Ethernet controller, as shown in Figure 12.8. This device represents a modern, feature-rich gigabit Ethernet controller.

The Ethernet frame data path consists of the off-chip medium dependent interface (MDI), which represents an Ethernet port, and the PHY device (or transceiver), which manages the signal transmission and reception across the physical medium. The PHY connects to the MAC/controller, which

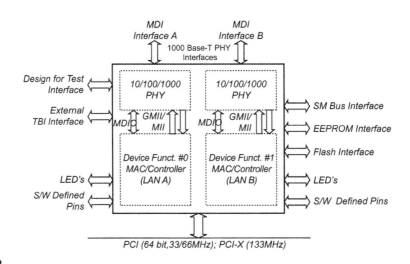

FIGURE 12.8

Block Diagram of the Intel® 82546-GB Dual Port Gigabit Ethernet Controller.

governs the operation of link-level Ethernet protocol across the gigabit media independent interface (GMII) with one bus going in each direction; GMII is clocked at 125 MHz with an 8-bit wide data path. GMII is backward compatible with MII, the corresponding bus interface for 10/100 Mbps Ethernet. The management data input/output bus (MDIO) is by the MAC to send controller information to the PHY. The MAC/PHY data path is reached from the host through the PCI bus.

Modern Ethernet silicon supports additional features intended to simplify use or improve performance and efficiency. Consider the following sample mechanisms supported by the Intel 82546GB.

Hardware support for receive and transmit ring management. Receive and transmit rings (i.e., circular FIFOs) in the MAC chip stage packets as they enter and leave the system. Traditional implementations require software on the CPU to read and write control registers on the device in order to manage the packet movement between ring buffers and main memory. This hardware support allows the system to post the addresses and sizes of main memory buffers and, with a few PCI commands, manage the transfers on its own. This frees the CPU to do other work and, in general, makes better use of PCI bandwidth.

Interrupt coalescing. Traditional NICs interrupt the operating system upon packet arrival. Under heavy load, frequent interrupts can degrade performance by trading useful work for interrupt handling. By aggregating packets as they arrive and issuing a single interrupt for a batch, the overhead due to interrupt processing can be reduced. Most operating systems enable interrupt coalescing hardware dynamically and only under times of load, in order to keep from increasing packet processing latency under lightly loaded conditions (when interrupt coalescing would delay a packet while awaiting the arrival of others).

Flash support for Preboot eXecution Environment (PXE). PXE is a protocol or booting a host with an image retrieved from the network. The Intel 82546GB provides a flash interface and associated logic for storing and booting from a PXE image.

Wake on LAN. Waking a sleeping machine from the network requires support from the NIC and BIOS. With this support, a system that is in a soft-off or sleep state (ACPI states G1 or G2; see Chapter 9 for more information) can be transitioned to the working state G0 upon receipt of a "magic packet." The magic packet is an Ethernet broadcast frame with a payload containing 6 bytes of all of 255 (all bits are one) followed by 16 copies of the destination machine's Ethernet MAC address.

WI-FI AND IEEE 802.11

Wireless LANS, and in particular Wi-Fi, have enjoyed robust popularity growth in recent years. The combination of Internet access via Wi-Fi and laptop computers has created a boom in mobile computing. In personal and business settings, the freedom and convenience associated with moving yourself, your work, and your information access and entertainment to wherever you choose have proven to have very broad appeal.

Beyond laptops, Wi-Fi has established a solid foothold in many categories of embedded systems, consumer electronics especially. From gaming systems such as the Nintendo Wii™ and DS to high-definition TVs and Blu-ray™ players, nearly all media-oriented consumer electronics feature Wi-Fi radios and Internet connectivity.

The term Wi-Fi is a trademark owned by the Wi-Fi Alliance, an organization of companies working to develop and promote wireless LANs based on the IEEE 802.11 family of protocol standards.

Wi-Fi has established itself as the dominant wireless LAN technology, and there are no serious challengers on the horizon. Like Ethernet, Wi-Fi has emerged as the only LAN of its type that matters.

History

The development of Wi-Fi relied on the availability of the unlicensed radio frequency spectrum and user demand for wireless computer networking. The use of the unlicensed spectrum in effect dictated the scale of wireless LANs; unlicensed frequency ranges tend to be high-frequency (and therefore do not penetrate walls well) and unpredictable (since no process governs the number of channel users).

The resulting scale was nearly ideal for offices and homes. The rise of laptop computers that users desired to move around with while remaining connected led businesses, universities, and homes to deploy Wi-Fi access points in North America and Europe at a robust rate. Healthy adoption rates drove further development and improvement of the early protocols.

Five 802.11 protocols have been standardized by IEEE, and while they've all been called Wi-Fi, they exhibit some substantial differences. The original protocol was introduced in 1997, but widespread adoption did not begin until 802.11b was released in 1999.

Protocol Description

Table 12.2 briefly summarizes each of the five standards. The protocols are primarily distinguished by their frequencies and modulation techniques. Two spread spectrum modulation techniques are used among the standards: direct-sequence spread spectrum (DSSS) and frequency-hopping spread spectrum (FHSS). Spread-spectrum techniques, whether employing direct sequence or frequency hopping, can be used for multiple access in a shared channel. In general, spread spectrum uses a noisy sequential signal structure, constructed by joining the original signal with a noise pattern known to sender and receiver, to spread the information signal over a wider spectrum of transmitting frequency than is found in the original signal. The receiver correlates the received signals to retrieve the original information signal.

Alternatively, frequency-division multiplexing techniques, such as orthogonal frequency-division multiplexing (OFDM), can be used to modulate the carrier signal. OFDM spreads the signal across multiple frequencies; spread spectrum techniques, on the other hand, help to effectively utilize the bandwidth within a single frequency.

The data rates are true physical layer bit rates and do not reflect the effective reduction in data rate due to the use of forward error correcting codes, which trade bandwidth for robustness. Accounting for this, 802.11g sustains a maximum data rate of around 22 Mbps under good conditions.

Table 12.2 IEEE 802.11 Standards

Standard	Date	Frequency (GHz)	Min/Max Data Rate (Mbps)	Modulation Technique
802.11	1997	2.4	1/2	DSSS, FHSS
802.11a	1999	5/3.7	6/54	OFDM
802.11b	1999	2.4	1/11	DSSS
802.11g	2003	2.4	1/54	OFDM, DSSS
802.11n	2009	2.4/5	7.2/150	OFDM

The 802.11 MAC protocol is designed to confront the two basic problems that arise in wireless communications. The first is the so-called hidden state problem. Suppose hosts A and B want to send to host C. Suppose further that A and B are within radio range of C but *not of each other*. If A and B simply listen for a clear channel before they begin sending, they may collide. The second problem is related and is known as the exposed station problem. Suppose A wants to send to C, while B is sending to another host. Further, suppose that A and B are in radio range, but B and C are not. If A senses the channel, it may falsely assume that it cannot send to C.

To deal with these two conditions, 802.11 provides two modes of operation. The Distributed Coordination Function (DCF) operates without centralized control. The Point Coordination Function (PCF) delegates all coordination within the cell to the base station.

DCF operates in a way very similar to the original Ethernet protocols, with a few additions. Senders wait for a clear channel before sending a request to send (RTS) frame. Any time a collision is detected, transmitters employ a binary exponential backoff strategy (if after a time the channel is still busy, wait for twice the previous time and repeat). The recipient receives and accepts the RTS by sending a clear to send (CTS) frame. The data are sent, and the receiver sends an acknowledgement frame to the sender upon completion. Neighboring stations that receive the RTS, CTS, or data frames know that transmission are underway or likely to start. In PCF, the base station controls who gets to send when, so most collisions are avoided.

The detailed operation of these protocols is, unfortunately, beyond the scope of this discussion. Most networking textbooks will introduce these in slightly greater detail; online tutorials are also a great way to learn the specifics of the protocols.

Frame Format

IEEE 802.11 defines three types of frames: data, control, and management. The organization of the data frame is shown in Figure 12.9.

The leading *Frame control* field contains a number of 1- to 4-bit flags. *Version* indicates the 802.11 version. *Type* identifies the frame as data, control, or management, and *Subtype* indicates RTS, CTS, or ACK control frames. The *To DS* and *From DS* fields indicate whether the frame originated from or is destined for an intercell connection, such as an Ethernet link. To decrease the likelihood of corrupted packets, the DCF mode previously described allows frames to be fragmented and sent with separate checksums; the *MF* field indicates whether more fragments follow this one. The *Retry* field indicates

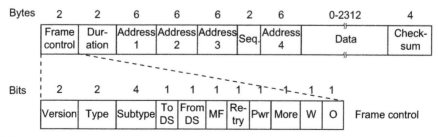

FIGURE 12.9

IEEE 802.11 Data Frame Format.

whether this frame is a retransmission. The *Power Management* bit can be used by base station to put the receiver into a sleep state or wake it up. The *More* bit signals whether the sender has more frames available to send. The *W* bit indicates that the wired equivalent privacy (WEP) encryption algorithm has been used to encrypt the payload. The *O* bit indicates whether a sequence of frames should be processed strictly in order.

The remaining fields are more straightforward. The *Duration* field indicates the expected transmission time for this frame. Four *Address* fields, each in the Ethernet MAC address format, indicate the source and destination hosts as well as the source and destination base stations in the case of traffic that travels between cells. The *Sequence* field is used to number fragmented frames. The *Data* field contains the payload. The *Checksum* field contains the 32-bit CRC value, as in Ethernet.

Management and control frames are subsets of the data frame format. Management frames have one fewer base station address (since they are limited to a single cell). Control frames lack data and sequence fields and have only one or two addresses.

A Wi-Fi Adapter and Its Features

As we saw in our Ethernet discussion, modern Wi-Fi silicon and network adapters will support the standard protocols, along with a range of enhancements intended to ease use or improve efficiency.

Consider, for example, the Intel Centrino® Ultimate-N 6300 network adapter, as shown in Figure 12.10.

FIGURE 12.10

Intel Centrino Ultimate-N 6300 in a PCIe Half Mini Form Factor.

The adapter supports all 802.11 standards. It provides support for up to three antennas (the connectors can be seen at the top of the card in Figure 12.10), with multiple input multiple output support (MIMO) for 802.11n that can in principle support 450 Mbps of aggregate traffic.

The management features include Intel Active Management Technology, which enables administrators to remotely monitor and diagnose system state without the involvement of the operating system.

BLUETOOTH

Bluetooth is a different kind of wireless network technology. It is sometimes referred to as a personal area network (PAN). Bluetooth was developed for mobile handsets, so that they could easily connect to other devices without requiring wires.

Bluetooth headsets have sold in vast numbers over the past decade. It is also commonly used to synchronize handset data with PC applications, although this practice appears to be diminishing for certain types of data (calendar entries, e-mail messages, and so on) as web-based alternatives make it easy to access or synchronize with remote web data through a handset's default data connection (such as 3G or Wi-Fi).

Bluetooth has cost and power advantages that suggest that it will remain significant for mobile handsets and select other embedded systems for years to come.

History

In the mid-1990s, Ericsson organized a group of technology companies (IBM, Intel, Nokia, and Toshiba) in an effort to establish a wireless technology to connection mobile handsets to other devices. Bluetooth was the result. The name Bluetooth is taken from Viking king Harald Blaatand II.

What was originally envisioned to be a replacement for a single cable grew to be a networking technology. The original group of companies established the Bluetooth Special Interest Group (SIG), which still develops and promotes Bluetooth today. The IEEE based its wireless personal area network 802.15 on Bluetooth, but differences remain between the standards developed by the SIG and IEEE. Foremost, the Bluetooth SIG defines a standard for an entire network architecture, from the physical links to application interfaces, whereas IEEE only keeps the physical and data link layers in its purview.

Protocol Details

The Bluetooth architecture features a *piconet* as its basic unit of organization. A piconet consists of one master Bluetooth device and up to seven active slave devices within radio range of the master, typically 10 meters or less. All communication is between master and one slave, and time division multiplexing is used as the master switches rapidly between slaves. Bluetooth version 2.0 and above support link rates on the order of 3 Mbps.

Table 12.3 Some Bluetooth Application Profiles

Profile	Description
Advanced Audio Distribution	Streams high-quality audio
Audio/Video Remote Control	Controls A/V devices such as TVs and Blu-ray players
Basic Imaging	Sends, receives, resizes images
Basic Printing	Sends text messages, emails, and other items to printer
Cordless Telephony	Enables the handset to serve as a cordless landline phone
Fax	Provides communication between a phone and PC fax
File Transfer	Shares file systems with other devices
Headset	Hands-free voice communication with a wireless headset
Intercom	Enables push-to-talk between handsets
LAN Access	Enables access to a LAN
Service Discovery	Discovers services available on a remote device
Synchronization	Synchronizes personal information with another device
Video Distribution	Allows the transport of a video stream

Multiple piconets can exist and overlap; when connected via a bridge node, the resulting internetwork is called a scatternet. Master nodes can cause slave nodes to transition to an inactive low-power state, and a piconet can contain a large number, 255, of these nodes.

As a networking technology, Bluetooth is peculiar in that it defines the applications for which it can be used. It does so via the definition of *profiles*, which outline both the application and the subset of Bluetooth features needed to implement it. This profile-based approach arose, presumably, as a compromise between providing rich capabilities and executing in the context of a resource-constrained, battery-operated handset.

Table 12.3 lists some, but not all, of the profiles currently supported in Bluetooth.

The Bluetooth protocol stack, illustrated in Figure 12.11, differs from the TCP/IP protocol stack discussed earlier. The lowest three levels, radio, baseband, link manager (LMP), and link control adaptation (L2CAP), roughly correspond to the physical and link-level protocols we discussed in the context of the Internet architecture and Ethernet.

The other stack components differ. First, above RFCOMM (a layer that emulates a standard serial port) a TCP/IP stack can be found. Also, audio (which corresponds to voice data) has its own path through the stack that avoids further processing. The other layers, vCard, AT commands, TCS BIN, and SDP, are examples of profiles that have a discrete presence at the application layer.

Packet Format

The primary Bluetooth frame format is illustrated in Figure 12.12. The leading Access Code field includes a preamble pattern and a slightly coded representation of the address of the master node in the piconet. Addresses in Bluetooth are 48-bit Ethernet MAC addresses.

The header contains several subfields. The AM_ADDR field is the temporary piconet address of the active slave device currently communicating; an all zero field is a broadcast indicator. The *Type*

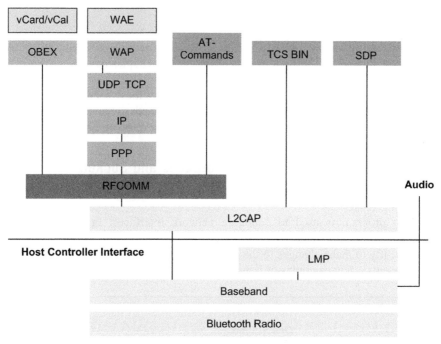

FIGURE 12.11

Bluetooth Protocol Stack.

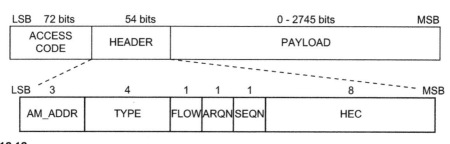

FIGURE 12.12

Bluetooth Frame Format. The Header is Repeated Three Times.

field specifies the Bluetooth packet type—synchronous connection-oriented (SCO), asynchronous connectionless (ACL), and so on. The *flow*, *arqn*, and *seqn* fields signal flow control, acknowledgment, and a sequence number (the discipline is stop and wait, so 1 bit is enough). For redundancy, three copies of the header are included, and, upon receipt, the majority value at each bit position is used.

LINUX NETWORKING

The popularity and open source nature of Linux make it a natural environment for networking education and development. All of the topics discussed in this chapter have a corresponding implementation in Linux.

In this section, we will briefly explore the networking utilities, sockets implementation, and networking kernel structures found in Linux, in order to bring depth to the discussion and to illustrate earlier concepts in a concrete way that the reader can further develop on his or her own.

Tools and Monitor and Control Network Interfaces and Sockets

As mentioned earlier, Unix-based systems like Linux offer a host of command line tools to interact with the networking subsystem.

The `ifconfig` program is used to configure network interfaces. In some distributions, this command is invoked during the boot process to initialize the system's interfaces, and it can be used at any time subsequently to make changes to the system.

Table 12.4 presents a few examples of how `ifconfig` can be used.

Table 12.4 Sample `ifconfig` Commands	
Command	**Description**
ifconfig -a	Displays details for all interfaces in the system
ifconfig eth0	Views the configuration, status, and statistics for interface eth0
ifconfig eth0 down	Disables interface eth0 (up is used to enable)
ifconfig eth0 128.252.160.10	Assigns specified IP address to eth0
ifconfig eth0 mtu 600	Changes the max transmission unit to 600 bytes; default value is 1500

The command `ifconfig` has long been used to control interfaces, but it is slowly being replaced by the `ip` command from the IPROUTE2 utility suite.

The `ip` command consolidates and normalizes a modestly large collection of network interface and routing tasks that had previously been implemented with a set of distinct set of command line utilities, such as `ifconfig`.

Table 12.5 demonstrates how the `ip` command can be used to replace the functionality of `ifconfig`.

The `netstat` utility can be used to both gather statistics from the network stack and to examine the current state of open and active sockets. It can also report the contents of network-related tables.

Table 12.6 includes several examples of `netstat` usage.

Programming Sockets in C

In our earlier discussion of networking basics, we walked through Python sockets implementations of simple UDP send and receive programs. At this point, after having discussed sockets, TCP/IP, and aspects of Linux programming, it will be instructive to revisit those programs in C, as shown in Listing 12.3.

Table 12.5 Sample `ip link` Commands to Be Used in Place of `ifconfig`

Command	Description
`ip link ls`	Displays details for all interfaces in the system
`ip link ls eth0`	Views the configuration, status, and statistics for interface eth0
`ip link set etho down`	Disables interface eth0 (up is used to enable)
`ip link set eth0 address 128.252.160.10`	Assigns specified IP address to eth0
`ip link set eth0 mtu 600`	Changes the max transmission unit to 600 bytes; default value is 1500

Table 12.6 Sample `netstat` Commands

Command	Description
`netstat -a`	Displays the status of all sockets
`netstat -t`	Displays the status of all TCP sockets; uses –u for UDP
`netstat -l`	Displays the status of all listening sockets
`netstat -r`	Displays the contents of the IP route table
`netstat -i`	Displays the table of network interfaces and their statistics
`netstat -a -c`	Displays the status of all sockets, continuously

```
1  #include <stdlib.h>
2  #include <stdio.h>
3  #include <errno.h>
4  #include <string.h>
5  #include <sys/socket.h>
6  #include <sys/types.h>
7  #include <netinet/in.h>
8  #include <unistd.h>
9
10 int main(int argc, char *argv[])
11 {
12   int sock;
13   struct sockaddr_in sa;
14   int bytes_sent, buffer_length;
15   char buffer[200];
16
17   buffer_length = snprintf(buffer, sizeof buffer,
18       "Mr. Watson--come here--I want to see you.");
19
20   sock = socket(PF_INET, SOCK_DGRAM, IPPROTO_UDP);
```

LISTING 12.3

Sending a UDP Packet: udp_sender.c.

```
21  if (-1 == sock) /*if sock creation fails, exit */
22  {
23    printf("Error creating socket");
24    exit(EXIT_FAILURE);
25  }
26
27  memset(&sa, 0, sizeof(sa));
28  sa.sin_family = AF_INET;
29  sa.sin_addr.s_addr = htonl(0x7F000001);
30  sa.sin_port = htons(7777);
31
32  bytes_sent = sendto(sock, buffer, buffer_length,
33              0,(struct sockaddr*)&sa,
34              sizeof (struct sockaddr_in));
35  if (bytes_sent < 0)
36    printf("Error sending packet: %s\n",
37        strerror(errno));
38
39  close(sock); /* close the socket */
40  return 0;
41 }
```

LISTING 12.3

(continued).

This program sends the same line of text to the localhost (IP address 127.0.0.1) at port 7777.

Lines 12–15: The required variables are all basic types, with the exception of the sockaddr_in structure, which is used to hold the socket details.

Lines 20–25: A new socket is created.

Lines 27–30: The sockaddr_in structure is first set to all zeros, then populated with the protocol, destination address, and destination port.

Lines 32–41: The sendto() socket function requires the socket, source buffer and its length, flags (0 in this case), and the populated sockaddr_in structure and its size. A successful send will return the number of bytes sent. To wrap up, the socket is closed.

The corresponding code listing for the UDP receiver follows in Listing 12.4.

```
1  #include <stdio.h>
2  #include <errno.h>
3  #include <string.h>
4  #include <sys/socket.h>
5  #include <sys/types.h>
```

LISTING 12.4

Receiving a UDP Packet: udp_receiver.c.

```
 6  #include <netinet/in.h>
 7  #include <unistd.h>
 8  #include <stdlib.h>
 9
10  int main(void)
11  {
12   int sock = socket(PF_INET, SOCK_DGRAM, IPPROTO_UDP);
13   struct sockaddr_in sa;
14   char buffer[4096];
15   ssize_t recsize;
16   socklen_t fromlen;
17
18   memset(&sa, 0, sizeof(sa));
19   sa.sin_family = AF_INET;
20   sa.sin_addr.s_addr = INADDR_ANY;
21   sa.sin_port = htons(7777);
22
23   if (-1 == bind(sock,(struct sockaddr *)&sa,
24            sizeof(struct sockaddr)))
25   {
26    perror("Error: bind failed");
27    close(sock);
28    exit(EXIT_FAILURE);
29   }
30
31   for (;;)
32   {
33    recsize = recvfrom(sock, (void *)buffer,
34              sizeof buffer, 0,
35              (struct sockaddr *)&sa, &fromlen);
36    if (recsize < 0)
37     fprintf(stderr, "%s\n", strerror(errno));
38    printf("Bytes received: %d\n ",recsize);
39    printf("Data: %s\n",buffer);
40   }
41   close(sock); /* close the socket */
42   return 0;
43  }
```

LISTING 12.4

(continued).

   This program is similar in content to the previous one, so we only call attention to the meaningful differences.

   Lines 23–24: The call to bind enables the process to receive data on port 7777.

   Lines 33–34: The recvfrom call takes as parameters the socket, the character buffer and its length, flags (once again 0), the sockaddr struct, and its size.

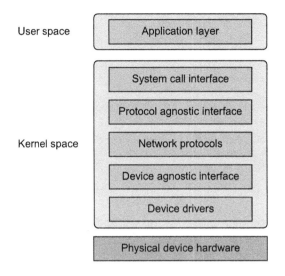

FIGURE 12.13

Conceptual View of the Linux Network Stack.

Linux Kernel Networking Structures

The preceding examples illustrate some of the C function prototypes and data structures found with user-level Linux network software. We now consider the same for kernel-based network software in Linux. Of course, we do not have the space available here for anything more than a brief introduction. Linux kernel networking is a large, complex, and fascinating subject. We recommend that interested readers dive into the Linux source code, and then after a bit of honest struggle leave the source code in favor of online tutorials and articles on the subject.

A high-level depiction of the Linux network stack is shown in Figure 12.13. Applications gain access to the kernel networking services via the system call interface. Through this interface, reads and writes on sockets occur, for example.

The layer marked *Protocol agnostic interface* refers to sockets. Applications communicate via sockets, and many interactions and data representations can be managed in a generic way. A socket data structure, `struct sock`, which is defined in linux/include/net/sock.h, is the unit of information that maintains the state of a connection in the stack.

The network protocols layer refers to the particular protocols that can be used via sockets. The available protocols are found in an array called `inetsw_array` of type `struct inet_protosw`. At boot time, the function `inet_init` in linux/net/ipv4/af_inet.c registers each available protocol by calling the `proto_register` function for each. An illustration of the protocol array, and the two types of additional structs—one protocol specific and one socket specific—can be found in Figure 12.14.

Packet data associated with sockets is stored in a socket buffer, with type `struct sk_buff`. The `sk_buff` holds packet payloads, headers from each of the network stack layers present in the packet, and additional management and logistical detail associated with the packet.

Figure 12.15 illustrates the organization of an `sk_buff`. As can be seen, they can be chained together via next and previous pointers. Helper functions exist to create, delete, and queue `sk_buffs`.

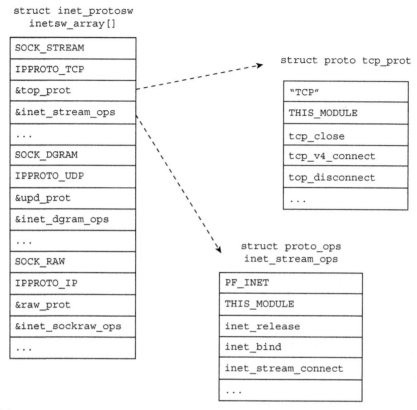

FIGURE 12.14

Organization of the Internet Protocol Array.

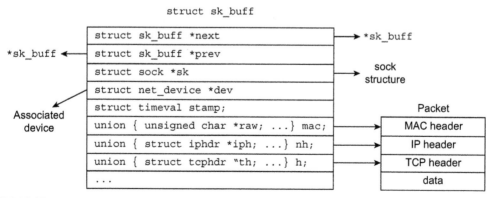

FIGURE 12.15

Organization of the struct sk_buff.

Beneath the protocols layer in Figure 12.13, there is another agnostic interface, one that generalizes underlying network devices. This layer provides a common set of commands that device drivers can use to interact with sockets in protocol-friendly ways.

The functions available to device drivers in this layer are defined in linux/net/core/dev.c. Device drivers can invoke `register_netdevice` or `unregister_netdevice`, to add or remove themselves. The caller provides a populated `net_device` struct (defined in /linux/include/linux/netdevice.h), which identifies, among other things, an initialization function that the kernel calls. The kernel also creates a `sysfs` entry for the device.

Functions `dev_queue_xmit` and `netif_rx (or netif_receive_skb` in Linux versions using the new NAPI organization), both of which interact with `sk_buffs`, are used to send and receive packets to device drivers, respectively.

Finally, device drivers are device-specific routines that manage individual network interfaces. During initialization, a device driver populates the `net_device` structure. This includes defining key functions, such as `hard_start_xmit`, which is responsible for transmitting an `sk_buff` out of this type of interface. Likewise, the driver must provide implementations for receiving packets through `netif_rx` or `netif_receive_skb`.

SUMMARY

This chapter has introduced the concepts of network connectivity and discussed the technologies and systems that are most significant for networked embedded systems. The basic concepts of networking, the Internet architecture, sockets, Ethernet, Wi-Fi, and Bluetooth all represent the most important areas in computer communications.

If you are new to networking, this chapter has likely improved your literacy and understanding of modern networking. However, you will soon recognize if you have not already that there is considerably more to learn. Entire textbooks and multi-semester course sequences exist to convey all of the important introductory ideas in networking. We have only scratched the surface.

Clearly, it will be worth your time to continue to develop your networking knowledge and practical skills. Even given the tremendous advances in the area seen thus far, the future of connected devices and the possibilities presented by their application will usher in new paradigms of networking and communications that will make our current technology and the world that it affects transform in ways we are only beginning to glimpse.

Application Frameworks

13

Much of the benefit of modern embedded systems comes from software-defined feature sets. In nearly all ways, shifting the engineering investment from hardware design to software design improves the financial health of product development.

Our detailed discussions of software to this point have focused on systems software, the software that defines the basic operations and capabilities of the platform. Above the systems software lies application software, and it is at the application layer that device features, services, and interfaces will be realized.

OVERVIEW

For reasons of developer productivity and overall quality, the vast majority of application development activity targets existing application frameworks. An application framework offers developers a well-defined model for application architecture along with common patterns for accessing and sharing system resources, organizing and managing user-interface elements, and adapting to changes to the underlying platform over time. Application frameworks are designed to increase code reuse and portability, characteristics that lead to improved developer productivity.

Application frameworks for embedded systems are evolving rapidly. In this chapter, we will introduce two popular frameworks that embody different philosophies, Android™ and Qt™.

Android is a comprehensive, integrated software platform that includes an application framework. Android is built on top of embedded Linux and has a substantial presence in mobile handsets and tablets. Android is integrated in the sense that Android applications can only run on the Android platform.

Qt is a traditional application framework that offers platform portability. Unlike Android applications, Qt applications can run on Microsoft Windows™, Apple Macintosh™, and Linux operating systems. Qt has a substantial presence in mobile handsets and other classes of embedded systems such as digital signage and fitness equipment.

In the following sections, we will introduce both Android and Qt and illustrate their organizations, features, and development environments.

ANDROID

Since launching in late 2007, Android has achieved something exceedingly rare: it has become a dominant, globally significant software platform. As of 2010, several industry marking reports have ranked Android as the number one or number two platform for smart phones globally.

379

Like many technologies, this was initially the vision of a startup company. Android Inc. was launched in 2003 by the founders of Danger Inc. (maker of the once-popular T-Mobile Sidekick smartphone) and WebTV. The startup was purchased by Google in 2005, under circumstances that may fairly be described as secretive since few knew specifically what Android Inc. was building or what interest Google may have had in mobile phone software.

In late 2007, Google announced both the existence of the Open Handset Alliance—whose members included, in addition to Google, semiconductor manufacturers, handset manufacturers, and wireless network operators—and the availability of the Alliance's first product: the Android platform for mobile phones.

Android is an open-source software platform for mobile devices. As we will see, it is based upon a modified version of the Linux kernel. In 2008, Google released the full source code of the platform under an Apache open-source license. Google does maintain Android as a copyrighted term and only licenses use of the Android copyright for devices that have adhered to a Google-managed certification process. Similarly, certain critical Android applications provided by Google are closed-source and only available for license to certified manufacturers, perhaps most notably the Android Market, which hosts the vast majority of the Android App ecosystem.

Android is first and foremost a platform for mobile phones. To date, however, Android has also shipped in tablets, netbooks, and set-top boxes such as those compatible with Google TV. Neither Google nor the Open Handset Alliance has expressed an ambition to see Android evolve to become a platform for a broader set of embedded systems. However, many of the technical strengths that have aided its success in the mobile handset market suggest that it could be successfully evolved in this way.

As will be described in greater detail, Android has been designed with a number of features and characteristics that make it a compelling embedded software application framework. These features include the following:

- *A modern software architecture.* The Android architecture enables the construction of applications in an object-oriented style with novel methods for achieving code reuse and component-level concurrency.
- *A familiar development language on an optimized runtime system.* Android applications are written in Java and adhere to Java interface definitions, but the underlying runtime system is not based on the Java virtual machine or Java bytecodes. Android applications are compiled for execution on the Dalvik virtual machine, which is optimized for battery-constrained and connected mobile devices.
- *A familiar development environment.* Android's best supported development tool chain is built upon Eclipse and includes a handset emulator and other development tools.
- *Substantial reliance on other open-source technologies.* As mentioned previously, a modified version of the Linux kernel forms the foundation of the Android platform. The integrated web browser is based on WebKit, the same engine used in the Chrome and Safari browsers.
- *Integrated library support.* A library layer is provided to insulate application developers from many of the hardware- or vendor-specific details of interacting with units that support 2D/3D graphics, audio/image/video formats, telephony, wireless network links, and a rich variety of mobile peripherals, including cameras and GPS receivers.

There is growing support for Android on IA-32-based platforms such as Intel® Atom™. At present, there is a vigorous and growing community of developers and maintainers of Android ports to IA-32 systems.

Android Framework Architecture

The purpose of this section is to describe the software elements that form the Android Application Framework. Our purpose is to clarify what paths an application has to system resources, and how those resources are shared among distinct applications. Because Android includes the Linux kernel at the bottom of its software stack, many of the system-level architecture features will be familiar.

Android is a software platform for mobile devices that includes an operating system, systems software including libraries and drivers, an application framework, and core applications. The Android software development kit (SDK) includes the tools and documentation required to develop software for Android.

Figure 13.1 illustrates the organization of the Android platform architecture. The layering illustrated here is an entirely traditional one. Android, in traditional language, can be described as a Linux kernel–based operating system for mobile devices.

Android is in all respects an operating system in its own right. From the bottom up, we will now consider its layers in greater detail.

Linux Kernel

The Android operating system kernel is based on Linux, and in particular kernel version 2.6. The kernel provides the basic architectural model for isolation, resource and process scheduling, memory management, networking, and device driver interfaces and organization. The kernel is the first layer of abstraction in the platform that insulates software from hardware-specific details.

In Android, running applications have unique Linux user IDs. Within an application, there is a single process and at least one thread of execution. As we will see, most application components will utilize their own threads to keep from dominating use of the main thread of execution.

Communications between applications, which is a frequent activity as a consequence of the structure of Android applications, is achieved via a system-wide broadcast mechanism.

While Linux kernel developers can translate their knowledge and skills to Android readily, not all kernel-facing code can be utilized directly. Google has maintained their own fork of the Linux kernel specifically for Android since early 2010. The prevailing view for why a fork was necessary derives from Google's inability to get a collection of changes (evidently concerning security and power management) accepted into the mainline kernel.

A major consequence of this Android-specific fork is that some systems software, including device drivers, must be written and compiled against the Android fork rather than the mainline one. For efficiency reasons, a common kernel would be better for all those maintaining, contributing, and relying on systems software.

Libraries

The Android system libraries are the layer immediately above the Linux kernel in userspace. The library LibC provides the interface between the Linux kernel and Android userspace libraries. These libraries are implemented in C or C++ and individually represent a system capability or resource that is exposed to the application framework but binds to the Linux kernel. These libraries include the following:

- *Surface Manager.* A subsystem for managing shared access to the display from among concurrent applications and services.

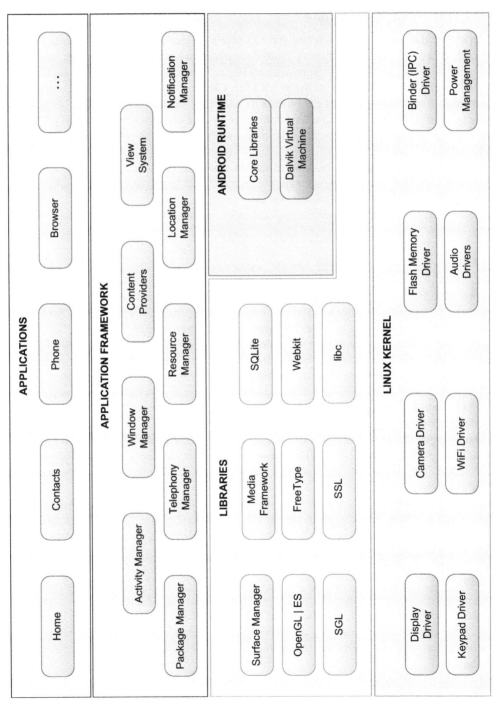

FIGURE 13.1

Android Platform Architecture.

- *OpenGL.* A 3D graphics implementation based on OpenGL ES 2.0 APIs. The OpenGL library includes a highly optimized 3D software implementation but can also take advantage of hardware support when available.
- *SGL.* A 2D graphics engine.
- *Media Libraries.* These media libraries are based on PacketVideo's OpenCORE™ libraries. They support the encoding and decoding of common multimedia formats for images, audio, and video including JPG, PNG, AAC, MP3, and H.264.
- *FreeType.* Bitmap- and vector-based font rendering subsystem.
- *SQLite.* A lightweight relational database subsystem for persistent structured data storage.
- *WebKit.* An open-source web browser engine.
- *C library.* A lightweight BSD-derived implementation of the standard `libc` system library. A nonstandard library is used to reduce usage of memory and compute resources.

The libraries and the Android runtime environment comprise the interface against which the application framework is built.

Android Runtime

While Android applications are written in the Java programming language, the execution environment is not based on the Java virtual machine. By eschewing Java bytecodes and the JVM, the Android platform is both free of Java licensing requirements and able to tailor its runtime environment to the constraints and requirements of mobile platforms.

Of course, this greater freedom comes at the cost of developing a new runtime environment. And, in the case of Android, the Dalvik virtual machine is that environment. The Android platform includes a set of core libraries within Dalvik that provide most of the functionality available in the core libraries of the Java programming language.

As mentioned previously, each Android application exists within its own Linux process. Additionally, each process includes its own Dalvik virtual machine instance. The Dalvik VM defines its own program file format and features a register-based execution model in contrast to the JVM's stack-based instruction set. The implementation of systems-software functions, such as access to I/O devices, permissions, threading, and memory management, is based on support provided in the Linux kernel.

Application Framework

While applications are written in Java and are executed on a Dalvik VM hosted in a Linux process, they do not typically interact directly with either of these lower layers. Rather, applications are written to interact with the Android application framework. The framework is organized to support and encourage code reuse and to make it easy to develop applications that bring together features already found in existing applications.

As we will see, the framework API prescribes an application structure that allows applications to share their component-level capabilities with other applications. Naturally, this structure also allows an application to import the components of other applications. Since the framework API was used to build the core Android applications, application developers have a rich set of components available to support new development.

The framework also provides system-level managers for shared resources. These managers are used to manage device displays and windows, interapplication communication, and access to hardware resources, among others. Some of these resources are elaborated on below.

- *User interface elements.* The framework includes a set of components (implemented as *views,* as described later) for display and user interaction. These include traditional UI widgets such as buttons, images, and checkboxes along with an embedded web browser and other feature-rich GUI elements.
- *Content providers.* Applications that share data, or access shared data, can do so via content providers. The core applications include examples such as contact lists, photographs, and videos. By leveraging the content provider interfaces, applications can integrate data from other applications without being responsible for capturing, curating, or maintaining the data set.
- *Resource managers.* Some aspects of an application will be common to all devices and users, and others will be specialized. Resource managers provide application localization support and enable applications to cleanly separate these two. For example, one application can use resource managers to manage user-facing application resources, such as text strings and icons, and specialize them to specific devices (phones versus tablets) and user languages (English versus Spanish).
- *Notification manager.* The notification manager serves as the device-wide alert and notification interface for the user. For example, most phones have a status bar that displays application and system notifications in a consistent way.
- *Activity manager.* The activity manager keeps track of the life cycle of application instances. As we will see, Android takes a much more proactive role in shutting down applications in response to resource constraints as compared to traditional operating systems. The activity manager maintains a view of how application components are connected to one another and the current state of each component. Using this information, the manager maintains a prioritized list of components that is used to make termination decisions when resources run low.

Applications

Finally, the top-most layer in the Android architecture is the application layer. The Android platform includes a set of core applications that represent the typical set of smart phone applications. These include clients for email and SMS messaging, a contact list manager, and a web browser. Each of these applications is written in Java and relies upon the framework API.

Android Application Architecture

Android applications are organized in an object-oriented fashion. As has been discussed above, Android applications are written in the Java programming language but do not execute on a JVM. For programmers familiar with Java, this difference is largely invisible. However, while the language is well known, the structure of Android applications is nontraditional, and even experienced Java programmers will spend time learning the principles and APIs.

Foremost, the Android application architecture has been organized to make it easy for distinct applications to share components. In traditional systems, this is done through static or dynamic linking. In the Android model, however, this is enabled by allowing one application to invoke a specific subset of another application. For example, application A can invoke the map-drawing functionality of application B, without needing to know about the entirety of application B. This allows substantial code reuse but implies serious changes to the way applications are organized.

Android applications differ from traditional applications in internal organization, interapplication communication, application packaging, and application life cycle. We will consider each in turn.

Application Organization

Android applications are organized as a collection of *components*. There are four types of components, and applications can be composed of one or more of each type. A dynamic instance of a component corresponds to an application subset that can be executed independently of the others. So, in many ways, an Android application can be thought of as a collection of interacting components. Android application components come in four flavors:

- *Activities.* User-facing components that implement display and input capture.
- *Services.* Background components that operate independent of any user-visible activity.
- *Broadcast receivers.* A component that listens for and responds to system-wide broadcast announcements.
- *Content providers.* Components that make application data accessible to external applications and system components.

We elaborate on each of these below.

Activities. An *activity* component implements interactions with the user. Activities are typically designed to manage a single type of user action, and multiple activities are used together to provide a complete user interaction.

For example, a mapping application may consist of two activities: one that presents to the user a list of locations to map, and one to display a map graphic that includes the chosen location. An activity includes a default window for drawing visual elements. An activity will use one or more *view* objects, which are organized hierarchically, to draw or capture user input. Views can be thought of as widgets, or user-interface objects, such as check boxes, images, and lists that are common to all types of GUI-based development environments. The Android SDK includes a number of views for developer use.

Services. Long-running or background components that do not directly interact with the user are expressed as *service* components. For example, I/O operations that are initiated by an activity may not complete before the user-facing activity disappears. In this instance, a service component can be used to carry out the I/O task, independent of the lifetime of the UI elements that initiated it. Services define and expose their own interfaces, which other components bind to in order to make use of the service. As is common with UI elements in GUI environments, services typically launch their own threads in order to allow the main application process thread to make progress and schedule threads associated with other components.

Broadcast receivers. As previously discussed, system-wide broadcast events can be generated by the system software or by applications. Components that listen to these broadcasts on behalf of applications are *broadcast receivers*. An application can include multiple broadcast receivers listening for announcements. In response, a broadcast receiver can initiate another component, such as an activity, to interact with the user or use the system-wide notification manager.

Content providers. Components that provide access to an application's data are *content providers*. Base classes are provided in the Android SDK for both the content provider (that is, the content provider component must extend the base class) and the component seeking access. The content provider is free to store the data in whatever back-end representation it chooses, be it the file system, the SQLite service, or some application-specific representation (including those implemented via remote web services).

Android applications consist of combinations of these component type instances. The invocation of components is managed through a system-wide broadcast mechanism based on *intents*.

Intercomponent Communication: Intents

To see how multiple components are referenced and invoked to form an application, we will now consider the essential Android concept of intents.

In Android, intents are asynchronous messages that name the activity, service, operation, or resource being requested. Intents are a dynamic binding mechanism that enables applications to specify what operations they want performed (optionally with some input data), without having to explicitly specify what component will carry out the operation. For example, this binding indirection would allow a user to change his or her default email client application without needing to reconfigure any existing applications that rely on an email client to compose or receive email messages.

The Intent class defines and implements the intent mechanism in the Android platform. It is an important and substantial class, consisting of 168 constants and 111 public methods, so our discussion of it will be limited to its high-level characteristics and its common usage.

While not comprehensively true, it is easiest to think about intents as being pairs of operations and data. Both operations and data are specified via names. Operation names are defined as constants in the Intent class. Data names are URIs. We now consider a few examples.

- Action: `ACTION_VIEW`. Data: `content://contacts/people/1`. Display information about the person whose identifier is "1."
- Action: `ACTION_VIEW`. Data: `mailto://contacts/people/1`. Invoke an email client and compose a message populated with this person's contact information.
- Action: `ACTION_EDIT`. Data: `content://contacts/people/1`. Launch an editor for this person's contact information.
- Action: `ACTION_DIAL`. Data: `tel:12345678`. Launch a phone dialer populated with the number passed as data.

In the examples above, the names of the provided data suggest that these are easily recognized types. Indeed, when intents get resolved to a target component, the data portion of the request is examined in order to find a best match. In fact, as we will see, component declarations include statements (intent filters) that indicate which actions the component can support. In this way, component requests and providers can be matched.

Implicit resolution is not always possible or desirable, however, so the Intent class includes additional attributes beyond the action and data that can be used to exert greater control over intent resolution (at either the time of request or declaration). These include the following.

- *Category*. The Intent constants also define categories of actions, most commonly used to determine when and where a given component appears as an option. For example, the `CATEGORY_LAUNCHER` category indicates that a component should appear in the application launcher as a user-invoked application.

- *Type.* This additional attribute can be used to specifically identify the data's MIME type. It is most common for the intent resolution to dynamically determine the MIME type based on an examination of the data provided. This implicit resolution is avoided when the type is provided in this way.
- *Component.* Similar to the Type attribute, the Component attribute can be used to explicitly identify a target component. Rather than allowing the system to dynamically identify a target component (or displaying a list of options to the user), this attribute disables implicit resolution and invokes the named component, for example, targeting a specific email application instead of the default email client.
- *Extras.* Additional information can be passed along in an intent via the Extras attribute. This is used in an action-specific way that typically requires some knowledge of the target component. For example, additional personal contact details, such mailing address and alternate phone numbers, could be sent via the Extras attribute for pre-population in a contacts editor view.

To see how components and intents interact, Figure 13.2 illustrates a timeline of how Android coordinates the interactions between two activities and a service.

In the example, Activity 1 publishes an intent via the `startActivityForResult()` method. The action and data associated with the request are packaged into `intentA`. Along with the intent, Activity 1 passes along a `reqCode` parameter that will be used to identify the result of this request when it eventually arrives.

The Android application framework resolves this intent to a target component and launches an instance of that component as Activity 2. Activity 2 retrieves the content of its originating intent and

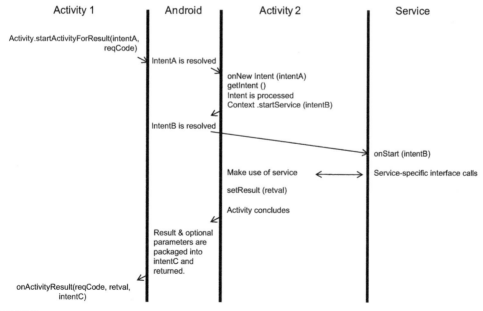

FIGURE 13.2

Example of Interaction between Components.

determines that it must invoke an external service to complete the request. Activity 2 creates `intentB` for this purpose, which Android resolves to a target component that is invoked as Service.

When the result is obtained, Activity 2 communicates its result via the `setResult()` method. Android packages this return value into an intent and invokes the `onActivityResult()` method within Activity 1. The `reqCode` value is provided in this invocation so that Activity 1 can identify which asynchronous request this result belongs to.

To keep the user experience orderly, such a sequence of activities is ordered into a stack-based *task* by Android. The activity on the top of the stack is the one currently interacting with the user.

Application Packaging

As a consequence of their unique organization, Android applications are packaged in a nontraditional way. The component-level organization of an application requires greater annotation as compared to traditional executable files. In traditional programs that have a single point of entry, this is unnecessary. Since each component within an Android application can be invoked independently, each must be specified within the package. In addition, some components may need to execute in their own process.

These details, along with others such as the application's name in the Java package namespace, are included in the application's manifest XML file, named AndroidManifest.xml. The manifest file provides the following information.

- *Component description.* The manifest explicitly identifies the activities, services, broadcast receivers, and content providers in the application. For each of these, it names the Java classes that implement each component and describes the Intent messages they can handle. Each component declaration can include a specification of which process should be used to host the component.
- *Permissions.* The manifest itemizes the permissions required to execute the application and its components. It also specifies what permissions are required of other applications in order to use this application's components. Permissions include access to contacts, network I/O, and the file system.
- *API version.* The manifest describes the minimum version of Android required to execute the application.

All resources comprising an Android application are combined into an Android package file with an .apk file name extension. The SDK provides a tool to produce the package, but most developers will rely on the Eclipse IDE support described below to produce their package files. Additionally, all Android applications must be signed with a private key associated with the application author. Cryptographic signatures are used to uniquely identify and verify application authors and to enable trust relationships between applications.

Application Life Cycle

The Android application framework manages the life cycle of applications in a novel way, one that has consequences for how applications are structured.

Due to the tighter memory constraints that exist in mobile devices, the Android framework requires that applications be prepared to stop executing and record their state at almost any time. This philosophy differs dramatically from traditional application development, where application termination is typically initiated by the user.

Each component type has its own life cycle. Content producers are purely reactive and do not have a life cycle in the sense that activities, services, and broadcast receivers do.

We begin with activities, which can be in one of three states.

- *Active.* When the activity is at the top of the display stack and facing the user, it is in the active state.
- *Paused.* An activity is paused when it is no longer on top of the display stack, but can still be seen by the viewer (that is, through a transparent overlay activity, or one that does not fill the display). Under low memory conditions, a paused activity may be terminated by Android.
- *Stopped.* An activity that can no longer be seen by the user is in the paused state. In this state, its resources are likely to be reclaimed by Android.

Figure 13.3 illustrates the life cycle of activity components.

Two methods are critical for saving the state of an activity. The `onPause()` method should be used to save persistent component state. This method is called every time an activity becomes eligible for termination. For transient state, which need not be persisted but that a user would expect to see should he or she return to the activity shortly, the `onSaveInstanceState()` method can be used. The difference between the two is that `onPause()` is always be invoked as part of the life cycle process, whereas `onSaveInstanceState()` is only to be invoked when the system, rather than the user, is about to cause an activity to become eligible for termination. Transient state can be recovered if your class defines `onRestoreInstanceState()`.

Services and broadcast receivers have simpler life cycles, ones that are not complicated by direct user interaction. Services are invoked in one of two ways: an initial `startService()` call or a subsequent `bindService()` call made against an active service. A service remains active until (1) all previously bound components have called `unBindService()` and (2) the service is stopped via an external `stopService()` or an internal `stopSelf()` call.

Broadcast receivers can only be invoked via `onReceive()` method invocations. When `onReceive()` returns, the broadcast receiver becomes inactive. One consequence of this design decision is that time-consuming `onReceive()` tasks should be handled outside the main thread of execution; however, doing so allows the `onReceive()` task to move to the inactive state, which risks process termination prior to receive completion. This problem is solved in Android via an idiom. Long-lived received tasks are typically implemented and invoked within services, so that the receive operation can complete despite the possible disappearance of the requesting broadcast receiver component.

Android Development Environment

The preferred and best-supported environment for Android application development is via Eclipse and the Android Development Tools (ADT) plug-in. While the Android SDK includes some documentation describing how to use alternative development environments, developers new to Android development should stick to Eclipse.

Eclipse is an integrated development environment (IDE) that is very popular among Java developers. Embedded systems developers unfamiliar with IDE-based project management will undergo a slight shift in perspective when using an IDE Eclipse. Just as makefiles and CTAGs can help keep

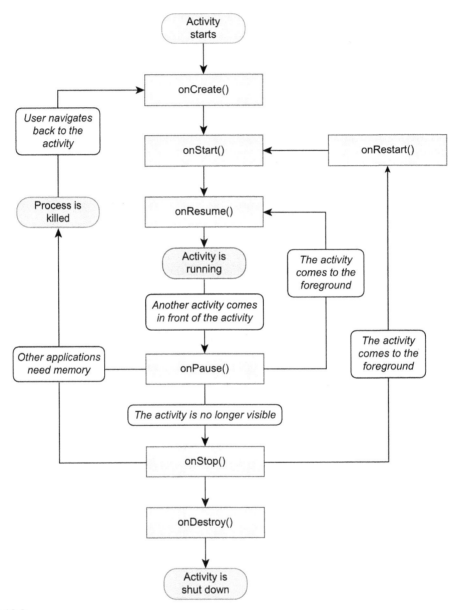

FIGURE 13.3

Android Activity Life Cycle.

build processes and source code relationships clear, a GUI-based IDE provides systematic support for software project management tasks.

The ADT plug-in and Eclipse together yield a highly productive development environment, with many attractive characteristics.

- *New project wizard.* The new project wizard is a dialog-based feature that sets up a new Android application project by creating the directory structure and template-driven versions of all of the required source files.
- *Automated build support.* With the project and its source code managed through the IDE, the build process can be fully automated by the tool and invoked through GUI elements such as menu items.
- *Device emulation.* The ADT includes a device emulator that can be customized to create devices with varying characteristics and features. The ADT includes an Android Virtual Device (AVD) Manager that is used to configure AVDs for use in the emulator. AVD emulation is the primary means of development and debugging for Android.
- *Device debugging.* The ADT can also be used to install and debug applications running on physical Android devices.
- *Automated packaging support.* Within Eclipse, your project can be packaged into a .apk file for debugging or deployment. The ADT can also generate certificates and sign applications.

Each version of the Android SDK (available at http://developer.android.com) describes the minimum Eclipse version required to operate. The SDK installation instructions include installation instructions for Eclipse and the ADT plug-in. Once installed, the full Android SDK and documentation will be available on your machine.

While this section has introduced the important Android developer concepts at a high level, a more comprehensive introduction is available within the SDK documentation. In fact, the Android developer documentation is unusually clear and well-organized. Developers accustomed to poor documentation are in for a very pleasant experience.

Deployment

In principle, Android applications can be distributed in many ways. In practice, Android applications are deployed via Google's Android Market.

Fortunately for developers, publishing applications in the Android Market is relatively straight-forward. As a developer, the first step is to ensure that you are signing your application with a real private key. For debugging purposes, debugging keys can be used, but deployment to users onto real devices will require a real key. You can use the ADT to generate a private key if necessary.

Other details become important when you deploy to other users. Your application must have a version number explicitly included in its manifest file. Commercial applications will need to include the Licensing Verification Library, which is used to enable the Google Android Market application to interact with Google's application licensing server to verify that a given user and device has permission to install and use your application.

To publish your application (and to arrange for license management), you must register as an Android Market publisher. For many, it is a tremendous benefit that Google provides a channel for application publishers to reach users. The challenge, of course, is making it easy for potential users to find your application among the growing assortment of applications available there.

QT

Qt (commonly pronounced "Q T" but officially pronounced "cute") is a cross-platform development framework for GUI-based applications. Qt, like Android, is an object-oriented development environment, but based on C++ rather than Java.

Qt is arguably the most successful cross-platform application framework in the world. Since 2008, Nokia has supported the development of Qt and made available both open-source and proprietary licenses for application developers. Nokia maintains supported ports of Qt to most major operating systems, including all versions of Windows (including CE), Mac OS X, the X11 window system for Linux, and Symbian.

Like Android, Qt was created by a small company, Trolltech, in 1991. Qt began its existence as a GUI library for both Windows and Linux/X11. In the subsequent 17 years, prior to Nokia's acquisition of Trolltech in 2008, Qt matured as an application framework and proliferated across platforms.

In 2008, Nokia took over Qt development and announced its intention to make Qt the primary development framework for the Symbian mobile phone operating system.

Qt Application Development Framework

Qt is a framework for developing applications, whereas Android is a fully specified platform, including everything beneath the application framework layer. Consequently, Qt is only concerned with the internal structure of applications.

To summarize the difference in perspectives, the deepest sophistication in Android aims to achieve graceful system-level resource utilization, whereas the deepest sophistication of Qt aims to make multi-platform application development efficient and natural for developers.

Qt Modules

Qt is an object-oriented, event-driven framework. To developers familiar with GUI-based applications, the architectural concepts are for the most part recognizable. Its applications make use of library modules organized around specific types of functionality, such as the following:

- *QtCore.* The QtCore module contains the core framework classes. These implement the event loop and the interobject communications mechanisms described below. The core classes also provide much of Qt's support for platform independence, including threads, shared memory, and Unicode support.
- *QtGui.* The QtGui module includes the GUI classes, including widgets and canvases. Aggregate layouts, such as grids, lists, and trees that make use of multiple panes, are included and are organized around the familiar model-view-controller (MVC) design pattern.
- *QtMultimedia.* This module provides platform-independent access to media display and capture.
- *QtNetwork.* The QtNetwork module includes classes for TCP/IP networking, including high-level protocols such as HTTP and IP services such as DNS.
- *QtOpenGL.* Platform-independent OpenGL 3D graphics rendering is provided via classes in the QtOpenGL modules.
- *QtSql.* The QtSql module contains classes that provides access to relational databases. It also includes an implementation of SQLite.
- *QtWebKit.* The QtWebKit module provides a web browser layout engine based on the WebKit open-source project.

While Qt is natively programmed in C++, language-specific bindings are available for all relevant programming languages (and more than a few irrelevant ones).

Signals and Slots

Communication between objects in Qt is achieved by the use of a novel mechanism based on signals and slots. This idea is best motivated by considering the relationship between GUI events, such as button clicks, and the corresponding object method invocation to carry out the activity associated with the event.

The typical way of relating GUI events to method invocations is to use callback functions. With a callback function, a pointer to the method is registered with the GUI object; this method is invoked in the GUI handler code. A major drawback of this approach is the lack of parameter checking: with this method, there is no language-based method available to verify that the GUI handler code provides the right typed parameters to the callback function.

To address this, Qt uses signals and slots. A slot is the name of a function that can be invoked at runtime (such as the name of class method); a signal corresponds to an event that invokes slots that have been connected to it. The standard QObject::connect() method is used to connect one object's signal to another object's slot. This connect method makes all the difference: it gives the system the opportunity to enforce parameter correctness.

To see how this works, consider the specific example of a basic Qt application illustrating slots and signals shown below.

```
1 #include <QtGui>
2 #include <QApplication>
3
4 int main(int argc, char *argv[])
5 {
6     QApplication a(argc, argv);
7
8     QPushButton quitButton("Quit");
9
10    QVBoxLayout layout;
11    layout.addWidget(&quitButton);
12
13    QWidget window;
14    window.setLayout(&layout);
15
16    QObject::connect(&quitButton,
17            SIGNAL(clicked()),
18            &a, SLOT(quit()));
19
20    window.show();
21
22    return a.exec();
23 }
```

In this example, the QtGui and QApplication modules are used to create an application containing a window and a single button widget. The QVBoxLayout class arranges all widgets assigned to the layout object on a single vertical column.

On line 16, the `clicked()` signal of the button object is connected to the `quit()` slot of the application object.

Aside from illustrating a generic use of slots and signals, this example also represents a complete and portable stand-alone Qt application. Of course, few interesting applications will be implemented in a single source document. For genuine code development, we now consider the Qt development environment.

Qt Creator

Given Qt's emphasis on programmer productivity, it should come as no surprise that both the open-source and commercial Qt development environments ship with a feature-rich, highly integrated development environment.

Qt Creator is a Qt-specific IDE that supports Qt application development for both desktop and mobile target platforms. The IDE includes everything needed for cross-platform development with Qt, for both novices and experts.

Novices experience accelerated learning curves in Qt Creator due to its integrated tutorial projects and samples. Due no doubt to its maturity as a platform, gentle introductions are provided in the form of annotated source code projects covering every aspect of Qt development.

In addition to introductory materials, Qt Creator is completely customizable and enables experienced developers to tailor the environment and project templates to specific needs.

Qt Creator and Eclipse provide similar IDE features, with two notable exceptions. First, Qt Creator includes a GUI-based UI designer that greatly simplifies UI design. Second, Qt Creator lacks the flexible device emulation that Eclipse and the ADT plug-in provide for Android. Qt Creator does include an emulator for the Nokia N900 tablet, but that is the only emulator available.

OTHER ENVIRONMENTS

While Android and Qt are arguably the most widely accessible application frameworks for embedded systems due to their open-source nature, they are certainly not the only ones.

In particular, iOS™ from Apple and the various flavors of Windows for embedded systems from Microsoft are extremely strong platforms for embedded systems application development.

Apple iOS and its development environment power Apple's iPod, iPad, iPhone, and Apple TV™ products. When combining the total units sold per year for iPods, iPhones, and iPads, there can be little doubt that iOS-based devices represent a significant fraction of the overall mobile embedded systems market. However, iOS is of diminished interest to embedded systems developers because only Apple products can use the system. While the application development environment is open to developers, none of us will be developing new embedded systems with iOS unless we work for Apple.

Embedded operating systems from Microsoft—including Windows CE, Windows 7 Embedded, and their descendants—have established a substantial presence in some embedded markets. Relative to iOS, moreover, embedded Windows is available on a diverse range of hardware platforms from a variety of manufacturers. In the coming years, we expect embedded Windows and Windows Phone 7 to play an even larger role in the marketplace. For pedagogical reasons, however, we prefer to base this book's material around open-source software when possible, in order to retain the ability to look into the implementation to clarify how things work.

MORE RESOURCES

For more information on Android, visit the information clearinghouse at http://developer.android.com. This site is home to the latest version of the Android SDK, and all official announcements and news items can be found there. Since the SDK is available under an open-source license, all aspects of Android development and operation can be explored free of charge.

More information on Qt is of course available online, although it is not as centralized. Nokia's official Qt site, where links to the open-source and proprietary releases of Qt Creator can be found, is located at http://qt.nokia.com. The most vigorous user community focused on Qt development is found in the forums hosted at Nokia (http://www.forum.nokia.com). Open-source Qt development is centered at http://qt.gitorious.org.

SUMMARY

In this chapter, we have discussed application frameworks and their role in modern embedded systems development. In many ways, the choice of an application framework for use in an embedded platform is the most important design decision. At least in the case of embedded systems with human users such as mobile handsets, most contemporary users seem to exhibit strong opinions about which application environment their chosen handset supports.

After all, with feature sets determined by software, most users want the assurance of a vigorous application ecosystem that will deliver the most exciting and useful applications in the timeliest and most cost-effective manner.

The two frameworks we discussed in detail, Android and Qt, represent substantially different philosophies. Qt is the older, more mature framework that views applications as stand-alone entities. Android, by contrast, is a young, rapidly evolving platform that defines everything in the software stack, from the OS kernel up to the application framework, in terms of how it can be reused and managed in order to effectively manage overall system resources.

No one application framework or software platform dominates embedded systems classes. In fact, at this point in time, it is impossible for us to predict with any confidence what the landscape will look like in five years. What is certain, however, is that the stakes are high.

Platform and Content Security

Informed users of embedded systems typically want answers to three fundamental questions:

1. Does it work?
2. What will it cost?
3. Is the system secure?

The first two questions differ from the third—which is the focus of this chapter—in more ways than one.

First, questions of correct function and cost are well within the traditionally recognized boundaries of embedded systems engineering. Engineers are trained to build things correctly, and engineers play an essential role in determining the cost of systems, both directly, by designing systems and choosing their components whose costs factor into the total system price, and indirectly, via their compensation for time spent on the development of the system. (Better engineers are paid higher wages and, hence, develop more costly technology!) But security? Historically, security has been someone else's concern.

Consider the traditional separation between development and quality assurance. In many engineering practices, development of a functional system is assigned to one group of engineers, and testing and quality assurance of that system are assigned to another type of engineer. In traditional organizations, both groups are focused on establishing the correct operation of the device or system. Security has more often than not been an attribute to be observed and considered once the system has been built.

The second difference is more important, and qualitatively more troublesome. The question "Is the system secure?" is far more vague and subject to interpretation than the first two questions.

The questions "Does it work?" and "What will it cost?" have reasonably straightforward interpretations. Each device or technology has an intended purpose and a cost of manufacture. The answers to these questions may be complicated, particularly when standards compliance must be validated, but the questions themselves are easy to understand, and two similarly informed people are likely to understand them in the same way.

What about security? What might the question "Is the system secure?" mean? As it happens, there are many possible interpretations to this question. Let's consider some possibilities.

- Can anyone else access my data?
- Can I control who uses the device?
- Can anyone interfere with or prevent my usage of the device?
- Can someone spy on my usage of the device?
- Can someone delete or corrupt my data?
- Can anyone see the data I send or receive on a network?

Most would agree that each of these questions would be a reasonable interpretation. Moreover, most would agree that more could be added to the list! So, in order to answer "Is the system secure?" do we need to enumerate and answer all such possible interpretations? Let's hope not, because it turns out that answering just one is hard enough. To see why, let's consider the first.

"Can anyone else access my data?"

The complexity-inducing culprit in this question is the indefinite pronoun: someone. The question asks, quite plainly, is there anyone who is able to steal my information or data?

To be sure we are casting the net wide enough, let us begin by dividing all living beings on the planet into two categories: those with authorized access to our mythical device, and those without authorized access. The device may or may not have a built-in notion of users, but presumably at least the owner of the device has authorized access. Given this distinction, we can explore the space of data access with the following questions.

- **Does the device have authenticated users? Is it a multi-user device? Are data access control mechanisms in place?** If users sign in, how do they do so? Is it possible for someone to trick the system into accepting a false user identity?
- **Can unauthorized users gain access?** Has the device been determined to be hack-proof and impervious to unauthorized access through technical means? If so, what standard of security applies?
- **Can authorized users delegate access to their data?** If a user can grant data access to another user, does the original user have any control over who else might get access?
- **Is there an administrative user account that can create and modify user accounts?** If so, then whomever controls the administrative account can control access to data.
- **Can the system be reset to factory defaults without destroying data?** Some systems provide a means to reset a system following a lost account credential that keeps the original data intact.
- **Is the data archived on a backup service or device?** If so, how is access to that data managed?
- **Do local laws require a back door for access by government authorities?** If so, can a user verify either that such an access request is legitimate, or whether such accesses have taken place?

You can see that none of these questions reach the bottom of the issue, and we're already three levels down.

Clearly, "Is the system secure?" is a different kind of question, and, as such, it requires a different perspective, an increased level of understanding, and a common vocabulary of security to go with it. The purpose of this chapter is to help you develop a point of view that enables you to answer this question despite all the uncertainty surrounding what it may mean to a person not versed in the vocabulary of security.

To this end, we will explore the core principles of computer and information security. We will also walk through specific approaches and concrete examples of securing Linux-based embedded systems.

We begin with a discussion of principles that will inform our perspective and better prepare us to answer the question: "Is the system secure?"

SECURITY PRINCIPLES

This is important: Security is a consequence of people, process, and technology. So security is more than a technical concern. While at first blush, it may appear that this fact simplifies the role of the

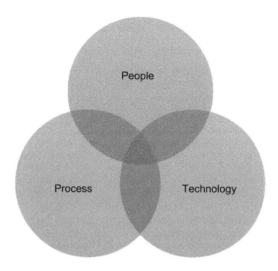

FIGURE 14.1

Security is a Consequence of People, Process, and Technology.

engineer, this is most certainly not the case. Evidence suggests that no matter the cause of the security failure, technology and its creators are the intuitive and popular culprit.

To see why, let's dig a little deeper.

People. If an embedded system has users, then those users have an impact on the operation and security of the device. For example, if users of a device have accounts and associated passwords, then users must understand that their passwords must be kept secret and should be difficult for someone else to guess.

Process. By process, we mean the rules and procedures that people and systems must follow. For example, your employer may have a process that requires that you change your password every 90 days and that a new password can only be accepted if it meets difficulty criteria.

Technology. The system itself, along with the collection of automated tools, technologies, and services put in place to secure it, represents the technological contribution to system security.

Hence, the challenge to designers and engineers is to create technologies that encourage more secure user action and encourage the creation of more secure processes. Increasingly, the notion of an affordance—a term borrowed from architecture and design that suggests that the natural and obvious uses of a design will be the most common uses—is implied in the design of embedded systems.

Ultimately, we want to translate these high-level notions into something concrete that leads to the development of secure embedded systems. We have a bit more to review before we can walk through a practical example, but we can take a step in that direction by considering how this people-process-technology perspective relates to securing or subverting a system. Consider Table 14.1.

Clearly, to secure a system, our attention must cut across these domains. In other words, to answer the question "Is the system secure?" our answer, or at least the evidence we provide to justify our answer, must address each of these aspects.

We are getting close to returning to the concrete world of software and systems, but we have still more background understanding to develop before we start looking at concrete solutions.

Table 14.1 Examples of the Relationships between People, Process, Technology, and Security

Factor	Security Measure	Attack
People	Provide training periodically to ensure that users have an understanding of security risks and are aware of common pitfalls.	Fool users into divulging their access credentials by sending convincing email messages that appear to be legitimate requests. These tactics are known as phishing attacks.
Process	Design rules and procedures for users and systems that are intended to improve security and increase the effort required on the part of any attacker. For instance, a policy may dictate that a user account be locked out after five unsuccessful login attempts. Such a policy will make it impossible for remote attackers to gain access by submitting large numbers of possible passwords.	In systems that provide remote access and also lock out accounts after some number of failed attempts, attackers can disrupt service and cause problems by assembling a list of user account names and then launching failed login attempts in order to lock all the accounts out. Then, the attacker can send immediate phishing messages with false instructions for re-enabling their account.
Technology	Software-defined systems typically pull together a large number of libraries and applications to provide functionality. Each of these libraries and applications represents a point of attack; hence, systems should be designed with the means to regularly update and apply any security-related patches.	Software with an exploitable weakness is the primary attack target in Internet-connected systems because they can be sought and attacked in an automated fashion. Some attackers discover and exploit weaknesses; others simply wait for exploits to be published then find and attack systems susceptible to the exploit.

There is much to be said about security principles. Unfortunately, many books and papers on the subject verge on the brink of philosophy and are therefore difficult to rely upon for developing a practical understanding. For the purposes of this chapter, we can get by with the following discussion of additional ideas and illustrations. These will serve as an adequate preparation for our specific security examples to follow.

Confidentiality, Integrity, and Availability (CIA)

If you are comparatively new to thinking about security and associated risks, some of the discussion above may have felt disingenuous. Gaining unauthorized access to a system (i.e., hacking into a system) seems like a different kind of security concern as compared to interfering with an authorized user's ability to access that system. So it feels a bit like sleight of hand when both types of examples are raised as risks in the same scenario. By extension, what is to keep up us from including all possible unanticipated events in the discussion of security?

The field of information security has emerged as a result of such questions being asked over time. Of course, information security is more encompassing than our specific focus on embedded systems security, but most of the time-tested observations and principles we rely upon to secure embedded systems come from information security principles.

In particular, the security of information is said to be due to its confidentiality, integrity, and availability. These three characteristics, often referred to as the CIA triad, derive from viewing the security of information in a manner analogous to the security of physical objects. That is, if information has some discrete existence (i.e., it exists just like diamonds or treasure maps), how can we characterize its security? To see one way of doing so, let us consider the components of the triad.

Confidentiality. Information is kept confidential when it can only be observed by authorized individuals. Those with permission can see it; those without it cannot. The meaning is clear, but there are some difficult consequences to reckon with. For example, observation must be limited to authorized users, no matter the form of the information. Your system may store user names and passwords in encrypted files, but if either is transmitted in plain text over a network that others may be monitoring, then confidentiality is violated. This most certainly includes web sites that transmit user names and session keys in unencrypted HTTP traffic. The use of user names and passwords is an example of an authentication mechanism, by which a system verifies that a user has rightful use of a digital identity. There are other such mechanisms, and we will discuss the topic in greater depth below.

Integrity. The integrity of information is preserved if it has not been altered in any unintended way. Note that this is a notion quite distinct from that of observing information. From an attacker's perspective, disruption or deception may be the goal, in which case altering or destroying information may be the most effective means. Attackers aside, reliable and robust information systems should keep users from being able to accidentally violate the integrity of their own data. For instance, a secure and reliable word processor should not corrupt a document in an unrecoverable way when the system crashes.

Availability. If we view information as an asset to keep secure, then it follows naturally that access to the information is an important component in its security. If my information has been kept in a confidential manner and its integrity has been preserved but someone can interfere with my access to it, then it is not secure. Alas, ensuring absolute access and availability is a very deep commitment, and one that illustrates the practical challenge in precisely characterizing information security.

These common components have endured in the information security community for many years. While a few refinements have been suggested that separate concerns into additional top-level elements, the CIA triad remains the conceptual core of information security.

One vexing challenge confronting this core, as well as the refinements, is the issue of time. How long must these characteristics be maintained? Forever? The atemporal nature of these components perhaps suggests an ill-defined characterization.

For example, when information is shared among multiple users, there is a qualitative change to the nature of confidentiality. Suppose that users A and B have been granted rightful access to some information. After some time passes, suppose B's access rights are withdrawn (e.g., B has changed employers and no longer has access to corporate information.) Can we be sure that B no longer has access to the information? Perhaps B can no longer log in to an information system, but did B make copies of files? Does B have memory of widely shared passwords and pass phrases that she can perhaps unlawfully give to others?

This issue—the revocation of access rights—is one that does not fit cleanly within most conceptual frameworks but must certainly be addressed in real-world systems. Fortunately, in this chapter, there is no need to make absolute definitions of information security watertight. It will suffice for us to be attentive to the important issues and develop a perspective that enables us to develop systems that are as secure as we can make them.

SECURITY CONCEPTS AND BUILDING BLOCKS

With some principles established, we can now explore some of the important ideas and practical concepts in computer security. There is an enormous body of knowledge that can be considered in this area. Indeed, there are entire degree programs and career paths devoted to the subject. Needless to say, our exploration will only serve as an introduction.

Our purpose here is to introduce the key ideas in sufficient depth to get started in securing the design and implementation of your embedded systems and software.

Encryption and Cryptography

For most, thoughts of computer and network security immediately turn to encryption, decryption, and cryptographic message transfers. Yet, here we are well into this chapter and we are only now getting around to discussing them!

Perhaps surprisingly, while critically important, encryption and cryptography occupy only a small part of the practical experience of securing real-world systems. This is mostly due to the fact that encryption represents one of the reliable aspects of security, and, hence, it is generally better understood by engineers.

Cryptography can be loosely defined as the art of keeping secrets with mathematical guarantees. When information is encrypted, it should be indistinguishable from random data. For our purposes, we need not explore the mathematics of encryption; rather, we will discuss how the mechanisms can be used to enable the secure storage and transfer of information.

We begin with single-key encryption. Suppose you have information in the form of a file on your computer that you want to keep secret. Encryption techniques make that easy.

First, you generate a repeatable secret (the "key" such as a pass phrase) that only you know. Second, the crypto algorithm translates that secret into a numerical form that is used to randomize the bits in the file you want to encrypt. The mathematical guarantee provided by "encryption algorithms" is that the bits in your encrypted file appear to contain no statistically discernable information. Of course, there are differences between encryption algorithms, and it is possible to get it wrong. As long as you are using an up-to-date open source crypto package with a large and active user community, such as GPG, you'll be OK. A simple transcript using gpg for single-key encryption and decryption follows.

```
$ gpg -c data.txt
Enter passphrase:
Repeat passphrase:
$ # data.txt.gpg now exists
$ rm data.txt
$ gpg data.txt.gpg
Enter passphrase:
$ # data.txt now exists
```

In this way, we can restrict direct access to data in files to only those people who know the secret pass phrase. This method is referred to as single-key encryption because the same key is used to both encrypt and decrypt. As we can see, single-key cryptography is based on the idea of a shared secret, and that idea has been around for a very long time.

Establishing and maintaining shared secrets can be cumbersome. A revolutionary idea emerged in the 1970s that forever changed the practice of cryptography. That idea was asymmetric-key cryptography, also known as public-key cryptography. In asymmetric-key cryptography, one key is used to encrypt (the public key) and another is used to decrypt (the private key).

To begin, a user generates a key pair, which consists of a public and private key. The private key is a secret, for example, a long, hard-to-predict pass phrase, known only to the user. The public key is freely available. When anyone wants to send a private message to the user, they encrypt it with the public key. Once this is done, the only one who will be able to make sense of the apparently random bits in the encrypted message will be the holder of the private key. While these public and private keys are mathematically related, the relationship only goes in one direction; knowing the public key gives no insight into what the private key might be.

In 1978 the cryptographers Rivest, Shamir, and Adelson published a description of a cryptosystem for public-key encryption that provides the functionality described above, plus a few other features. Their system, referred to as RSA from the concatenation of the first letters of their family names, was not the first such scheme, but it was the first one publicly described and implemented in a practical way. Consequently, it is supported by most public-key encryption systems in use today.

One very notable aspect of RSA is its ability to support authentication and integrity. We know that a public key may be used to encrypt a message in such a way that only the holder of the private key can decrypt it. It is also typically useful to establish the authenticity of the one who encrypted the message and determine their integrity. If I get an encrypted message from Alice, I would like some assurance that Alice is indeed the source of the message before I take it seriously. Additionally, I would like to know that the message has not been tampered with.

To achieve both, RSA allows a user to sign a message with their private key. In our example, Alice will sign the message with her private key before she encrypts it with my public key. In practical terms, a signature is a separate file that is derived from both the source file and Alice's private key. Upon receipt, I decrypt the message using my private key. Once decrypted, I can see that it comes with a signature. RSA will allow me to use Alice's public key to verify the signature. If the signature does not match, I know that either Alice was not the source or the file has been altered after signing.

The mathematical assurances of public-key cryptography, and the demonstrated effectiveness of RSA, may suggest that we can relax a little. Alas, there is one major issue remaining, and it is a significant one.

Consider how such a secure communications scheme might begin. Suppose I want to communicate with Alice. How do I get a copy of her public key? One way would be to invite her over and have her install her public key on my system herself. That would get the job done, but it doesn't scale.

What is needed is some objective assurance that a given public key in fact belongs to the personal identity it claims to represent. There are two broad approaches to this issue, one centralized and one decentralized.

The centralized solution—and the one that dominates use today—relies on the existence of so-called Certificate Authorities, or CA. A CA is a trusted source of identity information.

The term certificate refers to a collection of information:

- a public key,
- the name of the owner of the public key,
- the name of the attesting CA,
- and the signature of the CA.

Before a CA will sign someone's certificate, they will take some steps to establish their identity. Typically, they collect personal information and charge a handsome fee.

If you have studied philosophy, you may be familiar with the notion of "begging the question." It is natural to raise that notion here. How do we know if we should trust Certificate Authorities, and, assuming we trust one, how do we verify its public key? These are the right questions, but they are effectively moot. Practically speaking, effective Certificate Authorities are those whose certificates are included by default in the major web browsers. Mozilla, Microsoft, Apple, Google, and Opera choose to include a default set of certificates from CAs in their browsers (i.e., the "root" certificate authorities). So, the globally trusted CAs are the ones that the web browser vendors have elected to trust.

Given the stakes, it is reasonable to assume that the browser vendors take care to only include reputable and reliable CAs. VeriSign is one such trusted CA, and it is guilty of having committed the only publically discussed incident of CA subversion. In March 2001, VeriSign issued two certificates to someone fraudulently claiming to be a Microsoft employee. As a result, an unidentified fraudster has a certificate signed by VeriSign that associates a public key with the name "Microsoft Corporation." As you might expect, this created quite a stir. These particular certificates can only be used to sign code (such as Active X controls in this case), so the window of risk for most has passed. But the story serves as a reminder of where trust is placed.

The alternate, decentralized approach is to rely on a web of trust. Rather than relying upon the single certifying signature of an authority, the web of trust model allows signatures to be signed by multiple parties. The idea is that you may accept the authenticity of someone's certificate if other people you already trust have vouched for them by signing their certificate. This process is boot-strapped via "signing parties" where people gather together for the purpose of reciprocal signings. This method provides more trust, but it has not established any kind of foothold in the world of commerce.

As an aggregate, any scheme by which digital identities are managed is referred to as a public-key infrastructure, or PKI. One of the challenges in building an effective PKI is revocation: how do you remove authentication authority once it has been granted? This has proven to be a difficult challenge to overcome. Most revocation solutions are, in one way or another, based on the idea that, periodically, participants in the PKI should compare the keys and certificates they hold against a revocation list. A revocation list, published by a CA or key server, enumerates the keys that are no longer valid. This scheme can be made to work, but it is not entirely satisfactory. After all, if we should really consult a revocation list before we accept a certificate, how is that different from keeping all of our certificates in a central location? And, what happens if access to the revocation list is interrupted?

As you might guess, based on the preceding discussion, no PKI scheme has achieved Internet-scale success. There have been pockets of success in e-commerce, in governments, and within corporations, but the majority of Internet users lack personal certificates and the means by which to participate as an authenticated user in a public-key-based cryptosystem.

Secure Web Communications: TLS

In today's World Wide Web, secure communications are provided by a protocol called Transport Layer Security, or TLS. TLS is the name of the latest variant of the Secure Sockets Layer, or SSL, which was originally created by Netscape Corp. SSL has been called TLS since version 3.1.

TLS, despite its name, is effectively an application-level security protocol, and support for it must be built into applications like web browsers and web servers. Network-level security protocols, like IPSec, do not require application-level support. TLS is an IETF standards-track protocol, and its most recent description can be found in RFC 5246.

In TLS, we find most of the principles discussed above assembled in a form that enables web security. In particular:

- Public-key encryption is used to authenticate clients and servers.
- Single-key encryption is used to secure communications between two applications.
- Cryptographic signatures are used to ensure message integrity.
- Certificates and Certificate Authorities are used to associate names with public keys in a trusted manner.

TLS is best known for its use in securing HTTPS, the secure variant of HTTP. Support for TLS is built into all modern browsers and servers. As an increasing fraction of Internet communications occurs via web services and HTTP, we can expect the use of TLS to grow.

In fact, for most use cases outside of deeply embedded systems, most data-oriented Internet communications will be managed via web services and HTTP, and, in the future, most of those will be secured via HTTPS and TLS. So, let's take a look at how TLS works.

TLS begins with a handshaking protocol that, when successful, concludes by creating a secure communications channel that is guaranteed to be private and immune to tampering. The handshake protocol proceeds as follows.

The client sends the server a message (ClientHello, as described in the RFC) requesting a secure connection. This message contains the client's supported TLS version, along with a list of cryptographic algorithms for symmetric cryptography, asymmetric cryptography, and signature generation that it can use (the so-called cipher suite). The message also indicates what, if any, forms of compression it can support.

The server responds with a message (ServerHello) containing both its choice from among the intersection of versions and algorithms that both support and a random number.

The server follows with another message (Certificate) containing its certificate, which, as we know, contains its identity, its public key, and the identity and signature of a Certificate Authority.

The server then sends a hand-off message (ServerHelloDone), indicating that it is finished with its portion of the handshake.

The client replies with a message (ClientKeyExchange) that contains a *pre-shared secret* and a second random number encrypted with the server's public key. Note that two random numbers have been generated: one by the server and sent across the wire in the clear, and one by the client and sent across the wire encrypted so that only the server can decrypt it. Both the client and server compute a shared secret based on the pre-shared secret generated by the client, and the two random numbers (the two random numbers serve as "nonces" or numbers used once that ensure that these communications cannot be replayed again in the future). This shared secret is used to encrypt, using single-key cryptography, the channel between client and server.

The client next sends a ChangeCipherSpec message that signals that all following messages will be encrypted with the shared secret.

The client makes good on its previous message by sending an encrypted Finished message, which includes a signature computed over all of the previous handshake messages.

The handshake concludes when, after having verified the integrity of the client's Finished message, the server replies with its own ChangeCipherSpec and Finished messages.

From now own, messages between client and server will be encrypted and authenticated.

This protocol walk-through conveys the high-level behavior of TLS, but we can also examine the protocol in action. In particular, we can use the curl command-line utility to examine the protocol operations that occur when accessing a secure web server.

Let's examine TLS by visiting Gmail with curl. Consider the following console trace.

```
1  $ curl -v https://mail.google.com
2  * About to connect() to mail.google.com port 443 (#0)
3  *   Trying 72.14.204.83... connected
4  * Connected to mail.google.com (72.14.204.83) port 443 (#0)
5  * successfully set certificate verify locations:
6  *   CAfile: none
7     CApath: /etc/ssl/certs
8  * SSLv3, TLS handshake, Client hello (1):
9  * SSLv3, TLS handshake, Server hello (2):
10 * SSLv3, TLS handshake, CERT (11):
11 * SSLv3, TLS handshake, Server finished (14):
12 * SSLv3, TLS handshake, Client key exchange (16):
13 * SSLv3, TLS change cipher, Client hello (1):
14 * SSLv3, TLS handshake, Finished (20):
15 * SSLv3, TLS change cipher, Client hello (1):
16 * SSLv3, TLS handshake, Finished (20):
17 * SSL connection using RC4-SHA
18 * Server certificate:
19 *    subject: C=US; ST=California; L=Mountain View; O=Google Inc;
         CN=mail.google.com
20 *    start date: 2009-12-18 00:00:00 GMT
21 *    expire date: 2011-12-18 23:59:59 GMT
22 *    common name: mail.google.com (matched)
23 *    issuer: C=ZA; O=Thawte Consulting (Pty) Ltd.; CN=Thawte SGC CA
24 *    SSL certificate verify ok.
25 > GET / HTTP/1.1
26 > User-Agent: curl/7.19.7 (i486-pc-linux-gnu) libcurl/7.19.7 OpenSSL/0.9.8k zlib/
      1.2.3.3 libidn/1.15
27 > Host: mail.google.com
28 > Accept: */*
29 >
30 < HTTP/1.1 200 OK
31 < Cache-Control: private, max-age=604800
32 < Expires: Wed, 29 Jun 2011 14:25:10 GMT
33 < Date: Wed, 29 Jun 2011 14:25:10 GMT
34 < Refresh: 0;URL= https://mail.google.com/mail/
35 < Content-Type: text/html; charset=ISO-8859-1
36 < X-Content-Type-Options: nosniff
37 < X-Frame-Options: SAMEORIGIN
38 < X-XSS-Protection: 1; mode=block
```

```
39 < Content-Length: 234
40 < Server: GSE
41 <
42 <html><head><meta http-equiv="Refresh" content="0;URL= https://mail.google.com/ma
43 il/" /></head><body><script type="text/javascript" language="javascript"><!--
44 location.replace ("https://mail.google.com/mail/")
45 --></script></body></html>
46 * Connection #0 to host mail.google.com left intact
47 * Closing connection #0
48 * SSLv3, TLS alert, Client hello (1):
49 $
```

Let's see how this output matches with our understanding of the TLS protocol.

Lines 1–7: The first several lines of output make clear what's happening. We're attempting to contact mail.google.com, which corresponds to IP address 72.14.204.83, on port 443. That's the port to which HTTPS is bound. Next, we can see where curl found the cryptographic certificates (i.e., the CA certificates) on this Ubuntu Linux system. We will later be receiving a certificate from the server, and curl will expect that certificate to be signed by one of the root certificates stored in /etc/ssl/certs.

Lines 8–16: These lines correspond to the handshake protocol steps described above.

Lines 17–24: The next lines give insight into what the protocol negotiation yielded. The RC4-SHA algorithm will be used to secure the communications channel. Also, the server certificate details are given, along with an indication (on line 24) that the CA signature was verified by one of the roots certificates present in the system.

Lines 25–49: The remainder of the output represents the HTTP protocol details (our user agent in curl, …), some of which we can manipulate in curl via other command line options, and the corresponding HTML that is returned. In this case, our request is redirected via embedded JavaScript code to https://mail.google.com/mail/.

Secure Shell (SSH)

The secure shell utility and protocol, ssh, enables users to log in to a Linux or Unix-inspired system remotely. This protocol, like TLS, is an application-level security protocol that relies upon public-key cryptography for authentication and secure communications. While ssh is primarily used to enable secure remote command line sessions, it can also be used to copy files securely (via scp) and execute remote commands. As we'll see, ssh is a great help in remotely administering machines.

When ssh is installed on your system, a host keypair is created. More precisely, one keypair is created for each encryption algorithm supported. These public and private keys are typically found in /etc/ssh. Under normal circumstances, the public keys are world-readable and the private keys are only readable by root.

When using ssh to log in to a server host from a client host for the first time, the client begins by requesting a copy of the server's public key. By default, the ssh program will print to the screen a signature of the public key and ask, "User, do you believe that this is a legitimate public key for the server you requested?" As user, you either know it is legitimate (because someone sent you the signature beforehand) or assume it is legitimate. With no additional knowledge, it is impossible to know. The threat here is that someone on the network path between your client machine and the server machine is masquerading as the server machine in an attempt to sit in the middle of your conversation. Once you've logged into the machine, you can verify that the public key on that machine matches the one you saw.

Once accepted, the public key for the remote host will be appended to your ~/.ssh/known_hosts file. Next time you ssh into this remote machine, this public key will be used directly.

Once your client machine has authenticated the remote server and gotten its public key, it can use it to encrypt your communications. By default, this means that it will allow you to enter your password and try to log in to the remote machine. The ssh tool also lets you log in via a public key associated with you.

To do so, you must first generate a public-private keypair to represent your account name. The ssh package includes a utility, ssh-keygen, that generates public-private key pairs. On your client machine, you execute the ssh-keygen program with a command like the following to generate a keypair and enter a pass phrase to encrypt your private key:

```
$ ssh-keygen -t rsa
```

Unless directed otherwise, your newly created keys will be installed in your .ssh directory as in the following example:

```
$ ls -l ~/.ssh
total 16
-rw------- 1 ubuntu ubuntu 398 2011-06-06 19:33 authorized_keys
-rw------- 1 ubuntu ubuntu 1679 2011-06-06 19:34 id_rsa
-rw-r--r-- 1 ubuntu ubuntu 397 2011-06-06 19:34 id_rsa.pub
-rw-r--r-- 1 ubuntu ubuntu 842 2011-06-06 19:35 known_hosts
$
```

The public key, id_rsa.pub above, can now be copied to the remote server. In particular, once it is appended to the ~/.ssh/authorized_keys file on the remote server, you will not need to enter a password to log in via ssh. In this case, the remote system does not need a password from you, because it can authenticate you based on your public key.

Of course, your client machine may prompt you for the pass phrase that has been used to encrypt your private key, which naturally causes one to wonder: how exactly is this better? Rest assured, it is better in at least two ways.

First, you can use yet another helper program called ssh-agent to authenticate once when you log in to your local machine, and, once having done so and for as long as ssh-agent is running on your system, subsequent ssh actions will not require a pass phrase. Second, it turns out that the pass phrase is optional! When prompted by ssh-keygen, you can hit "return" and provide an empty pass phrase. This method is used whenever scripts must both execute in an unsupervised fashion and require remote access. For example, consider a cron job that executes periodically on a local machine but checks the size of a log file on a remote system.

Security Architecture for IP: IPSec

TLS and ssh are secure protocols that operate over IP, which is a protocol that lacks security features such as authentication and privacy. If the IP layer did offer security services, then, quite naturally, the need for and features of higher-level security protocols would change dramatically.

IPSec is the IETF standards-track architecture (RFC 2401 is a good starting point) for securing IP. It was developed as part of IPv6, but also includes protocol extensions for IPv4. To date, its deployment is trivial in relation to TLS and ssh, but it has important uses, particularly with virtual private networks (VPNs).

IPSec is another way to secure the traffic between two hosts that is distinguished from the protocols we've discussed so far due to its location at the network layer, the IP layer. When IPSec is in use between two hosts, all IP traffic between the two machines is secured. All protocols based on TCP or UDP would automatically inherit the security benefits of IPSec.

Due to the point-to-point nature of IPSec, it finds its greatest uses in enterprise-network-oriented applications. For example, within one company's network, each host can use IPSec to access servers on the company network. Similarly, to provide secure access to remote employees and machines, a network can provide a secure IPSec gateway through which remote machines access the local network. Traffic between the IPSec gateway and remote machines is kept secure, despite being carried over a wide-area network like the Internet.

In fact, these two uses correspond to the two operating modes supported by IPSec.

- **Transport mode.** In transport mode, security is applied to upper layer protocols and their data contents. The IP header itself is not encrypted and so is available for external observation. Transport mode is used in point-to-point fashion between end hosts.
- **Tunnel mode.** In tunnel mode, the original IP packet is encapsulated inside another IP packet. It is intended to be used to secure communications between hosts and security gateways, and between security gateways.

A key design goal and attribute of IPSec is to operate without requiring wholesale changes to the routing and forwarding infrastructure of existing networks. Traditional IP routers and switches forward IPSec packets in exactly the same way that IP packets are forwarded.

Before we look at the operation of the protocol itself, it is important for us to understand one more difference between IPSec and other protocols we've discussed. SSL (on which TLS is based) and ssh were protocols originally designed by individuals or small teams. By contrast, IPSec was developed by a committee—in particular, a working group consisting of several individuals representing several companies and industries—in the IETF. As such, the protocol had to satisfy many perspectives and apply to many use cases. For this reason, and surely others, the IPSec protocol is complex and has many narrowly defined pieces.

Consequently, no one has yet figured out how to describe IPSec succinctly yet deeply in a manner comparable to what can be done with, say, TLS and ssh. Alas, we must confess that we can be counted among that number because we have not been able to crack this problem of concise exposition either. So, our exploration of the protocol must remain at a high level, yet this will still require that we introduce and rely upon what feels like too many pieces of jargon that do not seem important enough to have their own names. Having issued this *mea culpa*, let's look at the protocol.

IPSec services are provided in the context of two distinct security protocols, each with a different aim. The first, and simpler, protocol is called the **IP Authentication Header**. If you think that's a strange name for a protocol because it looks like the name for a header, please understand that we agree.

The Authentication Header, or AH, provides authentication and integrity, but not privacy. When using AH, the communications between two systems are guaranteed to be authenticated and not tampered with. There are no guarantees that provide, or attempt to provide, data privacy. While this may sound strange, it is true that many communications services only require authentication from the network because, for instance, privacy can only adequately be provided by a higher-level protocol. Moreover, it is in many cases a vast improvement simply to be able to authenticate the end hosts in a conversation (something that IP itself does not enable). And, from a design and implementation perspective, a simpler protocol is a better protocol.

The second IPSec protocol is named the Encapsulating Security Payload, or ESP. ESP is the protocol that provides the security features of AH, as well as encrypted payloads. Most IPSec deployments rely upon ESP.

Fortunately, IPSec relies on the same categories of cryptographic and identity mechanisms to provide security as the protocols we have already discussed. In particular, IPSec relies upon the following.

Asymmetric key cryptography is used to authenticate and establish shared secrets.

Symmetric key cryptography enables communicating end hosts to encrypt communication payloads via a shared secret.

Cryptographic signatures are used to verify data integrity.

The IPSec protocol is designed in a modular fashion that allows implementations to choose from cryptographic algorithms and key management schemes. The protocol introduces the notion of a **security association**, or SA, that groups together the collection of keys, parameter choices, and algorithms used to secure an individual flow of information. In fact, before a packet can be transmitted by an IPSec-enabled network stack, its associate SA must be found. We will see how shortly.

It is valid to think of an SA as the dynamically negotiated security details associated with the flow of information between host A and host B. The SA is established in IPSec through a protocol called the **Internet Security Association and Key Management Protocol**, or ISAKMP. For our purposes, it is sufficient to think of this as the secure handshake protocol by which two hosts negotiate the cryptographic details of their secure communications. This exchange includes the establishment of shared secrets and the trading public keys, and there is a menu of options supported by the protocol.

Once an SA has been negotiated between two hosts, secure packets can be sent. Note again that these packets can be either between end hosts (transport mode) or secure gateways (tunnel mode), and can be either authenticated (AH) or authenticated and encrypted (ESP).

Once the collection of options and choices has been determined, they are stored in a security associations database and referred to by a number, the security parameters index, or SPI. To uniquely identify a specific security association, you need an SPI, a destination IP address, and the protocol identifier (AH or ESP).

When a packet is being transmitted from the host, this triplet is used to determine what security operations should be performed on the packet payload prior to transmission.

This level of indirection enables IPSec to support a very flexible and granular security management scheme. Between two hosts, IPSec can be configured to use separate encrypted tunnels for each IP-level flow; alternatively, it can be configured to use one secure tunnel for all traffic. The choice between these two is a security management choice, and the IPSec protocol defines a concrete management interface and scheme for enabling such choices.

IPSec is a tremendous work of engineering, and we could devote an entire textbook to its design and implementation. IPSec is well-supported in MS Windows since Windows Vista, Mac OS X, and Linux. IPSec is the primary protocol used to enable VPN access to remote networks. While this discussion has limited length and depth, the introduction to concepts should prepare you to dive into an existing implementation should the opportunity to do so ever arise.

Two-Factor Authentication

In computer-related security, often the desired goal is to make security violations impossible. Alas, we know that security is a consequence of people, process, and technology, and as long as this is the case security violations will always be possible.

A more practical goal is to make security violations more difficult to commit and therefore less common through time. One of the most practical steps that can be taken is to increase the difficulty of appropriating a digital identity.

In secure communications, a digital identity—whether it belongs to a person, machine, or other resource—must be authenticated. Previously, we discussed authentication method–based passwords and keys. We don't know who first said it, but it is often said that authentication methods can be based on the following categories.

- **Something you know.** Examples include passwords and pass phrases.
- **Something you have.** Private keys paired with public keys and cryptographically shared secrets are examples. Other examples include physical devices with similar secrets inside, such as smart cards and security dongles.
- **Something you are.** Examples include biometric traits such as fingerprints and iris patterns.

In an attempt to increase the difficulty involved with defrauding authentication schemes, some organizations and systems rely upon two-factor authentication in which users must authenticate their identity using evidence from two of the categories above.

For instance, a user upon login may need to provide both their personal pass phrase and a piece of information signed with their private key. In this way, an impersonator would need to both know the password and have possession of the private key.

Why two factors and not three, or more? Well, it turns out that the biometric factors are either too unreliable or too costly to gain widespread adoption. So, while multi-factor authentication may be an appropriate generalization, two-factor authentication is the practical and more specific name.

Two-factor authentication is worth considering in the design of embedded systems. The use of both passwords and keys can make an attacker's job harder, and that is a positive step as long as the intended use of the system is not diminished substantially, say, by burdening users with so much authentication effort that it reduces the utility of the embedded system.

Major Categories of Security Attacks

The preceding discussion has introduced methods and protocols for securing digital information and communications. We now turn out attention to the methods of attack that are most commonly exploited. Our aim is not to convert you to the dark side, but to inform you of how machines are exploited in order to help you engineer more secure systems.

In the following discussion, we will cover four significant categories of attack: buffer overflow, SQL injection, denial of service, and social engineering. All but the last are technically oriented attacks that target deficiencies in systems. The final one, social engineering, is non-technical in nature and seeks to subvert people or processes.

Buffer Overflow

The first category of attacks is stack buffer overflow, in which the stack-based execution model of many programming languages, like C and C++, is subverted to transfer control of execution to an externally provided program. The earliest and most public Internet-based security violation, the so-called Morris worm, which was a first in many categories beyond stack buffer exploits, relied upon it. Buffer overflow attacks are, alas, alive and well today, so they make a good starting point for this discussion.

To begin, consider the following typical implementation of the C standard library function strcpy, which copies the contents of a string to a destination string variable.

```
1 char *strcpy(char *dest, const char *src)
2 {
3     unsigned lcv;
4     for (lcv=0; src[lcv] != '\0'; ++i)
5         dest[lcv] = src[lcv];
6     dest[lcv] = '\0';
7     return dest;
8 }
```

This code works as advertised. The buffer dest will contain whatever buffer src contains, up to the first occurrence of the null character '\0', which is used to terminate strings in C.

The trouble with this code is that it takes no steps determine whether the buffer dest, the destination variable, is large enough to contain the string contents of src. And it is precisely this trait that can be exploited.

In a language like C, local variables are allocated on a stack data structure. Indeed, as you may understand very well if you have had a systems software course, C and other programming languages use a stack to implement procedure calls. Each invocation of a function gets its own region of a stack dynamically at run time; these regions on the stack are called stack frames. To implement function calls, the C compiler adds setup and teardown code before each function call, with the purpose of managing the stack. When a function uses local variables, those are allocated by the compiler on the stack frame. It is in this way that functions can call themselves without getting confused about what each occurrence of a local variable should contain. The shape of a stack and its frames are illustrated in Figure 14.2A.

One piece of information that must be included in any stack frame that calls another function is the return address: the address of the instruction that should be executed once the function call has finished.

Now, we come to the intersection of the destination buffer in strcpy and the stack. The variable dest, if it is a local variable, has a static declaration and some fixed size. If that size is sufficient to contain the string data found in buffer src, then all is well. This situation is depicted in Figure 14.2B.

If, however, the buffer dest is too small, then the contents of src will overrun dest and begin to overwrite data that immediately precede it on the stack. This type of buffer overflow of stack-based variables can easily corrupt the stack-management information stored on the stack, including the return address.

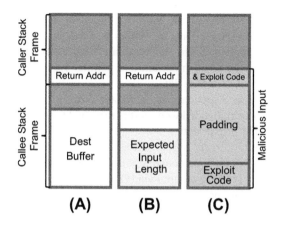

FIGURE 14.2

Illustration of Stack Buffer Overflow. (A) A normal stack frame. (B) A stack frame with an input variable within the bounds of the allocated stack buffer. (C) A stack frame with an input variable that is longer than the allocated stack buffer. In this case, the malicious input begins with assembly encoded executable exploit code, some padded bytes, and ends with the address of the beginning of the exploit code. This final address overruns the return address of the previous stack frame and, hence, will turn control of the flow of execution over to the exploit code.

As illustrated in Figure 14.2C, if an attacker has the ability to provide arbitrary input to a program that calls strcpy in this way (it can be something as innocuous as asking for a user name on a web form), the attacker can assemble an input string that contains malicious executable code at the beginning and the starting address of that executable code at the end and that is just long enough to ensure that the malicious address overwrites the return address in the previous stack frame.

Of course, it may be difficult for an attacker to know in advance what address on the stack will be used for the destination variable. Ultimately, an attacker targeting a buffer overflow vulnerability needs to know two things: (1) how to get input to the vulnerability and (2) how to control a return address. Some programs, particularly older ones, have easily reverse-engineered stack behavior. More recently, methods have been used to randomize stack locations and activities in order to prevent such attacks.

Ultimately, however, the best way to avoid such attacks is to always check the bounds of arrays and buffers. As an embedded systems developer, you will want to make sure that none of the software you've written, and that none of the software you include in your system that has been written by others, copies input strings from one buffer to another without verifying that the destination buffer is large enough.

In fact, this introduces a principle worth remembering: always verify input values. Whenever possible, you should never trust that any assumptions made about user input are true. Instead of trusting assumptions, validate those assumptions with dynamic verification in your code. This principle applies to our next attack type as well.

SQL Injection

Many of today's information services and devices rely on databases to keep structured information organized. Structured Query Language, or SQL, is the domain-specific language used to create, manage, and interact with database systems. More specifically, SQL is the language for relational databases, which are databases in which information is decomposed and represented by tables with columns that refer to one another in order to express relationships between data. For many years now, relational databases have been the most important and popular type of database; hence, SQL is the language of choice for managing structure data.

In particular, web sites and web applications are database driven. As mentioned previously, many classes of embedded systems use embedded web servers to provide user interfaces, to provide access to service APIs, and to export and import data.

In web applications that require user logins and associate stored data with individual users, this information and their relationships will be concretely managed by the use of a database. When a user signs in on a web form, one that is likely secured via HTTPS and TLS, the user name and password are compared to what is stored in the application's database. If a matching user name and password are found in the database, then the user is allowed to log in.

To do this, the database could, for example, contain a table called Users with columns Userid, First_Name, Last_Name, and Password. Given this table layout, the web application might include a string like the following that contains the SQL query that returns the table record associated with this user.

```
login_stmt =
"SELECT *
  FROM Users
 WHERE Userid = '" + userid_input + "';"
```

In this SQL statement, the variable userid_input would come from the input form. If the user enters 'alice' as the login ID, then userid_input would be set to that value and the query would correspond to the following.

```
login_stmt =
"SELECT *
  FROM Users
 WHERE Userid = 'alice';"
```

So, as you can see, this query changes based on the input assigned to the variable userid_input. Let's suppose for a moment that someone were to enter the this string: '; DROP TABLE Users;--' ?

```
login_stmt =
"SELECT *
  FROM Users
 WHERE Userid = ''; DROP TABLE Users;-- ';"
```

The resulting SQL query is a dangerous one! Thanks to this 'injection of SQL' into the query, it is now a compound statement that contains two SQL statements. The SELECT statement is terminated by the first semicolon. The second SQL statement, as is clear even if you are new to SQL, proceeds to drop the Users table. In SQL, a double-dash is the comment operator; so, the double-dash following the second semicolon turns the rest of the line into a comment. Hence, there are no SQL syntax errors.

The vulnerability here, as with the buffer overflow example discussed above, is due to the unexamined use of user input. In this case, the user input is used in its literal form as a string input to an SQL query. Any database system that does this is vulnerable to SQL injection attacks. In addition to destroying information, as in the example above, SQL statements can be inserted that create new users, write new files to web directories, or modify user names, passwords, or email addresses.

As you might expect, an attacker still has work to do. For example, an attacker must somehow learn about table and column names used in the database. However, many important and otherwise well-protected systems have fallen prey to this attack. The key in avoiding this vulnerability is to sanitize and verify all user input before putting it to use.

Denial of Service

A denial of service attack has a different aim as compared to the attack types we have discussed so far. Rather than attempting to violate the confidentially or integrity of a system, a denial of service attack, or DOS attack, targets its availability.

There are at least three broad categories for DOS attacks: resource exhaustion, resource interruption, and active interference. Let's consider each in turn.

The most public, and arguably most common, DOS attack aims to exhaust a resource. For example, consider a modestly provisioned web server. Many web server applications will exhibit sharp performance drop-offs as the number of concurrent connections approaches 1000 or so. To perform this style of DOS attack on such a server, an attacker must find a way to generate many thousands of connection requests per second. This can be achieved by writing high-performance software to generate such requests from a few machines or by directing a large number of hosts to make lower-rate requests of the server. Either can achieve the desired effect, because it is the product of the number of machines and their average request rate that determines the level of traffic seen at the server.

An excessive and ultimately disabling load on a web server is one form of resource-exhausting DOS attack, and there are others. A similar method can be used to exhaust the network bandwidth available to a target server or network; all that is required is that that attacker have greater aggregate network bandwidth than the target.

A subtler form of resource exhaustion attack targets an end host's operating system. By sending carefully malformed TCP packets, it is possible to create a large number of TCP connections on a target computer that are in a semi-open state. In one particular method, called a SYN flood, the attacker sends TCP/SYN packets to the target machine with false (or "spoofed") source IP addresses. By adhering to the TCP protocol, the machine under attack sends a TCP/SYN-ACK packet to the forged address. These packets, of course, never get a reply, and so the connection sits in a semi-open state until a timeout expires.

Ultimately, any end host has capacity for a fixed number of open TCP connections, and if an attacker can a open a large number of illegitimate connections, then legitimate communication requests on the host may be denied.

With resource interruption DOS attacks, a target is rendered ineffective by interrupting access to a key resource or service. With Internet-connected devices, the Domain Name Service, or DNS, is a critically important service. DNS, as we know, translates between Internet names and addresses, and if an attacker is able to a interrupt a device's or network's access to DNS, then many services will be rendered unavailable and many remote systems will become unreachable.

The final form of DOS attack concerns active interference. Most well-known instances of this attack once again rely upon features of the TCP protocol. If an attacker has the ability to both identify the destination IP addresses and ports used by a target machine and forge illegitimate packets that appear to come from those destination IP addresses, then the attacker can shut down individual TCP connections. This is done by sending to the machine under attack a TCP/RESET packet with a forged packet appearing to come from a legitimate destination machine. If the machine under attack has an open TCP connection with the forged address, the TCP/RESET packet will terminate it immediately.

Social Engineering and Phishing

What is the best way for attackers to obtain unauthorized access to systems or information? Evidence increasingly suggests that simply asking for it is the best attack. This approach is particularly attractive when a specific individual or organization is the target.

Social engineering refers to largely non-technical attacks that aim to trick suspects into divulging their secrets. Such scams are often perpetrated via telephone. Consider the following script.

> *Hello, my name is Bob Lastname with Big Credit Card, Co. We've noticed an irregularity in your account and we have temporarily suspended it in order to protect you. To unlock your account, I just need to ask you some questions about your recent purchases. First, however, I need to make sure that I am talking to the right person. Let's verify your name, then I'll need to verify your account number, expiration date, and CVV code....*

Now, you may not fall for such a trick, but some certainly may. And, more to the point, how many attempts across 100 arbitrary users would you expect to be successful?

Such tricks are far more effective than we would like them to be. In recent decades, there has been a dramatic rise in email-based social engineering incidents. After all, it is now quite easy to send 1 million email messages or have VoIP systems make 1 million automated phone calls. When someone sends a forged digital message in an attempt to get you to divulge secrets, we call that a phishing attack. Rather than requesting an email reply, such requests typically include links to web forms where personal information is solicited. In such attacks, both the email message and the corresponding web form are typically designed to look legitimate.

Attacks like these are extremely difficult to prevent because they derive their leverage from tricking uninformed, confused, busy, or unlucky people.

Firewalls

Some of the attack types discussed above appear to exploit inherent characteristics of the Internet protocols. DOS attacks, for example, are possible by virtue of how the Internet works. In the Internet, any machine can send packets to any other machine, and the protocols are designed to make that not only possible but also scalable and efficient. DOS attacks, particularly the resource exhaustion exploits, leverage this fact.

Firewalls block packets. A firewall is a device or software layer that filters out packets based on a set of rules that define which packets can be allowed through and which should be dropped.

Firewalls are perhaps best known as stand-alone network appliances that are placed at network boundaries and enforce the network's access policies. In addition, most operating systems ship with host-based firewall software that can be used to limit what type of network traffic can reach the host operating system. These firewalls operate within the system software, beneath the operating system networking stack. You might argue that it is still part of the operating system, which is technically true, but it is low enough in the packet processing sequence that drop decisions can be made before any system resources are allocated or consumed to handle arriving packets. This is low enough, for example, to avoid the threat of SYN flood attacks.

Linux includes a flexible and effective firewall. In fact, not only do most production Linux machines rely on it in one way or another, many organizations deploy a Linux-based device as their production firewall! Such systems cannot match the performance or range of features of some custom-designed firewall systems, but the price-performance cannot be beat. If your embedded system is Linux-based, it is likely that iptables will play an important role in its security.

The Linux iptables subsystem is built around the concepts of rules and chains. A rule is a combination of a packet filter and an action. The filter describes how it matches a packet; the action specifies what to do when a match is found. A chain is simply a linear sequence of rules. Let's look at an example of a command line that makes these ideas concrete.

```
$ sudo iptables -A INPUT -p tcp --dport 80 -j ACCEPT
```

In this line, the iptables command (which requires admin privileges, and typically lives at /sbin/iptables) is appending (-A) to a chain called INPUT, which is one of the five pre-defined chains. To match this rule, a packet must be a TCP packet (-p tcp) destined for port 80 (--dport 80), regardless of the interface on which it arrived. When a packet matches the rule, it is accepted into the system for protocol processing (-j ACCEPT). If a packet does not match the rule, it is evaluated against the next rule in the chain.

We will shortly walk through a scenario that secures access to a Linux machine under a sample set of access policy assumptions, but first we need to discuss some additional iptable concepts and details. First, as previously mentioned, there are five default chains created by the system. As admin, you can create additional chains, but the default chains correspond to the packet entry points in the system. They correspond, in fact, to the API of the underlying packet filtering mechanism, Netfilter, in Linux. The default chains are as follows.

- **INPUT.** Packets that have arrived at the system and are destined for the local IP address are processed by the INPUT chain.
- **OUTPUT.** Packets created on this host and sent from it are processed by the OUTPUT chain.
- **FORWARD.** When the system is configured as a router, packets may arrive at the machine that are destined for another. Such packets are processed on the this chain.
- **PREROUTING.** Before the system can decide whether an arriving packet is destined for this host or whether it needs to be forwarded elsewhere, a routing decision must be made. Before this routing decision is made, the arriving packet is processed by the PREROUTING chain.
- **POSTROUTING.** Before a packet is transmitted, it is processed by the POSTROUTING chain. This is true for both packets generated on this machine and those that are forwarded by this machine.

The preceding explanation makes clear that each packet will be processed by multiple chains. Upon arrival, all IP packets will be processed by the PREROUTING chain, and then, if it hasn't been dropped, either by the INPUT or FORWARD chains. Likewise, on output, all IP packets will be processed on the POSTROUTING chain after making their way through either the OUTPUT or FORWARD chains. As an introduction, this description will suffice. As you may later discover, Linux networking has a rich set of features, including network address translation, and a deeper exploration would reveal that each packet traverses these chains more than once.

Packet matching conditions, or filters, can be expressed in terms of packet header-level details, such as addresses and ports. In iptables, they can also include the state of connections. When a firewall supports rules that are depending on the state of TCP/IP connections, it is said to be a stateful firewall. Otherwise, it is a stateless firewall.

In the example command line above, the action was to accept (-j ACCEPT) the packet for further network stack processing. The command line switch –j, in fact, means "jump." In addition to specifying a final decision like ACCEPT, the switch also allows the transfer of processing to another user-defined chain. When –j is used in this way, the target chain will be processed, and unless an authoritative decision is reached there, it will return to this point in the original chain for further process. If this behavior is undesired, the –g or "goto" switch can be used to avoid returning to the original chain. These call and branch mechanisms allow the creation of extremely expressive packet processing routines.

There are several authoritative decisions that can be made, but the most important for us to understand at this point are ACCEPT, DROP, REJECT, and LOG, as described below.

- **ACCEPT.** The ACCEPT target directs iptables to allow the matching packet to continue along the packet processing path. Conceptually, this means allowing the packet to continue to work its way through the Linux network layer.
- **DROP.** The DROP target indicates that the system should delete the packet without sending any return notification to the sender.
- **REJECT.** The REJECT target, by contrast, attempts to send a failure notification to the sender. The specific type of notification can be declared explicitly or can be determined by default in some chains. For example, the system can generate an icmp-host-unreachable message. Most secured systems eschew used of the REJECT target, because it can serve as an aid to a probing attacker.
- **LOG.** The LOG target directs iptables to emit a system log message and continue processing the chain. You can set a log level (–log-level) and prefix (–log-prefix) that will determine which system log the message will appear in and how it should appear. Log level 7, perhaps the most common choice, will cause the messages to appear in /var/log/debug. To avoid filling logs unnecessarily, parameters are available to limit how often each type of message should be logged within a time interval.

With this background understanding in place, we can now consider an example of how to use iptables to secure access to a Linux-based, Internet-connected device.

Let's suppose that our target system is an embedded one that provides a secure, HTTPS-based web interface to its users, whose Internet addresses change through time. Furthermore, let's assume that we are responsible for the remote management of the device and that we will use ssh for remote login and administration.

To secure our system, we begin by checking the current configuration of the rules in iptables. If you are using a freshly installed system that has not been administered by anyone else, you will likely see the following.

```
$ sudo iptables -L
Chain INPUT (policy ACCEPT)
target   prot opt source          destination
Chain FORWARD (policy ACCEPT)
target   prot opt source          destination

Chain OUTPUT (policy ACCEPT)
target   prot opt source          destination
$
```

By using the –L switch, we see that our there are no rules currently active on the default chains. Moreover, we see that the default behavior on each chain is to ACCEPT. So, Linux accepts traffic by default. To see the contents of the PREROUTING and POSTROUTING chains, you must also add the "–t nat" switch.

The following listing of iptables commands will configure our firewall according to our policies.

```
1 sudo iptables -A INPUT -m conntrack --ctstate ESTABLISHED,RELATED -j ACCEPT
2 sudo iptables -A INPUT -i lo -j ACCEPT
3 sudo iptables -A INPUT -s 10.10.10.10 -p tcp --dport 22 -j ACCEPT
4 sudo iptables -A INPUT -p tcp --dport 443 -j ACCEPT
5
6 sudo iptables -P INPUT -j DROP
7 sudo iptables -P FORWARD -j REJECT
8 sudo iptables -P OUTPUT -j ACCEPT
```

The first four lines append rules to the INPUT chain and explicitly indicate which forms of traffic we want to actively admit to our system.

The first line contains a stateful matching rule (-m conntrack). Specifically, the rule says that any connections with a state that is established and related to an existing connection will be allowed. This allows connections originated by our device to receive inbound traffic; it does not allow externally initiated connections to pass.

The second line makes use of the interface switch, -i lo, and admits all inbound traffic on the local interface. This allows processes and programs active on the machine to communicate with one another. If we did not explicitly allow this, our later restriction rules (i.e., line 6) would ensure that processes could not communicate with one another over IP.

The third and fourth lines are like the ones we have seen earlier. Traffic on port 22, ssh traffic, is accepted provided that it is from remote IP 10.10.10.10 (this is a non-routable, private IP address used here for illustration only) and using the TCP protocol. Line 4 allows anyone to send TCP packets to port 443, in order to enable Internet access on the HTTPS port.

The first four rules express what types of traffic we want to admit into the system. The final three lines cover the remainder. Line 6 tells the system to drop all inbound traffic that has not already matched our accept rules. Line 7 ensures that the device does not act as a router. Line 8 explicitly enables outbound traffic.

Over time, the rules in iptables can grow complex. One way to keep track of its state, and the intention of the rules, is to maintain a commented script that includes everything. The utilities iptables-save and iptables-restore can also be used to save and restore snapshots of the currently active iptables configuration.

Servers and Logs

We conclude our discussion of building blocks and concepts with what amounts to a mention of good habits.

Even if you take every available precaution, and put in place every available preventative measure, you should expect the unexpected. The very nature of emerging security vulnerabilities is that they were not known prior to their exploitation. As such, you should prepare your systems as best you can, but be prepared to quickly respond to the unexpected.

One of the best ways to be prepared to respond is to maintain orderly logs of system activity. As you likely know, all major operating system features and applications optionally maintain logs of their activity. While each logging feature has its own set of configuration options, there is no better way to keep tabs on your system and its operation than by maintaining and monitoring logs of system activity. The following list represents a starting point for what your embedded system should probably be logging and monitoring.

- **Failed login attempts.** All operating systems maintain logs of login attempts. In Linux, you will likely find the log in /var/log/auth.log.
- **Web server and database access logs.** Attempts to extract information from web-based services are most likely to leave some indication in web server logs and any related database logs. The popular combination of Apache and MySQL would by default lead to logs left in /var/log/apache2 and /var/log/mysql, respectively.
- **Firewall logs.** As described above, logs can be maintained for the iptables firewall, in order to keep track of how often various rules are matched.

A good practice is to put in place an automated system for collecting, analyzing, and archiving these logs. For attacks that involve probing and brute force password guessing, often the size of the log file alone can serve as an alarm.

By extension, you should also consider the logging features of any application or systems software you develop yourself. As developers, we think of logs primarily as debugging tools, but, increasingly, they are proving to play an important role in system security.

PLATFORM SUPPORT FOR SECURITY

Given the importance of security in modern embedded and computer systems, it is natural to ask if hardware support in the platform can play a role in assisting or accelerating security related tasks. The answer is certainly yes! There are two broad categories of platform support for security.

In the first category, hardware implementations of security mechanisms are provided in order to reduce the computation burden of encryption. In modern systems, we know that most secure data are transmitted after having been encrypted via symmetric-key cryptography. By their nature, cryptographic algorithms are computationally heavy. Since multiple computations are carried out for each byte of the payload, the computational overhead for medium-to-large data volumes can be substantial. Many systems include hardware accelerators to aid in these bulk encryption/decryption tasks. Other hardware assists include random number generators, cryptographic signature units, and public-private key pair generators.

The second category is a broader one, one that not only supports cryptographic algorithms, but aims to manage and orchestrate a platform-wide security solution. The best known such solution goes by the name Trusted Computing, and is the outspring of a collaboration of many of the largest companies in the Windows and PC ecosystem, referred to collectively as the Trusted Computing Group, or TCG. The stated goal of Trusted Computing (which may well also apply to the lower-case version of the phrase) is to enable systems to consistently behave in expected ways and to enable the system hardware and software to verify the correct behavior and the integrity of the system. In other words, their goal is to enable systems to boot into an authenticated and known state and to allow the system software and operating system to continue to bring the system up to known secures states free of any tampering.

The core leverage of the Trusted Computing specifications comes from hardware-based trust. The Trusted Platform Module, or TPM, is a hardware component added either to the motherboard of computer system or as a unit on a system-on-a-chip. The Trusted Computing Group's specifications for a TPM include the hardware support for cryptographic algorithms as discussed above. They also include additional operational features critical to achieving the stated goal of verifiable system integrity.

First, the TPM module includes a built-in, burnt-in public-private key pair. This fact, coupled with the ability to sign data provided to it, means that the TPM is capable of authenticating its unique identity. This ability is referred to as remote attestation in the TCG specifications (but we simply think of it as authentication).

The TPM module specifications have other features and roles, but, to date, it seems that the dominant use of TPM has been to support full-disk encryption in recent MS Windows OS versions.

The Trusted Computing movement has its critics. The main objection offered by some observers is that the mechanisms provided by Trusted Computing can potentially be used for other ends, beyond maintaining the integrity of the end system. For instance, who has the authority to request that a remote system authenticate itself via the TPM remote attestation scheme? While there are many valid scenarios one can imagine, it is also possible that this scheme could be abused and used for end host and user tracking, which is beyond the scope of Trusted Computing.

SUMMARY

In this chapter, we have introduced some of the major concepts and tools that all embedded engineers should understand. This discussion has only scratched the surface but will provide you with the literacy and orientation needed to explore individual subjects more deeply in your future coursework and projects.

When developing embedded systems, correct function is rightly a primary concern, but all developers should consider security to be a major component of the "correct function" of a system. The reason is simple: a major security weakness may render a system unusable, even if it does all else.

Unfortunately, there are few absolutes in the security of computer systems. There is no security silver bullet, and there is no such thing as an impermeable security barrier. Instead, engineers must make the best of it, given the understanding and tools of the day.

Advanced Topics: SMP, AMP, and Virtualization

15

Relentless competition in computing-related markets naturally creates an intense pressure on developers to increase product functionality or decrease cost. Often, both new functionality and lower cost are central goals in a product development strategy.

Embedded systems are no exception. While some classes of embedded systems have long product lifetimes relative to personal computers and hence do not experience the same pace of innovation, many embedded device categories have even shorter development and deployment cycles.

The preceding chapters have provided a comprehensive introduction to the design and use of embedded systems based on the Intel® Atom™ architecture. Beginning with this chapter, we will now consider some advanced topics that represent critical aspects of modern embedded system design; indeed, most of these subjects are growing in importance.

As we have seen, the Intel Atom architecture closely integrates many aspects of system functionality into a small number of platform-oriented integrated circuits. The decision to include a hardware accelerator, for example, represents a substantial commitment of design resources to a system task that has some substantial combination of constraints along the dimensions of performance and power efficiency.

While such hardware assists can greatly improve system efficiency, the vast majority of system functionality will be determined by software. Indeed, as embedded devices of all kinds take on ever-increasing feature sets, nearly all of the new features will be expected to have software implementations rather than specialized ones designed into the hardware.

In this chapter, we consider the system design strategies that are used to meet this growing demand for product functionality in a cost-effective way. The two dominant methods—multiprocessing and platform virtualization—are complementary approaches for improving performance and manageability, respectively. As with many other developments, these first appeared in general-purpose computer systems and then quickly migrated to the design of chipsets for embedded systems.

Multiprocessing has always provided a path to higher performance. During the PC era, however, rapid, reliable advances in microprocessor performance diminished the need in many domains to develop a multiprocessing implementation strategy. These microprocessor performance improvements were primarily driven by clock and single-processor microarchitectural enhancements. In the early 2000s, however, the consistent increases in clock frequency and processor pipeline complexity ceased. The reason for this is that while subsequent design generations provided better performance, they also consumed dramatically more power. Ultimately, clock frequencies plateaued as a result of power dissipation limits. To improve performance without requiring increases in clock frequency, most microprocessor designs have become parallel processors by the addition of multiple processor cores. In this chapter, we discuss why this helps, as well as the consequences for software.

423

Platform virtualization was introduced for, in many respects, the opposite reason: first and foremost, platform virtualization is a benefit for underutilized systems that do not need the full resources of a dedicated machine. Platform virtualization allows one computer system to simultaneously host multiple machine instances, where a machine instance can be thought of as an operating system and all of the applications and services it executes.

The need to virtualize a platform in this way is a consequence of how most computing services are implemented. In most enterprise computing settings, servers are the basic unit of composition. Historically, major services have been implemented with one or more dedicated servers. Within an organization, email, the HR databases, and file systems would all be installed and operated on different physical server machines. Medium and large organizations can have hundreds or thousands of such services.

Using discrete physical servers in this way creates several problems. First, the organization must operate multiple servers, even if each of those servers is only lightly utilized. Second, when each service is tied to one physical machine, recovering from hardware failures can be cumbersome and require that an inventory of similarly configured hardware platforms be kept in reserve. Platform virtualization allows multiple distinct operating system instances to execute on the same hardware platform, directly addressing each of these problems. Platform virtualization and its unique advantages in embedded systems will be discussed later in this chapter.

While multiprocessing and platform virtualization address important problems and open new paths for future system design, they hold strong consequences for software and service architecture. In this chapter, we discuss these software architecture impacts, along with the communication mechanisms that are most effective for use within applications that are expected to be distributed across several processes and system instances.

MULTIPROCESSING BASICS

Before discussing how multiprocessing concepts are making their way into embedded system designs, it will be helpful for us to introduce some basic concepts and briefly discuss the recent history of multiprocessing. Gaining this context is essential for understanding why today's systems are organized as they are. After all, most system design and implementation decisions are the result of the evolutionary push and pull between the needs of users and the capabilities of underlying technologies.

History and Motivation

Small-scale multiprocessor systems emerged hand-in-hand with the use of microprocessors in server-class computer systems. Systems referred to as shared memory, symmetric multiprocessors, or SMP systems for short, appeared as viable PC-based competitors to servers built around dedicated server processors.

Prior to the PC era, and for a mercilessly short time during the PC area, a separate industry existed, consisting of multiple companies that provided hardware components, software, and systems for specialized supercomputers, servers, and high-end workstations. Much of the classical work in parallel computing was carried out in the context of such computers, which were designed to be parallel from the start. The PC era, and the dominant economic success of PC microprocessors, effectively eliminated these systems along with most of the companies that produced them.

In SMP systems, multiple CPU chips share both a memory controller and main memory. SMP machines are typically small-scale systems, with CPU counts in the single digits. With multiple CPUs, the system can execute multiple processes in parallel. Naturally, the operating system must be organized to keep its internal data structures and functions correct in the presence of multiple CPUs and to schedule multiple processes at a time rather than just one. Larger-scale parallel systems, consisting of tens, hundreds, or thousands of machines, appeared through the use of high-speed local area networks that interconnect individual machines (which may or may not be organized as SMPs).

While SMP systems have always been popular, they have historically taken a second seat behind uniprocessor systems, until recently. The recent trend in multicore CPU design has resulted in SMP architectures becoming the dominant computer system architecture. While most machines on the planet still contain just one CPU, that CPU is now organized as an SMP, itself containing two or more processor cores.

Adding multiple cores to a CPU increases the peak instruction bandwidth, and hence system throughput, without requiring an increase in operating clock frequency. This is important because dramatic increases in operating frequency must be avoided in order to keep thermal design power reasonable for general-purpose computing platforms. Indeed, merely maintaining current processor frequencies has required substantial semiconductor innovation.

As a simple example, two cores operating at 2 GHz have a combined instruction completion bandwidth equivalent to a single 4-GHz processor core. However, two concurrent programs, or threads of execution, are needed to realize the increased performance. This requirement of a multiple process workload in order to realize performance gain mirrors that which has always held for SMP systems.

In other words, if the program that you care about consists of a single thread of execution, then you will see only indirect performance benefits when moving to a CPU with more cores. These indirect benefits are due to reduced sharing; your program will share its core with fewer other programs and hence might experience some speedup. But single-threaded programs receive no direct performance benefit on a CPU with multiple cores.

Today's general-purpose processors feature two, four, or eight processor cores. Will tomorrow's CPUs feature tens or hundreds of cores? The future is unclear and very much depends on how well various application domains can leverage multiple processor cores.

Some domains are already dominated by multicore-friendly, thread-parallel software architectures. If your favorite software runs on a cluster or a compute cloud, then you are already in a strong position to benefit from multicore processors (and, happily, you do not really care about the details of a single computer).

Perhaps most extreme are those illegal, decentralized systems such as botnets that manage to make efficient use of large-scale parallel resources without the benefit of legal access to the individual computers.

At a lower level of system abstraction, high-performance embedded processors such as network processors have for years leveraged multiple cores to meet I/O-intensive real-time constraints. Cisco, for example, has designed a 192-core processor for its high-end router line-cards; each line-card features two of these processors, and they have been shipping since 2004.

So given that multiple processors and multiple processor cores can be used to scale performance, how do structure systems and software architectures take advantage of them?

Systems and software must be organized to carry out their work in parallel, in distinct threads of execution, in order to take advantage of multiple processor cores. There are two major approaches for parallel application structure, and we can introduce them with a simple generic example.

Suppose we begin with a single-threaded application that can be functionally decomposed into tasks A, B, and C, as indicated in Figure 15.1.

Single-Threaded Application: Maps to One Core

FIGURE 15.1

Single-Threaded Application: Maps to One Core.

The first approach we will consider for parallelizing this application is to *pipeline* it. Each task is factored out into its own thread of execution and mapped to a different processor core. Neighboring tasks must communicate data and control information to one another with some mechanisms, such as through the use of shared memory or by sending explicit messages. This pipelined organization is illustrated in Figure 15.2.

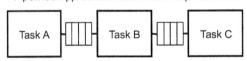

Pipelined Application: Each Task Maps to a Core

FIGURE 15.2

Pipelined Application: Each Task Maps to a Core.

How does this parallelization impact performance? Well, if we assume that each of the three tasks takes approximately the same amount of time to complete, then our execution throughput should increase linearly with the number of pipeline stages. In this case, a balanced pipeline with three stages would yield a 3x increase in performance.

As an alternative to this pipelined approach, a multithreaded approach may be used. Rather than decomposing the application into parallel subtasks, multithreading replicates the entire application. By doing so, each thread instance is able to execute on a different processor core at the same time. The application must be augmented with some dispatch code to assign work to the individual threads, as well as some cleanup code at the end to bring together the work done in parallel. This approach is illustrated in Figure 15.3.

The performance impact of this parallel organization is similar. Provided that the three thread instances can proceed in parallel, an increase in throughput on the order of 3x would be expected. Of

Multi-Threaded Application: Each Thread Maps to a Core

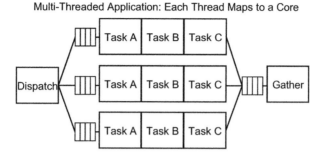

FIGURE 15.3

Multithreaded Application: Each Thread Maps to a Core.

course, the "dispatch" and "gather" blocks are not parallelized, so their contributions to total runtime reduce the effectiveness of the parallelized application.

To see how much of an impact this may have on achievable speedup, we can consider Amdahl's Law. Let's call S the fraction of the application that must run in serialized fashion. Amdahl's Law can be used to estimate the total impact on theoretical speedup when the application is parallelized. If we let N be the number of parallel tasks, then we can express Amdahl's Law as follows:

$$ParallelSpeedup(S, N) = \frac{1}{S + \frac{(1 - S)}{N}}$$

For example, if 1% of an application must be executed in serial fashion, but the remaining 90% can execute in four parallel processes on distinct processor cores, then we can expect the following maximum speedup.

$$ParallelSpeedup(0.1, 4) = \frac{1}{0.1 + \frac{0.9}{4}} = \frac{1}{0.32} = 3.1$$

So, with just 10% of an application serialized, we can expect a speedup of at most 3.1x, down from the 4x speedup that would be suggested by the presence of four processor cores.

Figure 15.4 illustrates the peak theoretical speedup over a range of processors and serialization percentages.

These numbers are sobering! With just 5% of an application serialized, Amdahl's Law yields an upper bound on speedup of around 16x, regardless of the number of processors. Note that the chart is drawn with a logarithmic scale on the vertical axis. It may appear that the 1% curve nearly matches ideal speedup represented by the 0% curve, but it does not; it achieves less than 50% of the peak speedup at 128 processors.

Amdahl's Law in general advises developers to focus their optimization on those portions of a program that contribute the most to total execution time. This is the right advice in all cases. When applied to parallel software, the most significant consequence is that even seemingly small amounts of serialization in an application can limit the scalability of a parallel implementation.

Of course, Amdahl's Law provides bounds to peak theoretical speedup. There are, in addition, many practical issues that reduce achievable speedups. For instance, the creation and management of

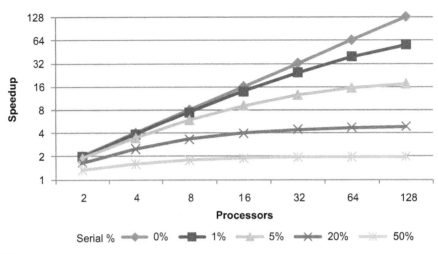

FIGURE 15.4

Theoretical Speedup over a Range of Processors and Serialization Percentages.

parallel threads can represent an overhead that is not present in a single-threaded implementation. When calculating speedup based on wall-clock measurements, these must sometimes be considered.

Given the preceding discussion, it is clear that applications that can be completely parallelized are qualitatively different from those that have even a small amount of serialized code: they can be scaled indefinitely!

While it may appear that few such applications exist, there is in fact a large category of applications that fit this task. Suppose, for example, you have a generic task that takes as its input a continuous stream of independent pieces of data to be processed. Suppose further that the processing of each of these data items is completely independent of one another. These classes of applications are often referred to as *throughput-oriented applications*.

For a specific example, consider the batch processing of large numbers of digital images. Suppose each digital image needs a color correction routine to be applied to it; this can be done for each image in a completely independent fashion. Since this application can be configured in advance of the processing of the first image, it is possible to create independent processes when the system is first initiated so that the cost of creating the independent processes can be amortized over the entire session.

Many large-scale or performance-intensive information processing tasks can be characterized this way. In the context of embedded systems, any task that resembles signal or media processing is a prime candidate for this style of parallelization.

A Concrete Example

Given the importance and ubiquity of multi-core processors, most programming environments include considerable support for organizing and executing applications in parallel fashion.

We will now examine a sample application in Python that performs data processing in a parallel fashion. Logically, the application's function is simple. It takes as input data files that contain one string of text per line, and each string of text is an integer between 1 and 999,999. The application reads the strings, converts them to integers, multiplies them all by the prime number 3571, divides the products by the prime number 1511, and writes the results to an output file with a name similar to the name of the input file.

This application, shown below, is organized to first operate serially, and then to operate in parallel over a range of parallel processes that is automatically determined by the number of CPUs in the system that is executing the program. In particular, the application is run with k parallel processes, where k ranges from 2 to $n \times 3$, where n is the CPU count of the system.

The following code can be executed on any system with Python version 2.6 or later.

```
1 import multiprocessing as mp
2 import random, time
3
4 DATA_CNT = 100000
5 FILE_CNT = 6
6
7 def read_file(fname):
8     f = open(fname, 'r')
9     data = f.readlines()
10    f.close()
11    return data
12
13 def conv_data(data):
14    # Convert strings to integers
15    numbers = []
16    for val in data:
17        numbers.append(int(val.strip()))
18    return numbers
19
20 def mult_data(data):
21    # Multiply integers by 3571
22    products = []
23    for val in data:
24        products.append(val * 3571)
25    return products
26
27 def div_data(data):
28    # Divide integers by 1511
29    quotients = []
30    for val in data:
31        quotients.append(val/1511)
32    return quotients
33
34
35 def process_file(fname):
36    outfname = fname.replace(".txt","_results.txt")
37    results = div_data(mult_data(conv_data
```

```
38                    (read_file(fname))))
39   f = open(outfname, 'w')
40   for val in results:
41     f.write("%i\n" % val)
42   f.close()
43
44
45 if __name__ == '__main__':
46   # Write an output file with DATA_CNT integers
47   # We could manipulate this in memory, but
48   # dumping it to a file allows us to verify
49   # correctness.
50
51   random.seed(1)
52
53   # Generate filenames
54   fnames = []
55   for fnum in range(1,FILE_CNT+1):
56     fnames.append('test_data_100k_%i.txt' % fnum)
57   # Create and fill files
58   for fname in fnames:
59     f = open(fname, 'w')
60     for i in range(0,DATA_CNT):
61       f.write('%i\n' % random.randint(0, 1000000))
62     f.close()
63
64   tottime = time.time()
65   for fname in fnames:
66     t1 = time.time()
67     process_file(fname)
68     print "Time to process input file %s: %.4f" \
69         % (fname,time.time() - t1)
70   one_p = time.time() - tottime
71   print "**************************"
72   print "Time with one process: %.4f" % (one_p)
73
74   cpu_count = mp.cpu_count()
75   print "System has %i processors." % cpu_count
76   # Now, measure performance with 1,
77   # ..., 3*cpu_count processs
78   for proc_count in range(2, cpu_count*3+1):
79     pool = mp.Pool(processes=proc_count)
80     t1 = time.time()
81     pool.map(process_file, fnames)
82     n_p = time.time() - t1
83     print "Time with %i processes: %.4f (%.2f)" \
84         % (proc_count, n_p, (one_p/n_p))
85
```

We can make the following comments on this code.

Lines 1–5: The `multiprocessing` module in Python provides classes for creating and controlling distinct operating system processes for your code to execute in. Python also provides a `threading` library, which, like many other language-specific threading libraries, cannot directly take advantage of multiple cores in an SMP system. By using separate processes, the operating system scheduler can migrate those processes to lightly loaded CPU cores.

Also, the constants `DATA_CNT` and `FILE_CNT` control the number of data items in each file and the number of total files, respectively.

Lines 7–42: These functions implement the core tasks of the application: reading a file, converting the strings to integers, multiplying the integers by a constant, dividing the products by a constant, and writing the results as strings to an output file.

Lines 45–62: To keep this example simple, the application generates its own test data in the form of files created in the current working directory. The list `fnames` is used to record the file names that get created; as we will see, work will be distributed among processes in the form of file names. Into each file is written `DATA_CNT` random integers drawn from the range between 0 and 999,999. In total, `FILE_CNT` distinct files are created.

Lines 64–72: To establish a baseline, all of the files are processed in a single process. The `time.time()` function is called before and after the function invocation to measure the time spent.

Lines 74–84: The `cpu_count()` function, which is implemented in the `multiprocessing` module, returns the number of CPUs that that operating system knows about. In this application, the CPU count is used to automatically determine how many processes to create. The purpose of this program is to measure the effect of multiprocessing, so measurements are gathered over a range of process counts. The range is defined to be 2 to $3 \times n$, where n is the CPU count.

The `Pool()` method instantiates a specified number of independent processes that can be assigned work. The `map()` method takes two arguments, a function to invoke within a process, and a list of arguments. For each argument in the list, a (function, argument) pair is used to invoke the function within a process. When a given process has completed an invocation it becomes available to receive a new (function, argument) pair for processing.

When executing the program above on a system with 2 CPUs, the results looking something like the following.

```
Time to process input file test_data_100k_1.txt: 0.2870
Time to process input file test_data_100k_2.txt: 0.2870
Time to process input file test_data_100k_3.txt: 0.2850
Time to process input file test_data_100k_4.txt: 0.2870
Time to process input file test_data_100k_5.txt: 0.2860
Time to process input file test_data_100k_6.txt: 0.2880
***************************
Time with one process: 1.7220
System has 2 processors.
Time with 2 processes: 1.0620 (1.62)
Time with 3 processes: 1.0490 (1.64)
Time with 4 processes: 0.9780 (1.76)
Time with 5 processes: 0.9630 (1.79)
Time with 6 processes: 1.0400 (1.66)
```

As these results illustrate, a speedup of 2 is never achieved. However, as the number of parallel processes are increased from two to six, the speedups range from 1.6 to 1.7 without any monotonic relationship between the times as the number of processes increase. There are a number of possible sources of measurement variation. This application, while simple, involves a significant amount of I/O, and variations in I/O completion times can vary with the degree of concurrent activity. Briefly, frequent I/O activity typically reduces CPU utilization as a process sleeps awaiting I/O completion. In the example above, four processes may have higher speedup than two because CPU utilization is lower when just one process is active; four processes in this case can get slightly more work done than two. The operating system scheduler will also vary its behavior from one execution to the next. Overall, however, a large number of these experiments would reveal the speedup to be between 1.6 and 1.7 with four, five, and six processes having the highest overall average by a small margin.

Physical versus Logical Cores

In addition to multiple CPU cores and multiple CPUs in SMP systems, Intel CPUs include Intel Hyper-Threading Technology (Intel HT Technology), also known as simultaneous multithreading, that allows a single processor core to appear as two. Consequently, a CPU can have more logical cores than physical ones.

Intel HT Technology works by replicating some state within a CPU core, thus allowing two threads of execution to be present and executing at the same time. While some per-core hardware resources are replicated, not all are. Figure 15.5 illustrates the relationship between hardware-support thread contexts, the memory hierarchy, and multiple cores. Not all multi-core CPUs from Intel have Intel HT Technology, nor do all on-chip cores share an L2 cache, but most do.

The operating system makes no distinction between logical and physical cores. In most instances, it is the logical core count that the operating system is aware of. Thus, both the operating system scheduler and tools that report CPU utilization will do so based on logical core counts.

Impact on Systems and Software

As we conclude this general introduction to multiprocessing, the most important point to emphasize is that the multiprocessing trend emphasizes the development of parallel and distributed software. If you

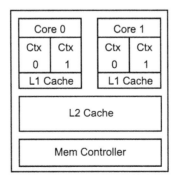

FIGURE 15.5

High-Level Depiction of Logical Processor Organization.

are developing software and systems that need to scale or migrate to future platforms, then you should be adopting a parallel and distributed software architecture.

As we will now discuss, the organization of the operating system and systems software can have a major impact on both performance and mechanisms that must be used to enable interprocess communication.

SYMMETRIC MULTIPROCESSING

The preceding discussion of multiprocessor systems has been implicitly made in the context of symmetric multiprocessing systems. In symmetric multiprocessing systems, all CPUs in the system can be used in the same way and are under the control and management of the same operating system. This is in contrast to asymmetric multiprocessing systems, which will be discussed shortly.

Overview

A symmetric multiprocessor system requires a multiprocessor-aware operating system. All mainstream operating systems today support multiprocessing, but this was not always the case.

Conceptually, the extension of a single-CPU operating system to a multiprocessor one is simple: the primary obligations are to schedule processes to run on each CPU and to provide communication and synchronization mechanisms between processes. Figure 15.6 illustrates the conceptual organization of a multiprocessor-aware operating system.

To be sure, scheduling processes on more than one CPU increases the complexity of the scheduling task: rather than choosing *what* to schedule, the scheduler must now also decide *where* to schedule a given process. Communication and synchronization mechanisms, however, were already largely present in all preemptive multitasking operating systems.

The greatest challenges in developing an SMP variant of an operating system have to do with details in the system software, with issues ranging from the boot processor to the management of I/O devices. None of these issues are conceptually formidable, but they do involve substantial engineering efforts.

Linux SMP Support

Multiprocessing support has been available in the Linux kernel since version 2.0, which was released in the mid-1990s. As support has improved over the past 15 or so years, substantial improvements in

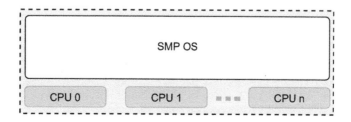

FIGURE 15.6

Organization of a Multiprocessor-Aware Operating System.

performance and reliability have been made. The main advances seen in major kernel upgrades have had to do with transitioning coarse-grained kernel locks to finer-grain ones, to reduce the amount of needless stalling. Today, Linux SMP is extremely robust and used in personal and enterprise systems around the globe.

In Linux, you can easily determine how many CPU cores are presented in the systems with a command like this one:

```
cat /proc/cpuinfo
```

which creates output like the following on a dual-core Intel Core™ 2 CPU.

```
$ cat /proc/cpuinfo
processor       : 0
vendor_id       : GenuineIntel
cpu family      : 6
model           : 23
model name      : Intel(R) Core(TM)2 Duo CPU   P8700 @ 2.53GHz
stepping        : 10
cpu MHz         : 2527
cache size      : 3072 KB
fpu             : yes
fpu_exception   : yes
cpuid level     : 13
wp              : yes
flags           : fpu vme de pse tsc msr pae mce cx8 apic sep mtrr pge mca cmov pat pse36
clflush dts acpi mmx fxsr sse sse2 ss ht tm pbe pni dtes64 monitor ds_ cpl vmx smx est
tm2 ssse3 cx16 xtpr pdcm sse4_1 xsave osxsave lahf_lm
TLB size        : 0 4K pages
clflush size    : 64
cache_alignment : 64
address sizes   : 36 bits physical, 48 bits virtual
power management:
processor       : 1
vendor_id       : GenuineIntel
cpu family      : 6
model           : 23
model name      : Intel(R) Core(TM)2 Duo CPU   P8700 @ 2.53GHz
stepping        : 10
cpu MHz         : 2527
cache size      : 3072 KB
fpu             : yes
fpu_exception   : yes
cpuid level     : 13
wp              : yes
flags           : fpu vme de pse tsc msr pae mce cx8 apic sep mtrr pge mca cmov pat pse36
clflush dts acpi mmx fxsr sse sse2 ss ht tm pbe pni dtes64 monitor ds_cpl vmx smx est tm2
ssse3 cx16 xtpr pdcm sse4_1 xsave osxsave lahf_lm
TLB size        : 0 4K pages
clflush size    : 64
```

```
cache_alignment : 64
address sizes    : 36 bits physical, 48 bits virtual
power management:
```

Linux supports concurrent processes both within the kernel and among applications. There is an unfortunate mixture of terms in Linux. Linux really only deals with processes; that is, applications that take advantage of user-level threads such as with the pthreads POSIX threads package do so within the context of a single process. Processes are the entities that are scheduled on CPUs. Except within the kernel! Within the kernel, kernel threads can be created and operated in parallel. Confusing term usage aside, it is important to note that in Linux, user-level threads cannot be used to take advantage of multiple CPU cores in an SMP system. To do that, you must use multiple processes. The Python example presented earlier in this chapter is an example of how to use multiple processes within an application.

Linux and other operating systems provided interfaces for expressing CPU affinity, so that developers and users can control which CPUs processes execute on. The Linux system call API includes `sched_set_affinity()` and `sched_set_affinity()` for this purpose.

Interprocess Communication

Independent processes exist in separate, protected address spaces. So, for processes to interact, mechanisms must be used to achieve interprocess communication.

These mechanisms are familiar to most of use, because they are the same ones that are used to provide communication between processes in single-processor systems. In Linux and other operating systems, the mechanisms include the following:

- *Pipes:* Most commonly used at the command line to connect the output of one process to the input of another. The same mechanism is available programmatically.
- *FIFOs:* Pipes with names.
- *Signals:* Identifiers sent between processes at the application layer and the kernel to indicate a state change or system condition.
- *Message queues:* Operate like pipes and FIFOs except they can have multiple readers and writers.
- *Shared memory:* Linux and other operating systems allow processes to share memory regions, either in memory or through the file system.
- *Semaphores:* A generic mechanism used to keep access to shared resources orderly and consistent. Semaphores are counters that get decremented when a process gains access to a shared resource and incremented when a process is finished using the resource. The initial counter value can be set to indicate how may processes may access the resource at the same time. The operating system typically allows a process to sleep and be awakened and reschedule when the state of a semaphore changes.

ASYMMETRIC MULTIPROCESSING

A multiprocessing system in which different CPUs have different characteristics is said to provide asymmetric multiprocessing.

Concepts and Motivation

Historically, this arrangement prevailed in small-scale multiprocessor systems such as dual-processor systems in which one CPU core was limited to running system software while the other could run applications as well. In past chipset, CPU, and operating system generations, this was the best that could be done to utilize multiple CPUs.

Modern systems, however, utilize asymmetric multiprocessing for performance or efficiency reasons. Perhaps the clearest example of an asymmetric multiprocessing system can be seen in networking, in which one or more CPU cores will eschew operating system control in favor of a custom, lightweight microkernel for handling network I/O tasks.

System Organization

This can be an attractive system organization in I/O-intensive applications due to the legacy overheads that typically burden operating systems and keep them from achieving high levels of performance in a deterministic fashion.

An early notable example of this organization can be seen in the ETA packet processing prototype developed by Intel engineers. A block diagram of the prototype ETA system mapped onto a dual-CPU Intel Xeon® computer system can be seen in Figure 15.7.

In Figure 15.7, the host CPU runs Linux and an abstraction layer that moves network processing functionality onto CPU 1, the packet processing engine (PPE). The PPE itself is based on a modified, lightweight Linux kernel that is only capable of managing the creation and operation of TCP/IP

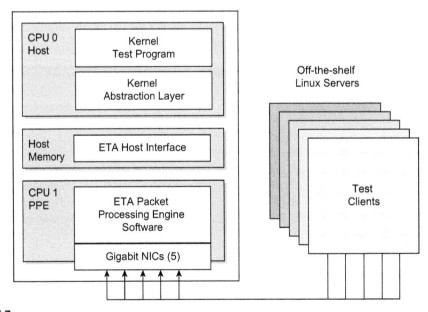

FIGURE 15.7

Prototype ETA System.

connections. Evaluations of the prototype reveal significant performance gains, of around 2x, relative to a baseline symmetric system, along with better overall CPU utilization.

The benefits of an asymmetric organization come at the cost of code complexity and management. Whenever part of a system is specialized in some way relative the rest of the system, this heterogeneity increases the range of code that must be developed, maintained, and ported to future systems.

VIRTUALIZATION BASICS

Computer system virtualization allows multiple machine instances to share a physical hardware instance. Virtualization has been a dominant general-purpose computing trend in recent years, and there is every indication that it will become one in embedded computing as well.

History and Motivation

One of the tensions that arise in software development is the need to port applications forward to new operating system versions through time. Often, these porting decisions are made naturally and are synergetic with the application's development regardless of how the underlying operating system may change through time. Other times, however, it may be inconvenient or impossible to port an application to a new version of an operating system, due to varied reasons including obsolete library dependencies, missing source code, or lack of programmer expertise with the application software. These situations can be exacerbated in asymmetric multiprocessing system organizations like those discussed in the previous section.

Computer system virtualization has been developed, in part, to help with these issues. Platform virtualization allows a single physical computer to run multiple, distinct operating systems in a fully isolated fashion at the same time.

This capability allows applications that cannot be changed or ported to continue to execute in the context of older operating systems, without requiring either that the underlying hardware be dedicated to the task or that all applications in the system remain on an outdated operating system version.

Aside from this management perspective, and just as important, is the ability for virtualized hosts to be collocated on a physical machine in order to increase the utilization of server hardware. In many respects, this technology development can be seen as a brave one to support on the part of system vendors. It is clear that helping customers make maximum use of their physical compute resources through virtualization at least runs the risk of reducing their demand for future physical resources.

Basic Concepts

Virtualization operates by use of the oldest trick in the computing book: the addition of a level of indirection. Operating systems are written to execute directly on hardware resources. In a system that provides platform virtualization, the operating system interacts with a virtualization substrate, which in turn acts as an intermediary between multiple operating systems and the underlying hardware resources.

Several methods exist for achieving this indirection, but they all share core concepts. In a virtualized platform, whenever an operating system thinks it is interacting with or observing or modifying

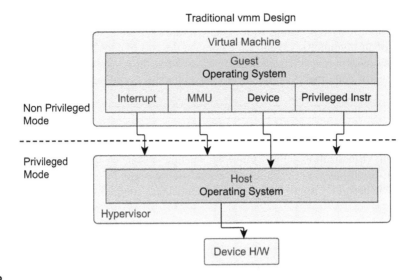

FIGURE 15.8

Basic Organization of a Virtual Machine Monitor.

hardware resources, it is actually doing so with a portion of the virtualization subsystem that is designed to simulate the operation of the underlying hardware (although some recent chipsets do have mechanisms that enable direct interaction with I/O hardware). While doing so, the virtualization substrate enforces isolation and correct operating among the operating systems hosted on the machine.

This basic organization is illustrated in Figure 15.8.

In a traditional design, a hypervisor (sometimes referred to as a virtual machine monitor) acts as the system supervisor for one or more guest operating systems. Each guest operating system can be referred to as a virtual machine; these machines are given the abstraction of having exclusive control of the machine's physical resources.

The hypervisor effectively intercepts all hardware-level events and interactions and multiplexes them through the underlying hardware in a manner that is operationally transparent to the guest operating systems.

METHODS FOR PLATFORM VIRTUALIZATION

The additional level of indirection in a virtualized platform can have substantial performance impacts. For this reason, a variety of virtualization variants and implementation techniques have been created.

Paravirtualization

The earliest instances of platform virtualization required modifications to the guest operating systems. When a guest operating system must be modified, or in some way an active participant, we characterize the system as one that offers *paravirtualization*. This is typically in contrast to systems with *full virtualization* that require no modification or active participation from the guest operating systems.

One of the earliest and most popular commercial virtualization systems, VMware™, relied upon binary rewriting in which certain code sequences (that is, those that would otherwise interact directly with hardware resources) are detected and modified either statically or dynamically in order to achieve virtualization without requiring others to modify operating systems. This is still considered para-virtualization, however, since the method is only distinguished based on how the change to the operating system is achieved.

While perhaps convenient for operating system vendors and users who want to virtualize the systems that they already own, binary rewriting suffers from substantial performance overhead.

Hardware Support for Virtualization

In response to the rising popularity of virtualization, Intel and AMD both added hardware support to their processors to provide full virtualization without requiring changes to operating systems. The hardware support is similar in spirit to binary rewriting, but rather than rewriting code sequences above the application binary interface, hardware support can be built in to the CPU to trap and virtualize hardware-specific operating and code sequences beneath it, in the CPU's microarchitecture.

Providing hardware support for virtualization involves very little runtime overhead but may lead to considerable resource additions in the microarchitecture to more effectively share internal CPU state that in a nonvirtualized context does not need to be shared.

Linux VServers

Linux provides a related mechanism known as VServers that can provide some, but not all, of what platform virtualization provides. In particular, Linux VServers enable resource isolation between distinct Linux instances running on the same physical machine. Resources that are shared among processes in Linux, such as CPU time, the file system, memory, and network resources, can be partitioned and securely assigned to distinct VServers. Unlike platform virtualization, however, VServer instances are limited to the Linux operating system.

Xen™

Xen is the dominant open-source platform virtualization system. Developed as an academic project at the Cambridge University Computer Systems Lab in 2003, Xen is now a community-sponsored project with commercial support and offerings from Citrix systems. Both free and for-license versions are available.

Xen and other platform virtualization solutions can be used in either a symmetric or asymmetric organization. A symmetric virtual platform is one that hosts multiple instances of the same operating system version. An asymmetric virtual platform, on the other hand, may run a variety of guest operating system types.

Figure 15.9 illustrates an asymmetric Xen system that, somewhat akin to the ETA prototype, uses a lightweight packet-processing system in one guest operating system to offload network processing tasks form the operating system instance that implements an intrusion detection application.

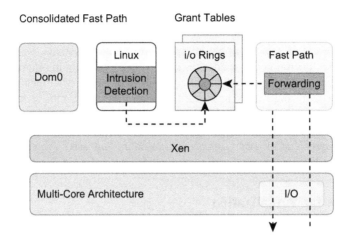

FIGURE 15.9

An Asymmetric Xen System.

As indicated in Figure 15.9, this type of arrangement makes the most sense when the underlying CPU supports not only virtualization, but also multiple CPU cores. We should also note that in Xen, Dom0 (short for Domain 0) refers to the management OS for the platform. Such a system needs multiple CPU cores to enable parallel operation, hardware support for virtualization to keep operating system performance at native levels, as well as carefully crafted I/O solutions (illustrated here as I/O rings) to enable high-performance communication between operating systems.

Xenomai

Xenomai is a Linux-based real-time operating system and virtualization platform. Linux is not a hard real-time operating system, as it does not guarantee that a task will meet strict deadlines. The kernel can suspend a task when its time slice has completed, and it can remain suspended for an arbitrarily long time (for example, when an interrupt is getting serviced).

The goal with Xenomai is to achieve real-time performance without throwing away the benefits of Linux. To achieve this goal, Xenomai adds a level of indirection between normal Linux and the underlying hardware. In particular, a small real-time kernel is inserted between Linux instances and the underlying hardware so that real-time processes can be scheduled in a real-time manner, while all others are scheduled in the typical Linux fashion. This organization is illustrated in Figure 15.10.

The real-time scheduler of the real-time kernel treats the standard Linux kernel as an idle task, which when given a chance to run executes its own scheduler to schedule normal Linux processes. But since the real-time kernel runs at a higher priority, the normal Linux processes can at any time be preempted by a real-time task. Interrupt management is another factor handled by the real-time kernel. When an interrupt gets triggered during the execution of a real-time task, it is first received by the real-time kernel and stored. When the real-time kernel is done, the interrupt is handed over to the standard Linux kernel. If there is an associated real-time handler for the interrupt, it is executed by the real-time kernel. Otherwise, if there are no more real-time tasks to run, the stored interrupt is passed to normal

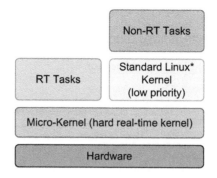

FIGURE 15.10

Xenomai.

Linux. Different mechanisms are used to pass the interrupts from real-time kernel to normal Linux kernel. Xenomai uses an interrupt pipeline from the ADEOS project.

Additionally, Xenomai supports what they refer to as a nano-kernel approach. While similar to a microkernel in that it also provides a real-time kernel layer between the standard Linux kernel and hardware, it effectively operates as a hardware abstraction layer that is capable of multiple real-time and non-real-time Linux operating systems. This organization is illustrated in Figure 15.11.

Perhaps most impressively, Xenomai also provides APIs for creating real-time tasks, timers, and synchronization objects. It also emulates popular real-time operating system APIs through an abstraction they call *skins* to ease the porting of existing real-time applications, including those that that use the POSIX interface, VxWorks, and others. The net result is a system that enables real-time functionality in a Linux-based, virtualized environment. Figure 15.12 depicts in a more specific and less conceptual manner the relationship between skins, the Xenomai core, and hardware.

The Xenomai core is an abstract RTOS that provides operating system resources and generic building blocks to support different RTOS interfaces in the form of skins. Xenomai uses the ADEOS real-time nano-kernel to handle real-time interrupt dispatching.

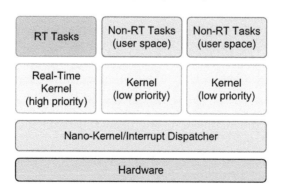

FIGURE 15.11

Xenomai Nano-Kernel Approach.

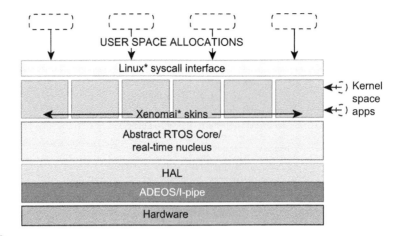

FIGURE 15.12

Skins, the Xenomai core, and Hardware.

SUMMARY

This chapter has introduced the concepts of multiprocessing and virtualization. These concepts may not have substantial deployment in embedded systems beyond networking platforms, but the scalability and manageability characteristics are so compelling relative to the alternatives that it requires neither creativity nor bravery to predict that most forms of future embedded systems will feature both.

The impact of these trends on software organization is substantial. The overriding requirement is for software to be organized in a distributed fashion that can scale across processes and/or machine instances.

Developing an Embedded System

Example Designs

At the risk of this chapter being perishable and out of date before you read it, we felt that at least one chapter in the book should go into a specific embedded design using a specific processor. For this purpose, the Intel® Atom™ Processor E6XX Series SOCs are used, with platform expansion through an interface device known as a platform controller hub.

As an embedded systems programmer, you should be able to read schematics for the platform you are operating on. You probably don't need to understand the detailed clocking or power control aspects of the design, but at a minimum you must understand the platform at a block level: which interfaces are used to connect devices, which GPIO pin is connected to the LED, and so on. It's always preferable to be able to refer to the schematics rather than high-level documents describing the platform; these can contain errors, and reading schematics is like looking at source code—it's unlikely that it does not represent what you are looking at in reality (ignoring any post-fabrication changes). In this chapter we outline the high-level feature sets of a number of components in the system. The intent is to call out capabilities that you as an embedded system programmer should be cognizant of. In many design cases you will be expected to understand the subtleties in the capabilities of a device, not just the first-order data sheet bullet list.

INTEL ATOM E6XX SERIES PLATFORMS

The Intel Atom–based E6XX Series processors come in a number of SKUs. This is quite common in the embedded field. Manufacturers create a number of devices in a family. Each device in a family is usually based on the same CPU but at a range of frequencies, and often different family members provide specific I/O or acceleration capabilities. The family usually starts off with a slower speed processor, adding features and performance as the range extends. This is also the case for the E6XX family of devices, the details of which are below. As a system designer or a software engineer providing input into the design, it's a good idea to ensure that there is a future scalability option on the platform, particularly in terms of CPU performance, because this can often be updated with a pin-compatible device. *Pin-compatible* refers to the fact that all the connections on the SOC are the same between two devices (electrical compatibly is also inferred).

The capabilities of the E6XX series devices are the following:

- One Intel Atom Core: 600 MHz, 1 GHz, 1.3 GHz, and 1.6 GHz
- Two-wide instruction decode and in-order execution
- 32-kB four-way Level 1 instruction cache and 24-kB six-way Level 1 data cache
- 512-kB Level 2 cache, eight-way
- Two hardware threads
- Primary expansion via PCI Express™ (PCIe): Gen 1.0a 4 x 1 lane

445

- Memory speed DDR2 800, maximum 2 GB, 1 channel, 32-bit interface, supports 1 or 2 ranks, proactive page-closing policies to close unused pages, supports partial writes through data mask pins
- CPU virtualization support: Intel Virtualization Technology (Intel VT–x)
- Advanced power management features including Enhanced Intel SpeedStep Technology
- Deep Power Down Technology (C6)
- Intel Streaming SIMD Extension 2 and 3 (Intel SSE2 and Intel SSE3) and Supplemental Streaming SIMD Extensions 3 (SSSE3)
- Lithography: 45 nm
- Available in commercial and industrial temperature ranges
- The datasheet for the part is available at http://download.intel.com/embedded/processor/datasheet/324208.pdf.

Architecture Overview

Throughout this book, we have provided detailed descriptions of many of the capabilities instantiated in the SOC. In this section we briefly describe the parameters of the interfaces on the E6XX series devices.

The SOC shown in Figure 16.1 is characterized by having an integrated memory controller, integrated 2D/3D graphics, dual display, and video encoder/decoder capabilities. It also includes all the required elements to be platform compatible with previous Intel architecture platforms (specifically, interrupt controllers, timers, watchdog timer, real-time clock, ACPI control, and so on). The platform can run all traditional IA-32 operating systems (with the inclusion of the appropriate device drivers).

As with all Intel platforms, I/O coherence is maintained with the processor caches. The internal coherent fabric ensures coherence between all I/O transactions to and from memory and the CPU(s) caches.

The integrated 2D/3D graphic engine performs pixel shading and vertex shading within a single hardware accelerator. The processing of pixels is deferred until they are determined to be visible, which minimizes access to memory and improves render performance. The graphics engine and display controller all use system memory (known as stolen memory). The following lists the key features of the 3D graphics engine:

- Two-pipe scalable unified shader implementation
- Fill rate: two pixels per clock
- Vertex rate: one triangle 15 clocks (transform only)
- Vertex/triangle ratio average = 1 vtx/tri, peak 0.5 vtx/tri
- Texture maximum size = 2048 x 2048
- Programmable 4x multisampling anti-aliasing (MSAA)
- Rotated grid
- Optimized memory efficiency using multi-level cache architecture
- Shading engine key features:
- Unified programming model
- Multithreaded with four concurrently running threads
- Zero-cost swapping in/out of threads
- Cached program execution model—unlimited program size

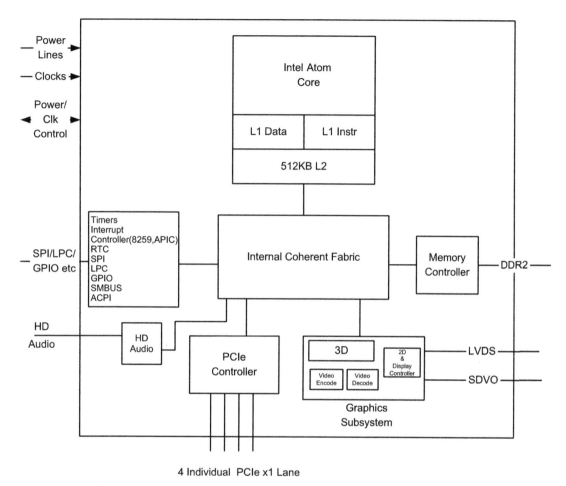

FIGURE 16.1

E6XX Series SOC.

- Dedicated pixel processing instructions
- Dedicated vertex processing instructions
- SIMD pipeline supporting operations

The hardware video decoder supports MPEG2, MPEG4, VC1, WMV9, and H.264 (main, baseline at L3 and high-profile level 4.0/4.1)[†], while the video encoder engine supports MPEG4, H.264, and H.263. It supports LVDS and serial DVO display ports permitting simultaneous independent operation of two displays.

The SOC supports a high-definition audio interface. The interface can support up to four multi-channel audio streams. Each channel within the audio stream can support a 32-bit sample depth, with a sample rate up to 192 kHz.

The SMBus host interface allows the processor to communicate with SMBus slaves. This interface is also compatible with most I2C™ devices.

An SPI interface is provided and is used to boot the processor. The BIOS/firmware for the processor must be stored in an SPI-attached flash device.

The SOC has 14 general-purpose I/O pins (GPIOs). Five of these are powered by the core power rail and are turned off during sleep mode (S3 and higher). Nine of these GPIOs are powered by the suspend power well and remained active during S3. All the GPIOs in the suspend power well can be used to wake the system from the suspend-to-RAM (S3) state. The GPIO pins can also be configured to generate an interrupt to the CPU.

A JTAG interface is provided for debug using a JTAG debugger, as described in Chapter 17.

A key expansion feature is the provision of PCIe interface(s) to expand the capabilities of the SOC. It provides four x1 lane PCI Express root ports supporting the PCI Express Base Specification, Revision 1.0a. The processor does not support the "ganging" of PCIe ports. The four x1 PCIe ports operate as four independent PCIe controlled links.

Most of the internal SOC blocks that need to be visible to software are presented logically as PCI devices on PCI bus zero. They are known as *root complex integrated endpoints*. Figure 16.2 shows the enumeration of devices within the SOC, along with possible devices enumerated from the external PCIe buses.

Platform Controller Hub(s)

A key philosophy of the E6XX service devices is the ability to extend the platform through industry standard PCIe interfaces. At the time of writing there are a number of expansion devices, targeted at differing use cases from different suppliers. The intent here is not to replicate the data sheet but to call out some of the key attributes of the interfaces.

Intel Platform Controller Hub EG20T

The Intel Platform Controller Hub is developed as a generic device for use in general embedded cases. Its features include the following:

- Peripheral Component Interconnect (PCI)-Express, the interface to the host processor
- Universal Serial Bus (USB) Host, Interface (EHCI) (1.0) and Open Host, Controller Interface (OHCI) 1.0a, six ports (two USB 2.0 hosts; three ports for each host); provides USB port that supports high-speed (480 Mbps), full-speed (12 Mbps), and low-speed (1.5 Mbps) operations
- Universal Serial Bus (USB) device, complies with USB 2.0 and USB 1.1 protocols. Up to four IN and four OUT physical endpoints (EP0-3), which can be tied to different interfaces and configurations to achieve logical endpoints
- Gigabit Ethernet Media Access Controller (GbE MAC); conforms to IEEE802.3
- Serial Advanced Technology Attachment (SATA), SATA 1.5 Gbps Generation 1 speed and 3 Gbps Generation 2 speed, two ports (two ports with one AHCI SATA controller)
- Secure Digital (SD) host controller, conforms to Secure Digital Host Controller (SDHC) speed class 6, two SD host controllers; one port for each host), SD bus transfer mode (1-bit/4-bit/high-speed), MMC transfer mode (1-bit/4-bit/8-bit/high-speed)

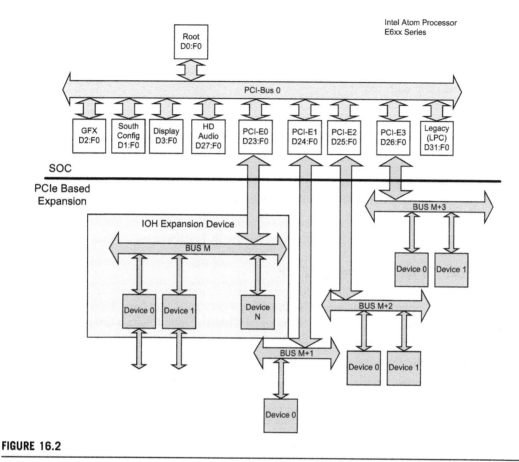

FIGURE 16.2

PCI Logical View.

- IEEE1588 block (clock synchronization), provides the hardware assist logic for achieving precision clock synchronization, conforms with the IEEE1588-2008 standard, supported on Ethernet and CAN interface
- Serial Peripheral Interface (SPI), up to 5 Mbps, bus-master function (includes a shared DMA), performs full-duplex data transfer, operates as master mode or slave mode
- Controller Area Network (CAN), CAN protocol version 2.0B Active, bit rate up to 1 Mbps, 32 message objects, priority control by each message object, detection/identification of bit error, stuff error, CRC error, form error
- Inter-Integrated Circuit (I2C) bus controller, Philips I2C Bus Specification 2.1 conformant controller; Standard mode (100 kHz) and Fast mode (400 kHz); the I2C transmitter and receiver support both master and slave devices
- One Universal Asynchronous Receiver-Transmitter (UART) with an 8-wire interface; 256-byte transmit and receive FIFOs, interoperable with 16550, modem control signals are configured

with CTS (Clear To Send), RTS (Request To Send), DSR (Data Set Ready), DTR (Data Terminal Ready), RI (Ring Indicator), and DCD (Data Carrier Detect), supports the following programmable serial interface characteristics, maximum baud rate: 4 Mbps

- Three UARTs with a 2-wire interface, 64-byte transmit and receive FIFOs, maximum baud rate: 1 Mbps, interoperable with 16550
- GPIO: 12-bit general-purpose I/O ports. Input or output can be specified for each port. Interrupts can be used for all of the bits. Interrupt mask and interrupt mode (level/edge, positive logic/negative logic) can be set for all bits. GPIO0-7 correspond to WAKE-ON (GPIO8-11 does not support wake features)
- JTAG; supports boundary scan mode
- Serial ROM I/F; supports access to the option ROM of each function, loading of a parameter required for initialization of each function (GbE MAC and SATA AHCI initialization), SPI interface

Figure 16.3 shows the allocation of functions to PCIe devices/functions.

A number of other vendors provide application-centric PCH devices.

OKI Semiconductor ML7213 and ML7213V

OKI Semiconductor has created a device for general applications, for example, in vehicle infotainment. The standard interfaces support PCI Express 1.1 x1, USB 2.0 host, USB 2.0 host/device switchable (only with ML7213), SD host (SDIO), serial ATA II, gigabit Ethernet (MAC), UARTs, SPI, I2C, I2S, and GPIO. The application-specific capabilities are the following:

- Time Division Multiplex interface (supports Multichannel Audio Serial Port, a popular interface used to connect to digital signal processors)
- Media LB™ (only with ML7213), interface to Media Oriented Systems Transport (MOST; http://www.mostcooperation.com) physical interfaces
- Security acceleration: 3DES, AES, SHA1/265/MD5 (acoustic/line echo, noise canceller)
- BT656/RAW video capture input
- SDVO input with digital RGB output

ST Microelectronics

ST Microelectronics has created an in-vehicle infotainment targeted system. The device will include automotive targeted capabilities such as Controller Area Network (CAN), Ethernet AVB (audio video bridging), and Media Oriented Systems Transport. The device also supports the traditional interfaces such as USB and SATA.

CAN is a robust slow-speed network used in most vehicles; it is used to exchange messages between the many embedded controllers found in modern vehicles. A high-performance in-vehicle network is needed to exchange multimedia content between devices such as the head unit (the primary infotainment display visible to the driver). There are many special considerations required in the automotive environment and networks based on Ethernet AVB, a set of IEEE 802.1 standards for distributing audio and video over an Ethernet network. MOST, a high-speed network (25/50 and 150 Mbps) over an optical ring carrying both synchronous and best effort traffic, and Firewire™ are deployed. The key attribute of these networks for use in audio and video distribution is quality of service, all of which are addressed.

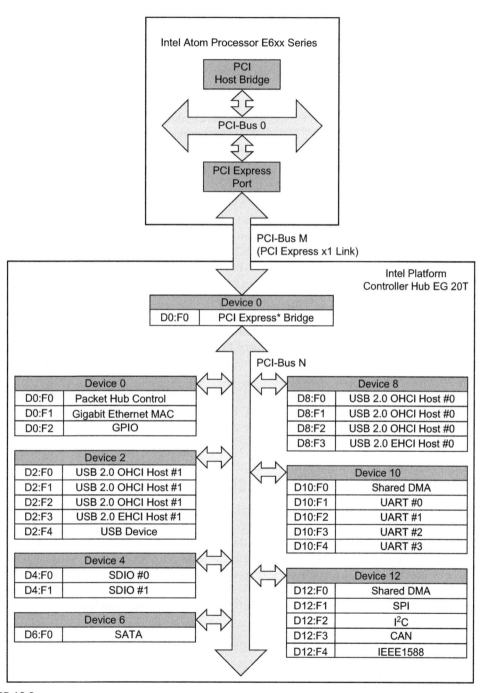

FIGURE 16.3

EG20T Platform Controller Hub.

Discrete Device Expansion

You are not required to use a Platform Controller Hub. Given that the Intel Atom SOC provides standard PCIe interfaces, you can add almost any PCIe discrete device to the platform. For example, a SATA controller could be added with a Silicon Image SiI3132 SATALink PCI Express to a 2-Port Serial ATA II Host Controller. The devices can be soldered down on the platform or added as an add-in card through standard interfaces such as Mini PCI or PCI connectors. In fact, adding a PCIe-based module is the most typical mechanism for adding wireless capability to the platform. The development of a wireless module requires a specialized wireless skill set that may not be the core competency of the team developing the embedded system. The purchase of a wireless module significantly eases and reduces the risks of adding a wireless capability to an embedded platform.

FPGA Expansion

Most FPGA devices include PCIe interface capability at this point; you can add specific capabilities via FPGA should you need to. This is a very common expansion option used in embedded systems. Intel has released a part with a pre-integrated FPGA. The devices were formerly code-named Stellarton and are released as the E6x5C series, shown in Figure 16.4. You can, of course, use any discrete FPGA that supports PCIe. The device consists of an E6XX services Intel Atom processor along with an Altera FPGA.

The FPGA contains a PCIe hard IP block. A *hard IP block* is a block on the FPGA developed without using any of the configurable resources within the device. It is called hard IP because the functions cannot be modified. This provides the PCIe endpoint and is discovered by the PCIe enumeration process. The FPGA logic behind the endpoint block provides the configurable expansion capability. In some cases you may have a bandwidth requirement that exceeds that provided by a single PCIe x1 lane; then the programmable blocks can be attached to the processor via the second PCIe link to the FPGA. This requires that you use a soft IP PCI endpoint. The endpoint uses up some of the configurable elements in the FPGA to provide the connectivity.

MULTI-RADIO COMMUNICATIONS DESIGN

Connectivity to a device is an increasingly important aspect of embedded systems. In many cases the device has a specific embedded function and connectivity is used to provision and manage the device remotely. In many other embedded applications the purpose of the device is to mediate communications between devices and networks. A simple example of such a device is the residential gateway or wireless router in your home. This section describes the hardware and software design of a machine-to-machine (M2M) gateway design. The design has a number of communications interfaces and the associated software stacks to route between the different communication modalities.

Hardware Platform

The reference platform must communicate between 3G/4G modules. The capabilities can be provided by a using a pre-certified 3G/4G module. Having the module pre-certified can save time because certification by the appropriate certification bodies can take quite some time. The module selected for

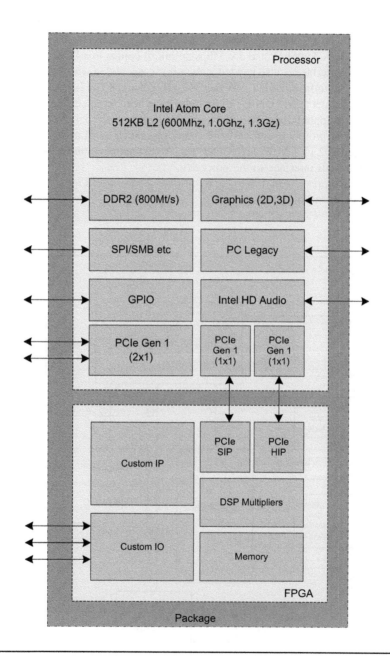

FIGURE 16.4

E6x5C Series (Formerly Code-Named Stellarton) Package Partitioning.

this example is an Ericsson F5521gw module. The module offers high-speed connectivity with HSPA evolution speeds: 21 Mbps downlink and 5.7 Mbps uplink. It comes in a PCI Express mini-card form factor. A local wireless interface is also needed, and in this case, both a wired Ethernet interface (from the PCH) and a Wi-Fi™ interface (which provides 802.11b/g/n and 802.11a through a Mini PCIe Wi-Fi card, in our example, an Intel 4964AGN Wi-Fi module) have been selected. The platform also requires a radio for local sensor applications. The platform requires an 802.15.4 WPAN transceiver, which supports a wide range of protocols and network topologies, such as 6LoPAN, Wireless HART, and ZigBee, using a unique 802.15.4 MAC layer interface. An example of such a radio is the TI CC2530. The device provides a USB interface to the processor.

All other platform features are similar to the traditional capabilities. Figure 16.5 shows an example of a multi-radio communications gateway.

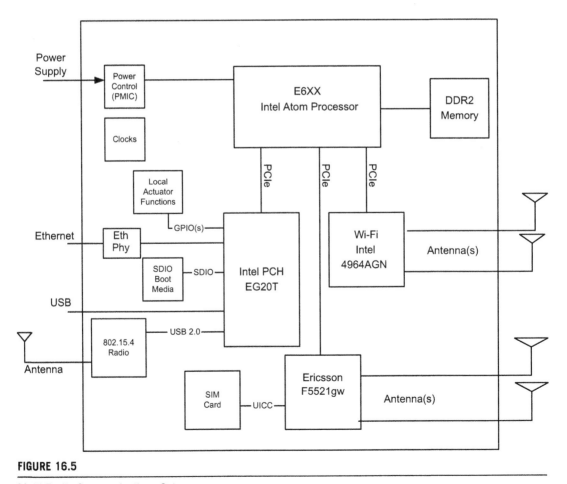

FIGURE 16.5

Multi-Radio Communications Gateway.

The platform includes a 3G/4G wireless module, and as such is using licensed spectrum. In order to use this wireless module, a subscription is required. In the case of 3G/4G standards that are defined by the 3FPP organization you must have a subscriber identity module. This SIM takes the form of a Universal Integrated Circuit Card. The UICC smart card contains a CPU, ROM, EEPROM, and I/O. In mobile phones, it usually takes the form of a removable SIM card. In embedded platforms, the SIM function is provided by embedded IC (such as an Infineon SLM76). This device can be soldered down on to the platform.

The radios often use a number of antennas to support better, more reliable connectivity. In some cases the antennas are used for diversity, and the strongest signal will be selected from the appropriate antenna. In newer systems multiple-input and multiple-output (MIMO) schemes are used, where multiple antennae at the transmitter and receiver are used to significantly improve the performance and range of the radio.

Yet another consideration can apply if multiple radios are sharing the same wireless spectrum. This can often be the case in the unlicensed 2.4-GHz spectrum, where Wi-Fi, Bluetooth, DECT, Zigbee, and many other radios operate. In many cases the protocols are designed to gracefully degrade (each other), but the spectrum is shared. It is a good idea to read the relevant papers on Wi-Fi and Bluetooth) and Wi-Fi and Zigbee to better understand coexistence issues for the shared spectrum.

Software Platform

The Linux platform offers an excellent baseline to start development of a multi-radio gateway platform. Linux has a rich networking infrastructure that is covered in Chapter 12. Starting with the device drivers, device drivers need to be obtained for all the required radios. This has become much easier in recent times, as vendors have come to realize the importance of Linux for such systems.

Device Drivers

The status of Linux drivers is an ever-moving target. In some cases you can only get the drivers directly from the radio module provider: in others the code is staged in a project repository on a server such as SourceForge, and ideally the driver has already been upstreamed and is part of the kernel trees. If you have flexibility in device selection, it's recommended that you identify the quality and support and distribution of the wireless drivers before selecting the hardware—a piece of hardware without a driver is not much use.

The Wi-Fi radio is supported and upstreamed in the kernel at drivers/net/wireless/iwlwifi/. More details can be found at http://intellinuxwireless.org/.

The Ericsson F5521gw drivers are (at the time of writing) in the kernel but also use a staging area at SourceForge. The project is known as Mobile Broadband Modules.

The availability of 802.15.4 drivers is a little less mature then the other subsystems but they are being actively developed. The IEEE paper "How to become an IEEE 802.15.4 expert" is an excellent introduction to IEEE 802.15.4.

The device selected above to provide the 802.15.4 radio capability is the Texas Instruments CC2531, which provides a USB device interface that is presented to the host as a standard USB Communication Device Class (CDC) capability. As such, the standard Linux CDC Class driver provides the serial abstraction to the devices. The ZigBee stack itself is an open source stack such as FreakZ (http://www.freaklabs.org).

Network Stack

The networking stack is a critical element of a gateway function. The stack supports bridging (at Layer 2) between Wi-Fi and Ethernet attached devices. For packets targeted at the gateway, the packets are routed up the TCP/IP stack. The stack can also perform IP routing and network address translation for packets to and from the WAN (3G/4G) interface.

Host Access Point

You may wish to allow 802.11 wireless devices to connect to the gateway. This can be supported in two ways; the first is through a peer-peer connection, but it is more typically done by supporting access point mode in the gateway. The HostAP module allows many Wi-Fi modules to be configured in access point (infrastructure) mode. This allows appropriately configured Wi-Fi–based devices to connect to the gateway.

Connection Management

It is useful to provide a mechanism to manage the connection on the platform. A number of open source projects support the configuration aspects of wireless connections and maintain such communications. The connman (http://www.connman.net) project is one such project, and network manager (http://projects.gnome.org/NetworkManager/) is another.

Security is an important aspect of any platform that provides remote access capability. It best to use OpenVPN to secure communication between the device and any remote user.

802.15.4 Stacks

There are a number of different protocols that all use the 802.15.4 layer: 8LoPAN, Ipv6 Over Low Power Wireless Personal Area Networks, and Zigbee. At the time of writing, the 802.15.4 stack development, device support, and upper layer support are still an active area of development within the kernel.

Web Server

A web server process is a straightforward mechanism to communicate with the gateway remotely. The platform must run a web server. Apache is a mainstream web server that is widely deployed; however, it may be too resource heavy for embedded systems. There are many servers targeted at embedded platforms, such as `lighttpd`. The ability for a server to support CGI or PHP scripts is important because it allows a simple mechanism to convert actions performed on the web page into actions on the gateway device itself. The support for https is also a key consideration to allow secure communications with the web server.

Application

The routing functions of packets will take place automatically by the Linux infrastructure once set up. The setup can be controlled by scripts and managed by the web server though a component such as `webmin` (with the appropriate plug-ins). If the application must translate between commands on the web interface into messages directed toward PAN devices, then it is likely that the application must mediate and translate between these domains. The translation function can be written in a native application using C, or as often the case, in a scripting language. The language Lua is popular for such embedded control applications.

Figure 16.6 shows the some of the key components used to create a web-managed multi-radio gateway device.

In many cases, a large number of embedded devices (as in millions) need to be managed remotely. To facilitate large-scale remote management, a vast range of web-based management agents are available that can be overlaid on such a platform. The traditional 3G/4G device management is carried out through OMA-DM standards defined by the Open Mobile Alliance (OMA). In wire-based applications such as DSL modems or cable set-top boxes, the Broadband Forum Technical Report 069,

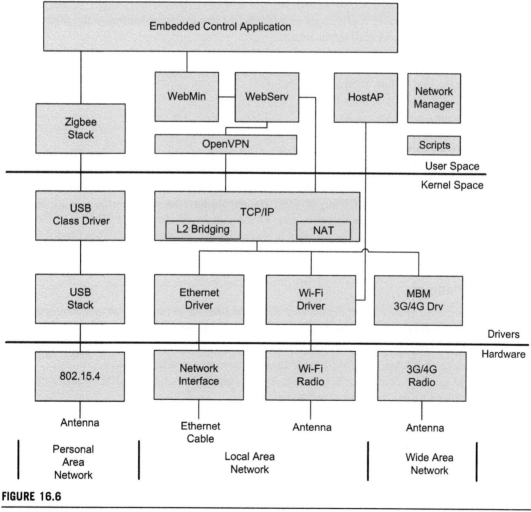

FIGURE 16.6

Multi-Radio Gateway Components.

known as the TR-069 specification, defines the protocol and mechanisms to manage customer devices by the infrastructure providers.

MULTIMEDIA DESIGN

Many embedded systems are convergent with consumer devices. High-resolution displays with touch control are now commonplace; examples can be found in in-vehicle infotainment systems, home automation/security systems, and media phones. A media phone is a cross between a traditional phone and a tablet. The attributes of these reference designs are similar to many embedded devices. Let's first outline some high-level features for the platform:

1. Support for downloadable applications or widgets to extend the capabilities of the platform
2. Support for calendar and mail applications
3. Playback of high-quality media from local and remote streaming from local and Internet sources
4. Web browsing support
5. Enable intent applications such as Pandora
6. Provide DECT-based telephony handset
7. Support voice over IP telephony
8. Video telephony
9. Local speakerphone support
10. Voice mail messaging service

This is just an overview; in reality, a product in this class would have a product requirements document (PRD). This is the starting point for any project; you should have an idea of what you are building before you start. In many cases you will also integrate through the design so the PRD is an active living artifact that you update as you go. The first step is to identify the hardware capabilities needed to meet the high-level feature set.

Hardware Platform

The first item to select is the base line processor. Since the Intel Atom processor is the reference in this book, the design will be based on the E6XX service device, along with the general embedded PCH (EG20T). This will provide the following:

- Core processor (Intel Atom); offers a large range of software to select from
- Display and graphics controller; high-resolution display with sophisticated 3D transitions along with alpha blending are common expectations
- Hardware decode engine; smooth playback of high-definition streams are computationally expensive, and the use of a hardware decode pipeline makes it possible to free up CPU cycles for other aspects of the application
- Hardware video encode engine; video encode can be even more costly (in terms of CPU computes) than video decode. The video encode can be used to encode a captured video stream from a local camera
- Mass storage interfaces; SDIO or SATA can be used to provide OS, application, and data storage for the platform

- Ethernet connectivity; it is beneficial to offer a physical connectivity option to the design; in some environments the use of Wi-Fi to provide telephony services does not work well (particularly in cases of interference or a loaded network)
- HD audio interface; can be used to locally connect speakers and microphones

The platform still requires a touchscreen interface, a DECT, and Wi-Fi interfaces.

A touchscreen interface chip depends on the selection of touchscreen technology; for consumer-oriented cases, capacitive touchscreens are commonplace. The touch controller interfaces to the core processor via the SPI or I2C interface. This example employs the SPI interface using the ST Microelectronics STMT07 S-Touch™ FingerTip multi-touch capacitive touchscreen controller. The recognition of gestures (particularly multi-touch) on the touch device is often carried out by the controller, so you should consider the features supported prior to selection.

The DECT controller can be attached via USB or SPI. We have chosen a USB controller to allow both data and voice to be transferred to the DECT handler. We don't go into the DECT handset design at this point. When using USB we must ensure that the voice is carried over isochronous endpoints to ensure low-latency deterministic voice data transfer. In some designs, SPI may be a better choice.

We also need some simple push button controls for some aspects; these are attached via GPIO pins.

Putting it all together gives the diagram shown in Figure 16.7.

The following section will delve into the software component selection.

Software Platform

In many modern software development challenges you will not be developing the entire system software from scratch. In fact, that is a very poor use of your time. The objective should be to reuse as much preexisting software as possible and focus on what differentiates your particular product. This reused software could take the form of open-source software, driver or enabling software from the different silicon vendors, or purchased software components.

The software within the platform can be broken down into layers within the overall software design:

- Core platform software, operating system, and all associated device drivers, power management, file systems, and display system.
- Platform middleware and frameworks, the collection of libraries and frameworks that can be used to build higher-level applications, for example, a media framework such as GStreamer, telephony solutions such as Telepathy, optimized libraries for DSP voice processing, and 3D/2D APIs. An interprocess communication (IPC) framework is also critical in developing and coordinating the activities of the higher-level applications; DBUS provides such a capability.
- The overall user experience is generated by a number of separate applications, each written to support a specific feature/user experience. For example, a media player is separated and distinct from the telephone dialer. It is very useful to use a Model View Controller (MVC) design pattern when developing applications that are run on such a system. For the media player example, the application should consist of a separate media playback engine that takes care of rendering/playback of media on the required outputs, while taking all control input via

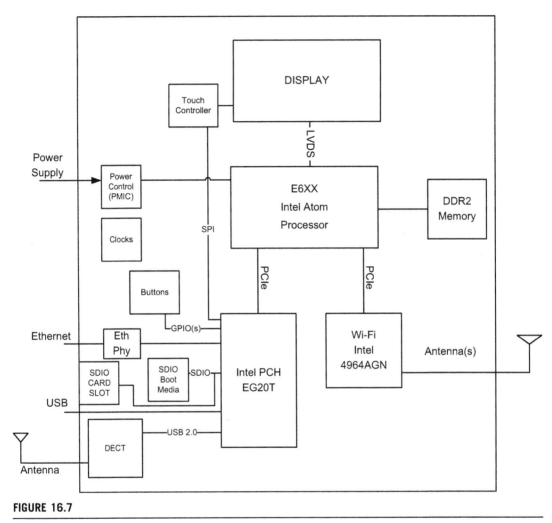

FIGURE 16.7

Media Phone Reference.

an IPC mechanism. The user interface of the media player can then be written and developed (personalized/skinned) separately. It allows for sophisticated use-case behavior to be integrated into the overall experience—for example, the telephone stack can pause the media when an incoming call occurs.

- Home screen and application coordinator. At least one primary application should take ownership of the home screen; it will contain a mechanism to launch applications. In many cases portions of the screen will continue to be owned by the home application (for example, a banner).

Figure 16.8 shows the components selected and their relative positions in the stack.

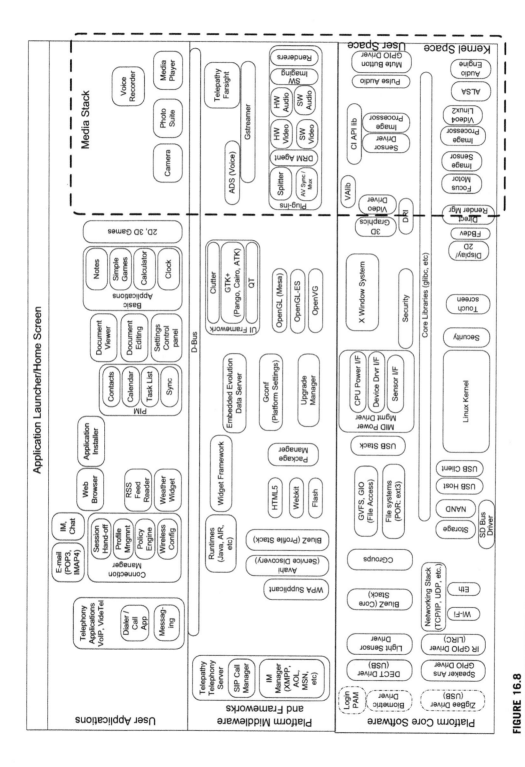

FIGURE 16.8

Multimedia Software Platform (Based on Linux).

Figure 16.8 is an extreme simplification of the overall system; it can take considerable effort to select the capabilities and integrate them into an overall solution.

Figure 16.9 shows a high-level overview of the audio path interactions in the system. The incoming audio samples are captured from the DECT device driver and then routed through the Linux ALSA and PulseAudio frameworks. The application routes the audio samples to the telephony/VOIP stack where the packets are encoded using a codec such as G.729a. Once encoded, the samples are sent to a real-time protocol (RTP, a transport protocol for real-time applications—IEFT RFC 3550) stack to be encapsulated in packets to be streamed toward the Internet VoIP service provider (such as Vonage in the United States).

As you can see, the system is built up from a large number of components with complex interactions. There is a truly staggering amount of code that can be reused in the creation of sophisticated embedded systems. This is particularly true for IA-32-based systems because the vast majority of the code has already been targeted to IA-32 systems, albeit desk/notebook/netbook–based systems. Having said that, many of the packages are also validated on other CPU architectures.

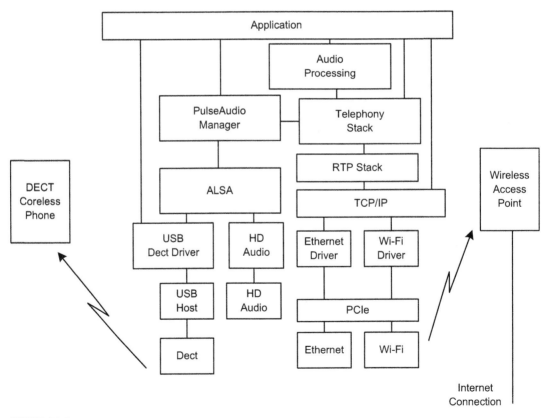

FIGURE 16.9

Audio Data Path from DECT to VOIP Interface.

MODULAR REFERENCES

A variety of modular form factors are used in embedded systems. Such systems define a key interface connector between the compute board and the expansion or application specific board. The compute boards are offered with a variety of CPU configurations, which allows the embedded system designer to upgrade the capabilities of the system without a significant redesign of the application-specific design each time. There are a number of such connector standards, two examples being Com Express (http://www.picmg.org/) and QSeven.

The Inforce computing (http://www.inforcecomputing.com) E6XX series module is a good example of the type of module available. Figure 16.10 shows the module break down.

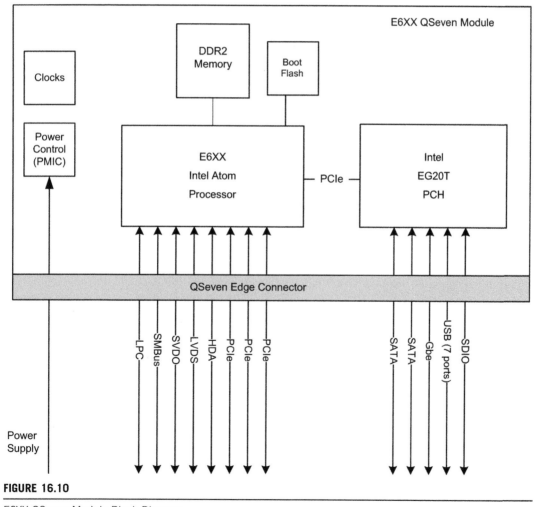

FIGURE 16.10

E6XX QSeven Module Block Diagram.

The platform is then expanded using various base boards. Because the connector is standard, different carrier boards can be used.

Given that the board shown in Figure 16.10 exposes many of the standard Intel architecture platform interfaces, the platform just requires a BIOS/firmware image (provided) and will boot a standard Linux, Windows, or RTOS as needed.

SUMMARY

There is such a broad range of embedded applications, it is impossible for any chapter or book to do justice to the entire landscape. In this chapter we have touched upon just a tiny subset of such embedded platforms, attempting to select some key attributes of modern embedded systems.

It is key as an embedded systems developer to understand the system at a component level and to integrate the subsystems into an overall functional system. In many cases this involves device and component selection. When doing so it is important to also consider the software availability or development costs for devices/components selected. In many cases, the required device drivers are available from the device provider; however, it is often the case in embedded systems that no such driver is available and you must develop it yourself. All such considerations should be incorporated into the overall system design.

Platform Debug

17

Once you eliminate the impossible, whatever remains, no matter how improbable, must be the truth.
—**Sir Arthur Conan Doyle**

The rapid pace of innovation in the development of embedded systems can be exhilarating, but it is not without its consequences for developers. Balancing the thrill of working with new processors, sensors, and circuit boards is the fact that new hardware, like new software, is often buggy. Moreover, new hardware platforms and system software have the unique characteristic of failing in ways that stable systems do not. Application-level software developers targeting general-purpose computers are not typically accustomed to hardware or system-level faults; when they debug errors, they know the problem lies within the bounds of their application development environment. Not so with embedded systems.

When developing an embedded system, it is highly likely that most aspects of the system will be reused from a previous one. This is important because developing new software on new hardware can be a challenging task, because when things break there are many possible culprits. When some portions of the system are stable and known to function, whether it is software, like the OS kernel or a previous device driver implementation, or hardware, such as a circuit board layout that is known to be correctly implemented, these likely correct components can be used to help eliminate debug targets and hence reduce the subsets of the system that must be systematically examined for correct function.

In this chapter, we will explore a process for debugging an embedded platform. As we will see, platform debug is more art than well-defined process, but after working through the chapter, you should be capable of diagnosing and identifying the most important classes of errors that, for example, keep embedded systems from booting correctly to an operating system.

To do so, we will first discuss a perspective and methodology that form the foundation for debugging an embedded platform. Then, we will discuss the tools and chipset features that aid and enable debugging. Finally, we will consider the platform debug process in detail.

DEBUGGING NEW PLATFORMS

Suppose you are one of a small number of embedded systems engineers who have formed a startup company around your new embedded device concept. The team has completed its first circuit board design, and a fully built-out board—including the Intel® Atom™ processor and all the burnt-in components—has been delivered from the third-party vendor, and it is time for first boot. It is a Linux-based platform, and the system has been designed to boot from a USB device. The team assembles, the

465

USB memory stick is inserted, power is turned on, and … nothing. No flashing LEDs, no indicators of any kind. The team was expecting a celebration, but got nothing but inert disappointment. What's wrong? Is the problem serious or trivial? How will you know?

Of course, in this fictional scenario and in every other real-world platform debug effort, there are an extraordinary number of possible causes. Was the power supply plugged in? Was memory inserted and properly seated? Is some component configured for debugging rather than operation? Is there a short on the circuit board? The fully enumerated list would be a very long one, indeed. Rather than working with a flat checklist, however, we will follow a process, one that is designed to systematically identify what works and what is faulty or misconfigured.

Before jumping in, it will be constructive to consider your mindset and perspective as you debug. Debugging is an open-ended activity, in which neither the ultimate explanation nor the time that will be needed to find it is known in advance. What is certain, however, is that you must ultimately find the problem. Given this, for most it is highly productive to adopt a positive, inquisitive mindset as you begin debugging. Not only will this make you feel better as you work, but it will make you better at what you are trying to do. Debugging, whether at the platform level or the application level, requires a careful, systematic effort to reduce possible causes until the problem is identified. Debugging in frustration or in haste is not conducive to careful, systematic work. So, before you start debugging, make sure you begin with the right frame of mind: be calm, systematic, and curious.

A PROCESS FOR DEBUGGING A NEW PLATFORM

The modify-compile-debug pattern so familiar to programmers is of little use when your platform will not boot. This traditional practice is a productive one, because with each change there is a high probability that any problems observed in the newly compiled program will be related to the most recent changes. When a system will not boot, while there is a possibility that only a small number of changes have been made that help to locate the source of the failure (that is, "all we changed was the power supply!"), but it is more likely that trouble with a brand new embedded system cannot *a priori* be confined to a small set of locations.

To tackle the search systematically, you can rely upon a structure process like the one presented in this chapter. The process can be characterized in three high-level steps:

1. Visual examination. Look at the system. Verify that external cords, cables, and I/O devices are attached. Remove the cover and examine the circuit board for damage and properly seated components.
2. Hardware evaluation. Are the hardware components, such as power supplies, voltage regulators, and integrated circuits, in their proper state and operating normally? As we will see, this step is subdivided into a number of specific, ordered substeps to uncover possible hardware faults or misconfigurations.
3. Software evaluation. Are the BIOS and OS kernel properly configured and able to boot? Are you aware of all known bugs from the most recent data sheet? Once the hardware has been determined to be operating properly, the next step is to verify that the systems software is properly configured and is being invoked correctly. This step, too, is subdivided into further substeps.

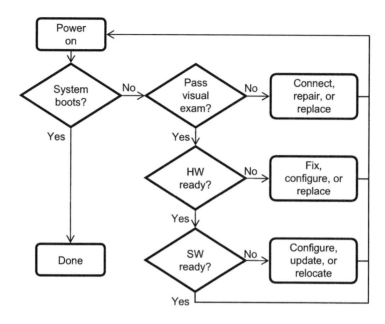

FIGURE 17.1

Platform Debug Process.

These three steps are illustrated in an overall platform debug flowchart in Figure 17.1. We will soon discuss these debug steps in detail, but before doing so we must first review some tools and chipset features essential to platform debug.

DEBUG TOOLS AND CHIPSET FEATURES

Debugging at the platform level requires inspection of system state that is not typically visible to the user or programmer. Consequently, a variety of tools may be needed in the course of a debugging session. In this section, we will discuss the classes of tools that are typically employed in the platform debug process. These include both hardware probes and analyzers and software tools.

Additionally, we will discuss some processor and chipset features that provide access to internal chip state for the purposes of debug and test that would otherwise be inaccessible.

Observing the output characteristics of hardware devices implies the measurement of fundamental electrical characteristics such as voltage and current. While voltmeters and multimeters can offer such measurements, it is typically necessary to observe these characteristics as they change through time.

To do this, hardware probes are required. Such probes come in several varieties and device specializations. Regardless of the power levels and time domains in which your system operates, hardware probes have been produced to meet your needs. Often, however, extremes of both very high and very low power and frequency come at a steep price. For most classes of embedded systems, however, reasonably affordable, USB-based measurement devices can be obtained in the cost range of hundreds of dollars (USD). At the high end, some probes can cost hundreds of thousands of dollars. Most university and digital design laboratories will be stocked with these devices.

Oscilloscopes

Oscilloscopes are a ubiquitous form of hardware probe that primarily provides voltage levels as a function of time for one or more inputs. For example, leads can be attached to CPU pins to watch the change in voltage level as power is applied to a system. This simple example illustrates the type of observation required to verify that the various power levels required by a CPU are being provided and are arriving in the correct order.

Logic Analyzers

Logic analyzers are a related form of hardware probe whose purpose is to capture hardware protocol-level information being communicated across one or more connections. While oscilloscopes report analog values, logic analyzers are designed to work with digital systems, where information and system state are expressed at discrete voltage levels.

The user of the probe has complete control over how the logic analyzer is used. The user chooses the points of observation within the system under test, provides names for the input signals, and then expresses when information should be captured in terms of the values observed among the input signals. In this way, a logic analyzer can be programmed to observe a precise subset of system state under specific system conditions. Logic analyzers, like oscilloscopes, come in a variety of forms, from stand-alone units to more modest USB-based ones.

As an example, a logic analyzer can be used to capture a trace of memory addresses that are transmitted between a CPU and DRAM. For a given application, a logic analyzer must be capable of capturing the required number of inputs (for example, one for each pin under observation) and must operate at an adequate frequency to observe the state transitions on the pins.

Bus Analyzers

Important computer I/O bus types, such as PCI Express™, are popular enough to warrant their own logic analyzer specialization. A PCI Express bus analyzer can capture and analyze PCI traffic in a much more straightforward way than a comparably capable logic analyzer would. Logic analyzers are generally more expensive, but also may be widely applicable.

Power-On Self-Test (POST) Cards

In IA-32-based devices, power-on self-test (POST) routines run immediately after power is applied to the system. These routines are defined by the BIOS vendor and are the part of the pre-boot sequence intended to catalog system resources and identify easily recognizable classes of system errors.

PC users may be familiar with the so-called "beep codes" that can be used to diagnose some hardware problems during system boot. For example, booting a PC with heavy book on the keyboard (which presses down multiple keys continuously) will, in many machines, result in a sustained series of beeps as the system boots.

In addition to reporting errors through the system speaker, most BIOS vendors report error numbers through I/O port 0x80, which is mapped to a PCI location that can be observed by a PCI card. These cards, sometimes called POST cards or port 80 cards, can be used to collect a finer grain of BIOS-defined error conditions.

JTAG Adapters

The Joint Test Action Group, or JTAG, standard defines a process for testing boards and controlling processor execution. A CPU or chipset supporting JTAG must support a minimum set of commands to reset the system, read and write system state, and read and write test data. The most basic usage is to send test vectors into a system via the JTAG interface. Such an interaction can be used to test logic correctness that cannot be definitively verified in pre-silicon simulation.

In addition to system test, the JTAG interface and command set can be used to control the CPU and its software. In this context, JTAG can be used as a systems-level debugger, enabling breakpoints, stepping, and source code correlation at the systems software level. JTAG can also be used to initialize devices or program a boot loader into ROM for systems that are powering up for the first time and do not have code in ROM to control the boot sequence. As a debug interface, JTAG can be invaluable because it is available regardless of the soft state of the system.

A JTAG adapter connects to the system under test via the JTAG interface and through a debug machine through some other interface, such as USB.

Most chip vendors provide their own extended version of JTAG. Intel processors, including Intel Atom, feature extended debug ports (XDP), which implement JTAG and some proprietary extensions.

DEBUG PROCESS DETAILS

Given the preceding high-level overview and discussion of tools, we are now ready to consider the steps of the platform debug process in detail.

Visual Examination

The first step of the process, visual examination, is at once the most obvious and the least familiar of the steps in the platform debug process. The step is unfamiliar because most software-level debugging can be carried out in ignorance of the physical state of the computing device. New embedded systems, and new digital systems of all kinds, must be methodically examined for physical correctness and proper component inventory.

Depending on the enclosure, removing covers to get at the underlying circuit board may be a challenge in and of itself. Sometimes rare screw heads are used, requiring rare screwdrivers; other times, no screws are used at all and the proper sequence of squeezes, pressures, and pries must be applied to separate pieces of an enclosure.

Assuming that the circuit board can be uncovered, the next step is to take a physical inventory of proper components while noting signs of physical damage. It is certainly possible for assemblers to leave pieces out, use the wrong pieces, or accidentally damage components or metal traces during assembly. If the design includes jumpers or other forms of switches, verify that they are in their proper state for system boot.

During the visual examination, signs of shorts or burning should be noted as well. Faulty design and components can lead to shorts or exceeded capacity, resulting in burnt-out, broken components and devices.

Ensure that all cabling, both power and I/O, is properly seated and interconnected. For components that include visible or audible cues, such as LEDs or fans, take note of what functional indicators are present during an attempted boot. These indicators, when present, can dramatically shorten the time needed to identify where in the system boot process failure occurs.

Hardware Evaluation

After a successful visual examination, the next step is to examine the state of the hardware components and to observe their proper operation through time. The high-level steps of this process are illustrated in Figure 17.2 and elaborated on below.

Verify Real-Time Clock. Computing devices built around the Intel architecture generally include a 3.3 V lithium battery to power a real-time clock (RTC). If this battery is missing, damaged, or dead, the system will not come out of reset. You can verify that the RTC is operating properly by examining

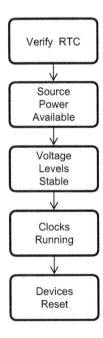

FIGURE 17.2

Steps in Hardware Evaluation.

the SUSCLK signal from the I/O controller hub (ICH) RTC oscillator circuit. This signal should exhibit a square waveform at 32 kHz.

Since the RTC logic is stateful, it is also good practice to remove the battery and reinsert it to return to a known starting state when experiencing problems booting or resetting platform.

Source Power Available. Most Intel architecture systems included ATX power supplies. The ATX power supply will provide DC power at several voltage levels from an AC wall outlet. The ATX signal PS_ON# indicates that the power supply should supply the voltage levels and the power supply will assert the PWR_OK signal when all voltages are available and stable.

The voltage levels are provided in sequence from high to low, as indicated in Figure 17.3. The timings T1, T2, and T3 are specific to the power supply vendor and can be found in the supply's datasheet.

Voltage Levels Stable. Once the power supply is verified to be providing power, the next step is to determine whether the chipset is powering on with properly conditioned standby voltage levels. The detailed levels and timings are specific to a PCH or system-on-chip device, but a representative illustration is provided in Figure 17.4.

At this point in the boot process, the system is in the S5 system sleep state. The RTC is running, but the system itself is not operating. To begin wakeup, an external event such as a power button press is required.

Given that the system is in a proper standby state, a power button press will transition the system from S5 ultimately to S0. Along the way, the chipset will assert the PS_ON# signal to turn on the ATX power supply. The specific timings between these events are, as expected, chipset specific, but a representative illustration of the relative timing can be found in Figure 17.5.

There is an additional signal, SKTOCC#, which indicates whether a CPU is found in the CPU socket. If the socket is empty or if the chip is improperly seated, this signal will not be deasserted and neither will PS_ON#.

Regardless of the chipset and CPU in your design, voltage regulators and their associate status signals will be present to ensure proper levels before the system attempts to generate and apply the core

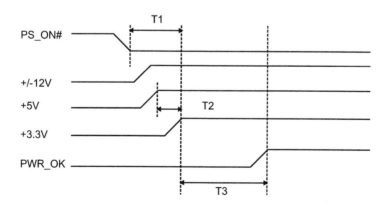

FIGURE 17.3

ATX Power Supply Timing Diagram—Timings T1, T2, and T3 Are Model Specific.

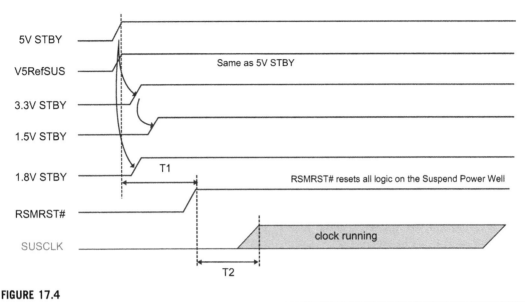

FIGURE 17.4

Representative PCH Power-On Timing Diagram.

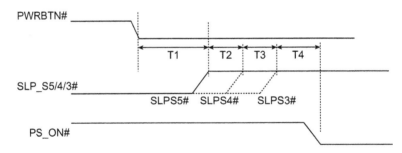

Note: T1, T2, T3 and T4—refer to component specification for timing requirements

FIGURE 17.5

Power-On Signal Timing.

CPU voltage. There will be a signal named something along the lines of VCCP_PGOOD to indicate that the core voltage, VCC_CPU, is available and properly conditioned.

Clocks Running. Once the power supplies are known to be stable, the next milestone is to verify that the system clocks are operating correctly. Intel architecture devices will feature a clock chip for the CPU (for example, CK505) and chipset and one or more clock chips for I/O devices (for example, DB1200).

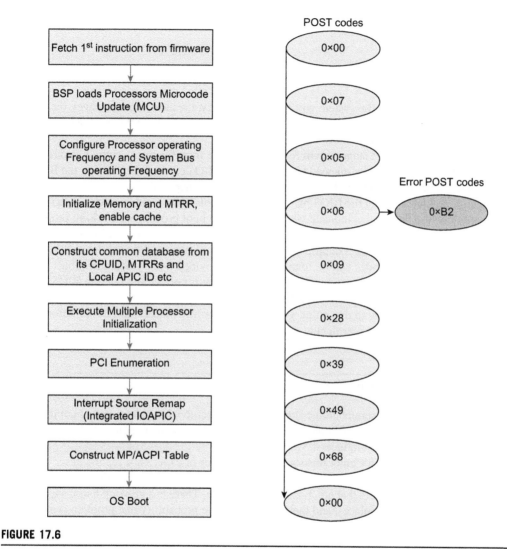

FIGURE 17.6

Power-On Signal Timing for AMI BIOS.

The CPU frequency is indicated by the BSEL clock chip input signals. The BSEL signals and the resulting clock source outputs can be examined for correct signal timing. For design-specific clock distribution problems, timing can be checked at clock signal termination points.

Devices and CPU Reset. If power and clock signals are present and stable, the PCH will attempt a system reset to bring all devices into an operating state. After PWR_OK is asserted, the PCH will assert PLTRST#. Then the PCH will send a CPU reset packet. Once that message is acknowledged, CPURST# will be deasserted, and this will cause the CPU to begin executing at its reset vector, physical address 0xFFFFFFF0. If your system gets this far, it is ready to begin executing its first instruction.

Software Evaluation

If the hardware is in order and the system will not boot properly, the next step is to check the software configuration of the platform. This includes the BIOS settings, which affect the pre-boot operation of the device, as well as the OS itself.

As the CPU leaves the reset stage, it will fetch and execute from the reset vector, physical address 0xFFFFFFF0. This address will be mapped to firmware or an I/O device, depending on the BIOS boot settings. A normal boot sequence will proceed as described in Chapter 6.

To diagnose problems during the BIOS phase of system boot, BIOS vendors output POST codes as described previously. These codes indicate which steps of the boot process are working properly and which step hangs the system. POST codes can be observed via PCI cards or via LEDs built into the platform. Figure 17.6 provides an example of a generic boot sequence and associated POST codes. Specific examples of POST codes can be found in vendor-provided BIOS documentation.

At this stage, it is important to verify that the BIOS version is correct and that the BIOS boot and configuration options are appropriate for the system under test.

If the system boots properly to this point, you have successfully transitioned from platform debug to operating system or device driver debug.

ADDITIONAL RESOURCES

This brief chapter has merely scratched the surface with respect to what can be said about debugging new and faulty hardware platforms. Of course, there is no better way to learn platform debugging skills than to learn from experienced engineers.

The Intel Embedded Design Center hosts a growing number of experience reports describing both specific and general examples of debugging platforms and specific hardware faults.

Table 17.1 lists a few pointers that are available at this time. There is a growing list of such articles on the Intel web site and other places, and there is a reasonable probability that problems you may be encountering with your embedded system have been found and written about by others.

Table 17.1 Further Platform Debug Resources

Title	URL
Debug Methodology for Intel Architecture-Based Platforms	http://download.intel.com/design/intarch/papers/321053.pdf
Processor Reorder Buffer (ROB) Timeout	http://download.intel.com/design/intarch/papers/324353.pdf
Debugging Machine Check Exceptions on Embedded IA Platforms	http://edc.intel.com/Link.aspx?id=3565

In fact, if you find that you have stumbled upon a seemingly unique platform error, you should be sure to write it up for the benefit of your fellow engineers!

SUMMARY

In this chapter, we have explored the basics of platform-level debugging. Debugging a brand-new hardware design is a necessarily open-ended activity. Through rigorous design and careful simulation, many system errors can be avoided. However, not all faults and errors can be designed around, so embedded systems engineers need to be prepared to debug a system with very few preconceived notions about what operates correctly.

Of paramount concern is your frame of mind as you begin debugging. Careful, methodical evaluation is needed for productive platform debug, and hasty action and poor documentation are counterproductive in this context.

This chapter has introduced a simple process for system-level platform debugging. Through visual examination of the system components and a careful walk-through of the hardware and software boot sequences, it should be possible to pinpoint the source of platform boot errors through systematic trial and observation.

Performance Tuning

18

Performance tuning is one of the black arts of embedded system development. You will almost certainly spend some portion of your development schedule on optimization and performance activities. Unfortunately, these activities usually seem to occur when the ship date is closing in and everyone is under the most pressure.

However, help is at hand. We have developed a useful toolbox of tricks and techniques for performance tuning, which are summarized in this chapter. These best-known methods are presented in "pattern" form. Most of the techniques described here are generic performance tuning techniques. The optimization and performance tuning patterns have been organized under the following headings:

- General approaches
- Code and design
- Processor specifics
- Networking techniques

WHAT ARE PATTERNS?

Each performance improvement suggestion is documented in the form of a pattern (Alexander, 1979; Gamma et al., 1995). A pattern is "a solution to a problem in a context," a literary mechanism to share experience and impart solutions to commonly occurring problems. Each pattern contains these elements:

- *Name*—For referencing a problem/solution pairing.
- *Context*—The circumstance in which we solve the problem that imposes constraints on the solution.
- *Problem*—THE specific problem to be solved.
- *Solution*—the proposed solution to the problem. Many problems can have more than one solution, and the "goodness" of a solution to a problem is affected by the context in which the problem occurs. Each solution takes certain forces into account. It resolves some forces at the expense of others. It may even ignore some forces.
- *Forces*—The often-contradictory considerations we must take into account when choosing a solution to a problem.

A pattern language is the organization and combination of a number of interrelated patterns. Where one pattern references another pattern we use the following format "(*see* Pattern Name)."

You may not need to read each and every pattern. You certainly do not need to apply all of the patterns to every performance optimization task. You might, however, find it useful to scan all of the context and problem statements to get an overview of what is available in this pattern language.

477

GENERAL APPROACHES

This first set of patterns proposes general approaches and tools you might use when embarking on performance tuning work. These patterns are not specific to any processor or application.

Defined Performance Requirement

Context: You are a software developer starting a performance improvement task on an application or driver.

Problem: Performance improvement work can become a never-ending task. Without a goal, the activity can drag on longer than productive or necessary.

Solution: At an early stage of the project or customer engagement, define a relevant, specific, realistic, and measurable performance requirement. Document that performance requirement as a specific detailed application and configuration with a numerical performance target.

- "Make it as fast as possible" is not a specific performance requirement.
- "The application must be capable of 10-gigabit per second wire-speed routing of 64-byte packets with a 600-megahertz CPU" is not a realistic performance requirement.

Forces:

- A performance target can be hard to define.
- Waiting to have a goal might affect your product's competitiveness.
- A performance target can be a moving target; competitors do not stand still. New competitors come along all the time.
- Without a goal, the performance improvement work can drag on longer than is productive.

Performance Design

Context: You are a software developer designing a system. You have a measurable performance requirement (*see* Defined Performance Requirement).

Problem: The design of the system does not meet the performance requirement.

Solution: At design time, describe the main data path scenario. Walk through the data path in the design workshop and document it in the high-level design.

When you partition the system into components, allocate a portion of the clock cycles to the data path portion of each component. Have a target at design time for the clock cycle consumption of the whole data path. Ganssle (1999) gives notations and techniques for system design performance constraints.

During code inspections, hold one code inspection that walks through the most critical data path.

Code inspections are usually component based. This code inspection should be different and follow the scenario of the data path.

If you use a polling mechanism, ensure that the CPU is shared appropriately.

It can also be useful to analyze the application's required bus bandwidth at design time to decide if the system will be CPU or memory bandwidth/latency limited. If available, you should use performance modeling environments during this phase.

Forces:

- It can be difficult to anticipate some system bottlenecks at design time.
- The design of the system can make it impossible to meet the performance requirement. If you discover this late in the project, it might be too difficult to do anything about it.

Premature Code Tuning Avoided

Context: You are implementing a system, and you are in the coding phase of the project. You do have a good system-level understanding of the performance requirements and the allocation of performance targets to different parts of the system because you have a performance design (*see* Performance Design).

Problem: It is difficult to know how much time or effort to spend thinking about performance or efficiency when initially writing the code.

Solution: It is important to find the right balance between performance, functionality, and maintainability.

Some studies have found that 20% of the code consumes 80% of the execution time; others have found less than 4% of the code accounts for 50% of the time (McConnell, 1993).

KISS—keep it simple and straightforward. Until you have measured and can prove that a piece of code is a system-wide bottleneck, do not optimize it. Simple design is easier to optimize. The compiler finds it easier to optimize simple code.

If you are working on a component of a system, you should have a performance budget for your part of the data path (*see* Performance Design).

In the unit test, you could have a performance test for your part of the data path. At integration time, the team could perform a performance test for the complete assembled data path.

The best is the enemy of the good. Working toward perfection may prevent completion. Complete it first, then perfect it. The part that needs to be perfect is usually small.

—Steve McConnell

For further information, see Chapters 28 and 29 of *Code Complete* (McConnell, 1993) and question 20.13 in the comp.lang.c FAQ web site (Summit, 1995).

Forces:

- Efficient code is not necessarily "better" code. It might be difficult to understand and maintain.
- It is almost impossible to identify performance bottlenecks before you have a working system.
- If you spend too much time doing micro-optimization during initial coding, you might miss important global optimizations.
- If you look at performance too late in a project, it can be too late to do anything about it.

Step-by-Step Records

Context: You are trying a number of optimizations to fix a particular bottleneck. The system contains a number of other bottlenecks.

Problem: Sometimes it is difficult when working at a fast pace to remember optimizations made only a few days earlier.

Solution: Take good notes of each experiment you have tried to identify bottlenecks and each optimization you have tried to increase performance. These notes can be invaluable later. You might find you are stuck at a performance level with an invisible bottleneck. Reviewing your optimization notes might help you identify incorrect paths taken or diversionary assumptions.

When a performance improvement effort is complete, it can be very useful to have notes on the optimization techniques that worked. You can then put together a set of best-known methods to help other engineers in your organization benefit from your experience.

Forces:

- Writing notes can sometimes break the flow of work or thought.

Slam-Dunk Optimization

Context: You have made a number of improvements that have increased the efficiency of code running on the processor core.

Problem: The latest optimizations have not increased performance. You have hit some unidentified performance-limiting factor. You might have improved performance to a point where environmental factors, protocols, or test equipment is now the bottleneck.

Solution: It is useful to have a code modification identified that you know should improve performance. For example:

- An algorithm on the data path that can be removed temporarily such as IP checksum.
- Increase the processor clock speed.

In one application, we implemented a number of optimizations that should have improved performance but did not. We then removed the IP checksum calculation and performance still did not increase. These results pointed to a hidden limiting factor, an unknown bottleneck. When we followed this line of investigation, we found a problem in the way we configured a physical layer device, and when we fixed this hidden limiting factor, performance improved immediately by approximately 25%. We retraced our steps and reapplied the earlier changes to identify the components of that performance improvement.

Forces:

- Increasing the processor clock speed improves performance only for CPU-bound applications.

Best Compiler for Application

Context: You are writing an application using a compiler. You have a choice of compilers for the processor architecture you are using.

Problem: Different compilers generate code that has different performance characteristics. You need to select the right one for your application and target platform.

Solution: Experiment with different compilers and select the best performing compiler for your application and environment.

Performance can vary between compilers and versions of the compiler. GCC is an excellent compiler for general use, but vendors often support highly optimized processor-specific micro-architecture optimizations. The difference can be in the order of 5–10% for certain applications

Forces:

- Some compilers are more expensive than others.
- Some compilers and operating systems might not match. For example, the compiler you want to use might generate the wrong object file format for your tool chain or development environment.
- A particular compiler might optimize a particular benchmark better than another compiler, but that is no guarantee that it will optimize your specific application in the same way.
- You might be constrained in your compiler choice because of tools support issues. If you are working in the Linux kernel, you might have to use GCC. Some parts of the kernel use GCC-specific extensions.

Compiler Optimizations

Context: You have chosen to use a C compiler (*see* Best Compiler for Application).

Problem: You have not enabled all of the compiler optimizations.

Solution: Your compiler supports a number of optimization switches. Using these switches can increase global application performance for a small amount of effort. Read the documentation for your compiler and understand these switches.

In general, the highest-level optimization switch is the -O switch. In GCC, the switch takes a numeric parameter. Find out the maximum parameter for your compiler and use it. Typical compilers support three levels of optimization. Try the highest. In GCC, the highest level is -O3. However, in the past -O3 code generation had more bugs than -O2, the most-used optimization level. The Linux kernel is compiled with -O2. If you have problems at -O3, you might need to revert to -O2.

Moving from -O2 to -O3 made an improvement of approximately 15% in packet processing in one application tested. In another application, -O3 was slower than -O2.

You can limit the use of compiler optimizations to individual C source files.

Introduce optimization flags, one by one, to discover the ones that give you benefit.

Other GCC optimization flags that can increase performance are

- `-funroll-loops`
- `-fomit-frame-pointer`

Forces:

- Generally, optimizations increase generated code size.
- Some optimizations might not increase performance.
- Compilers support a large number of switches and options. It can be time consuming to read the lengthy documentation.
- Optimized code is difficult to debug.
- Some optimizations can reveal compiler bugs, as they are not as frequently used as the normal default options.
- Enabling optimization can change timings in your code. It might reveal latent undiscovered problems.

Data Cache

Context: You are using a processor that contains a data cache. The core is running faster than memory or peripherals.

Problem: The processor core is spending a significant amount of time stalled waiting on an external memory degrading performance. You have identified this problem using the performance monitoring function on your chosen processor quantifying the number of cycles the processor is stalled for.

In some applications, we have observed that a significant number of cycles are lost to data-dependency stalls.

Solution:

In general, the most efficient mechanism for accessing memory is to use the data cache. Core accesses to cached memory is several times faster than accessing it from the DRAM In addition, it does not need to use the internal/external bus, leaving it free for other devices such has high speed I/O.

The cache unit can make efficient use of the memory bus. On the IA-32 processors the core fetches an entire 64-byte cache line, using special memory burst cycles when accessing memory. This is far more efficient than when compared to issuing separate 32-bit data reads.

The cache supports several features that give you flexibility in tailoring the system to your design needs. These features affect all applications to some degree; however, the optimal settings are application dependent. It is critical to understand the effects of these features and how to fine-tune them for the usage model of a particular application. We cover a number of these cache features in later sections.

In one application (using an RTOS) that was not caching buffer descriptors and packet data, developers enabled caching and saw an approximate 25% improvement in packet-processing performance. Choose data structures appropriate for a data cache. For example, stacks are typically more cache efficient than linked list data structures.

In most of the applications we have seen, the instruction cache is very efficient. It is worth spending time optimizing the use of the data cache.

Forces:

- On IA-32 systems, if you cache data-memory that the core shares with another bus master, the cache coherence with I/O is maintained; however, on some architectures you must manage cache flush/invalidation explicitly.
- If you use caching, it is best to ensure that two distinct data sets never share the same cache line. Inadvertent cache line sharing, popularly called false cache sharing, arises when two agents (either CPU threads or IO devices) attempt to access the same cache line. In such a case, the cache coherent based architecture like Intel has to resolve the cache conflict. This may result in a temporary stall in execution, leading to performance degradation.
- Be careful what you cache. Temporal locality refers to the amount of time between accesses to the data. If you access a piece of data once or access it infrequently, it has low temporal locality. If you mark this kind of data for caching, the cache replacement algorithm can cause the eviction of performance-sensitive data by this lower-priority data.
- The processor implements a round-robin line replacement algorithm.

CODE AND DESIGN

This section covers some general code tuning guidelines that are applicable to most processors. In many cases, these optimizations can decrease the readability, maintainability, or portability of your code. Be sure you are optimizing code that needs optimization (*see* Premature Code Tuning Avoided).

Reordered Struct

Context: You have identified a bottleneck segment of code on your application data path. The code uses a large struct.

Problem: The struct spans a number of cache lines.

Solution: Reorder the fields in a struct to group the frequently accessed fields together. If all of the accessed fields fit on a cache line, the first access pulls them all into a cache, potentially avoiding data-dependency stalls when accessing the other fields. Organize all frequently written fields into the same cache line.

Some architectures are sensitive to variable address alignment on a particular address boundary. Whenever possible, align variables at the right address boundary using complier pragmas.

Forces:

- Reordering structs might not be feasible. Some structs might map to a packet definition.
- Multiprocessor access to the same cache line will generate additional interprocessor traffic. If possible, data shared by a process should be split into separate instances.

Supersonic Interrupt Service Routines

Context: Your application uses multiple interrupt service routines (ISRs) to signal the availability of data on an interface and trigger the processing of that data.

Problem: Interrupt service routines can interfere with other ISRs and real-time processing work such as packet processing code.

Solution: Keep ISRs short. Design them to be re-entrant.

For example, an ISR should just give/release a semaphore, set a flag, or en-queue a packet. You should de-queue and process the data outside the ISR. This way, you obviate the need for interrupt locks around data in an ISR.

Interrupt locks in a frequent ISR can have hard-to-measure effects on the overall system.

For more detailed interrupt design guidelines, see *Doing Hard Time_* (Douglass, 1999).

Forces:

- Posting to a semaphore or queue can cause extra context switches, which reduce the overall efficiency of a system.
- Bugs in ISRs usually have a catastrophic effect. Keeping them short and simple reduces the probability of bugs.

Assembly-Language-Critical Functions

Context: You have identified a C function that consumes a significant portion of the data path.

Problem: The code generated for this function might not be optimal for your processor.

Solution: Re-implement the critical function directly in assembly language.

Use the best compiler for the application (*see* Best Compiler for Application) to generate initial assembly code, then hand-optimize it.

Forces:

- Modern compiler technology is beginning to out-perform the ability of humans to optimize assembly language for sophisticated processors.
- Assembly language is more difficult to read and maintain.
- Assembly language is more difficult to port to other processors.

Inline Functions

Context: You have identified a small C function that is frequently called on the data path.

Problem: The overhead associated with the entry and exit to the function can become significant in a small function, frequently called on by the application data path.

Solution: Declare the function inline. This way, the function gets inserted directly into the code of the calling function.

Forces:

- Inline functions can increase the code size of your application and add stress to the instruction cache.
- Some debuggers have difficulty showing the thread of execution for inline functions.
- A function call itself can limit the compiler's ability to optimize register usage in the calling function.

Cache-Optimizing Loop

Context: You have identified a critical loop that is a significant part of the data-path performance.

Problem: The structure of the loop or the data on which it operates could be "trashing" the data cache.

Solution: You can consider a number of loop/data optimizations:

- Array merging—the loop uses two or more arrays. This merges them into a single array of a struct.
- Induction variable interchange. Induction variables are variables that get increased/decreased by a fixed amount each iteration of a loop (e.g., For i).
- Loop fusion

Forces:

- Loop optimizations can make the code harder to read, understand, and maintain.

Minimizing Local Variables

Context: You have identified a function that needs optimization. It contains a large number of local variables.

Problem: A large number of local variables might incur the overhead of storing them on the stack. The compiler might generate code to set up and restore the frame pointer.

Solution: Minimize the number of local variables. The compiler may be able to store all the locals and parameters in processor registers.

Forces:

- Removing local variables can decrease the readability of code or require extra calculations during the execution of the function.

Explicit Registers

Context: You have identified a function that needs optimization. A local variable or a piece of data is frequently used in the function.

Problem: Sometimes the compiler does not identify a register optimization.

Solution: It is worth trying explicit register hints to local variables that are frequently used in a function.

It can also be useful to copy a frequently used part of a packet that is also used frequently in a data path algorithm into a local variable declared register. An optimization of this kind made a performance improvement of approximately 20% in one real application.

Alternatively, you could add a local variable or register to explicitly "cache" a frequently used global variable. Some compilers do not work on global variables in local variables or registers. If you know the global is not modified by an interrupt handler and the global is modified a number of times in the same function, copy it to a register local variable, make updates to the local, and then write the new value back out to the global before exiting the function. This technique is especially useful when updating packet statistics in a loop handling multiple packets.

Forces:

- The register keyword is only a hint to the compiler.

Optimized Hardware Register Use

Context: The data path code does multiple reads or writes to one or more hardware registers.

Problem: Multiple read-operation-writes on hardware registers can cause the processor to stall.

Solution: First, break up read-operation-write statements to hide some of the latencies when dealing with hardware registers. For example:

Read-operation-writes on hardware registers:

```
*reg1ptr |= 0x0400;
*reg2ptr &= ~0x80;
```

Optimized read-operation-writes:

```
reg1 = *reg1ptr;
reg2 = *reg2ptr;
```

```
reg1 |= 0x0400;
reg2 &= ~0x80;
*reg1ptr = reg1;
*reg2ptr = reg2;
```

This modified code eliminates one of the read dependency stalls.

Second, search the data path code for multiple writes to the same hardware register. Combine all the separate writes into a single write to the actual register. For example, some applications disable hardware interrupts using multiple set/resets of bits in the interrupt enable register. In one such application, when we manually combined these write instructions, performance improved by approximately 4%. This is particularly important on IA-32 systems with strongly ordered memory models.

Forces:

- Manually separated read-operation-write code expands code slightly. It can also add local variables and could trigger the creation of a frame pointer.

Avoiding the OS Buffer Pool

Context: The application uses a system buffer pool.

Problem: Memory allocation or calls to buffer pool libraries can be processor intensive. In some operating systems, these functions lock interrupts and use local semaphores to protect simultaneous access to shared heaps.

Pay special attention to buffer management at design time. Are buffers being allocated on the application data path?

Solution: Avoid allocating or interacting with the RTOS packet buffer pool on the data path. Pre-allocate packet buffers outside the data path and store them in lightweight software pools/queues.

Stacks or arrays are typically faster than linked lists for packet buffer pool collections because they require fewer memory accesses to add and remove buffers. Stacks also improve data cache utilization.

Forces:

- OS buffer pools implement buffer collections. Writing another light collection duplicates functionality.

C Language Optimizations

Context: You have identified a function or segment of code that is consuming a significant portion of the CPU clock cycles on the data path. You might have identified this code using profiling tools (*see* Profiling Tools) or a performance measurement.

Problem: A function or segment of C code needs optimization.

Solution: You can try a number of C language level optimizations:

- Pass large function parameters by reference, never by value. Values take time to copy.
- Avoid array indexing. Use pointers.
- Minimize loops by collecting multiple operations into a single loop body.
- Avoid long if-then-else chains. Use a switch statement or a state machine.

- Use int (natural word size of the processor) to store flags rather than char or short.
- Use unsigned variants of variables and parameters where possible. Doing so might allow some compilers to make optimizations.
- Avoid floating-point calculations on the data path.
- Use decrementing loop variables, for example,

```
for (i=10; i--;) {do something}
```

or even better

```
do { something } while (i--)
```

- Look at the code generated by your compiler in this case.
- Adjust structure sizes to the power of two.
- Place the most frequently true statement first in if-else statements.
- Place frequent case labels first.
- Write small functions. The compiler likes to reuse registers as much as possible and cannot do it in complex nested code. However, some compilers automatically use a number of registers on every function call. Extra function call entries and returns can cost a large number of cycles in tight loops.
- Use the function return as opposed to an output parameter to return a value to a calling function. Return values on many processors are stored in a register by convention.
- For critical loops, use Duff's device, a devious, generic technique for unrolling loops. See question 20.35 in the comp.lang.C FAQ (Summit, 1995).

For other similar tips, see Chapter 29 in *Code Complete* (McConnell, 1993).

Forces:

- Good compilers make a number of these optimizations.

Disabled Counters/Statistics

Context: Many applications have a large number of statistics/counters associated with the data path in the application. You have completed integration testing of your application.

Problem: The software keeps a number of counters and statistics to facilitate integrating and debugging of both the components and the system as a whole. These counters usually incur a read and write or increment in main, or possibly cached, memory.

The access layer also contains code that checks parameters for legal values. This feature facilitates the integration and debugging of the software and the system as a whole. These checks usually test conditions that never occur once the system and customer code have been fully tested and integrated.

Solution: You can identify if there are macros in the code to disable the incorporation of debug counters. Doing so also removes many of the internal parameter debug checks.

In one application, use of this pattern increased packet-processing throughput by up to 4%.

Forces:

- Disabling counters and statistics removes useful debugging information.
- Removing parameter checks can obfuscate an issue, making it harder to detect incorrect parameter checks in customer code.

PROCESSOR-SPECIFIC

For IA-32-specific platforms, Intel has developed Intel® 64 and IA-32 Architectures Optimization Reference Manual. In particular, Chapter 12 covers specific Intel Atom™ optimizations.

Stall Instructions

Context: You have run some tests using performance measurements (for example, the Intel VTune™ Performance Tools of your target) that indicate that a large number of core cycles are being lost due to data dependency stalls.

Problem: You might find a large portion of the cycles is lost to stalls on fast processors. You need to identify the pieces of code that are causing these stalls.

Solution: One simple way to identify "hot instructions" is to use a program counter sampler. The sampler would run at a regular interval and count the number of times each instruction or program-counter executes while running the networking performance test.

- To reduce the impact of these stalls you could use the Prefetch instruction (*see* Prefetch Instructions). You could also move code that won't cause a stall before the code that does.

Forces:

- Adding sampling code can affect the behavior of the system under test.

Profiling Tools

Context: You are at an early stage of performance improvement. You have not identified a specific bottleneck but you have proven tht the current bottleneck is the speed of execution of the code on the processor core.

Problem: You have a working system that is not meeting a performance requirement. You suspect that raw algorithmic processing power is the current bottleneck; you need to identify the bottleneck code.

Solution: A number of profiling tools exist to help you identify code hotspots. Typically, they identify the percent of time spent in each C function in your code base.

- Intel Vtune tools are performance characterization tools; these provide significant detail on the application behavior.
- Rational Quantify™ contains an excellent performance profiler, not to mention Purify™, the memory corruption/leak checker. You instrument your code and then execute that code on the target platform.
- Gprof is available for many Linux-based systems.
- Some JTAG debug tools contain profiling features.

Forces:

- Profiling tools can affect the performance of the system.
- Some tools might not be available for your RTOS.
- Some profiling tools cost money.
- Each of these tools has a learning curve but could pay back the time and money investment.

Prefetch Instructions

Context: You have identified a stall instruction (*see* Stall Instructions).

Problem: You want to reduce the time the processor spends stalled due to a data dependency.

Solution: The IA-32 has a number of temporal prefetch load instructions called PREFETCH™. The purpose of these instructions is to preload data into multiple levels of the cache hierarchy. The prefetch instruction is a hint.

Data prefetching allows hiding of memory transfer latency while the processor continues to execute instructions. The judicious use of the prefetch instruction can improve throughput of the processor.

Look at the line of C code that generates the stall instruction (*see* Stall Instructions).

Insert an explicit assembly language prefetch instruction some time before the stall instruction (*see* Stall Instructions). Data prefetch can be applied not only to loops but also to any data references within a block of code.

Using prefetches requires careful experimentation. In some cases performance improves, and in others the performance degrades. Overuse of prefetches can use shared resources and degrade performance.

Spread prefetch operations over calculations so as to allow bus traffic to free flow and to minimize the number of necessary prefetches.

Forces:

- Overuse of prefetches can use shared resources and degrade performance.
- The placement of a prefetch instruction can be CPU speed specific. The latency to external memory when measured in cycles changes when you change the CPU speed.
- The placement of the prefetch instruction can depend on the previous data pattern access to the data.

Separate DRAM Memory Banks

Context: You have completed a performance measurement. These data have identified a significant percentage of cycles lost due to data dependency stalls.

Problem: DRAMs are typically divided into four or eight banks. Thrashing occurs when subsequent memory accesses within the same memory bank access different pages. The memory page change adds three to four bus clock cycles to memory latency (tens of nanoseconds).

Solution: You can resolve this type of thrashing by either placing the conflicting data structures into different memory banks or paralleling the data structures such that the data resides within the same memory page. Either action can reduce the latency reading data from memory and reduce the extent of many stalls.

Allocate data buffers in their own bank. The DRAM controller can keep a page partially open in four/eight different memory banks. You could also split data buffers across two banks.

It is also important to ensure that instruction and data sections are in different memory banks, or they might continually thrash the memory page selection.

In one networking application, this technique increased packet-processing performance by approximately 10%. In another, it had no effect.

Forces:

• Write code to use different banks for code and data or spread data across multiple banks. Either action will complicate your BSP and configuration code.

Line-Allocation Policy

Context: You are using data cache for data or packet memory. You have enabled the cache.
Problem: The cache line-allocation policy can affect the performance of your application.
Solution: The logic a processor uses to make a decision about placing new data into the cache is based on the line-allocation policy.

If the line-allocation policy is read-allocate, all load operations that miss the cache request a 64-byte cache line from external memory and allocate it. Store operations that miss the cache do not cause a line to be allocated.

With a read/write-allocate policy, load or store operations that miss the cache request a 64-byte cache line from external memory if the cache is enabled.

In general, regular data and the stack for your application should be allocated to a read-write allocate region. Most applications regularly write and read this data. Again, it is worth experimenting to see if your processor architecture supports it.

Write-only data—or data that is written and subsequently not used for a long time—should be placed in a read-allocate region. Under the read-allocate policy, if a cache write miss occurs, a new cache line is not allocated and hence does not evict critical data from the data cache.

In general, read-allocate seems to be the best performing policy for packet data. One application had an improvement of approximately 10% when packet memory was set up read-allocate.
Forces:

• The appropriate cache line-allocation policy can be application dependent. It is worth experimenting with both types of line-allocation policies.
• Not all processors allow you to configure the allocation policy.

Cache Write Policy

Context: You are using data cache for data or packet memory. You have enabled the cache.
Problem: The cache write policy can affect the performance of your application.
Solution: Cached memory also has an associated write policy. A write-through policy instructs the data cache to keep external memory coherent by performing stores to both external memory and the cache. A write-back policy only updates external memory when a line in the cache is cleaned or needs to be replaced with a new line.

Generally, write-back provides higher performance because it generates less data traffic to external memory. However, if your application is making a small number of modifications, for example, to packet data or message buffers, write-through may be more efficient.

In a multiple-bus/master environment, you might have to use a write-through policy or explicit cache flushes if data are shared across multiple masters.

Forces:

- The appropriate cache write policy can be application dependent. It is worth experimenting with both types of write policies.
- In systems with multiple hierarchies of cache (L1 and L2), the inclusion of L2 may dictate the write policy (probably the best, because having an L2 cache improves processor performance).

Cache-Aligned Data Buffers

Context: Your application/driver caches packet buffers and buffer descriptors.

Problem: You need to use the cache as effectively as possible. On some systems, the descriptors might be larger than a cache line.

Solution: Allocate key data on cache line boundaries. This action maximizes the use of cache when accessing these data structures.

You must make sure the descriptors and packet storage for different packets do not share the same cache line.

Forces:

- You might waste some memory if the size of these data structures in your operating system is not divisible by the cache line size. Typically, this memory wastage is worth the increase in performance.

On-Chip Memory

Context: Your data path code makes frequent reference to a specific table or piece of data.

Problem: Accesses to these data are causing stalls because the cache is heavily used and the data are being frequently evicted. Most processors employ a round-robin/or least-recently-used replacement cache policy; all cache data that is not locked is eventually evicted.

Solution: Some processor architectures support cache locking. You could consider locking key data/code elements into the cache.

Locking data from external memory into the data cache is useful for lookup tables, constants, and any other data that are frequently accessed.

Forces:

- Locking data into the cache reduces the amount of cache available to the processor for general processing.

Optimized Libraries

Context: You are optimizing an application for the target processor. Your application uses some of the C functions for key vector algorithm elements in the system.

Problem: Some compilers do not take full advantage of SIMD type instructions such as Intel® SSE/AVX when targeting vector-based code.

Solution: Intel and other silicon vendors provide optimized libraries that take full advantage of the SIMD engines available. The Intel libraries are known as Intel Integrated Performance Primitives (Intel IPP).

Modulo/Divide Avoided

Context: You are writing code for a processor.

Problem: The processor does not directly support modulo or divide instructions. When compiled, the code generates a call to a library support function.

Solution: You can translate some modulo or divide calculations into bit masks or shifts.

For example, modulo for dimensions that are a power of 2 can use a mask, such as instead of (var % 8), use (var & 7). Likewise, you can convert some divisions by constants into shift and add instructions.

Most compilers should be capable of generating this optimization, but it might be worth examining generated code for any modulo or divide on your data path.

Forces:

• Bit masks/shifts are less readable code than division or modulo.

NETWORKING TECHNIQUES

The following patterns can be applied to networking performance in general.

Bottleneck Hunting

Context: You have a running functional system. You have a performance requirement (*see* Defined Performance Requirement). A customer is measuring performance lower than that requirement.

Problem: You can have a number of performance bottlenecks in the designed system, but unless you identify the current limiting factor, you might optimize the wrong thing. One component of the system might be limiting the flow of network packets to the rest of the system.

Solution: Performance improvement really starts with bottleneck hunting. It is only when you find the performance-limiting bottleneck that you can work on optimizations to remove the bottleneck. A system typically has a number of bottlenecks. You first need to identify the current limiting bottleneck, then remove it. You then need to iterate through the remaining bottlenecks until the system meets its performance requirements.

First, determine if your application is CPU or I/O bound. In a CPU-bound system, the limiting factor or bottleneck is the amount of cycles needed to execute some algorithm or part of the data path. In an I/O-bound system, the bottleneck is external to the processor. The processor has enough CPU cycles to handle the traffic, but the traffic flow is not enough to make full use of the available processor cycles.

To determine if the system is CPU or I/O bound, try running the processor at a number of different clock speeds. If you see a significant change in performance, your system is probably CPU bound.

Next, look at the software components of the data path; these might include the following:

- Low-level device drivers specific to a piece of hardware. These device drivers could conform to an OS-specific interface.
- A network interface service mechanism running on the CPU core. This mechanism might be a number of ISRs or a global polling loop.
- Encapsulation layers of the networking stack.
- The switching/bridging/routing engine of the networking stack or the RTOS.

If some algorithm in a low-level device driver is limiting the flow of data into the system, you might waste your time if you start tweaking compiler flags or optimize the routing algorithm.

It is best to look at the new or unique components to a particular system first. Typically, these are the low-level device drivers or the adapter components unique to this system.

Concentrate on the unique components first, especially if these components are on the edge of the system. In one wireless application we discovered that the wireless device driver was a bottleneck that limited the flow of data into the system.

Many components of a data path can contain packet buffers. Packet counters inserted in the code can help you identify queue overflows or underflows. Typically, the code that consumes the packet buffer is the bottleneck.

This process is typically iterative. When you fix the current bottleneck, you then need to loop back and identify the next one.

Forces:

- Most systems have multiple bottlenecks.
- Early bottleneck hunting—before you have a complete running system—increases the risk of misidentified bottlenecks and wasted tuning effort.

Evaluating Traffic Generator and Protocols

Context: You are using a network traffic generator and protocols to measure the performance of a system.

Problem: The performance test or protocol overheads can limit the measured performance of your application.

Solution: Identifying the first bottleneck is a challenge. First, you need to eliminate your traffic generators and protocols as bottlenecks and analyze the invariants.

Typical components in a complete test system might include the following:

- Traffic sources, sinks, and measurement equipment
- The device under test (DUT) for which you are tuning the performance
- Physical connections and protocols between traffic sources and the DUT

Your test environment might use a number of different types of traffic sources, sinks, and measurement equipment. You need to first make sure that they are not the bottleneck in your system.

Equipment, like Smartbits™ and Adtech™ testers, is not typically a bottleneck. However, using a PC with FTP software to measure performance can be a bottleneck. You need to test the PC and FTP software without the DUT to make sure that your traffic sources can reach the performance you require.

Running this test can also flush out bottlenecks in the physical media or protocols you are using.

In addition, you need to make sure that the overhead inherent in the protocols you are using makes the performance you require feasible. For example:

- You cannot expect 100 megabits per second over Ethernet with 64-byte packets due to interframe gap and frame preamble. You can expect to get at most 76 megabits per second.
- You cannot expect to get 8 megabits per second over an ADSL link; you can expect to get at most 5.5 megabits per second.
- You cannot expect to get 100 megabits per second on FTP running over Ethernet. You must take IP protocol overhead and TCP acknowledgements into account.
- You cannot expect 52 megabits per second on 802™.11a/g networks due to CTS/RTS overhead and protocol overhead.

Characteristics of the particular protocol or application could also be causing the bottleneck. For example, if the FTP performance is much lower (by a factor of 2) than the large-packet performance with a traffic generator (Smartbits), the problem could be that the TCP acknowledgement packets are getting dropped. This problem can sometimes be a buffer management issue.

FTP performance can also be significantly affected by the TCP window sizes on the FTP client and server machines.

Forces:

- Test equipment typically outperforms the DUT.

Environmental Factors

Context: You are finding it difficult to identify the bottleneck.
Problem: Environmental factors can cause a difficult-to-diagnose bottleneck.
Solution: Check the environmental factors.

When testing a wireless application, you might encounter radio interference in the test environment. In this case, you can use a Faraday cage to radio-isolate your test equipment and DUT from the environment. Antenna configuration is also important. The antennas should not be too close (<1 meter). They should be erect, not lying down. You also need to make sure you shield the DUT to protect it from antenna interference.

Check shared resources. Is your test equipment or DUT sharing a resource, such as a network segment, with other equipment? Is that other equipment making enough use of the shared resource to affect your DUT performance?

Check all connectors and cables. If you are confident you are making improvements but the measurements are not giving the improvement you expect, try changing all the cables connecting your DUT to the test equipment. As a last resort, try a replacement DUT. We have seen a number of cases where a device on the DUT has degraded enough to affect performance.

Polled Packet Processor

Context: You are designing the fundamental mechanism that drives the servicing of network interfaces.

Problem: Some fundamental mechanisms can expose you to more overhead and wasted CPU cycles. These wasted cycles can come from interrupt preamble/dispatch and context switches.

Solution: You can categorize most applications as interrupt or polling driven or a combination of both.

When traffic overloads a system, it runs optimally if it is running in a tight loop, polling interfaces for which it knows there is traffic queued.

If the application driver is interrupt based, look to see how many packets you handle per interrupt. To get better packet processing performance, handle more packets per interrupt by possibly using a polling approach in the interrupt handler.

Some systems put the packet on a queue from the interrupt handler and then do the packet processing in another thread. In this kind of a system, you need to understand how many packets the system handles per context switch. To improve performance, increase the number of packets handled per context switch.

Other systems can drive packet processing, triggered from a timer interrupt. In this case, you need to make sure the timer frequency and number of packets handled per interrupt are not limiting the networking performance of your system. In addition, this system is not optimally efficient when the system is in overload.

Systems based on Linux usually support a combination of both interrupt and polling based for network drivers (NAPI is such a mechanism used for network drivers).

Forces:

- Reducing wasted CPU cycles can complicate the overall architecture or design of an application.
- Some IP stacks or operating systems can restrict the options in how you design these fundamental mechanisms.
- You might need to throttle the amount of CPU given to packet processing to allow other processing to happen even when the system is in overload.
- Applying these techniques might increase the latency in handling some packets.

Edge Packet Throttle

Context: The bottleneck of your system is now the IP forwarding or transport parts of the IP stack.

Problem: You might be wasting CPU cycles processing packets to later drop them when a queue fills later in the data path.

Solution: When a system goes into overload, it is better to leave the frames back up in the RX queue and let the edges of your system, the MAC devices, throttle reception. You can avoid wasting core cycles by checking a bottleneck indicator, such as queue full, early in the data path code.

For example, on VxWorks™, you can make the main packet-processing task (netTask) the highest-priority task. This technique is one easy way to implement a "self-throttling" system. Alternatively, you could make the buffer replenish code a low-priority task, which would ensure that receive buffers are only supplied when you have available CPU.

Forces:

- Checking a bottleneck indicator might weaken the encapsulation of an internal detail of the IP stack.
- Implementing an early check wastes some CPU cycles when the system is in overload.

Detecting Resource Collisions

Context: You make a change and performance drops unexpectedly.

Problem: A resource collision effect could be causing a pronounced performance bottleneck. Examples of such effects we have seen are the following:

- TX traffic is being generated from RX traffic; Ethernet is running in half-duplex mode. The time it takes to generate the TX frame from an RX frame corresponds to the interframe gap. When the TX frame is sent, it collides with the next RX frame.
- The Ethernet interface is running full duplex, but traffic is being generated in a loop and the frame transmissions occur at times the MAC is busy receiving frames.

Solution: These kinds of bottlenecks are difficult to find and can only be checked by looking at driver counters and the underlying PHY devices. Error counters on test equipment can also help.

Forces:

- Counters might not be available or easily accessible.

References

CHAPTER 2

Intelligent transport systems. http://www.its.dot.gov/
Advanced Telecommunications Computing Architecture. http://www.picmg.org/
PC/104 specification. http://www.pc104.org/pci104_Express_specs.php
COM Express. http://www.picmg.org
QSeven Standard. http://www.qseven-standard.org/
15 billion Internet-attached devices by 2015. http://www.bbc.co.uk/news/technology-13613536
Security of SCADA systems. http://www.truststc.org/scada/
Worm distribution. http://voices.washingtonpost.com/securityfix/2008/06/malware_silently_alters_wirele_1.html

CHAPTER 3

Bell, G. (March 3–5, 1997). *The Laws of Prediction.* San Jose, CA: ACM97 Conference.
Moore, G. (April 19, 1965). "Cramming More Components onto Integrated Circuits," *Electronics, Vol. 38*(No. 8). http://download.intel.com/research/silicon/moorespaper.pdf
Moore, G. E. (1975). *Progress in Digital Integrated Electronics, pages 11–13, International Electron Devices Meeting.* ftp://download.intel.com/museum/Moores_Law/Articles-Press_Releases/Gordon_Moore_1975_Speech.pdf
http://www.readwriteweb.com/archives/verizon_att_cisco_internet_of_things.php
OECD Broadband statistics. http://oecd.org/sti/ict/broadband
Key World Energy Statistics. (2010). *International Energy Agency.* http://www.iea.org/textbase/nppdf/free/2010/key_stats_2010.pdf
http://www.diabetes.org/diabetes-basics/diabetes-statistics/
http://www.myomnipod.com/about-omnipod/see-how-it-works/

CHAPTER 4

http://www.pcisig.com
http://www.onfi.org
http://www.usb.org
http://www.intel.com/technology/usb/ehcispec.htm
http://www.jedec.org/standards-documents/docs/jesd84-a441
http://www.picmg.org
http://www.serialata.org
http://www.intel.com/technology/serialata/ahci.htm
http://www.nxp.com/documents/user_manual/UM10204.pdf
http://www.maxim-ic.com/app-notes/index.mvp/id/476
http://www.intel.com/design/chipsets/hdaudio.htm
http://www.nxp.com/acrobat_download2/various/I2SBUS.pdf
http://www.columbia.edu/Kermit
http://www.bluetooth.com

CHAPTER 5

Intel® 64 and IA-32 Architectures Software Developer Manuals. http://www.intel.com/content/www/us/en/processors/architectures-software-developer-manuals.html

http://www.kerneloops.org

https://sites.google.com/site/x32abi/

http://www.arm.com/products/processors/cortex-a/cortex-a9.php

http://www.jedec.org

CHAPTER 6

http://msdn.microsoft.com/en-us/windows/hardware/gg463119

http://www.uefi.org

Zimmer, Rothman, Hale. *Beyond BIOS.* Intel Press, 2006. http://www.intel.com/intelpress/sum_efi.htm [UEFI Main Specification]; UEFI Specification, Version 2.3, http://www.uefi.org

Rothman, Lewis, & Zimmer, Hale. *UEFI Shell.* http://www.intel.com/intelpress/sum_eshl.htm. Intel Press, 2009.

Zimmer, Rothman, Hale. "UEFI: From Reset Vector to Operating System," Chapter 3 of *Hardware-Dependent Software.* Springer, February 2009.

UEFI Platform Initialization (PI) Specifications, Volumes 1–5, Version 1.2. http://www.uefi.org

EFI Developer Kit. http://www.tianocore.org

Implementing Firmware on Embedded Intel® Architecture Designs. http://download.intel.com/design/intarch/papers/321072.pdf

Minimal Boot Loader for Intel. http://download.intel.com/design/intarch/papers/323246.pdf

CHAPTER 7

http://www.gnu.org

http://www.kernel.org

http://www.uclinux.org

http://www.ntp.org

http://www.bluetooth.org

http://www.linuxfoundation.org/collaborate/workgroups/networking/napi

http://www.yaffs.net

http://www.xenomai.org

http://lxr.linux.no/linux+v2.6.37/Documentation/scheduler/sched-design-CFS.txt

CHAPTER 8

http://www.kernel.org

http://www.gnu.org

http://crosstool-ng.org/hg/crosstool-ng

http://www.busybox.net

http://www.sco.com/developers/devspecs/abi386-4.pdf

http://www.x86-64.org/documentation/abi.pdf

http://www.arm.com

refspecs.freestandards.org/elf/elf.pdf
http://refspecs.linuxfoundation.org/fhs.shtm
http://buildroot.uclibc.org/
http://www.yocto.org
http://www.linuxfoundation.org/collaborate/workgroups/yocto
http://www.openembedded.net
http://www.linaro.org
http://www.lanana.org/docs/device-list/devices-2.6+.txt
http://lxr.free-electrons.com
http://lxr.linux.no/linux/
http://lwn.net/Kernel/LDD3/
Google I/O 2008 – Anatomy and Physiology of an Android – YouTube (17:50)

CHAPTER 9

PowerTOP. http://www.lesswatts.org/projects/powertop/
ACPI. http://www.acpi.info
ACPI 4.0 Specification. http://www.acpi.info/spec40.htm
Intel® Atom™ Processor Z6xx Series. Datasheet. http://www.intel.com/content/www/us/en/processors/atom/
    atom-z6xx-datasheet.html
Python Programming Language. http://www.python.org/

CHAPTER 10

http://embedded.communities.intel.com/servlet/JiveServlet/download/5522-1766/IEGD%20Framebuffer.pdf
http://www.vesa.org
http://www.digital-cp.com/
http://edc.intel.com/Software/Downloads/IEGD/#download
http://www.opengl.org
http://www.khronos.org
http://www.iso.org/iso/home.htm
http://download.macromedia.com/f4v/video_file_format_spec_v10_1.pdf
http://www.freedesktop.org/wiki/Software/vaapi
http://www.itu.int/rec/R-REC-BT.656/en
http://freedesktop.org/wiki/Software/vaap
http://www.khronos.org/files/openmax/whitepapers/OpenMAX_IL_with_GSstreamer.pdf
http://www.Gstreamer.net

CHAPTER 11

http://software.intel.com/en-us/articles/intel-integrated-performance-primitives-code-samples
Feldkamper, H. T., et al. "Low Power Delay Calculation for Digital Beamforming in Handheld Ultrasound
    Systems."
http://downloadcenter.intel.com/Detail_Desc.aspx?agr=Y&DwnldID=17427

CHAPTER 12

http://www.cisco.com/web/go/vni
http://tools.ietf.org/html/rfc1122
http://tools.ietf.org/html/rfc1123
http://www.iana.org/assignments/port-numbers
http://download.intel.com/design/network/datashts/82546GB_ds.pdf
http://download.intel.com/network/connectivity/products/prodbrf/323017.pdf

CHAPTER 13

Android acquisition by Google. http://www.businessweek.com/technology/content/aug2005/tc20050817_0949_tc024.htm
Open Handset Alliance. http://www.openhandsetalliance.com/
http://developer.android.com
WebKit. http://www.webkit.org
Trolltech acquisition by Nokia. http://labs.qt.nokia.com/2008/01/28/nokia-to-acquire-trolltech/
http://qt.nokia.com
Embedded Windows. http://www.microsoft.com/windowsembedded/en-us/windows-embedded.aspx
Apple iOS. http://developer.apple.com/devcenter/ios/index.action

CHAPTER 14

http://www.microsoft.com/technet/security/bulletin/MS01-017.mspx
http://tools.ietf.org/html/rfc5246
http://en.wikipedia.org/wiki/IPsec
http://www.ietf.org/rfc/rfc2401.txt
http://www.trustedcomputinggroup.org/

CHAPTER 15

Will Eatherton's ANCS. (2005). *keynote presentation*. http://www.cesr.ncsu.edu/ancs/slides/eathertonKeynote.pdf
http://www.faqs.org/docs/Linux-HOWTO/SMP-HOWTO.html
Regnier, G., Minturn, D., McAlpine, G., Saletore, V. A., & Foong, A. (Jan.–Feb. 2004). "ETA: Experience with an Intel Xeon Processor as a Packet Processing Engine." *Micro IEEE, Vol. 24*(No. 1), 24–31
Homogeneous Multi-Core. http://download.intel.com/design/intarch/papers/321062.pdf
http://www.xenomai.org/index.php/Main_Page
Xenomai. http://download.intel.com/design/intarch/papers/322386.pdf
Adoption of SMP w/ VxWorks. http://download.intel.com/design/intarch/papers/321307.pdf

CHAPTER 16

http://download.intel.com/embedded/processo/datasheet/324208.pdf
http://www.mostcooperation.com

http://www.linuxfordevices.com/c/a/News/RTS-Hypervisor-and-STMicroelectronics-ConneXt-IOH
http://www.freaklabs.org
http://www.qseven-standard.org/fileadmin/spec/Qseven-DG_08_Release_Candidate.pdf
http://www.inforcecomputing.com
http://download.intel.com/embedded/chipsets/datasheet/324211.pdf
http://sourceforge.net/apps/mediawiki/mbm/index.php?title=MBM
http://sourceforge.net/apps/trac/linux-zigbee/
http://www.hp.com/rnd/library/pdf/WiFi_Bluetooth_coexistance.pdf
http://www.ieee802.org/15/pub/TG4Expert.html
http://www.zigbee.org/imwp/idms/popups/pop_download.asp?contentID=13184

CHAPTER 17

Joint Test Action Group (JTAG) IEEE 1149.1 Standard Test Access Port and Boundary-Scan
System won't boot. Methodology. http://download.intel.com/design/intarch/papers/321053.pdf
System crashes. ROB timeout. http://download.intel.com/design/intarch/papers/324353.pdf
System doesn't have debug-friendly interface. Meego debug. http://software.intel.com/en-us/articles/debugging-
    meego

CHAPTER 18

Forces and Context (Alexander 1979)
Consequences (Gamma et al., 1995)
Ganssle (1999)
McConnell (1993) *Code Complete.*
Summit (1995)
Douglass (1999) *Doing Hard Time.*
http://www.intel.com/Assets/PDF/manual/248966.pdf

Index

Note: Page numbers followed by *f* indicate figures and *t* indicate table.

Printed and bound by CPI Group (UK) Ltd, Croydon, CR0 4YY

03/10/2024

01040310-0008